Clinical Case Formulations

Clinical Case Formulations

Matching the Integrative Treatment
Plan to the Client

BARBARA LICHNER INGRAM

WILEY

JOHN WILEY & SONS, INC.

Library of Congress Cataloging-in-Publication Data:

Ingram, Barbara Lichner.
    Clinical case formulations : matching the integrative treatment plan
to the client / Barbara Lichner Ingram.
        p.   cm.
    Includes bibliographical references.
    ISBN-13: 978-0-471-74314-9 (pbk.)
    ISBN-10: 0-471-74314-3 (pbk.)
    1. Psychotherapists, training. I. Title.
    [DNLM: 1. Psychotherapy—methods.   2. Mental Disorders—therapy.
    3. Models, Psychological.   4. Psychological Theory.   WM 420 I54c
    2006]
    RC459.I54   2006
    616.89′14—dc22

                                                          2005029941

Printed in the United States of America.
10   9   8   7   6   5   4   3   2

To the memory of my parents,
Rose and Sydney Lichner,
to Tony, Sami, and Paul,
and to all my students, past and future.

Contents ————————————————————————

Appendix III: Skill-Building Activities   547

Appendix IV: Examples   579

References   599

Author Index   617

Subject Index   623

Tables

Preface

This book's creation began over 25 years ago, continuing throughout my career as professor of psychology in Pepperdine University's graduate clinical psychology program. My challenge as a teacher and practicum supervisor was to have my students achieve very specific objectives: mastery of the skills of case formulation as well as feelings of competence and confidence as a beginning therapist.

Each class contained between 10 and 18 students (a small enough size for me to become familiar with each person's learning process and to find ways to make my methods clearer). From review of case formulation reports and suggestions from students, I was able to improve this book by reorganizing the sequence, breaking skills into smaller components, and providing more examples and opportunities for practice. Feedback from former students has assured me that this book meets its intended goals:

- To bridge the gap between graduate school and clinical placement.
- To provide tools for the development of effective treatment plans that match the client's needs.
- To teach a method for integrating ideas and techniques from different theories in a coherent way.
- To enhance the quality of clinical conceptualizations, promoting the integration of textbook knowledge with creativity.
- To serve as a reference book for clinical hypotheses from biological, cognitive-behavioral, psychodynamic, humanistic-existential, family systems, and sociocultural frameworks.

I shared drafts of this book with professionals and found that it met their needs as clinicians. Although a majority of therapists call themselves *eclectic* or *integrative* (Lambert, 2004), they lack a clear conceptual framework for drawing on the wisdom of all approaches. Therapists who may want to learn how to create integrative case formulations may lack a methodology. This book will help.

Regardless of their years of clinical practice, experienced therapists have probably never received systematic training in how to create an integrative clinical case formulation. My interest in case formulation skills stemmed from my own frustration as a trainee and new therapist. My supervisors did not teach me how to think critically and creatively about cases but either expected me to follow a set of rules by rote or threw me into sessions with clients, expecting me to figure it out by trial and error. When I expressed my anguish, supervisors assured me that most beginners had similar feelings and that I was doing fine. My humanistic supervisor said that developing a good relationship with clients was enough. My psychodynamic supervisor said that I should explore the countertransference issues surrounding my need for structure and control, and my intolerance for ambiguity. When I worked in a behavioral clinical setting, I found structure, but I knew I would never be satisfied unless I could integrate ideas from all the theories I had studied. Although *eclectic* was a disreputable idea (as it still is in a few professional circles), I had already formed in my mind the principle that is the core of the method in this book:

> You must create a formulation that fits the client rather than try to squeeze the client into your preferred formulation.

I made a promise to myself when I began teaching graduate psychology students: I will spare them the misery I went through and help them learn a framework for combining ideas, coherently, from different models.

Only people who have gone through psychotherapy training can understand the levels of anxiety and self-doubt felt by a beginning therapist. The more compassionate and responsible you are, the more you worry about doing harm. The more you worry, the harder it is for you to draw from your academic knowledge and feel calm and confident as you face clients. The transition from classroom to therapy room is a momentous change in the life of a future psychotherapist. Many students experience a sharp disconnect between what they learn in the classroom and what is expected in their face-to-face contacts with clients. I open Chapter 1 with a question that is at the back of all beginners' minds: *How will I know what to do when I face a client?*

The answer to that question is that you need a specific set of skills that are not taught in most graduate programs or clinical training sites. *Case formulation skills* refer to the ability to conceptualize your client's needs in a way that leads to effective treatment plans. With the use of these skills, which this book presents, you will be able to think intelligently, critically, and creatively. You will draw from your personal understanding of clients as well as your academic knowledge base, to develop a treatment plan that is tailor-made for each client.

In trying to determine why there is this void in the formal education of future counselors and psychotherapists, I concluded that several elements of training programs give the illusion that students are being adequately taught to conceptualize their client's problems and needs when, in fact, they are not:

- The emphasis on learning to use the *Diagnostic and Statistical Manual of Mental Disorders,* fourth edition, text revision (*DSM-IV-TR;* American Psychiatric Association, 2002) leads to the faulty assumption that psychiatric diagnosis, a labeling, categorization process with a specific set of inclusion criteria, is equivalent to a case formulation, which is the creation of an individualized conceptual framework for a single, unique client.

- The message to "choose an orientation" from well-established theoretical approaches results in the adoption of a ready-made formulation that is chosen before the therapist lays eyes on a new client. Despite the evidence that most therapists combine ideas from different approaches and that no single model is comprehensive enough to incorporate biological, psychological, interpersonal, and social factors in human functioning, faculty and supervisors often discourage an integrative approach.

- The complicated, time-consuming paperwork in clinical settings focuses on meeting legal and administrative requirements without developing the trainee's conceptualization skills. Busy clinicians are not going to be able to find time for such intensive focus on individual clients.

CASE FORMULATION SKILLS CAN BE SYSTEMATICALLY TAUGHT

Teachers, supervisors, and program administrators are not aware that it is possible to teach case formulation skills in a systematic, structured way because they learned their skills in a haphazard way in the apprenticeship model of clinical training, through mentorship relationships with supervisors and their own trial-and-error learning. They believe that a beginner's self-doubt and frustration is a normal developmental stage in the learning process and that the ability to conceptualize develops naturally, over time, and with clinical experience. Even those professionals who themselves integrate ideas from different theoretical models in their session-to-session decision making urge their students to stick to one orientation.

Many kind-hearted practitioners advise trainees that your first session is a success if you just get through it, maintain your composure, and instill enough hope in the client so that he or she will come back. The idea that you should leave your first session with a set of relevant clinical hypotheses in your mind would seem overly ambitious to them.

An assumption underlying this book is that conceptualization skills can be systematically taught. This may be the first book in this field that teaches these skills in a structured, systematic manner. Therapists are rarely taught how to think and conceptualize: These abilities are assumed to flow naturally from native intelligence, experience, and unstructured conversations with supervisors. Although the personality and innate qualities of a therapist are important, it is a mistake to allow therapists to face clients relying solely on their intuitions and hunches. They need skills—both interpersonal and conceptual skills. This book presents an alternative to "choosing an orientation"—a coherent model for integrating ideas from a comprehensive range of theoretical frameworks and mental health models.

TREATMENT QUALITY IS ENHANCED BY INTEGRATING DIFFERENT APPROACHES

This book teaches how to conceptualize clinical cases by integrating ideas, skills, and techniques from a variety of theoretical perspectives to design treatment plans that are the best match for the needs of a client. Although some approaches to integration lead to the development of a new integrative theory (called a *transtheoretical* approach), this book keeps theories separate, extracting their core ideas, and then allowing the creative clinician to combine or choose those ideas that lead to the best treatment plans.

A list of 28 *core clinical hypotheses* offers a metatheoretical framework that embraces all theories, orientations, and mental health intervention models. Combining and recombining these hypotheses leads to new discoveries about effective treatment, without contributing to the proliferation of new theories. Because the description of each hypothesis is free of technical jargon, this framework has the potential to break down barriers among orientations and professional guilds and to unify the knowledge base of all of the professions that provide psychotherapy and other mental health services. With 28 different clinical hypotheses available, the clinician has more "ingredients" to make individualized "recipes" of treatment plans.

For each hypothesis, I have provided a summary of what I consider to be key ideas, some examples and guidelines for when this hypothesis is a good match, and a set of treatment suggestions. I know that I will not please everybody: Experts will complain that I have oversimplified, whereas novices will complain that some sections are overly complicated. I hope that the references and suggested readings will serve the important function of steering readers toward sources with more complete and comprehensive presentations of the different models.

This book encourages readers to consult the research literature, use empirically supported treatments when appropriate, and to individualize treatment to the client's needs. Lambert, Garfield, and Bergin (2004), in a massive review of empirical literature in psychotherapy over the past 10 years, offered an opinion that supports the use of core hypotheses instead of abstract theories:

> We do not foresee any major new theoretical developments along the line of global, comprehensive theories that attempt to explain all aspects of personality, psychopathology, and psychotherapy, as we have in the past. It is more likely that the trend toward minitheories centered on specific problem domains and empirical evaluations will continue. (p. 819)

EMPIRICAL VALIDATION CAN COME FROM CLINICAL, SINGLE-CASE METHODOLOGY NOT JUST FROM RANDOM CLINICAL TRIALS

The current emphasis on empirically validated treatments (EVTs) gives disproportional power to academic researchers, who randomly assign large groups of patients to different, manualized treatment methods, and devalues the knowledge and wisdom of experienced practitioners who work in clinical settings. Clinicians need to convince the researchers—and managed care companies—that the effectiveness of a treatment plan can be validated by monitoring progress in an individual case, not just by traditional quantitative research studies. It is sound scientific practice to evaluate the effectiveness of a treatment plan by implementing it with a client and monitoring, by data collection, the changes in the client's functioning.

To assure rigor in the use of the case formulation method, I provide a list of 33 *standards for evaluating case formulations*. When you read the rules, you will see familiar guidelines for the use of the scientific method: Keep data separate from speculation, test the validity of hypotheses with data, and treat interventions as experiments. The method in this book guides therapists not only to evaluate the effect of therapeutic interventions right from the beginning but also to have the flexibility to modify their conceptualization and plans if they discover that what they are doing is not working.

WE NEED TO ADDRESS THE NEEDS OF CULTURALLY AND RELIGIOUSLY DIVERSE CLIENTS

Within the list of 28 hypotheses, several address cultural factors and the religious/spiritual dimension. More important, this book teaches that each person exists in a specific cultural/social/historical context, and that therapists must understand the client's multiple identities, including gender, race, ethnic group, sexual orientation, religion, and age cohort, to create the best treatment plan.

WE NEED A SYSTEM TO COMMUNICATE MORE EFFECTIVELY WITH CASE MANAGERS IN MANAGED CARE AND INSURANCE COMPANIES

Currently, most books on treatment planning emphasize meeting the needs of the case manager. This book helps therapists focus on the client's needs, while using a language that will have the clarity and specificity that insurance and managed care companies require. The *problem-oriented method* taught in this book is already widely practiced, using the SOAP (i.e., subjective data, objective data, assessment, and plan) format for organizing a case formulation. This simple structure provides a framework for integrating hypotheses. The method in this book is not just window dressing to pacify case managers. This system promotes a commitment to accountability that will satisfy our own professional, ethical desire to provide the highest quality services to our clients.

The case formulation skills taught in this book require a foundation of professional study and good intellectual abilities. This book is clearly not a cookbook for nonprofessionals. There are no shortcuts to becoming a competent psychotherapist: Case formulation skills are just part of the package of abilities, knowledge, and judgment that is necessary for professional practice. No single book can possibly substitute for the quantity of reading and the variety of supervised clinical experiences that contribute to clinical competence.

BARBARA LICHNER INGRAM

Acknowledgments

I am grateful to the competent and creative students who served as my assistants over the years: Andi Cupp, Nicole Crouch, Natalie Feinblatt, Amy Jones, Michal Mayo-Dvir, Michelle Logvinsky, Laura Paulson, and David Schafer. The following students gave valuable feedback and suggestions: Ardell Broadbent, Arlene Cruz, Gunilla David, Cori Day, Charles Dvorak, Nicola Flinn, Michelle Friedman, Matt Keener, Tamara Kline, Merry Lambert, Tom Rankin, Alice Richardson, Bruce Singer, Greg Spano, Alvin Sandjaja, Marilyce Srugies, Chantelle Thomas, Gail Wilburn, Renee Wilkinson, Wendi Williams, and Amanda Wood (I apologize for inadvertent omissions). I also thank anonymous students and trainees who provided material for case examples.

Many teachers, colleagues, and professionals contributed to my knowledge, reviewed portions of this book, or gave me encouragement: Kathi Borden, Ros Byrne, Kathy Castle, Richard Chung, Anat Cohen, Leslie Eichenbaum, Steven Frankel, Barbara Fritz, Nick Ingram, David Levy, Francie Neely, Michelle Pearce, Mary Jane Rotheram-Borus, Daryl Rowe, and Jerome Singer. The name of George Saslow appears several times in the text; if he hadn't chosen to take a confused psychology intern into his education program for psychiatric residents, I would not have become the passionate proponent of coherent case formulations that I am today.

My appreciation goes to all the people at John Wiley & Sons who contributed to the creation of this book with special thanks to Tracey Belmont, who acquired it and improved it with the help of well-selected reviewers; to Christy Croll, copyeditor, who made many helpful suggestions; and to Pam Blackmon and the staff at Publications Development Company. My special thanks go to Heather Turgeon for her editing skills and her sound advice.

Finally, I thank three friends who gave me inspiration and emotional support—Anita Bavarsky, Ruth Blaug, and Nao Hauser—and my husband, Paul, a very special, one-of-a-kind person, who brought humor, insights, and love into my life while I was working on this book.

BLI

PART I

GETTING STARTED

The first chapter is an overview of the case formulation method, including definitions of key concepts (e.g., case formulation, integrative, core clinical hypothesis, and the problem-oriented method), descriptions of the steps in creating a case formulation, and two important lists that are repeated in Appendix II (Charts 11.A and 11.B):

1. Twenty-Eight Core Clinical Hypotheses.
2. Thirty-Three Standards for Evaluating Clinical Formulations.

These two charts become reference tools to help write case formulation reports by combining the core hypotheses when they fit the data. (Part II will take you through each of the 28 hypotheses.) The framework of the problem-oriented method (POM) organizes the case formulation report into sections: problem title, outcome goal, two kinds of data, an explanatory assessment essay, and detailed treatment plans. As you write the report, you can check each step by referring to the standards. (Part III will take you through each of the 33 standards.)

At the end of Chapter 1, you are introduced to the first activity: An invitation to write a "baseline" formulation, using the ideas from Chapter 1. To build *case formulation skills,* you are encouraged to stop and do the activities in Appendix III if a box announcing an activity appears in the text. An alternate approach is to first complete the book, and then use the activities as a method of review.

Chapter 2 addresses the topic of data gathering. The quality of a case formulation and your ability to be integrative both depend on gathering a comprehensive, unbiased database. Many different charts and tools are presented in Chapter 2 to assure that you gather and organize data in a way that will make it easy to apply the clinical hypotheses and develop good treatment plans.

When you have completed Part I, you have two choices: (1) You can proceed to Part II where each chapter addresses one of the seven categories in which the core hypotheses are organized. (2) You can go directly to Part III (Chapters 11 through 15) to learn the details of the case formulation method.

Chapter 1 ――――――――――――――――――――――――

A FRAMEWORK FOR CASE FORMULATIONS

As a beginning therapist, facing your first clients, you probably ask yourself: *How am I going to know what to do?* When your training begins, you may wonder: *What should I do with this specific client?* With more experience, you will grasp a more important need: *When I face any new client, how do I create a treatment plan that is the best match for that client?* Even experienced therapists face this challenge. Thus, you need skills to create case formulations—the focus of this book.

> A clinical case formulation is "a conceptual scheme that organizes, explains, or makes clinical sense out of large amounts of data and influences the treatment decisions" (Lazare, 1976). A formal clinical case formulation is an oral or written presentation that communicates the treatment plan along with the conceptual rationale and justification for that plan.

Jerome Frank (Frank & Frank, 1991) defined two components of a case formulation: (1) A plausible explanation for the patient's symptoms, in the form of a conceptual scheme or even a myth, which provides a rationale for (2) the prescription of a ritual or other type of procedure for resolving them. Based on this definition, a case formulation includes the following elements:

- Symptoms or problems that need to be changed.
- A large amount of information that needs to be organized.
- A conceptual scheme that provides an explanation.
- Treatment decisions that lead to specific procedures.

A clearly articulated case formulation is essential for communicating with supervisors and treatment team members, as well as with case managers representing the companies who pay for treatment. Other benefits for learning how to create clinical case formulations include:

3

- Increased confidence and reduced anxiety at the thought of facing new clients.
- Tools and skills for evaluating the needs of clients and understanding clients from multiple perspectives.
- A coherent strategy for applying what you have learned in the classroom to your work with clients.
- A framework for developing appropriate treatment plans.
- A structure for bringing your creativity and academic education to the rewarding process of helping people.

HOW AM I GOING TO KNOW WHAT TO DO?

To create a formulation, you can either choose an orientation and follow its rules or develop a unique, integrative formulation for each client.

Choose an Orientation

By choosing an orientation, you develop case formulations using the theories of your preferred theoretical model. This may be an attractive approach because it offers structure, guarantees you consistency and coherence among your ideas, and wins you approval from members of the profession who have followed this path. Furthermore, if you choose an orientation, it removes ambiguity and stress from clinical decision making, helps you feel prepared for job interviews, and gives you access to professional organizations and training programs with like-minded professionals. If your orientation is the best match to the needs of a specific client, it serves you well; however, there is a tendency to squeeze clients into your preferred model even when other clinical hypotheses might lead to more effective treatment.

Develop Unique, Integrative Formulations

In an alternative process, the therapist integrates ideas, skills, and techniques from different theoretical approaches to create a unique formulation that is tailor-made for each client's problems, personality, and sociocultural context. This approach recognizes that every theory has something of value to offer but is not sufficient as a sole guide for therapy.

This book supports the second approach and teaches an integrative method for creating case formulations. Table 1.1 describes the two key features of the method.

Though many therapists shy away from using the word *eclectic,* studies have shown that a majority of therapists integrate ideas from different models (Lambert & Ogles, 2004).

> An integrative treatment plan combines concepts and techniques from different therapy approaches, in a systematic, coherent way, to meet the needs of a unique client.

Table 1.1   Two Features of Case Formulations

The integration of ideas from the 28 *core clinical hypotheses*.

The list of hypotheses is in Appendix II, Chart II.A. The chapters in Part II present each hypothesis in turn. These hypotheses:

- Extract the essential explanatory ideas from all theories and approaches to therapy;
- Permit combination and integration of components of different theories; and
- Lead logically to treatment plans.

A structured framework called the problem-oriented method.

A list of 33 standards for evaluating the application of this method is in Appendix II, Chart II.B. The chapters in Part III explain each of these standards. The problem-oriented method (POM) requires:

- Identification of the *problem*, which is the target for treatment;
- Specifications of the *outcome goal*, the desired change in the client's functioning;
- Well-organized summaries of the collected information about the client (the *database*);
- A coherent explanation of each problem, integrating clinical hypotheses (*assessment*);
- Recommended treatment *plan*, consistent with the explanation, and focused directly on achieving the outcome goal.

In applying the POM, you will learn to SOAP each problem that you identify for a client. SOAP stands for Subjective Data, Objective Data, Assessment, and Plan.

The system in this book differs from other approaches to integrating theories—samples of which are listed in the *Suggested Reading* section at the end of this chapter. You learn to select and combine core clinical hypotheses based on how you believe they explain a clearly defined problem. Using a problem-oriented method (POM) and integrating multiple hypotheses helps you think intelligently, critically, and creatively to develop a treatment plan that is tailor-made for each client. You may still have normal anxieties as a beginning therapist, but, with these case formulation skills, you are more likely to feel challenged and focused rather than confused, overwhelmed, and inadequate. If you are an experienced therapist, you will find that, using this framework, you integrate new ideas into your customary approach and have tools for troubleshooting when interventions fail to produce the expected benefits.

CORE CLINICAL HYPOTHESES

Lazare (1976) provided a clear definition:

A *core clinical hypothesis* is a single explanatory idea that helps to structure data about a given client in a way that leads to better understanding, decision making, and treatment choice.

Every theoretical orientation can be broken down into core hypotheses. When we examine these hypotheses, it is apparent that different theorists use the same ideas, but package them with different jargon. For instance, cognitive-behavioral, existential, and narrative therapists all explain problems as faulty cognitive constructions of life experiences. Chemistry provides an analogy: A theoretical orientation is like a complex chemical compound and a single hypothesis functions like a pure chemical element. The same element (hypothesis) can appear in many different formulas (orientations), and a compound (single orientation) can be broken down into component elements (hypotheses).

Lazare (1976) recommended using a list of hypotheses to

> help the clinician make efficient use of limited time, guard him from coming to premature closure in the collection of data, and provide a stimulus for the exploration of relevant but neglected clinical questions. . . . In the process of bringing these partial formulations to the interview for consideration, they become hypotheses to be tested. The clinician, by thinking in terms of hypotheses, keeps himself from being bombarded or overloaded with large amounts of unstructured data. Each new observation can now be considered in terms of its relevance to a limited number of hypotheses under consideration instead of being one out of thousands of possible facts. (pp. 96–97)

If you use these hypotheses with a scientific attitude, you understand that a formulation is tentative and you do not need to stick to it if it does not lead to beneficial change in the client's functioning. If you only have one hypothesis, you are wedded, dogmatically, to a single orientation. If you choose one orientation, but want to avoid the mistake of imposing an inappropriate treatment plan on your new client, you need two hypotheses:

1. My approach is a good fit for this client, so I can proceed with my preferred type of therapy.
2. My approach does *not* fit this client, and therefore I should refer the client to another therapist.

I have been developing and reshaping a list of *core clinical hypotheses* ever since my first exposure to Lazare's suggestion. The essential ideas from different theoretical approaches and mental health intervention models are extracted and freed from theoretical jargon; given names, codes, and brief descriptions; and organized into seven categories:

   I. **Biological Hypotheses (B)**
  II. **Crisis, Stressful Situations, and Transitions (CS)**
 III. **Behavioral and Learning Models (BL)**
 IV. **Cognitive Models (C)**
  V. **Existential and Spiritual Models (ES)**

VI. **Psychodynamic Models (P)**

VII. **Social, Cultural, and Environmental Factors (SCE)**

Although 28 seems like an excessive number of hypotheses to learn, with familiarity, the list becomes a helpful tool for examining the data of a new case. In addition, the list is useful when you are exposed to what appears to be a new approach to psychotherapy: See if you can deconstruct the new model down to three or four core hypotheses from my list; if a new idea doesn't fit, you should expand the list to contain 29 hypotheses.

Table 1.2 contains 28 hypotheses, which are explained in detail in Chapters 3 through 9.

When you shift from espousing theoretical orientations to using clinical hypotheses, you discover that (a) all theories comprise multiple hypotheses and (b) there are multiple treatment possibilities for all problems and diagnoses. The following examples illustrate both those points:

Gestalt Therapy's Core Ideas Represent Multiple Hypotheses

- **B3 Mind-Body Connections:** Gestalt therapists recognize mind-body connections when they comment on the message in the movement of a leg or have the client pay attention to breathing.

- **P1 Internal Parts and Subpersonalities:** Gestalt therapists identify polarities—inner parts in conflict, such as "top dog" and "underdog"—and encourage their dialogue.

- **P2 Reenactment of Early Childhood Experiences:** Gestalt therapists help clients deal with unfinished business from the past so that they don't remain stuck, like a broken record, reenacting the same dysfunctional pattern.

- **ES2 Avoiding Freedom and Responsibility:** Gestalt therapists help clients to confront their freedom instead of using childhood manipulations to get other people to provide support.

Treatment for Posttraumatic Stress Disorder Is Consistent with Multiple Hypothesis

- **B2 Medical Interventions:** Medication is available for symptoms and there is research in progress to create a medication that will prevent PTSD.

- **B3 Mind-Body Connections:** The symptoms of both reexperiencing (flashbacks) and avoidance have underpinnings in brain function and how memories are encoded; a method like Eye Movement Desensitization Reprocessing (EMDR; F. Shapiro, 1996) attempts to integrate neural pathways.

- **BL2 Conditioned Emotional Response:** Emotional deconditioning methods are used—either a desensitization or flooding model of treatment—or in vivo exposure, if possible.

Table 1.2 Twenty-Eight Core Clinical Hypotheses

I. Biological Hypotheses (B)

B1 Biological Cause	The problem has a **Biological Cause:** The client needs medical intervention to protect life and prevent deterioration, or needs psychosocial assistance in coping with illness, disability, or other biological limitations.
B2 Medical Interventions	There are **Medical Interventions** (e.g., medication, surgery, or prosthetics) that should be considered.
B3 Mind-Body Connections	A holistic understanding of **Mind-Body Connections** leads to treatment for psychological problems that focus on the body and treatment for physical problems that focus on the mind.

II. Crisis, Stressful Situations, and Transitions (CS)

CS1 Emergency	The client's symptoms constitute an **Emergency:** Immediate action is necessary.
CS2 Situational Stressors	The client's symptoms result from identifiable recent **Situational Stressors** or from a past traumatic experience.
CS3 Developmental Transition	The client is at a **Developmental Transition,** dealing with issues related to moving to the next stage of life.
CS4 Loss and Bereavement	The client has suffered a **Loss and** needs help during **Bereavement** or for a loss-related problem.

III. Behavioral and Learning Models (BL)

BL1 Antecedents and Consequences	A behavioral analysis of both problem behaviors and desired behaviors should yield information about **Antecedents** (triggers) **and Consequences** (reinforcers) that will be helpful in constructing an intervention.
BL2 Conditioned Emotional Response	A **Conditioned Emotional Response** (e.g., anxiety, fear, anger, or depression) is at the root of excessive emotion, avoidant behaviors, or maladaptive mechanisms for avoiding painful emotions.
BL3 Skill Deficits or Lack of Competence	The problem stems from **Skill Deficits**—the absence of needed skills—**or** the **Lack of Competence** in applying skills, abilities, and knowledge to achieve goals.

IV. Cognitive Models (C)

C1 Utopian Expectations	The client is suffering from the ordinary "miseries of everyday life" and has unrealistic **Utopian Expectations** of what life should be like.
C2 Faulty Cognitive Map	Limiting and outdated elements in the **Faulty Cognitive Map** (e.g., maladaptive schemas, assumptions, rules, beliefs, and narratives) are causing the problem or preventing solutions.
C3 Faulty Information Processing	The client demonstrates **Faulty Information Processing** (e.g., overgeneralization, all-or-nothing thinking, and mind reading) or is limited by an inflexible cognitive style.
C4 Dysfunctional Self-Talk	The problem is triggered and/or maintained by **Dysfunctional Self-Talk** and internal dialogue.

Table 1.2 *(Continued)*

V. Existential and Spiritual Models (ES)

ES1 Existential Issues	The client is struggling with **Existential Issues,** including the fundamental philosophical search for the purpose and meaning of life.
ES2 Avoiding Freedom and Responsibility	The client is **Avoiding** the **Freedom** and autonomy that come with adulthood **and**/or does not accept **Responsibility** for present and past choices.
ES3 Spiritual Dimension	The core of the problem and/or the resources needed for resolving the problem are found in the **Spiritual Dimension** of life, which may or may not include religion.

VI. Psychodynamic Models (P)

P1 Internal Parts and Subpersonalities	The problem is explained in terms of **Internal Parts and Subpersonalities** that need to be heard, understood, and coordinated.
P2 Reenactment of Early Childhood Experiences	The problem is a **Reenactment of Early Childhood Experiences:** Feelings and needs from early childhood are reactivated and patterns from the family of origin are repeated.
P3 Immature Sense of Self and Conception of Others	Difficulties stem from the client's failure to progress beyond the **Immature Sense of Self and Conception of Others** that is normal for very young children.
P4 Unconscious Dynamics	The symptom or problem is explained in terms of **Unconscious Dynamics.** Defense mechanisms keep thoughts and emotions out of awareness.

VII. Social, Cultural, and Environmental Factors (SCE)

SCE1 Family System	The problem must be understood in the context of the entire **Family System.**
SCE2 Cultural Context	Knowledge of the **Cultural Context** is necessary to understand the problem and/or to create a treatment plan that shows sensitivity to the norms, rules, and values of the client's cultural group.
SCE3 Social Support	The problem is either caused or maintained by deficiencies in **Social Support.**
SCE4 Social Role Performance	Difficulty meeting demands for **Social Role Performance** contributes to the client's distress and dysfunction.
SCE5 Social Problem is a Cause	A **Social Problem** (e.g., poverty, discrimination, or social oppression) **is a Cause** of the problem. Social problems can also exacerbate difficulties stemming from other causes. You must avoid *blaming the victim.*
SCE6 Social Role of Mental Patient	The problem is causally related to disadvantages or advantages to the **Social Role of Mental Patient.**
SCE7 Environmental Factors	The problem is explained in terms of **Environmental Factors.** Solutions can involve modifying the environment, leaving the environment, obtaining material resources, or accepting what can't be changed.

- **C3 Faulty Information Processing:** Cognitive distortions need to be corrected.
- **P4 Unconscious Dynamics:** The dissociative symptoms represent unconscious processes—the lack of memory for events that were experienced. Random, intrusive flashbacks can be eliminated if memories are encoded verbally and brought under conscious control.
- **SCE3 Social Support:** The social support of others who have gone through the same trauma can be helpful. For instance, groups of veterans can share stories of what happened and relive painful memories.

THE PROBLEM-ORIENTED METHOD

This book uses a problem-oriented framework for integrating clinical hypotheses into a coherent conceptualization that leads to effective treatment. The problem-oriented method (POM; Weed, 1971) requires a set of skills, which includes defining problems, setting goals, and designing plans focused on the achievement of those goals. Fowler and Longabaugh (1975) describe the benefits of this method:

- Problems are clearly defined and delimited at the level of data, not diagnosis.
- Problem lists require clinicians to be accountable for all problems.
- The problem title provides the target for treatment plans.
- Progress notes document that plans are being followed.
- By separating data from assessment, the clinician can document the processes of clinical judgment.
- The method clarifies and simplifies peer and utilization review functions.

> The term *problem* refers to difficulties, dysfunctions, complaints, and impairments that are identified by the client, by others with whom the client interacts (e.g., family members, courts, or school systems), or by the professionals who evaluate the client's functioning.

We are in the business of helping people resolve problems and become better problem-solvers on their own. Mental health clinics and psychiatric hospitals invariably use *Presenting Problem* as one of the required sections of an intake report. Managed care and insurance companies ask providers to specify the problem that is the target of treatment.

Once you master this method, it seems like common sense because you have a foundation in problem-solving skills from your everyday life. When you take your car to a mechanic, you expect to see a demonstration of problem-solving skills. Mechanics *identify the problem* (e.g., car will not start; funny noise when brakes are applied), seek out *explanations* (e.g., fuel pump is broken; brake pads are worn down), and *implement a plan* to resolve the problem (e.g., replace bad parts with new parts). The quality of their work is evaluated not by the elegance of their theory or by research findings from studies of other cars but by the attainment of the *desired outcome* with this particular car: It starts when you turn the key, and it stops when you step on the brakes.

> The POM framework embraces all possible theories and organizes the clinician's thinking, setting no limitation on the choice of explanatory hypotheses or treatment methods.

The terms *problem-oriented* or *problem-solving* have been associated with directive, short-term approaches such as cognitive-behavioral therapy (CBT) and strategic family therapy. Therefore, you may mistakenly assume that using the POM means you must use these problem-focused therapies. On the contrary, the POM also supports the application of psychodynamic and humanistic-existential models, providing an effective format for communicating treatment recommendations. The treatment strategy could be a directive, problem-solving approach, such as the cognitive therapy of Aaron Beck; a nondirective client-centered approach, such as that used by Carl Rogers; or a creative integration of both. A quick glimpse at the four major orientations will show how the POM will be a useful tool for integrating theories.

1. **Behavioral and Cognitive-Behavioral:** Therapists who work in behavioral and cognitive-behavioral orientations already use a problem-oriented approach. The POM will give them a framework for integrating ideas from psychoanalytic and existential theories (e.g., explanations for why "maladaptive schemas" are resistant to change).
2. **Family Systems:** Practitioners from family systems orientations feel comfortable with the idea of a problem-oriented approach. Therapists who describe their therapy as "solution-focused" will appreciate that the POM requires clear specification of the desired future goals.
2. **Psychodynamic:** Students who are attracted to psychodynamic theories will find that both cognitive and family systems frameworks can shed light on the early family dynamics that are usually the focus of this kind of therapy.
3. **Humanistic and Existential:** Many therapists from these orientations have already developed integrative approaches (Cain & Seeman, 2001; Gendlin, 1996; Greenberg, Watson, & Lietaer, 1998). Although words like *case* and *data* may seem dehumanizing, these terms do not imply a way of treating the client, but rather they refer to the clinician's formulating process. The POM framework permits the treatment plans to include a focus on an authentic human relationship.

SOAPing Each Problem

One of the distinguishing features of the POM is the way you organize data and your formulation. You do not write an overall discussion of the whole client but, rather, first give titles to his or her problems and then provide material, organized into four categories, under each problem title. Table 1.3 presents a description of

Table 1.3   How to SOAP a Problem

Problem title: A statement of the difficulties, dysfunctions, complaints, and impairments for which the client seeks help. The problem title must be clear, specific, and free of theoretical jargon.

Outcome goal: A statement of the desired state at the end of therapy. The outcome goal is directly related to the problem title and contains no description of how the goal will be attained.

THE DATABASE

S   Subjective Data

This section contains data that the client reports to you (the word **story** is another word beginning with **s** to remind you what belongs in this section). Factual information that is learned from the client goes in this section (e.g., age, number of years in school, number of children). Information from family members also goes in this section. It is helpful to selectively provide direct quotations from the client. This section must be complete for purposes of the formulation because no additional data can be introduced in the A and P sections. Subjective data is organized by topics, without reference to when and how you got the information. You must be careful that conceptualizations and theoretical constructs do not appear in this section.

O   Objective Data

The primary source of data in this section is the therapist's **observations** (another word beginning with **o** to remind you what belongs in this section). The therapist uses technical terminology to describe the client's mental status and the nature of the interpersonal process between client and therapist. Other examples of objective data are test results, reports from professionals, and written records.

THE FORMULATION

A   Assessment

This section contains the clinician's conceptual scheme for understanding the problem based on clinical hypotheses. *Assessment* encompasses much more than a diagnostic label or a summary of data. This section contains a well-organized essay, which thoroughly discusses **your analysis of the problem, including explanations, hypotheses, conceptualizations, and theoretical speculation.** The ideas in this section must be consistent with the data and should lead to plans that will resolve the problem. New data may not be introduced in this section. However, data that were previously presented may be repeated to make a specific point. Revise your final written product several times to improve the quality of your case conceptualization.

P   Plan

This section describes a treatment strategy that follows logically from the previous conceptualization. The plan describes how the therapist will work with the client to achieve the goals of treatment and resolve the problem. **Process goals and intervention strategies** are discussed. Every recommendation must have a foundation in the assessment section. A plan addresses the goals for different stages of therapy and recommends techniques and creation of a productive therapist-client relationship. The plan may address how to evaluate progress toward goals, as well as considerations about an appropriate time to terminate treatment.

these four categories, which make up the acronym SOAP (subjective data, objective data, assessment, and plan): The database has two categories (*subjective* and *objective* data) and the formulation has two components—an explanatory discussion (which fits under *assessment*) and treatment recommendations (*plan*).

The SOAP format organizes all your data about a specific client and provides a structure for presenting a formulation in which the database is separate from the formulation. Therefore, you can present a clean database when you are communicating with supervisors and team members. The assessment (conceptualization) is separate from the plan (prescribed treatment) so that you can design different interventions based on the same conceptualization.

The term *assessment* has many meanings in clinical practice, including the administration and interpretation of psychological tests. I use the term *assessment* because the SOAP acronym is easy to remember and is in wide clinical use. The word *formulation,* strictly speaking, refers to the conceptualization, but you must include an "assessment-plan" combination if asked, "What is your formulation of the client's problem?"

TASKS AND PROCESSES OF CASE FORMULATION

Formulating, as a verb, refers to the creative cognitive processes of developing an official formulation. You are formulating when you sit face-to-face with the client and generate hunches about the causes of problems or structure questions to test a specific hypothesis. You are formulating when you spend time between sessions thinking about the client. Formulating is different from writing progress notes in a chart. The notes that you write in charts—which are legal documents open to scrutiny in many different contexts—emphatically do *not* contain the creative speculation that is part of a good formulation.

Unlike the final product (a report in a linear format), the tasks and processes of creating a formulation can occur simultaneously; you can go back and forth between steps. Figure 1.1 is a diagram of the six tasks of formulating:

1. Gather Data.
2. Define Problems.
3. Specify Outcome Goals.
4. Apply Hypotheses.
5. Plan Treatment.
6. Monitor Effects of Interventions.

Gather Data

The term *database* (S-O in the SOAP) refers to the entire body of information available for a specific client. *Subjective data* refers to what the client tells you and *objective data* refers to what you see and hear during the session. Chapter 2 presents

Gather Data

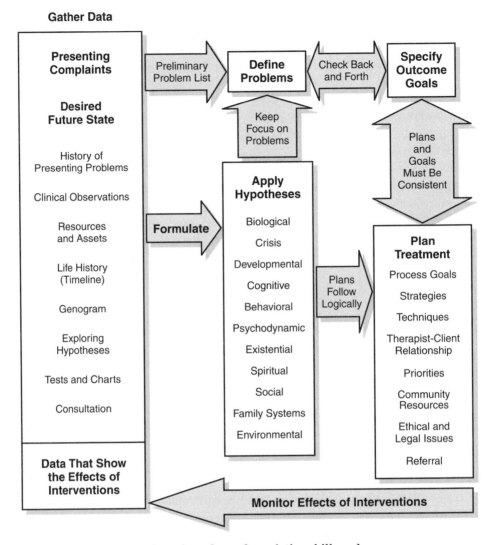

Figure 1.1   Overview of case formulation skills and processes.

techniques and suggestions for gathering a comprehensive, unbiased database, and Chapter 13 presents guidelines for presenting a well-organized database.

The term *data* is sometimes associated with scientific models (e.g., the medical-psychiatric model and the research-based cognitive-behavioral model) and might sound cold or businesslike. However, the terms *data* and *database* are theory free and refer to the information you gather about the client.

The contents of the database must be uncontaminated by theoretical assumptions, inference, and interpretation: Different professionals would agree about the content of the database, regardless of their orientation.

Data gathering starts before the therapist sets eyes on the client, often with a phone call. Although the first session (often called the intake) is a major source of information about the client, the data-gathering process occurs in every session.

In the beginning, your focus is on identifying and exploring problems. Later in therapy, data gathering is the tool for evaluating whether the plan is effective in helping the client make progress toward outcome goals.

The therapist may gather data not only through interviewing but also by reading charts, communicating with family members, consulting with other professionals, administering and interpreting tests, and giving homework assignments. The process of testing hypotheses to see which ones fit the data is a task that requires thorough knowledge of the 28 core clinical hypotheses, plus the ability to gather data in an open and unbiased way.

The first session can be overwhelming if the therapist believes that all important data must be gathered immediately. This attitude can be disastrous for developing rapport with the client, and it can distort the data. View the first session as a chance to rule out two important hypotheses: biological causes (**B1**) and emergency issues (**CS1**) that require immediate action, such as hospitalization, warning intended victims, or instituting crisis intervention strategies. Once you are convinced that there is no pressure to act immediately, you can continue the intake process into the second and third sessions. Three sessions is a reasonable period to gather sufficient data for a preliminary, tentative case formulation.

Because the clinical interview is the main tool of data gathering, the clinician must be a competent interviewer or the validity of the database is compromised. Therapists need to become aware of their personal values, biases, and possible countertransference issues that could contaminate data. In actual training, the building of case formulation skills should be integrated with the development of interviewing skills, including the following: attentive nonverbal behaviors, accurate observation of the client's nonverbal behavior, reflection of feelings, accurate paraphrasing and summarizing, effective open-ended questions, and focused questions that achieve specific data-gathering and hypothesis-testing goals. Table 1.4 presents the major components of the database.

Define Problems

We all have a tendency to rush to explanations and solutions, instead of spending time identifying the problem or problems. The ability to create good problem titles might be the most important skill taught in this book. The definition of the problem helps to focus the discussion in the assessment section and keeps it from becoming an abstract discussion of the client's personality or the therapist's pet theory. A "good" title means that the therapist and the client have agreed on a target for change that leads to achievable, realistic, and desirable outcome goals. Chapter 11 explains the problem identification process, and how to write specific problem titles, teaching you to make the following distinctions:

- **Specific problem title:** *Lack of control of anger while disciplining children.*
- **Vague problem title:** *Anger problems.*
- **Faulty problem title that contains formulation ideas:** *Unresolved issues with abusive father.*

Table 1.4   Components of the Database

Presenting Complaints

The therapist must note and explore the reasons why the client came to therapy, described in the client's own words. In addition, the therapist might be able to identify additional problems or reframe the presenting problems into a more solvable form.

History of Presenting Problems

A detailed timeline of recent history is essential for understanding the onset and development of the presenting complaints. Therapists seek the answer to questions (e.g., *Was there an identifiable onset of the problem?* and *Why is the client seeking help now, instead of sooner or later?*), along with information about past efforts to resolve problems.

Clinical Observations

The therapist attends to the client's appearance, speech and behavior, and uses a specialized vocabulary to describe the client (e.g., see Chart II.C, Mental Status Exam, in Appendix II). The "here and now" of the session provides samples of the client's style of relating.

Desired Future State

Therapists probe to discover what the client wants in the future, assuring that it is a reasonable, attainable goal that will not cause damage.

Life History with Timeline

Organizing information about the client's personal history shows the stages and transitions of a unique life. By using a visual timeline, therapists recognize gaps in their information and how seemingly unconnected events coincide in time. It is also very useful to match the individual's life history timeline with a timeline of historical events to grasp some of the social, economic, and cultural factors in a person's history.

Resources and Assets

Therapists need information about success, support networks, strengths, and talents. It is important to assess competence as well as weakness.

Genogram

This is a diagram of the family tree going back at least to the grandparent generation. A visualization of this information, along with details about culture, relationships, and family dynamics, can be enormously helpful.

Tests and Charts

Data may be available in preexisting medical records. The therapist can seek additional data through testing or structured data-gathering homework assignments.

Consultation

Information is sometimes obtained by consulting with people who have had contact with the client.

Effects of Interventions

When a plan is implemented, it is essential to gather data to see if it is working as predicted. Trial interventions are useful, before a formal case formulation is developed, to evaluate their effectiveness.

The starting point in the case formulation process is the development of a comprehensive list of problems. Give each problem a clear, specific, and understandable title, worded without theoretical jargon. A preliminary list of problems is derived from the client's initial complaints, as well as from your focused questions and clinical observations. Occasionally, problems are identified through complaints from people who know the client. In defining problems, you will make many judgments and decisions. Certain complaints need to be "normalized," instead of targeted for treatment. As new data are gathered, problem definitions may change.

People frequently define problems in ways that cannot be solved; for example, "I want my boyfriend to change." The therapist must avoid that trap. Every problem title must lead to an outcome that is possible and you need to be sure that the problem is defined so that the focus is on what the client has control over. Be careful not to impose your values and try to change the client in ways that the client does not want.

After years of academic training in psychology, it is hard to resist jumping to clinical explanations before clearly defining the problem. To avoid letting your conceptualization creep into the problem title, you must keep reminding yourself to word problem titles in simple, ordinary language that is free of theoretical concepts. Problem titles must be agreeable to practitioners of all orientations, so it is incorrect to include theoretical terms that are specific to one orientation. Save the explanations for the assessment (the A in the SOAP).

Specify Outcome Goals

Chapter 12 discusses how to specify outcomes—the desired state at the end of therapy. Outcome goals refer to the client's behavior outside of the therapy session—in real life—and are described in language that is free of theoretical jargon. The method taught in this book is both problem and goal oriented—defining a problem leads to specification of goals and sometimes goal setting comes first and helps you define a problem.

Outcome goals must be defined in a way to allow outside evaluators to verify whether they were attained or not. Outcome goals do not contain any clues about the "how" of therapy or the techniques used in the process. Therapists from different orientations will agree on what a successful outcome is, even as they prepare to use different treatment strategies to attain it. Outcome goal statements must be clear, realistic, and free of theory. For instance, "to make the unconscious conscious" or "to become a fully actualized person" are faulty outcome goals: They (a) contain theoretical constructs and (b) are too idealistic and utopian to be achieved. The wording of these goal statements must be changed so that the goal is specific and attainable.

By specifying outcome goals, we determine *how we know that we have achieved problem resolution and that it is appropriate to terminate therapy.* Reference to outcome goals in the plan helps to focus your intervention strategy.

If you only use a problem focus, you are stuck exploring "what's wrong." Therapists sometimes refer to outcome goals with other terms, such as the *preferred scenario* and the *future vision.*

The definition of problems and the specification of outcomes are bidirectional processes. As the vision of the desired future becomes clearer, the wording of the problem may be modified.

There is a logical relationship between a problem title and a goal. When you write a clear problem title, the outcome goal often seems self-evident, as in this example:

Problem: *Lack of friends*
Outcome: Initiate and maintain a friendship

However, the identification of the desired outcome can shape the wording of the problem title. The following examples illustrate how you can start with the outcome goal and work backward to the problem title.

Outcome: Develop a support network
Problem: *Social isolation* or *Lack of friends*
Outcome: Decide on career goal
Problem: *Indecision and ambivalence about career goals*

Often, going back and forth between problem title and outcome statement helps you clarify both.

During therapy, you will continually reassess the goals of treatment. As goals are met, you can cross problems off the problem list. As new problems are defined and new data are gathered, outcome goals can be specified and changed. Certain goals may be recognized as too costly in time and effort.

In creating goals for clients, distinguish between outcome goals and process goals. *Outcome goals* refer to desired client functioning at the termination of therapy such as "develop social skills." Like problem titles, outcome goals must be completely free of theory in their wording.

Process goals (described later) refer to desired in-session experiences and are based on the therapist's conceptualization. Process goals will reveal the theory of the therapist (e.g., ventilation of feelings, demonstration of insight, free association, or building a hierarchy of feared situations). If the goal refers to the therapist's actions and intentions (e.g., to help, to facilitate, to support, or to challenge), it is a process goal. In the section of the case report called Outcome Goals, eliminate all process goals and focus on the client's functioning at the end of therapy, without reference to how this will be achieved. This rule allows therapists of all theoretical persuasions to agree on outcome goals.

To assure that something is a good statement of an outcome goal, ask:

- *Will achievement of this goal produce positive out-of-therapy changes?*
- *Will I be able to verify that this goal has been achieved?*
- *If the client achieves this goal, will that be sufficient to resolve the problem?*

Apply Hypotheses

The application of relevant hypotheses involves multiple tasks and competencies. First, learn the hypotheses by reading Chapters 3 through 9. Then, practice applying them through the activities in Chapter 10. Of all the skills taught in this book, applying hypotheses is the most complex. It involves the following:

- *A search for the "best-fit" hypotheses:* The clinician sorts through the available clinical hypotheses that are compatible with the data about this specific client.
- *"Testing" the fit of a specific hypothesis:* The focus of the interview becomes gathering data to rule "in" or "out" that hypothesis. If you commit to a specific hypothesis too quickly, the search for information will be biased by your expectations.
- *Selecting and combining hypotheses:* You will not include every possible hypothesis that fits but instead seek a combination that will lead to a good plan. This process includes examination of cost-effectiveness: Given hypotheses of equal merit, determine which ones lead to a plan that is more economical in time, money, and effort.

Once you have selected hypotheses, you need to develop the integrative, explanatory discussion that goes in the A section of the SOAP (see Chapter 14). Every idea in the assessment must be consistent with and justified by the data. You cannot ignore significant data nor can you apply hypotheses that are not supported by data. There is no reason to retain a hypothesis that does not direct you to a treatment strategy.

Plan Treatment

The end product of a formulation and the reason that you are bothering to develop these skills is the creation of a treatment plan, designed for a specific individual, which describes a strategy for attaining the desired outcome goals (Chapter 15). The plan cannot be created by a computer program or by a nonprofessional, just based on a problem title. The plan must be tailor-made for each client. Even if you choose to use a treatment package that involves systematic instructions, it is still necessary that you administer this treatment with empathy, flexibility, and sensitivity to cultural and relationship factors.

The prescribed interventions in the plan follow logically from the ideas in the assessment. The bridge between the assessment and the plan consists of *process goals.*

WHAT ARE PROCESS GOALS?

Process goals describe events and conditions that occur in the therapy sessions. They answer two questions:

1. How will I achieve the outcome goal (i.e., by empathizing, challenging cognitions, teaching skills, restructuring the family system, or creating a trusting relationship)? These goals may reveal the therapist's theory.
2. What interventions follow logically from the chosen hypotheses?

Skill deficit	Build new skills
Dysfunctional self-talk	Modify self-talk
Unconscious dynamics	Make the unconscious conscious

Process goals may contain language that belongs to a specific theory and refer to constructs that cannot be observed or verified (e.g., *utilize the transference, integrate disowned parts of the personality,* and *resolve unfinished business with parents*).

Every important idea in the assessment section must be followed by process goals and a specific strategy in the plan section. Eliminate ideas in the assessment section that do not merit a plan. If you write ideas in the plan that were not addressed in the assessment essay, go back to that section and insert the rationale for the plan.

To reach many outcome goals, it is necessary to set *intermediate objectives*—short-term goals that are steps toward achieving outcome goals. Process goals and intermediate objectives can overlap. For instance, if the outcome goal is for the client to be appropriately assertive with his boss and coworkers, an intermediate objective might be for the client to role-play an assertive encounter in the session. This is a process goal, because it refers to activity in the session, and it is also an intermediate objective, because the client is demonstrating attainment of new skills that would transfer outside of therapy and contribute to achievement of his outcome goal.

There can be many different strategies for achieving a process goal, and your choices will depend on multiple factors, including your own training and level of competence, the abilities and preferences of the client, and the institutional context. The written plan is a guide, but, as therapy progresses, new choices will be made. Although the clinical case formulation is organized in a linear structure, the implementation of plans is fluid, flexible, and creative. There is room for intuition, trial and error, and snap decisions that bubble up from our unconscious, which—as explained by Gladwell (2005) in *Blink,*—stem from both expert knowledge and the ability to process information faster than we code our thoughts into words.

Monitor Effects of Interventions

The effectiveness of therapy is judged by a comparison of pretherapy (problem) and posttherapy (outcome) functioning, with three possible outcomes: (1) improvement (successful therapy), (2) deterioration (harmful therapy), and (3) no change (ineffective therapy). The POM helps therapists be accountable for the effectiveness of their treatments by forcing them to specify the goals that they are working toward and monitor their success in reaching those goals.

The quality of a formulation is evaluated by examining the impact treatment has on the client's real-life, outside-of-therapy functioning. The interventions in the treatment plan can be viewed as an experiment: "If my hypothesis is correct, this strategy should resolve the problem and achieve the desired outcome." Does it work? Does it help? Does it lead to the desired outcome? You gather data about the change in the client's functioning and if he achieves the desired goals, then you confirm the formulation's merit. If not, then you must cycle back through the formulation tasks. You should watch for signs that the interventions are making problems worse or creating new problems. What you may label as "resistance" must be viewed as a source of useful data and a powerful clue that you need to improve the formulation.

Two important criteria for evaluating the quality of formulations are *effectiveness* and *cost-effectiveness:*

1. *Effectiveness:* A formulation is effective when its prescribed interventions lead to desired change in the client's functioning and achievement of the client's goals.

2. *Cost-effectiveness:* A formulation is cost-effective when, compared to alternative effective approaches, it achieves the desired outcome with less time and effort and in a more economical manner. This criterion is especially important when resources are scarce or when third parties such as insurance or managed care companies are providing payment.

When you understand how to monitor the effects of treatment, you will worry less that you might inflict harm on clients because of inexperience. This scientific attitude means that you are as concerned about empirical validation for treatment as are researchers in large institutions who are conducting random clinical trials.

Report Writing

The case formulation method in this book is a tool to help you to think creatively and develop good treatment plans. It is not a method of keeping chart notes or writing official reports. However, to develop skills, it helps if you make a commitment to write reports that take considerable time and effort (see Chart II.J in Appendix II for the outline that I recommend). You will have achieved competence when your report meets the 33 standards listed in Table 1.5.

Table 1.5   Thirty-Three Standards for Evaluating Case Formulations

Problem Definition

1. Problems are defined so that they are solvable targets of treatment.
2. Titles refer to the client's current, real-world functioning.
3. Titles are descriptive, designed for a specific client, and are justified by the data.
4. Problem titles do not contain theoretical, explanatory concepts.
5. The therapist is not imposing cultural or personal values in problem definitions.
6. *Lumping* and *splitting* decisions are justified in that they lead to good treatment planning.
7. The problem list is complete and comprehensive.

Outcome Goals

8. Outcome goals are directly related to the problem title and are consistent with the client's values.
9. Outcome goals refer to real-world functioning and do not contain formulation ideas.
10. Outcome goals are realistic and are not utopian.
11. Outcome goals do not contain the "how" of the treatment plan.

Presentation of Database (S and O)

12. The database is thorough, comprehensive, and complete: There are sufficient data so that multiple hypotheses can be applied.
13. Subjective and objective data are appropriately distinguished.
14. Good quotations from the client are included in the subjective data section.
15. The subjective section does not include formulation concepts (unless they are quotations from the client).
16. There is no reference to how and when the information was gathered in the subjective data section; this information, if relevant, goes in the objective section.
17. The subjective section is well organized and appropriately concise: There is selection, summarization, and condensation of details.
18. The objective section does not contain theoretical concepts, biased opinions, or formulation discussion.

Assessment (A)

19. The assessment integrates hypotheses that are consistent with the prior database.
20. The assessment does not introduce new data.
21. The focus of the assessment is on the specific problem of the specific client: This is not an abstract essay about a theory.
22. The writer is not including all possible hypotheses, just the ones that are useful in developing intervention plans.
23. If theoretical jargon is used, it enhances rather than detracts from understanding and does not contribute to tautological explanations.
24. The writer is integrating material from the highest level of education thus far attained. Commonsense ideas are appropriate but are not sufficient for explaining the problem.
25. The writer demonstrates professional-level thinking and writing skills to provide a coherent conceptualization.

Table 1.5 *(Continued)*

Plan (P)

26. The plan is focused on resolving the identified problem and achieving outcome goals.
27. The plan follows logically from the assessment discussion and does not introduce new data or hypotheses.
28. There is clarity regarding process goals, intermediate objectives, strategies, specific techniques, relationship issues, and sequencing of interventions.
29. The plan is tailor-made for the specific client: Such factors as gender, ethnicity, and personal values are considered.
30. The plan is appropriate for the treatment setting, contractual agreements, and financial constraints.
31. When there is more than one problem, the therapist addresses issues of priorities, sequencing, and integration of plans.
32. The therapist considers community resources and referrals, if appropriate.
33. Legal and ethical issues are addressed appropriately, if relevant.

THE LEARNING PROCESS

Learning case formulation skills can be fun, interesting, creative, and rewarding. The biggest obstacle to this being a pleasurable learning experience is that most students, by the time they get to graduate school, want to earn grades of A on their first try. It is hard to adjust to a learning-by-doing process. Although detailed instructions are necessary and useful, the way to learn is by submitting samples of your work and getting detailed feedback. Here is a piece of advice that former students asked me to pass on: "Do *not* put pressure on yourself to get it right the first time you try."

The long list of standards can make the method seem overly complicated and difficult. However, the method is actually familiar to most professionals: We have all had extensive prior experience with the scientific method and with the development of problem-solving skills. You are not starting with a blank slate but instead are building on abilities and attitudes that you probably already have, including:

- The ability to distinguish between *data* and *theory* and between *evidence* and *conclusions*. This skill can also be described as the ability to differentiate between *sensory experience* (what you saw and heard) and *conceptualization* (what you think).
- The ability to generate hypotheses consistent with available data and to identify data needed to test hypotheses.
- An attitude of *relativism* rather than *dogmatism*, which allows you to realize that there is more than one way to work with a client.

Sometimes prior professional training has created habits that interfere with initial success with this method. For instance, attorneys integrate their reasoning and evidence, whereas the method in this book requires the evidence (data) to be presented first, without any reasoning (assessment). Mental health workers who write concise chart notes and protect the client's privacy by not providing too much specific content find it difficult to expand at length on both the client's content (data) and their own thought processes (assessment).

The learning process is much smoother when we accept that, as with most skills (as discussed under **BL3 Skill Deficits or Lack of Competence**), competence comes with experience, practice, and feedback. The development of case formulation skills is an ongoing, continual process, and improvement will occur in stages, as you gain more clinical experience and learn more about the clinical hypotheses. Chapters 3 through 9, on the clinical hypotheses, serve as an introduction or a review; they are not sufficient for learning a theory that you have never studied. Reading about ideas for treatment is not the same as learning how to implement those plans in therapy. Nevertheless, as a trainee, you will benefit from practicing conceptualization skills even when you are not yet skilled in all of the treatment approaches you will want to recommend.

One thing that this book does not teach is how to convince your supervisors to endorse an integrative approach if they do not already lean in that direction. Many training programs will limit your ability to implement an integrative treatment plan. Luckily, the method in this book, while intended to promote integration of hypotheses, also serves well as a format for organizing your thoughts and plans in a single theoretical orientation.

An anonymous student shared his thoughts about mastering case formulation skills:

> The improvement of my case formulation skills cannot be measured because I had none when this course began. To this point, I had not had any professor ask me to structure an analysis of a client in the way we did in this class. The method is reminiscent of my experience learning how to compose music. Without knowing how, I one day found myself writing music skillfully. I look back and realize that I learned to believe in myself. I feel the same way now about my case formulation skills.

Developing an integrative case formulation is a task that requires a comprehensive knowledge base, strong analytic skills, and creativity. This creative process must occur anew with each client—that is what this book is going to teach.

ACTIVITY 1.1 _____

Writing Your Baseline Case Formulation Report

Appendix III contains instructions for you to select a personal problem and write your first case formulation report, using the SOAP format on Form I.A in Appendix I. This will give you a chance to apply the ideas in this chapter and evaluate your baseline performance before studying the 28 hypotheses in Part II and the skills and standards in the chapters of Part III.

SUGGESTED READINGS

American Psychiatric Association. (2002). *Diagnostic and statistical manual of mental disorders* (4th ed., text rev.). Arlington, VA: American Psychiatric Association.

Lambert, M. J. (Ed.). (2004). *Bergin and Garfield's handbook of psychotherapy and behavior change* (5th ed.). Hoboken, NJ: Wiley.

Theories of Psychotherapy

Corsini, R. J. (2005). *Current psychotherapies* (7th ed.). Itasca, IL: F. E. Peacock.

Gurman, A. S., & Messer, S. B. (2003). *Essential psychotherapies: Contemporary theory and practice* (2nd ed.). New York: Guilford Press.

Prochaska, J. O., & Norcross, J. C. (2002). *Systems of psychotherapy: A transtheoretical analysis* (5th ed.). Belmont, CA: Wadsworth.

Sue, D. W., & Sue, D. (2002). *Counseling the culturally diverse: Theory and practice* (4th ed.). Hoboken, NJ: Wiley.

Integrative Approaches

Beitman, B. D. (1987). *The structure of individual psychotherapy.* New York: Guilford Press.

Beutler, L. E., & Harwood, T. M. (2000). *Prescriptive psychotherapy: A practical guide to systematic treatment selection.* New York: Oxford University Press.

Frances, A. J., Clarkin, J. F., & Perry, S. (1984). *Differential therapeutics in psychiatry: The art and science of treatment selection.* New York: Brunner/Routledge.

Frank, J., & Frank, J. (1991). *Persuasion and healing: A comparative study of psychotherapy* (3rd ed.). Baltimore, MD: Johns Hopkins University Press.

Gendlin, E. (1996). *Focusing-oriented psychotherapy: A manual of the experiential method.* New York: Guilford Press.

Hubble, M. A., Duncan, B. L., & Miller, S. D. (Eds.). (1999). *The heart and soul of change: What works in therapy.* Washington, DC: American Psychological Association.

Lazarus, A. (1976). *Multimodal behavior therapy.* New York: Springer.

Norcross, J. C. (Ed.). (1987). *Casebook of eclectic psychotherapy.* New York: Brunner Mazel.

Norcross, J. C. (Ed.). (2002). *Psychotherapy relationships that work: Therapist contributions and responsiveness to patient needs.* New York: Oxford University Press.

Norcross, J. C., & Goldfried, M. R. (2005). *Handbook of psychotherapy integration* (2nd ed.). New York: Oxford University Press.

Stricker, G., & Gold, J. R. (1993). *Comprehensive handbook of psychotherapy integration.* New York: Plenum Press.

Guides for Reports and Treatment Planning

Johnson, S. L. (2003). *Therapist's guide to clinical intervention: The 1-2-3's of treatment planning* (2nd ed.). San Diego, CA: Academic Press.

Jongsma, A. E., & Peterson, L. M. (2003). *The complete adult psychotherapy treatment planner* (3rd ed.). Hoboken, NJ: Wiley.

Kennedy, J. A. (2003). *Fundamentals of psychiatric treatment planning* (2nd ed.). Washington, DC: American Psychiatric Association.

Maruish, M. E. (2002). *Essentials of treatment planning.* Hoboken, NJ: Wiley.

Zuckerman, E. L. (2000). *Clinician's thesaurus: The guidebook for writing psychological reports* (5th ed.). New York: Guilford Press.

Chapter 2

GATHERING DATA

The quality of the entire case formulation rests on the therapist's ability to gather a complete, unbiased database. This chapter addresses the clinical interview, which is the primary source for building a client database in outpatient settings. This chapter also provides helpful frameworks and tools for gathering and organizing data.

DATA-GATHERING TASKS

In an interview with a client, the tasks of gathering data, testing hypotheses, and providing helpful interventions are intertwined. This fluid and often circular process contrasts with the linear organization of data, explanations, and interventions in the formal case formulation report. Because the client undergoes change from the very first contact with the therapist, it is impossible to construct a pure database of how things were before the therapist entered the scene. For instance, the instillation of hope that occurs from making a phone call and setting an appointment with a therapist alters slightly the emotions and beliefs that are part of the client's presenting problem (the data). Furthermore, the very nature of the relationship, the personality of the therapist, and the context and setting of the interview all influence the data. In the context of seeking help from a culturally designated expert, the client will take the most neutral message from the therapist—a head nod, silence, or "uh-huh"—as an opinion, instruction, or advice. Even Carl Rogers selectively reinforced certain material and responded with less enthusiasm to other material; not surprisingly, the reinforced content increased in frequency and the other types of content decreased. The idea that the therapist can be a "blank screen" has largely been abandoned because it is widely recognized that a therapist's distant, removed manner is far from neutral. Instead, clients experience this as cold and hostile.

Part of your training should include feedback to develop an awareness of how other people perceive and respond to you. You also need to be aware of your values, emotional reactions, cognitive filters, defensive tendencies, and cultural factors (which may differ from those of the client) to prevent contaminating and biasing the data. Through supervision and consultation with more experienced therapists, as well as peers in a training program, you will learn how to interpret data from the unique interpersonal dynamics of your relationship with a specific client.

Data Gathering from a "Not-Knowing" Position

In many clinical settings, trainees are taught to conduct an intake from a predetermined outline, often with a questionnaire in hand. Even if not following a written outline, many interviewers structure questions according to the categories of the report they know they are going to have to write. These approaches not only restrict and shape the client's *content* but also neglect the importance of the client's *process:* The "how" of the client's storytelling is a significant part of the database. It is important to gather data about how the client relates to a stranger, how she organizes her story, her approach to the help-seeking role, her degree of initiative or passivity, and so on.

Freedman and Combs (1996) wrote:

> When we meet people for the first time, we want to understand the meaning of their stories for *them*. This means turning our backs on "expert" filters: not listening for chief complaints; not "gathering" the pertinent-to-us-as-experts bits of diagnostic information interspersed in their stories; not hearing their anecdotes as matrices within which resources are embedded; not listening for surface hints about what the core problem "really" is; and not comparing the selves they portray in their stories to normative standards. Instead, we try to put ourselves in the shoes of the people we work with and understand, from their perspective, in their languages, what has led them to seek our assistance. (p. 44)

Expert filters and problem identification tasks are necessary, but they must be postponed until you grasp what it is like to be *inside* the client's reality.

Empathic Relationship

Research has consistently found that therapeutic success is facilitated by therapists who show warmth, understanding, and acceptance (Beutler, Machado, & Neufeldt, 1994; Lambert & Ogles, 2004). Empathic listening not only is a tool for effective data gathering but also a potent therapeutic factor. Lambert and Ogles (2004) even noted in their comprehensive review of the literature that relationship factors (e.g., trust, warmth, understanding, acceptance, kindness, and human wisdom) may have a greater effect on therapeutic change than do specific techniques (p. 181). People feel better when they have a chance to ventilate and to talk at length, without being rushed, while having the full attention of an empathic, patient listener who is calm, interested, respectful, concerned, and focused. If clients begin to trust that you are a caring human being, they are more likely to reveal parts of themselves that are usually hidden from others. However, when a therapist is working with a client from a different culture, the challenge to achieve and demonstrate understanding is greater and requires not only the knowledge found in texts on cultural diversity (e.g., T. B. Smith, 2004; D. W. Sue & Sue, 2002) but also the willingness to do research after your first encounter with a new client.

Although the words *gather data* and *interview* probably evoke thoughts of *asking questions,* and questions are necessary for data gathering, they are not sufficient; questions must be balanced by statements—paraphrases, summaries, and reflections—that show your understanding of what the client is expressing. Such empathic reflection is powerful and effective because it accomplishes the following goals:

- It develops rapport and helps the client feel understood, respected, and valued.
- It gathers data with statements and serves the same function as an open question, getting the client to elaborate on a topic.
- It makes clear to clients that they are the sole source of data regarding their internal world of feelings and thoughts.

Avoid Premature "Fixing"

Therapists' techniques fall into two broad categories:

1. *Exploring:* You are receptive and curious, gathering data without trying to produce change. Your *no-change agenda* is to discover *what is* and to re-mind yourself of the explorer role with the saying, "take only photos and leave only footprints."
2. *Intervening:* You are consciously trying to intervene and help the client achieve goals. You have a *change agenda.*

Restrain yourself from intervening until you have a formulation to guide you.

In my experience, the biggest challenge for beginning therapists is to resist the impulse to *fix* the client. In my practice sessions, trainees are asked to go 15 minutes in pure exploratory mode and to end with a summary. The vast majority of trainees find it difficult to abstain from a change agenda and will sneak some advice and suggestions into their final sentences.

Rushing to action violates the principles of good problem solving: *gather data, identify problems, decide on goals, test hypotheses, and then move toward solutions.* Intervening too quickly will cut short your data gathering, distort the data that you do gather, and, if your attempted solutions fail, undermine the client's confidence in your abilities. Premature fixing may even send a disrespectful message to the client—as if the problem is so easy and he is so incompetent—that you can solve in 1 hour what he has possibly struggled with for months. You must start with data gathering and hypothesis testing as your primary tasks, and know that the interventions you plan will benefit from your patience.

Exploratory Questions Produce Change

When you engage in competent data gathering, staying in a receptive, exploring mode, you are already engaged in a helpful process that will result in beneficial change. There is a paradox about exploring: The very act of patiently engaging in exploration is actually already an action. The metamessage is: *Your problem can be understood and if we think together, we will find solutions.*

From the client's point of view, the data-gathering process can be the beginning of new insights and ideas for constructive action. A skilled therapist blends listening and questioning in a way that causes important information to become explicit, exposing the complexity of a situation while also achieving clarity. Certain techniques of data gathering are challenging enough to produce beneficial change in the client because they get the client thinking in new ways. For instance, questions about past behavior, *Did you ask him about your feelings?* carry the metamessage, *If you do that, things will be better.* Basic questions like *When did you first feel that way?* followed by *What was happening in your life at that time?* make the client curious about causation. Furthermore, in the process of gathering information, you are teaching problem-solving skills—that before you can come up with plans, you need to gather information and then think about it. You are even modeling impulse control when you resist your client's demands to tell her, immediately, what to do.

Use of Clinical Hypotheses

There is no such thing as a complete database, and it takes experience to know what is "good enough." Beginners normally err in two directions: (1) jumping to a formulation with insufficient information or (2) postponing action while they pursue details that are not necessary for creating a good formulation. The use of clinical hypotheses helps you judge what data are necessary to evaluate the utility of various hypotheses and gives you a sound basis to decide that you have enough data to support a specific formulation.

At the beginning of the first session, the client speaks freely and you begin to recognize that certain hypotheses seem to fit. As more information is revealed, some hypotheses are ruled out, while others are supported. As you explore these hypotheses, you focus the clinical interview on specific topics. If you recognize that several hypotheses fit the data, you begin to make judgments about which hypotheses will lead to the best treatment plans. To help in making these judgments, you need to gather even more data. New data appear in every session, providing information about the effectiveness of the treatment strategy, changes in the client's life situation, and new problems or goals that should be a focus of therapy.

Trial Interventions

Trial interventions allow the therapist to walk the line between data gathering and a change agenda. Such interventions are based on a specific hypothesis and are intended to gather data and test the validity of that hypothesis. Table 2.1

Table 2.1   Examples of Trial Interventions for Data-Gathering Purposes

What would your husband say if he were here?

Data desired: Does the client know the husband's point of view or has she been mind reading (**C2**)? Does the client understand that two people have different points of view and that her view is not the "truth" (**P3**)?

Possible benefits: The client could develop empathy for the husband. Possibilities for compromise and problem solving may become apparent.

How would you feel about role-playing this situation? I'll pretend to be your coworker and you can express whatever you think would be an effective approach to solving this problem. Then we can switch roles and you can show me how you think she will respond.

Data desired: What is the quality of the client's communication skills (**BL3**)? How much anxiety does the client have about confrontation (**BL2**)? The activity can give data about what the other person's behavior is like, which is useful for checking the validity of the client's interpretations (**C3**).

Possible benefit: The client could become less anxious and more confident, recognize that she is exaggerating the level of her coworker's hostility, and change some beliefs about how scary it is to confront a coworker.

I wonder if there is a similarity between the feelings you have with the group you are working with and feelings you had with your brother and sisters when you were little.

Data desired: The therapist is exploring whether there is a reenactment of the dynamics in the family of origin (**P2**). If there is a similarity, there is a likelihood of a self-fulfilling prophecy (**C2**).

Possible benefit: The client could recognize that his response is part of a lifetime pattern.

---

gives examples, with hypotheses indicated by their codes (refer to Chart II.A in Appendix II for the list of hypotheses with codes).

Cultural Issues and Data Gathering

Appendix I of the *Diagnostic and Statistical Manual of Mental Disorders,* fourth edition, text revision (*DSM-IV-TR*) provides guidelines for developing a cultural formulation, requiring that data be gathered in four categories:

1. *Cultural identity:* Ethnic or cultural reference groups, degree of involvement with both host and original culture, and language abilities and preferences.
2. *Cultural explanations of illness:* Idioms of distress, the meaning and perceived severity of symptoms, perceived causes and explanations; and preferences and experiences with types of care.
3. *Cultural factors related to psychosocial environment and levels of functioning:* Social stressors, supports, and role of religion and kin networks.
4. *Cultural elements of the relationship between the individual and the clinician:* Differences in culture and social status and possible difficulties these differences may cause in diagnosis and treatment.

Part of cultural competence is learning the importance of overcoming your unconscious biases and prejudices. You must treat each client as a unique individual and not make assumptions or impose stereotypes. When you gather data, you learn from the client's own words how he describes his cultural identification, and you gather data to establish the level of acculturation of the client and his family members. You can learn about the specific cultural messages that have been internalized as well as those that have not been. You cannot generalize from the textbook summary of a culture to an understanding of the specific client in front of you.

During the first session, you must not only gather important cultural data but also create good rapport and establish your credibility in a manner that is sensitive to the client's culture. After the first session with the client, it is important to start doing research on the cultural factors relevant to your client. For instance, if the client is a Japanese American who was born in this country in the past 65 years, you need to be aware of the impact of internment camps during World War II, not only on the people who endured the experience but also on their descendents. If the client comes from another country, you need to be eager to learn about that country's history and culture (the topic of cultural competence is also addressed under hypothesis **SCE2** in Chapter 9).

Self-Report Questionnaires

An inventory of depression or anxiety, such as Beck's Depression Inventory, provides a baseline of distress and can be readministered at various intervals to monitor progress and at the end of therapy to measure outcome and document improvement. The use of such scales is common with managed care companies seeking to increase accountability and researchers wanting to find empirical support for treatments. Other examples of questionnaires include a reinforcement survey, which allows the client to identify potential pleasurable experiences and rewards for behavioral interventions (**BL1**), and Adler's Lifestyle Questionnaire, which elicits information about the early family constellation (**P2**).

Note Taking

When therapists take continual notes throughout the intake, they interfere with the empathic, genuine human connection that facilitates the optimal flow of the client's story. A few notes are fine and shared note-taking activities are often productive. Some clients appreciate note-taking because it shows that an expert is listening and taking them seriously. However, a therapist who sits with a pad in hand, frantically trying to get down every word, is damaging the database, as well as the therapeutic rapport. In training settings, the ability to tape-record your therapy sessions reduces anxiety about, and usually builds trust in, the quality of your memory.

INTAKE PROCESSES

The term *intake* is commonly used for the initial session. In some mental health clinics, a staff member conducts a single intake interview, writes up an intake report, and presents the case at a staff meeting, where the client is assigned to a therapist. This separate intake process is necessary for screening for emergencies and for selecting an appropriate therapist, especially when there are trainees of differing levels of experience or when there are staff therapists with varying specializations.

If this is the setup at your clinic, then from the client's point of view, the first meeting with you represents a second intake session, and he may feel frustrated at having to start over again. Although the database already in the chart is useful, it would be a mistake for you to rely on it. Gather your own database, regardless of how much information you receive in a chart or staff meeting.

Begin the first contact with a client by asking for the whole story to be told from the beginning. You should view your first two or three sessions as the intake: Inform the client that these sessions are an *assessment phase,* after which you will offer recommendations for treatment. At that point, the client can accept, reject, negotiate, and learn about alternatives. With the "informed consent" of the client, a verbal contract exists for a certain type of therapy, and therapy begins.

Realizing that there are a few sessions to arrive at a formulation takes the pressure off the first session; however, you still must use the first session to test the emergency hypotheses (**B1** in Chapter 3 and **CS1** in Chapter 4). You need to rule out the need for crisis intervention, medical referral, hospitalization, mandated reporting, and other types of required action on your part. Once hypotheses of this nature are eliminated, you can view the data-gathering and hypothesis-generating process in a more leisurely and creative fashion. There are several sessions to get to know the person and to test relevant hypotheses, so you can create a pace that is "in tune" with the individual client. Otherwise, you are so preoccupied with the data-gathering task that it is easy to turn into an interrogator.

Structuring Time

A good initial session generally has three phases, providing a balance between structure and ambiguity. In the beginning, you should be as nondirective as possible, encouraging the client to tell the story, responding with empathy and interest. Then you can shift into focused exploration, gathering data while continuing to be empathic. Table 2.2 describes the phases in more detail.

Interviewing Skills

Because the clinical interview is the chief tool of data gathering, the quality of the data is dependent on the quality of the interviewer's skills. Therapists must have the capacity for empathy and the ability to make the client feel understood and valued. They must have the ability to describe the client's process and understand the relationship, to gauge the credibility of the client as a source of in-

Table 2.2   Three Phases of First Interviews

Phase 1: Nondirective Data Gathering

Open-ended questions help the client begin his story without direction or structure. If a prompt is needed, invite the client to tell you what is troubling him or why he is seeking help at this time. You want the client's story to flow, unobstructed, in his own words and style. To see if the client feels understood, check with him by paraphrasing periodically. If you ask a direct question, it must be vague enough to let the client choose the direction. In the first phase of the first interview, try to let go of expert filters and to keep an open mind so that you gather data without influencing it. Good rapport is your first priority.

Phase 2: Focused Exploration

Your goal is to begin to identify problems and outcomes and get relevant information for the timelines of recent and past history. When you choose to probe a specific area, it is important to create a bridge to what the client has been saying, rather than to switch into an interrogator mode. The therapist processes the client's information through the filters of hypotheses. When a specific hypothesis seems to fit, the therapist focuses the interview to gather specific data to test that hypothesis.

Phase 3: Closing

The therapist keeps track of time without being rude or distracting (it helps to have a table or wall clock that you can see while facing the client.) Near the end of the session, if an important topic, such as substance abuse, has been overlooked, you can ask direct questions. You might give a summary of what you've learned about the client, allowing the client to react to it and correct it, if necessary. Part of what you say may include elements of the case formulation: You can clarify problem titles and outcome goals and offer your own formulation hunches. At the end of the session, address certain business issues such as scheduling the next appointment, information about clinic policies and procedures, and fees.

formation, and also to glean data from the client's behavior. They also need skills to ask focused questions, without biasing the answers, to explore hypotheses.

As a therapist, you need to be competent in two styles and to be aware of the process in which you are engaged:

1. *Tracking:* You follow what the client says, with minimal intervention on your part, allowing the client to tell the story freely, in his or her own style, without interference. Your verbal responses follow directly from what the client just said; you do not make a leap to a different topic. You make efforts to match the client's tempo, choice of language, and body posture.

2. *Leading:* You direct the client toward a focus of your choosing so that you can gather specific data, test hypotheses, make necessary evaluations, and develop your formulation. You have the ability to use both open and closed questions, as well as statements, to direct the flow of the interview.

Although those styles may mingle in your exploration, each response you make should be clearly one or the other, or the client will pick up mixed messages. In addition, you need to be able to tolerate silence—not only permitting several beats after the client stops talking but also allowing a period of a minute or more, for the client to reflect on what is said and have a pause, which allows her to take the initiative. When you feel it appropriate to break a silence, your prompt should invite the client to share what was going on inside rather than introduce a change of topic.

Exploring a Specific Problem

When you are ready to sit down and start working on your case formulation, your first two tasks will be *problem identification* and specification of *outcome goals,* so the most important topics during the intake process are what brings the client to therapy right now and what he or she hopes to gain. Table 2.3 shows four "frames" (Linden, 1998) for exploring a specific problem: (1) the *problem,* (2) the *outcome,* (3) the *obstacles,* and (4) the *resources.* The most commonly used frame in clinical practice is the problem frame, focusing on "what's wrong" and the etiology of the problem—events in the past that help explain causation. Often neglected is the outcome frame—the picture of the desired future. Clarifying realistic, achievable goals helps define the problem, provides specific goals for treatment, and instills hope in clients. Once a problem is explored and a desirable future state is identified, some clients will realize they already have the resources to attain their goals. However, when there is a *gap between the present problem state and the desired future,* it is useful to focus on obstacles and resources. What barriers, both internal and external, exist? What would it take for the client to achieve the desired outcome?

One of the most useful tools for organizing data about the presenting problem and its development is the use of a recent history timeline—a horizontal line with the right end representing the present moment in time and the left end a designated amount of time prior to now. In inpatient settings, using the acronym PTA (prior to admission) is convenient shorthand for reporting time sequences. The following is a sample for a client referred for problems with handling stress.

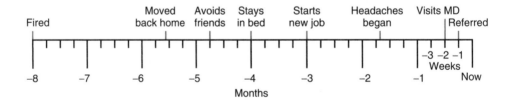

Using the BASIC SID

Arnold Lazarus (1981) created the acronym, BASIC ID, which stands for seven modalities: **B**ehavior, **A**ffect, **S**ensation, **I**magery, **C**ognition, **I**nterpersonal, and **D**rug/Biology (the letter D instead of B was chosen for the last letter as a humorous reference to the id of Freudian theory). A growing awareness of the spiritual and religious issues that come up in therapy (Richards & Bergin, 2000; Shafranske, 1996; Sperry, 2001) supports the addition of the Spiritual domain to the BASIC ID, making the acronym BASIC SID. Table 2.4 explains the eight do-

Table 2.3   Four Frames for Exploring a Specific Problem

Problem What's wrong? Since when? Why now?	**Description of the problem:** What are the complaints, symptoms, signs of distress? What is the "operational definition" of the problem behavior? **When and how was the onset?** Are there specific precipitating events? External stressors? Positive changes that tax an individual's coping abilities? What was time and cause of onset (if acute)? A specific event that triggered the presenting problem? A turning point when the problems began? **What has been the course of development of the problem?** If the problem seems to be chronic, look for the point in time when things started becoming worse. **Specific details of progressive deterioration:** Look for evidence of downward spirals. Do poor efforts to solve problems create new problems? Does increased stress lead to greater cognitive distortions followed by increased disorganization of behavior? **What is the history?** Are there prior episodes and early relevant experiences? When has the problem not occurred? Are there examples of successful coping? **What has the client already done to try to solve this?** What has been helpful? What has made things worse? Are there examples of independent use of resources?
Outcome What do you want?	How would things be different if the problem were resolved? What do you desire for the future? What is your vision of how it would be if the problem were solved? What are the outcome goals? If you woke up tomorrow morning and the problem was gone, how would your life be different? Describe what the day would be like.
Obstacles Barriers to getting what you want.	What prevents the achievement of your desired goals? What stops you? How do you stop yourself? Are there internal barriers in the form of thoughts or feelings? Are there external, environmental obstacles and barriers? Are there family members who are creating obstacles? Are there social or cultural barriers?
Resources What would help you get what you want?	What coping skills do you already have that can be applied to solving the problem and achieving the desired outcome? What strengths and assets have you demonstrated in the past that will help you with this problem? Have you been successful before in a similar situation? What social supports are available? Are there environmental changes or material tools that would help? What knowledge do you need? What community resources could help? What new skills are needed?

Table 2.4   The BASIC SID: An Adaptation of Lazarus's BASIC ID

Category	Examples of Data
B **Behavior** What the person is doing and not doing; what others can observe; the quality of skills.	Specific description of observable behavior. Excessive behaviors—occur too intensely or frequently. Skills that are present or absent. Activities that are engaged in or avoided.
A **Affect** Internal experience and overt verbal and nonverbal expression of feelings.	The term *affect* in the Mental Status Exam refers to observed manifestations of feelings; here it has a broader meaning. Mood (the subjective state) and congruence or incongruence with outward expressions. Level of awareness of own feelings. Level of expression of feelings to others. The labels for feelings that are experienced.
S **Sensation** Awareness of the body; use of senses; sensory data with minimal filtering through cognition.	Functioning of sensory organs. Presence of hallucinations or perceptual illusions. Presence of pain or muscular tension. Excessive sensitivity to environmental stimuli. What the person heard (use quotations) and saw (concrete experiential data).
I **Imagery** Mental imagery, about past, present, or future; fantasies and dreams.	Obsessive mental images. Disturbing nightmares. Distorted body image. Flashbacks of past trauma. Responses to guided imagery activity.
C **Cognitive** Constructed meaning; self-talk; beliefs and schemas; information-processing skills and other mental abilities.	Content of thought (e.g., ideas expressed; self-talk). Process of thought (e.g., tangential or circumstantial). Style of thinking (e.g., rigid or flexible). Errors of logic and reason (e.g., overgeneralization). Quality of cognitive skills (e.g., problem solving). Cognitive symptoms (e.g., obsessions about contamination). Description of beliefs, standards, assumptions, expectations, and rules.

Table 2.4 *(Continued)*

	Category	Examples of Data
S	**Spiritual** Spirit or soul; religion as well as non-religious aspects of spirituality; creativity; moral issues; and the lack of spirituality.	Beliefs regarding Supreme Being. Identification with religious group. Spiritual and religious practices, private and communal. Spiritual resources and activities (e.g., meditation, nature, and creativity). Conscience, moral code, guilt, forgiveness.
I	**Interpersonal** Relationships with others; family; membership in social groups; cultural factors; and issues of social injustice.	Degree of social isolation and social support. Quality of relationships: family, friendship, and work. Presence of socially unacceptable behavior. Cultural/ethnic/racial identity. Level of acculturation. Experiences with racism and social oppression. Level of interpersonal skills.
D	**Drug and Biological** Physiology, biology, genetics, medical issues; use of legal and illegal drugs, including alcohol.	Use of alcohol and illegal substances. Use of prescription medications. Degree of compliance with medical instructions. Symptoms of delirium or dementia. State of health, presence of illness. Problems with weight, eating, or biological effects of stress.

mains, providing examples of data. Form I.B in Appendix I is a blank chart for you to copy and use with your clients.

Having an acronym assures that you are being thorough and comprehensive in your data gathering. We all have a tendency to view client problems through a preferred lens, and by using eight different lenses, you are less likely to overlook important information. Use the BASIC SID between sessions to review the data you have gathered and to set goals for future exploration. It can also operate as a template in your mind as you face the client. When you are ready to focus the exploration, you mentally review the acronym: *Which modalities has the client already described? What other modalities would I like to learn about?* Remember that it is less important to identify the "right" category for a specific bit of information than it is to be thorough. For instance, descriptions of social behavior fit under **Behavior** as well as **Interpersonal;** hallucinations are a disturbance of sensory processing (**Sensation**) as well as the creation of mental images (**Imagery**).

Table 2.5 gives an example of the BASIC SID as a data-gathering guide for a client whose main complaint was "procrastination"—defined with the problem title: *Difficulty completing an important project.*

ACTIVITY 2.1

Practice with the BASIC SID

This activity in Appendix III asks you to use the BASIC SID on yourself and then with a partner.

Internal Processing

It is important to have tools to understand the client's *internal processing*—how the client links thoughts, feelings, images, and sensations. The founders of Neurolinguistic Programming (NLP; Bandler & Grinder, 1990; Cameron-Bandler, 1985) were interested in how people encode and *program* their experience, through words, pictures, sounds, emotions, movements, and sensations. They use the term *representational systems* (*rep system* for short) for the different modalities for storing and processing experiences. A small proportion of experience is represented through taste and smell; the majority of our sensing occurs through sight (visual), hearing (auditory), and awareness of emotions and the body (kinesthetic). For therapists to communicate and organize these types of data, it is convenient to use the letters **V, A, K** as shorthand.

- **Visual (V):** What we see in the external environment and our internal visual imagery.
- **Auditory (A):** External and internal sounds, including the voices of our internal speech.
- **Kinesthetic (K):** Experiences in our bodies, including emotions, bodily sensations, movement, and the sense of touch.

Laborde (1987) provides a metaphor that explains how rep systems work:

It is as if each of us were an elaborate television set with five recording devices tuned to pick up five different stations. One station transmits only sound, another only pictures. One sends feelings, and the last two stations send tastes and smells. We have only one screen for our conscious mind. We switch from station to station, favoring one at a time over the others. All the information from the other four channels is being recorded, but not tended to consciously. (p. 52)

To continue this metaphor, consider the possibility that people tend to trust one station more than the others. They pay attention to data, retrieve memories, and communicate with words from their preferred modality.

Table 2.5   Data Gathering, Using the BASIC SID, for *Difficulty Completing Project*

Behavior

What specifically does she do to avoid working on the project?

What exactly are her behaviors when she enters her office and faces the computer?

What writing skills might she be lacking?

Does she know how to use practical skills of time and project management? Can she break the task into "baby steps" and set reasonable goals for a specific time period?

Identify specific excess behaviors: what are antecedents (triggers) and consequences (reinforcers)?

Identify deficient or absent (desired) behaviors: Are they in the client's behavioral repertoire?

Affect

Insert feeling words to fit in this frame: You feel _____ , _____ , _____ because of your difficulties completing your project.

Are there symptoms of depression or anxiety interfering with her work?

Is her productivity related to specific mood states?

Does she have control over the ability to access a confident, productive emotional state?

What are sources of her fears?

In what ways does anger, towards self and towards others, contribute to her difficulties?

Sensation

What form does the anxiety take? Where in her body does she experience tension?

Is there physical discomfort associated with sitting at the computer?

What visual input from the environment affects the problem?

What auditory input from the environment affects the problem?

Has she gathered sensory data about her assumptions? What specifically has she been told would happen if she doesn't complete it by a certain date?

Imagery

Are there visual images that either impede or facilitate the process?

Can she visualize herself actually holding the completed document in her hand?

What images come to mind when she thinks of earlier experiences in her life working on a major project?

Has she had any dreams lately?

Cognitive

What kind of self-talk does she have when she sits down to work on the project?

What does completing this project mean to her?

Does she value other activities more than completing the project?

What kinds of underlying schemas does she have about success, achievement, and perfectionism?

What is her explanation for her difficulties? What ideas does she have about the problem and a possible solution?

What *shoulds* and *can'ts* are involved?

(continued)

Table 2.5   *(Continued)*

Spiritual

Is she forcing herself to work every day, or is she allowing herself a guilt-free Sabbath day of rest?

Does she believe in a higher power and can that belief serve as a resource in dealing with this problem?

What spiritual needs are being neglected during this period of hard work and stress?

Is it possible that there is a moral dilemma that is keeping her "stuck"?

Interpersonal

What rewards and punishments do people in her social world offer her, related to working or not working on her project?

What do other people actually say to her about her work, her problem, her topic?

In terms of her culture, what does completion mean?

Will her social role change when she completes the project?

Does "finishing" and "not finishing" have an impact on her family system?

How does her relationship with boss and/or coworkers affect completion of this project?

Drug and Biology

Are there health issues that might be interfering?

How is her sleep and appetite?

Is she using alcohol or drugs?

Could she benefit from some kind of pharmacological agent?

Beginner therapists commonly ask, *How do you feel?* This practice taps into the client's kinesthetic modality. Instead, it is preferable to ask neutral questions such as *What are you experiencing?* so that you do not unintentionally direct the client into a particular sensory modality. Therapists should learn about their own preferred rep system, develop skills in identifying the preferred rep system of a client, and have the flexibility to create verbal responses from all rep systems. Table 2.6 presents five important applications of V-A-K awareness for the data-gathering process.

More about internal processing is discussed in Chapter 5 under **BL1 Antecedents and Consequences:** In conducting a behavioral analysis, consider not only the client's self-talk and other cognitive mediation but also how her internal processing of sensory information affects both problem and desired behaviors.

Metamodel Questions

The developers of NLP made a huge contribution when they explained how people create faulty mental maps of reality, failing to test their linguistic/cognitive models against the experience of their senses. Neurolinguistic Programming practitioners use the term *metaperspective* to describe the understanding that a representation of reality is not the same as reality—"the map is not the territory" and "the menu is not the meal."

Table 2.6   Representational Systems (V-A-K) and Data Gathering

Identifying the Client's Leading Representational System

Some clients will tell their story using all possible modalities. Others will rely primarily on one, which can be called the "primary" or leading representational (rep) system. As clients tell stories, without direction or interruption, you can identify the leading system and recognize which modalities are neglected.

Developing Good Rapport

Good rapport is developed by matching the *rep system* that the client is using. For instance, when a therapist wants to communicate understanding, there are different ways to word the message:

V: I see what you mean or I can picture that clearly.
A: I hear you or That sounds right.
K: I grasp what you mean or That feels right.

People who rely on the visual modality are forming pictures in their minds. It is possible that if you lock eyes with such a client in an attempt to make good eye contact, you will be interfering with her internal processing.

Exploring Underused Representational Systems

At an appropriate time, you can lead the client with a specific question into the underused system. For instance, you can ask a person who leads with the auditory system, What pictures come to mind? What are you feeling right now? A person who is very emotional and describes events in colorful visual impressions could be asked auditory questions: What were you hearing during the argument? What were you saying to yourself? You can also give homework assignments that force a person to attend to a neglected modality. By leading the person into a different modality, you gather data and at the same time, expand awareness. The underused rep system often carries the very resources that the person needs to solve a problem.

Responding after a Period of Silence

If the client is barraged with your questions and quick verbal responses, there is no time for internal processing during the session. Explain to the client that you will not always have a response and that it is okay to take time to process (a neutral word) what is being experienced. If you break the silence with an invitation, you can word it neutrally, yet show your interest in understanding the internal experience:

I wonder what you're experiencing now?

Would you be willing to share what's going on inside?

Eye Movement as Clues to Internal Processing

NLP practitioners suggest eye movements provide clues to the type of internal data that is being accessed. Upward eye movements reflect visual processing, and lowered eyes occur when the person is either experiencing feelings or accessing internal speech. By attending to the client's eye movements as they correspond to the different types of content in the session, you can determine if there are reliable eye movement clues for this particular individual's internal processing. When the client is silent, it is useful to attend to eye movement for two reasons: (1) It convinces you that "something is going on in there." Many beginning therapists get anxious during silence because they think "nothing is happening," and then think "it's my responsibility to make something happen." (2) It gives you clues on how to break a silence and show empathic attunement. For instance, if you know your client's eyes go up when she is visualizing, and you see that movement during silence, you can gently ask, Are you picturing something you'd care to share with me?

Bandler and Grinder (1990) explain that because we use words to store, file, and retrieve our experiences, there is a natural tendency to *delete* (eliminate information), *generalize* (ignore differences), and *distort* (classify information arbitrarily or erroneously). Furthermore, because we code in words, we can only code those events for which we have words.

> There is an inevitable gap between a person's model of the world (recognized through the use of language) and his or her real-world experiences.

To reduce this gap, the therapist needs a set of tools for recognizing, exploring, and challenging the information presented by the client. To meet this goal, Bandler and Grinder created a set of linguistic information-gathering tools that they called the *Metamodel*. They defined a set of nine categories of deletion, overgeneralization, and distortion, which together can be called "metamodel violations" (the word "violation" means that there is an insufficiency in the verbalized cognitive map). The therapist's task is to search for specific data about concrete experience, moving the client from the cognitive level to sensory information.

For instance, when a client says that she is ending a friendship with her best girlfriend because *she betrayed me,* the therapist asks *How specifically did she betray you?* Here are examples of two different types of answers:

1. **Cognitive answer (no sensory data):** *She was very disloyal. She showed me that she is completely untrustworthy.*

2. **Sensory-specific answer:** *She told me that she is dating my ex-boyfriend.*

You want the client's answer to be "fully specified," containing enough concrete sensory data to be a clear statement about reality. Some clients reveal very little concrete information, seeming to be accessing stored language and meaning systems rather than sensory data. These clients *are* storing sensory experience but they will need direction to access it. Metamodel questions, presented in Table 2.7, provide tools for achieving this direction. They gather data and challenge the client to recognize her own faulty thinking, often leading to new discoveries. Consider the following response to the question above:

> **Insightful answer:** *I guess I'm wrong to say that she betrayed me. I broke up with him 10 years ago, and I never told her I still have any feelings for him.*

For each category of "violation," there is a specific type of question. Table 2.7 presents the *Metamodel* with sample questions and answers for each category. You will realize that the client's words can be classified in more than one category and could be responded to with different questions. Furthermore, the answers could be followed up with additional questions to get more specific sensory-specific data.

Table 2.7 Metamodel Questions

Metamodel Violation	Examples	
Deletion	**Client's Words**	I am afraid.
Some details are missing.	**Metamodel Question**	Of what, specifically?
Use brief information gathering questions like *where*, *when*, of *what*, by *whom*.	**Sensory-Specific Answer**	That he will say something mean to me.
Lack of Referential Index	**Client's Words**	Men can't be trusted.
Vague pronoun, vague plural or abstract noun.	**Metamodel Question**	Which man, specifically, can't you trust?
Ask for identification of the specific people or things that are being referred to.	**Sensory-Specific Answer**	I can't trust Joe, I caught him in several lies.
Unspecified Verb	**Client's Words**	He bullies other kids.
Vague about the observable actions and behaviors.	**Metamodel Question**	How specifically does he bully them?
Ask *how* to elicit specific actions and behaviors.	**Sensory-Specific Answer**	He threatens to hit them if they don't give him some of their lunch.
Nominalization	**Client's Words**	Our relationship is dull.
An ongoing process that is turned into a static thing by using an abstract noun.	**Metamodel Question**	How specifically are you relating?
Avoid repeating the noun and ask the unspecified verb question.	**Sensory-Specific Answer**	We spend the evenings and weekends in separate rooms watching different TVs.
Universal Quantifier	**Client's Words**	I'm never included.
Overgeneralization; all-or-nothing thinking.	**Metamodel Question**	Never? Have you *ever* been included?
Exaggerate the word or ask for an exception. In the answer, the client either recognizes it is as an overgeneralization or provides information to prove that it is valid representation of experience.	**Sensory-Specific Answer**	**Example 1:** I can remember two times when they invited me. **Example 2:** No, and once when I asked if I could come, they said, "No, we don't want your company."
Modal Operator	**Client's Words**	I. I can't tell him how I feel. II. I have to spend every Sunday with my mother.
Imposed limits; shoulds and can'ts.	**Metamodel Question**	I. What stops you? II. What would happen if you didn't?
I. For *can'ts*—Search for obstacle. II. For *shoulds*—Examine imagined consequences of not obeying "should."	**Sensory-Specific Answer**	I. I have a fear of discovering that I care more than he does. II. My mother will complain about what a bad son I am.

(continued)

Table 2.7 *(Continued)*

Metamodel Violation	Examples	
Mind Reading Making assumptions about another person's feelings, thoughts, or intentions. Search for sensory data which support the assumption; this can challenge the client to stop mind reading.	**Client's Words**	He wants me to fail.
	Metamodel Question	How specifically do you know?
	Sensory-Specific Answer	**Example 1:** I guess I don't really know, I never asked him how he feels about it. **Example 2:** He told me that he hopes I don't pass the test.
Cause-Effect Errors There is a faulty assumption that A causes B, or that A prevents B. A common example is "another person makes me feel something" or "I would do it but _____ ." Challenge the causal link and search for disconfirming data; you may need to ask several questions to get the client to recognize that there is no proof of causation.	**Client's Words**	She makes me feel guilty.
	Metamodel Question	How are *your* guilty feelings *caused* by her? (Have you ever not felt guilty when she said that? Could you imagine feeling differently?)
	Sensory-Specific Answer	I guess I let her get to me, I suppose I could just feel sorry for her.
Lost Performative Imposed values; an unexamined platitude. Inquire about source of belief. You want the client to challenge the truth of the statement or take responsibility for choosing it as a personal value or preference.	**Client's Words**	Vacations are a waste of money.
	Metamodel Question	According to whom?
	Sensory-Specific Answer	**Example 1:** My parents always said that, but they were very poor, and I have lots of money and can decide to spend it the way I want. **Example 2:** According to me. I prefer to spend money on remodeling my home.

It takes several hours of drill for metamodel skills to become automatic. You listen to a sentence and then practice asking the right kind of question remembering that each sentence probably can be challenged in different ways. An answer invites another question, until the answer is sufficiently concrete and specific or the client recognizes the gap between belief and evidence. You would not bombard a client with question after question, but in a practice drill, the goal is to learn the metamodel rather than to develop sensitive counseling skills. The reward for this effort is that you can never again *not* take the meta-perspective. At that point, you discover that there are many ways, besides metamodel questions, to move away from cognitive labeling and descriptions to the real experiences:

- *Tell me the whole story of the argument you had, starting from the beginning.*
- *If I were watching you on TV, what would I be seeing?*
- *What is your definition of that word?*
- *Could you give me some examples?*
- *What specific actions and behaviors were you observing?*

ACTIVITY 2.2 _____

Metamodel Practice

This activity in Appendix III asks you to practice the skills from Table 2.7 on a list of client statements.

EXPLORATION OF THE COGNITIVE DOMAIN

You may have noticed that the question "why" is not one of the metamodel questions. That is because "why" asks for the client's reasons and explanations, which are elements of the cognitive rather than the sensory domain. There are other tactics for exploring the extremely broad and complex domain of thinking. There are many types of cognitive *contents* (e.g., belief, delusion, or superstition) and cognitive *processes* (e.g., deciding, blaming, or judging) that therapists can help clients identify and explore. The following list, although no means complete, shows the wide variety of cognitive concepts:

Abstractions	Dogmas	Perceptions
Appraisal	Expectations	Philosophy
Aspirations	Evaluations	Prediction
Assumptions	Formulation	Premises
Attributions	Hypotheses	Presuppositions
Beliefs	Ideas	Principles
Categorize	Ideology	Processing of information
Classify	Inferences	Realizations
Comprehension	Insight	Reasoning
Conceptualize	Interpretations	Rules
Conclusion	Judgments	Stereotypes
Constructs	Knowledge	Superstition
Convictions	Logic	Theories
Decision	Meaning	Thoughts
Deductions	Obsession	Understanding
Delusions	Opinions	Values

Notice how in the following questions the insertion of a cognitive word makes it clear to the client that you are interested in his unique belief system and thought processes.

- *What are the **rules** you have regarding first dates?*
- *What are your **values** about spending money?*
- *What **inferences** (or **conclusions**) did you draw from his behavior?*
- *What **meaning** do you give Valentine's Day cards?*
- *What kind of **reasoning** led you to conclude that he intended to marry you?*
- *What kind of **philosophy** do you have regarding child rearing?*
- *How do you **interpret** that?*
- *Tell me about how you formed these **judgments** of him?*
- *On what do you base that **opinion?***
- *What **insights** did you gain from your prior therapy?*

These questions strengthen the awareness of the client that she is the one who is constructing her reality; they are very effective with people who let emotions dominate reason.

Cognitive Empathy

In learning the skill of *empathic reflection,* trainees recognize the importance of understanding the emotional domain and using feeling words. To help clarify the cognitive domain, the response should have a cognitive word preceding the summary of the client's core meaning.

Instead of saying *So you feel very hurt because he rejected you,* you insert a word that emphasizes the client's thinking, and say *So you feel very hurt because you **interpreted** his behavior to be rejection.*

If the client says "If he cared, he would have visited me in the hospital," you can respond: *Your **assumption** is that if a person cares, he would just want to come visit,* or *One of your **rules** for friendship is that "if you care about a person, when they're sick, you have to pay a visit."*

Personal Meaning

Another task in exploring the cognitive domain is to become familiar with your client's unique "dictionary." Be cautious about making assumptions that you understand what a person means just because you understand a word: The same word often means different things to different people. Ask for a definition or for examples when you wish to clarify a word's meaning. For instance, if the client says she wants to become more "independent," you could offer any of these responses:

- *Explain what you mean by independent.*
- *What are some things you would be doing if you were more independent?*
- *What's an example of a time when you did feel independent?*

Take the attitude that you want to learn and understand and be alert to the possibility that your client might construe your question as a criticism—as if he chose the wrong word. Often it helps to explain ahead of time the concept of "personal definitions" and the importance of not making assumptions but rather understanding *exactly* what the client means.

George Kelly (1955), one of the earliest modern theorists to explore the importance of the cognitive model of the world, used the term *personal construct.* His premise was that if you can make the client aware of how he has constructed his own meaning in life, you can give him the tools to choose alternate ways of viewing his existence. A *construct* is a bipolar dimension, or dichotomy, such as "good-bad," "strong-weak," and "active-passive." The constructs that a person uses have significance for what he views as possible and desirable. Kelly advises us:

> To understand what your client means by a certain word, ask what the polar opposite would be. Be sure that you understand which pole is good and which is bad.

As a demonstration of this idea, cover the words on the right with your hand. Then examine the adjectives on the left and write down a word that represents the opposite of each, for you. Don't just quickly respond with an automatic antonym but rather think about the meaning for your life experience.

Aggressive	Passive, supportive, polite
Humorous	Serious, boring, solemn
Lazy	Ambitious, driven, productive
Compulsive	Spontaneous, disorganized, flexible

Note whether your choice of opposite was listed. Kelly (1955) believed that the most important constructs were developed with our families of origin and could be discovered by examining all the important people in your childhood in groups of three, asking "How are two of them alike and different from the third?" By writing down the word that describes the similar pair and the word that describes the third person, you arrive at a list of the bipolar constructs through which you filter experience.

Cognitive Classification Systems

To fully explore an individual's unique cognitive map, you need to know his or her classification systems. Any word or concept is part of a "cognitive family tree": The word has a "parent" category (a broader, more abstract concept of which it is an example); it has "siblings" (other members of that category, which are analogous or parallel); and it has "children" (component attributes or concrete examples).

That means there are three directions you need to explore—up, across, and down—which in information-processing terms is *chunking*. Here is an example of the chunking process for the word *dog*.

- *Chunking down:* Getting more specific, giving concrete attributes or examples: *a brown dog, a tame dog, or a pug.*
- *Chunking up:* Finding superordinate categories into which the concept fits. The dog can be viewed as a *canine, a domestic animal, a pet, a beloved family member, an object of fear, an annoying responsibility that keep me from traveling, or a nuisance that makes noise and keeps me awake.* When you are given two examples of an event or behavior, and you ask "How are those two similar?" you are instructing the client to "chunk up."
- *Chunking across:* Seeking other examples in the same category: *Dog and cat (pets), Dog and airplanes (things I'm afraid of), Dog and wolf (canines).*

It is unlikely that the therapist and client have the same classification system for a word—this is especially true when the client comes from a different culture. Table 2.8 shows the kinds of questions you would ask to explore the cognitive space surrounding a specific concept.

Asking chunking-type questions balance exploring and intervening. You are looking for data from the client's classification system, but usually the answer isn't readily available for retrieval. Instead, the client is pushed to think in new ways. Your questions are modeling an analytic approach and will move the conversation toward effective abstract thinking. The technique of *reframing*, explained in Chapter 6, is based on the process of chunking. When you ask the client *Can you think of any way that this is a good thing, not a problem?* or *What is the positive intention underlying this negative behavior?* you are asking him to chunk up, but to move from the current frame (bad things) to a different one (good things).

THE CLINICIAN AS OBJECTIVE OBSERVER

One of the most important rules for the first interview is to start by letting clients tell their stories in their own way. By asking an open question about the client's reasons for seeking therapy, you provide some ambiguity. You can then observe how the client responds to the lack of structure: how coherent the story is, whether the thought associations are tight or loose, and whether the connections between ideas are tangential, circumstantial, or appropriate. Your task is to describe the *mental status* of the client and to evaluate the type of relationship the client forms with you, a stranger and a helping professional. The Mental Status Exam (MSE; see Appendix II, Chart II.C) provides the clinician with a specific vocabulary and set categories of information to describe a client. This information is not raw data, but rather data that an experienced clinician has processed and evaluated. You take the client's story, as well as your own observations, and form certain conclusions, applying a technical vocabulary. For in-

Table 2.8   Exploring Cognitive Classification Systems

THE CLIENT'S CONCEPT: "MY HUSBAND'S ANGER PROBLEM."

Chunking Down (Getting More Concrete)

Can you give me a specific example? (He punches his hand in the door and there is a hole there now.)

How, specifically, does he show anger? (He yells and hits property, but doesn't hit people.)

In what specific contexts does it occur: where, when, with whom? (At home with family, never at work.)

What is the entire sequence of events from the minute he walks in the door to the moment of the anger outburst? (Client describes events, including her own behavior, and may recognize how she provokes him.)

Chunking Up (Getting More Abstract)

How would you categorize that behavior? (It is abusive, infantile, or a risk factor for a heart attack.)

What is the significance of this problem to you? (Makes me want a divorce; leads me to avoid sex.)

Do you view this as something that can be changed? (No, it is an unchangeable personality trait; yes, if he chooses to exercise self control.)

You say he has this anger problem and earlier you said that he thinks you nag him too much. Can there be any relation between these two things? (Both are things we do that push the other away, both are ways that we resemble our parents, both are things that we want to change about the other.)

What does his anger stem from? (He has trouble putting his feelings into words. He can't handle any frustration. He had an abusive father.)

What need does it meet or what purpose does it serve? (He gets to blow off steam in a safe environment. It lets him put the blame on others and avoid responsibility. It allows him to feel powerful instead of weak. He really wants to divorce me but wants me to be the one who takes the first step.)

Chunking Across

Referring to higher category that has been mentioned: Are there other examples besides angry outbursts? (No, otherwise he's a kind and considerate husband; yes, he jeopardizes his health by unhealthy eating and lack of exercise.)

Looking for opposites and exceptions: Can you think of situations when he didn't get angry when you expected him to? (When he was drinking water instead of alcohol, when I cook him a special meal.)

Looking for metaphors and analogies: If you were to describe his style of anger as a particular animal, what would it be? (A shark, a Chihuahua.) When you feel the same way he does, how do you express it? (The same way that he does, the "silent treatment.")

---

stance, the term *mood* refers to the client's description of his feeling state, whereas the term *affect* refers to the reactions and expressions observed by the clinician. *Inappropriate affect* is a judgment that involves comparing the affect with the content of the client's story. Zuckerman (2000) wrote a guide to report-writing that provides numerous examples of terminology for putting clinical observations into words.

The MSE is often described as *assessment*. However, this does not mean that it belongs in the assessment (A) section of the SOAP. Remember that the assessment section contains explanations of the problem, leading to a plan. The MSE contains descriptive terms applied by a professional expert (you) without conceptualizing or diagnosing. It therefore belongs in the objective (O) section of the SOAP (subjective data, objective data, assessment, and plan).

Each clinical setting will have its own preferred outline for the MSE. Appendix II, Chart II.C presents 15 categories with examples. Because the MSE is usually taught for use with patients with severe pathology, it is generally more difficult to describe a "normal" client than to describe one with pathology. To build objective observation skills, it is helpful to practice perceiving and describing people outside of clinical situations—something you can do when you're at a social gathering or a staff meeting at work.

Objective data is only as good as the awareness and competence of the clinician. Therapists need training and experience to be able to describe their clients with accuracy. The objectivity of the therapist can be compromised for many reasons: The client may remind the therapist of someone else, the client's issue may be similar to the therapist's unresolved conflicts, or strong needs or fears of the therapist may be aroused in the session. The term *countertransference* is a useful label for the variety of reasons why experienced and well-trained therapists might distort, misperceive, and bias the database. Although this term originates with psychodynamic theorists, it has become a widely used label for personal reactions of therapists.

Countertransference is not necessarily an obstacle to professional competence. If the therapist has insight and self-control, these reactions can be a valuable source of data about the client. When therapists tune into their feelings and impulses with a client, they can access important information:

- *Clues to how other people may respond to the client.*
- *Clues to the role in which the client tends to put others.*
- *Clues to feelings that the client may not be acknowledging in himself.*

After a session, and preferably in front of a video recording of it, you can explore what you were truly thinking and feeling at various points of the interview. The skills of recognizing and understanding such countertransference must be built into every training program. Trainees can watch videos of clients expressing especially difficult emotions (e.g., hostility, rage, dependency, helplessness, or seductiveness) and compare the accuracy of their perception and their emotional reactions with other members of the training group.

CLIENT HISTORY

In the typical intake or case history report, the client's history is organized into categories such as those appearing in Appendix II, Chart II.D: *Identifying information, presenting problem (and reason for referral), current situation, prior psychological treatment, family history, educational and occupational history, social and sexual history,* and other topics, when relevant, such as *military history.* When using the problem-oriented method (POM), data that apply to a specific problem title should be placed in the S section under that title.

As discussed in the previous *Intake Processes* section, you are encouraged to allow the interview to flow in a way that keeps the focus on the client and allows information to be revealed as part of the spontaneous storytelling. Although you may worry that information needed on paperwork may be missed if you don't follow an outline of topics, even more information will emerge if you focus on rapport and creating a safe environment. Rapport-building questions, which also elicit data about the client's history, include open-ended questions (*Tell me about your family*), probing questions that flow naturally from what the client has been saying (*Does this experience remind you of anything when you were young?*), or focused questions that are a coherent part of hypothesis-testing (*Could there be a pattern here that was developed in your family?*). At the end of the session, if you feel that there are gaps in the history, you can pose your structured questions.

Life History Timeline

By far the most useful tool for noting life history data is a timeline. Whereas the recent history timeline, described previously, covers the immediate period of time prior to the client's seeking help, the life history timeline covers the entire life. Once you know the client's current age or year of birth, you can draw a horizontal line slightly longer than the client's life span. Indicate the year of birth near the left end, allowing space prior to birth for genealogical information, data about pregnancy, and the parents' situation prior to birth. Then plug in all the important information, anchored by the age of the client. Form I.C in Appendix I can be copied for use in preparing timelines.

Creating a timeline immediately after a session, when your head is flooded with information, will give you confidence that you have a good memory and do not need to take notes during the session or follow a structured outline. With a timeline, you have a visual aid to understanding the stages, transitions, and key events in the client's life. Constructing a detailed timeline helps you organize information and engages your creativity in developing good formulations and recognizing important gaps in the database. When writing the formal report, the narrative of the database is already outlined, and you can organize the flow of the story, using the client's age (see Standard 17 in Chapter 13).

In addition, a timeline helps you organize data that clients, when permitted to tell their story freely, will often present haphazardly. The following example of information from an intake performed in 2004 for a 37-year-old woman shows how to figure out the client's age when it is not explicitly stated.

- **The date:** *We moved to California in August of 1991*—13 years ago, subtract that from 37 and she was 24.
- **The amount of time prior to the present day:** *My divorce was final 2 years ago*—when she was 35.
- **Reference to other events and contexts:**

  —*When my younger brother was 3*—You pinpoint the clients age at 7 because you know there is a 4-year difference.

  —*My daughter is 10 years old*—The client was 27 when she had this child.

  —*When I finished high school*—You estimate 18.

  —*I stayed in that job for 3 years and then I quit. I've been unemployed for 4 years.*—She held the job from ages 30 to 33, when her daughter was 3 to 6.

Once that information is put on a timeline, the life history is easier to grasp; additional facts can be added as the therapist learns them.

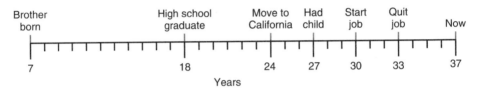

The events that you put on a timeline will depend on the client's life story. You definitely want to get information about past psychological problems, psychiatric treatment, medications, and so forth (remember that the recent history timeline has data about the onset and development of current symptoms). Here are some ideas about significant life history events:

- *Childhood and adolescence:* Births of siblings, deaths of grandparents, separations from parents, transitions in schooling, relocation to new neighborhoods, changes in school, changes in family composition from divorces and remarriages, special achievements, hobbies, activities, significant friendships, onset of puberty, first romantic relationship, driver's license, child-care responsibilities, beginning of sexual activity, first job.
- *Adulthood:* Move out of family home, post-high school education, employment milestones (e.g., change of jobs, promotion, periods of unemployment, retirement), marriage, separation, divorce, changes in family composition (e.g., birth of first child, birth of other children, last child leaves home), death of parents, special achievements, hobbies, activities, creative pursuits, geographic relocation, health problems, accidents, operations, chronic illnesses.

During case conferences and supervision groups, each person can draw a timeline and jot down notes as the speaker presents information. I regularly do this and find interesting connections or important gaps. Using a timeline side by side with the client during a session allows the client to discover important connections: *My mother must have been depressed at the time because my grandmother—her mother—had just died.*

A very effective way to develop a timeline is to instruct the client to create a list of "stepping stones" (Progoff, 1992). Here is how you might word your request: "Make a list of 10 to 12 turning points in your life: These should be events that were significant because they were the start of a new phase for you. They could be traditional milestones, like starting high school, but there should also be events that have personal meaning for you."

A person's life history needs to be understood in two different frameworks:

1. Psychological stages of development.
2. The historical and cultural context of a specific cohort.

Psychological Stages of Development

Form I.C in Appendix I contains notes to remind you of developmental stages, discussed later in Chapter 4, under **C3 Developmental Transitions** (review Tables 4.10 and 4.12). It is important to know what stage the person is currently grappling with as well as the relative success with which the tasks of prior developmental stages were accomplished. It helps to understand that normal development involves a disruption of the established personal equilibrium every 7 to 10 years for adults. This transition, sometimes a "developmental crisis," brings losses, challenges, and opportunities. In childhood and adolescence, the developmental tasks follow a predicted course, depending on age, but during adulthood in twenty-first century American culture, there is great variation in the sequence of developmental tasks. For certain cultural subgroups and cultures in other countries, there are very strict norms about the developmental stages of adulthood. People commonly evaluate where they are in life through comparisons with others and a yardstick of the age norms they have accepted.

The Client's Cohort and Culture

You need to contextualize your client's story in a broader social/cultural/historical context. If your client is the same age as you, and from the same culture, you can make assumptions that you are familiar with the historical and cultural events in this person's past history. Otherwise, it is important to have tools that help you understand the wider context of the life experience. *Cohort* refers to a group of people born at the same time. When you know a person's age, you also know the year of birth, and this gives you information about the person's life history in a specific historical context. An example of a cohort difference is age norms for marriage: In the 1950s, a woman who got married at 23 was older than expected—practically an "old maid," whereas in the present decade, 23 is considered fairly young to be a bride in many cultural groups.

Different cohorts can be given nicknames. The term *baby boomers* is applied to the cohort of people born after World War II who are now approaching 60. Sheehy (1996) called the cohort born between 1946 and 1955 the *Vietnam Generation* and those born from 1956 to 1965 the *Me Generation.*

When you know the cohort, you know the social, political, and economic factors that influenced life experience, including wars, the Depression, cultural movements (e.g., feminism or the civil rights movement), and so on. Different cohorts encounter different developmental challenges as they leave adolescence. You can speculate about the significance of entering the job market during the era of the Depression and the impact of feminism on women entering early adulthood during the late 1960s. Increased longevity and economic factors have radically changed the nature of development after the age of 50, as compared to what it was like for our parents. Years ago, age 70 was viewed as close to the end of life, whereas now it is often the beginning of a phase of at least 15 years, which can involve new friends and interests.

Part of your inquiry into the client's life history can be asking about key events: *Were there significant events in the world at that time that had an impact on you?* Members of one cohort will say the assassination of President Kennedy, whereas a younger cohort will say the explosion of the Challenger. Clinicians in future decades will need to be aware of the impact of September 11 and Hurricane Katrina, especially if their clients come from New York or New Orleans.

To facilitate an appreciation of how historical events and cultural changes impact each individual's life history, Form I.D in Appendix I provides an "American History Timeline" covering key events in history, entertainment, and technology from 1900 to 2005. In reviewing my choice of events, I recognize how my own life experience biased my judgments about what is important. The decade of the 1960s is extremely rich in detail because that was the period in my life when I experienced the most significant events for me (ages 14 to 24). I included the earthquake in LA, where I live, but not Hurricane Andrew on the East Coast.

To understand the relevance of cohort differences, imagine three different clients coming to you in the year 2000: (1) a 25-year-old woman, raised with a single mother; (2) a 55-year-old Black man (that's the term he prefers over African American); and (3) a 75-year-old upper middle-class widow. How do the events on the American History Timeline help a therapist understand their lives?

1. The 25-year-old woman was born in 1975. Her mother was probably influenced by the feminist movement. Divorce no longer carried a stigma. She may have grown up with expectations that, as a woman, she could make her own choices and function in life without depending on a husband.

2. The 55-year-old man was born in 1945 and was eligible for the draft during the Vietnam War. He might very well be a war veteran; he definitely

had friends who went to war and probably knew someone who was killed. The assassination of Martin Luther King when he was 23 probably was of enormous significance.

3. The 75-year-old woman who was born in 1925 was 35 in 1960. She could be the type of woman for whom Betty Friedan wrote her book, *The Feminine Mystique.* This woman has been raising children and keeping house, and did not experience other choices. Her husband might have wanted her to stay home and would have been embarrassed if she worked—people might think he wasn't an adequate breadwinner.

If the client is from a different country or culture, you will need to do research on significant sociocultural-historical events. For instance, if someone from Iran talks about geographic relocation in the late 1970s, you should know that there was a revolution at that time. When working with Jewish clients, the Holocaust may be a significant factor in their personal histories and identities, even if they were born after World War II. Armenian clients will appreciate your understanding that they were victims of genocide.

ACTIVITIES FOR DATA GATHERING

There are several ways of gathering data other than face-to-face conversation. The following examples are also explained under the designated hypothesis. These activities have many benefits: They bypass storytelling and access new sources of information; they allow for systematic exploring of hypotheses; and they engage the client's sense of play and tap into resources such as creativity, imagination, and humor.

Role-Play (BL3, P2)

You can ask the client to role-play himself in a designated situation so that you can gather data about the client's current level of skill. It is common to then ask the client to switch roles with you, and play the role of the other person in the interaction. In this way, you gather data either on how the other person really behaves, or on the client's imagined version. You can gather data about a past situation—*Pretend I'm your boss and show me exactly what you said and how you said it*—or a hypothetical situation—*What would you like to say? Imagine she's sitting in that chair.* You can have the client role-play herself at different ages, or role-play significant others from the family of origin.

An advantage of this approach to data gathering is that you are moving away from the recitation of narratives that the client may have repeated many times, and tapping into new sources of information.

Expression of Different Inner Parts (P1)

In the course of the interview, when the client and therapist have identified and discussed different parts or voices, it can be a very natural next step to invite the client to let each part speak for itself. For instance, you might say, *You mentioned that you have a very critical inner voice. How about talking directly with the voice of that inner critic.*

Request a Different Point of View (P3)

After the client has described an interpersonal situation (her own point of view; POV), you can ask her to take two different POVs—that of an impartial observer and that of the other person. *Imagine you are Susan. Okay, now Susan, how do you feel about the argument? Pretend that you are watching the argument between (client's name) and Susan on a videotape. How would you describe it?* Table 8.12 gives a demonstration of an exercise that can be used as a data-gathering activity.

Genogram (SCE1)

A genogram (Bowen, 1994; McGoldrick, Gerson, & Shellenberger, 1999) is a family tree that maps at least three generations of a family. You ask the client to provide information, sitting side by side, so the client can watch as you draw symbols. Starting with the family of origin, use circles for females and squares for men and draw symbols for the siblings, beginning with the oldest at the left. Write in dates of birth, death, marriage, divorce, and marital separation. Go back at least to the grandparent generation and get facts about culture and immigration. These diagrams can get quite complicated if there are remarriages of parents, with step- and half-siblings. The most interesting part comes when the client describes relationships and interaction patterns. If there is a coalition, you would put a circle around the people, and you can indicate close bonds or estrangement with appropriate symbols. For instance, you can indicate the quality of relationships by connecting two people with lines: three parallel lines for a very close relationship, a dotted line for a distant relationship, a zigzag line for a conflicted relationship, and a gap in the middle of a straight line for estrangement. With clients from cultures who have close ties to extended family and other community members, you can be innovative and create additional lines and symbols.

Couple and Family Enactments (SCE1)

When you are doing conjoint therapy—seeing more than one member of a relationship or family—you have the opportunity to instruct the clients to engage in a specific task together while you watch. For instance, you can ask a family with children of different ages to plan a vacation together. In this way, the interaction patterns are demonstrated rather than described.

HOMEWORK ASSIGNMENTS AS A SOURCE OF DATA

The use of homework contributes to a collaborative relationship by putting responsibility on the client to actively participate. The client's response to the assignment is a valuable piece of objective data. Is the client compliant or defiant? Dutiful or irresponsible? Careless, competent, or perfectionistic? Here are some examples of how homework assignments can be used to gather data.

Charting a Specific Behavior

An essential part of a behavioral analysis (**BL1**) is keeping a daily record of specific behavior to discover the frequency as well as the antecedents and consequences. For instance, if the goal is to stop smoking, the client would be asked to make an entry on a chart every time he smokes a cigarette, including the context (where? with whom?), the trigger (what precipitated the decision to light up?), and feelings before and after. The data-gathering goal is to get a baseline; however, the homework assignment contains a paradox. The instruction to *write down your behavior but don't change anything* contains contradictory messages: *Be the same* and *Be different by being very conscious and honest about what you do.* It is very likely that the client will smoke less that week, an example of how data gathering overlaps with intervention. See Table 6.12 for an example of a chart that focuses on self-talk.

Learning to Use the Subjective Units of Discomfort Scale

There are two main reasons why you will want to teach clients how to monitor their emotions with a quantitative scale. First, quantitative data about a presenting problem—excessive anxiety, depression, or anger—allows you to measure progress and evaluate the effectiveness of interventions. Second, by quantifying and monitoring her emotional state, the client increases self-awareness, takes responsibility for achieving control over emotional states, and has a powerful tool for developing skills of emotional regulation.

Behavior therapists came up with a name for an interval scale that can measure any type of problematic emotion and called it the *SUDS,* using an acronym for Subjective Units of Discomfort Scale. A scale of 1 to 10 is usually sufficient for most purposes although some therapists prefer a 100-point scale. When used for anger problems, the numerical scale is often called an "emotional thermometer."

The most common use of the SUDS is for anxiety: People need to learn relaxation for health reasons (**B3**), coping with stress and crises (**CS2**), deconditioning anxiety (**BL2**), or applying difficult interpersonal skills (**BL3**). The scale is used as a continuum from total relaxation (1), almost to the point of sleep, to an extreme amount of anxiety (10), as in a panic attack. The midpoint (5) is calibrated as a state of functional alertness—neither too tense nor too relaxed. A range of 4 to 6 represents good concentration, the ability to focus, alert attention, and a capacity to carry out complex thinking and behaviors—the desirable level for taking a test, negotiating a contract, and dealing with a conflict. When the scale value rises above 6, the emotional arousal is entering the dysfunctional zone.

Although therapists can give suggestions for experiences that correspond to numbers on the scale, it is important that the client develop the scale for herself and key the different scale values to familiar experiences. Before using the scale for a specific problem, the client should randomly sample experiences during the week, and practice assigning a SUDS number, as well as describing sensations, feelings, and thoughts that occurred at the time.

Identifying Thoughts

Homework charts are essential in teaching clients to identify their self-talk (**C4**) and implicit assumptions (**C2**). In this way, clients discover for themselves that their feelings are not caused by the situation but rather by how they think about it. Table 2.9 gives an example of a SUDS self-monitoring chart for a graduate student with Generalized Anxiety Disorder.

Instructions to Interact

The therapist can ask the client to talk to specific people (e.g., partners, parents, grandparents, or coworkers). The purpose could be to use these people as informants to gather specific data, for example, to assess the SUDS level and self-talk while interacting with that person, or to gather data to test the validity of an assumption about how the person would respond.

Table 2.9   Subjective Units of Discomfort Scale Self-Monitoring Chart

Day and Time	Situation (e.g., where, what, or with whom)	Body Sensations (e.g., heart, muscles, or breathing)	Thinking	Feeling Words	SUDS (1–10)
Tuesday 3 P.M.	First day of class, open square arrangement of tables, called on by teacher.	Chest feels tight, sweaty palms.	I'm going to sound stupid. Everyone is looking at me.	Anxious, self-conscious.	8
Thursday 8 P.M.	Having dinner with Charlie, talking about movie.	Warm hands, full stomach, smooth breathing.	He's fun. He likes me.	Comfortable, happy, amused.	5
Sunday 9 A.M.	Lying in bed, petting my dog.	Slow breathing, warm, relaxed.	Not aware of anything.	Sleepy, loving.	2

Use of a Journal

Journal writing has many useful functions; one of them is data gathering. The client can be asked to either write freely or address specific topics. It can be beneficial, with some clients, to give them the assignment to write their thoughts and feelings on a daily basis. Another approach might be autobiographical, life history writing. Here is a writing assignment from a book on "self-discovery" (Snow, 1992) that would be useful for a client who is examining a current or recently terminated relationship.

JOURNAL ACTIVITY

You will need a half hour to an hour of uninterrupted time.

A. Tell the story of how you fell in love. Include where you met, what attracted you, and what there was about the other person that resonated with some deep wish or need of yours.

B. Tell a little about the early stages of your relationship, your first date, your first brief interlude together. Write about the feelings you had at the time, and include your expectations. What did you expect would eventually occur in the relationship (don't think about what occurred, but go back to the original time and the original feelings and expectations)?

C. At the beginning of a relationship, there is a little clue that registers (and is subsequently disregarded) that something will go wrong eventually or that the relationship isn't going to last forever. Write about this *clue of failure*.

SUGGESTED READINGS

Bandler, R., & Grinder, J. (1990). *The structure of magic: A book about language and therapy.* Palo Alto, CA: Science and Behavior Books.

Egan, G. (2002). *The skilled helper* (7th ed.). Belmont, CA: Brooks/Cole.

Groth-Marnat, G. (2003). The assessment interview. In *Handbook of psychological assessment* (pp. 69–101). Hoboken, NJ: Wiley.

Ivey, A. E., & Ivey, M. B. (2003). *Intentional interviewing and counseling: Facilitating client development in a multicultural society* (5th ed.). Belmont, CA: Wadsworth.

McGoldrick, M., Gerson, R., & Shellenberger, S. (1999). *Genograms: Assessment and intervention* (2nd ed.). New York: W. W. Norton.

Rigazio-DiGilio, S. A., Ivey, A. E., Kunkler-Peck, K. P., & Grady, L. T. (2005). *Community genograms: Using individual, family, and cultural narratives with clients.* New York: Teachers College Press.

Zuckerman, E. L. (2000). *Clinician's thesaurus: The guidebook for writing psychological reports* (5th ed.). New York: Guilford Press.

PART II

TWENTY-EIGHT CORE CLINICAL HYPOTHESES

The following chapters address seven categories of hypotheses:

Chapter 3: **Biological Hypotheses (B)**

Chapter 4: **Crisis, Stressful Situations, and Transitions (CS)**

Chapter 5: **Behavioral and Learning Models (BL)**

Chapter 6: **Cognitive Models (C)**

Chapter 7: **Existential and Spiritual Models (ES)**

Chapter 8: **Psychodynamic Models (P)**

Chapter 9: **Social, Cultural, and Environmental Factors (SCE)**

The complete list of hypotheses was presented in Table 1.2 in Chapter 1 and is available in a one-page chart in Appendix II, Chart II.A.

The capital letters in parenthesis are abbreviated codes to identify each hypothesis. These codes will make absolutely no sense to anyone who has not read this book; however, for people who are using this method, the codes will facilitate communication.

Each hypothesis is discussed, using the following outline.

- *Introductory chart with title, description, and three clinical vignettes:* Once you are familiar with the hypothesis, this chart will serve as a reminder of when to use the hypothesis. The first row of the chart contains a code (e.g., **B1**—the combination of letters for the model and a number for the hypothesis), followed by the official title of the hypothesis (e.g., **Biological Cause**). The title is followed by a formal definition of the hypothesis. The second row in the chart provides explanations that are central to understanding and using the hypothesis. In the third row, three clinical vignettes show when the hypothesis is an appropriate match.

- *Key Ideas:* I have chosen ideas that I think are central to understanding the hypothesis, realizing how much more could be said. The selection process was guided by the audience for whom I am writing: practitioners who want to use these ideas with their clients. The size of this section varies, depending on the breadth and complexity of the hypothesis.

- *When Is This Hypothesis a Good Match?* This section presents suggestions for recognizing the relevance of the hypothesis, including specific client data, problem titles, and *DSM-IV-TR* diagnoses, when appropriate.

- *Treatment Planning:* This section provides a selection of ideas for treatment. It is not all-inclusive: There will be effective treatment ideas that are overlooked, and that does not mean that they are of lesser value than those that have been included. Some approaches that are mentioned have strong support by respected groups of clinicians; others are controversial or are so recent that they are not widely known. This section is not intended to instruct you about what to put in your treatment plan but rather to provide a range of possibilities. The plans that you create will be based on the facts of a specific case, your professional judgment, the research literature that applies, your client's preferences, and your competence.

- *Integration of Hypotheses:* To see samples of how hypotheses are integrated, go to Chapter 10. Otherwise, the title of this section might not make sense: It contains a list of those hypotheses that will often be combined with the hypothesis in question. At first reading, it may not be very helpful because you may not have reached the chapter that discusses the hypothesis in depth. However, when you are using this book as a reference in preparing a case formulation, this section should be useful.

Each chapter concludes with a *Suggested Reading* section, which contains a selection of books that will expose you to the diversity of contributors to that single hypothesis.

HOW TO APPROACH THE HYPOTHESES

You need to understand each hypothesis before you can use it appropriately. It may seem overwhelming to face 28 hypotheses, but you probably will recognize most of them. There are three phases of learning the hypotheses: first, skim through the material quickly to get the key ideas; second, read more slowly and identify your own strengths and interests; finally, when you have client data to work with, go back and study the relevant hypotheses more closely, with attention to treatment plan ideas.

When you sit down with a new client, there are only a few clinical hypotheses that must be addressed in the first session: You need to recognize issues that require immediate attention to prevent irreversible negative consequences. If you want to jump immediately to the hypotheses that are essential for intakes, they are **B1 Biological Cause** and **CS1 Emergency Issues.** You need to rule out (or rule in) medical problems and substance abuse, emergency and trauma issues, obligations for legal reporting, and diagnoses of severe mental disorders.

When you see the same problem mentioned under different hypotheses, you can conclude that those hypotheses can be effectively integrated. For instance, chronic pain is addressed under **B2 Medical Interventions** because it can be treated by medication and also under **B3 Mind-Body Connections** because it responds to stress-management techniques and body-focused interventions such as biofeedback training. Broad problems like "depression" and "difficulty establishing intimate relationships" will be mentioned under many hypotheses.

Confusion might result from seeing the name of a theorist listed under several hypotheses. We usually think of therapeutic approaches as a bundle of ideas belonging under the name of the founder of a theory, so it may be surprising to see the contributions of a single person unpackaged and placed in different bins. For instance, Jung's contributions are mentioned under three hypotheses: **P1 Internal Parts or Subpersonalities** because his model of the self included subselves, such as the Ego and Persona, which are in conscious awareness; **P4 Unconscious Dynamics** because his theory includes both the personal unconscious and the *collective unconscious;* and **ES3 Spiritual Dimension** because his theory has a strong spiritual emphasis.

Chapter 10 provides examples of how the different hypotheses can be applied and integrated. If you are a person who likes to dig right in, go to Activity 10.1, and see how well you can apply hypotheses to clinical vignettes and propose strategies to gather relevant data for hypothesis-testing.

Chapter 3 ——————————————————————————

BIOLOGICAL HYPOTHESES

The field of medicine is gradually acknowledging the advantages of the biopsychosocial model over the traditional biomedical model, whereas the field of psychology is increasing its interest in neuroscience and the functioning of the body.

The mind and body are inseparable. Every emotion, thought, and behavioral impulse has underpinnings in the activities of the brain, making it impossible to view psychological symptoms as distinct from biology. We understand that there are bidirectional influences between the physical and mental domains, but we currently have very limited ability to make assertions about causality because of the fact that physiological and psychological processes are simultaneous rather than sequential. For instance, we know that low levels of serotonin correspond with depression, but we can't say which comes first—the depressed mood or the inadequate amount of neurotransmitter at the synapse.

Sometimes causation is relatively clear. Biological causation is demonstrated when brain trauma, disease, and ingestion of toxic substances are followed by mental symptoms such as memory impairment, anxiety, depression, confusion, and personality change. There is also strong support for the proposition that psychological states affect the chemistry of the brain and can both boost and lower immune system function. For instance, the placebo effect shows that positive expectations in the absence of an active chemical in the pill can produce physical benefits; psychological stress, such as academic pressure, divorce, and unemployment, can increase the probability of becoming ill; and group therapy can result in reduced recurrence and mortality rates in cancer patients. Recently, research demonstrated that the activities of psychotherapy—putting experiences into words, emotional attunement, and helping clients confront their fears—is effective in building neural networks and changing the chemical activity of the brain: The "talking cure" changes the brain (Cozolino, 2002).

Decisions about treatment plans must be based on knowledge of both physiological and psychosocial factors, with attention to the complex connections of the mind and body. The three biological hypotheses offer different templates for examining client problems (see Table 3.1). Only the **Biological Cause** hypothesis (**B1**) is based on clear biological causation. The **Medical Interventions (B2)** and the **Mind-Body Connections (B3)** hypotheses assume that mind-body connections are complicated, but that attention to the physical and somatic realm is

Table 3.1   Biological Hypotheses

B1 Biological Cause	The problem has a **Biological Cause:** The client needs medical intervention to protect life and prevent deterioration, or needs psychosocial assistance in coping with illness, disability, or other biological limitations.
B2 Medical Interventions	There are **Medical Interventions** (e.g., medication, surgery, or prosthetics) that should be considered.
B3 Mind-Body Connections	A holistic understanding of **Mind-Body Connections** leads to treatments for psychological problems that focus on the body and treatments for physical problems that focus on the mind.

necessary for treatment planning. In some cases, more than one of these hypotheses will fit, and can be combined in the formulation. If you find yourself struggling to decide which of the two seems more appropriate, the odds are that both should be included.

The treatment of anxiety can illustrate the differences among the three biological hypotheses.

B1: After a medical examination and a complete blood panel, the client is diagnosed with a thyroid condition. After taking thyroid medication to bring her hormone levels back to normal, she no longer complains of anxiety.

B2: A medical examination did not reveal any abnormalities. The client had gone to many therapists but has not been able to successfully reduce the anxiety. A referral to a psychiatrist for medication evaluation leads to a prescription for antianxiety medication.

B3: A medical examination did not reveal any abnormalities. The client is constantly on the go, handling work and family responsibilities without any time taken for relaxation. After scheduling an hour every weekend for a massage, half an hour every day for relaxation practice, and a five-minute pause every hour for a deep breathing and positive imagery exercise, the client is no longer bothered by anxiety.

The following example shows a client for whom all three hypotheses are integrated:

A 66-year-old retired man suffered a spinal cord injury as a teenager that left him a partial paraplegic. As he ages, his physical disabilities have become more severe, and he uses an electric scooter to get around (**B1**). Recently, he has become increasingly depressed because of his declining mobility, as well as the death of his best friend and the termination of a close relationship, and has been staying home and avoiding the few activities that bring pleasure and social interaction. His therapist recommended a trial of antidepressants (**B2**), and he had begun to respond positively when he suffered a leg injury. He is now dealing with daily pain, but doesn't want to take a recommended medication because a possible side effect is loss of balance. His therapist taught him a method of self-hypnosis that helps reduce the pain (**B3**).

B1 BIOLOGICAL CAUSE

Definition

The problem has a **Biological Cause:** The client needs medical intervention to protect life and prevent deterioration or psychosocial assistance in coping with illness, disability, or other biological limitations.

Explanation

This hypothesis applies to a wide range of physical problems that produce psychological symptoms and impairments, including strokes, brain tumors, spinal cord injuries, Alzheimer's syndrome, transient toxic states, drug and alcohol intoxication, AIDS, vitamin deficiency, and endocrine disorders. It should also be used when the client needs help coping with a medical condition or physical disability or dealing with limitations from biological sources such as genetics or aging.

Examples

Pamela, a psychology graduate student, was experiencing fatigue and difficulty concentrating, symptoms that she attributed to "stress" and "depression." Despite her loss of appetite, she was gaining weight and her waistband was getting tighter and tighter. A thorough medical examination and testing revealed a huge malignant tumor growing in her abdomen.	George was diagnosed with Schizophrenia 2 years ago, but never responded to medication. In a "psychotic episode," he murdered his girlfriend and then committed suicide. The autopsy revealed that he had a huge brain tumor. If the tumor had been diagnosed 2 years ago, surgery would have eliminated his mental symptoms and prevented two unnecessary deaths.	Teresa and Pedro came to therapy because of Teresa's hurt over her husband's emotional withdrawal and avoidance of sex for a year. Pedro was very embarrassed about discussing the problem, saying that he was overloaded with work and always exhausted. A referral to a physician led to a diagnosis of diabetes and the discovery that his lack of erection was physiologically-based.

KEY IDEAS FOR B1 BIOLOGICAL CAUSE

The status of medical research at a specific point in history will determine whether the **B1** hypothesis is used correctly. Sometimes what clinicians believe to be a biological cause of illness is later proven to be false. In some cases, the cause is not biological at all; in others, the cause is biological but not what was initially hypothesized.

Faulty Diagnoses from Lack of Scientific Knowledge

The *Madness of King George,* produced in 1996, is a movie that illustrates the faulty diagnosis of the mental illness of George Ill of England, the monarch at the time of the American Revolution. The clinical case formulations of the experts of the time are demonstrated as the drama unfolds:

B1 *Hypothesis in the Eighteenth Century*

The physicians believe that the body contains "humors" and that mental problems result from an excess of humors in the brain. Based on this hypothesis, the treatment is to dip glass jars into a flame and then place their round edges on the King's back and legs to create blisters that should draw humors away from the brain.

Nonbiological, Psychosocial Hypothesis

When the painful blistering method doesn't work, a more "modern" expert is found. This doctor, previously a clergyman, believes that the King's madness developed from getting his way all the time and therefore developing a "weak character." His hypothesis is that the madness will be cured when the character is "curbed, stood up to, and thwarted." The treatment for misbehavior is strapping the King in a chair and keeping him in restraints until he becomes docile.

B1 *Hypothesis in the Twentieth Century*

At the end of the movie, after the credits, two sentences on the screen reveal the hypothesis based on modern medical science: "The color of the King's urine suggests that he was suffering from porphyria, a physical illness that affects the nervous system. The disease is periodic, unpredictable, and hereditary."

As viewers read these words, we remember that a servant brought the doctors a basin of the King's urine, exclaiming over the fact that it was blue. This information supports the diagnosis of porphyria, but it was meaningless to the physicians of the late eighteenth century.

Medically Unexplained Symptoms

Sometimes clients are referred to therapists when physicians cannot find a diagnosis for symptoms. The assumption will usually be that the person is a "somatizer," converting psychological distress to physical symptoms, which therefore do not have biological causation. However, we need to leave room for the possibility that the symptoms have a medical cause that has not yet been discovered by medical science. Chronic Fatigue Syndrome used to be called "neurasthenia" and was viewed as a form of neurosis, whereas it is now accepted as a physical illness for which there is no definable cause. In the future, research might find that the cause is a virus, environmental toxins, or neuroendocrine malfunction. The term *medically unexplained symptoms* (MUS) is useful because it does not assume psychiatric disorder as does the term *somatization*.

The Importance of Diagnostic Skills

"Differential diagnosis" is a systematic approach for inclusion or exclusion of diagnoses, based on preliminary examination of the data. The diagnoses on the list of possibilities must then be subjected to tests to rule out diagnoses for which there are no confirmatory data. One of the biggest errors that a therapist can make is failing to detect symptoms of a possibly fatal or disabling medical disorder, thus failing to include the medical problem in the differential diagnosis. If you are not a physician, you are not expected to be a diagnostician of medical problems, but as a licensed psychotherapist you are required to be competent in recognizing the *DSM-IV-TR* criteria for biologically-based disorders and to know when referral to a physician is necessary. You need to be aware that psychological symptoms (e.g., anxiety, depression, memory impairments, and changes in personality) can be caused by both biological and psychosocial disorders. Procedures for confirming a medical diagnosis include analyses of blood and urine, X-rays, and brain scans. Clinical psychologists with competence in neuropsychological assessment can pinpoint locations in the brain that are associated with specific functional deficits caused by stroke, brain trauma, or degenerative brain diseases.

Biological Causation with Co-Occurring Disorders

Medical problems may coexist with other types of psychiatric disorders. To complicate matters, the same symptoms may stem from both biological and psychosocial causes. The most common example of this is the coexistence of depression and medical illness. Depression can be a symptom of the illness and a consequence of difficulty coping with the illness—and the same person can have depression stemming from both causes. One third of medical patients have at least moderate mood symptoms. Depression in elderly clients is very common because of their multiple physical impairments, social isolation, and grief from many losses, and therefore often coexists with dementia, complicating the diagnostic process. Anxiety disorders and substance abuse also can accompany biologically-based disorders.

WHEN IS THIS HYPOTHESIS A GOOD MATCH?

DSM-IV-TR lists various mental disorders such as Delirium, Dementia, and Amnesia that stem from such medical conditions as vascular disease (stroke); intracranial injury (head trauma); HIV disease; and a variety of diseases named after their discoverers—Alzheimer, Parkinson, Huntington, Pick, and Creutzfeldt-Jakob. There are also disorders in the *DSM,* such as Obsessive-Compulsive Disorder (OCD) and Attention-Deficit/Hyperactivity Disorder (ADHD), for which recent brain scan research finds evidence of correspondence between activation of parts of the brain and manifestation of behavioral symptoms. Until research firmly establishes causation, these disorders are best addressed under **B2.**

Although the primary importance of this hypothesis is in recognizing biologically-based disorders that might be misdiagnosed and untreated, it also fits when the client needs help in coping with a medical condition or dealing with impairments in functioning that stem from physiological causes. Another application of this hypothesis is to help your client identify those biological "givens," such as temperament, talents, physical disability, or body type, which limit choices or determine the type of environmental niche that would be most beneficial.

The need for medical referral is recognized by such data as impaired memory, concentration, and consciousness; the use of alcohol, drugs, and medications;

changes in appetite, weight, sleep patterns, mood, and personality traits; events such as head injury, illnesses, and accidents; and family members' reports of poor grooming, neglect of home and health, and loss of competence at work.

Substance-Related Disorders

Problems with drugs and alcohol are extremely common and should be considered with every client. The ingestion of alcohol and drugs can result in a transient, reversible syndrome called intoxication. The term *dependence* refers to a physiological condition where the body needs the drug and without it will develop a group of symptoms called withdrawal. Clinicians need to probe for specific details of frequency and quantity of consumption. Recognition of substance use is especially important with pregnant women and clients who need intact impulse control, such as potentially suicidal clients. The consequences of prolonged alcohol abuse are illustrated in this case example:

> A 40-year-old man, a successful writer, denied that alcohol was a problem in his life. Even after he broke his leg in an alcohol-related accident, he claimed that it was an exceptional circumstance. Finally, he was arrested for driving under the influence, and was forced to attend AA meetings. He successfully terminated alcohol use and attended AA until completion of his probation. Six months later he was found dead by his neighbor, holding a bottle of vodka. The autopsy report showed severe liver damage and extreme cardiomyopathy—"his heart looked like that of a man twice his age," the pathologist explained.

Medical Conditions that Masquerade as Mental Disorders

Medical disorders can cause any of the following symptoms: anxiety, depression, mania, psychosis, delirium, dementia, uncontrollable rage, and personality changes. If a client presents with dementia or psychotic symptoms, clinicians are usually alert to the fit of the **B1** hypothesis. However, more commonplace symptoms, such as anxiety or depression, may be treated as purely psychological when, in fact, they might be caused by medical conditions such as thyroid disorders, renal failure, an autoimmune disease like lupus, or electrolyte imbalance.

Client Needs Help Coping with Medical Condition or Physical Disability

Biologically-based conditions involve emotional, behavioral, and cognitive dimensions including subjective level of pain, intensity of emotional distress, the need to develop new skills, alterations in cognitive maps, demands to make difficult decisions, social isolation, and disruption to the functioning of the family. Often just receiving a serious diagnosis can overwhelm a person's ability to cope. Conditions that therapists might encounter include aphasia following a stroke, amputation following war service, paraplegia from an accident, and partial or complete loss of functioning in one of the sense organs. The aging process involves physical changes that interfere with mobility and can cause chronic pain.

Opportunities for Prevention

Often clients describe behaviors or lifestyle choices—smoking, overeating, excessive drinking, unprotected sex, and reckless driving—that put them at risk for developing medical problems. For instance, a lifestyle of high stress, workaholism, overeating, and no exercise can contribute to heart conditions. Excessive smoking can result in serious, irreversible damage to the lungs. Anorexia Nervosa and the accompanying weight loss and condition of starvation affects metabolism, heart rate and pulse, blood pressure, skin and hair, and bone density. For bulimics, the effects of purging include electrolyte imbalance, which can cause heart attack and brain damage. Therapists can formulate problems in ways that promote prevention and early interventions. For instance, if your client is a postmenopausal woman who works 14 hours a day at a high-pressure job, neglecting nutrition and exercise, you can explain the connection between lifestyle and health, bring the risk of osteoporosis to her awareness, encourage proper diagnostic tests (e.g., bone-density test), and support her making a commitment to better self-care.

Coping with Genetic "Givens"

Without minimizing the role of nurture and the freedom of people to make choices, we must recognize that genetic factors do set limits on freedom and influence psychological and behavioral functioning. Clients benefit from recognizing that varied factors are hardwired into their makeup, the makeup of a child, or that of a significant other. Examples include character traits like introversion/extraversion, aptitudes and talents for things like mathematics or music, sexual orientation and gender identity, and aspects of physical appearance such as height and body type. Although you might think telling a client to accept genetic limits is discouraging, many clients experience an increase in self-acceptance when they realize that they are not at fault for difficulties that they have been unable to resolve. This hypothesis is very useful when counseling parents who want their violinist son to be an athlete or their athletic daughter to be a bookworm. When parents are able to acknowledge their child's core, unchangeable characteristics, their frustration is reduced and the psychological well-being of the child is enhanced. Parents who have trouble accepting the sexual orientation of their gay, lesbian, or bisexual child need to understand that same-sex attraction is an innate part of a person's makeup to stop blaming their child or themselves.

As genetic research progresses, there will be greater understanding of inherited characteristics and discoveries of gene therapies that will overcome genetic limitations. An interesting new issue for therapists will be counseling clients who need to make choices about genetic testing. For instance, if a Jewish woman of Eastern European background with family history of breast cancer discusses her indecision about whether to get tested to see if she carries the gene associated with breast cancer, the therapist will need to explore the pros and cons and how she would cope if the news were bad.

Many aspects of sexual functioning are part of our biological hardwiring. Some of these factors, although evolutionarily adaptive, can result in considerable emotional pain. It makes sense (in terms of preserving the species) that a middle-aged man should have a stronger sexual attraction for an attractive woman of childbearing years than for his postmenopausal wife, but this does not provide consolation for the wife and family if the husband acts on these biologically-based impulses. For women, sexual intercourse creates the same bond to the sexual partner as that which occurs with their newborn infant, thus securing protection for mother and baby; however, this bond is unfortunate for a woman who finds it difficult to sever an unsatisfactory relationship. In both those examples, the head says "this is not good for me," but the body and emotions have a different agenda.

TREATMENT PLANNING

When biologically-based issues are involved, one of the problem titles should be the name of the disease, disorder, or disability that will be treated by medical professionals. The other problems that you define might be consequences of the medical problem, concurrent psychological problems, or lifestyle problems that increase health risk. Table 3.2 lists some examples of useful problem titles.

Referrals

You need to have the flexibility to leave the traditional role of psychotherapist and take on roles of social worker, case manager, advocate, and supportive cheerleader. In your initial intake, when you recognize signs of a biologically-based condition such as impaired memory, confusion, or personality changes, you need to arrange for the client to get a medical evaluation. Depending on the level of impairment, you should involve family members or call an ambulance. If the client does not already have a primary care physician, you can help the client find someone who is suitable, considering constraints of geography, financial means, and health insurance guidelines. It is helpful to establish good professional relationships with physicians in the community.

Use of Community Resources

It is essential to have access to printed or online directories of resources and services. Fortunately, psychosocial treatment programs are often available in hospitals or in the community to help patients and their families deal with specific disorders such as breast cancer, strokes, spinal cord injuries, prostate cancer, heart disease, Alzheimer's disease, and HIV/AIDS. Substance abusers usually need multiple resources—residential programs, Twelve Step groups, and religious or social organizations that allow them to build new substance-free social networks.

Table 3.2   Useful Problem Titles for Biologically-Based Issues

Problems Associated with Brain Damage

Inadequate self-care
Risk of violence or injury
Frustration over inability to communicate needs

Difficulties Coping with Medical Disorders

Refusal to modify work schedule despite debilitating weakness from chemotherapy
Noncompliance with doctor's instructions
Difficulty asserting needs with medical personnel

Problems of Caretakers

Need for respite from caregiver responsibilities
Engaging in elder abuse
Difficulty coping with spouse's loss of memory

Problems Associated with Terminal Illness

Indecision about entering hospice program
Refusal to face grief over impending death (for patient as well as family)
Difficulty coping with family members' refusal to talk about death

Problems Associated with Drug Addiction

Drug-seeking, criminal behavior
Inability to fulfill occupational obligations
Inability to sustain healthy relationships
Legal problems stemming from sale of illegal substances

Problems That the Addict Had before Use of Drug

Difficulty maintaining intimate relationships
Difficulty coping with painful emotional states
Difficulty committing to future goals that require work, persistence, and frustration tolerance

Becoming Informed

Unless you are a medical doctor, you will frequently be confronted with your ignorance about your client's condition. To provide your client the highest level of care, you will need to gather information and educate yourself. Thanks to Internet search engines, such as Google, it is easy to find medical information and support groups for sufferers of a specific disease. The following electronic databases provide access to medical research and critical reports of the research: Cochrane Library, Medline, Healthstar, and EMBASE. Allow your client to educate you about the medical disorder and consult with physicians and health psychologists to broaden your knowledge base and understanding of the client's particular situation. Because most medical patients get very limited time with physicians and nurses, a well-informed psychotherapist can provide a valuable service by helping the client understand the medical condition—however, be sure to uphold professional ethics and make it clear that you are not a medical authority.

Working in Interdisciplinary Teams

The coordination of care is of huge benefit to the client. If you are working in a health setting, you need to be familiar with different professional roles: What does each team member do, and what can they provide the client? Collaboration with a team of rehabilitation specialists is an important part of treatment of people with irreversible impairments such as loss of speech in stroke victim and loss of mobility for quadriplegics. Being an effective advocate for quality care for terminally ill individuals and their families involves working as part of multidisciplinary teams to ensure that individual needs and quality of life issues are understood and addressed, such as the need for increased pain control.

Family Involvement

It is important to involve family members in treatment discussions, especially if the client has serious impairments that are expected to worsen. Caregiver stress is a common problem that can lead to mistreatment of the client and the development of emotional and health problems in the caregiver. When a child has a serious illness and is getting the majority of the parents' attention, siblings can develop conduct problems or mood symptoms as a result of neglect. The treatment plan needs to attend to the needs of the whole family to help prevent these consequences. Referral to family therapy may be advisable when the therapist notices new problems developing in the already stressed family unit, as illustrated by the following example:

> A 45-year-old woman insisted on having her mother, a brain trauma victim with lack of speech and severe paralysis, move into the small house she shared with her husband and 13-year-old daughter. Four years later, the patient showed little improvement, despite many different kinds of rehabilitation programs. Her daughter refused to let go of the fantasy that her mother would eventually show miraculous improvement and neglected her obligations to her husband and child; the husband suffered from many stress-related complaints that seemed to be related to anger; and the patient's granddaughter had two car accidents within 3 months of getting her driver's license.

Working with Terminally Ill Clients

The web site for the American Psychological Association (www.apa.org) offers guidelines for end-of-life counseling. Here are a few key points:

- When working with people who are dying, it is essential to assess the overall quality of care they are receiving, to identify sources of suffering and ways of alleviating them, and to determine what decisions need to be made and who needs to be involved in making and implementing them.

- You can help dying persons raise and resolve issues of meaning in their individual lives through values clarification and life review. Religious and spiritual issues often arise and need to be discussed. There may be issues of unresolved grief from prior losses, such as the deaths of parents.

- Themes that frequently arise in counseling dying persons are loss of autonomy, control, dignity, and meaning as well as fears of dependency and being a burden to others emotionally, physically, or economically. Those factors often contribute to requests for assisted suicide and euthanasia, even more than pain and depression.

- Some patients and families may turn to you for help with decision making regarding death-related issues such as advance care directives, designating a guardian or health-care proxy, and details of the desired funeral or memorial service.

Ethical and Legal Issues

You always need to be aware of legal and ethical issues that affect your practice; with clients who have medical problems, it is especially important to have a good resource for understanding your responsibilities and risks (e.g., Sales, Miller, & Hall, 2005). Zuckerman (2003) provides useful forms for professional practice, such as release forms that clients must sign so that you can share information and coordinate treatment plans with other health professionals. The ethical principle "limits of competence" is especially important when working with populations for whom specialized training is necessary. If you are treating an elderly person in an assisted living setting, you must be screening for any signs of abuse that will need to be reported.

INTEGRATION OF HYPOTHESES

One or more of the following hypotheses are often combined with the one just reviewed to create an integrative formulation for a specific problem. The decision about whether a specific hypothesis should be integrated is based on your professional judgment.

CS4 Loss and Bereavement

This hypothesis is useful when people deal with the emotional pain of losing abilities and functions. Therapists can help patients express and explore the roots of their anger, which can otherwise be manifested as hostility toward medical professionals. When people have terminal illnesses, clinical work may focus on grief, mourning, loss, and feelings about dying and death. The patient and family members need help coping with sorrow, depression, anger, guilt, and anxiety. Unresolved grief over the earlier deaths of loved ones is likely to arise as some dying people relive past losses in preparation for losing everything.

BL1 Antecedents and Consequences

A thorough behavioral analysis is necessary for health-related behaviors, such as *poor medication compliance.* For example, a client can identify triggers to appropriate use of medication, such as counting pills once a week and using a plastic container with compartments. Be aware that clients experience negative side effects as punishment for taking pills and need help in focusing on the rewarding consequences. A behavioral intervention designed to increase "activity level" in small increments from a baseline, using contingency contracting, is an appropriate treatment for Chronic Fatigue Syndrome (Demitrack & Abbey, 1999).

BL2 Conditioned Emotional Response

Medical patients with fears of hospitals or certain procedures may benefit from a desensitization paradigm to reduce their fears, preferably through *in vivo* contact with the hospital, staff, and equipment.

BL3 Skill Deficits or Lack of Competence

Social skills training may be helpful for learning how to elicit social support and deal with medical professionals. The field of rehabilitation overlaps with psychotherapy: People with brain damage from strokes or tumors need to develop cognitive and independent living skills.

C2 Faulty Cognitive Map

The client needs to have accurate information about the disease and may require help in making rational decisions. Cognitive distortions need to be identified, as when the client is catastrophizing ("If I can't walk, I'll never be happy again") and overgeneralizing ("Cancer is always a terminal disease"). Attitudes toward taking medication and adhering to other treatment recommendations need to be addressed.

C4 Dysfunctional Self-Talk

Dysfunctional self-talk is an important target of treatment, especially because there is evidence that positive thinking enhances health outcomes.

ES1 Existential Issues

Patients are often dealing with loss of meaning in life and are questioning "why me?" Discussing the question of suicide is often relevant, either because of concurrent depression or because the quality of life is so greatly diminished and the prognosis so poor that patients want to make decisions about dying with dignity.

ES3 Spiritual Dimension

Spiritual activities, such as prayer or meditation, may have a positive effect on the course of the illness. With dying patients, spiritual and religious issues are very important. Collaborative relations with members of the clergy can be very helpful at that time.

SCE3 Social Support

One of the most important functions of a therapist will be assuring that there is a support network for the person who is experiencing a medical crisis or adjusting to physical disability. A common problem with cancer and AIDS is that even well-intentioned friends withdraw from the patient, finding it too painful to see physical changes and feeling that what they have to offer is inadequate. Support groups are extremely useful for both patients and caregivers. Patients may initially resist the idea of listening to other people suffering from the same disease, but if they can agree to try a group for a few sessions, they often will report surprising benefits from the therapeutic factors that Yalom (1995) describes, including practical advice, instillation of hope from people who are coping successfully, and the chance to be altruistic and offer help to others.

SCE7 Environmental Factors

When clients are faced with irreversible disabilities or the givens from their genetic makeup, they need to recognize that their happiness can be enhanced by choosing a satisfying environmental niche and obtaining needed environmental resources. For instance, people can choose to move to dry and warm states like Arizona if they have difficulty breathing in other climates. Electric scooters and elevators in homes can vastly improve the lives of people who are unable to walk. Relapse prevention for addicts involves avoiding places where drugs are available. The client's need to obtain financial resources and to utilize legal assistance is something that you should be ready to address.

KEY IDEAS FOR B2 MEDICAL INTERVENTIONS

Two movies, both starring Jack Nicholson, show the appropriate and inappropriate application of this hypothesis:

As Good as It Gets

The main character suffers from OCD, as well as from misanthropic attitudes and terrible social skills. He becomes deeply attached to a waitress and demonstrates

B2 MEDICAL INTERVENTIONS

Definition

There are **Medical Interventions** (e.g., medication, surgery, and prosthetics) that should be considered.

Explanation

The primary application of this hypothesis will be when the use of psychotropic medication is indicated for a psychiatric disorder. Other medical interventions (e.g., surgery, or the use of appliances and prostheses) and interventions from alternative medicine can also be used to alleviate psychological symptoms.

Examples

Gerald is a chronic pain patient, suffering from a cycle of pain, anxiety, and tension. He is in a treatment program with a multidisciplinary treatment team. One professional is teaching him biofeedback for the tension but, at the same time, he has been prescribed pain medication and tranquilizers.	Tipper Gore, wife of the candidate for president in 2000, went through a very difficult time when her young son was severely injured in a car accident. Seeking help, she received the diagnosis of clinical depression and was prescribed medication for her condition.	Marian, an obese woman who had struggled with weight problems since childhood, opted for gastric bypass surgery. The surgeon required a psychological evaluation to assure that she had realistic expectations and would be able to handle lifestyle changes after the surgery.

his caring by helping her son get appropriate treatment for an illness. Nevertheless, his annoying behaviors and severe anxieties appear to be insurmountable obstacles to a successful romantic relationship. The happy ending of the film corresponds to his admission that he has resumed taking antianxiety medications.

One Flew Over the Cuckoo's Nest

The main character is a malingerer who feigns mental illness in order to be sent to a mental hospital rather than prison. His behavior is disruptive to the smooth management of the ward, but we see it as a healthy response to the repressive, dehumanizing behavior of the head nurse, as well as therapeutic for the other patients on the ward. At the end of the movie, a surgical procedure on his brain renders him docile and takes away his essence as a human being.

Medical Research

The acceptability of medical treatment for psychological complaints depends on the status of medical research at a particular point in history. Today, Schizophrenia is a disorder for which medication is widely accepted as a necessary component of treatment. A few decades ago, however, it was respectable to claim that Schizophrenia could be caused by double-binding, schizophrenogenic mothers. Today, the treatment of ADHD is controversial, with many parents and practitioners strongly opposed to the use of medication despite the fact there is much research evidence of the benefits of medication and that, furthermore, brain scans show differences in the brains of children with this diagnosis when compared to controls. With further research in neuroscience, the use of medication may become more widely accepted. As brain physiology research progresses, the **B2** hypothesis will be more widely used, and the scope of the **B1** hypothesis will likely expand.

Biases about Medical Interventions

All practitioners have the following obligations: (a) Understand your prejudices and values about medical interventions, some of which are absorbed, without reflection, from teachers and supervisors; (b) stay abreast of the research literature (e.g., Thase & Jindal, 2004); and (c) maintain a *biopsychosocial,* integrative perspective rather than exercise either-or thinking. Nonphysician therapists often view medication as a last resort when psychotherapy has failed to produce expected progress, or as a useful adjunct to psychotherapy, but not something that alone could be sufficient. In contrast, physicians, as well as cost-conscious managed care companies, find treatment with medication, without concurrent psychotherapy, to be satisfactory, and neglect the benefits that come from empirically supported psychotherapy interventions.

In addition to medication, surgical and medical interventions elicit strong personal biases. In our culture, we value self-reliance, admire demonstrations of what we call "willpower," and scorn the idea of "relying on crutches." Therefore, an operation like gastric bypass surgery or the use of a methadone maintenance treatment for drug addiction may be disapproved of, even by professionals. There are also strong personal values regarding the desirability of "aging naturally," versus taking advantages of aesthetic surgery to look younger.

Training in Psychopharmacology

Psychopharmacology training is important for all psychotherapists; it is critical that you understand when medication might be appropriate and that you are able to communicate intelligently with the psychiatrist involved in the case. Some of the competencies that need to be developed are (a) the ability to recognize symptoms and syndromes that justify referral to a psychiatrist for a medication evaluation, (b) an understanding of the therapeutic effects and side effects from the most common types of psychotropic medications, and (c) the ability to discuss medication with clients with an understanding of factors that promote and impede medication compliance. Because new medications are continually being developed, have the most recent edition of a concise psychopharmacology guide (e.g., J. Johnson & Preston, 2004) and the current *Physician's Desk Reference* (*PDR*; Medical Economics, 2005) available to keep abreast of current research developments in psychopharmacology. Psychologists who take advanced training in psychopharmacology may not yet have prescription privileges, but they are considered experts for purposes of consultation.

The Split-Treatment Model

Gitlin (1996) used the term *split-treatment model* for the common practice of having one professional, typically a nonphysician therapist, provide psychotherapy while another (e.g., a psychiatrist, internist, or family practice physician) prescribes medication. The nonprescribing psychotherapist needs to be a knowledgeable participant in the pharmacological treatment. This includes talking to clients about medication and also communicating directly with the prescribing professional. Every nonprescribing therapist should create a good professional relationship with a psychiatrist for referral purposes: someone who is highly competent, shares your values, and respects your strengths. Effective collaboration provides the client with the strongest combination of skills and resources.

The split-treatment model is not ideal, but exists for two reasons: (1) an insufficient number of psychiatrists to perform therapy with all clients who need medication and (2) the lack of prescription privileges for psychotherapists in other professions. Wiggins (2004) summarizes the research evidence in support of psychologists' attainment of statutory authorization to write prescriptions, as they now have in the military.

WHEN IS THIS HYPOTHESIS A GOOD MATCH?

We need to be aware that for severe disorders, such as Schizophrenia and Mania, psychopharmacological treatment is not considered optional, but is rather a part of the "standards of care" for physicians (see Agency for Healthcare Research and Quality at www.ahrq.gov and American Psychiatric Association at www.psych .org) and that "to knowingly withhold pharmacotherapy from patients with these disorders thus could amount to malpractice" (Thase & Jindal, 2004, p. 756).

Thase and Jindal (2004) cite strong research support for combining medication and psychotherapy for Schizophrenia, Major Depressive Disorder, OCD, and Bipolar Affective Disorder. Other disorders for which medication is effective include panic attacks, other anxiety disorders, eating disorders, Attention Deficit Disorder (ADD), and substance abuse disorders.

Target Symptoms That Respond to Psychotropic Medication

It is through a competent differential diagnosis process that you will recognize when to recommend referral for medication. In the intake interview, you will be screening for target symptoms that are criteria for the disorders listed above:

- Signs of thought disorder (e.g., loose associations or incoherent speech); psychosis (e.g., hallucinations or delusions).
- Depression (e.g., negative self-appraisal, suicidal ideation, and vegetative symptoms such as sleep disturbance, appetite disturbance, weight gain or

loss, fatigue, decreased sex drive, agitation, psychomotor retardation, diurnal variation in mood, and anhedonia).

- Mania (e.g., flight of ideas or grandiose delusions).
- Anxiety (e.g., restlessness or impaired concentration).

Medication evaluation is also indicated when the client reports panic attacks or meets diagnostic criteria for ADHD and OCD. Sometimes presenting symptoms that suggest Anxiety or Attention Deficit Disorder stem from either caffeine consumption or withdrawal or are effects of taking medications. Table 3.3 provides indications that strongly support referral for medication evaluation.

Addictions

Medical intervention can be very helpful in the initial stage of detoxification and withdrawal and for assistance during the recovery stages. Therapists should be knowledgeable about the existence of medical interventions: nicotine patches for smoking cessation; methadone programs for heroin addiction; Antabuse (disulfiram), which produces nausea when combined with alcohol, and a newer

Table 3.3 Indications for a Referral to a Psychiatrist for Medication Evaluation

The Client Is Actively Suicidal or Has Severe Functional Impairments

The client's symptoms are interfering with basic functioning—the ability to get out of bed in the morning, go to work, feed herself, and bathe—or the therapist considers the client to be a suicide risk or a risk to others if symptoms are not aggressively treated.

The Symptoms Have Persisted despite Psychotherapeutic Interventions

The client has been in therapy with the current therapist or another therapist for a significant period of time and symptoms have not been alleviated.

The Client Is Self-Medicating

When the client reports the use of alcohol, prescription pain medication, street drugs, herbal remedies, or over-the-counter medicine, it is important to find out specifically what benefits are derived from the chemical. For instance, diet pills can improve concentration and productivity for school assignments, and alcohol can help overcome shyness or reduce sexual inhibitions. This information will tell the therapist that the client may have an underlying condition that could be addressed with medication.

Psychotropic Medication Worked for the Client in the Past

The client has a psychiatric history and medications have worked to alleviate symptoms in the past. Prior success with a medication is one of the strongest reasons for using it with the current symptoms.

Psychotropic Medication Has Worked for Family Members with Similar Symptoms

A family history of similar psychiatric symptoms should be taken as strong evidence that the client might respond to medication, especially if family members have been successfully treated with medication.

drug, Acamprosate, which helps to maintain abstinence from alcohol by reducing cravings. Nonphysician psychotherapists must be careful not to recommend the treatments but rather to recommend a referral to a qualified physician for further evaluation. When clients have received advice from physicians to use a prescribed substance to overcome dependency on another substance, they may be obstinately opposed, as was demonstrated in the movie *Ray,* which dramatized Ray Charles's decision to go through heroin withdrawal cold turkey.

Medication for Physiological Conditions

Conditions related to eating, sleeping, and sexual functioning respond to medication. For example, Viagra can correct erectile dysfunction and sleep medication can treat insomnia. For people who are struggling to lose weight, there are medications to suppress appetite and stimulate metabolism, which can help jumpstart a weight loss program, but which will not lead to long-term success unless the person learns to change eating habits and maintain those changes after the medication is terminated.

Other Medical Interventions

Therapists need to be knowledgeable about the array of interventions on the physical level that can produce mental health benefits. When you discuss these options with clients, note the following caveat for nonphysicians:

> Be careful not to exceed the scope of your practice by doing anything that could be construed as medical advice.

Acupuncture

Acupuncture was formerly considered a fringe treatment, yet now it is commonly integrated into group medical practices and receives reimbursement from health care companies. A common application is in an integrated pain management treatment program for such problems as headaches, back pain, and arthritis. It also has been effective with addictions, weight problems, and depression.

Invasive Treatment of the Brain

It may come as a surprise that psychosurgery is still used, though infrequently: Eskander, Cosgrove, and Rauch (2001) estimate fewer than 25 operations annually in the United States and Great Britain. Rodgers (1992) describes the successful treatment of uncontrollable violent rage episodes: Fortunately, the methods are more advanced than the lobotomy method of the 1940s—an icepick in the orbit of the eye. Modern methods of psychosurgery, including deep brain stimulation and irreversible lesioning, have been used successfully with refractory OCD (Husted & Shapiro, 2004). Electroconvulsive therapy (ECT) is still practiced on patients with severe mood disorders or subtypes of Schizophrenia that have not responded to medication. Electroconvulsive therapy is considered when there is an imminent risk of suicide, because it has more immediate results than antidepressant medication. The name of this treatment still evokes horror, so the patient needs to understand that the seizure activity is carefully monitored and controlled, while patient comfort is assured with medication during the procedure.

Optional Surgery

When surgery offers benefits to the client's mood, functioning, or life satisfaction, the therapist can help the client make a decision and cope with the adjustments that follow. Surgeons frequently require psychological evaluation before deciding whether to provide the requested surgery. Table 3.4 lists several examples of optional surgeries that can improve psychological functioning:

Appliances and Prostheses

Clients may need to consider devices to reduce symptoms or help compensate for loss of functioning. Many clients refuse to consider devices that could improve their quality of life; for example, a person who misses half of conversations, but will not get a hearing aid, or an elderly person who cannot walk without pain but refuses to use a wheel chair because she does not want the negative attention of people who would view her as "crippled." Sometimes the issue is the need for information and access, other times there is a need to explore opposition to use of an appliance that is based on beliefs and assumptions.

TREATMENT PLANNING

An effective approach to case formulation would be to define one problem, for instance, *acute depressive episode,* so that the medical intervention is the main feature of the plan. Then assign other problem titles for issues that do not require a medical intervention. For instance, for a depressed client, other problems could be *excessive discouragement in response to being passed over for promotion; difficulty accepting support from friends and family; difficulty coping with loss and separation.*

How to Handle a Medication Referral

When the need for a medication referral is recognized, the therapist must take steps to ensure that it will be a productive experience.

Presenting the Suggestion

Describe specific target symptoms when explaining the rationale for suggesting a referral for a medication evaluation; assume that the client is wondering *why now*? When you describe the potential value of medication, you must be

Table 3.4   Optional Surgeries to Improve Psychological Functioning

Physical Treatments for Erectile Dysfunction

Erectile dysfunction can have physical and psychological causes. In an otherwise healthy man, this condition may be due to the following: (a) neurological or hormonal abnormalities prevent the initiation of an erection, (b) blockage of arteries prevents the erection chambers from filling with blood, or (c) scarring of the erection chambers prevents them from storing blood. Well-known medications for erectile dysfunction (Viagra, Levitra, and Cialis) are appropriate for the first cause but will be ineffective for the other two. Therapists, even if not specializing in sex therapy, should be knowledgeable about the options available: (a) a vacuum constriction device, (b) insertion of a medicated pellet into the urethra, (c) self-injection therapy, (d) penile prosthesis insertion (penile implant) and, rarer than the other choices, (e) the option of penile revascularization (bypass) surgery. Evaluation of the need for this surgery should involve a team approach, including an urologist and a sex therapist.

Gastric Bypass Surgery

Surgeons generally require prospective patients to undergo a psychological evaluation prior to gastric bypass surgery to rule out psychological issues that might negatively affect the results of the surgery, such as depression, substance abuse, or eating disorders. The evaluation assesses whether the patient has realistic expectations, understands the seriousness of the procedure, and is capable of the lifestyle changes that are necessary after surgery.

Sex Reassignment Surgery

Transsexualism, a problem of gender identity, needs to be distinguished from homosexuality (sexual attraction to the same gender) and fetishistic cross-dressing (achieving sexual arousal while wearing the clothes of the other gender, without desiring to actually be that gender). A client who is considering surgical reassignment needs to be referred to a responsible expert who would require psychological evaluation as well as an extended time period living in the role of the desired gender. Generally, the drastic intervention of a sex change operation would not be considered unless the following criteria are met: (a) conviction since childhood of having been born into the wrong sex, (b) repugnance towards one's sexual characteristics, and (c) a wish to be accepted in the community as belonging to the opposite sex.

Cosmetic (Aesthetic) Surgery

When reconstructive surgery is medically necessary (e.g., after burns, mastectomies, trauma, or severe acne scarring), it belongs under **B1.** Cosmetic surgery is not covered by health insurance and is chosen for the benefits of physical enhancement, as with these problem titles: *Excessive embarrassment and discomfort in social situations* or *Extreme dissatisfaction with physical appearance.* Therapists can help evaluate the client's reasons for the surgery and help challenge unrealistic expectations and misconceptions about how plastic surgery will improve the client's life. Utopian expectations (**C1**) can be identified if the client thinks that a straight nose will bring happiness and instant success with dating. Deeper issues of self-loathing, social anxiety, or inability to accept aging gracefully may be uncovered in therapy. Alternatively, opposition to the idea can come from a set of schemas (**C2**) that oppose vanity: The thought that "you should accept the body that God gave you," or "there are better ways to spend your money."

careful not to state or imply that medication is necessary. You are not telling the client that she needs medication, just that you think it is a good idea to have an evaluation from someone with the expertise to make that decision. You should discuss client fears and beliefs, and help shape realistic, positive expectations.

Exploring the Client's Reaction

Exploring a client's reaction should be a two-way dialogue. What meaning does the client attach to the suggestion? Is the therapist admitting defeat? Is this a rejection? The client might ask: *Does this mean that I'm crazy?* Many clients are very resistant to the idea of taking medication because they fear the stigma, as if medication officially stamps them as having "mental illness," or they have personal rules that prohibit relying on external substances for emotional well-being. If the client is worried about the cost of medication, the therapist should explain that psychiatrists have free samples and that many drug manufacturers have programs for free or reduced cost medication.

Explaining the Roles of the Two Professionals

Make clear to the client that you will continue to provide psychotherapy, while the prescribing psychiatrist will monitor the effect of medication on target symptoms. Two copies of a two-way release of information form should be signed and the client should understand that the two professionals will communicate to best coordinate care.

The Referral

The therapist provides the psychiatrist with a short history and reasons for requesting the evaluation prior to the appointment and expects to receive a follow-up report and phone conversation following the appointment.

Debriefing the Evaluation with the Client

The therapist invites the client to talk about reactions after the evaluation. The roles of the two professionals are again clarified, and boundaries are explained.

When the Client Is on Medication

Whether the client was already on medication when entering therapy or has just begun medication following a referral, you need to be prepared to deal with the following: (a) issues specific to medication, such as experiencing side effects as well as other reasons for desiring to be noncompliant, (b) issues that arise from seeing two different professionals, and (c) new problems that emerge after symptom reduction is obtained. You should encourage the client to discuss questions and concerns with the prescribing professional. Although you will reinforce and explain what the other professional has communicated, you must be careful not to overstep the bounds of your competence. Sometimes, you may have to explain that you will no longer be able to see the client, because of the limits on the scope of your practice, if the client's severe symptoms are not controlled by medication. Table 3.5 lists some common medication issues.

Table 3.5   Common Medication Issues

Onset of Clinical Action

Clients need to understand that it will sometimes take several weeks before they are expected to experience improvement and they should not quit taking the drug because they are not noticing any positive effects.

Dealing with Side Effects

A major cause of discontinuation is distress over side effects. Urge the client to talk to the prescribing psychiatrist if he or she experiences side effects from the medication. Giving the medication a little more time might be recommended by the physician, with specific predictions of normal side effects. If troublesome side effects persist, they are usually managed by adjusting dosage or switching to another medication.

Understanding and Following Instructions

Clients need to understand that they must not discontinue taking medication because they feel better, but instead should do so under the guidance of the psychiatrist. Sudden discontinuation can produce withdrawal symptoms. Clients should understand and follow rules for avoiding light, getting required blood tests, discussing intention to become pregnant, and not combining prescribed medication with alcohol, drugs, or herbal remedies.

Relapse Prevention

There are many conditions that require long-term maintenance on medication to prevent recurrence of symptoms. Therapists can help clients to do a cost-benefit analysis of maintenance versus discontinuation, comparing the negative effects of medication with the consequences of a recurrence of the disorder. Clients may have been taught that medication is only a temporary measure. However, it is common practice now, when the client has a third recurrence of the disorder that responded to medication, to consider continuous rather than intermittent use.

Direct Communication between Professionals

Effective coordination of care requires ongoing communication. Therapists need to be aware of the possibility of the client telling different stories in the two settings. In one case, a client told the therapist that she was drinking and taking street drugs but denied this to the psychiatrist. The two professionals, after comparing notes, decided that the psychiatrist would order drug testing.

"Splitting"

This is a psychodynamic term for the interpersonal dynamic where the client sees people as all good or all bad. This can occur when the client is seeing two professionals: One becomes idealized and the other devalued. The therapist needs to be aware of the potential for this dynamic, and make it a focus of therapy if it occurs. The professional who is being idealized must recognize this process and not collude with the client's efforts to denigrate the other professional. To deal effectively with splitting, the two professionals must already have a good working relationship.

Emergence of New Problems

These may be problems that were ignored because of the severity of the symptoms, or new ones that emerge as symptoms subside. Common problems include:

- *Suicidal risk:* Clients with severe depression do not have the energy to mobilize resources to kill themselves. When antidepressants begin to work, the risk of suicide may increase.

- *Deficits in life skills:* Although the clients' symptoms were extreme, she was relieved of responsibilities for life tasks or excused for impairments in functioning. Now that the symptoms are clearing up, it becomes clear that there are deficits that need to be addressed, for instance, poor job skills.

- *Problems in interpersonal relationships:* When a client is stabilized on medication, many interpersonal problems may be identified (e.g., lack of a good friendship network, poor communication skills, or difficulty coping with conflict).

INTEGRATION OF HYPOTHESES

You should always consider the following hypotheses when clients are evaluated for psychotropic medication.

C2 Faulty Cognitive Map

The client's attitudes and schemas about medication are important factors. Some clients want a quick fix when a better approach would involve developing new skills or working patiently on long-standing emotional issues; other clients reject the idea of medication because of the meaning they attribute to taking it (*I'm weak, crazy, mentally ill*) or faulty beliefs (*My boss will find out*). If taking medication means that the illness is physical rather than mental (*I'm just correcting a neurotransmitter imbalance, it's like a person with diabetes taking insulin*), it can be very comforting, removing the stigma of being severely mentally ill.

SCE2 Cultural Context

Cultures and subgroups differ in their values and prejudices about medication and psychotherapy. Psychotherapists may believe that medication carries more stigma than psychotherapy, whereas many clients may believe the opposite.

SCE6 Social Role of Mental Patient

Knowledge that a person is taking psychotropic medication can put the person into the social role of mental patient, which can influence the reaction and judgments of others, as well as the client's self-appraisal.

B3 MIND-BODY CONNECTIONS

Definition

A holistic understanding of **Mind-Body Connections** leads to treatment for psychological problems that focus on the body and treatment for physical problems that focus on the mind.

Explanation

This hypothesis is a good fit for clients classified as somatizers, for many types of stress and tension complaints, and for sexual disorders. Clients often need to increase their awareness of and control over their bodies and to develop a somatic awareness of feelings. Many body-centered therapies have utility for psychological problems. Psychological states can affect the brain, autonomic nervous system, and immune system. Health problems, such as cancer and AIDS, are benefited by positive mental states.

Examples

Paul had difficulty expressing emotions and was incapable of spontaneity. Even though he had read unfavorable things about it, he chose Reichian therapy. The therapist worked directly on his body's musculature. While experiencing physical pain, Paul recovered memories from childhood that he had repressed. Following treatment, his capacity to express feelings and feel close to his fiancée was greatly improved.	Nick's gastrointestinal pain began when his wife began neglecting him, to pay attention to her newly divorced sister's children. The physician ruled out a medical cause for the pain. In psychotherapy, he discovered that the somatic symptoms were caused by emotional tensions. Nick was feeling angry and abandoned, but never communicated these feelings. When he learned to express his needs, the symptoms disappeared.	Barbara described herself as "living entirely in her mind." She didn't know what she felt or what she truly wanted, and she operated solely on "shoulds" and automatic submission to the demands of other people. She went to a therapist who integrated Eugene Gendlin's focusing method into therapy. She learned the skill of focusing on her bodily experience and waiting for a "felt sense" to occur. This method helped her resolve a major dilemma.

KEY IDEAS FOR B3 MIND-BODY CONNECTIONS

The bidirectional connections of mind and body have been documented in numerous ways (e.g., brain scans of people with symptoms of ADD or OCD, health outcomes of cancer patients in support groups, the effective use of imagery in pain management, and the reduction of blood pressure from biofeedback techniques). The professional specializations of health psychology, behavioral medicine and liaison psychiatry are based on the application of the **B3** hypothesis.

Stress

The term *stress* has multiple meanings. Sometimes it means "external environmental stressors," as when I say *"There's a lot of stress in my life now,"* referring to academic pressure, divorce, or unemployment. It also refers to the physiological responses involved in "fight-flight" reactions: activation of the sympathetic nervous system, biochemical changes in the brain and glands, and avoidant responses. Stress can manifest in somatic symptoms such as stomach aches, muscle tension, headaches, fatigue, nausea, dizziness, and skin rashes. The mind-body relationships are bidirectional: Psychological factors influence muscle tension and autonomic responses, while the arousal level of the body leads to the subjective experience of anxiety, anger, or panic.

Psychological Trauma

When Freud developed his theory of neurotic mechanisms, he included conversion reactions, where unconscious defenses repress emotional pain while producing a symptom in the body, such as paralysis or blindness, often symbolic of the underlying psychic conflict. Wilhelm Reich (1980) focused on the way the child's body developed rigidity as a defense against emotional pain, using the term *character armor* for these enduring self-protective mechanisms. Levine (1997) describes how "survival energy" from the fight-flight reaction, which was not appropriately discharged at the time of the trauma, remains "stuck" in the body and the nervous system; the various symptoms of trauma result from the body's attempt to manage and contain this unused energy. Neuroscientists describe Posttraumatic Stress Disorder (PTSD) in terms of dysregulation of the central nervous system involving chronic hyperarousal, the intrusions of sensory, somatic, and emotional memories into current consciousness as if they were happening in the present (*flashbacks*), dissociation and amnesia in extreme situations, and inhibition of language centers.

Psychoneuroimmunology

Psychoneuroimmunology (PNI) is the field that studies the interactions among the neural, immune, and endocrine systems; most commonly, PNI refers to the link between someone's state of mind and her health, with special attention to the evidence that mental activities can promote healing. The well-known *placebo effect,* referring to improvement in members of the control group of a drug study who have been given an inert substance instead of medication, demonstrates that positive expectancies have measurable physiological benefits. Norman Cousins (1979) popularized the view that positive emotions, particularly humor, can produce dramatic benefits to physical health. The Simonton Cancer Center in California reports evidence that guided imagery and meditative techniques produce positive changes in cancer patients. Participation in support groups has been associated with better life expectancies for cancer patients as compared to patients who did not participate. When patients have a sense of control over the management of their illness, they are likely to have a more positive outlook.

Negative psychological experiences can depress the immune system. A wide range of stressful events have been associated with lowered immune system function, including school examinations, divorce, and bereavement. Research has confirmed the commonsense belief that we are more susceptible to the common cold when we are experiencing higher levels of stress. It follows that people who use good coping strategies and have social support when faced with stressful events will have better-functioning immune systems. There is even research showing that people can learn to suppress overreactive immune responses, which cause such diseases as lupus.

Although it is important to understand the progress made in this new field, be aware of two risks: (1) fueling unrealistic faith in the power of positive mental states, possibly leading to the rejection of medical care; and (2) triggering guilt in medical patients who may blame themselves (e.g., for poor stress management or excessive anger) for causing their disease.

Physiological States

Physiological conditions, such as sexual arousal, hormonal changes, and fatigue, can greatly influence mental states. For instance, adolescent, menopausal, premenstrual, and postpartum hormonal states can be extremely disruptive to emotional, cognitive, and behavioral functioning. The very common experience of jet lag occurs from disruption of sleep and waking cycles. The release of endorphins produces a pleasurable effect, which serves as positive reinforcement for the behavior that elicited this biological response. This reinforcing effect can be beneficial when it helps people develop healthy habits of regular exercise. However, the release of endorphins also reinforces harmful behavior, such as self-mutilation.

Abilities and Capacities for Optimal Body Functioning

Individuals possess a variety of abilities and capacities that contribute to good physical and mental health. Table 3.6 presents a list of abilities and capacities for optimal body functioning. By understanding the components of positive health, therapists can identify problems and set outcome goals.

WHEN IS THIS HYPOTHESIS A GOOD MATCH?

From the previous topics, we can develop problem titles for impairments and dysfunctions: A few examples are *Inability to relax and enjoy leisure time; difficulty focusing on body sensations during sexual intercourse;* or *difficulty accessing and labeling emotions.* The following categories provide a wide range of common applications.

Stress, Anxiety, and Tension

Clients need help with stress reactions whether they are coping with difficulties from a current, temporary situational stressor, dealing with chronic stress conditions that put health at risk, or coping with the aftereffects of severe trauma. The client needs to learn how to enter a physiologically relaxed state, putting the body's arousal level under voluntary control. This goal fits a variety of problems including anxiety symptoms and disorders, anger management issues, stress-related physical disorders, difficulty falling asleep, and overeating because of emotional factors. Difficulty relaxing and enjoying breaks from work is a common complaint of workaholics and perfectionists.

Table 3.6   Abilities and Capacities for Optimal Body Functioning

The Ability to Take Care of the Needs of Your Body

Eating, sleeping, bathing, providing for shelter, enhancing immunity from disease, social contact, and sexual fulfillment are all essential processes in maintenance of physical health and well-being. We also need behaviors that improve health: good nutrition, exercise, medical check-ups, and relaxing leisure. Caring for the body can also include luxuries like massages, facials, and aromatherapy.

Coordination of the Body

Ideally, the movement of the body is smooth and fluid, the muscles are loose and free of tension, and the posture is upright with the head balanced loosely on the spine. These qualities are especially important for people engaged in performance arts or sports as their occupations or hobbies. The body bears the imprint of early experiences with stress and trauma in the form of tightness, rigidity, and loss of spontaneity.

Sensory Awareness of Cues from the Body

It is important to be able to assess one's level of arousal, distinguish between physical hunger and emotional cravings for food, and recognize the difference between emotional and physical pain. Attention to the body should be under voluntary control. During sex, it is desirable to be able to attend fully to specific sensations in the body and tune out external stimuli. However, you want to be able to ignore signals from the body, such as pain, if you are facing an external threat.

The Capacity to Regulate Arousal

When the fight-flight reaction is triggered, it is essential to be able to distinguish real danger from conditioned or symbolic threat. In the latter case, you need the ability to lower your arousal. The ability to induce in yourself a state of relaxation, at will, is probably one of the most important coping skills you can develop. It also may be necessary to voluntarily increase your arousal, as when you need higher levels of concentration to complete a project or higher levels of sexual arousal when you so choose.

The Ability to Put Your Emotional and Somatic Experiences into Words

This behavior is associated, on a neural level, with integration between cognitive and emotional processing networks and communication between both hemispheres of the brain. Lack of this ability, which means lack of neural integration, results in problems such as *poor affect regulation* and *dissociative states*. When emotional experiences are not verbalized, the risk of somatization—replacing awareness of feelings with somatic symptoms—is increased.

The Capacity to Register What You Want and Feel, versus What You "Should" Want and Feel

What a person thinks she feels and wants can be completely at odds with a deeper body sense that carries a more valid expression of true desires. The technique of *focusing* (Gendlin, 1982) teaches how to access a "felt sense" in the body.

The Ability to Experience Pleasure and Contentment at Moderate to Low Levels of Arousal

There are people who associate high levels of stimulation with pleasure and feel bored or anxious at lower levels. This is problematic in a committed relationship: New lovers are exciting, but will no longer be appreciated when a sense of familiarity and comfort develops. Some people find that if they stay busy and stressed, they maintain a good mood, but when they get more relaxed, they feel terrible. For instance, "workaholics" can't enjoy vacations and "stimulus junkies" get depressed when operating at normal levels of stimulation.

(continued)

Table 3.6   *(Continued)*

The Ability to Tolerate Unpleasant Emotions

Anxiety can cause an increased heart rate and sweaty palms, anger reddens the face and blurs vision, and grief overwhelms the body with lethargy and aches. It is not easy to sit with these feelings and simply endure them; people find strategies for either eliminating awareness of these feelings or immediately acting out on them to make them go away. These tactics can lead to countless problems: distortions of reality through projection and displacement, obsessions and compulsions, agoraphobia, kleptomania, aggressive acting out behavior, addictions to substances as well as to unsatisfying relationships, and suicide.

The Awareness of and Ability to Control Nonverbal Messages

Our bodies send messages through facial expressions, posture, gestures, and movements that are interpreted by the viewer to have social meaning. Often, these messages are incongruent with our internal thoughts and feelings, creating an unintended impact. If a client wishes to be warm and friendly to strangers but unintentionally sends uninviting messages, he may need help in changing nonverbal messages.

The Ability to Appraise and Evaluate the Appearance of Your Body Realistically

There are many ways that people hold distorted body images: A person of average weight sees a "fat person" in the mirror; an anorectic person views her emaciated body as normal, and an obese person describes himself as "somewhat overweight."

Chronic Pain

Pain is usually a temporary state that either goes away naturally or is a signal of a medical disorder that can be treated. When the pain is continual or recurring and interferes with daily functioning, and the person has to learn to live with it rather than hope for a medical cure, the term *chronic pain* is used. Chronic pain is both physical and psychological. Psychotherapists can be part of an interdisciplinary treatment team or receive referrals when pain medication is not appropriate or sufficient for dealing with chronic pain. A theoretical model of pain, like that of stress, involves interactions of physiological changes, cognitive appraisal, and muscular tension. Sufferers of chronic pain are at risk for substance abuse and often experience depression.

Medical Complaints without Medical Cause

Therapists may receive referrals from physicians of patients who insist that there is something physically wrong with them, even after multiple tests produce normal findings. The term *hypochondriasis* applies when the patient overreacts to bodily sensations, convinced that there is a serious disease. The term *somatization* is used when patients fit the following profile: Their health problems began at an early age, covering a variety of organ systems, and they pursue surgeries even when clinical findings are in the normal range. These people are not consciously malingering; the mechanism for substituting physical and somatic symptoms for psychological issues is outside of their awareness and not under conscious control. The symptoms give the person an entrance ticket to attention, care, and nurturing from the health professionals and provide a means of indirectly controlling other family members. The clinician must refrain from suggesting "it's all in your head," an attitude that destroys the therapeutic alliance, but instead validate that the suffering is real. Because real medical problems can coexist with somatization complaints, the therapist cannot eliminate the need for medical evaluations.

Problems with Eating, Sleep, and Sexual Functioning

Problems with eating can include severe disorders, such as Anorexia Nervosa and Bulimia, as well as common frustrations of failure to attain a desired weight and lack of control over one's eating or drinking behaviors. These clients need to learn to monitor body sensations of hunger and fullness, as well as to identify bodily sensations that are signs of emotions other than hunger. Sleep disturbances include the occasional by-product of worry and stress, symptoms of depression and anxiety disorders, and more complicated conditions requiring referral to sleep disorder clinics, such as sleep apnea, the intermittent cessation of breathing during sleep.

Problems in sexual functioning involve complex interactions between mind and body. Therapists need to be able to talk comfortably about sex with clients: Many trainees feel embarrassed to probe in this area, and clients might not feel comfortable talking about it without encouragement. Therapists should be ready to refer clients to competent sex therapists.

Dissatisfaction with Body

The client may directly express dissatisfaction with some aspect of the body and its functioning. *Body Dysmorphia* is a *DSM* diagnosis for people who have a distorted view of the size of their own body. Athletes, singers, musicians, and dancers may need psychological interventions because of problems with their performance. For instance, a tennis player may need tools for focusing concentration and a concert pianist may suddenly have debilitating attacks of stage fright. In addition, medical patients may need psychological help adjusting to the impact of the disease on their body. For instance, ostomy patients adjusting to the use of an external bag have difficulties in coping with the loss of dignity and fear of public humiliation.

Difficulties with Awareness and Expression of Emotions

Excessive emotional arousal, with lack of awareness of sources of emotions or tools for appropriate management and expression, is an extremely common problem in therapy. Patients diagnosed with Borderline Personality Disorder show extreme emotional instability and need help with emotional regulation. People with lack of control over expressions of anger may end up in therapy through a court referral.

At the other extreme, there are people who are out of tune with how they feel and have no idea about how to access internal states for information about their own feelings and desires. A person may talk in a monotone and verbalize feelings with a lack of congruence in the bodily signs of that emotion. Excessive rigidity in the body and shallow breathing can cut off the experience of feeling.

Mental States and Behaviors That Put Health at Risk

When the client has already been diagnosed with a medical illness, he or she may need help in bolstering the immune system through positive, health-enhancing attitudes. The choices that a person makes regarding environment, social contacts, and occupation, as well as decisions about smoking, alcohol, diet, exercise, protected sex, and leisure affect the level of risk for physical problems such as accidents, infectious disease, stroke, heart attack, HIV/AIDS, and cancer.

Conditions That Respond to Reputable Body Therapies

Descriptions of therapies that focus on the body give ideas about when to consider referral for one of those treatments. For instance, neurofeedback has been found to be effective with ADHD and Eye Movement Desensitization Reprocessing (EMDR) is widely used for PTSD.

TREATMENT PLANNING

Many body-focused treatment strategies require advanced training, supervision, and even certification. You must decide whether you are qualified to implement a desired plan or whether you need to offer the client a referral.

Strategies to Increase Awareness of the Body

For some clients, especially those with eating disorders, lack of sexual arousal, and tendencies to intellectualize, a primary element of the treatment plan is to increase awareness of their bodies. This awareness can be developed a number of ways, including through journaling, feedback, and focusing.

Diary

A compulsive overeater needs to learn to identify the difference between eating from physical hunger (stomach hunger) and eating to fulfill an emotional need (mouth hunger) a daily monitoring chart (see Table 2.9) could be designed where the client can keep track of the time of day, the situation, the exact amount of food consumed, thoughts and feelings, and also have a column to indicate whether the eating was triggered by "stomach hunger" or "mouth hunger." Discussion in therapy of these diaries can help clients identify the functions of their eating and assist them in finding alternate ways of dealing with their emotions.

Feedback about Messages from the Body

The client's movements, gestures, tics, posture, and facial expression all carry messages. The therapist pays attention to the body and comments on body movements, even asking the person to exaggerate them, to understand their meaning. The painful, tense, and tight areas of a client's body may carry psychological messages. For instance, a stiff neck may mean that he thinks someone is a "pain in the neck" while curved, tense shoulders may show how burdened the client feels.

Focusing

The *focusing* method, developed by Eugene Gendlin, involves specific guided instructions to help people move from their mental definitions of problems to a physically felt body sense. Therapists can use this method in sessions and clients can learn focusing skills independently or with peers.

Treatments for Stress Management

A number of strategies can be integrated in teaching clients to control emotional responses that contribute to physiological stress.

Psychoeducation

Therapists teach the client about stress, explaining how psychological factors influence muscle tension and autonomic responses and how the arousal level of the body leads to the experience of anxiety, anger, or panic. There are many useful books that clients can read about stress, for example, Benson's book, *The Relaxation Response*. The client learns that by directing the mind toward relaxation instead of tension, he or she can directly affect the brain, hormonal activity, blood pressure, and other physical processes and simultaneously alter the subjective sense of anxiety, stress, or panic.

Physical Movement

Any form of physical activity can help to reduce stress. In addition, exercise can allow a client to take a break from stressful activities and gain some perspective on his situation. T'ai chi—one of the martial arts from Asia that is performed in very slow motion—is a technique that reduces stress and produces a sense of confidence and self-mastery. The practice of yoga includes meditation, a focus on breathing, and gentle stretching and simulation of every part of the body, including internal organs.

Use of the Subjective Units of Discomfort Scale

The use of the SUDS was described in Chapter 2. The most common use of this scale is for intense emotional arousal, either from anxiety or anger. Through use of diaries as homework, the client learns to use SUDS numbers for various events during the week and to discriminate different bodily states and emotional reactions. The client then is taught tools to lower discomfort levels during stressful situations, such as taking a "time out" or engaging in deep breathing.

Relaxation Training

As part of your assessment you must determine whether the client can voluntarily lower the SUDS level with simple advice. If not, you should directly teach skills of relaxation. Table 3.7 offers examples of diverse ways of teaching clients how to get control over their level of physiological arousal.

Biofeedback

Learning to lower stress and induce a state of relaxation can be enhanced by the use of physiological monitoring devices. Sensors are attached to the client to measure blood pressure, skin temperature, heart rate, muscle tension, or perspiration. Then the client concentrates on a relaxation technique, paying attention to the feedback from the monitoring equipment to learn if he is successful in changing the body's processes. For instance, learning how to raise the temperature in one's fingers can be beneficial for vascular (migraine) headaches and learning how to reduce the muscle tension in the frontalis muscle is helpful for reducing tension headaches.

Alteration of Brain Functioning

Progress in the field of neuroscience will lead to innovative ways to modify the brain to get changes in thinking, feeling, and behaving. *Neural integration* or *new neural pathways* are outcomes in the brain of effective psychotherapy and other learning experiences. Four methods illustrate ways of directly modifying the brain and states of consciousness to achieve positive clinical results.

Neurofeedback

Like biofeedback, neurofeedback is a technique that uses physiological monitors. However, instead of getting feedback on blood pressure, galvanic skin response (GSR), or body temperature, the feedback is from an electroencephalogram (EEG), which gives information on brain wave activity. Through use of a video display and audio signals, the client learns to match the video display to a desirable frequency band of brain activity. This technique has been used with many types of problems, including sleep problems, addiction, chronic pain, and mood disorders.

Hypnosis

During hypnosis, the practitioner uses verbal suggestions to induce the client to enter and deepen a trance state, which involves intense absorption in the object of concentration, lack of awareness of other experiences, and suggestibility to the instructions and guidance from the person who induced the trance. With practice, the client learns to enter the trance quickly and to use self-hypnosis for therapeutic aims. Hypnosis can help pain sufferers by reducing the perceived level of pain as well as help people lose weight and give up smoking. For hypnosis to work, the client has to meet a threshold of suggestibility and be motivated for the type of change being sought.

Table 3.7 Techniques of Relaxation Training

Progressive Relaxation Training (PRT)

The client is instructed to focus attention on specific muscle groups (e.g., hand or forehead) and to first tighten and then release (relax) them. When those muscles are "completely relaxed," attention is directed to the next group. She repeats this with each muscle group, moving systematically throughout the body, until every muscle group is covered. At the end of the process, the entire body is relaxed. With practice, the client can produce a relaxed state by recall or by counting. It is helpful to have the client make an audio recording of the relaxation instructions for home practice until the method becomes automatic.

Autogenic Training and Self-Hypnosis

The use of suggestion, first from the therapist and then by the client, can induce a relaxed state. *Autogenic training* is a method of passive concentration on bodily sensations, such as heaviness, warmth, coolness, or breathing, without tensing muscles. Another method (not to be used for elevator phobics) is: *Imagine that you are going down an elevator in a tall building, and as you go to each lower floor, you become more and more relaxed, until, when you get to the bottom floor, you are completely relaxed.*

Meditation

Techniques derived from Asian religions are used for producing physiological relaxation and a peaceful mental state. The client learns to discipline the mind to focus on the present moment and to create a sense of stillness, free of the usual chatter that occurs in the mind. The term *mindfulness* refers to awareness, without judgment, of ongoing internal and external experience. In Transcendental Meditation, the person repeats a mantra—a silent word or phrase—to quiet the stream of internal dialogue. However, any type of quiet focused attention on sensory and bodily experience can be considered a form of meditation. People who enjoy knitting describe the pleasurable meditative state they achieve through the rhythmic, repetitive clicking of needles and the visual and tactile pleasure from attending to the yarn.

Breathing Focus

Often a part of other methods, this can be used alone: As the breath is released, it carries tension from the body. By simply focusing on breathing, and increasing the depth of breathing, and hence the intake of oxygen, the client calms mental processes, which achieves a bodily state of relaxation. Learning to breathe from the stomach (diaphragm) rather than from the upper chest helps people reduce anxiety. Here is an example of a simple set of instructions to induce relaxation and to teach the client how to self-relax: *Close your eyes and get comfortable. . . . Take a deep breath in through your nose. . . . Put your hand on your stomach and feel it expand as you inhale again, breathing into the diaphragm rather than into the chest. . . . Exhale through your mouth and feel the diaphragm lower. . . . Focus on the breath and continue a few more times.*

Imagery

The therapist asks the client to remember a place where total relaxation was experienced. The therapist can offer suggestions—the beach with the sound of the ocean, a cool mountain forest, or a hammock under a tree—but the client has to choose something that works for him. The client closes his eyes and imagines himself in that place. The therapist provides verbal suggestions that direct the client's attention to visual, auditory, tactile or olfactory sensations, until total relaxation is achieved. A tape can be made so that the client uses this technique as a self-management tool.

Eye Movement Desensitization Reprocessing

Developed by Francine Shapiro (1996) in 1987, and now called Reprocessing Therapy, this approach teaches clients to stay out of "bad trances" that they experience as symptoms and uncomfortable psychological states. The therapist creates alternating stimulation to the two sides of the brain, while the client brings to mind a past negative incident and links it with a desired future outlook. In treating PTSD, past traumatic events are recalled and processed with a protocol that involves focus of attention on cognitive, emotional, and sensory domains, combined with the therapist stimulating alternate sides of the body, either by hand movements or touch. Alternative activation may enhance neural connectivity and integration of traumatic memories into normal, explicit memory processes.

Phototherapy (Light Therapy) for Depression

There is substantial medical research (e.g., Lundberg, 1998; Terman & Terman, 2005) documenting the benefits of a machine emitting the amount of light that is equivalent to standing outdoors on a clear spring day, for the treatment of Seasonal Affective Disorder, a pattern of major depressive episodes that occur and remit with changes in seasons. Light is registered by the eyes through the retina, which then transfers impulses to the hypothalamus in the brain to normalize the circadian rhythm. There is research supporting the use of light therapy with other conditions, such as nonseasonal depression, premenstrual syndrome, Bulimia Nervosa, difficulties adjusting to night-shift work, and circadian rhythm sleep disorder. A light machine does not require a prescription and can be bought on the Internet.

Body-Centered Therapies

These approaches are rarely covered in the graduate curriculum, but students can find information in the web sites of associations for body psychotherapies in Europe (www.eabp.org) and the United States (www.usabp.org). Some therapies focus on the body through verbal techniques and others involve physical touching. Because they attempt to bypass the defenses and coping strategies of the conscious mind, they carry risks for negative effects, especially when the client has been a victim of severe trauma, and they should only by used by people with extensive specialized training. For practitioners who implement techniques that involve touching the client and/or having the client remove clothing, there is risk of violating laws and ethics, or of being maliciously accused of doing so.

Releasing Old Traumas

Reichian Therapy and *Rolfing* are two approaches (derived from Wilhelm Reich and Ida Rolf, respectively) that involve touching the body of the patient, often in very painful ways, to release emotional pain, sometimes triggering recall of forgotten experiences. Levine (1997) describes a method of "somatic experiencing": The client develops an inventory of resources and then is helped by the therapist to shift back and forth between the high activation of traumatic material and the calming effect of resources.

Alexander Technique

This method is popular in England as a treatment for physical and emotional problems, but is much less known in the United States. An Alexander teacher is not a psychotherapist but someone who has been trained to teach clients to re-structure their posture to recover the spontaneity and coordination that was lost in childhood. The student lies or sits fully dressed while the teacher gently aligns the body into its natural, correct posture, repeating brief verbal instructions. The student learns the verbal instructions and experiences what correct posture feels like, and then is expected to practice the technique between sessions.

Energy Approaches

Many approaches attribute psychological benefits to changes in the flow of energy in the body. In *Bioenergetics* the client assumes postures that lead to trembling and shaking, attributed to the flow of energy. Acupuncture and acupressure are treatments that have been found to have psychological as well as somatic benefits.

Treatment of Chronic Pain

Treatment for chronic pain integrates many of the techniques described earlier, as well as clinical techniques drawn from cognitive therapy and behavior therapy. A multidisciplinary approach in an inpatient treatment program lasting 2 to 4 weeks at Johns Hopkins Pain Treatment Program includes the following components in addition to medications and physical therapy:

Psychoeducation

Includes lectures about chronic pain, mind-body relationships, and treatment modalities.

Psychotherapy

Individual, group, and family therapy to explore how pain affects feelings and feelings affect pain, to deal with the grief and loss from chronic pain, and to increase coping skills and interpersonal relationships.

Therapeutic Group Activities

Involvement in recreational and vocational activities that decrease social isolation and give positive experiences.

INTEGRATION OF HYPOTHESES

One or more of the following hypotheses are often combined with the one just reviewed to create an integrative formulation for a specific problem. The decision about whether a specific hypothesis should be integrated is based on your professional judgment.

CS2 Situational Stressors

Whereas **B3** deals with the bodily state of stress, **CS2** focuses on the stressors from the environment that impinge on the person and create demands to cope adaptively. The concept of *trauma* links an external cause and an internal, often physiological, response.

BL3 Skill Deficits or Lack of Competence

Many adults lack competence in differentiating messages that signal exhaustion, hunger, and thirst. A person who overeats in response to all bodily sensations of discomfort needs to learn to recognize hunger. Many types of skills help people reduce body tension: relaxation skills, time management skills, even skills for reducing clutter in their living space.

P1 Internal Parts and Subpersonalities

Consider that the body needs a spokesperson to articulate its needs. A goal of therapy could be strengthening a self-nurturing part that takes good care of the body.

SCE2 Cultural Context

Eastern religions provide a completely different mind-body perspective from Western culture. In Chinese medicine, organs in the body represent specific mental or emotional conditions. Cultural conditioning affects attitudes toward our bodies, including comfort with nudity, sexuality, and aging. Many cultures use dance, touching, and rituals involving the body to enhance mental health and reduce suffering. Cultures differ in their encouragement of open expression of feelings. Somatization is more common in cultures where emotional expression of stress and anxiety is discouraged.

SCE3 Social Support

Social support brings emotional comfort, and it can reduce stress and boost the immune system.

ES3 Spiritual Dimension

Prayer and other spiritual activities have been found to have positive effects on health and are beneficial resources when coping with stress, chronic pain, and trauma.

SUGGESTED READINGS

Heilman, K., & Valenstein, E. (Eds.). (2003). *Clinical neuropsychology* (4th ed.). New York: Oxford University Press.

Kalat, J. W. (2003). *Biological psychology* (8th ed.). Belmont, CA: Wadsworth.

Pinel, J. P. J. (2005). *Biopsychology* (5th ed.). Boston, MA: Allyn & Bacon.

B1 Biological Cause

Morrison, J. (1997). *Psychological problems mask medical disorders: A guide for psychotherapists.* New York: Guilford Press.

Taylor, R. L. (1990). *Distinguishing psychological from organic disorders: Screening for psychological masquerade.* New York: Springer.

Zarit, S. H., & Zarit, J. M. (1998). *Mental disorders in older adults: Fundamentals of assessment and treatment.* New York: Guilford Press.

Neuropsychological Assessment

Groth-Marnat, G. (Ed.). (2000). *Neuropsychological assessment in clinical practice.* New York: Wiley.

Lezak, M. D. (2004). *Neuropsychological assessment* (4th ed.). New York: Oxford University Press.

Health Psychology

American Psychiatric Association. (2001). *Practice guideline for the treatment of patients with HIV/AIDS* (American Psychiatric Association Practice Guidelines). Arlington, VA: Author.

Baum, A., & Andersen, B. L. (Eds.). (2001). *Psychosocial interventions for cancer.* Washington, DC: American Psychological Association.

Derogatis, L. R., & Wise, T. N. (1989). *Anxiety and depressive disorders in the medical patient.* Washington, DC: American Psychiatric Press.

Gatchel, R. J., & Oordt, M. S. (2003). *Clinical health psychology and primary care: Practical advice and clinical guidance for successful collaboration.* Washington, DC: American Psychological Association.

Holland, J., & Lewis, S. (2001). *The human side of cancer: Living with hope, coping with uncertainty.* New York: Quill.

Langer, K. G., Laatsch, L., & Lewis, L. (Eds.). (1999). *Psychotherapeutic interventions for adults with brain injury or stroke: A clinician's treatment resource.* Madison, CT: Psychosocial Press.

Nezu, A. M., Nezu, C. M., Friedman, S. H., Faddis, S., & Houts, P. S. (1998). *Helping cancer patients cope: A problem-solving approach.* Washington, DC: American Psychological Association.

Spiegel, D., & Classen, C. (1999). *Group therapy for cancer patients: A research-based handbook of psychosocial care.* New York: Basic Books.

B2 Medical Interventions

Bezchlibnyk-Butler, K. Z., & Jeffries, J. (Eds.). (2002). *Clinical handbook of psychotropic drugs* (12th ed.). Cambridge, MA: Hogrefe & Huber.

Johnson, J., & Preston, J. D. (2004). *Clinical psychopharmacology made ridiculously simple* (5th ed.). Miami, FL: Medmaster.

Medical Economics. (Ed.). (2005). *Physicians' desk reference* (59th ed.). Montvale, NJ: Thomson Healthcare.

Thase, M. E., & Jindal, R. D. (2004). Combining psychotherapy and psychopharmacology for treatment of mental disorders. In M. J. Lambert (Ed.), *Bergin and Garfield's handbook of psychotherapy and behavior change* (5th ed., pp. 743–766). Hoboken, NJ: Wiley.

B3 Mind-Body Connections

Benson, H., & Klipper, M. Z. (2000). *The relaxation response* (Reissue ed.). New York: HarperTorch.

Bernstein, D. A., Borkovec, T. D., & Hazlett-Stevens, H. (2000). *New directions in progressive relaxation training: A guidebook for helping professionals.* Westport, CT: Praeger.

Cozolino, L. (2002). *The neuroscience of psychotherapy: Building and rebuilding the human brain.* New York: W. W. Norton.

De Alcantara, P. (1999). *The Alexander Technique: A skill for life.* Wiltshire, England: Crowood Press.

Erickson, M. H., & Rossi, E. L. (1989). *The February man: Evolving consciousness and identity in hypnotherapy.* Philadelphia: Brunner-Routledge.

Evans, J. R., & Abarbanel, A. (Eds.). (1999). *Introduction to quantitative EEG and neurofeedback.* San Diego: Academic Press.

Lowen, A. (1994). *Bioenergetics* (Reissue ed.). New York: Penguin.

Rossi, E. L. (1993). *The psychobiology of mind-body healing: New concepts of therapeutic hypnosis.* New York: W. W. Norton.

Rothschild, B. (2000). *The body remembers: The psychophysiology of trauma and trauma treatment.* New York: Norton.

Schore, A. (2003). *Affect regulation and the repair of the self.* New York: W. W. Norton.

Schwartz, M. S., & Adrasik, F. (1998). *Biofeedback* (2nd ed.). New York: Guilford Press.

Selye, H. (1978). *The stress of life* (2nd ed.). New York: McGraw Hill.

Shapiro, F. (1996). *Eye movement desensitization and reprocessing (EMDR): Basic principles, protocols and procedures.* New York: Guilford Press.

Siegel, D. J. (2001). *The developing mind: How relationships and the brain interact to shape who we are.* New York: Guilford Press.

Smith, E. W. L. (2000). *The body in psychotherapy.* Jefferson, NC: McFarland.

Totton, N. (2003). *Body psychotherapy: An introduction.* Berkshire, England: Open University Press.

Chapter 4 ————————————————————

CRISIS, STRESSFUL SITUATIONS, AND TRANSITIONS

A crisis often pushes people to seek therapy, and, at their first session, they face the therapist with urgency, intense emotions, and doubts about their ability to cope. The therapist needs to remain calm, respond empathically to emotional stories, and use assessment skills to determine: *Is this someone who needs an immediate, active intervention, or is this a client who can safely wait a week for a second session?* There are two errors that must be avoided: (1) Failing to prevent serious consequences, including death, destructive actions, and long-term pathology by not promptly responding in crisis mode, and (2) pathologizing a condition that, while painful and debilitating, is best understood as a normal, expectable response to the stressors, traumas, and transitions of living. The four hypotheses listed in Table 4.1 are useful in preventing these errors.

Although each of these hypotheses can be used alone, there will be many opportunities to integrate them. For instance, the death of a spouse involves **Situational Stressors (C2),** triggers the psychological experience of **Loss and Bereavement (CS4),** and initiates the **Developmental Transition (CS3)** to widowhood. If the grieving spouse becomes suicidal, **Emergency** interventions **(CS1),** such as breaking confidentiality and hospitalization, are needed.

Table 4.1 Crisis, Stressful Situations, and Transitions

CS1 Emergency	The client's symptoms constitute an **Emergency:** Immediate action is necessary.
CS2 Situational Stressors	The client's symptoms result from identifiable recent **Situational Stressors** or from a past traumatic experience.
CS3 Developmental Transition	The client is at a **Developmental Transition,** dealing with issues related to moving to the next stage of life.
CS4 Loss and Bereavement	The client has suffered a **Loss and** needs help during **Bereavement** or for a loss-related problem.

CS1 EMERGENCY

Definition

The client's symptoms constitute an **Emergency:** Immediate action is necessary.

Explanation

This hypothesis must always be considered in the first session because of the severe negative consequences for not taking action. It applies to situations where patients must be hospitalized, and where there are legal requirements for reporting abuse or intended violence. It also fits when the client is about to take an irrevocable action.

Examples

Charles recently lost his family in an acrimonious divorce and states to his therapist, in an agitated voice, "I don't want to go on living." He has a gun at home and has given away his prized baseball card collection. You judge him to be a danger to himself and take immediate steps to get him hospitalized.	Angela is about to take an impulsive, irreversible action—quit her job in a fit of anger over someone else getting a promotion she desired. You switch to a directive and active style of intervention because you want to assure that she takes her time in making such a major decision.	Tom is in therapy for help with "anger management" because of his poor self-control at work. As you ask him how he vents his frustration outside of work, he reveals that he often beats his 6-year-old child. You explain to him that you must report child abuse to the proper authorities.

KEY IDEAS FOR CS1 EMERGENCY

The Emergency hypothesis leads you to take immediate action and to use crisis models instead of leisurely approaches to therapy. Your first task is to stabilize the client's condition. You then need to develop a problem list for issues that caused the emergency and for problems that will continue once the emergency is over: For example, *difficulty coping with loss of significant other* for a person who made a suicide attempt; *poor parenting skills* and *lack of control over anger* for a perpetrator of child abuse, which you had to report; and *poor medication compliance* and *need for supervised living situation* for someone having a psychotic episode.

Knowledge of Community

It is not enough to know about hospitalization and day treatment as abstract topics; you need to be prepared with a clear flowchart of necessary actions, starting with the hospital you will use, the phone number you will dial, the consultants you can count on, and, if possible, the hospital staff member who will work with you if you do not have staff privileges.

Legal and Ethical Issues

Licensed practitioners are required to know the laws and judicial decisions that affect psychotherapy in their state, such as the laws requiring a prompt report of

Table 4.2   Managing a Violent Client

Maintain a demeanor of calm and confidence; take your time—do not hurry the situation.

If the client has a weapon, insist that it be removed from the scene.

Frame your role: I want to help you get control over these feelings; I want to help you find a better means of handling the situation.

Do not block the client's access to the door.

Have support people available—leave the door open, have someone else present, or have an alarm system.

Lower the client's emotionality: Talk in simple direct language, help put words to feelings, and ask factual questions.

Provide structure and limits: Make it clear that violence will not be tolerated.

Give praise for signs that the client is keeping his temper under control.

Call police or psychiatric emergency team, if needed.

Do not hesitate to do what you need to feel safe, even if you think it will offend the client.

child abuse, the criteria for involuntary hospitalization, and legal decisions that mandate notification of intended victims. Ethical issues that are particularly relevant in emergencies are the limits on confidentiality and the requirement to work within the limits of your competence. Sales et al. (2005) provide a useful text on laws affecting clinical practice.

Managing Violent Clients

It is important to have the knowledge and skills to deal with a client who enters your clinic or office in a violent state. Ideally, in your training program, you had the opportunity to role-play these scenarios and will work in a setting with buzzer systems for safety and a staff that is trained to deal with this type of emergency. Table 4.2 gives guidelines from Hipple and Hipple (1983) for this situation.

WHEN IS THIS HYPOTHESIS A GOOD MATCH?

To recognize emergency situations, screen for three conditions: (1) danger to self, (2) danger to others, and (3) inability to take care of basic needs. You need to assess whether emergency action is needed, as well as manage the interview in a constructive way when you are going to take actions that the client may object to, such as breaking confidentiality to notify family members or report child abuse. Assessing suicide risk is automatically part of initial sessions and is always performed when there are signs of depression. Be assured that it is a myth that talking about suicide puts the idea in someone's head: Avoiding the topic is riskier than approaching it. Trainees should role-play the assessment of suicide potential, as described in Table 4.3.

Table 4.3   Assessment of Suicide Potential

Be direct in a discussion of suicide, showing comfort in dealing with the topic: *Have you had thoughts about taking your life?*

Ask about specific suicidal thoughts, asking follow-up questions to assess the duration and intensity: *How often do you think about shooting yourself?*

Inquire about the presence of a plan: *Have you thought about how you would kill yourself? What steps have you already taken?*

Assess lethality of the chosen method: The more specific the plan, the higher the rating of lethality. Does the client have the means? Is there a possibility of rescue?

Explore suicidal behavior as communication. What message is the person communicating? What response is hoped for? Is there a specific person from whom a response is desired? Has the person severed communication and lost hope of any help?

Gather details of past attempts: *Have you ever tried to take your life? Tell me about that.*

Assess social support resources: How isolated is the client? Who can be turned to for help? Is the significant other a helpful resource or a part of the problem?

Assess the level of current substance abuse—a factor that diminishes impulse control.

Assess the level of depression and the possibility of psychosis—factors that increase risk.

Explore precipitating factors. Is there an acute stressor in the life of a stable person or is there a pattern of chronic suicidal behavior?

Evaluate the level of ambivalence: How strong is the "death" side versus the "stay alive" side?

Has anyone else in the family attempted or completed suicide?

Have there been final preparations for death, such as making a will, giving away valuables, or making arrangements for pets?

Risk of Violence against Others

In assessing the client's potential for violence use these criteria: past history of violent behaviors, specificity of plan, possession of weapon, diagnoses of psychosis, current state of intoxication, demonstration of agitation, presence of threatening behaviors, and capacity to control anger in your presence.

Recognition of Child, Spousal, and Elder Abuse

The American Medical Association has guidelines for detecting and responding to various kinds of abuse—child abuse, child sexual abuse, elder abuse, domestic violence, and sexual assault—at http://www.ama-assn.org/ama/pub /category/3548.html. A frustration for professionals is that victims lie to protect their abusers. Children internalize messages that they deserved what they got, or they may be silenced by threats from the perpetrator. When the abuser is a parent, children also fear the loss of that relationship. In elder abuse by a family member, the victim has many reasons to deny a problem—the biggest being the fear that being put in an institution is worse than the suffering caused by the abusive spouse or child. Walker (1984) was one of the first to describe "battered woman syndrome," suggesting that women do not report abuse because of (a) the "honeymoon" phase after an episode of violence when the man is repentant, (b) the fear of danger to self or children for reporting the abuser, and (c) the belief that the violence was her fault.

Judgments about abuse can be made from clues dropped by the client, even if the victim of abuse is not present. For instance, while discussing how she is trying to meet eligible men, a divorced mother may say that she left her young child at home without a babysitter, locking her in the bedroom so that she wouldn't get into trouble. A caretaker of his mother, a stroke victim, may reveal how he has cut off her telephone access to her daughter, who lives in a distant state, "because it gets her upset," without realizing that he is denying her a basic right.

Small Emergencies

There is no dispute about taking immediate directive actions for "big" emergencies. However, many therapists are willing to ignore the client's real-life crises so that they can proceed calmly and patiently with their theory of choice. For instance, a student in a practicum class reported that her supervisor wanted her to help a client develop insight into early childhood dynamics. Meanwhile, the client was involved in a custody dispute and was about to lose her children. Every member of the practicum group agreed that the first priority should be a focus on real-world actions that the client could take, such as immediately getting a lawyer.

TREATMENT PLANNING

In managing emergencies, unlicensed trainees must remain in close contact with supervisors; even experienced licensed professionals should seek consultation for both expert guidance and emotional support. Be sure to document assessment and actions in charts and memos.

The "right thing to do" is not always clear, despite numerous laws, rules, and guidelines. There will be complicated grey areas, and you will need to weigh costs and benefits. For instance, hospitalization might mean you'll sleep easier at night, but perhaps the patient can get through the crisis in a less restrictive environment as long as he knows he can call you at any time during the night. The "best interests of the client" may conflict with your own need to do what is easiest and most comfortable for you.

The Decision to Hospitalize

You need to determine whether the client and his support system can manage the client's emotional state and protect the client and others from harm. After a period of emotional ventilation, empathic and soothing responses, and structured, crisis management problem-solving efforts, the risk level may be much lower than it seemed at first. The guiding principle is to try to keep the client in the *least restrictive environment.*

If hospitalization is judged to be necessary, you can encourage voluntary admission, before seeking an involuntary hold. Hipple and Hipple (1983) recommend the following steps:

- Explain to the client and family why you believe hospitalization is the best choice at this time.
- Provide information, including a description of the admissions process, ward activities, and treatments that will be offered.
- Offer reassurance and help create realistic expectations.
- For voluntary hospitalization, call ahead and let staff know when the client will be arriving; provide the intake staff with your written notes.
- If involuntary hospitalization is necessary and client will be transported by police, help him understand what procedures to expect, such as the mandatory use of handcuffs.

Maintaining the Therapeutic Alliance

When your legal duties involve breaking confidentiality, the therapeutic alliance is jeopardized; informing the client in the first session of the limits of confidentiality does not protect you from the client's sense of betrayal. You need to be able to tolerate anger and work to restore trust.

Suicidal Clients

Therapists need skills and sensitivity for working with suicidal clients. Therapists must consider their own needs for support and back-up. Countertransference is an inevitable part of working with these clients, and, if unexamined, might lead to inadvertently sending the message that you wish the client would disappear, which would increase the client's suicidal potential. Jongsma and Peterson (2003) list a variety of therapeutic interventions for suicidal ideation, including the following:

- Notify family and significant others of the suicidal ideation. Ask them to form a 24-hour suicide watch until the crisis subsides.
- Assist the client in developing an awareness of his or her cognitive messages that reinforce hopelessness and helplessness.
- Draw up a contract with the client identifying what he or she will do when experiencing suicidal thoughts or impulses.
- Assist the client in finding positive, hopeful things in his or her life at the present time.

- Assist the client in developing coping strategies for suicidal ideation (e.g., more physical exercise, less internal focus, increased social involvement, and more expression of feelings).
- When suicidal ideation is connected with survivor guilt, implement a "penitence ritual."
- Assist the client in becoming aware of life factors that were significant precursors to the beginning of his or her suicidal ideation.

Reporting Abuse and Intended Violence

Mental health professionals are mandated reporters of child and elder abuse and need to know the laws and procedures of their states. For instance, in California, Section 11166 of the Penal code requires a mandated reporter

> who has knowledge of, or observes, a child in his or her professional capacity or within the scope of his or her employment whom he or she knows or reasonably suspects has been the victim of child abuse to report the known or suspected instance of child abuse to a child protective agency immediately, or as soon as practically possible, by telephone and to prepare and send a written report thereof within 36 hours of receiving the information concerning the incident.

Similarly, knowledge or reasonable suspicion of elder abuse requires you to make a report. When you are aware that a client intends violence against an identifiable person, you have a duty to contact the intended victim as well as the police, a duty established by the Tarasoff decision in California (*Tarasoff v. Regents of the University of California,* 17 Cal. 3d 425, 1976). A recent court ruling in California extended the duty to include knowledge that comes from family members of the client.

These responsibilities and duties can be very anxiety-provoking for therapists and the wisest thing to do is to consult with experts. Fortunately, the major professional organizations have consultation available. For instance, members of the American Association of Marriage and Family therapists can arrange for telephone consultation with a legal expert through their web site, http://www.aamft.org.

Ensuring Safety for Battered Women

It is not a simple task to persuade a battered woman to leave her home and seek shelter for herself and her children. One strategy is to have a woman from a shelter come talk to the client because of the credibility of someone who has gone through the same experience. You can guide the client through steps to get a protective order from the court. A useful intervention is to help the victim draw up a formal written safety plan, which she can consult at a time of future need. The Alaska Network on Domestic Violence and Sexual Assault provides a very clear and thorough template at http://www.andvsa.org/safety.htm. The opening statement affirms positive action:

> This is my plan for increasing my safety and preparing in advance for the possibility of further violence. Although I do not have control over my partner's violence, I do have a choice about how to respond to him and how to best get myself and my children to safety.

The document includes phone numbers of emergency hotlines and shelters, advice for handling an assault, steps for leaving home safely, a list of items to take, and suggestions for including neighbors as resources.

INTEGRATION OF HYPOTHESES

All of the following hypotheses are relevant for assessing and managing emergencies.

B1 Biological Cause

Psychiatric symptoms with a biological basis, such as signs of a stroke, may require emergency action. A client with Anorexia may require immediate hospitalization.

B2 Medical Interventions

Evaluation for psychotropic medication is often necessary, especially when an emergency situation is being managed outside of a hospital.

SCE3 Social Support

Family members and other members of the client's support network need to be contacted and involved in the planning of emergency actions.

SCE6 Social Role of Mental Patient

One reason for choosing an environment that is less restrictive than a psychiatric hospital is to reduce the stigma involved in putting someone in a mental patient role when they are experiencing a temporary psychological emergency.

ES3 Spiritual Dimension

Spiritual emergency is a term for psychological difficulties stemming from spiritual practices and spontaneous spiritual experiences. An example would be a psychotic episode following intense immersion in spiritual practice (yoga and meditation). Additionally, spiritual resources such as prayer and support from clergypersons and congregations can help individuals and families cope with emergencies.

CS2 SITUATIONAL STRESSORS

Definition

The client's symptoms result from identifiable recent **Situational Stressors,** or from a past traumatic experience.

Explanation

It is important to evaluate whether the client's symptoms and impairments are proportional to the level of stress. You need to specify the external stressors, which may range from life-threatening traumas to the accumulation of daily hassles of living, and have an objective way of measuring their severity. Crisis intervention techniques can prevent crisis reactions from developing into long-term disorders. Adult survivors of early abuse and trauma and people with PTSD need specialized treatment modalities.

Examples

Rachel was visiting her family and friends in Israel, where she grew up. She was sitting at a beachfront café when a suicide bomber exploded in front of the restaurant. She and her friends were unharmed, but she was sprayed with blood and body parts. She took a flight home the next day and refused to talk about the experience in order not to upset her husband. She is troubled by intense anxiety symptoms and nightmares.	At first, Grant's depression seemed to stem from being passed over for a promotion a year ago. However, the symptoms didn't develop until 2 months ago, after his wife called his father and discussed his condition behind his back. You realize that "situational stress" is not an adequate hypothesis; the wife's "betrayal" is a symbolic stressor, which taps into vulnerabilities from his early relationship with his father.	Lisa came to a sex therapist with her husband because she was unable to have sexual intercourse. She enjoyed hugging and kissing, but as soon as he touched her genitals, she froze, had severe anxiety symptoms, and started crying. The therapist arranged to meet separately with each partner. Lisa admitted that she had been a victim of incest as a child. She had never told anyone and was afraid to tell her husband.

KEY IDEAS FOR CS2 SITUATIONAL STRESSORS

Stressors are a normal part of life; when they are in manageable limits they are viewed as stimulation and challenges. However, when stressors increase in intensity, they can overwhelm an individual's ability to cope and disrupt her psychological equilibrium. During the intake process, you need to ask questions about situational stressors that might have served as *precipitating factors* in the development of the presenting problems.

Severity of Stressors

It is useful to have an objective rating of the severity of stressors to recognize whether the reaction of an individual is a typical, appropriate response to the situational stressor, or if it is excessive compared to others (real or hypothetical) in the same situation. Is the stressor objectively dangerous (a lion escapes his cage and approaches you) or harmless, but appraised as dangerous (a cat howling outside your window)? Losing a job entails serious financial and emotional costs but having a boss who frowns all the time does not result in objective harm.

Vulnerability and Resilience

Situational stressors alone cannot explain the response of individuals; there is wide variation in how people deal with the same precipitating factors. The concept of *predisposing factors* refers to individual difference variables influenced by biological endowment and prior history—vulnerabilities and weaknesses on one hand and hardiness and resilience on the other. Internal sources of resilience include easy temperament, social competence, ability to problem-solve, optimism, self-directedness, sense of humor, intelligence, and emotional and behavioral adaptability (Katz & Pandya, 2004). In children, important protective factors are an inner capacity for emotional regulation, an effective use of social systems for support, and the protective influence of caring and competent adults (Koplewicz, Cloitre, Reyes, & Kessler, 2004). According to Myers (1989), factors that make individuals vulnerable to extreme reactions to a disaster include the following:

- Lack of verbal ability to describe experiences.
- Disabilities that limit ability to get needed resources.
- Preexisting stresses.
- Previous traumatic life events that were not successfully resolved.
- Lack of adequate social support.
- Poor coping skills.
- Separation from family.

Crisis Theory

People usually find their coping and defensive processes effective in resolving problems of living and thus sufficient to maintain their psychological equilibrium. However, when the difficulty of a problem exceeds the available repertoire of coping resources, a crisis may be precipitated. The immediate precipitant could be a severe personal trauma such as rape or a diagnosis of cancer; a negative life event such as divorce or unemployment; the accumulation of stress from hassles of daily living; or a major disaster that affects an entire community. Caplan (1964) described the development of a crisis in four phases:

1. *Rise in tension:* In response to stressful stimuli, there is an initial rise in tension and discomfort.
2. *Unsuccessful coping efforts:* When there is a lack of success in coping, the stressful stimuli and discomfort increase.
3. *Mobilization of emergency resources:* A further increase in tension mobilizes internal and external resources and emergency problem-solving mechanisms are tried.
4. *Disorganization:* If the problem continues and can be neither solved nor avoided, tension increases and a major disorganization occurs.

Crisis theorists find it useful to refer to the Chinese character for crisis, which combines *danger* and *opportunity*. The danger is the risk of a temporary crisis developing into a long-term psychological disorder; the opportunity comes from increased flexibility and openness to new learning during a state of disequilibrium, which can result in a higher level of functioning than the pre-crisis condition. Caplan believed that prompt and effective interventions during a crisis would achieve goals of primary and secondary prevention of mental disorders:

1. *Primary prevention:* lowering the rate of new cases of mental disorder among people at risk.
2. *Secondary prevention:* prevention of long-term consequences in individuals who are experiencing early symptoms and dysfunctions.

Crisis Intervention

Crisis intervention is a method of therapeutic treatment that focuses on resolving an immediate crisis, which has overwhelmed a person's abilities to cope, with the goals of relieving symptoms and returning the person to the precrisis level of functioning. The goals of crisis intervention usually include the following: reduce harmful pressures on the individual or family, help to strengthen coping skills, and muster environmental and social support. Wilkinson and Vera (1989) summarize five concepts of crisis intervention:

1. The coping skills of the client are temporarily overwhelmed.
2. Rapid and specific help from others can restore the person to the precrisis level of functioning.
3. Only those functions that the person cannot handle should be handled by others.
4. The help offered must be congruent with the usual coping style of the person.
5. Help should be discontinued as soon as possible.

Aguilera (1998) describes two approaches to crisis intervention:

1. *Generic approach:* Focuses on the characteristic course of the particular kind of crisis rather than on the unique characteristics of each individual in crisis. It can be carried out by nonmental health professionals.
2. *Individual approach:* Emphasizes assessment by a mental health professional of the interpersonal and intrapsychic processes of the person in crisis. It differs from brief psychotherapy in that the focus is exclusively on the immediate causes for disturbed equilibrium. The therapist takes an active and directive role in the intervention.

Balancing Factors

Aguilera (1998) frames crisis intervention as problem solving and identifies three balancing factors between the stressful situation and resolution of the problem, as shown in Table 4.4. In each category, strengths will lead to resolution of crisis, and weaknesses may exacerbate the crisis and create new problems.

Disasters

Disasters are traumatic events that happen to groups of people and disrupt the functioning of a community as well as the individuals directly involved. They

Table 4.4   Crisis Intervention Framework

PERCEPTION OF THE EVENT

Perceptions that facilitate crisis resolution:

The perception of the stressful event is realistic.

The person understands the relationship between the event and emotional responses.

The person has a sense of *self-efficacy* (Bandura, 1989), judging herself competent for the situation.

An expectation of a successful outcome, leading to confidence, optimism, and persistence in the face of obstacles.

Perceptions that increase stress:

The event has a meaning that threatens an important life goal or value.

The environmental demands are perceived as exceeding coping abilities and endangering well-being (Lazarus & Folkman, 1984).

The stressor threatens self-esteem or a sense of control, disrupts attachments and commitments, and contains uncertainties and unpredictable elements (Houston, 1987).

SITUATIONAL SUPPORTS

Social isolation increases vulnerability. House (1981) developed a framework for social support that included four components:

1. **Social support:** esteem, affection, trust, concern, and listening
2. **Appraisal support:** affirmation, feedback, and social comparison
3. **Informational support:** advice, suggestion, directives, and information
4. **Instrumental support:** supplies, tools, and money

COPING MECHANISMS

People use different methods to reduce anxiety and tension and maintain psychological integrity when their normal equilibrium is disrupted:

- **Attack:** attempting to remove or overcome obstacles,
- **Flight:** removing the threat or removing oneself from the situation, and
- **Compromises:** accepting substitute goals or changing values and standards.

People also have tension-reducing defense mechanisms such as rationalization, regression, or denial.

Adapted from *Crisis Intervention: Theory and Methodology,* 8th ed., by D. C. Aguilera, 1998, St. Louis, MO: Mosby.

are divided into natural disasters (e.g., hurricanes, tsunamis, and tornados) and man-made ones (e.g., airplane crashes, terrorist attacks, and nuclear power plant accidents). Factors in a disaster that increase the severity of survivors' difficulties include lack of warning, the belief that the event could have been prevented, the presence of human error, fear of recurrence, scope and intensity of the event, degree of personal loss, traumatic stimuli such as dead bodies, lack of opportunity for effective action, and the deprivations and frustrations of the postdisaster environment (Myers, 1989). Disaster victims with severe emotional reactions and functional impairments should receive psychological interventions to prevent the development of disorders in the future, such as Posttraumatic Stress Disorder (PTSD), phobias, or generalized anxiety disorders. Educational material about coping with disasters is available from the Red Cross, Federal Emergency Management Agency (FEMA), the American Psychological Association (APA), and from county mental health agencies.

Victims of Crime

Violent crime is one of the most traumatic situational stressors imaginable. Victims include not only the person who was criminally attacked but also, in cases of homicide and kidnapping, family members, friends, and classmates. Even crimes that affect property rather than persons, like having a car stolen or a house burglarized, are traumatic personal violations. M. A. Young (1989) notes that victims experience "second assaults" by the criminal justice system, the media, helping agencies, and insurance companies, and lists the intangible losses following a violent crime: loss of sense of control over one's life, loss of trust in people, loss of sense of justice, and for some, loss of identity or sense of future. Furthermore, family and friends may withdraw from the victim, whose emotional pain is unbearable, or blame the victim for not having avoided the crime, as in rape, kidnapping of children, or "battered wife syndrome." The terrorist attacks on September 11, 2001, combined the worst elements of both disasters and violent crime, adding the loss of both the sense of security within the national borders and the fantasy of America's invulnerability.

Survivors of Trauma

Since the Vietnam War, there has been increased understanding of the long-term effects of exposure to trauma; in 1980, the American Psychiatric Association added PTSD to the *DSM-III*. The syndrome of PTSD has received extensive study: A web site for veterans (www.ncptsd.va.gov) provides a thorough review of epidemiology, diagnosis, and treatment. The traumatic events most often associated with PTSD for men are rape, combat exposure, childhood neglect, and childhood physical abuse. The most traumatic events for women are rape, sexual molestation, physical attack, being threatened with a weapon, and childhood physical abuse. About 30% of the men and women who have spent time in war zones experience PTSD. There are four major risk factors for development of PTSD:

1. *Severity of stressor:* magnitude and intensity, unpredictability, uncontrollability, sexual (as opposed to nonsexual) victimization, real or perceived responsibility, and betrayal.
2. *Prior vulnerability factors:* genetics, early age of onset and longer-lasting childhood trauma, and concurrent stressful life events.
3. *Subjective threat level:* greater perceived threat or danger, suffering, terror, and horror or fear.
4. *Lack of social support:* lack of functional social support or a social environment that produces shame, guilt, stigmatization, or self-hatred.

Adult Survivors of Child Abuse

Adult survivors of childhood abuse, especially survivors of incest, are a population with a high incidence of PTSD symptoms, as well as disorders such as depression, borderline personality, substance abuse, and eating disorders. They frequently have problems trusting and permitting closeness in relationships and engage in self-destructive behaviors. All forms of child abuse inflict two levels of trauma on the child: (1) the trauma of the abuse and (2) the effects of blaming themselves, protecting the perpetrator, and experiencing the betrayal of other adults who fail to help them. Incest by a parent is considered the worst type of child abuse because of the loss of innocence and betrayal of trust by someone who is responsible for the safety of the child.

Holocaust Survivors and Second- and Third-Generation Members

Children who survived the Holocaust are now in their 60s and 70s and therapists who work with them are well aware of their unique history of trauma. However, therapists also need to recognize that children and grandchildren of Holocaust survivors carry scars that would not be understood without putting it in the context of their family's history. Such *transgenerational transmission of Holocaust trauma* has been studied, leading to a body of literature and a network of support groups. Issues presented by the second and third generation include depression, anxiety, symptoms of PTSD, separation anxiety, and guilt. This framework provides a valuable template for making sense of a client's suffering.

Job-Related Burnout

It is important to understand *burnout* not only for the sake of the clients you will be helping but also to protect yourself from its effects. Helping professionals (including psychotherapists, nurses, teachers, and hospice workers) have the unique job demand of attending to the emotional needs of others, many of whom are emotionally traumatized, in a nonreciprocal relationship where their own needs must be put aside. Maslach (2003) developed an inventory in 1981 to measure a *burnout* syndrome in human service professionals that included feelings of emotional exhaustion, diminished interest, apathy, physical complaints, and symptoms of depression. This burnout syndrome also includes the development of a dehumanizing attitude toward clients, replacing the original compassion, dedication, and idealism with callousness, dislike, and detachment. There is often a reduced sense of personal accomplishment and resentment over the futility of and lack of appreciation for one's efforts. Burnout can lead to substance abuse, suicide, and incompetent and negligent professional behaviors, which in turn can lead to legal problems, ethical sanctions, and loss of license.

Currently, the term *burnout* is used for all types of jobs (Leiter & Maslach, 2005). Personal factors that contribute to burnout include lack of interests, hobbies, and friendships that are unrelated to work; overwork and lack of self-care activities; and disengagement from family. Risk factors in the work environment include lack of opportunities to share problems and get support from work colleagues, understaffing, and bureaucratic rules and procedures that undermine effective service delivery.

WHEN IS THIS HYPOTHESIS A GOOD MATCH?

Holmes and Rahe (1967) developed a scale of stressful events and gave them numerical scores to indicate their intensity. Positive and desired events as well as negative ones are included because both kinds of events tax the individual's capacity to adjust to change. By adding up the scores for every life change in the prior year, the therapist and client can discover that there is ample justification for the symptoms and impairments in functioning. Table 4.5 gives samples of the scores for selected items.

The term *hassles* was used by R. Lazarus and Folkman (1984), referring to daily negative interactions with the environment. An accumulation of these

Table 4.5   Items from the Holmes and Rahe Life Change Index Scale

Event	Points
Death of spouse	100
Divorce	73
Detention in jail or other institution	63
Marriage	50
Retirement from work	45
Gaining a new family member	39
Foreclosure on a mortgage or loan	30
Outstanding personal achievement	28
Troubles with the boss	23
Changing to a new school	20
Christmas	12

Adapted from "The Social Readjustment Rating Scale," by T. H. Holmes and R. H. Rahe, 1967, *Journal of Psychosomatic Research, 11,* pp. 213–218.

mundane, minor events can result in disruptions in functioning. For instance, a student had a mini-breakdown during finals week when her car broke down and her dishwasher flooded the kitchen on the same day.

DSM-IV-TR Diagnoses

These diagnoses incorporate situational stressors:

- *Adjustment Disorders (309):* Clinically significant symptoms develop within 3 months after the onset of the stressor and are resolved within 6 months; more time is allowed if the stressor is chronic, as in a serious illness, or has enduring consequences, as with divorce or loss of a job.
- *Acute Stress Disorder (308.3):* The client has been exposed to a traumatic event, which involved actual or threatened death or serious injury, and responded with fear, helplessness, or horror. Symptoms include dissociation, avoidance, anxiety, and reexperiencing the event, lasting between 2 days and 4 weeks. If the duration is longer, the diagnosis is changed to PTSD.
- *Posttraumatic Stress Disorder (PTSD; 309.81):* The traumatic event may be recent or in the past; the symptoms are the same as Acute Stress Disorder, but have lasted for more than 1 month.
- *Brief Psychotic Episode with Marked Stressors (298.8):* This disorder was called Brief Reactive Psychosis in *DSM-III-R*. The symptoms do not last more than 1 month, and the person returns to a premorbid level of functioning.

Variety of Reactions to Stress

Reactions to stress fall into three categories:

1. *Somatic:* fatigue, nausea, insomnia, bruxism (grinding of teeth), loss or increase of appetite, migraine, muscle tremors, twitches, rapid heart rate, difficulty breathing, thirst, visual difficulties, vomiting, weakness, dizziness, profuse sweating, or chills.
2. *Cognitive and emotional:* anxiety, depression, guilt, fear, intense anger, suspiciousness, irritability, nightmares, confusion, poor attention, poor decisions, heightened or lowered alertness, poor concentration, memory problems, or poor problem solving and abstract thinking.
3. *Behavioral:* Changes in activity, social withdrawal, emotional outbursts, or substance abuse.

Table 4.6 presents a list of trauma-related stress symptoms published by the Arizona Department of Health Services (www.azdhs.gov/bhs/traumal.pdf).

Children show different symptoms from adults. A review of the child trauma literature by Lubit, Rovine, Defrancisci, and Eth (2003) found that preschoolers tend to express fear through avoidance of new activities, middle school children avoid school and become preoccupied with danger and reminders, and adolescents engage in new or increased aggression and substance abuse.

Table 4.6 **Signs of Trauma-Related Stress**

Recurring thoughts or nightmares about the event

Having trouble sleeping or changes in appetite

Experiencing anxiety and fear, especially when exposed to events or situations reminiscent of the trauma

Being on edge; being easily startled or becoming overly alert

Feeling depressed, sad, and having low energy

Experiencing memory problems including difficulty in remembering aspects of the trauma

Feeling "scattered" and unable to focus on work or daily activities

Having difficulty making decisions

Feeling irritable, easily agitated, or angry and resentful

Feeling emotionally numb, withdrawn, disconnected, or different from others

Spontaneously crying, feeling a sense of despair and hopelessness

Feeling extremely protective of, or fearful for, the safety of loved ones

Not being able to face certain aspects of the trauma, and avoiding activities, places, or even people that remind you of the event

Greenstone and Leviton (1993) describe the profile of a person whose inability to cope with stressful situations has pushed him to the crisis point:

- Confusion: *I can't think clearly.*
- Impasse: *I feel stuck; nothing I do helps.*
- Desperation: *I've got to do something.*
- Apathy: *Nothing can help me.*
- Helplessness: *I can't take care of myself.*
- Urgency: *I need help now!!!!!!!!*
- Discomfort: *I feel miserable, restless, and unsettled.* (p. 6)

TREATMENT PLANNING

Stress management has two components: (1) active problem solving and (2) coping with negative emotions. Therapists help clients, on an individual basis, to discover strategies for reducing painful emotions and finding respite from the stress of coping with problems. When active coping is not possible, "passive coping" requires serenity and patience. The tools that people use for making themselves feel better are varied and include the following: relaxation techniques such as deep breathing and meditation, exercise, yoga, enjoying a hobby or sport, watching TV, talking with friends, music, reading, hot baths, massage, aromatherapy, changing one's attitude, humor, prayer, ventilating feelings by screaming or having a "good cry," and seeking pleasurable activities. A creative imagery technique is to visualize the stress, portraying it as a monster, and then express feelings to this imaginary character. The use of food and drink for relaxation can be very appropriate, as long as the client is not creating new problems such as substance abuse and undesired weight gain.

Crisis Intervention

Table 4.7 presents steps in crisis intervention, incorporating ideas from Hipple and Hipple (1983), Aguilera (1998), and Greenstone and Leviton (1993).

Posttrauma Debriefing

One popular intervention after a disaster is the Critical Incident Stress Debriefing (CISD; J. T. Mitchell & Everly, 2001). A form of crisis intervention, it aims to reduce initial distress and to prevent the development of later psychological problems.

A typical debriefing session is a single group meeting lasting about 2 hours that takes place 2 to 3 days after the trauma. It has two parts:

1. *Ventilation and normalization:* Clients are encouraged to give a detailed narrative account of the trauma, including facts, cognitions, and feelings. During the CISD, the facilitator asks each participant to describe the trauma "to make the whole incident come to life again in the CISD room." Emotional reactions are addressed in some detail with an emphasis on normalization—assuring them that they are responding normally to an abnormal event.

2. *Preparation for possible future experiences:* Clients are taught how to deal with their reactions and where to find further support, if necessary.

There is controversy over CISD, because it lacks empirical validation (Bisson & Deahl, 1994; McNally, Bryant, & Ehlers, 2003) and carries the risk of possibly retraumatizing the client through intense imaginal exposure to the traumatic event. For rape victims, reexposure to the event may increase their sense of shame. Another concern is that when a counselor describes possible future symptoms to the trauma victim, the intervention might create a self-fulfilling prophecy for people who might not otherwise have had those problems. Mandatory debriefing can lead to passive participation and resentment in victims.

According to Brom, Kleber, and Hofman (1993), victims needs general information about psychological reactions following a serious traumatic event, a safe and quiet environment so they can realize the traumatic event is over, the opportunity to go over the experience again and again to reconstruct the event and to regain their sense of control, and proper referrals, if necessary. Ideally, there should be several sessions, the last of which should be at least 2 to 3 months after the event.

Table 4.7 Steps in Crisis Intervention

Goal	Therapist Actions
Improve emotional state	Instill hope, and give reassurance to the client. Show that you are calm and confident and that you believe that there will be a positive outcome. Use nonverbal and verbal messages to lower the level of emotionality. Normalize the experience to counteract the fear that symptoms mean weakness or "going crazy."
Set direction	Be in charge of the interview, provide structure, and present yourself as a problem-solving expert. Include family members or other members of the social network, if available. Help the client begin to reorder the chaos and confusion in his mind.
Assessment of the crisis	Use active focusing techniques to obtain an accurate assessment of the precipitating event. Assess for the balancing factors described in Table 4.4, such as perception of the event, the social supports, and the coping mechanisms that have been used and, if not used, are available. Inquire about past successful coping experiences to identify resources. Assess both realistic and symbolic meanings of the crisis event. Discover how much the crisis has disrupted the client's life and the effects of this disruption on others.
Screen for emergency	Evaluate whether the client is a danger to self or others and rule out the need for hospitalization. If person has suicidal ideation, use a no-suicide contract and increase the frequency of the sessions.
Help client to understand the crisis	Explain the connection between stressors or trauma and the intensity of the emotional reactions. Provide education about possible phases in emotional reactions following a trauma. Explain the theory of crisis, using concepts of equilibrium and disequilibrium. Help the client realize that the crisis state is temporary.
Facilitate emotional expression	Encourage the client to express feelings. Show understanding of emotional reactions, using feeling words in your responses to help the client label emotions (e.g., shock, confusion, anger, overwhelmed, or guilt). Help the client access feelings that may be suppressed, such as anger towards loved ones—an emotional catharsis with a caring listener can help reduce tension. The opportunity to repeatedly put experiences in words may help in preventing the avoidance that characterizes PTSD.
Use cognitive restructuring	Cognitive restructuring techniques can change appraisals of the stressors as well as the client's capacity to cope. Clients may have faulty assumptions that certain traumatic events could have been predicted and prevented if they had acted differently, and therefore may be inappropriately blaming themselves.

(continued)

Table 4.7   *(Continued)*

Goal	Therapist Actions
Develop action plan	Model problem-solving skills. List alternatives and help the client to evaluate pros and cons: Assure that the plan is consistent with the client's personal and cultural values. Break the plan into steps that are simple, concrete, realistic, and appropriate for the client's functional level. Intermediate objectives should be set in terms of hours and days. If other agencies are involved, make sure that there is proper coordination.
Shore up social supports	Social support can come from the individual's social network, other sufferers going through the same crisis, and community organizations. If possible, include family members in the treatment process. Intervene if there are signs of family crisis developing from the personal crisis. Encourage participation in group activities that provide support and channel energy towards appropriate goals.
Monitor progress	As positive changes occur, summarize the progress and help the client understand which coping strategies have been most effective. Provide reinforcement and encouragement. Use problem-solving skills to handle unforeseen obstacles.
Anticipatory planning	After the current crisis is managed, help the client develop insights and skills to prevent future crisis situations and to cope better with them if they do occur.
Terminate	Terminate crisis intervention when the client is restored to prior equilibrium and is handling problems effectively. If further help is needed, make the appropriate referral or discuss a psychotherapy contract for identified problems.

Treatment for Posttraumatic Stress Disorder

Table 4.8 provides an overview of the major treatment methods for PTSD (Foa, Keane, & Friedman, 2000), which draws from several different hypotheses.

Treatment of Adult Survivors of Childhood Abuse

Several organizations provide information, support, and access to self-help groups for these victims, such as Adult Survivors of Child Abuse (ASCA; www.ascasupport.org); Survivors of Incest Anonymous (www.siawso.org); and Voices in Action, Inc. (www.voices-action.org).

There is consensus that one of the most important components of treatment is the quality of the therapist-survivor relationship (e.g., Courtois, 1996). Therapists need to create a warm and safe environment and show great sensitivity to the survivor's fear of closeness and difficulty with trust. Incest survivors bear the extra burden of secrecy and shame, so it is especially important to help clients express the emotional truth of the experience and correct the distorted perception that they were in any way responsible. If the survivor is in a stable relationship, the partner can be included in treatment (Graber, 1991), although this

Table 4.8   Treatment Interventions for Posttraumatic Stress Disorder

Education

The therapist educates the trauma survivor and his family that PTSD is a disorder that occurs in normal individuals exposed to extremely stressful conditions, and that probably all people would develop PTSD if they were involved in a severe enough trauma. This message normalizes the symptoms and counteracts the belief that PTSD symptoms are a sign of weakness. The therapist explains facts about PTSD and gives the rationale for the different treatment approaches.

Exposure (BL2)

The client engages in careful, repeated, detailed imagining of the trauma (exposure) in a safe, controlled context to face and gain control of the fear and distress that was overwhelming during the trauma. After learning relaxation techniques, the client progresses gradually up a hierarchy of trauma-related stimuli (systematic desensitization). In some cases, trauma memories or reminders can be confronted all at once (flooding).

Cognitive-Behavioral Therapy Methods (C2, C3, C4)

The therapist gives the rationale that PTSD is, in part, caused by the way we think. Cognitive-behavioral therapy (CBT) can help change the way we think (cognitive restructuring) by exploring alternative explanations and assessing the accuracy of our thoughts. Even if we are not able to change the situation, we can change the way we think about a situation. CBT for trauma includes strategies for processing thoughts about the event and challenging negative or unhelpful thinking patterns

Eye Movement Desensitization and Reprocessing (B3)

Eye Movement Desensitization and Reprocessing (EMDR), a method developed by Shapiro (1996), combines elements of exposure therapy and CBT. The client follows instructions to focus thought and move his or her eyes, while the therapist creates an alternation of attention back and forth across both brain hemispheres. Although this is a newer treatment, favorable research support is accumulating.

Group Therapy

PTSD patients can discuss traumatic memories, PTSD symptoms, and other problems with people who have had similar experiences. As survivors discuss and share how they cope with trauma-related shame, guilt, rage, fear, doubt, and self-condemnation, they prepare themselves to focus on the present rather than the past. The group leader's task is not to interact therapeutically with each group member but to create a safe and supportive environment in which members interact therapeutically with one another.

Medication (B2)

Medication can reduce anxiety, depression, and insomnia and can help survivors participate in therapy. Researchers are searching for effective medications to prevent PTSD.

Coping Skills (BL3)

Skills are taught for coping with anxiety (e.g., breathing retraining or biofeedback), managing anger, preparing for stress reactions (i.e, stress inoculation), handling future trauma symptoms, resisting urges to use alcohol or drugs when trauma symptoms occur, and communicating and relating effectively with people (i.e., social skills or marital therapy). Clients are encouraged to increase recreational, artistic, or work activities that help distract a person from memories and reactions, without using this tactic as a substitute for therapy.

should be determined on a case-by-case basis, depending on the nature of the abuse and the sensitivity and shame of the victim. Courtois (1996) described three stages in the treatment process:

Stage I: Alliance-building, safety, and stabilization.

Stage II: Deconditioning, mourning, and resolution of the trauma.

Stage III: Reconnection; self and relational development.

The ASCA also recommends a three-part recovery framework in its literature and groups:

Stage 1: Remembering

The survivor acknowledges the truth of the physical, sexual, or emotional abuse, makes a commitment to recovery, agrees to reexperience memories as they surface, and accepts "that I was powerless over my abusers' actions which holds *them* responsible."

Stage 2: Mourning

The survivor identifies problem areas, faces feelings of shame and anger, identifies faulty beliefs and distorted perceptions, recognizes self-sabotage, accepts the right to make free choices about how to live, and affirms "I am able to grieve my childhood and mourn the loss of those who failed me."

Stage 3: Healing

The survivor commits to strengthening self-esteem, improving behavior and relationships, resolving issues with the offenders "to the extent that is acceptable to me," and transforming the self-image from survivor to "thriver."

The group modality offers the benefit of sharing stories with people who have endured similar traumas, thus relieving the shame and feelings of aloneness and providing the inspiration of people who are further along on the path toward healing. Therapists can also recommend helpful books (e.g., Bass & Davis, 1988; Bass & Thornton, 1983).

Coping with HIV/AIDS

Receiving the diagnosis of a serious illness is always stressful; however, testing positive for HIV brings an array of problems and stressors that easily outpace an individual's capacity to cope. Despite advances in treatment, there is still no cure for AIDS, so news of positive HIV status is often interpreted as a death sentence. Although AIDS sufferers are now protected against discrimination and covered by the Americans with Disability Act (ADA; www.usdg.gov/crt/ada/adahom1.htm), there is both a stigma attached to the disease and a risk of

Table 4.9   Helping Clients Cope with HIV Diagnosis

Assure the client that confidentiality will be protected, and abstain from judging, blaming, interrogating, or making decisions for the client.

Provide empathy and support, allowing the client to express the emotional impact of the diagnosis (possibly disbelief, anger, fear, or betrayal). Recognize that intense emotional reactions may prevent the client from understanding the information received about the diagnosis and the need to prevent transmission.

Impart needed information and clarify misconceptions. The therapist should be knowledgeable about transmission and prevention, natural history of HIV, and prevention and support services.

Address the need to notify others and how to do this. The therapist can help the client assess if there is physical danger in sharing results. Otherwise, you might help the client role-play how to share the information.

Help the client access medical and other support services. It is important to know about appropriate resources in the community.

Help the client create a plan for mobilizing social support, including finding a support group at a local AIDS resource center. Make sure the client understands the need for ongoing support and counseling.

Emphasize the importance of preventing transmission of the disease and ensure that the client has specific behavioral goals for protecting others. Explain that she needs to protect not only others from infection but herself from being exposed to a different strain of HIV.

Help the client to maintain hope and realize he can live well. This goal is facilitated by contacts with people who are living full and satisfying lives with HIV/AIDS.

losing social connections when there is the greatest need for social support. Counselors who work with AIDS patients face unusually demanding challenges and need support for themselves, including a forum for sharing experiences with colleagues.

Although most HIV/AIDS counseling will occur in settings where the testing is performed or in clinics that specialize in that population, all practitioners need guidelines for helping people cope with this disease. Table 4.9 offers suggestions for helping a client cope with news of HIV positive status, based on guidelines from the Centers for Disease Control and Prevention (2001) and The Synergy Project (2005).

Community Resources

It is essential to know how to access resources in your community. For instance, in California, the Resource Directory Group, Inc. (www.resourcedirectory.com) publishes the *Social Service Rainbow Resource Directory* for major counties, in printed volumes and electronic versions. As you gain experience dealing with crises, keep a Rolodex or electronic file of people in the community with whom you can consult, for specific types of crises, and of services to which you can refer clients in crisis.

Making a Referral

When making a referral, take into consideration that the crisis state has overwhelmed normal adult coping abilities. If necessary, place the call and make the appointment for the client. Write instructions down and check to see if there are any anticipated obstacles to keeping the appointment. Be sure to follow up with the client to see how the contact with the referral agency went.

INTEGRATION OF HYPOTHESES

Sometimes you can help the client cope with stress and trauma solely through empathic listening, clarification, and psychoeducation. Otherwise, the integration of other hypotheses is necessary. Many of the following hypotheses have already been integrated in the previous tables and discussions.

B2 Medical Interventions

People coping with trauma can benefit from an evaluation for the use of prescription medication.

B3 Mind-Body Connections

Psychological trauma affects mind and body. Early prolonged trauma causes many brain and hormonal changes that affect memory, learning, and regulating impulses and emotions. Posttraumatic Stress Disorder has many biological correlates, including abnormal levels of cortisol, epinephrine, and norepinephrine. The fight-flight reaction of stress results in physiological arousal, which, if prolonged, can negatively impact health. Stress management tools such as relaxation training and meditation are presented under **B3.**

BL2 Conditioned Emotional Response

Reactions to current stressors can be excessive because of past conditioning. Furthermore, the current trauma creates new maladaptive conditioning. Following a traumatic event, anxiety responses are generalized to new stimuli, leading to excessive fear and avoidance, and possible development of an anxiety disorder. Counter-conditioning techniques such as desensitization and flooding are very useful interventions.

BL3 Skill Deficits or Lack of Competence

It is important to evaluate the coping skills of the client. These skills include cognitive skills (e.g., planning, problem solving, or decision making), life skills (e.g., job search, financial management, project management, or time management), communication skills (e.g., the ability to say "no" when new tasks and commitments are offered), and stress management skills. Therapists assess whether the client already has skills in her repertoire for dealing with this particular stressor; if not, treatment plans include strategies for acquiring new and better skills.

C3 Faulty Information Processing

The way the client appraises the stressor is an important predictor of whether a stressful situation turns into a crisis. Paraphrasing the prayer that is used in Twelve Step programs (e.g., Alcoholics Anonymous) *Is this a situation that requires courage to take action to change something, or serenity to accept something that can't be changed?*

ES3 Spiritual Dimension

Traumatic experiences can result in anger toward God and a loss of meaning. At the same time, spiritual resources can be of tremendous benefit in coping. Beveridge and Cheung (2004) describe a spiritual framework for treatment of incest survivors, using a definition of forgiveness as "no longer wanting revenge on the perpetrator" (p. 113), and countering the belief of being defective with spiritual responses: "God offers unconditional love for all."

P2 Reenactment of Early Childhood Experiences

Clients are helped when they can distinguish between emotional reactions that are appropriate to the stressor and those that carry baggage from early experiences. The reactions to current stressors can be affected by stress and abuse that occurred in childhood. Past experiences with parents can explain why, for one person, an unpleasant boss is a trigger for so much anger that his job performance deteriorates, while for another, the boss's behavior is a minor nuisance.

P4 Unconscious Dynamics

Dissociation, considered an unconscious mechanism, is a major component in the development of PTSD. The controversy over recovered "repressed memories" of childhood sexual abuse should be understood through available research (e.g., Pope & Brown, 1996).

SCE1 Family System

A family can be a source of either support or additional stress. Furthermore, the crisis or trauma in one member has repercussions for the entire family. For instance, in families of soldiers returning from combat experience, children may develop school problems and spouses may engage in verbal or physical violence. Therapists need to educate families on how to cope with crisis and to intervene in ways that serve both treatment and prevention goals.

SCE2 Cultural Context

The meaning of stressors will be dependent on the cultural context. For instance, the accidental "outing" of a gay person would be extremely traumatic when the ethnic or religious group ostracizes gays but could be a relief in a very liberal, supportive context. There are cultural differences in how support should be provided following a disaster or trauma: Ventilation (talking through the trauma) may not be useful outside of Westernized groups. For example, talk therapy approaches were ineffective among some Taiwanese natural disaster victims but traditional religious practices were beneficial (Marsalla & Christopher, 2004). Interventions with victims should use their language and communication patterns.

SCE3 Social Support

As discussed previously, social support is a major buffer against crisis and is an important ingredient in action plans. The presence of a confidante, and the feeling that one is not all alone in the struggle, can prevent a normal reaction to stress from turning into more serious mental and emotional problems. In addition to the support of the existing social network, victims of trauma often benefit from support from people who have had similar experiences, and they can derive hope from people who have healed.

SCE5 Social Problem Is a Cause

Stressors that affect an entire community may stem from a social problem. For instance, when the economy is in a recession and unemployment is at a high level, difficulties of the job search process are very much greater than when the economy is doing well. When there are social causes, the most effective plans may be those that benefit the entire group, such as joining in a lawsuit or creating a neighborhood-watch group. The suffering of victims of Hurricane Katrina was compounded by inequities in our socioeconomic system and malfunction of our governmental entities.

SCE7 Environmental Factors

Action plans for coping with stress and crisis can include changing or leaving the environment.

KEY IDEAS FOR CS3 DEVELOPMENTAL TRANSITION

Healthy maturation involves change, tension, stress, and a disruption of harmonious living, followed by periods of consolidation and stability. Erik Erikson

CS3 DEVELOPMENTAL TRANSITION

Definition

The client is at a **Developmental Transition,** dealing with issues related to moving to the next stage of life.

Explanation

Every 5 to 10 years, a developmental transition is inevitable because of the interactions among biological maturation, personality growth, and society's role expectations for people of different ages. This hypothesis normalizes dramatic disruptions and leads to interventions that prevent a maturational crisis from becoming a long-term disorder. Individuals need support for making personal choices and accomplishing developmental tasks in their own timeframe.

Examples

Henry recently turned 45 and the second of his two children went away to college. He described his problem as a "midlife" crisis: Symptoms included job burnout, loss of meaning, impulsive wishes to dramatically change his lifestyle, perhaps by running off with his 23-year-old personal trainer. When asked about his wife, he said "we've just gone in different directions."	Kent, a 26-year-old accountant, is living with his parents. He is resentful of their rules and demands and frequently thinks of finding his own apartment, which he could easily afford, but then he decides, "It's just easier to let Mom take care of me." None of his relationships with women have lasted longer than 3 months because he thinks that they will expect him to "get serious."	Edward, a 62-year-old corporate executive, complained constantly about his job and was thrilled to accept a very generous early retirement package. However, after a few months, he sunk into a depression, staying in his pajamas all day. He was angry at his wife for not quitting her job to travel with him whenever he felt like it.

(1993) created a well-known eight-stage model of development, which identified core psychological issues at each stage throughout the life span. Erikson made us aware that periods of upheaval bring the possibility of both positive and negative outcomes: The disequilibrium of each new stage brings opportunities to correct deficiencies that occurred in earlier stages along with stressors that can impede progression to the next stage.

Developmental transitions are triggered by physical growth, psychological maturation, and social pressures and expectations. Furthermore, the push toward change often springs from a subjective sense of stagnation and dissatisfaction, combined with a yearning for more creativity, fulfillment, and meaning. When we think of movement through the life span, we tend to think of *marker events* such as the first tooth, entering preschool, first communion or Bar/Bat Mitzvah, graduation from high school, first job, marriage, childbirth, empty nest, and retirement. However, there are also transitions for which there are no markers, such as the movement from psychological dependence on the approval of others to a state of self-acceptance.

The concept of *developmental task* is more flexible than a model of fixed stages. The term *stage* implies a fixed, linear sequence where one stage is completed before the next begins, whereas the idea of a *task* implies that the sequence may vary, phases can overlap, and tasks can be revisited in later stages of life. If a specific age is used as a standard for normal development, unnecessary stress is created when an individual deviates by being "late" or "early," as when a child is behind his playmates in saying his first word, a young adult finishes college at age 25, and a woman doesn't get married until 35.

With the caveat to not pathologize people who do not fit into a neat model of stages, therapists are advised to understand, in depth, the models of developmental stages for which there have been many contributors. Research on child development by Mahler and others (Mahler, Pine, & Bergman, 1975; Stern, 1985) expanded understanding of the transitions of the first 3 years of life. Piaget defined stages in terms of cognitive development, showing that "egocentrism" is normal in early childhood, and abstract thinking does not begin to develop until adolescence (Piaget, 2002). Harry Stack Sullivan (1968) noted that an intimate relationship with a same-sex "chum" during preadolescence provided a corrective experience of being seen through another's eyes and experiencing love in an honest, sharing relationship. Carl Jung's theory helps us understand changes in midlife and old age. In an era where most authorities saw old age as a period of decline, degeneration, and disengagement, Jung saw that "even in old age we are growing toward realization of our full potential" (Stevens, 1999, p. 225). Levinson (1986) described the transitions in the lives of men as occurring every decade and involving discomfort, questioning, reassessment, and redirection, while Sheehy (1977) built on his research to discuss the lives of both men and women.

With changes in our culture and people living much longer than in the past, the typical timeline of transitions has been altered. Sheehy (1996) discusses how the stage of adolescence seems to be prolonged into the 20s, after which young adults enter committed relationships and solidify their careers closer to the age of 30, and a "second adulthood" stage begins in the late 40s. Pipher (1999) gives credit to Bernice Neugarten (1996) for describing a new developmental stage called "young-old"—a period when people lead vigorous lives with expanding interests and activities—in contrast to "old-old," when they suffer from impaired health and loss of capabilities. Table 4.10 gives a description of the stages and subphases of development, integrating contributions from these different theorists and researchers.

Cohort Differences

As explained in Chapter 2, a cohort is a segment of the population born at the same time, and therefore they pass through stages of the life span together. Changes in the economy, as well as cultural and historical events, will make the experience of each cohort different. It is predicted that the cohort of "baby-boomers," which experienced the feminist revolution, birth control pills, and the Vietnam War in their late adolescence and early adulthood, will put its own stamp on old age, in view of longer life spans and the degree of political power this large group will have.

Table 4.10   Stages of Development

Erik Erikson's Stages	Sub-Phases	Description
Basic Trust versus Mistrust (Hope) Birth to 1 year	Normal infantile autism Birth to 2 months	The child responds to internal needs—shielded from environmental stimulation. The mother is calm and attends to needs, holds, soothes, and hugs.
	Symbiosis 3 to 8 months	The child exhibits social smiles and eye-to-eye contact. There is undifferentiated fusion with the mother; a sense of "oneness" and harmony; attachment bond formed—mother is empathically attuned.
	Differentiation 6 to 9 months	The child is aware of the boundaries of the body, directs attention outward, uses transitional objects and reacts to strangers because the mother is now experienced as a unique person. The mother is ready to resume her boundaries.
Autonomy versus Shame and Doubt (Will) 10 months to 4 years	Practicing 10 to 18 months	Begins when the child walks; elated investment in the exercise of autonomous functions to the near-exclusion of the mother. "Love affair with the world," using the mother as a refueling station.
	Rapprochement 18 to 24 months	The child experiences the attachment as secure when the mother responds empathically to alternate needs for separateness and closeness. Demonstrates the use of words; object permanence attained; signs of empathy appear; internalization of rules and demands; adjusts to preschool.
	Consolidation of individuality	Emotional object constancy—the child can maintain positive feelings in absence of love object. Language development; interest in playmates and adults other than mother; negativism is a sign of individuation; risk of power struggles; achievement of bladder and bowel control.
Initiative versus Guilt (Purpose) 3 to 5	Phallic (Oedipal) stage (Freud)	The child makes stories with structure of narrative; active play, fantasy, and imagination. Learning to cooperate, lead, and follow; coping with jealousy; sexual curiosity, gender role; guilt felt for thoughts as well as deeds.

(continued)

Table 4.10 *(Continued)*

Erik Erikson's Stages	Sub-Phases	Description
Industry versus Inferiority (Competence) 5 to 10	"Latency" period (Freud)	Concrete operations begin; end of egocentrism; transition to school. Structured play with rules and teamwork; mastering school subjects; self-discipline with homework; recognition for producing things.
	Preadolescence	Intense relationship with a best friend of the same sex contributes to positive self-appraisal and open self-disclosure.
Ego Identity versus Role Confusion (Fidelity) Adolescence	Early Adolescence 10 to 13	Begin shift from concrete to abstract thinking; puberty; concern with body; peer influence increases.
	Middle Adolescence 14 to 16	Growth of abstract thinking; risk-taking behavior; challenges to authority; close relationships with peers; sexual attractions.
	Late Adolescence 17 to 19	Capacity for realistic risk assessment; sexual identity established; serious intimate relationships; transition to work or college; development of ideals.
Intimacy versus Isolation (Love) Young adult	Provisional Adulthood 18 to 30	Extended financial dependence on parents; extended schooling; launching career; dating without being ready to settle down.
Generativity versus Stagnation or Self-Absorption (Care) Adulthood	First Adulthood 30 to 45	Commitments to career, marriage, and parenthood. Some women have first children, others enter "empty nest," and others choose to be childless.
	Begin Second Adulthood 45 to 65	Midlife transition and crisis of meaning; may begin second career; coping with layoffs; gender roles become more flexible. Caring for elderly parents. Jung's *Individuation:* increased spirituality, integrating disowned parts of the personality, and seeking wholeness and balance.
Ego Integrity versus Despair (Wisdom) Maturity	Young-Old Age 65 to Failing health	Retirement. If healthy, life expectancy is 20 to 30 more years; Freedom (with minimal physical limitations) for travel and play. Acceptance of one's life, serenity, new sources of meaning; deaths of friends; loss of spouse; possibility of new loves.
	Old-Old Age Mid 80s +	Health problems and disabilities. Dependent on children or living in assisted living facilities. Outliving friends, siblings, and possibly children. Preparation for death.

Gender and Cultural Differences

Psychosocial stresses and opportunities of aging are different for the two genders and for different cultures. For instance, women need to consult their "biological clock" regarding decisions about motherhood, whereas men are known to father children into their 80s. Men's self-esteem may be more tied to the amount of money they earn and their job status than is women's. As they age, men and women tend to accept those qualities in themselves that did not fit society's sex role stereotypes. Older men are more comfortable with vulnerability and emotion, and older women are more comfortable with their power, aggression, and ability to please themselves rather than sacrificing for the needs of others. Cultural differences are apparent in the nature of developmental stages. In some cultures, women become mothers shortly after puberty, and the oldest generation is revered instead of devalued.

Stages of Intimate Relationships

By understanding the stages that romantic relationships go through, committed couples have a framework for weathering certain predictable storms and periods of mismatched needs. In their book, *In Quest of the Mythical Mate,* Bader and Pearson (1988) examine the stages of intimate relationships using Mahler's framework for separation-individuation. Table 4.11 describes five stages.

Pittman (1998) offers his view of the maturational achievements in successful marriages with the challenging title, *Grow Up!*

Parenting

Most models of developmental stages focus on the path of an individual through the life span. It is useful to examine the transitions from the parental point of view. As they cope with the development of their first child, parents experience these stages as uncharted territory. However, for later-born children, parents can be more competent, either because of their track record of success or because they have a chance to learn from their mistakes. Table 4.12 presents Galinsky's (1987) model of the six stages of parenthood.

Parents are coping with their own developmental transitions at the same time that they need to be experts on handling their children's developmental transitions. Therapists often straddle dual roles: child-rearing consultant and therapist.

Childlessness

The normative stages of development include parenthood, and, for most women, motherhood is a central part of their identity. Women can be childless by either circumstances or choice; developmental transitions are very different for these two categories. However, all childless women have to deal with a societal prejudice in favor of motherhood. Those couples who question whether to have children, or have already firmly decided to remain childless, have very little

Table 4.11 Developmental Stages of Intimate Relationships

Symbiosis

The first stage is being madly in love, merging lives, and overlooking differences, with high levels of mutual nurturance and avoidance of behaviors that would jeopardize the sense of unity. Failure to progress beyond this stage results in two dysfunctional types of relationship: (1) *enmeshed,* with avoidance of conflict and minimization of differences, and (2) *hostile-dependent,* dominated by anger and conflict, with the partners "too terrified to end the relationship and not mature enough to end the battles" (Bader & Pearson, 1988, p. 10).

Differentiation

Many relationships end at this stage because differences emerge, and lovers are taken off their pedestals, or one or both of the partners wants "space." Awareness of differences and disillusionment over flaws also develop. Partners who stay together are giving up the fantasy of perfect harmony and total gratification.

Practicing

Each partner directs attention to the external world: Developing the self is more important than developing the relationship. Conflicts intensify and the couple needs to learn to resolve them to maintain an emotional connection.

Rapprochement

After each partner has developed a well-defined, competent identity, it is safe to be vulnerable and look to the relationship for intimacy and emotional sustenance. Partners seek comfort and support from each other. Needs for intimacy and independence may be out of sync, but the partners learn to negotiate and are not anxious about abandonment or engulfment.

Mutual Interdependence

Two well-integrated individuals find satisfaction in the security of being loved and "have built a relationship based on a foundation of growth rather than on one of need" (p. 12).

---

societal support. Fortunately, people who have decided to be "childless by choice" have developed web sites that can be accessed by using those three words on Google. For instance, *No Kidding!* (www.nokidding.net) is a group that helps people throughout the United States and Canada to form local social groups. As mental health professionals, we need to examine our biases about parenthood and voluntary childlessness. Ireland (1993) studied childless women and found that those who made a conscious decision to be childless in their 30s had an easier time of creating new identities and channeling their energy into creative and occupational challenges than did those who waited until their childbearing years were over to come to terms with childlessness.

WHEN IS THIS HYPOTHESIS A GOOD MATCH?

The *DSM-IV-TR* diagnosis Phase of Life Problem (V62.89) is used when the focus of clinical attention is a problem associated with a particular developmental phase or some other life circumstance. These problems may pertain to an individual (*difficulty making a career decision*), a couple (*difficulty deciding whether to get engaged*) or a family (*difficulty coping with adolescent child's increased indepen-*

Table 4.12   Six Stages of Parenthood

Parent's Stage	Child's Stage	Developmental Tasks
Image-Making Stage	Prebirth	Accepting the pregnancy
		Preparing for parenthood
		Preparing for the birth
Nurturing Stage	Birth to Toddler	Reconciling images of birth with reality
		Facing the feelings of attachment
		Redefining relationships
Authority Stage	Toddler to School Age	Developing authority
		Gaining distance
		Dealing with sex roles and identity
Interpretive Stage	Starting School to Middle School	Interpreting oneself as a parent
		Separating and connecting
		Interpreting the world to the children
		Deciding how involved to be
		Anticipating the teenage years
Interdependent Stage	High School	Adapting to a new authority relationship
		Dealing with sexuality
		Accepting the teenager's identity
		Forming new bonds with the almost-grown child
Departure Stage	High School to College and Beyond	Preparing for departure
		Adapting to the departure
		Changing images
		Loosening control
		Taking stock of successes and failures

dence). The client may present with the transition as the desired focus, or suffer from anxiety or depression of unknown origins, and need the therapist to discover the precipitating circumstances. The problem *difficulty establishing or maintaining a healthy committed relationship* can often be understood by identifying developmental issues. The movie *Moonstruck,* offers multiple examples of developmental challenges: a man cheats on his wife because he's trying, symbolically, to avoid death; a college professor goes out with young students to avoid facing his age; another man cannot marry while his mother is alive because he's never separated from her; and a widow becomes engaged to a man she doesn't love to avoid repeating the pain of her prior grief.

Major Life Decisions

The emotional upheaval of a maturational crisis is not conducive to clear-sighted, rational decision making. For instance, difficulties dealing with the aging process can lead people to divorces, career changes, and elective surgeries without an understanding of the deeper needs and fears that are motivating their behavior. Clients can sometimes get more objectivity to guide their decisions when they realize that they have been in a phase of stability that has lasted more than 7 years, and that a push toward some kind of change is inevitable: The expression "seven-year itch" conveys that marital boredom sets in after a long period of familiarity. Clients need to explore the costs and benefits of acting on impulses toward change.

TREATMENT PLANNING

Table 4.4 presented a model of three balancing factors that apply to developmental and situational crises: (1) perception, (2) situational supports, and (3) coping mechanisms, and Table 4.7 described the steps of crisis intervention. In dealing with maturational crises, the therapist must understand the stages of development and also be aware that situational stressors interact with changes that are prompted by biological and psychological growth.

Psychoeducation

Educating the client and family members about developmental stages is essential. Parents need to have realistic expectations for what their child is capable of and understand the types of disturbances that are stage appropriate.

Using Films and Books

Movies and books can be prescribed to help clients understand developmental transitions. For instance, the movie *Mother,* with Albert Brooks, can help people discuss transitions in the relationship between adult children and parents. *Metroland,* with Emily Watson, shows a new father having difficulty facing responsibilities. Pittman (1998) uses examples from movies to illustrate the maturational level of marriages. Daniel Stern's book, *Diary of a Baby* (1998) helps new parents imagine the inner world of their child from birth to age 4 years, increasing the likelihood of empathic attunement and realistic expectations. Enter the words "Stages of Life" for an online search for books (e.g., at Amazon.com), and you will see the variety of topics that are viewed as developmental.

Group Support

Group modalities are especially useful for people going through the same developmental transition. Hearing people describe similar feelings and experiences is beneficial; moreover, people receive concrete suggestions and tools and develop networks that help them meet their goals. Examples of useful groups include single people looking to find a committed relationship; middle-aged workers who are engaged in the job search process; and parents who are having difficulty coping with the changes in their adolescent child.

INTEGRATION OF HYPOTHESES

One or more of the following hypotheses are often combined with the one just reviewed to create an integrative formulation for a specific problem. The decision about whether a specific hypothesis should be integrated is based on your professional judgment.

BL3 Skill Deficits or Lack of Competence

Not surprisingly, transition to a new stage of life can confront an individual with challenges for which she lacks skills. A learning model, including coaching and identification of competent role models, can be useful.

C2 Faulty Cognitive Map

Each developmental stage represents new territory and the need to update the cognitive map. At many points during the life span, outdated and inappropriate beliefs and assumptions set limits and create stress. People often have expectations that the move to a desired new stage, such as marriage or retirement, will bring instant happiness, whereas it instead involves a stressful period of adjustment. People who believe that they are old, and that old age means a decline until death, have much lower quality of life than those who believe that old age is a time of freedom, growth, and play. People have rigid ideas about the age at which it is normal to be at a particular developmental marker, and negative judgments and self-imposed limitations result from not doing things on schedule: *I should be married by age 30, or something is wrong with me. I'm too old to start graduate school at 45.*

P2 Reenactment of Early Childhood Experiences

The transitions in adulthood can reactivate unresolved issues from early childhood stages. For instance, adjusting to certain phase-appropriate separations (e.g., empty nest) can be more difficult for people who had problems with separation in early childhood. Furthermore, as children move to a new stage, parents may find that buried feelings and conflicts are stimulated. On one hand, this process provides a positive opportunity for the adult to work through unresolved issues, and, on the other, it creates risks for children that parents will treat them inappropriately. For instance, when a teenage daughter is beautiful and popular, one mother may be relieved and happy, feeling compensated for her own pain at having been a wallflower, whereas another might feel jealous and competitive, as she did toward her more successful peers in high school.

P3 Immature Sense of Self and Conception of Others

When adults fail to progress beyond Margaret Mahler's stages of separation-individuation, they have immature intimate relationships and provide inadequate parenting. The developmental approach of Bader and Pearson (1988), described in Table 4.11, illustrates how couples who progress through developmental stages together can achieve higher levels of maturation and correct deficits from early childhood.

SCE1 Family System

Families, as well as individuals, go through developmental stages; the birth of the first child and the departure from home of the last child are important milestones. These transitions disrupt the equilibrium of the family system. The symptoms in one individual (the identified patient; IP) can be caused by developmental changes that other individuals or subsystems of the family are going though. Family therapy may be the treatment of choice for many developmental transitions.

SCE2 Cultural Context

"Normal" life span development must be placed in a cultural and historical context. In our own culture, the norms for adult development changed dramatically over the past 25 years. In cultures where people have fewer choices, transitions are smoother and there is no role confusion; for many cultures, elders are highly respected and adult children are obligated to take care of them; and in Buddhism, isolation is viewed as rewarding, not as a failure to achieve intimacy. It is the culture that establishes whether the new phase is more or less desirable. The frequency of divorce, the availability of second careers, and the tolerance for young adults remaining in residence with their parents are all dependent on the cultural context. Some cultures do a much better job than others in providing rites of passage to smooth transitions to the next developmental stage.

SCE4 Social Role Performance

Becoming a parent is a new stage and involves a new social role. The availability of role models makes transitions easier. When the culture is changing, young people reach new stages without good models. As the life span has gotten longer, new roles need to be created for the elderly.

KEY IDEAS FOR CS4 LOSS AND BEREAVEMENT

Bereavement is the state of having suffered a loss, such as the death of a family member or close friend; grief is the reaction to the loss, with affective, cognitive, behavioral and somatic components; and mourning is a term that embraces

---

CS4 LOSS AND BEREAVEMENT

Definition

The client has suffered a **Loss and** needs help during **Bereavement,** or for a loss-related problem.

Explanation

Losses can be external (e.g., from death, divorce, or natural disaster), internal (e.g., loss of capacities due to illness or aging), or combinations (e.g., loss of job triggers loss of identity as breadwinner). Knowledge about typical stages of grief is useful, as long as individual and cultural differences in the mourning process are recognized. Sometimes the loss is recognized as the precipitating cause of emotional symptoms; other times, the client is not aware of the connection.

Examples

Deborah, a woman in her 40s, had been estranged from her father ever since her marriage 20 years ago. She received a call from her sister that he was in the hospital; when she arrived at his bedside, he had just died. She told everyone that she didn't feel anything because he had ceased to be important in her life; nevertheless, she has developed symptoms of depression and cries uncontrollably several times a week.	Max, a college junior, came to the counseling center 3 months after his mother's sudden death. He was unable to concentrate, started crying at random moments, had lost interest in social activities, and questioned the point of working hard at school when death was so final. His counselor explained that his experiences were normal parts of grieving and helped him make plans so that he did not fail his courses.	Christine, a 63-year-old professional woman, had a stroke 4 years ago. Despite the efforts of many speech therapists, she never regained the capacity for speech and can only say three or four words. Her family members tell her "it takes time" and keep searching for new speech therapists. Christine cries frequently when she is alone, because she knows she will never fully regain her lost capacities.

---

grieving as well as coping and adapting, and often involves cultural and religious customs and rituals.

Bereavement usually involves **Situational Stressors (CS2)** and often coincides with **Developmental Transitions (CS3),** as when the loss of a spouse initiates the stage of widowhood. However, there are special characteristics of the grieving process that justify treating **CS4** as a separate hypothesis. The bereaved person's responses reveal the level of dependency, intolerance of separation, and basic problems with attachment (M. S. Stroebe, Hansson, Stroebe, & Schut, 2001). Loss of a spouse, intimate partner, or child requires major transformation of the sense of self. The death of a child is one of the most difficult losses to cope with because it violates assumptions about the world and deprives the parent of a relationship and role that was likely a major source of identity (Braun & Berg, 1994).

Addressing complex and multiple stressors, Stroebe and Schut (2001) developed a dual-process theory for bereavement:

- *Loss-oriented processes:* Both confronting and avoiding the loss as one goes through the grieving process.

- *Restoration-oriented processes:* Coping with problems and responsibilities resulting from the loss and finding one's place in a world without the deceased.

The tasks of restoration do not just occur in the final phase of multistage grieving, but begin immediately, oscillating with the loss-oriented processes.

Stages of Grief

There are several popular models of the "normal" stages of grieving. Lindemann (1944) gets credit for the earliest stage theory, with his three phases of mourning:

1. Shock, disbelief, and numbness.
2. Facing the loss and experiencing pain and yearning.
3. Resolving the loss and achieving acceptance.

Horowitz (1992) described a different four-stage model: (1) outcry, (2) denial and intrusion, (3) working through, and (4) completion. Worden (1991) describes four tasks of grieving:

1. Accept the reality of the loss.
2. Work through the pain of grief.
3. Adjust to an environment without the lost person or thing.
4. Emotionally relocate that which was lost and move on with life.

Table 4.13 integrates ideas from these models and from other studies of bereavement (Muller & Thompson, 2003; Parkes & Weiss, 1995; Servaty-Seib, 2004).

Variation in Grieving Process

Models of stages are helpful when they can normalize clients' experiences and help them understand why the process of healing is taking so long. However, we must be careful not to assume that there is only one right process of grieving; for instance, there is no evidence that expressing and sharing emotions is a necessary process in adjusting to loss in normal bereavement (M. Stroebe, Schut, & Stroebe, 2005).

Therapists need to accept that there are different possible healthy resolutions to grieving, with varying degrees of connection maintained to the deceased. An assumption often explicit or implicit in models of healthy grieving is that a person must disengage from the deceased to form new relationships. Countering this view, Klass, Silverman, and Nickman (1996) argue that creation of a continuing bond with the deceased is a healthy, rather than pathological, outcome, and this view is supported by study of bereavement in other cultures. The bereaved person accepts the death and begins to take some comfort in positive memories, establishing a permanent sense of connection to the person who died. It becomes possible to reengage in activities and relationships while still maintaining a sense of closeness to the deceased. Examples of ways of maintaining the connection to deceased parents in our culture include dreaming, talking to the parent, believing that the parent is watching us, keeping mementos, and visiting the grave. People who have suffered a major loss appreciate it when other people accept and respect their desire to remain connected.

Table 4.13   Stages of Grieving

Shock, Disbelief, and Outcry

First reaction to the death often includes shock, disbelief, and numbness, lasting from a few hours to days or weeks.

The initial response may be screaming, yelling, crying, or collapsing. These feelings may be expressed publicly or kept private. Numbness and outcry may alternate.

There is preoccupation with thoughts or images of the deceased.

Symptoms of somatic distress occur in waves: tightness in throat, choking, shortness of breath, sighing, empty feeling in abdomen, and lack of muscular power.

There may be a slight sense of unreality, emotional distance from people, and feeling shut off from the world.

Denial may be evident when dealing with loss through disabilities such as spinal cord injury or stroke, with refusal to accept that the loss could be irreversible.

Confronting the Loss

After the rituals of the funeral and the initial arrangements are over, the numbness wears off. People need most support during this phase, which may last from weeks to months.

Reactions include: pain and despair, persistent yearning, weeping and feelings of helplessness, trouble thinking and remembering, and difficulty doing day-to-day activities.

Symptoms of depression are common: loss of appetite, sad appearance, depressed mood, loss of weight, restlessness and anxiety, difficulty sleeping, and feeling tired and weak.

People often feel distant from others and all alone: they may express anger or envy at seeing others with their loved ones, and may withdraw from social activities.

Preoccupation with death and the deceased: dreams of the deceased and experiences while awake of hearing and seeing the deceased; thoughts of death and reflection on one's own mortality; searching for reasons for the loss, sometimes with guilt; and dwelling on mistakes made with the deceased.

People alternate between periods of disengagement, when they don't think about the loss, and periods of engagement, when feelings are as strong as the outcry stage. People bounce between these poles of engagement and disengagement, and may feel guilty about disengaging.

There is a need to face the feelings, rather than bury or avoid them. However, people differ in their need to express the feelings to others.

Resolving the Loss

The swings between denial and intrusion slow down, with less time spent feeling overwhelmed by the loss. Feelings are less painful and no longer interfere with functioning, although temporary reactivation of grief feelings may occur from time to time.

The bereaved person adjusts to everyday life without the relationship. After many life changes, life starts to feel normal again. The person reinvests in life and finds new fulfilling relationships and activities.

When coping with permanent loss from disability, the person must learn to live with the abilities that remain, by compensating for what is lost, accepting dependence on wheelchair or ventilator, and learning to ask for and accept help.

Often, bereaved people seek activities and causes that will keep the deceased's memory alive and somehow create meaning in the death. For instance, parents of children killed by violence (e.g., drunk drivers or sex offenders) have started organizations (e.g., Mothers Against Drunk Driving) and pursued legislation (e.g., Megan's law; Amber alert system), to spare other parents the pain of loss.

Complications in the Grief Process

The judgment that the process of grieving is problematic should be based on the symptoms and impairments of the bereaved person rather than theoretical models of grief. The term *incomplete grieving* often is used when someone seems "stuck," and has not progressed through a grieving process to a satisfactory resolution. Although this concept makes sense for persistence of acute symptoms, we should avoid assuming that a lack of "normal" emotional expression means a problematic "delayed" or "absent grief." First, it is possible that the person had a very limited attachment to the deceased. Second, he may be coping in a way that is appropriate for him. For instance, expressions of pain would be absent if a person had a firm spiritual belief that she would be reunited with the deceased in Heaven.

Bonanno and Field (2001) challenge the assumption that unless people show overt signs of grief and make efforts to "work through" the loss, they will develop problems in the future. They identified a group of people who, 6 months after a loss, were not showing overt emotional signs of grieving and found that 5 years later, they were functioning as well as people who had been more expressive of their pain and loss. Nevertheless, W. Stroebe, Schut, and Stroebe (2005) continue to include the absence of overt grief in their description of three types of complicated bereavement:

1. *Chronic type:* Too much focus on loss; prolonged experience of symptoms of acute phase such as anger, sadness, bitterness, or depression; maintenance of a fantasy relationship with the deceased with feelings that he or she is always present and watching; continuous yearning and searching for the deceased; lack of progress in tasks of restoration.

2. *Delayed, inhibited, or absent type:* Too little focus on loss with exclusive focus on restoration tasks.

3. *Traumatic type:* Highly intense and persistent confrontation with loss combined with avoidance; experience of symptoms characteristic of PTSD such as persistent flashbacks, nightmares, or intrusive memories.

Risk factors for complications fall into six categories:

1. *Type of relationship with the deceased:* Very close or complicated; extreme dependency or ambivalence; insecure rather than secure attachment (Bowlby, 1988); high level of guilt in the history of the relationship.

2. *Circumstances of death:* Sudden, rather than expected; perceived as unfair or unjust; violent death; multiple losses; suicide, which carries stigma and

brings guilty self-questioning; a loss that other people negate or minimize such as a miscarriage or a partner that is not a spouse; uncertainty of loss, as with missing children or soldiers; guilt over events in time period surrounding loss.

3. *Grieving process:* Attempts to avoid experiencing the pain; belief that decreasing grief is a betrayal of the deceased.

4. *Individual personality and history:* Poor coping skills of the grieving person; prior history of depression; traumatic experiences in childhood.

5. *Concurrent life stressors:* Either caused by the death or coming from different sources.

6. *Lack of adequate social support:* Includes lack of available support, withdrawal from social relations; poor choice of response by people in support network.

Terminal Illness

Kubler-Ross (1997) interviewed over 500 dying people and developed a model of the stages of dealing with one's own impending death: denial, anger, bargaining, depression, and acceptance. There is no evidence that people go through all of those stages in sequence, but the model is helpful in recognizing the experience of coping with a terminal diagnosis: *This can't be true* (denial), *It's not fair, why me?* (anger), *God, I'll be a good person and do whatever you want if you make me better* (bargaining), *I'll never see my grandchildren, I wasn't as good as I should have been, my whole life has been a waste* (depression), *It's a fact, I'm going to die, I might as well get my affairs in order and make my last months as comfortable as possible* (acceptance). Kubler-Ross advocated to Congress that rather than isolating and institutionalizing dying people, we should provide them with palliative care at home. Her efforts contributed to the development of the Medicare benefit for hospice care and changes in society's attitudes about caring for the dying (National Hospice and Palliative Care Organization, 2005). The concept of "dying with dignity" includes the right to be involved in decision making, and to have the opportunity to share with loved ones feelings and thoughts about the final transition of life.

Knowledge of a terminal diagnosis gives family members a chance to prepare for the loss, which can reduce the intensity and duration of the bereavement process after the person dies. However, sometimes the belief that they will feel prepared is disproved by the shock of the emotional reaction to the actual death. The risk of starting to grieve early is that the person may emotionally disengage from the loved one while he or she is still alive and needs the connection.

Aging, Illness, and Disability

Changes in functioning caused by age are experienced as losses. Initially the losses are small—needing reading glasses, stiffness in the morning, more easily fatigued—but often there is a loss that symbolizes the beginning of a decline.

An episode with a life-threatening illness such as cancer, even if treatment has been successful, represents a loss of one's identity as a healthy person. Coping with a chronic illness or disability represents the loss of comfort and activities that were likely taken for granted.

Members of the "old-old" population are dealing with a terminal diagnosis, even if they do not yet know the eventual cause of death. As Pipher (1999) vividly describes, the final stage of life for an elderly person with serious health problems and functional impairments is full of losses in every dimension of living, in addition to the loss by death of spouse, friends, and siblings:

- The loss of access to hobbies and interests (e.g., reading, physical activities like gardening, cooking, dancing).
- The loss of independent living (e.g., needing others to drive, buy groceries, or, with further physical decline, needing assistance for toileting and bathing).
- The loss of days in which one is without pain, exhaustion, and physical symptoms.
- The loss of home, when one is forced to live with relatives or move to an assisted living facility.

Loss of a Relationship

Grief is a response to the loss of significant relationships by causes other than death. When the relationship ends by the loved-one's choice, it can be more difficult to cope with than the death of a loved-one. Even the person who makes the choice to terminate the relationship may experience bereavement.

Limbo

Colgrove, Bloomfield, and McWilliams (1976) describe situations where there is uncertainty about whether there is a loss: Awaiting results of medical tests, someone missing in action, lovers after a quarrel, a marriage that seems to be on the brink of divorce, or a project that may or may not fail. In some cases, uncertainty is ended: Divorce papers are filed, the missing person comes home, or the boyfriend marries another woman. In other instances, the client denies the loss by keeping hope alive when there is little basis in reality to do so. The most painful condition is a limbo that never ends: A teenager runs away and the parents never give up hope that their child will contact them.

Can't Let Go

The course of an unhappy romantic relationship can include many episodes of loss and grief followed by reconciliation; the relationship is never fully lost. There is intense ambivalence, inability to let go, a lack of reality testing, and a roller coaster of hope and pain. The resolution may be *letting go:* terminating a relationship and making a firm decision to say no if the other person makes contact. With that step, the process of grieving can begin. Hence the refusal to let go functions as protection against the pain of grieving and coping with the tasks of restoration.

Other Losses

There are many losses for which the grieving individual lacks cultural rituals and adequate social support to ease the pain.

Pregnancy Losses

When a mother fails to bring a pregnancy successfully to term—through miscarriage, stillbirth, or induced abortion—people often do not understand the gravity of the loss and the complexity of the mourning process. Summarizing the literature, Ney (1994) explains that an incomplete pregnancy represents many losses: loss of a significant person, loss of some aspect of the self, loss of a stage of life, loss of a dream, and loss of creation. The mother, herself, may not grasp the significance of the bereavement.

Infertility

Spector (2004) describes the stressors for an infertile couple, including the pain of attending the rituals associated with child rearing such as baby showers, birthday parties, and graduations; the tensions in the marital sexual relationship; and the cycle of hope and disappointment. Support and advice for people facing infertility is available through the National Infertility Association (RESOLVE) at www.resolve.org.

Adopted Children

Many experts believe that even children who were adopted in early infancy and who never knew the birth parent will experience lifetime consequences from the loss of connection to their biological parents (Brodzinsky & Schechter, 1990; Klass et al., 1996; Reitz & Watson, 1992). They may have low self-esteem, fears of abandonment, questions about identity, feelings of rejection, avoidance of intimate commitments, and fears of hurting their adoptive parents' feelings if they reveal their true thoughts and feelings. Feelings of loss are invalidated by the adoptive parents' efforts to put a positive spin on the adoption process. According to Axness (1998), adoptive mothers, especially those who adopted after unsuccessful efforts to get pregnant, would affirm their child's reality by putting into words these thoughts: *"I'm sorry, too, that you didn't grow in my tummy. . . . But I am happy that you and I ended up together."*

Pet Loss

When people lose their beloved companion animal, the grief reaction is often the same as that for the death of a person, but their embarrassment and the lack of understanding of other people may lead to suppression of feelings. Neiburg and Fischer (1982) describe issues of pet loss, including the difficulties of the decision for euthanasia and the timing of finding a replacement pet.

WHEN IS THIS HYPOTHESIS A GOOD MATCH?

There are three circumstances under which this hypothesis is a good choice:

1. *Recent loss:* The client has suffered a recent loss, either from death, divorce, disability, or other cause, which serves as a precipitating factor in emotional distress.

2. *Past loss:* The client is suffering from a loss in the past and has not achieved a resolution of the grieving process.

3. *Hypothesized past or symbolic loss:* The client presents with symptoms and problems that do not relate to an identifiable loss, but there are data supporting the hypothesis of incomplete or unresolved grieving for a loss in the past or the presence of a recent symbolic loss of which the client is unaware.

Normal Grief Process

The symptoms and problems may be typical of a normal grief process. The client and family may be concerned that this is a pathological condition, but once they are educated, there may be no need for any formal counseling.

When reactions to the death of a loved one are the focus of therapy, the *DSM-IV-TR* diagnosis is *V62.82 Bereavement.* The client may have symptoms that are severe enough to be characteristic of a Major Depressive Episode such as sadness, insomnia, poor appetite, and weight loss. However, these reactions are viewed as part of normal bereavement during the 1st month following a loss.

The diagnosis of Major Depressive Episode would be warranted if there are certain symptoms that are not characteristic of a normal grief reaction, or if the severe grief symptoms are present 2 months after the loss:

- Guilt about things other than actions at the time of death.
- Thoughts of death other than survivor feelings.
- Morbid preoccupation with worthlessness.
- Marked psychomotor retardation.
- Prolonged and marked functional impairment.
- Hallucinatory experiences other than transient experiences related to the deceased person.

Incomplete Recovery from Past Losses

When an individual's reaction to a loss is extreme and disproportionate in its intensity, the explanation could be that she avoided adequately grieving a prior loss, perhaps by keeping busy or immediately starting a new relationship. The concept of *incomplete recovery* may also fit when the client's current problem does not have a recent loss as a precipitating factor. The presenting problems might be depression, severe anxiety, difficulty developing an intimate relationship, or inability to maintain stable employment. With appropriate supporting data, the clinical formulation can be that a loss in the distant past was not adequately grieved. Some examples of this application are the following:

- A new mother has difficulty bonding to her baby because she did not sufficiently grieve a prior miscarriage, abortion, or stillbirth (Ney, 1994).
- People dealing with postpolio syndrome and other problems of aging may have complications in their ability to cope because of never having adequately grieved the losses from the original disability (Genskow, 1996).
- A woman who was never able to "properly grieve" her sister's death several years earlier, in part because her role as caregiver did not allow her to let go (M. Miller et al., 1998), responds to the retirement of her husband with depression.
- Rape survivors experience major losses that persist long after the trauma: loss of control, trust, healthy sexual functioning, sense of safety, virginity, and faith in a just world (Koss & Harvey, 1991; Metzger, 1976). Matsakis (2003) describes the need for mourning rituals to help with long-term healing from rape.

Termination of Therapy

When clients who have been in long-term therapy decide with their therapist that it is time to terminate, they feel anxiety about the impending loss of an extremely important relationship. There is often a recurrence of symptoms as a way of prolonging treatment and thereby warding off the anticipated grief.

TREATMENT PLANNING

You need to provide the bereaved individuals and family members with information about grief and its symptoms, course, and complications. The American Cancer Association web site (2005) provides simple and clear explanations:

> When a person loses someone important to them, they go through a normal process called grieving. Grieving is a natural and expected process which, over time, can allow the person to accept and understand their loss. Grieving involves feeling many different emotions over a period of time, all of which help the person come to terms with the loss of a loved one. . . . Many people think of grief as a single instance or very short period of pain or sadness in reaction to a loss—for example, the tears shed at a loved one's funeral. However, the term grieving refers to the entire emotional process of coping with a loss. Normal grieving allows us to let a loved one go and continue with our lives in a healthy way. Though grieving is painful, it is important that those who have suffered a loss be allowed to express their grief, and that they be supported throughout the process. Each person's way of grieving for a loved one will be different. The length and intensity of the emotions people go through will also vary from person to person.

It can be helpful to suggest reading books such as *How to Survive the Loss of a Love* (Colgrove et al., 1976), which combines poetry, information, encouragement, and advice:

- You will survive.
- Nature has a healing process, but it takes time.
- You are much more than the emotional wound you are currently suffering.
- An emotional wound requires the same priority attention as a physical wound.
- Expect ups and downs, not a smooth progression.

Counseling the Bereaved

The therapist needs to evaluate the nature and intensity of distress as well as assess for troubling problems that are created by the loss, such as impairment in work functioning, neglect or overprotection of children, substance abuse problems, and practical issues related to handling an estate. It is important to monitor suicide risk and other self-destructive behaviors. The guidelines for crisis intervention presented previously in Table 4.7 are very relevant for working with bereaved clients.

You need to demonstrate empathy and patience while allowing the bereaved person to talk about the loss at his own pace. The client will be grateful that you do not commit the errors of well-intentioned friends, such as saying, "I know exactly how you feel," "You're so strong," or "Isn't it time to move on?" These responses invalidate the uniqueness of suffering and imply that weakness and intense distress will not be tolerated. Many clients need to tell their stories over and over and may feel that they have exhausted their friends' capacity to bear the repetition. They will be reminiscing about positive memories, reviewing details of the final days, and describing the character of the deceased. You might want to ask the client to bring mementos to the session or even have a meeting at the client's home.

Conversations with the bereaved client often will focus on meaning. Neimeyer (2000) suggests that the survivor's personal meaning system was altered by the loss, and therapy can assist her in finding significance in the death and in her own life. Bereaved people often talk about how their experience with death changes priorities and gives clarity about values. Some clients will be struggling with the unfairness of an untimely death, needing philosophical and spiritual direction that Kushner (1981) discusses in *When Bad Things Happen to Good People*. Existential, narrative, and CBT approaches all have effective methods for helping clients create new meaning (Servaty-Seib, 2004).

There is diversity in the way that people mourn their loss and therapists should not impose arbitrary rules for how to grieve. Muller and Thompson (2003) describe differences in the type of counseling sessions that bereaved people need. Some prefer a "companioning" approach, where the therapist abstains from analyzing and advising, whereas others benefit from direct assistance in coping. Expressing feelings is assumed by many researchers and therapists to be necessary for healthy adjustment (Lindemann, 1944; Worden, 1991); however, other professionals have found that it is not a necessary condition for long-term adjustment (Bonanno & Field, 2001).

Guidance for Coping

An important task of the grief counselor is to help the bereaved person and family members with concrete suggestions for how to cope during the grieving process. Psychotherapy trainees are so frequently told to avoid giving advice that it may be hard for them to fill this needed role. Table 4.14, which can be copied and given to clients, provides suggestions for coping with loss from the American Cancer Society (2005).

Therapeutic Interventions

Using the dual-process theory for bereavement (M. S. Stroebe & Schut, 2001), interventions will focus on either *loss-oriented processes* or *restoration-oriented processes,* depending on the needs of the individual client.

Loss-Oriented Processes

The following techniques help clients deal emotionally with their loss.

Gestalt empty chair: The client can speak directly to the deceased and express feelings, say what there was no opportunity to speak during the deceased's life, and possibly forgive or seek forgiveness. The act of saying "good-bye" is often avoided, but it is important for accepting the reality of the loss.

Guided imagery: The therapist can guide the client through a set of experiences that may culminate in speaking to the deceased. The process is internal and silent; the therapist may or may not ask the client to share what happened.

Writing letters, poetry, or a journal: Lepore and Smyth (2002) provide many examples of how writing activities can be helpful with bereaved clients.

Making art: M. A. Hill (2005) describes a range of benefits for bereaved people from art activities: Bringing to consciousness feelings that are below the surface; giving form to incoherent emotions; freeing up energy for daily life; cathartic release of feelings that are difficult to express to people, such as rage; and enjoying a pleasurable and relaxing activity.

Commemoration: The client can create a scrapbook with letters, photos, and other mementos from the deceased's life. The art-making activities can lead to a lasting memorial.

Healing rituals: J. W. James and Friedman (1998) give instructions for completing the grieving process, including a ritual for saying good-bye not only to the person but also to the pain of the loss.

Table 4.14   Guidance for Coping during Bereavement

Be Patient with the Process

Don't pressure yourself with expectations. Accept that you need to experience your pain, your emotions, and your own way of healing. Don't judge your emotions or compare yourself to others.

Express Your Feelings

All your feelings are okay. Suppressing them can make it harder to progress. Let yourself cry. It's normal to have very strong feelings and to sometimes be overwhelmed by the intensity. Some people find benefit from writing letters to the person they lost.

Get Support from Your Friends, Family, and Religious Community

Talk about your loss, your memories, and your experience of the life and death of your loved one. Do not protect your family and friends by not expressing your sadness. Ask others for what you need. Others can give encouragement, information, guidance, comfort, practical suggestions, and can help you feel less alone.

Get Support from Other People Going through a Similar Loss

Consider joining a bereavement support group. There are many organizations with useful websites, such as Compassionate Friends for bereaved parents (www.compassionatefriends.org), WidowNet for widows (www.widownet.org), and Griefnet (www.griefnet.org). You can get more out of a self-help group if you also socialize with members outside of the group.

Try to Maintain Your Normal Lifestyle

Avoid major life changes in the first year of bereavement. This will allow you to maintain roots and some sense of security. It is helpful to keep to a schedule and routine for a sense of order and control.

Take Care of Yourself

Let yourself get sufficient rest. Eat well and exercise. Use spiritual resources. Physical activity is a good way to release tension. Nurture yourself: Allow yourself small physical pleasures that help you replenish yourself like hot baths, naps, and favorite foods. Don't neglect your own needs to be strong for others. Avoid excessive alcohol, which can harm your body, slow your recovery, and may cause new problems. Don't start smoking.

You Will Be Developing a New Relationship with Your Loved One

You are changing the relationship from one of presence to one of memory. You will be able to maintain a bond and connection if you choose. Accepting that he or she is dead does not mean that you have forgotten your loved one or are minimizing the importance of the relationship.

Forgive Yourself, If Necessary

Compassion and forgiveness for yourself and others is important in healing. Forgiveness is necessary for all the things you said or didn't say or do. Not dealing with your guilt will make things worse and lead to complications such as depression.

Take a Break from Grief

Although it is necessary to work through grief, you do not need to constantly focus on it. It is healthy to find appropriate distractions like going to a movie, dinner, or a ball game, reading a good book, listening to music, and getting a massage or manicure.

Prepare for Holidays and Anniversaries

Decide if you want to continue certain traditions or create new ones. Plan in advance how you want to spend your time and with whom. Do something symbolic in memory of your loved one.

Books Can Be Very Helpful

You can get more suggestions for coping from books. It also can be helpful just to read the words of people who have gone through the type of loss with which you are dealing. Religious and spiritual readings might provide what you need.

Restoration-Oriented Processes

The following approaches help clients cope with life without the deceased.

Narrative therapy: The therapist helps the client to create a coherent narrative of a future life without the presence of the deceased but with a connection in memory and freedom to pursue new activities and relationships.

Cognitive-Behavioral therapy (CBT):   The therapist challenges limiting beliefs and schemas and helps the client create ones that support competence in new roles and tasks and gives permission to "move on." The therapist can use a structured problem-solving model and help the client develop and implement an action plan.

Skill development: There are many situations and challenges following a loss that may require new skills, such as financial management, becoming self-supporting, and forming new friendships. The therapist can help the client identify strengths and weaknesses, provide practice for interpersonal situations through role-playing, and encourage the client to seek appropriate informal or professional help.

Complicated Bereavement

In a recent study, Shear, Frank, Houck, and Reynolds (2005) demonstrated that their complicated grief treatment (CGT) was more effective than interpersonal therapy (IPT; Klerman & Weissman, 1993), for people who had severe grief symptoms over 6 months after the loss. Complicated grief treatment used the dual-focus approach. For the restoration focus, patients defined life goals and developed concrete plans for working toward these goals. For the loss focus, there were two innovative techniques:

1. *"Revisiting" exercises:* The therapist asks the patient to close her eyes and tell the story of the death so it can be tape-recorded and then listened to at home between sessions.
2. *Promoting a sense of connection to the deceased:* The therapist has the patient, with eyes closed, speak to the deceased and then switch roles to answer. The patient also completes a questionnaire focused primarily on positive memories.

Complicated grief treatment (CGT) resulted in improvement for 51% of patients compared to 28% for IPT. The fact that 49% did not benefit shows the need for continued clinical research on effective treatment for complicated grief.

Countertransference Issues

When counseling grieving clients, be aware of your countertransference issues around death and prolonged emotional distress. If working with the client triggers your own unresolved losses, you may act in ways to shut off expression of pain to the detriment of the client's treatment.

INTEGRATION OF HYPOTHESES

One or more of the following hypotheses are often combined with the one just reviewed to create an integrative formulation for a specific problem. The decision about whether a specific hypothesis should be integrated is based on your professional judgment.

B2 Medical Intervention

An evaluation for medication may be necessary when emotional symptoms are very severe, prolonged, and interfere with sleep and normal functioning.

C2 Faulty Cognitive Map

The client may have schemas that serve to catastrophize a loss: *I'll never find anyone else to love me.* There are maladaptive schemas that interfere with progression through the grieving process or increase risk of suicide: *If I start enjoying my life, it's a betrayal of my dead husband,* or *If I can't walk, life is not worth living.*

ES1 Existential Issues

Death and other major losses make people consider their own mortality and question the meaning of life. They recognize the value of their own remaining days and the preciousness of those things that have not been lost.

ES2 Avoiding Freedom and Responsibility

Many losses are events that are imposed on us, rather than chosen: We are victims of circumstances or other people's choices. However, we have freedom to choose our response to the loss: how to interpret it, cope with grief, and reconstruct our lives. Clients need to be aware of the consequences of choices—to seek support or isolate themselves, to begin to date or to remain loyal to the memory of the spouse, or to remain obsessed with their dead child or pay attention to the needs of the surviving children.

ES3 Spiritual Dimension

As part of the mourning process, people often need to explore issues of religion and meaning. Clergymen are often better resources than psychotherapists for helping people cope with losses.

P1 Internal Parts and Subpersonalities

A grieving person will probably have internal parts in conflict: One part may be grief-stricken, while another part may feel relieved, especially if a loved one died after prolonged deterioration. When bereavement is complicated by intense guilt, the therapist can work with the punitive, unforgiving part of the person and help the client dialogue with it, either seeking forgiveness or disputing its irrational blame.

P2 Reenactment of Early Childhood Experiences

Unfinished business surrounding grief and loss makes a person more vulnerable to complicated bereavement and depression. The early attachment style of the individual (i.e., secure, anxious, or avoidant) predicts the nature of adult attachments as well as the bereavement experience.

P3 Immature Sense of Self and Conception of Others

The maturity of the person's capacity for healthy object relations will influence the nature and course of the grief reaction. People who have not progressed past the narcissistic stage of development may have intense feelings of abandonment if the deceased functioned as a *selfobject*, a term for a person who shores up the other person's empty and vulnerable sense of self. However, they may find a replacement very quickly: someone else to fill the same functions. In contrast, a mature person creates a bond to a unique and special person, and loves the person for herself, not for the functions she serves; this individual is more likely to have the prolonged grief process described in the bereavement literature.

SCE1 Family System

The family system is an important factor in bereavement. The loss of a member will stress the system and disturb its equilibrium; family members will be induced into different roles, often including "the strong one," who is expected to hold everything together. At the same time, families are a major source of support and, whenever possible, should be included in the treatment process.

SCE2 Cultural Context

The duration and expression of "normal bereavement" varies considerably among cultural groups. Culture-bound syndromes may occur in association with a major loss. For instance, an *ataque de nervios,* an idiom of distress for Latinos from the Caribbean, frequently occurs as a result of news of a death. Ghost sickness, a preoccupation with death and the deceased, is frequent among members of many Native American tribes. A "spell" is a trance state in which individuals communicate with deceased relatives. In many cultures, including Japanese and Native American, the deceased continues to live in some form after death, and there are rituals that facilitate a continuing connection. Widowhood in our culture is viewed as a temporary phase with remarriage as an expected and desirable outcome. In other cultures, it is acceptable to remain connected to the lost spouse, to keep the house full of his possessions, and to talk to him, perhaps asking his guidance. In addition, you need to be aware that there are culturally based gender differences in grieving styles and that gays and lesbians have additional stressors in the loss of a partner when society does not accord them the status of "spouse."

SCE3 Social Support

Isolated people typically have a more difficult time with the grief process than do people with social support. Support can come from friends, family, and community resources such as religious organizations and support groups for people sharing a common loss. At a time when people most need social support, others may back off and not be available. For instance, a woman whose child dies often finds that her friends start to avoid her, finding contact to be too painful. Support groups for this and other types of bereavement are extremely effective (Kyrouz, Humphreys, & Loomis, 2002).

SCE4 Social Role Performance

Role change can be associated with loss, even if the change is positive. The empty-nest stage involves the loss of the role as active parent; retirement is a loss of the role as active worker. When women cope with infertility, they grieve the loss of the role of pregnant woman and biological mother. People who function as spouses without being legally recognized as having that role will have additional stressors during their bereavement, without the comfort that comes from role-related social rituals.

SUGGESTED READINGS

Recommendations are provided for each hypothesis.

CS1 Emergency

Blumenreich, P. E., & Lewis, S. (1993). *Managing the violent patient.* New York: Brunner-Routledge.

Davies, J. M., Lyon, E., & Monti-Catania, D. (1998). *Safety planning with battered women.* Thousand Oaks, CA: Sage.

Jacobs, D. G. (Ed.). (1999). *The Harvard Medical School guide to suicide assessment and intervention.* San Francisco, CA: Jossey-Bass.

Kleespies, P. (Ed.). (1997). *Emergencies in mental health practice: Evaluation and management.* New York: Guilford Press.

Maris, R. W., Berman, A. L., & Silverman, M. M. (2000). *Comprehensive textbook of suicidology.* New York: Guilford Press.

Roberts, A. R. (1998). *Battered women and their families* (2nd ed.). New York: Springer.

Sales, B. D., Miller, M. O., & Hall, S. R. (2005). *Laws affecting clinical practice*. Washington, DC: American Psychological Association.

Schneidman, E. S. (1996). *The suicidal mind*. New York: Oxford University Press.

Shea, C. S. (2002). *The practical art of suicide assessment*. Hoboken, NJ: Wiley.

Walker, L. (1984). *The battered woman syndrome*. New York: Springer.

CS2 Situational Stressors

Aguilera, D. (1998). *Crisis intervention: Theory and methodology* (8th ed.). St. Louis, MO: Mosby.

Briere, J. (1989). *Therapy for adults molested as children*. New York: Springer.

Courtois, C. A. (1996). *Healing the incest wound: Adult survivors in therapy* (Reprint ed.). New York: W. W. Norton.

Davis, M., McKay, M., & Eshelman, E. R. (2000). *The relaxation and stress reduction workbook* (5th ed.). Oakland, CA: New Harbinger.

Elkin, A. (1999). *Stress management for dummies*. New York: For Dummies.

Gist, R., & Lubin, B. (Eds.). (1999). *Response to disaster: Psychosocial, community, and ecological approaches*. New York: Brunner-Routledge.

Kanel, K. (2002). *A guide to crisis intervention* (2nd ed.). Belmont, CA: Wadsworth.

Psychological Trauma

Chu, J. A. (1998) *Rebuilding shattered lives: The responsible treatment of complex posttraumatic and dissociative disorders*. New York: Wiley.

Foa, E. B., Keane, T. M., & Friedman, M. J. (Eds.). (2000). *Effective treatments for PTSD*. New York: Guilford Press.

Foa, E. B., & Rothbaum, B. O. (2001). *Treating the trauma of rape*. New York: Guilford Press.

Foy, D. W. (Ed.). (1992). *Treating PTSD: Cognitive-behavioral strategies*. New York: Guilford Press.

Herman, J. L. (1994). *Trauma and recovery*. London: HarperCollins.

Parkinson, F. (2000). *Posttrauma stress: A personal guide to reduce the long-term effects and hidden emotional damage caused by violence and disaster*. New York: Perseus.

Raphael, B., & Wilson, J. (Eds.). (2000). *Psychological debriefing: Theory, practice and evidence*. Cambridge, England: Cambridge University Press.

Resick, P. A., & Schnicke, M. (1993) *Cognitive processing therapy for rape victims*. Thousand Oaks, CA: Sage.

Salter, A. C. (1995). *Transforming trauma: A guide to understanding and treating adult survivors of child sexual abuse*. Thousand Oaks, CA: Sage.

Schiraldi, G. R. (2000). *Posttraumatic stress disorder sourcebook*. New York: McGraw-Hill/Contemporary Books.

Wright, H. N. (2003). *The new guide to crisis and trauma counseling*. Ventura, CA: Regal Books.

CS3 Development Transition

Brodzinsky, D. M., & Schechter, M. D. (1990). *The psychology of adoption*. New York: Oxford University Press.

Haley, J. (1980). *Leaving home: The therapy of disturbed young people*. Boston, MA: McGraw-Hill.

Kaplan, L. J. (1978). *Oneness and separateness: From infant to individual.* New York: Simon & Shuster.

Mahler, M. S., Pine, F., & Bergman, A. (1975). *The psychological birth of the human infant.* New York: Basic Books.

Pittman, F. (1998). *Grow up! How taking responsibility can make you a happy adult.* New York: St. Martin's Griffin.

Santrock, J. W. (2005). *Life-span development.* New York: McGraw Hill.

Sheehy, G. (1977). *Passages: Predictable crises of adult life.* New York: Bantam Books.

Sheehy, G. (1996). *New passages: Mapping your life across time.* New York: Ballantine Books.

Stein, M. (1983). *In midlife: A Jungian perspective.* Putnam, CT: Spring Publications.

CS4 Loss and Bereavement

Bernstein, J. R. (1998). *When the bough breaks: Forever after the death of a son or daughter.* Lenexa, KS: Andrews McMeel.

Finkbeiner, A. K. (1998). *After the death of a child: Living with loss through the years.* Baltimore, MD: Johns Hopkins University Press.

Grollman, E. A. (Ed.). (1996). *Bereaved children and teens: A support guide for parents and professionals.* Boston, MA: Beacon Press.

Kubler-Ross, E. (1997). *On death and dying.* New York: Scribner.

Neimeyer, R. A. (Ed.). (2001). *Meaning reconstruction and the experience of loss.* Washington, DC: American Psychological Association.

Parkes, C. M., Laungani, P., & Young, B. (Eds.). (1996). *Death and bereavement across cultures.* New York: Routledge.

Rando, T. A. (1991). *How to go on living when someone you love dies.* New York: Bantam.

Schiff, H. S. (1978). *The bereaved parent.* New York: Viking Press.

Shernoff, M. (Ed.). (1997). *Gay widowers: Life after the death of a partner.* Binghamtom, New York: Haworth Press.

Staudacher, C. (1987). *Beyond grief: A guide for recovering from the death of a loved one.* Oakland, CA: New Harbinger.

Stroebe, M. S., Hansson, R. O., Stroebe, W., & Schut, H. (Eds.). (2001). *Handbook of bereavement research: Consequences, coping, and care.* Washington, DC: American Psychological Association.

Wass, H., & Neimeyer, R. A. (1995). *Dying: Facing the facts.* Washington, DC: Taylor & Francis.

Worden, J. W. (1991). *Grief counseling and grief therapy: A handbook for the mental health practitioner* (2nd ed.). New York: Springer.

Chapter 5 ———————————————————

BEHAVIORAL AND LEARNING MODELS

Common sense and decades of debates on the roles of nature and nurture have led to the conclusion that a major cause of human problems is faulty and incomplete learning. Logically, treatment should provide new and corrective learning experiences. *Behavior therapy,* developed by systematically applying the principles from experimental and social psychology, corrects faulty learning to alleviate suffering and improve the functioning of people who seek help in mental health settings. Table 5.1 presents three major paradigms of learning and useful terminology from behavioral therapy.

Behavioral principles operate even when you are not aware of them. You will selectively reinforce specific client behaviors during therapy sessions. The expression on your face will be a discriminative stimulus for certain responses from clients. You will function as a role model. Research demonstrates behavioral principles at work:

- When behaviorists studied transcripts of Carl Rogers's therapy, they found that he, like all therapists, provided positive reinforcement for desirable client behaviors, and he was less interested, warm, and emotionally present when the client engaged in less desirable behaviors.

- Bandura studied *countertransference* as the therapists' avoidance of those specific client themes or issues (e.g., dependency or anger) that were their personal areas of personal conflict.

Therapists also need to be aware that *clients shape the behavior of their therapists.* For instance, a client can reinforce a therapist's dream interpretation by producing the therapist's preferred kind of dream imagery. Therapists with strong needs for approval, or who have difficulty tolerating conflict or anger, may be making treatment decisions based not on the best interests of clients but rather on their need to get clients' approval and avoid clients' anger or disappointment.

The three behavioral and learning hypotheses are listed in Table 5.2.

Frequently, two or three of these hypotheses will be integrated to develop a comprehensive treatment plan for a given problem. The following is an example of how a doctoral student in a clinical psychology program applied three hypotheses to the problem title: *Difficulty completing dissertation.*

Performing a behavioral analysis (**BL1**), Jennifer identified the desired behavior as "sitting at my desk, concentrating on the task of writing, for 3-hour blocks of

Table 5.1 Major Learning Paradigms

Classical Conditioning

Pavlov's experiments demonstrated how pairing a bell sound with food could result in a dog salivating when a bell rings. In this paradigm, food is the unconditioned stimulus and the bell is the conditioned stimulus.

Unconditioned stimulus: Causes a response without any learning or training (e.g., blink at bright light, flinch at loud noise, or salivate at sight of food).

Conditioned stimulus: Meaningless in themselves, these stimuli have been paired with an unconditioned stimulus (e.g., ringing of bell, words, or money).

Stimulus generalization: The response will occur in situations that are similar to the original learning experience.

Operant Conditioning

B. F. Skinner demonstrated that behavior could be experimentally increased if it is followed by rewards (reinforcers).

Positive reinforcement: The experience of a rewarding, pleasurable consequence following the behavior will lead to the behavior being repeated.

Negative reinforcement: Behavior is repeated if it results in the cessation of an unpleasant stimulus, such as a painful shock.

Discriminative stimulus: A cue or signal that indicates that performance of the behavior will lead to reinforcement. The absence of this stimulus means that no reinforcer will be forthcoming for a particular behavior. The behavior is *under stimulus control* when a certain cue needs to be present for the behavior to occur, and therefore triggers the occurrence of the behavior.

Social Cognitive Theory

Bandura described the *cognitive mediation* that occurs in learning.

Expectancy: The subject develops a belief about contingencies between behavior and reward, which leads to rules for achieving rewards and minimizing punishment: *If a white light is on and I press the bar, I'll get shocked, but if a red light is on and I press the bar, I'll get food.*

Vicarious learning: Learning occurs by observing another's performance and discovering the contingencies for reward and punishment for that other, who serves as a model.

time" and listed undesired behaviors as going to the refrigerator, cleaning files, making telephone calls, and watching TV. She decided that antecedents of productive work were a tidy desk, lumbar support for her back, and encouraging inner talk like "stick with it, you're making progress." Antecedents of dysfunctional behavior were excessive clutter, physical pain, and negative inner talk like

Table 5.2 Behavioral and Learning Models

BL1 Antecedents and Consequences	A behavioral analysis of both problem behaviors and desired behaviors should yield information about **Antecedents** (triggers) **and Consequences** (reinforcers) that will be helpful in constructing an intervention.
BL2 Conditioned Emotional Response	A **Conditioned Emotional Response** (e.g., anxiety, fear, anger, or depression) is at the root of excessive emotion, avoidant behaviors, or maladaptive mechanisms for avoiding painful emotions.
BL3 Skill Deficits or Lack of Competence	The problem stems from **Skill Deficits**—the absence of needed skills—or the **Lack of Competence** in applying skills, abilities, and knowledge to achieve goals.

"it'll never be done, I don't deserve a doctorate." She set up a contingency contract: For every 3 hours of work, she would reward herself with a snack and reading one chapter in a novel. For failing to complete the 3-hour time block, she would write a $10 check and send it to a political party that she detested. This plan was successful: Two months later, and $50 poorer, she had a completed draft to show the chair of her committee. Her professor liked the content, but pointed out a skill deficit (**BL3**) in her writing skills: Her paragraphs were poorly organized and her ideas did not flow in a logical order. Jennifer bought a book on writing and, after studying it diligently, she began to make improvements. As she was nearing the end, she started to experience intense anxiety, sweaty palms, loss of concentration, shaking hands, and a feeling of dizziness. She realized she was having an excessive emotional reaction (**BL2**) to the idea of completion. She knew there were deep issues about success and independence, but she didn't want to deal with them—she just wanted to eliminate the anxiety. So she practiced relaxation techniques and implemented them when she noticed the earliest sign of rising anxiety. She completed the dissertation the next month.

Table 5.3 lists suggestions for assessment and treatment that apply to all three hypotheses.

BL1 ANTECEDENTS AND CONSEQUENCES

Definition

A behavioral analysis of both problem behaviors and desired behaviors should yield information about **Antecedents** (triggers) **and Consequences** (reinforcers) that will be helpful in constructing an intervention.

Explanation

A comprehensive behavioral analysis will uncover antecedents and consequences for behaviors. Specific hypotheses about the relations among variables will lead to strategies for change. The application of principles from learning theory will lead to both the elimination of problem behaviors and the institution and maintenance of desired behaviors. In your behavioral analysis, you need to assess whether the desired skill is in the repertoire, and if it is not, you need to integrate **BL3**.

Examples

Sarah developed what she calls a "freeway phobia" after a minor fender-bender. When her husband realized how frightened she was, he began coming home early from work so he could take her shopping. Her boss was very understanding, and allowed her to work at her home computer. You speculate that she is getting payoffs and rewards for having the symptom. In fact, she will be punished for getting over the phobia.

You would like to help Jamal, an inner-city youth, succeed in school and develop positive goals for the future. Whenever there has been some progress, it is immediately followed by a major setback (e.g., truancy, disruptive behavior, a poor grade on a test for which you know he studied). You discover that he is a member of a group that ridicules him when he gets praise from teachers, and rewards him when he gets in trouble.

Jesse is referred by the court for anger management therapy after committing assault in a road rage incident. You help him identify the triggers for his excessive rage reactions. He describes an external trigger (the driver gave him "the finger" and forced him off the road) and an internal trigger (the thought "someone is disrespecting me"). He also notes that his road rage is worse on hot days because his car doesn't have air conditioning.

Table 5.3   Suggestions for Applying Behavioral and Learning Hypotheses

Start with a Competent Behavioral Analysis

The terms *functional analysis* and *applied behavioral analysis* refer to the process of clearly identifying a problem behavior, and then discovering the principles that will allow you to bring this behavior under control. The process of behavioral analysis combines data gathering and hypothesis testing. Cognitive data are included in the analysis; the Dysfunctional Self-Talk hypothesis (**C4**) should be integrated with Antecedents and Consequences hypothesis (**BL1**).

Function as an Educator

The client is viewed more as a student, trainee, or apprentice than as a client or patient. Thus, this hypothesis removes the stigma of many other mental health models. The treatment plan must attend to stages of learning, build tolerance for being a beginner, and provide many opportunities for practice. Explain the rationale for treatment in language that your client will understand. Suggest that the client read books that explain principles of learning and behavior change (e.g., Pryor, 1999). The literature from the field of teacher training can be helpful for understanding different learning styles. At times, you will feel like a classroom teacher, and at other times, an athletic coach.

Treat the Client as a Collaborator

The client should be actively involved in planning and implementing the treatment. Homework assignments are intrinsic parts of treatment, especially the use of charts such as Table 2.9 in Chapter 2. Encourage the client to interpret the data and apply behavioral principles to build skills for behavioral management of future problems. For instance, the client can seek relevant books, find good role models among acquaintances, and make plans for practice between sessions. A useful book is *Self-Directed Behavior: Self-Modification for Personal Adjustment* (Watson & Tharp, 2001).

Implement Behavioral Techniques with Empathy and Flexibility

Behavior therapists structure the session, typically beginning with an agenda and ending with a homework assignment. Although in most circumstances it is appropriate to stick to this structure, there will be times when something is happening in the client's life that takes priority. There is evidence that clients who rate their therapist as warm and caring at the beginning of therapy will have better outcomes.

Be Knowledgeable about Research Literature on Empirically Validated Treatments

The research literature on cognitive behavior therapy provides clinicians with many examples of treatments that have been empirically validated for specific problems and disorders. These empirically validated treatments (EVTs) are discussed in review articles (Lambert, 2004). Many manual-based treatments have received empirical support in controlled clinical trials, for example, panic control treatment (PCT) for Panic Disorder and agoraphobia (Barlow, 2001).

KEY IDEAS FOR BL1 ANTECEDENTS AND CONSEQUENCES

The process of a behavioral analysis, or assessment, involves defining behaviors, clarifying antecedents and consequences, and using a linear model of causation.

$$\text{Antecedent} \rightarrow \text{Behavior} \rightarrow \text{Consequences}$$

Although behavior therapists originally took a "black box" approach to human functioning, completely disregarding what happened inside, the role of cognition, primarily as internal speech, including its effect on emotions, was included in this model:

Antecedent → Cognitive Mediation → Feelings → Behavior → Consequences

This linear model is a very simplified representation of human functioning. For instance, cognitive activity does not just occur after the antecedent; it also occurs between the emotional response and the behavior, after behavior, and after the environmental consequences.

Therapists need to ask clients to tell very detailed stories of their experiences and help clarify the sequences. Review the summary of the BASIC SID (Table 2.4) and the concept of representational systems (Table 2.6) to be sure to have a thorough database to work with. The data for the analysis come not only from clinical interviews but also from client homework, behavioral observation, and self-report surveys.

Behavioral analysis is so powerful because it simplifies human functioning: Analysis helps clinicians focus on specific variables amidst complexity, and thereby design treatments that can be empirically validated. The result of the behavioral analysis is the development of specific hypotheses about the functional relations among variables for a specific client; these hypotheses lead logically to a specific treatment plan. Here are some of the functional relations for *failure to meet deadlines:*

- Dysfunctional self-talk triggers maladaptive feelings (guilt) as well as inappropriately timed relaxation.
- Television and coffee are reinforcers that should be scheduled after the work is completed, not before.
- Uncluttered desk would be a cue for desired work behavior.
- Music is an antecedent for desired work behavior (shuts out dysfunctional self-talk and lowers anxiety level).

Steps in a Behavioral Analysis

The steps of the analysis leading up to selection of the treatment plan are: defining behaviors, identifying antecedents, identifying consequences, discovering potent reinforcers, clarifying social and cultural supports, conducting a cost-benefit analysis of "change" versus "no change," clarifying the sequences, and doing a functional analysis. The details of each step follow.

Defining Behaviors

The beginning of the analysis is clear definition of behaviors: the *problem behavior* (often called the *maladaptive behavior*) and the *desired behavior* (the outcome goal). In further clarifying the problem, a distinction is made between *excess behaviors,* which need to be reduced or eliminated, and *deficient behaviors,* which need to be increased. The behaviors need to be *operationalized:* described with enough clarity so that the occurrence or nonoccurrence can be recognized and measured. A vague and general definition of a problem would be "overeating." Three different operational definitions would be:

1. *Consumes portions at a meal that are three times the recommended size.*
2. *Eats food between the conclusion of dinner and falling asleep.*
3. *Exceeds 1,200 calories per day.*

In clarifying a desired behavior, it is essential to determine whether such behavior has ever occurred. Determining if the desired behavior is in the client's behavior repertoire has important implications for the treatment plan. You cannot increase a behavior if it is never performed. Instead, you need to apply the **BL3 Skills Deficits** hypothesis and focus on shaping and training the desired behavior from scratch.

Identifying Antecedents

Antecedents are stimuli that precede a behavior in time and function as cues or triggers for the occurrence of a behavior. You need to search for antecedents to both the problem and desired behavior. For instance, the refrigerator is a trigger for overeating and a trigger for self-control could be a picture of a smaller-size dress that you would love to wear. The term *antecedent* can apply to a context or a situation, such as work, school, home. Furthermore, antecedents come from both inside the person and from the external environment, as shown in the following:

- *Biological conditions:* The behavior could occur during certain phases of the menstrual cycle, above a certain threshold of pain, under the influence of alcohol, or above a certain level of sexual arousal.
- *Emotional states:* The behavior might only occur with a certain type of emotion and when the emotion is above a certain level. The SUDS should be used for quantitative measure of emotions.
- *Cognitive triggers:* As discussed later under **C4 Dysfunctional Self-Talk,** internal speech can function as a trigger for behavior. Other types of cognitive triggers are expectancies, evaluation of self-efficacy, attributions, and appraisals of threat.

To clarify antecedents, it is important to discover circumstances under which the problem behavior does not occur. You can ask: *Can you think of a time when you were in that situation and the problem didn't occur? What was different about that situation?*

Identifying Consequences

Consequences are those events that follow the specified behavior. A *reinforcer* is anything that, occurring in conjunction with an act, tends to increase the probability that the act will occur again.

- *Positive reinforcer:* Something you like (food, money, praise, good grade, smile).
- *Negative reinforcer:* An aversive event—the removal of which is rewarding (loud noise, frown, painful sensation).

There are several questions that help clarify consequences:

- *What follows the behavior?* This can be environmental events as well as self-talk and changes in emotional states.
- *How do significant others respond to the problem?* You want to see if there is social reinforcement for the problem.
- *How do they respond when you begin to improve?* It is very common for there to be punishments in the social environment for positive change.
- *What are some payoffs and benefits for having this problem?*

Although clients may say initially that they are unambivalent about wanting to change, further exploration often reveals that there are advantages of staying the same, and eliminating the problem might result in loss of certain satisfactions and benefits. For instance, other people may take over responsibilities and obligations, the problem might provide an excuse for failure, or emotional closeness with its risks and vulnerabilities can be avoided.

Discovering Potent Reinforcers

For planned reinforcement to be effective, the therapist and client must select the most powerful reinforcers for that individual. Although there are many things with a high probability of being pleasurable and rewarding, it is important not to make assumptions. Elementary school teachers realize that public praise can be a reward for one child but a punishment for another. There are individual differences in the strength of social needs, such as the need for recognition, approval, control, sociability, and solitude, which will affect the choice of reinforcers. Furthermore, the rewards need to be appropriate for the client's goals: M&M candies are not an appropriate choice for people attempting to reduce their consumption of sweets. You can recognize reinforcers by identifying behaviors that the person voluntarily spends time doing—like watching TV, reading a book, listening to music, or going to a shopping mall. If someone is willing to endure physical discomfort to do something pleasurable (standing in the rain to wait for concert tickets), it is probably a strong reinforcer. What are the aversive stimuli that the client will seek to evade? For instance, wearing tight clothes provides a negative reinforcer for weight loss: By eating less, the client can attain physical comfort.

Clarifying Social and Cultural Supports for the Problem Behavior

This next step in the behavioral analysis is often neglected, but it is extremely important not only for planning treatment but also in preparing for possible sabotage of the client's improvement. Clarify the following questions with the client:

- *Who objects to the behavior?*
- *Who persuaded the client to seek help?*
- *Which persons or groups have the most control over current behavior, either by supporting and encouraging problem behaviors or punishing desired behaviors?*
- *What are the norms in the client's sociocultural milieu for the problem behaviors? For the desired behaviors?*
- *Are there conflicts between norms in different settings?*
- *How would others be affected if the problems were resolved?*
- *Who else in the family/social network should be included in therapy?*

Cost-Benefit Analysis: Change versus No Change

Any time therapists set goals with clients, it is important to examine the pros and cons of change and consider the possibility that the benefits of staying the same outweigh the benefits of changing. Instead of waiting for "resistance" to appear in the implementation of the plan, it is wiser to explore, up front, sources of ambivalence, secondary gains, and fears of change:

- *What satisfactions would be gained by changes in problematic behavior?*
- *What new problems in living would be created by a successful outcome?*
- *What (from the client's point of view) are the risks, dangers, and feared consequences of changing?*

Clarifying the Sequences

Once you have clarity about the behaviors you want to reduce or eliminate and the behaviors you want to elicit or increase, you need to clarify sequences of external and internal events:

- *What precedes the problem behavior* (e.g., cues, triggers, settings and contexts, behavior of others, self-talk, moods, or biological states)?
- *What is the internal process* (e.g., sequences among feelings, bodily sensations, thinking, and imagery)?
- *What follows the behavior* (e.g., responses of people, reduction of anxiety, or the impact the behavior has on the environment)?

The Functional Analysis

Having gathered data in the preceding categories, you are ready to develop hypotheses about relations among variables that will lead you logically to a treatment plan. When the client understands behavioral principles and has several weeks of homework charts to examine, she can recognize functional relations such as those seen in the following example:

> A person who wants to quit smoking discovers that she tends to smoke with coffee, when she smells smoke, and when she is in the company of other smokers (triggers). The result of smoking is that she feels more relaxed (negative reinforcement from the reduction of anxiety) and has pleasant interactions with strangers (positive reinforcement from the occurrence of social rewards).

The phrasing of the functional hypotheses should be very specific for the individual client. This is the most creative part of the process:

[B] ehavior Is a Function of [A] ntecedents and [C] onsequences

Here are examples of functional hypotheses for the problem:

Excessive eating.

Hypotheses related to antecedents:
- Her excessive eating is a function of being in the kitchen with a full refrigerator, while tired, after work.
- Excessive eating is under the stimulus control of the place, the availability of food, the state of fatigue, and the time of day.

Hypotheses related to consequences:
- Her excessive eating is maintained by pleasant feelings of fullness, pleasurable tastes in her mouth, and the belief that she is nurturing herself.
- Excessive eating is maintained because it terminates feelings of anger and injustice.
- Excessive eating terminates the boring and frustrating experience of working at her computer.

Cognitions can fall in any of the three categories in a functional analysis:

Cognitions as antecedents:
- Her excessive eating is a function of negative self-talk, "I'm so fat, what difference does it make?"
- Adaptive self-talk is a trigger for desired self-control: "This is not my last chance on earth to eat chocolate cake. If I turn it down, I'll feel good about myself."

Cognitions as problem behavior:
- Her negative self-talk ("I'm so fat, what difference does it make?") is the problem behavior that needs to change: The problem behavior is reinforced by the pleasure of eating that follows.

Cognitions as consequences:
- Her excessive eating is rewarded by the self-talk: "I've already eaten too much so now I might as well eat as much as I want, because tomorrow is another day."
- She learns to reward self-control behavior by saying: "I stuck to my plan. Good for me!"

WHEN IS THIS HYPOTHESIS A GOOD MATCH?

Table 5.4 illustrates four situations in which the **BL1** hypothesis is used.

Using Trial Interventions

As long as you are able to operationalize the behavioral target of change as well as the outcome goal, then you are able to use the **BL1** hypothesis. The skills of behavioral analysis can be included in every intake (e.g., clear definition of problems, identifying antecedents and consequences, and exploring cognitive mediation), and you can judge whether the functional analysis leads to promising intervention plans. A trial intervention based on a specific hypothesis can be implemented:

> A businessman who has trouble working on his project decides to hang a poster of Hawaii in his office, play his favorite music, and after 2 hours of work, drink coffee and watch TV for 10 minutes.

If this plan leads to increased time on task and reduced anger and guilt, it is a good match. If change does not occur as expected, gather more data to create an improved functional analysis.

Table 5.4   Uses of BL1 Antecedents and Consequences Hypothesis

The Client Is a Collaborator in a Program to Voluntarily Change His Own Behavior

The client wants to eliminate behaviors (e.g., smoking, drug use, or gambling,) or reduce behaviors (e.g., overeating, alcohol consumption, social avoidance, procrastination, or yelling at children); The client wants to increase behaviors: self-care activities, time spent exercising, speaking up in meetings, or time spent removing clutter from house. A couple wants to reduce conflict and increase enjoyable time together.

The Client Is Learning Behavioral Principles to Change Another Person's Behavior

The client can be taught the skills of behavioral analysis, and can be helped to design a behavior change strategy: a parent wants to increase child's cooperative behavior; a classroom teacher wants to reduce acting out behaviors. Knapp and Jongsma (2004) and Barkley (1997) integrate behavioral techniques in their approaches to building parenting skills.

The Therapist (or Other Interventionist) Uses Behavioral Principles in Client's (and/or) Society's Best Interest

Clients (singly or as members of a group) are reinforced for medication compliance or the use of condoms during sexual relations for HIV positive persons. A program that integrates behavioral principles is developed to help welfare mothers return to work.

The Therapist Uses Behavioral Principles during the Session

The therapist praises the client's efforts to meet new people; gives warm nonverbal reinforcement when the client opens up about painful experience; refuses to extend the session when the client brings up important topic during the last 5 minutes.

TREATMENT PLANNING

There are two broad goals of intervention: (1) increasing desired behavior and (2) reducing or eliminating undesired behavior. The outcome goal is best if it is stated in positive terms, describing what will be occurring at the successful end of therapy. This principle is incorporated into the standards for outcomes in case formulation reports (see Chapter 12). Sometimes the desired behavior is obvious—more exercise, time studying, medication compliance—but other times it requires effort to clarify: What would the client do instead of the negative behavior? For instance, if a person wants to give up smoking, what activity will she substitute when her friends are sitting and smoking over coffee?

A treatment plan would usually combine the elimination or reduction of undesired behavior with the increasing of desired behavior. When the goal is to eliminate a behavior completely—to *stop doing it*—then it is important to find something to fill the void: The goal of *doing nothing* is impossible to achieve.

If the desired behavior is not in the repertoire, then principles of *shaping* are used; these are explained under **BL3.**

Pryor (1999), in an entertaining book on dog training, explains the principles and tactics of behavior change in a format that is accessible to both clients and to therapists who need a quick review. That book guided the list of principles and tactics in Table 5.5. Therapists should apply a self-modification program to themselves (Watson & Tharp, 2001) and consider teaching clients how to set up their own behavioral interventions.

Evidence-Based Treatments

You will find evidence-based treatments that incorporate behavioral principles by reading review articles (see Bergin & Garfield, 1993; Lambert, 2004), searching abstracts, and reviewing journals listed on page 189. The following problems are often resolved through behavior therapy.

Marital or Relationship Distress

Datillio (1998) reviews cognitive behavioral principles and provides cases where behavioral interventions are integrated with systems approaches. A behavioral assessment usually reveals that the partners are exchanging many negative behaviors and few positive behaviors. The therapist adds behavioral observation of the couple's interaction in the office to their separate self-reports. Because each spouse probably has a different behavioral definition for love, they need to define the loving behaviors they desire from their spouse. Then each spouse agrees to voluntarily provide those behaviors, perhaps scheduling "caring days" (Stuart, 1980) or making contracts to exchange these positive behaviors. The increase of positive behaviors leads to the growth of affection and the cessation of hostility that has caused misery and loss of sexual interest. Christensen and Jacobson

Table 5.5   Principles and Tactics of Behavior Change

INCREASING DESIRED BEHAVIOR

Positive Reinforcement

Identify potent reinforcers and schedule these rewards to follow the desired behavior: When the child completes homework, she gets to watch her favorite TV show.

Negative Reinforcement

Arrange for an unpleasant event or stimulus to be halted or avoided when the desired behavior occurs: When the child apologizes to his mother, he gets to leave the time-out corner.

Contingency Contracting

Set up an agreement where performance of specific behaviors is rewarded or punished. Using a written contract increases the effectiveness. You buy a new dress when you maintain your desired eating plan for seven days.

Planning Reinforcement

A detailed plan will specify the timing and size of the reinforcer and schedules of reinforcement. If a behavior is rewarded every time it occurs, there is a good chance that the behavior will extinguish when the rewards stop. However, if the schedule of reinforcement is intermittent and random, the behavior will be very resistant to extinction. The 1st week on the exercise program, reward yourself every day if you complete 15 minutes of exercise. On the 2nd week, you need to exercise 20 minutes to get a reward. On the 6th week, reward yourself once a week if you completed 30 minutes on 4 days.

ELIMINATING AND REDUCING UNDESIRED BEHAVIOR

Stimulus Control

Determine the antecedents and triggers for the undesired behavior and then remove those stimuli (or learn to avoid those situations, contexts, and people). To reduce overeating, the client ate at sushi bars instead of Italian restaurants, asked the server to remove bread from the table in other restaurants, and replaced junk food snacks at home with cut-up vegetables.

Extinction

Remove the rewards so that the undesired behavior produces no results. You need to figure out exactly what is rewarding the behavior: What looks like punishment to one person can be a reward for another—getting someone in the family to yell and be upset can be rewarding to another member. Also, what you think is "no reward," like ignoring a behavior, can be a punishment (rudeness and neglect) from the other person's point of view. Whenever their child got out of bed and came to their room, the parents would cuddle her for half an hour, then take her back to bed and read her a story. They decided to lead her back to bed immediately and say, "see you in the morning," and return to their room. In a few days, the child was staying in her own room.

Punishment

This is defined as an aversive event following the undesired behavior. When used on another person, it has negative effects such as producing anger and desires for revenge. However, it can be very effective when part of a freely chosen self-change program. Every time the client had an obsessive thought, he snapped a rubber band on his wrist.

Reward an Incompatible Behavior

Use rewards to increase a behavior that is physically incompatible with the undesired behavior. A behavior that produces a physiological response of relaxation will prevent behaviors associated with anger and anxiety. At the simplest level, a person cannot be in two places at the same time. A mother was worried that her son was spending too much time at the computer. She enrolled him in a karate class. At first, she planned to give him rewards for attendance, but then she discovered that there were plenty of rewards built into the program: feeling good physically, getting praise from the teachers, making a good friend, and moving to the next color belt.

(2000) emphasize the importance of differentiating behaviors in the spouse that can be changed and those that need to be accepted.

Depression

One behavioral approach to depression is that depression is caused or maintained by the absence of positive reinforcement in a person's life (Ferster, 1973; Lewinsohn, Antonuccio, Steinmetz, & Teri, 1984). Depression is associated not only with inertia and low energy but also with social withdrawal, which deprives the person of positive social reinforcement. *Behavioral activation* (BA; Martell, Addis, & Jacobson, 2001) is a treatment program for depression with two components: (1) increasing behaviors that lead to positive affect and a sense of mastery, and (2) replacing avoidance patterns with alternate coping responses. Because most depressed clients believe that their mood must improve before they can become more active, therapists must persuade them that if they increased activity first, a more positive mood would follow. An example of a simple activity that produces a spark of pleasure with minimal effort is watching baby animals play.

Chronic Fatigue Syndrome

The following behavioral intervention for CFS (Demitrack & Abbey, 1999) can be used with other conditions (e.g., depression, chronic pain, obesity, and health problems) for which the goal is increased activity level.

Assessment

Have the client keep an hour-by-hour diary to obtain a baseline of the current activity level. The diary should include activities, rest, and sleep.

Evaluate Benefits

Help the client evaluate the potential benefits of increasing his or her activity level. Potential benefits for CFS include more energy, increased productivity, and improved self-esteem.

Develop Plan

Work with the client to design a plan for an increased activity level. The new activity level should be (a) at a reasonable and tolerable level for the patient; (b) consistent day to day; (c) increased in small, graded increments; and (d) rewarding for the patient.

Review and Modify

At each session, make a contract with the client for small changes and then review the results in the next session.

Addictions

Emmelkamp (1994) describes a self-control program for reducing alcohol consumption that contains the steps that are typical of most self-control training: (a) functional analysis using daily drinking records; (b) strengthening of nondrinking activities; (c) training in self-management techniques, which include self-monitoring, self-evaluation, and self-reinforcement; and (d) a prepaid commitment fee that is refunded for program compliance. The same treatment approach can be used whether the goal is abstinence or moderation in drinking. Emmelkamp (1994), in fact, found that many individuals who were randomly assigned to an abstinence group "rejected this goal from the outset" (p. 403) and that, at the 10-year follow up, a substantial number of alcoholics in abstinence-oriented programs were successful moderate drinkers.

School and Work Problems

Behavioral interventions are appropriate for increasing study behaviors, task completion, and even job search activities. For instance, students or workers can discover the contexts and stimuli that promote effective on-task behavior and establish contingency contracts to reward blocks of time during which they worked productively.

Impairments in Psychiatric Inpatients

Common goals for people with chronic mental disorders are positive social behaviors, participation in activities, and completion of graduated tasks leading toward more independent living. A token economy can be instituted in an inpatient setting so that the patient can earn points or tokens, which can be cashed in for chosen rewards. The staff person administering the rewards also provides social reinforcement.

INTEGRATION OF HYPOTHESES

Every hypothesis can be combined with **BL1;** only 5 are included in this section.

C4 Dysfunctional Self-Talk

Cognitive mediation is part of every behavioral assessment; therefore **BL1** and **C4** should always be integrated.

P1 Internal Parts and Subpersonalities

When clients do not complete behavioral assignments, or in other ways fail to cooperate in the plan, there are two reasons that should be considered:

1. The task was too big a step, and something easier should be assigned.
2. The client might be ambivalent about achieving the outcome and it would be useful to hear from the subpersonality that wants something different. For instance, "the drinker" is in conflict with "the abstainer."

P4 Unconscious Dynamics

Many of the concepts of psychodynamic theory can be explained by using concepts from learning theory:

- Psychoanalytic methods provide clients with an *extinction* paradigm: The client comes closer and closer to the dangerous emotional experience, without the occurrence of the feared catastrophic consequences, and so becomes able to tolerate emotions and relinquish extreme defensive measures.

- The psychodynamic concept of *secondary gains* is compatible with principles of reinforcement: The problematic behavior is maintained because it is rewarded by positive consequences such as sympathy, not having to fulfill adult responsibilities, and getting other people to submit to one's will.

- The psychodynamic concept of defense mechanisms can be explained by the *avoidance learning* experimental paradigm. The animal who has been shocked learns a behavior to avoid pain and develops the expectancy of pain unless it completes the action. It will maintain the behavior even after the shock is discontinued, because by avoiding the situation, there is never an opportunity for new learning to occur.

- An explanation for resistance to change is that the problem behavior serves a defensive function, protecting the client from pain stored in the unconscious. For instance, because a doctoral degree represents achieving the highest level of achievement in the family, unconsciously the student might equate completion of the dissertation with shaming his father.

SCE3 Social Support

Adherence to behavior change programs is enhanced when there is social support, either informally or provided through an organization like Weight Watchers or Alcoholics Anonymous. The Weight Watchers program was created, in part, by a behavior therapist (Stuart, 1972), and incorporates suggestions for reinforcement and stimulus control methods.

SCE7 Environmental Factors

Environmental factors must be included in a behavioral analysis. The environment contains cues and reinforcers for certain behaviors. A behavioral treatment plan can be *leave the environment that contains the cues for undesired behavior,* as when recovering addicts are told to avoid people and places that trigger their substance use. Another plan can be *change the environment,* as when a person with insomnia moves the home office out of the corner of the bedroom so that the bedroom can be solely a cue for sleeping.

KEY IDEAS FOR BL2 CONDITIONED EMOTIONAL RESPONSE

Joseph Wolpe (1958), one of the founding fathers of behavior therapy, developed the treatment approach of *systematic desensitization,* which inhibited anxiety through counterconditioning. Wolpe (1995) described how he conducted a functional analysis with a man whose anxiety symptoms interfered with his job's requirement to visit managers of companies in their offices. The variables that determined the intensity of the anxiety were particularly important when it was time to prepare a hierarchy from "easy" (low anxiety) to most difficult situations:

> Anxiety was greater in the presence of unfamiliar people and if there was no easy access to a toilet. Other factors that increased it were the importance of the oc-

---

BL2 CONDITIONED EMOTIONAL RESPONSE

Definition

A **Conditioned Emotional Response** (e.g., anxiety, fear, anger, or depression) is at the root of excessive emotion, avoidant behaviors, or maladaptive mechanisms for avoiding painful emotions.

Explanation

The intense emotional response is not justified by the stimuli in the current environment, so we infer that prior learning involving classical conditioning explains the overreaction. The treatment will require new learning: extinction of the problematic emotions and counterconditioning of a more adaptive emotional response. People may avoid situations and experiences that are triggers for unpleasant feelings.

Examples

Zach needs to overcome intense public speaking anxiety to attain an important promotion. He can recall the traumatic situation in which the conditioning occurred: He was giving a speech to his eighth grade class when his mind went blank and he ran out of the room. Even thinking about standing in front of a group produces uncomfortable sensations: He blushes, sweats, and his heart beats faster.

Emily describes an intensely emotional reaction whenever she receives even mild criticism. She has no memory of any trauma; she says her parents were very loving and never criticized her. She wants to be able to stay calm, feel confident, and avoid crying whenever anyone points out a weakness. This emotional reaction seems automatic: She cannot report any self-talk regarding the criticism.

Hilary presents with symptoms that meet the criteria for a diagnosis of Panic Disorder with agoraphobia. She reported that her first panic attack occurred after her boyfriend broke up with her. After that, she began to attend to bodily sensations and worried constantly about having another panic attack. She developed a learned fear of her internal bodily sensations and began to fear any signs of impending panic.

casion and the importance of the other person. On the whole, there was more anxiety in anticipation of a meeting than at the meeting itself. . . . It was apparent that the duration of interviews with his clients was an important factor determining the strength of Mr. B.'s anxiety. (p. 112)

Imaginal or in Vivo Treatment?

In vivo refers to treatments occurring in the real world, outside of the therapist's office, as well as facing the real object, within the office. For instance, if the person is afraid of snakes, instead of using imagery, the therapist could bring a harmless caged snake into the office or go with the client to the snake exhibit at the zoo. Exposure to *interoceptive stimuli* is an in vivo method that occurs in the office: To help a person with panic disorder reduce her fear of dizziness, she is told to twirl around in a chair until she becomes dizzy. In vivo treatment should be used when possible; however, this may require that therapists leave their offices and schedule time more flexibly. There are circumstances when it is necessary to use imagery as when the client refuses to face the object in reality or the real situation is not available or is too traumatic, as with war-related trauma. A new development in behavioral treatment is the use of *virtual reality exposure.*

Knowledge of Causation Is Not Necessary

Effective treatment does not require discovery of the original conditioning situation or exploration of buried issues, quests that would require a lengthy amount of time. A short-term structured approach that targets the emotional overreaction and gives skills of emotional control achieves the desired outcome in a cost-effective way.

WHEN IS THIS HYPOTHESIS A GOOD MATCH?

There are many situations where extreme emotional reactions are justified, as with traumatic events (discussed under **C2**), deaths and other losses (**C4**), and social injustice (**SCE5**). Similarly, intense emotional reactions accompany developmental transitions (**CS3**), loneliness and social isolation (**SCE3**), and changes in one's social environment and required social role (**SCE4**). If your goal were only to reduce unpleasant emotions, you would fail to engage in necessary problem solving and action. It would be inappropriate to launch a behavioral approach to reduce emotional intensity without an understanding of the client's life situation. With many case formulations, the plan is for clients to fully feel their feelings rather than reduce the intensity.

However, there are circumstances where emotional intensity becomes problematic:

- *The emotional reaction has generalized from the original stimulus and is appearing in inappropriate contexts:* A woman who was raped is now frightened of sexual intimacy with her husband.

- *The emotional reaction is causing distress and impairing functioning:* A man with panic attacks is now developing agoraphobia or a woman with obsessive-compulsive symptoms cannot make appointments on time because she keeps returning to her house to check to see if she locked the front door.

- *There are negative social consequences:* A man who has road rage is arrested for assault.

Examples

The following list gives examples of clients for whom this hypothesis is a good fit:

- The client with a fear of dogs reports being bitten by a dog as a child.
- After September 11, 2001, the client is afraid to work in a tall building.
- After being left at the altar on her wedding day, the client refuses to go out with men.
- The client's wife complains that he responds with outbursts of rage to the mildest signs of being disrespected.
- The client feels depressed after the smallest amount of conflict with his spouse.
- The client feels intense anxiety and jealousy if her boyfriend is more than 10 minutes late.

Is There Cognitive Mediation?

In dealing with excessive emotional responses, it is important to gather data about cognitive triggers. If there are cognitive triggers, then **BL1** combined with **C4** will lead to a cognitive intervention: Develop more adaptive self-talk and the excessive emotional reaction will diminish. With many clients, however, the emotional reaction seems to occur unrelated to thought. The client already may know that the feelings—anxiety, fear, or anger—are irrational responses. Under those circumstances, a counterconditioning approach (**BL2**) is the best match.

Empirically-Supported Treatments

Emmelkamp (1994, 2004) found substantial research support for the effectiveness of *exposure in vivo* for Anxiety Disorders (simple phobia, panic disorder, agoraphobia, social anxiety or social phobia) and Obsessive-Compulsive Disorder (OCD). Posttraumatic Stress Disorder (PTSD) responds to *imaginal exposure* and Generalized Anxiety Disorder is improved through *relaxation training*. Division 12 of the American Psychological Association (APA), Society of Clinical Psychology, publishes books on evidence-based practice (see www.hhpub.com/index.php?content=books/ series/52.html).

TREATMENT PLANNING

Relaxation is a physiological and emotional state that is incompatible with distressing emotions. Wolpe's (1958) treatment model for anxiety, which he called reciprocal inhibition, was to pair relaxation with the cue for anxiety, thereby performing *counterconditioning* to supplant the original conditioning. The first part of many treatment plans is giving the client the opportunity to learn to relax. Table 3.7, in Chapter 3, explained several methods of relaxation training. The choice of approach is a pragmatic one: Use what works best for the client. The therapist teaches the method in the office, and assures that the client is mastering it. Then the client is given homework to practice it on a daily basis, sometimes with an audio tape provided, often recorded in the client's own voice. A goal of relaxation training, and the prerequisite for many interventions, is the ability of the client to enter a relaxed state (to lower the SUDS level) in a few seconds.

Develop a Hierarchy

The client and therapist develop a hierarchy of emotion-evoking stimuli. The lowest item is something that is very easy to deal with and each successive item should represent a very small step up the ladder toward the top of the hierarchy. Here are some examples of low, medium, and high items for several problems:

Fear of freeways

- *Low:* You are studying a map and planning a trip, running your finger over a major freeway.
- *Medium:* You are driving on a freeway very early on a Sunday morning, without any traffic.
- *High:* You are on a very crowded freeway during rush hour and need to change lanes to exit.

Anxiety about dating

- *Low:* You are studying in the cafeteria and notice a girl reading a book.
- *Medium:* You are asking a girl in your class to study together for an exam.
- *High:* You are having dinner with a girl and there is a long silence.

Easily provoked to road rage

- *Low:* You notice that someone several cars ahead of you changes lanes without signaling.
- *Medium:* Someone cuts ahead of you on the freeway.
- *High:* You are driving slowly and a car speeds past you with the driver pressing on the horn while the passenger gives you a rude hand signal.

Imaginal Desensitization

In this technique, anxiety-producing cues are imagined vividly while the client stays in a relaxed state, thereby successfully pairing that set of stimuli with a relaxation response instead of anxiety. The therapist structures the sessions, starting with the lowest item on the hierarchy. When the client can imagine it without a rise in anxiety, then the second item in the hierarchy is introduced. The therapist assures that the scenes are presented at an appropriate pace.

There can be different hierarchies for different components of the problem. In the previous example of Mr. B., Wolpe (1995) created a hierarchy for time spent with a manager. The lowest item was *Imagine that you have just entered the office of a manager who has a rule that no representative is permitted to spend more than 2 minutes in his office.* The length of time with the manager was gradually extended until the client, by the ninth session, could imagine a 60-minute meeting without anxiety. Then a new hierarchy for anticipatory anxiety was begun: The top level included imagining himself sitting in the waiting room for 2 minutes before the appointment.

Graduated in Vivo Exposure

Instead of or in combination with imagery techniques, the therapist creates a hierarchy of real-world situations and structures therapy so that the client must first successfully accomplish an activity before moving up the hierarchy. This approach is effective for phobias (e.g., plane; freeway driving) and situations where high anxiety interferes with performance (e.g., public speaking anxiety; social anxiety).

Implosion and Flooding

Instead of using a gradual hierarchy, this approach uses intensely distressing scenes from the beginning, and therapists use imagery to intensify the emotion. By forcing the client to face the feared image or object, the emotional response will be experienced and then extinguished. Therapists must be careful that they stay with a scene until the anxiety has been noticeably reduced and at least partly extinguished. If they were to end a session when the anxiety was still at its peak, they would actually be *sensitizing* the client, and the anxiety and avoidance might be worse. Wanderer and Ingram (1990) reported the use of flooding treatment for phobias with a blood pressure monitoring device to ascertain that anxiety reaches a peak and then diminishes with repetitious exposure to the feared stimuli.

Aversive Conditioning

The principles of emotional conditioning can be used as part of treatment when the client wants to stop doing a behavior that he or she enjoys. For instance, if someone wants to stop drinking alcohol, she could smell a nausea-inducing substance at the same time that she sips the beverage. To stop smoking, a person could sit in a very small closed space and continue to chain smoke until vomiting is induced.

Covert Sensitization

This technique is the same as aversive conditioning except that the paired stimulus and response are imagery. The client would imagine consuming an alcoholic beverage while the therapist describes disgusting scenes. This method can also be used when the client wants to stop being sexually aroused by certain stimuli. For instance, a criminal sex-offender might benefit from pairing imagery of painful experiences to the images that stimulate criminal behavior.

Response Prevention for Obsessive-Compulsive Disorder

An extinction method for people suffering from OCD is called response prevention. The compulsive rituals were assumed to have been conditioned by the negative reinforcement paradigm: They are maintained by reducing an aversive emotional state. As long as the rituals occur, the anxiety does not have a chance to be extinguished. When the compulsive ritual is prevented, the client initially feels a rise in distress. However, anxiety can then be extinguished. Hyman and Pedrick (2005) have a self-help manual for sufferers of OCD that integrates this technique.

Anchoring

Anchoring is a method of deliberately conditioning a relaxed state to a cue that is under the client's control. The cue can be a word ("calm"), a phrase ("let it go"), a visual image (picturing a waterfall), or the sense of touch (pressing a freckle on the hand). The imagery method at the end of Table 3.7 is very useful for this technique. To set up an anchor, use the following steps:

Conditioning Phase

Have the client enter the imaginary scene and use all of her senses to induce a very relaxed state. When that state is achieved, she uses the cue (e.g., pressing the freckle, for several seconds) and then returns to an alert state. The pairing of cue and relaxation is repeated two more times.

Testing

Now, the client is asked to just use the cue. The desired result is for there to be a sudden switch back to the relaxed state. If this does not occur, repeat the conditioning phase.

Homework

The client is instructed to practice the conditioning and testing at home, at least once a day.

Once the relaxed state is successfully anchored, the client has a very useful coping tool: The lowering of anxiety or anger is now under self-control. This technique is useful for therapists as well as clients: Once students and trainees have learned this method, they report using it successfully for exams, interviews, and public speaking.

INTEGRATION OF HYPOTHESES

The following hypotheses are the most useful ones to combine with **BL2.**

B2 Medical Interventions

Medication alone may be sufficient to reduce the problematic emotional state, or medication could be combined with behavioral approaches.

B3 Mind-Body Connections

The physiological benefits of the relaxation response and the harmful effects of excessive negative emotions are discussed under **B3.** In health-related situations, people can often benefit from exposure methods of extinction. For instance, pregnant women and their husbands are taken on a visit to the delivery room. Fear of dialysis could be treated with either imaginal exposure or an in vivo visit to the dialysis machine.

CS4 Loss and Bereavement

Normal grief responses, no matter how intense and disruptive, should not be treated as if they were inappropriate emotions. However, when the grief reaction is excessively prolonged, intense, and disruptive of daily life, techniques to help reduce emotional arousal would be indicated.

BL3 Skill Deficits or Lack of Competence

Relaxation skills are one of the most useful benefits that clients can get from therapy. Being able to relax, at will, is an extremely important life skill. Clients who have difficulty being assertive because of either excessive anger or excessive anxiety benefit from assertion training, which teaches effective communication skills. While the client role-plays scenarios, moving up a hierarchy, the emotions of calm and confidence are conditioned to the situational cues.

C2 Faulty Cognitive Map

Even when treatment is based on conditioning rather than cognitive models, there will be major change in the client's cognitive map. The client comes to believe: "Instead of being a passive victim to emotional storms that are out of my control, I can control my emotional response." Objects that were mislabeled as threatening are relabeled as harmless. Overgeneralization is replaced with appropriate discrimination: "Rapists are dangerous, but sex with my loving husband is not."

C4 Dysfunctional Self-Talk

Exposure techniques can be combined with cognitive restructuring. For instance, as the client engages in in vivo exposure, he not only produces the relaxation response but may also repeat adaptive self-talk to himself.

KEY IDEAS FOR BL3 SKILL DEFICITS OR
LACK OF COMPETENCE

All approaches to therapy produce new learning, whether or not the therapist formulates the approach in those terms. Rogerian therapy builds skills in self-exploration and self-direction. Psychoanalytic therapy teaches people the skills of tolerating painful affect without needing to distort reality. Existential therapy helps people develop the skills of creating meaning and taking responsibility. Almost any problem can be put in the frame of "needing to learn something new." Even if there is a biological cause, the individual needs to cope with impairments and required changes in lifestyle. When neuroscientists talk about

---

BL3 SKILL DEFICITS OR LACK OF COMPETENCE

Definition

The problem stems from **Skill Deficits**—the absence of needed skills—**or** the **Lack of Competence** in applying skills, abilities, and knowledge to achieve goals.

Explanation

The desired outcome is defined as new or improved skills or competencies. Treatment involves creating opportunities for new learning; therapists can function as teachers, coaches, and role models. Many problems that are initially viewed as pathology can be reframed as skill deficits. Therapists should not settle for goals of stabilization or maintenance but rather must set goals for recovery or improvement.

Examples

Jill has done very well in graduate school and has only one remaining hurdle: the dissertation. She reports intense anxiety and feelings of inadequacy, and admits she has been avoiding her dissertation chairperson. After exploring her various experiences with academic tasks, you conclude that she has never before done independent research and lacks many of the needed skills.	A former therapist diagnosed Gabe as having a narcissistic character disorder. You decide to do systematic empathy training to help him perceive and communicate understanding of another person's point of view. You also role-play situations where he feels hurt and angry so he can learn to ask for what he wants in an appropriate way, before the anger builds up.	Cindy is a 35-year-old woman who has been addicted to drugs and alcohol since she was 14. After a year of being "clean and sober," she had a relapse and went to a residential treatment facility. She realized that she would never succeed at sobriety unless she developed skills for soothing painful emotions. She also needs to develop skills for finding and keeping a job.

"new pathways in the brain," "neural integration," and "plasticity of the brain," they are describing the physiological underpinnings of new learning.

In explaining the goals of therapy, we sometimes refer to an often-quoted Chinese proverb: "Give a man a fish and you feed him for a day. Teach a man to fish and you feed him for a lifetime." As therapists, we want not only to help clients solve current problems but also to teach them skills for the future.

Evaluating Competence

Gather data about the client's competence and skills, through self-report and direct observation. The client's behavior with the therapist is an important source of data about interpersonal competence and cognitive skills.

You can also assign a specific task and evaluate the client's performance. In conjoint therapy, as you observe the family or couple trying to accomplish a task, you can evaluate their skills in communication, problem solving, negotiation, and delivering positive messages.

Be sure to evaluate if the skill is in the client's repertoire, distinguishing whether the client lacks the skill completely or if he or she is able to perform it with even a small degree of competence in at least one context. Sometimes the person has a very high level of skills in one context but not in another. For instance, a poor public speaker can be a very effective communicator in one-on-one dialogue.

When the presenting problem is anxiety or fear regarding a specific situation (e.g., public speaking, going on a blind date, or accepting a promotion at work), it is essential to evaluate the client's competence. If the person lacks competence, fear of failure is justified; if you reduce anxiety without helping the client improve performance, she may encounter very punishing and demoralizing consequences for risk taking.

When clients set goals for competence in certain areas, you may need to help them evaluate, honestly and courageously, their limits as well as their strengths. People have individual differences in their talents, abilities, and potential, and sometimes a client has reached the ceiling of competence. For instance, not all people will succeed in doctoral programs, sell their screenplays, or become successful entrepreneurs. According to the "Peter Principle" (Peter, 1969), corporations often promote people to positions for which they lack abilities. For example, a brilliant engineer might be an ineffective team leader.

Stating Goals as Competence Objectives

The target of learning becomes clear if you word your outcome goals in terms of skills, performance, behavior, and competence (see Chapter 12 for a more thorough discussion of outcome goals). The following goals for the problem *excessive conflict in marriage* show the progression from initial, abstract goals to specific competence objectives:

- Less conflict in marriage.

- Have tools to resolve conflict effectively.

- Have the skills to express anger and disagreement without hostility and blame, and have the ability to control defensive responses to criticism.

The Benefits of Skills Training and Educational Models

The advantages to framing the therapeutic strategy as *education* or *training* include the following:

- *Reduces stigma:* When you frame the problem as the "need for new skills and knowledge," you remove the stigma of pathology and reduce shame for participating in the intervention program. For many areas of functioning, you can say, "We're never taught these skills as we grow up, we're just left to use trial and error to figure it out." The invitation to learn new skills is face-saving for a client who is expecting the judgment of "there's something wrong with you."

- *Builds on familiar experiences:* Clients, through past experiences with learning a sport or how to drive a car, are aware that learning occurs gradually and requires practice. With this frame, there is acceptance of being a beginner, making mistakes, and receiving constructive criticism.

- *Taps into strengths:* To create a good plan, the therapist needs to evaluate strengths as well as weaknesses. What skills are already in the repertoire? Can the person perform a skill well in some contexts but not in others? The therapist designs assignments that are graduated so that there are small increases in difficulty, allowing the client to achieve repeated experiences of mastery.

WHEN IS THIS HYPOTHESIS A GOOD MATCH?

Table 5.6 illustrates the broad range of domains that can be treated with a skills-training approach. Note from the examples that the skills-training approach leads very naturally to integration of different hypotheses.

TREATMENT PLANNING

The "learner role" requires an acceptance that one is not currently competent and that achievement of proficiency requires effort, practice, and acceptance of mistakes. The learner must understand that there are stages to becoming competent: In medical school, the stages of learning a procedure are "see one, do one, teach one." A popular framework of four stages of competence is frequently used in skills-training programs to take the stigma out of *incompetence,* help normalize uncomfortable beginner feelings, and instill a hopeful attitude about the

Table 5.6 Skills-Training Domains

Problem Solving/Decision Making

These skills require a methodical, systematic approach:

1. Identify and clarify the problem.
2. Gather information and search for explanations.
3. Brainstorm alternative solutions.
4. Evaluate the costs and benefits of each and choose the best.
5. Implement action plan and monitor results.

Teach clients to make charts, listing all possible alternatives on the left and creating columns for "advantages" and "disadvantages." Recommend programs for children that use video models of good problem-solvers (Webster-Stratton & Hammond, 1997). Shure and Spivack (1980) developed a successful school-based program called "I Can Problem Solve."

Emotional Regulation

Linehan (1993a,1993b) combines techniques from CBT with a "technology of acceptance," teaching the skills of mindfulness derived from both Eastern Zen practices and Western contemplative spirituality (**ES3**). She created a program to teach stress tolerance and acceptance skills such as distracting, self-soothing, improving the moment, thinking of pros and cons, radical acceptance, turning the mind toward acceptance, and willingness versus willfulness.

Stress Management

To engage in effective stress management, people need to identify external stressors and internal responses. Clients learn skills of monitoring their feelings or SUDS level and modifying their emotional reactions. Relaxation training (Table 3.7) gives people tools for lowering their physiological level. Cognitive techniques (**C3, C4**) teach skills for changing patterns of thinking that contribute to excessive emotions. Clients learn to gather information to make choices about whether to take action or engage in passive acceptance.

Psychosocial Rehabilitation

Liberman (1992) was a pioneer in developing the field of psychosocial rehabilitation for chronic mental patients. Partial Hospital Programs or Day Treatment Programs are settings where people can get training in varied skills, including activities of daily living (e.g., how to cook, comparison shop, plan a menu, and budget money).These programs are relevant for groups such as the chronically mentally ill, including the homeless (Gonzalez, Gonzalez, & Aguirre, 2001), people recovering from strokes, and mentally ill substance abusers (Anderson, 1997).

Employment/School

For people with severe disabilities, development of vocational skills may include sheltered work experiences, placement into volunteer jobs, or transitional employment placement to learn work skills. Participants with chronic mental illness are taught how to complete a job application form, what they do and do not have to tell employers about their illness, and how to write a resume. You may discover skills deficits when the initial complaint is anxiety about failure. For instance, students with poor grades or test scores can make plans to build competence in that subject area as well as in test taking.

Basic Communication

There are many good texts on basic communication (e.g. McKay, Davis, & Fanning, 1995) that teach the following skills: (a) awareness of nonverbal behavior in other people as well as in oneself; (b) attentive listening (and overcoming blocks to listening); (c) expression of all

---

Table 5.6 *(Continued)*

facets of awareness, including thoughts, feelings, observations, and wants; (d) use of "I-messages"; and (e) empathic responding to other person's feelings and meaning. An activity for building skills of perspective taking is presented under **P3** (see Table 8.12). Tannen (2001) explained the differences in communication styles between men and women and gave tips for building skills of intergender communication. Intercultural communication requires specialized knowledge and skills **(SCE2).** Some clients will recognize a need to develop what Dresser (2005) calls *Multicultural Manners.*

Assertiveness

Effective strategies of *Assertiveness Training* (AT; Alberti & Emmons, 1995; Lange & Jakubowski, 1978; M. J. Smith, 1975) were developed to help people overcome both the passivity that stems from fear and lack of confidence, and the aggressiveness that comes from excessive anger. In addition to skills for managing emotions and restructuring thinking (e.g., building a sense of rights), AT teaches how to make requests, say no, and give and receive negative feedback. The goal of "setting interpersonal boundaries" **(P3)** can be broken down into specific skills (Whitfield, 1987).

Conflict Resolution and Negotiation

The ability to successfully manage conflict requires skills in several domains—communication, assertion, and problem solving—and specific skills of identifying individual and shared needs, negotiating with expectation of compromise, and designing win-win solutions. Many business books are available on the subject of negotiation, including those that teach aggressive, competitive approaches.

Anger Management

Anger management packages (e.g., Gottlieb, 1999; Williams & Williams, 1993) teach skills such as recognition of angry feelings while they are still at a low, manageable level; anger interruption techniques (e.g., relaxation, time-out, distraction, and modifying self-talk); assertive skills to express angry feelings appropriately; and problem solving to change situations that cause anger. Children often need help in controlling anger and handling disappointment appropriately. Robin, Schneider, and Dolnick (1976) developed a popular four-step "turtle technique": (1) recognize anger, (2) think "stop," (3) go into your shell and take three deep breaths and think calming thoughts, and (4) come out of your shell when you are calm and ready for problem solving.

Social Skills

Social-skills training fits the needs of varied clients at different levels of functioning. Chronic mental patients need social-skills training both for practical tasks (e.g., job interviews) and to increase their positive interactions. Autistic children are usually provided with intensive one-on-one therapy to shape their behavior. People who describe their problem as "shyness" or "loneliness" often benefit from approaches that teach skills of starting friendships. Social-skills training for adults combines anxiety reduction **(BL2)** with practice in skills of appropriate nonverbal behavior, initiating a conversation, offering appropriate self-disclosure, following up on "free information" that the other person gives, making small talk, and asking for a date. Social-skills groups for children are effective for conduct disorders (Alvord & Grados, 2005). Classroom programs like "Teaching Students to Get Along" (Canter & Petersen, 1995) can prevent mental health problems of children at risk.

(continued)

Table 5.6   *(Continued)*

Marital Relationship

Many of the prior topics are relevant for couples in committed relationships. Gottman (2002) teaches couples to avoid the "Four Horsemen of the Apocalypse": criticism, defensiveness, contempt, and stonewalling. Christensen and Jacobson (2000) teach couples to negotiate for change as well as to recognize what can't be changed, so they will practice "acceptance." Hendrix (1988) teaches skills of both expressing vulnerability and being sensitive to the partner's vulnerability to create safety and trust. Schnarch (1998) teaches couples to practice "hugging until relaxed" as the first step toward creating a fulfilling sexual relationship. There are community resources for couples who want to improve their relationships. For instance, the program called Practical Application of Intimate Relationship Skills (PAIRS; http://www.pairs.com) includes skills in confiding, building self-esteem, and "complaining without blaming."

Parenting

Competence in parenting includes the ability to be empathically attuned, to understand developmental stages, and to be a good role model of communication, emotional maturity, and intimacy. Parent training programs generally combine several skills components, such as communication, problem solving, anger management, stress management and self-control, and skills of behavior management (**BL1**). Knapp and Jongsma (2004) provide a treatment planner for parenting skills. When parents improve their skills at coping with their own stress, they interact more positively with their aggressive children, who then behave better (Kazdin & Whitley, 2003). If a client physically abuses a child, parenting skills and anger management skills should be mandated. A strict, consistent, directive parenting style, combined with warmth, increases academic achievement of inner-city children (McLoyd, 1998). Oliver and Ryan (2004) wrote *Lesson One: The ABCs of Life: The Skills We All Need But Were Never Taught* to help parents build the following skills in their children: "self-control time" (breathing to relax), self-confidence, responsibility and consequences, problem solving, and cooperation. Barkley (1997) provides a program for parents of defiant children.

Time/Life Management

Management skills apply not only in business but also in setting and achieving personal and family goals. Lakein (1996) provides tools of time management to achieve both short- and long-term goals. Covey (1994) also teaches life management skills, including how to discriminate between things in life that are important and those that are urgent. Another life management skill is "de-cluttering"—competence in creating a neat, orderly, and organized life space.

---

learning process. Prior to starting a skills-training program, the therapist explains the following stages of learning:

1. *Unconscious incompetence:* You were not aware that you didn't have the skill and that having more competence would be helpful.

2. *Conscious incompetence:* Now you realize that you lack skills that you need, but you don't yet know how to get them. This is an uncomfortable stage; nobody likes feeling incompetent.

3. *Conscious competence:* When you first learn how to do something new, it takes conscious effort and concentration, just like when you first learned

to drive a car. It might feel awkward and unnatural, like you're pretending to be someone else.

4. *Unconscious competence:* At this stage, you have had so much practice that the new skills are "second nature."

In developing interventions for skill deficits, you are able to be creative and make the experience fun. You need flexibility to take different roles—teacher, coach, model, or cheerleader.

Behavior Therapy Principles

The basic behavioral principles for building skills are summarized in three categories:

1. *Graduated tasks and homework:* The skill is broken down into components, and a step-by-step plan is developed. As with desensitization, discussed under **BL2,** there is a need to develop a hierarchy of difficulty, as we would expect when learning a sport or a musical instrument. An important principle in planning is that *success must be ensured at each step.* If the gap between consecutive steps is too great, the therapist must devise an intermediate step. With this approach, there is no failure for the client. If the client fails to do a homework assignment, the therapist will set a smaller goal for next time. Some of the tasks will be in the therapy session; for social skills training, group modalities are the treatment of choice so that clients can practice with peers. Other tasks will be assigned for in vivo practice between sessions.

2. *Modeling:* Bandura (1977, 1989) supplemented conditioning principles of learning by describing how people learn from *models.* The learner needs to observe and mimic a person who already has the skill. The model can be someone on videotape, the therapist giving a demonstration, a peer participant in a group who already has the desired level of competence, an acquaintance of the client, or characters in books and movies. The client can even be asked to create, in imagery, a model of competent performance. One important principle to remember is that *people learn better when the model is not "perfect,"* but rather is close to their current skill level. If the model is too far above them in competence, they will not be able to imitate successfully. As the client improves, more proficient models will be appropriate.

3. *Shaping:* Shaping consists of taking a very small tendency in the right direction and rewarding it. You start with the client's current level of functioning, finding something to praise about the performance. Then step-by-step, a higher standard is required to earn praise. The term *successive approximations* is used for this gradual progression toward the ultimate competence goal. When different components of a complex skill

have been learned separately, rewards are given for combining them together, a process called *chaining.* A planned shaping program follows established rules such as how to raise the criteria for reinforcement, training one aspect of a behavior at a time, and ending on a positive note.

Behavioral Rehearsal

Before implementing the actual behavioral rehearsal technique, take the following steps:

1. *Use of SUDS:* If the client has already learned the use of this scale, explain that you will be asking for SUDS numbers at various points in the rehearsal. SUDS level should be in the 4 to 6 range for the most effective performance (relaxation training methods are explained in **B3**). If the SUDS level is high, the client needs to repeat rehearsals without moving up to a more difficult level.

2. *Cognitive tools:* In preparation for rehearsal, help the client build a sense of *rights,* challenge *catastrophic fantasies* of a possible outcome (**C2**) and substitute *adaptive self-talk* for maladaptive self-talk (**C4**). During the rehearsals, it may be necessary to take a time-out from the rehearsal to discuss cognitive factors that interfere with good performance.

3. *Cultural awareness:* Be sensitive to cultural differences, showing awareness of what is appropriate in the specific situation for which the client is preparing (**SCE2**).

4. *Evaluate the client's developmental level:* Be sure that the client has the psychological maturity (**P3**) to differentiate role-playing from reality, and be ready to stop the activity immediately if the client seems to take the role-play for a real interaction. This is especially necessary if the therapist is going to play the part of someone who is hostile and critical.

5. *Establish a hierarchy of situations:* In preparing the client to face a particular encounter, start with easier situations and work up to the target situation.

Table 5.7 presents instructions for the technique that are adapted from *Clinical Behavior Therapy* (Goldfried & Davison, 1994) and *Responsible Assertive Behavior* (Lange & Jakubowski, 1978).

Community Resources

Once goals of skill development and competence are established, you will probably be able to recommend resources in the community for learning opportunities. For instance, parents who want to increase their competence can take parenting classes at schools and religious organizations, find web sites that provide information and support, and join support groups where advice and encour-

Table 5.7   Behavioral Rehearsal

Preparation

Clarify outcome: The client's behavior, not the other person's response, defines success.

Explain the technique: Keep the explanation brief and encourage the client to try it first and discuss it later.

Warm-Up

Set up a scenario: Ask for a description of the physical environment and be prepared to move furniture and use props.

Establish client's baseline: Start with a very brief role-play.

Role reversal: Have the client play the other person to teach you how to play that role realistically.

First Rehearsal

Positive feedback: After the rehearsal, ask the client for positive feedback: *What did you like about what you did?* Tell the client what you liked. If the format is a group, elicit positive feedback from members.

Small goal for improvement: Have the client say what she wants to do better and offer coaching suggestions.

Continue Rehearsals

Reverse roles: As a model, you show the client how to make an improvement that is a small step up from current performance.

Gradually increase difficulty: Playing the other person, you start with an easy-to-handle response and then make the response increasingly challenging for the client.

A variation: You can role-play the worst-case scenario—the "feared catastrophe." This can add humor and help the client feel that the realistic response will be manageable.

End of Activity

End on a positive note: You and the client (and the group) acknowledge the improvement in the performance.

Get commitment for action: Have the client make a commitment to do something in the real world between sessions. Remind her that "success" is defined as her own good performance, not as success in getting the other person to change.

agement is exchanged. An organization like Toastmasters helps build public speaking skills, university extension schools have courses in assertiveness and communication skills, and employers often offer training in time-management and supervisory skills.

INTEGRATION OF HYPOTHESES

The **BL3** hypothesis is easily integrated with most other hypotheses. The four hypotheses that follow would rarely be sufficient without focusing directly on building the client's competence.

CS2 Situational Stressors

Clients who are dealing with stress and trauma need coping skills to manage their own emotions and lower their stress reactions, engage in problem solving, and take needed actions.

CS3 Developmental Transition

As people move to a new developmental stage, they need new skills: Adolescents need dating skills, newlyweds need conflict resolution skills, and retired people often need skills for managing a life without the structure of work. Parents need new skills as their children progress through developmental phases.

P3 Immature Sense of Self and Conception of Others

Tables 8.8 and 8.9 in Chapter 8 list competencies for healthy functioning of the self and mature object relations, respectively. Although the titles of those tables are derived from psychoanalytic theory, the competences are described in behavioral terms and can be framed as skills, such as those described by Marsha Linehan (1993a, 1993b) in treatment for people diagnosed with Borderline Personality Disorder (see Table 11.5). The activity of taking alternate POVs (Table 8.12) is not only an assessment tool but also a method of teaching skills of taking different perspectives, which is a prerequisite for empathy.

SCE4 Social Role Performance

When people assume new social roles, they may not yet have the necessary skills. For instance, when someone receives a promotion at work to a supervisory or managerial position, they may need to develop skills in communication, leadership, and project management.

SUGGESTED READINGS

Barlow, D. H. (Ed.). (2001). *Clinical handbook of psychological disorders: A step-by-step treatment manual* (3rd ed.). New York: Guilford Press.

Cooper, J. O., Heron, T. E., & Heward, W. L. (1987). *Applied behavioral analysis*. Columbus, OH: Merrill.

Cormier, S., & Nurius, P. (2003). *Interviewing and change strategies for helpers: Fundamental skills and cognitive-behavioral interventions* (5th ed.). Monterey, CA: Brooks/Cole.

Craighead, L. W., Craighead, W. E., Kazdin, A. E., & Mahoney, M. J. (Eds.). (1993). *Cognitive and behavioral interventions: An empirical approach to mental health problems*. Boston, MA: Allyn & Bacon.

Emmelkamp, P. M. G. (2004). Behavior therapy with adults. In M. J. Lambert (Ed.), *Bergin and Garfield's handbook of psychotherapy and behavior change* (5th ed., pp. 393–446). Hoboken, NJ: Wiley.

Goldfried, M., & Davison, G. C. (1994). *Clinical behavior therapy* (Expanded ed.). New York: Wiley.

Haynes, S. N., & O'Brien, W. H. (1999). *Principles and practice of behavioral assessment.* New York: Plenum.

Hergenhahn, B. R., & Olson, M. H. (2004). *Introduction to the theories of learning* (7th ed.). Upper Saddle River, NJ: Prentice Hall.

Kanfer, F. H., & Goldstein, A. P. (Eds.). (1991). *Helping people change: A textbook of methods* (4th ed.). Boston, MA: Allyn & Bacon.

Martin, G., & Pear, J. (2000). *Behavior modification: What it is and how to do it* (7th ed). Upper Saddle River, NJ: Prentice Hall.

Pryor, K. (1999). *Don't shoot the dog! The new art of teaching and training* (Rev. ed.). New York: Bantam Books.

Stout, C. E., & Hayes, R. A. (2004). *The evidence-based practice: Methods, models, and tools for mental health professionals.* Hoboken, NJ: Wiley.

Self-Help Books

Baer, L. (1992). *Getting control: Overcoming your obsessions and compulsions* (Reprint ed.). New York: Penguin Putnam.

Hyman, B. M., & Pedrick, C. (2005). *The OCD workbook: Your guide to breaking free from obsessive-compulsive disorder.* Oakland, CA: New Harbinger.

Markway, B., Carmin, C. N., Pollard, C. A., & Flynn, T. (1992). *Dying of embarrassment: Help for social anxiety and phobia.* Oakland, CA: New Harbinger.

Markway, B., & Markway, G. (2003). *Painfully shy: How to overcome social anxiety and reclaim your life.* New York: St. Martin's Griffin.

Ross, J. (1995). *Triumph over fear: A book of help and hope for people with anxiety, panic attacks, and phobias* (Reissue ed.). New York: Bantam.

Watson, D. L., & Tharp, R. G. (2001). *Self-directed behavior: Self-modification for personal adjustment* (8th ed.). Belmont, CA: Wadsworth.

Recommended Behavior Therapy Journals

Advances in Behavior Research and Therapy
Behavior Modification
Behavior Research and Therapy
Behavior Therapy
Behavioral Assessment
Behavioral Psychotherapy
Child and Family Behavior Therapy
Journal of Applied Behavior Analysis
Journal of Behavior Analysis and Therapy (electronic journal)
Journal of Behavior Therapy and Experimental Psychiatry
Journal of the Experimental Analysis of Behavior

BL1 Antecedents and Consequences

Lewinsohn, P. M., Antonuccio, D. O., Steinmetz, J. L., & Teri, L. (1984). *The coping with depression course: A psychoeducational course for unipolar depression.* Eugene, OR: Castalia.

Stuart, R. B. (1972). *Slim chance in a fat world: Behavioral control of obesity.* Champaign, IL: Research Press.

Stuart, R. B. (1980). *Helping couples change: A social learning approach to marital therapy.* New York: Guilford Press.

BL2 Conditioned Emotional Response

Bernstein, D. A., Borkovec, T. D., & Hazlett-Stevens, H. (2000). *New directions in progressive relaxation training: A guidebook for helping professionals.* Westport, CT: Praeger.

Bourne, E. J. (1998). *Overcoming specific phobias.* Oakland, CA: New Harbinger.

BL3 Skill Deficits or Lack of Competence

Barkley, R. A. (1997). *Defiant children: A clinician's manual for assessment and parent training* (2nd ed.). New York: Guilford Press.

Knapp, S. E., & Jongsma, A. E. (2004). *The parenting skills treatment planner.* Hoboken, NJ: Wiley.

Liberman, R. P. (Ed.). (1992). *Handbook of psychiatric rehabilitation.* Boston: Allyn & Bacon.

Linehan, M. M. (1993a). *Cognitive-behavioral treatment of borderline personality disorder.* New York: Guilford Press.

Linehan, M. M. (1993b). *Skills training manual for treating borderline personality disorder.* New York: Guilford Press.

McKay, M., Davis, M., & Fanning, P. (1995). *Messages: The communication skills book* (2nd ed.). Oakland, CA: New Harbinger.

Assertion Training

Alberti, R., & Emmons, M. (1995). *Your perfect right.* San Luis Obispo, CA: Impact.

Lange, A. J., & Jakubowski, P. (1978). *Responsible assertive behavior: Cognitive/behavioral procedures for trainers.* Champaign, IL: Research Press.

Smith, M. J. (1975). *When I say no, I feel guilty.* Toronto, Ontario, Canada: Bantam.

Chapter 6

COGNITIVE MODELS

Cognitive hypotheses should be applied to every single problem that you en-counter because all problems and solutions are influenced by the unique cognitive map and thinking style of the individual. A large section in Chapter 2, *Explo-ration of the Cognitive Domain,* provides the foundation for this chapter. Table 6.1 lists the four hypotheses in this category.

In most cases, after ruling out **C1 (Utopian Expectations),** the remaining cognitive hypotheses are integrated, as shown in the following:

Catherine, a 62-year-old successful attorney, is very frustrated with her failure to lose weight and keep it off. Her therapist asked what her weight goal was to check out whether she had utopian expectations (**C1**) of regaining the figure she had when she young. However, Catherine's goal was realistic and losing 20 pounds would put her in the desired weight range for her age and height. She described how she brings low calorie frozen meals to work for lunch, but then tells herself "I'm working hard. I deserve to eat what I like" (**C4**). When her ther-apist asked her to talk about her childhood eating patterns, she recalled that her mother made her stay at the table, alone, with a plate of cold vegeta-bles, and not leave until her plate was clean. She discovered, suddenly, a core

Table 6.1 Cognitive Models

C1 Utopian Expectations	The client is suffering from the ordinary "miseries of everyday life" and has unrealistic **Utopian Expectations** of what life should be like.
C2 Faulty Cognitive Map	Limiting and outdated elements in the **Faulty Cogni-tive Map** (e.g., maladaptive schemas, assumptions, rules, beliefs, and narratives) are causing the problem or preventing solutions.
C3 Faulty Information Processing	The client demonstrates **Faulty Information Process-ing** (e.g., overgeneralization, all-or-nothing thinking, and mind-reading) or is limited by an inflexible cogni-tive style.
C4 Dysfunctional Self-Talk	The problem is triggered and/or maintained by **Dysfunc-tional Self-Talk** and internal dialogue.

Table 6.2   Cognitive Concepts from Diverse Theorists

Sigmund Freud	Making the unconscious conscious; ego functions; primary versus secondary process thinking
Harry Stack Sullivan	Parataxic thinking (primitive thinking style of young children)
Alfred Adler	Dogmatized guiding fictions; basic mistakes
Karen Horney	"Tyranny of the should"
Viktor Frankl	Search for meaning
Jean Piaget	Schemas; stages of cognitive development; egocentrism
George Kelly	Personal constructs
Albert Bandura	Self-efficacy
Carl Rogers	Conditions of worth
David Shapiro	Cognitive (neurotic) style
Jerome Frank	Assumptive world
Albert Ellis	Irrational thoughts, catastrophizing
Aaron Beck	Cognitive triad of depression (negative thoughts about self, future, and ongoing experience)
Michael White	Narratives and stories

element in her faulty cognitive map (**C2**): "I get it. I must have decided, 'When I grow up, no one is ever going to tell me what to eat'." The therapist pointed out that she was engaging in faulty information processing (**C3**): All-or-nothing thinking was demonstrated by her treating all rules about eating as if they were bad, instead of distinguishing the ones that she freely chose and were in her own best interest.

Very often, students and professionals, alike, assume that cognitive-behavioral therapy (CBT) is the automatic choice of treatment when faulty cognitions are identified. By understanding the role of cognitive factors in a variety of theories, we become more open to seeing that cognitive hypotheses integrate the thoughts of diverse thinkers and that techniques can come from many different sources. Table 6.2 gives examples of cognitive terminology.

KEY IDEAS FOR C1 UTOPIAN EXPECTATIONS

The term "utopian syndrome" comes from the very important book *Change* (Watzlawick, Weakland, & Fisch, 1974) and is very similar to one of Adler's "basic mistake"—a misperception of life and life's demands. Expectations for an easy, effortless, pain-free life actually cause more pain than just accepting the reality of the human condition. When people learn that effort, disappointment, and painful experiences are a natural part of life, they can cope better with whatever is bothering them.

In avoiding the utopian, it is important not to discourage people from pursuing goals that are difficult, but not impossible, by misusing the term *utopian* to deflate the ambitions of people who are idealistic and set high standards.

C1 UTOPIAN EXPECTATIONS

Definition

The client is suffering from the ordinary "miseries of everyday life" and has unrealistic **Utopian Expectations** of what life should be like.

Explanation

The client wants to eliminate the disappointments, struggles, and unpleasant emotions that are inevitable parts of living. In confusing normal life difficulties with problems that need therapeutic intervention, the client is seeking unattainable goals. Therapists need to avoid making contracts to pursue the goal of a perfect, problem-free life.

Examples

Michelle, a 35-year-old married dental hygienist and mother of three children under 12 years old, has the following complaints: She is not "living up to her potential in everything she does"; she loses her temper and yells at her children occasionally; and her sex drive has diminished from the early years of her marriage.	Nadya, a 28-year-old married doctoral student, sought therapy from a well-known existential therapist. She was dissatisfied with many aspects of her life: working too hard, no quality time with her husband, and anxiety about the job market. The therapist told her that her suffering was the inevitable consequence of the choice to get a doctorate.	Steve, a hardworking, responsible professional, is married and has one child. When he goes on vacation to a tropical island, he is completely relaxed, free of worry, and enjoys every minute of the day. "My life should always feel this way," he thinks. When he gets home, he thinks, "Why can't I always feel as relaxed as I did on vacation?"

WHEN IS THIS HYPOTHESIS A GOOD MATCH?

In the initial sessions, the Utopian Expectations hypothesis is intended to be a screening tool to help recognize when a person is mistakenly seeking therapy for difficulties that she is already coping with quite well. This hypothesis must be considered during the processes of problem definition (Chapter 11) and outcome goal setting (Chapter 12) to define solvable problems and set realistic goals. Because there is no disorder, *DSM* diagnoses should not be used at the same time as this hypothesis: You have a normal, healthy individual who just needs a reminder of life's realities. However, if the client continues to hold on to faulty illusions rather than readjust expectations, there is a problem that needs to be addressed and **C2 (Faulty Cognitive Map)** becomes the appropriate choice of hypothesis. Here are examples of how problem titles then might be worded:

- *Excessive bitterness and resentment over normal life difficulties*
- *Difficulty accepting normal limits and frustrations of life*

TREATMENT PLANNING

Therapists need to remember that sometimes "no therapy" is the treatment of choice. It may seem disrespectful, rude, and unprofessional to ever take the position "you don't need to be here," but in fact it can be a very positive message to a person who is feeling demoralized.

The following list provides guidelines for the therapeutic conversation:

- Focus on the discrepancy between *what is* and how the person wants life to be. You want the client to understand that disappointments, unpleasant emotions, misunderstandings, and conflict in relationships are a normal part of living.
- Be very empathic and supportive. Be careful not to shame clients by implying that they were stupid to have such utopian expectations.
- Discuss probabilities: *If you choose to marry a person of a different culture from your parents, what is the probability that they will instantly rejoice and embrace your partner as one of the family? What are the odds that a person of 55 will have the same weight, the same body, the same energy, the same athletic performance, as he did when he was 25?*
- Use humor when appropriate. People often challenge each other's utopian hopes with questions such as *What have you been smoking?* or comments like *When you die and go to Heaven.* You can judge when a joking comment or a humorous anecdote would be well received.

INTEGRATION OF HYPOTHESES

The concept of utopianism is especially useful when applying the following three hypotheses.

ES2 Avoiding Freedom and Responsibility

Mistaken assumptions about what is possible can prevent a person from taking responsibility to pursue realistic goals. For instance, a mediocre athlete who refuses to get a job but instead persists in training for the Olympics is operating with utopian expectations.

P3 Immature Sense of Self and Conception of Others

Standards of maturity can often be very utopian. For instance, Bowen's (1994) theory of "differentiation of self" may set expectations for independence that are unrealistic.

SCE2 Cultural Context

Expectations need to be examined in a cultural context. What is unrealistic in one culture may be normal in another (e.g., the expectations of parents to have control over the choice of a child's spouse and to be taken care of by children in old age).

C2 FAULTY COGNITIVE MAP

Definition

Limiting and outdated elements in the **Faulty Cognitive Map** (e.g., maladaptive schemas, assumptions, rules, beliefs, and narratives) are causing the problem or preventing solutions.

Explanation

Therapists need to help clients modify aspects of their thinking, not because of arbitrary standards of right and wrong, but because the faulty map limits choices, creates pain, and interferes with getting their needs met, achieving their goals, and enjoying their lives. There are maladaptive schemas, assumptions, rules, beliefs, self-fulfilling prophecies, and personal narratives that need to be identified, evaluated, challenged, and revised.

Examples

Tracy, a 30-year-old unmarried woman, has been attending self-help groups for "codependents" but feels that she needs individual therapy. With her therapist, she identifies underlying assumptions: "My needs are not important"; "the more I sacrifice, the more I will be worthy of love"; and "if I assert my needs or say no to others' demands, they will reject and abandon me."

Ralph, a 42-year-old attorney, admits that his "workaholism" is negatively affecting his health and his relationship with his family. He says he wants to change, but when he doesn't go into the office on weekends, he feels worthless and depressed. When he went with his wife and kids to Disneyland, he got angry over the waste of time.

Julia, a beautiful, intelligent, 40-year-old divorced woman feels "trapped" in a relationship with a "cold, withholding, and often cruel" man. Her therapist helps her to understand these elements of her cognitive map: "I can't survive without a relationship"; "any relationship is better than none"; and "deep down he needs me, and I'm responsible for his happiness."

KEY IDEAS FOR C2 FAULTY COGNITIVE MAP

Through the use of language, each person creates a personal reality. Many different terms are used for this concept: *model of the world, schemas, assumptive world, perceptual system, narrative, construct system, and cognitive map.* These cognitive models provide meaning and purpose, a rule book on how to behave in the world, and a framework that provides predictability and stability in our daily lives.

Cognitive Maps

The term *cognitive map* allows us to use a metaphor that is easily explained to clients. Bandler and Grinder (1990), integrating ideas from many theories and philosophies in *The Structure of Magic,* taught the slogan: "The map is not the territory." The "real territory," discovered through sensory experiences, refers to objects with a separate existence from our minds—roads, rivers, mountains, and bridges. A map is a representation of the territory. Laborde (1987) wrote:

> Once we have perceived the real world with our senses and coded experiences in our brains on a map or series of maps, then this coding or representation

determines our behaviors. Often people's frustration or unhappiness is the result of limitations in their coding, in their representation of the real world. Sometimes, the very thing to bring about their happiness is available once that thing (or person) is placed on their maps of reality.

Faulty cognitive maps create impossible goals and imaginary obstacles. A person might direct a lifetime of energy toward the goal of "finally winning my father's approval." The father may be incapable of expressing approval or may even be dead, yet the behavior directed toward an impossible goal persists. Imaginary obstacles may be beliefs like "I'm not smart enough to go to college"; "I need the approval of others to feel good"; and "men shouldn't show feelings."

Behavior Makes Perfect Sense

Cameron-Bandler (1985) wrote, "Human behavior, no matter how bizarre or resistant it may seem, makes sense when it is seen in the context of the choices generated by a person's map or model." Without the concept of a cognitive map, we would be unable to explain how different people go through the same experiences and end up with radically different feelings and behaviors. Whenever our clients' positions seems irrational or inexplicable, we have to stop ourselves from making judgments or trying to persuade them to a more rational point of view. We must first get inside their model of the world, and see how their choices make perfect sense. Cameron-Bandler explains:

> It is not that our clients are making the wrong choices, it is just that they do not have enough choices available when needed. Each of us makes the very best choice available to us from our model of the world. (pp. 223–224)

In working with a suicidal client, it is especially important to understand how the wish to take her own life can make perfect sense. People commit suicide over the breakup of a relationship, failing grades in college, and rejection letters from medical school not because of the events, but because of how they interpret them in terms of their self-worth and possibilities for future happiness. Here is a cognitive formula for suicide: A person experiences a thwarted need (which we all do in our lives), judges the need to be the most important, believes that there was only one way to satisfy it, concludes that it will never be satisfied, decides that life is not worth living without it, and evaluates the pain as unbearable. With this tunnel vision, suicide is the only logical choice.

Maps Must Be Updated

A map that inaccurately represents the territory will mislead and confuse rather than help. It is probably worse than no map at all, because the existence of the map carries an aura of authority and inhibits the explorer's willingness to trust his senses and rely on his own exploratory skills.

Maps become outdated because change is inevitable: New roads are built, empty fields are converted to housing developments, and a freeway can be severed by an earthquake. A map developed in childhood cannot be completely valid in adulthood, not only because of change in the world and in oneself, but because it was constructed with the cognitive capacity of a child.

- **Bridges we used to rely on no longer get us where we want:** *Throwing a tantrum no longer gets other people to take care of me.*
- **People still drive the same old bumpy roads, even though new super highways have been constructed:** *We select friends and partners who are difficult in the same way as our parents and siblings, when we can find others who are easygoing, comfortable, and fun to be around.*

The midlife crisis refers to the need for a major overhaul of the map. Failure to attain a deeply desired goal would lead to a permanent state of misery if people were not able to create a map toward a different goal where there is possibility of success. Successes and failures bring the need for new maps. Attainment of a desired goal, such as getting an advanced degree, marrying, or retiring, terminates the usefulness of the map that guided us toward that end.

Normal Resistance to Change

Before you rush in to change clients' maladaptive maps you need to realize that these models serve important needs. Stable models of reality provide guidelines on how to behave, how to predict consequences, how to maximize satisfaction, and how to reduce pain and anxiety. Models make life easier and allow people to function efficiently, because each new situation can be categorized as something familiar rather than treated as completely novel. Without understanding how a faulty cognitive map fills emotional needs, you will have difficulty dealing with the resistance people have to changing these maps.

To varying degrees, people fear the unknown and want to hold on to the familiar. Given the need for stability, some resistance to change is expected and adaptive. When people recognize the shortcomings of their map, they experience anxiety, tension, uncertainty, and confusion. These emotions interfere with openness to change. Furthermore, the recognition that much of their own suffering came from their own failure to update their maps leads people to feel foolish and become angry with themselves: "Why didn't I realize this sooner? What a childish, stubborn, and irrational fool I have been." The awareness of lost time and opportunities can awaken feelings of loss, sadness, grief, and self-blame.

Therapists need to understand the emotional issues in relinquishing old maps and creating new ones. Often, when the therapist explores the painful childhood context in which a child developed the cognitive map, it becomes easy to admire the child's resourcefulness, resilience, and intelligence. A client will be less resistant to challenges to faulty thinking when she has first experienced your appreciation

Table 6.3   Adler's Basic Mistakes

Basic Mistake	Examples
Overgeneralizations	People are hostile.
	Life is dangerous.
False or Impossible Goals of Security	One false step and you're dead.
	I have to please everybody.
Misperceptions of Life and Life's Demands	Life never gives me any breaks.
	Life is so hard.
Minimization of One's Worth (Inferiority Complex)	I'm undeserving.
	I am not capable of solving problems.
Exaggeration of One's Worth (Superiority Complex)	I am superior to others.
	My needs are more important than others' needs.
Faulty Values	Be first even if you have to climb over others.
	I'm better off if I can get other people to take care of my responsibilities.

Adapted from *Current Psychotherapies*, 6th ed., R. J. Corsini and D. Wedding (Eds.), 2000, Stamford, CT: Wadsworth.

for her creative, if outdated, solution to getting her needs met, reducing pain, and protecting her vulnerable self in difficult circumstances.

Alfred Adler's Cognitive Approach

Adler, an early follower of Freud, created his own theory of individual psychology, which emphasized the cognitive domain, and was an important influence on both Viktor Frankl and Albert Ellis. By studying Adler (e.g., Adler, Ansbacher, & Ansbacher, 1989), we remind ourselves that cognitive therapy did not begin as an offshoot of behavior therapy. According to Adler, the roots of neurotic functioning lie in the *dogmatized guiding fictions* and the *basic mistakes* of childhood. Adler used the term *lifestyle* for "the convictions individuals develop early in life to help them organize experience, to understand it, to predict it, and to control it" (cited in Mozak, 2000, p. 55). Table 6.3 presents Mozak's examples of Adler's *basic mistakes* (p. 73).

Albert Ellis's Rational Emotive Therapy

Albert Ellis, creator of Rational Emotive Therapy (now called Rational Emotive Behavioral Therapy [REBT]) believed that core irrational ideas are at the root of emotional disturbance. Table 6.4 presents a version of one of these lists from Ellis and Grieger (1977).

More than just teaching a list of faulty beliefs, Ellis provided an ABC model for teaching clients the role of cognitions in determining their emotional reactions. We usually operate on the assumption that events or people make us feel a certain way: "I got depressed because he didn't call." "She makes me mad when

Table 6.4   Albert Ellis's Core Irrational Ideas

It is a dire necessity for an adult to be loved by everyone for everything you do.

Certain acts are awful or wicked, and people who perform such acts should be severely punished.

It is horrible when things are not the way you would like them to be.

Human misery is externally caused and is forced on you by outside people and events.

If something is or may be dangerous or fearsome, you should be terribly upset about it.

It is easier to avoid than to face life's difficulties and self-responsibilities.

You need something other or stronger or greater than yourself on which to rely.

You should be thoroughly competent, intelligent, and achieving in all possible respects.

Because something once strongly affected your life, it should indefinitely affect it.

You must have certain and perfect control over things.

Human happiness can be achieved by inertia and inaction.

You have virtually no control over your emotions and you cannot help feeling certain things.

Source: "Table of Irrational Beliefs," in *Handbook of Rational-Emotive Therapy,* A. Ellis and R. Grieger (Eds.), 1977, New York: Springer. Reprinted with permission.

she asks where I'm going." "He told me I had to work on the weekend, so I snapped." This cause-effect assumption can be drawn with the letters A and C:

[A] Event → Causes → [C] Feelings

Then the therapist can explain why this isn't so: *The same event can cause different feelings. There is something that intervenes between A and B, and that's what you think:*

[A] Event → [B] Thinking → [C] Feelings

Once this model is understood, clients become collaborators in searching for the thoughts that cause their feelings. Their cognitive map undergoes a radical change from "I am controlled by my emotional responses" to "I have control over my thinking, and therefore I can alter the way I feel."

Aaron Beck's Cognitive Bases for Emotions

The ABC model is particularly powerful when the presenting problem is an extreme emotional state, such as depression, excessive anxiety or anger, or paranoid feelings. Aaron Beck and his associates (e.g., Beck, 2000; Beck, Emery, & Greenberg, 1985; Beck, Rush, Shaw, & Emery, 1979) used a similar framework, but instead of focusing on irrational thoughts, they helped people discover the deeper assumptions that laid the foundation for emotional reactions. For instance, the belief that *good things happen to good people, and bad things happen to bad people* is a core assumption shared by members of our culture, which states a principle that is frequently violated by experience, leading to extreme

Table 6.5   Cognitive Bases for Extreme Emotional States

Anxiety	**Core assumption:** I must be good or bad things will happen.
	Situation: Striving towards a future goal.
	Sample beliefs: This is the most important goal in my life, but I'm incompetent and I will probably fail. If I don't succeed, terrible things will happen: I will be shamed, ridiculed, and rejected.
Depression	**Core assumption:** If something bad happens, it must mean that I wasn't good.
	Situation: Something bad happened.
	Sample beliefs: Something necessary for my happiness has been lost irretrievably, so I will never be happy as long as I live. There is no forgiveness or redemption for what I have done: I am worthless and deserve to suffer.
Anger	**Core assumption:** If something bad happens, and I've been good, then life isn't fair.
	Situation: Something bad happened.
	Sample beliefs: God is not good and just, and I will never forgive him. Somebody else must be to blame; I am innocent, and that person deserves punishment.
Paranoia	**Core assumption:** The malicious motives of others are responsible for my failures.
	Situation: Something bad happened.
	Sample beliefs: I am special and important enough so that others want to keep me down. I have a special talent to detect hidden meanings behind what others are doing and saying.

reactions of anger or depression. Table 6.5 shows some associations between types of emotional experiences and the cognitive elements that support them.

Jeffrey Young's Early Maladaptive Schemas

Jeffrey Young (1999), a cognitive-behavioral therapist, developed a list of schemas for personality disorders, presented in Table 6.6. Schemas are the link between early childhood experiences and the cognitive map of the adult and can be the focus of treatment.

If the wording of the schema is softened, these schemas are typical of people who do not suffer from personality disorders but instead have problems with work, relationships, self-esteem, and emotional regulation.

Table 6.6   Jeffrey Young's Early Maladaptive Schemas

Disconnection and Rejection

The expectation that our needs for security, safety, stability, nurturance, empathy, sharing of feelings, acceptance, and respect will not be met in a predictable manner.

1. **Abandonment/Instability:** Perceived instability or unreliability of those available for support and connection.
2. **Mistrust/Abuse:** Expectation that others will hurt, abuse, humiliate, cheat, lie, manipulate, or take advantage.
3. **Emotional Deprivation:** Expectation that others will not adequately meet our desire for a normal degree of emotional support.
   a. **Deprivation of nurturance:** Absence of attention, affection, warmth, companionship.
   b. **Deprivation of empathy:** Absence of understanding, listening, self-disclosure, or mutual sharing of feelings from others.
   c. **Deprivation of protection:** Absence of strength, direction, or guidance from others.
4. **Defectiveness/Shame:** Belief that we are defective, bad, unwanted, inferior, or invalid in important respects; or that we would be unlovable to significant others if exposed; may involve hypersensitivity to criticism, rejection, and blame. Perceived flaws may be private or public.
5. **Social Isolation/Alienation:** Belief that we are isolated from rest of the world, different from other people, and/or not part of any group of community.

Impaired Autonomy and Performance

Expectations about the environment and ourselves that interfere with our ability to separate, survive, function independently, or perform successfully.

6. **Dependence/Incompetence:** Belief that we are unable to handle our everyday responsibilities in a competent manner without considerable help from others.
7. **Vulnerability to Harm or Illness:** Exaggerated fear that imminent catastrophe (medical, emotional, or external) will strike at any time and that we will be unable to prevent it.
8. **Enmeshment/Undeveloped Self:** Excessive emotional involvement and closeness with significant other at the expense of individuation or normal social development. Often involves the belief that at least one of the enmeshed individuals cannot survive or be happy without the constant support of the other. Often experienced as a feeling of emptiness and floundering, having no direction, or being smothered by or fused with the other.
9. **Failure:** Belief that we have failed, will inevitably fail, or are fundamentally inadequate relative to our peers in areas of achievement. Often involves the belief that we are stupid, inept, or untalented.

Impaired Limits

A deficiency in internal limits, responsibilities to others, or long-term goal orientation, which leads to difficulty respecting the rights of others, cooperating with others, making commitments, or setting and meeting realistic personal goals.

10. **Entitlement/Grandiosity:** Belief that we are superior to other people, entitled to special rights and privileges, or not bound by the rules of reciprocity that guide normal social interaction. Often involves insistence that we should be able to do or have whatever we want. Often involves asserting our power or controlling the behavior of others in line with our own desires, without empathy or concern for others' needs or feelings.
11. **Insufficient Self-Control/Self-Discipline:** The lack of beliefs necessary for the self-control and frustration tolerance needed to achieve personal goals or to restrain excessive expression of our emotions and impulses. Includes exaggerated emphasis on discomfort and beliefs that promote avoidance of pain, conflict, confrontation, responsibility, or overexertion.

(continued)

Table 6.6 *(Continued)*

Other-Directedness

An excessive focus on the desires, feelings, and responses of others (at the expense of our own needs) designed to gain love and approval, maintain our sense of connection, or avoid retaliation—usually involves suppression and lack of awareness regarding our own anger and natural inclinations.

12. **Subjugation:** Excessive surrendering of control to others to avoid anger, retaliation, or abandonment. Belief that we are coerced or required to suppress our preferences, decisions and desires (subjugation of needs) and/or our emotional expression, especially anger (subjugation of emotions).

13. **Self-Sacrifice:** Excessive focus on voluntarily meeting the needs of others in daily situations at the expense of our own gratification. The most common reasons are to prevent causing pain to others, avoid guilt from feeling selfish, or maintain the connection with others perceived as needy. Often results from acute sensitivity to the pain of others. Can lead to resentment of the recipients of our care.

14. **Approval-Seeking/Recognition-Seeking:** Excessive emphasis on gaining approval, recognition, or attention from other people, or "fitting in" at the expense of developing an internal source of self-esteem. Sometimes includes an overemphasis on status, appearance, social acceptance, money, or achievement.

Overvigilance and Inhibition

Excessive emphasis on suppressing our spontaneous feelings, impulses and choices or on meeting rigid, internalized rules, and expectations about performance and ethical behavior, often at the expense of happiness, self-expression, relaxation, close relationships, or health.

15. **Negativity/Pessimism:** Pervasive, lifelong focus on the negative aspects of life (e.g., pain, death, loss, disappointment, conflict, guilt, resentment, unsolved problems, potential mistakes, betrayal, or things that could go wrong) while minimizing or neglecting the positive or optimistic aspects. Because potential negative outcomes are exaggerated, there is chronic worry, complaining, or indecision.

16. **Emotional Inhibition:** Excessive inhibition of spontaneous action, feeling, or communication, usually to avoid disapproval by others, feelings of shame, or losing control of our impulses. Can include inhibition of anger, inhibition of positive impulses such as sexual excitement and play, difficulty expressing vulnerability, and excessive emphasis on rationality.

17. **Unrelenting Standards/Hypercriticalness:** Underlying belief that we must strive to meet high internalized standards of behavior and performance, usually to avoid criticism. Typically results in feelings of pressure, difficulty slowing down, and hypercriticalness toward others and ourselves. Often involves perfectionism, rigid rules, and "shoulds" in many areas of life, and preoccupation with time and efficiency to accomplish more.

18. **Punitiveness:** Belief that people should be harshly punished for making mistakes. Involves the tendency to be angry, intolerant, punitive, and impatient with those people (including ourselves) who do not meet our expectations or standards.

Source: Cognitive Therapy for Personality Disorders (pp. 12–25), 3rd ed., by J. Young, 1999, Sarasota, FL: Professional Resource Press. Reprinted with permission.

Narrative Therapy

Narrative Therapy is a relatively new school of therapy, but its core hypothesis of faulty cognitive maps is familiar. A *narrative* is a cognitive map extended through time. White and Epston (1990) explain:

> In striving to make sense of life, persons face the task of arranging their experiences of events in sequences across time in such a way as to arrive at a coherent

account of themselves and the world around them. . . . This account can be referred to as a story or self-narrative. The success of this storying of experience provides persons with a sense of continuity and meaning in their lives, and this is relied upon for the ordering of daily lives and for the interpretation of further experiences. (p. 10)

Unfortunately, the self-narratives do not only provide benefits; they also limit choices and create pain.

Success in helping people to change their narratives requires the ability to take a postmodern perspective. A comparison of three baseball umpires describing their job illustrates what postmodernism means:

First umpire: There's balls and there's strikes, and I call 'em the way they are.

Second umpire: There's balls and there's strikes, and I call 'em the way I see 'em.

Postmodernist umpire: There's balls and there's strikes, and they ain't nothin' until I call 'em.

The typical client is like the first umpire, believing that the stories she tells are accurate descriptions of reality. After listening and understanding the stories without trying to squeeze them into preexisting categories, the therapist helps the client to *deconstruct* them, which means to realize (a) they are not reality, (b) they have been influenced by stories available in the society and culture, and (c) there are alternate stories possible. Freedman and Combs (1996) explain that therapists help clients develop new narratives that offer "new self-images, new possibilities for relationships and new futures," noting:

in any life there are always more events that don't get "storied" than there are ones that do—even the longest and most complex autobiography leaves out more than it includes. This mean that when life narratives carry hurtful meanings or seem to offer only unpleasant choices, they can be changed by highlighting different, previously un-storied events or by taking new meanings from already-storied events, thereby constructing new narratives. (p. 32)

WHEN IS THIS HYPOTHESIS A GOOD MATCH?

It is hard to imagine any human situation that is not profoundly influenced by an individual's cognitive construction of reality. For example, according to McCullough (2005), the outcome of the Revolutionary War depended on the *interpretation* that the Battle of Trenton was a huge success and a major turning point for the Americans rather than on an objective measure of any military advantage accomplished by that small victory.

Therefore, you can apply this hypothesis with every single client. Although this hypothesis contains the word *faulty* in its title, the therapist must recognize the healthy, functional, and rational elements of the cognitive map, as well as the elements that lead to problems.

Table 6.7 Applying the C2 Faulty Cognitive Map Hypothesis

Examples of Problems

Anxiety, depression, stress, and anger problems: Cognitive-Behavioral Therapy has received substantial empirical validation as a treatment for phobias and other anxiety disorders, anger management problems, and depression. Table 6.5 gives examples of cognitive bases for extreme emotional reactions.

Personality disorders: Each personality disorder has a characteristic pattern of cognitive contents and processes (Beck, Freeman, & Davis, 2003). The early maladaptive schemas listed in Table 6.6 are associated with personality disorders. Reinecke and Freeman (2003) contrast the underlying schemas for two personality disorders:

>   **Dependent individual:** The world is a dangerous place; I am a flawed or incapable person; If I can maintain a close relationship with a supportive person, I can feel secure.

>   **Schizoid individual:** The world is a dangerous place; others are dangerous or malevolent; If I can avoid intimate relationships with others, I can feel secure.

Examples of Goals

To adhere to a weight loss program: I should be able to eat whatever I want, whenever I want it.

To learn to relax and reduce stress: Unless I'm busy and accomplishing something productive, I am worthless and unlovable.

To achieve a promotion at work: If I stand out and show my exceptional abilities, I will be rejected and isolated and feel lonely and embarrassed.

To be an effective parent: If I set limits and say no, my child won't love me.

To have a satisfying intimate relationship: There is a perfect partner out there somewhere who has no faults and who will always focus on my needs.

Table 6.7 gives examples of both problems and outcomes goals for which **C2** is especially fitting.

TREATMENT PLANNING

In *Persuasion and Healing,* Frank and Frank (1991) explain that the prescribed treatment (or therapeutic ritual) must match the belief system of the person who is seeking help: A pilgrimage to Lourdes is only beneficial to people who believe in the power of that location to produce miracles. A client who believes that "problems are resolved by following guidance from experts" needs a different therapeutic approach than one who believes "I need to find my own answers." When the treatment of choice is discrepant from the client's cognitive map, the therapist needs to address that issue and offer a rationale that the client will accept. This stage of persuasion is important when a somatizer is referred for psychotherapy. The client believes that the problem is medical and thinks that being "sent to a shrink" means that the doctor does not believe that the pain is real. The therapist needs to explain the beliefs of health professionals regarding the effects of stress on physiology, providing a link between psychological interventions and physical benefits. When the client comes from a different culture, therapists need to understand the beliefs about healing and the available indigenous healing rituals, and integrate them into treatment planning.

Cognitive-Behavior Therapy

Training in CBT will give tools for working with faulty cognitive maps and will build competence in cognitive formulations. The approach of CBT is to use an agenda, a didactic approach, and structured activities. However, an exclusive reliance on CBT will limit your treatment options. Reinecke and Freeman (2003) make the point that:

> Any intervention or technique that alters a patient's perceptions or beliefs might be viewed as cognitive. The number of techniques that are potentially available is virtually infinite. . . . The effective cognitive therapist is able to provide patients with experiences in a creative, flexible manner that will refute their maladaptive beliefs. (p. 245)

Create a Collaborative Relationship

In terminology from Transactional Analysis (TA), you want to "hook the Adult" in your client, or to use a Freudian term, you want to make an alliance with the client's "observing ego." In Aaron Beck's language, you are engaging in "collaborative empiricism," helping the client learn how to test beliefs against empirical reality and learn to function as a "personal scientist." Instead of taking the attitude that you have to change the client, assume that an adult of normal intelligence will want to make changes when he discovers that his own patterns of thinking are creating and maintaining problems. Monitor the process of the relationship and be able to switch to an empathic, responsive style when the alliance is threatened by ill-timed cognitive challenges.

In TA terms, it is essential to maintain an "Adult-Adult" alliance with the client, and to avoid slipping into the role of "Critical Parent" by criticizing or shaming the client for illogical or primitive thinking. Even when you are careful to avoid the pitfall of sounding like a Parent, clients may easily distort your intentions and react defensively. Catch yourself when you begin to lecture or preach to a client who appears bored, sullen, or uninterested. You can avoid Parent-Child dynamics by creating a contract or agenda with the client for each session, in which the client makes the choice about the desired target of change.

Use Metamodel Questions

Table 2.7 in Chapter 2 presented the nine types of metamodel violations and the specific questions for challenging them. These skills should become automatic: They serve not only as data-gathering tools but also as interventions for faulty cognitive maps. For instance, the belief "I have to try my hardest and never give up" is a *lost performative* and can be challenged by asking, *According to whom?*

This question leads to an understanding that (a) this is an arbitrary rule, not a statement of fact; (b) it is too rigid to be an adaptive approach to all situations; and (c) the client can create a new principle for how hard to work and when it's okay to quit.

Explanations and Teaching

Educate your client about the concepts of faulty cognitive maps and maladaptive schemas and teach the client how to evaluate beliefs by examining empirical evidence, effect on mood, rationality, or impact on achieving goals. For instance, you can explain Ellis's ABC model (described previously) and give examples of how thinking—attributing meaning to the event, or putting it into a category—affects feelings. Explain to the client that (a) it is her own thinking that is creating pain and frustration, and (b) she has control over how she thinks and therefore can choose to think differently. It is helpful to use an example of how the same event produces different emotional reactions.

Rejection letter from a graduate school

Three people can have very different reactions:

Person 1: It means a catastrophic proof of worthlessness, leading to depression.

Person 2: It is an unfortunate but impersonal event, understood as a reasonable outcome given the high number of applicants for few positions and the arbitrariness of admissions procedures. This person decides to apply again, this time to more schools.

Person 3: The rejection letter means that he is now free to pursue what he loves instead of pleasing his parents, so he feels relief and elation.

Persuasion and Direct Influence

Sometimes when clients uses absolutistic, inflexible thinking, therapists directly instruct them to substitute more flexible and realistic terms:

- Change *always* to *often.*
- Change *never* to *rarely.*
- Change *I need* to *I prefer.*
- Change *I must* to *I want to.*
- Change *I shouldn't* to *It would be preferable not to* or *I choose not to have the consequences of.*
- Change *I can't* to *I won't* or *I would find it difficult* or *I am afraid of.*

Therapists also teach clients about the cognitive concept of "rights" and about how beliefs about the rights of the self and others contribute to either unassertiveness or aggressiveness instead of an appropriate level of assertiveness. Lange and Jakubowski (1978) illustrate how socialization messages that are more commonly given to girls than boys can limit their sense of personal rights:

- I have no right to place my needs above those of other people.
- I have no right to do anything that would imply that I am better than other people.
- I have no right to feel angry or to express my anger.
- I have no right to make requests of other people.
- I have no right to do anything that might hurt someone else's feelings.

Here are some examples of rights that empower people to speak up and express their thoughts and feelings, ask for what they want, and say no to what they do not want:

- I have the right to assert my needs because they are as important as those of other people.
- I have a right to show my abilities, enjoy my accomplishments, and take pride in myself.
- I have a right to my angry feelings, and I have a right to express them appropriately at the time they occur so they won't build up and explode.
- If my rights are violated, I have the right to make demands for change.
- I have the right to express my thoughts and feelings, even if occasionally someone's feelings get hurt, as long as I am not deliberately trying to inflict hurt.

How to Challenge Schemas, Assumptions, and Beliefs

Very often, when clients actually see or hear their faulty beliefs, they spontaneously realize—sometimes as a dramatic epiphany—how irrational they sound. There are several approaches that will get the client to recognize and challenge faulty cognitive maps:

- **Discuss a list of faulty schemas:** Tables 6.3, 6.4, and 6.6 provide items that can be directly presented to the client, or the therapist can prepare an individualized list. The client can select the items that she identifies as her own way of thinking.
- **Interpretation:** The wording of a schema or belief is offered to the client after listening to what is said and observing the client's behavior: *I get the idea that you are expecting your boyfriend to meet the needs that your mother never met. You seem to have the expectation that I will provide you answers and that this problem can be solved without your having to expend any effort.* The wording and tone of voice show that the therapist is tentative, awaiting the client's agreement or disagreement.
- **Challenging questions:** The metamodel gives one approach to asking questions. The therapist can use variety in framing questions, to help the

client recognize faulty thinking. *Was there ever a time when you did confide in someone and it was a positive experience? That belief that you're not good enough—Where specifically does it come from?*

Conversations

Cognitive maps will be changed in the course of any type of therapeutic conversation. Sometimes the conversation is a philosophical discussion of the client's view of the world and an evaluation of its tenets in terms of truth, morality, expediency, and other values. Narrative therapists encourage clients to tell stories about their lives and use techniques that they call *externalizing* or *reauthoring* conversations. Therapists can tell stories of their own lives and struggles, talking about their own schemas and how they were changed through experiences and choices.

Reframing

This is a cognitive technique that helps the client shift the category in which an event or behavior is placed. Table 2.8 in Chapter 2 provides a foundation for the skills of this technique. The metaphor of frame is used because we know that the same picture can look very different in a different frame. When the client has created a frame that causes pain and limits choice, the therapist helps her shift to a new frame, which creates positive feelings and contributes toward achieving desired goals. Milton Erickson's therapy (Haley, 1993) gives many examples of this technique. Here is an example adapted from one of his cases:

> A woman in her 70s lives alone and spends a great deal of time keeping her house in perfect order. Whenever her children and grandchildren come to visit, they mess up her house, and she feels very angry, resentful, and helpless. The therapist asks her to use visual imagery and picture a time in the future when the house is perpetually spotless. After completing this visualization exercise, she reports feeling lonely and isolated. She realizes that the clean house is not that important and that what she values is the company of her family.

In reframing, the behavior or event is unchanged—it is the interpretation that is modified. In the original frame, "messy house" is part of the category *things people do which show lack of consideration and make my life more difficult.* In the new frame, "messy house" has shifted to the category *proof that I am part of a loving, connected family, and that my family members are comfortable, relaxed, and enjoying themselves when they visit me.* Reframing is a very appropriate technique for this case because the client's goal, "to have my family visit and keep my house perfectly neat every minute of their visit," was impossible—a perfect example of utopian thinking (**C1**).

Reframing, as a technique, carries the risk of making the client feel misunderstood and invalidated, as in this example: The client says, "My daughter fights me every step of the way," and the therapist responds, *At least you know that you brought up a strong and independent person.* Whether that response would be helpful to the client depends on the timing, the context, and the relationship between client and therapist.

A very effective approach to reframing is to ask questions about the purposes and benefits of a behavior that the client has framed as *a self-defeating and stupid behavior, over which I have no control.*

- *What purpose does this behavior serve?*
- *What benefits (payoffs, positive consequences) do you get?*
- *How does this behavior help you?*
- *When you were young, how did this behavior help you survive?*
- *Is there any other way of looking at this?*

The answers to these questions can help the client shift the behavior to a positive frame: protection, positive intentions, attempts to get my needs met, or things I do to survive and reduce pain. Once in the new frame, the negative feelings and self-blame are reduced, and the client can examine whether there are better ways to achieve those benefits.

Downward Arrow Technique

By repeating the same questions (*And that means? And then? And next?*), a series of responses lead the client from the original thought to deeper schemas and core beliefs. When the questions do not produce a "deeper" response, then the core belief has been identified and then the therapist can move on to challenging that belief. Once this technique has been demonstrated in a session with the therapist, the client is able to use it as a homework assignment. Drawing a downward arrow on paper as each successive response is written is helpful in showing that the movement is toward a deeper, fundamental level.

When the client identifies a negative thought that leads to anxiety about performance, good questions to ask are *If that thought were true, why would it be upsetting?* or *What would that mean to you?* A client will move from "I might make a mistake" to "My colleagues will think I'm stupid" to "They will know that I don't deserve this job" to "That would mean I'm worthless."

Clum (1990) provides an example of a person with panic attacks who has a fear of driving on the interstate.

Identifying the Irrational Belief

Therapist: *What will happen?*

Client: *I will have a panic attack.*

Therapist: *What will happen next?*

Client: *I will have to pull off the road.*

Therapist: *And next?*

Client: *I will be there forever.*

Challenging the Belief

Therapist: *How likely is it that you will be there forever?*

Client: *Of course I wouldn't be there forever. Either my panic attack would sub-side and I'd drive off, or someone would come to help me. Panic attacks always end, so I'll be able to drive away. And the police always stop to help cars stopped alongside the road.*

Cost-Benefit Analysis

Instead of addressing whether a core belief is rational or true, this method en-gages the client in an examination of whether it is useful to continue to maintain that belief. The belief is written down, and then under it are drawn two columns, one for advantages or reasons for maintaining and the other for disadvantages or reasons for changing. Then, when the two lists are finished, the client divides 100 points between the two columns to indicate the relative weight given to each argument. Burns (2005) provides an example for the belief "I need everyone's approval to be worthwhile."

Advantages

I'll work hard to get people to approve of me; I'll respect other people and pay careful attention to what they say and how they feel; I'll sell lots of life insur-ance and make lots of money; I'll be a people person and have lots and lots of friends. I'll feel great when people do approve of me.

Disadvantages

Other people will control my self-esteem; I'll get upset when people criticize me; I may try too hard and turn people off; I may not know what I believe in or stand for; My emotions will go up and down like a roller coaster depending on whether people like me.

In the example, the client gave 30 points to the advantages and 70 to the disadvantages.

Focus on Changing Behaviors

Behavior change can precede schema change. To change *poor self-esteem,* the person needs data that he or she is behaving in a way worthy of esteem. Get the person to break a task into small steps and succeed, and he or she will begin to view the self as competent and masterful. If the cognitive map creates fear by labeling many situations as "threatening and dangerous," it can be very benefi-cial to help the person engage in risky behaviors, doing what is difficult, in spite of fear. Then when the client masters those situations, the cognitive map will change and the situations will no longer be labeled dangerous. For instance, Albert Ellis gave this assignment to a client who had catastrophic beliefs about the consequences of appearing silly in public: *Take the New York subway and as you approach each station, shout out the name of the stop.*

INTEGRATION OF HYPOTHESES

The **C2** hypothesis is almost always a useful partner to the following hypotheses.

BL3 Skills Deficits or Lack of Competence

Therapists have a tendency to want to build self-esteem, instead of considering that low self-esteem is justified. Often people have negative beliefs about their competence and adequacy because they lack the level of competence expected of people at their age or in their occupation. The appropriate approach is to help the client improve his skills and competence, thereby earning a positive evaluation from others and the self.

ES1 Existential Issues

People who are struggling with existential issues are searching for a new cognitive map, a term that embraces *philosophy of life*. Whereas the original cognitive map provided meaning that was derived from parents and society, the therapist is helping the client create her own meaning and discover that she is free to choose her response to events that are imposed.

ES2 Avoiding Freedom and Responsibility

Freedom, limits, and responsibility are topics for cognitive exploration. Therapists help people relinquish their fictions, illusions, and self-deceptions to enjoy the benefits of freedom, recognize aspects of the world that cannot be controlled, and accept responsibility for the consequences of their actions. Existential therapists believe that adults can make the choice to think in more mature ways once they recognize their errors in thinking and the price they pay for them.

P1 Internal Parts and Subpersonalities

Different parts of the personality hold on to different cognitive maps of reality. It is a very common experience that people have a rational part that can recognize faulty thoughts, although there is an emotional part that continues to act as if they are true. When therapists find that cognitive therapy is not working, they should suspect that the Adult part of the personality is not as powerful as other parts. It is essential to engage the "Adult-in-the-Child" (the "little professor" from TA) because this could be the part that originated and still believes the maladaptive schema.

P2 Reenactment of Early Childhood Experiences

In gathering data about early childhood, you are not looking for disconnected facts, but are trying to learn specific information that helps explain how the client constructed the faulty cognitive map that directs his or her way of living. By tracing the roots of faulty schemas back to childhood and the dynamics of the family of origin, we can discover how they "make sense" and served survival functions for the little child. To relinquish them, the client must be able to tolerate painful feelings and to have more mature strategies for getting emotional needs met. It is also important to integrate **C2** with **P2** so that psychodynamic formulations do not remain vague and overly general. A formulation that states *She is bringing elements of her early experience into the present* needs to go further and describe the specific elements, for instance the belief that she is unlovable, the assumption that men can't be trusted, or the decision, "I'll make them sorry."

P3 Immature Sense of Self and Conception of Others

Clients will differ in their ability to separate thinking from the sense of self. If clients do not have the capacity to critically examine their own thinking, they will construe your efforts to challenge their model of the world as if they are personal attacks and failures of empathy. If that happens, the psychodynamic hypothesis **P3** should be considered.

Items 6, 8, and 10 from Jeffrey Young's list of maladaptive schemas (Table 6.6) are capturing what psychoanalytic psychotherapists would consider developmental defects, narcissistic disturbances, or character disorders.

SCE2 Cultural Context

Many terms that we use to describe culture are cognitive in nature: for example, norms, values, beliefs, rules, and expectations. An exploration of cultural issues involves many cognitive frameworks: How the person views his own culture, how he thinks others view his culture, how norms and rules for behavior differ between cultures, and how people from different cultures have different stories or narratives about the same historic periods. You must respect the diversity of cognitive maps stemming from culture and seek to increase choice and improve cognitive skills, not indoctrinate people with your preferred beliefs. Goals for cognitive change must be supported by specific problems and desired outcomes; otherwise, the judgment that certain patterns of thinking are dysfunctional can be driven by cultural and personal bias.

C3 FAULTY INFORMATION PROCESSING

Definition

The client demonstrates **Faulty Information Processing** (e.g., overgeneralization, all-or-nothing thinking, and mind reading) or is limited by an inflexible cognitive style.

Explanation

Effective living requires the ability to perceive accurately the data of experience and change schemas to accommodate new experiences. Adaptive information processing involves application of the rules of logic, practice of the scientific method, and the willingness to seek validation for thoughts, from either experiments or the consensual reality of other people. Problems can be traced to lack of cognitive skills and to cognitive styles that are inappropriate for the context and goals.

Examples

Corinne is extremely depressed and finds much evidence that life is not worth living. Her car broke down, proving "nothing ever works for me." Her best girlfriend didn't return a phone message, demonstrating "she doesn't give a damn about me." Her boss pointed out a small error she had made, leading her to conclude: "I guess I don't have what it takes to succeed at anything."	Tina developed the schema, "men cannot be trusted" when her high school boyfriend broke up with her in a humiliating way. When she dates a new man and he doesn't call her the next day, she concludes: "He is untrustworthy." If he calls on the third day, she acts very distant and cool. When he stops calling, she concludes: "See, I knew he would reject me."	John wants to get married and have a family, but his relationships with women never seem to work. When he meets a woman with a certain type of beauty, he is convinced that "she is my future wife." When she has sex with him, he interprets it as proof that she feels the same way. When she breaks up with him, he is convinced, "She's playing hard to get. She really loves me."

KEY IDEAS FOR C3 FAULTY INFORMATION PROCESSING

All thinking has distortions. The minute we impose meaning on the raw data of our senses, we call it *perception* instead of *sensation*. There are always different ways of perceiving the same events. We are bombarded with information from the environment as well as from our internal world; it would be impossible to attend to and process everything. When you sit on a park bench, reading a book, thoroughly absorbed, you are not hearing the birds or seeing the trees: There is always selective attention. Thus, the goal in using this hypothesis is not to aim for perfection in thinking; rather, you want to identify those patterns of thinking that result in psychological pain, poor problem-solving and coping skills, and interference with achieving goals. Furthermore, therapists need to be aware of their own tendencies toward faulty thinking. Levy (1997) teaches tools of critical thinking for clinicians—essential skills in developing effective case formulations.

Common Errors in Thinking

Therapists can help clients correct their faulty information processing and acquire tools for avoiding future difficulties by teaching them to recognize specific errors in thinking. Table 6.8 gives names and examples for some of the most common of these errors (Beck & Weishaar, 2000).

Maturation of Cognitive Capacities

Many problems of adults stem from their immature thinking: They are egocentric, concrete, rigid, and confuse fantasy and reality, as do young children.

Piaget's (2002) theory of cognitive development in children explains that children's cognitive capacities develop in stages: Styles of thinking that are normal at one age are considered immature at a later age. For instance, a little child may have the word "daddy" for all men. Then that term gets restricted to one man, and new labels are developed for other men. A 3-year-old child is naturally egocentric: Events are interpreted from one point of view—the self—and the child is unable to switch to the point of view of other people. The capacity for abstract thinking does not arrive until adolescence: At this stage, the individual can think of hypothetical situations and use the scientific method to gather evidence and test the validity of conclusions.

Piaget is the source of the term *schema,* which is commonly used for cognitive structures. When the data of experience are consistent with the schema, the schema *assimilates* the data and remains unchanged. However, when the data are inconsistent and cannot be assimilated without distortion of reality, the schema must undergo *accommodation* and change to be consistent with the data. *Cognitive dissonance* is a term for the inconsistency between preexisting beliefs and new information, and this state needs to be resolved, either by modifying beliefs or by screening out and avoiding the discrepant information. *Reality testing* is a process of checking the match between schema and the sensory data from reality. In healthy maturation, schemas are constantly revised. If the individual does not independently recognize that the schema is faulty, other people—parents, teachers, friends, police—give corrective experiences. If schemas fail to change despite confrontation with inconsistent data, the person is going to be ill equipped to deal with challenges of life.

Parataxic Distortions and Transference

Freud used the term *transference* for the client's distorted view of the therapist and Sullivan (1968) recognized the same process in all relationships, calling it *parataxic distortion.* A distorted perception of other people is a common experience: We meet a new acquaintance and respond based on similarity to someone we knew in the past. However, as we spend more time with that person, we are supposed to process the information that reveals who that person is in reality, not fantasy, and adjust our beliefs, expectations, and assumptions. When distortions are extreme and the adult cannot effectively test reality, there are likely to be severe problems in relationships. Examples include an adult woman who expects her boyfriend to meet the needs her father never met and a competent professional man who stammers with anxiety when his reasonable and friendly boss asks a question.

Table 6.8 Errors in Thinking

Overgeneralization	Using terms like *always* and *never* and ignoring any exceptions. Assuming that knowledge about one member of a group gives you knowledge about all members of that group. For instance, you had a teacher who was mean and so you act as if all teachers are enemies. A female client says, "Men are incapable of empathy."
Personalization	Assuming that external events refer to you without considering alternate explanations. When a person at work looks preoccupied, you think it's because he's mad at you for something.
All-or-Nothing Thinking	Known as dichotomous or polarized thinking in which everything is viewed as black and white; there are no shades of grey. You make one mistake and equate that with total failure. An admired person reveals a weakness and you label her as no good.
Arbitrary Inference	Commonly called jumping to conclusions—taking one bit of data and drawing a premature conclusion, without considering alternate explanations or gathering more data. European tourists conclude that restaurants close early in New York City because they walk for two blocks in a residential neighborhood and do not find any open restaurants.
Selective Abstraction	Using a "mental filter" to select only one kind of information from a complex experience and ignore everything else, including the total context. A person with an "angry" filter describes his day in terms of the bad things that other people did to him: Someone cut him off in traffic, his boss showed favoritism toward another employee, and the server made him wait too long.
Mind Reading	Assuming that you can accurately know what another person is thinking and feeling without any corroborating data. For instance, a woman saw a frown on her husband's forehead and said, "I know you're mad about how much money I spent."
Emotional Reasoning	Drawing conclusions based on feelings rather than facts. *I feel self-conscious, so people must be looking at me and ridiculing me. I'm feeling anxious, so there must be a real threat in this situation.*
Fortune Telling	Assuming that you can predict the future. Instead of dealing in probabilities, you take an attitude of certainty about what will happen. *I know I'll only get rejections.* This error can lead to self-fulfilling prophecies as you filter experiences and then find proof that your prediction was correct. *I know that people in my new neighborhood will be unfriendly.*
Magnification and Minimization	Judging something as far more significant or less significant than it is. *They're telling us to evacuate because of the fire, but I'm sure I can handle whatever happens. My heart is beating faster; it must be a heart attack.* The term *catastrophizing* is used for negative magnification.

There are two ways of clearing up parataxic distortions and transferences:

1. Get to know the real person, for who he or she is in reality, which involves listening to that person describe his or her internal process, intentions, and feelings, as well as observing behavior and drawing inferences from the facts of that behavior rather than from fantasies about the person.

2. Check out perceptions and assumptions with a group of other people. Group therapy is an effective modality because it provides the opportunity for a client to compare perceptions with a group of people, not just the therapist (Yalom, 1995). If others agree with the perception—yes, the person did insult you and treat you rudely—you have achieved *consensual validation* for your hunch, but if they disagree, then you need to correct your faulty thinking.

Cognitive Styles

People differ in their style of processing information, and a variety of theories and tools exist that classify these styles. Differences in cognitive styles have implications not only for defense mechanisms and pathology but also for talents, interests, preferred learning modalities, occupational choice, and creation of compatible relationships. Jung developed a typology for modes of processing— *sensing, intuition, thinking, feeling;* a personality assessment tool, the Myers-Briggs Type Indicator (MBTI), identifies sixteen personality types, based in part on those differences (Hammer, 1996):

- *Sensing:* Using physical senses of seeing, hearing, touching, smelling, and tasting.
- *Intuition:* Using past experiences and more abstract thinking.
- *Thinking:* Making decisions objectively and impersonally, based on laws, principles, and factual information.
- *Feeling:* Making decisions subjectively and personally, based on relationships and values.

An important distinction in cognitive style is whether a person thinks in global, undifferentiated terms or focuses on details, differentiating the whole into component parts. This difference can be assessed with the Rorschach test: Some people will respond to the whole card, with little attention to details, whereas others have many responses for details without forming a concept for the whole card. Although people have a preference for one style or another, the most effective individuals have the flexibility to use both styles, and make deliberate choices about which style is most adaptive for a specific situation. David Shapiro (1965) identified several "neurotic styles" and noted how people's style determines what they search for and attend to in the environment:

Compulsive individuals seek technical data; paranoid persons search for clues; and hysterics notice "the immediately striking, vivid, and colorful things in life" (p. 119). Shapiro describes individuals with the two most common styles as having the following characteristics:

- *Hysterical style:* Gives answers in terms of impressions rather than facts; lacks focus on detail; seems incapable of persistent or intense intellectual concentration; distractible; satisfied with relying on hunches and intuitions; lacks intellectual curiosity; highly suggestible; fails to see things that are obvious to others; and able to keep unpleasant experiences on the periphery.
- *Obsessive-compulsive style:* Attention has a sharp, intense focus; concentrates on detail; seems unable to allow his attention to wander; rarely seems to get hunches; seems incapable of a relaxed, impressionistic cognition; attempts to reach a decision by invoking a rule or principle; and alternates between uncertainty and dogma.

WHEN IS THIS HYPOTHESIS A GOOD MATCH?

Techniques of cognitive therapy have received strong research support (Reinecke & Freeman, 2003) for the following targets: depression, Generalized Anxiety Disorder (GAD), Panic Disorder, Posttraumatic Stress Disorder (PTSD), Social Anxiety, Body Dysmorphic Disorder, Obsessive-Compulsive Disorder (OCD), anger management, psychotic disorders, and eating disorders.

Table 6.9 presents the biases in information processing that Beck and Weishaar (2000, p. 251) have noted for various psychological disorders.

Table 6.9 Faulty Information Processing in Psychological Disorders

Disorder	Faulty Thinking
Depression	Negative view of self, experience, and future
Hypomania	Inflated view of self and future
Anxiety Disorder	Sense of physical or psychological danger
Panic Disorder	Catastrophic interpretation of bodily/mental experiences
Phobia	Sense of danger in specific, avoidable situations
Obsession	Repeated warning or doubts about safety
Compulsion	Rituals believed to ward off perceived threat
Paranoid states	Persist in believing others are prejudiced, abusive, and malicious
Anorexia Nervosa	Fear of being fat and misperception of body size
Hypochondriasis	Faulty attribution of serious medical disorder

Source: "Cognitive therapy" (p. 251), by A. T. Beck and M. Weishaar, in *Current Psychotherapies*, 6th ed., R. J. Corsini amd D. Wedding (Eds.), 2000, Itasca, IL: Peacock Press. Reprinted with permission.

A focus on faulty information processing is effective in marital therapy. For instance, partners need to distinguish between behaviors in each other that are volitional and therefore are able to be changed, and those characteristics that reflect genetics, personality, and core attributes and therefore need to be accepted (Christensen & Jacobson, 2000).

TREATMENT PLANNING

The following strategies focus directly on faulty thinking; be aware that errors in thinking or rigidity in cognitive style can also be modified indirectly, through therapeutic conversations.

Collaborative Empiricism

Aaron Beck encourages the client to function as a "personal scientist" and examine the data of reality to see if it fits the client's beliefs and predictions. He recommends:

- Teach the client about the relation of thoughts to feelings and behavior.
- Use questions to get the client to assess the validity of thinking.
- Give the client specific homework assignments.

Teaching

One treatment method is to teach the client about common errors in thinking, using an educational approach to correct errors and teach better reasoning skills, perhaps giving the client a copy of Table 6.8. Here is an example of how a therapist might present this strategy to the client: "People often make certain kinds of errors in the way they look at situations and these errors in thinking may contribute to arriving at premature or incorrect conclusions, which cause (insert the clients specific problem)."

Questions

The metamodel questions that were presented in Chapter 2, Table 2.6, are interventions to correct faulty information processing. They promote changes, not only as a result of helping the client to access information that has been ignored, but because you are teaching the client the metaperspective—that his cognitive map probably contains distortions and errors that create limitations and interfere with the range of opportunities and choices that are available. You may challenge the mind reading in the client's statement: "My husband feels resentful of my success" by asking, *How specifically do you know?* Three different kinds of change can result:

1. *Specific change:* I need to ask my husband how he really feels.

2. *Pattern change that generalizes to new situations:* I have this pattern of mind reading that gets me into trouble. I need to catch myself and remember to gather data from the other person.

3. *Ability to change other patterns:* I need to understand the map I've constructed and how I often distort my experience. I need to challenge my thinking and test reality on an ongoing basis.

Socratic Dialogue

The therapist asks questions that will help the client arrive at logical conclusions and process the data of experience more effectively, as in the following situations.

- **Consider alternate explanations:**
  —*So when she didn't invite you, you concluded that she doesn't want to be your friend any more. Can you think of any other possible explanations?*
  —*Could there be other reasons for the way she behaved, which had nothing to do with you?*

- **Test conclusions by examining evidence:**
  —*You say he loves you, but how does he treat you?*
  —*How do you know that the teacher won't give you an extension on your paper?*

- **Recognize distortions by examining experience:**
  —*You said you believe that if you try hard and are loving enough and anticipate all his needs, he will have to love you. You have been acting on that belief for a long time. What have you noticed about his behavior?*
  —*Has anyone else ever experienced that same event and reacted in a different way?*

- **Increase imagination and flexibility:**
  —*Could you imagine any other way of reacting?*
  —*What other kind of information would you need?*

Confrontation

In a *confrontation,* the therapist draws attention to contradictions and inconsistencies and allows the client to draw his own conclusions.

- *You say that you can't count on anybody, but hasn't your sister been there for you during this crisis?*

- *You say you don't need to study but last time you got a C on the test.*

By challenging faulty information processing you can help the client modify schemas and assumptions and update the cognitive map, as in this example:

- **The therapist confronted the client:** *You say that you have to be perfect to be loved; how did your boyfriend respond when you told him about your mistake?* When the client examines data of the boyfriend's response, she develops a new schema: "When I show my fallibility, flaws, and weaknesses, my boyfriend still loves me; in fact, he becomes even more loving in his behavior."

Homework Assignments

One helpful type of homework assignment is the use of structured journal keeping using a chart format (see Table 2.9 in Chapter 2 for an example). The client writes down a situation or event in the first column, and then writes down what he thought about it. Other columns are used to record the resulting feelings or Subjective Units of Discomfort Scale (SUDS) level and an alternate adaptive way of appraising the situation.

INTEGRATION OF HYPOTHESES

The recognition of faulty patterns of thinking will be very useful when you use the following hypotheses.

B3 Mind-Body Connections

The way a person processes the information from the environment affects the development of neural networks in the brain. Catastrophizing, an exaggerated response to perceived threat, results in fight-flight arousal states. Misinterpretation of bodily states is a component of Panic Disorder. The immune system may be affected by whether a person has positive or negative interpretations of experiences: Pollyannaism is better for your health than pessimism.

CS2 Situational Stressors

The interpretation of a stressor affects how a person copes and whether crisis develops. Table 4.4 includes "perception of the event" as one of the three factors that predict the response to stressors. Crisis intervention techniques include a focus on thinking processes. In dealing with trauma, attention is paid to helping victims process their experience in words to avoid an overgeneralization of affect to new situations and the magnification of threatening stimuli in the future.

BL3 Skill Deficits or Lack of Competence

Faulty information processing represents skill deficits in logic, scientific method, and analytic abilities. Therapist can directly teach problem-solving and decision-making skills.

P1 Internal Parts and Subpersonalities

We assume that in the client there is a part capable of competent information processing, rational reasoning, and effective scientific thinking, which can be labeled as the Adult or the personal scientist. The Child state engages in immature thinking and misinterpretations of reality. The Parent state carries arbitrary rules and dogma, plus the metarule: "Obey me without thinking."

P3 Immature Sense of Self and Conception of Others

Certain people are unable to separate their thinking from their sense of self. Therefore, when the therapist challenges the client's thinking, the person reacts defensively as if he, himself, rather than the faulty thinking, is being attacked. A good way to test the goodness of fit of hypothesis **P3** is to challenge faulty thinking and examine the client's responses.

P4 Unconscious Dynamics

When a client maintains faulty thinking despite the best tools of cognitive therapy, it is useful to consider the hypothesis that unconscious defense mechanisms are involved. For instance, a person who distorts social cues to mean rejection may be protecting herself from the vulnerability that accompanies trust, and is hence avoiding emotional pain and a repetition of early childhood situations.

C4 DYSFUNCTIONAL SELF-TALK

Definition

The problem is triggered and/or maintained by **Dysfunctional Self-Talk** and internal dialogue.

Explanation

There are many different terms for self-talk (e.g., self-messages, internal speech, internal voice, internal tapes, automatic thoughts, or interior monologue). Dysfunctional self-talk causes painful feelings and maladaptive behavior. Sometimes the person is very aware of the self-talk; at other times, you need to probe to discover inner speech.

Examples

José would like to date and form a lasting relationship that could lead to marriage, but he is troubled by debilitating shyness and fear of rejection. Before calling a girl, he thinks, "She wouldn't want to go out with someone like me"; he ruminates all the time, "I'll never find anyone to love me." When friends invite him to go to a party where he could meet women, he thinks, "It's too much effort."

Jake was arrested for an incident of "road rage" and was ordered, as a condition of probation, to attend anger management therapy. He learned to examine the way he talked to himself about other drivers. Instead of thinking, "He can't do that to me!" and "I'll get even!" he learned to tell himself, "This isn't personal, there are many lousy drivers in the world, and if I overreact, I'll just hurt myself and my family."

Marge teaches parent education courses at a local community center. She feels very confident and effective when she is working with groups of 6 or 8 people. However, when she gets up in front of large audiences, she is overcome by anxiety. She tells herself, "They'll be bored" and "They won't like me." As she feels her anxiety go higher, she thinks, "I'm going to forget what I want to say. They'll laugh at me."

KEY IDEAS FOR C4 DYSFUNCTIONAL SELF-TALK

When people are asked, *What were you thinking?* or *What did you say to yourself then?* they give an answer that describes internal speech. There are various ways of describing it: "A voice in my head tells me to be careful"; "I keep telling myself that something bad is going to happen"; or "It's like a broken record, saying over and over again, don't trust him."

This level of cognitive functioning is easy to identify and work with; some therapists focus on this level without getting into deeper layers of the cognitive map. Others, like Aaron Beck, stress the importance of connecting *automatic thoughts* to underlying schemas (**C2**).

Behavioral Approach to Covert Speech

Internal speech can be treated as an ordinary behavior and is part of every comprehensive behavioral analysis. In addition to being the identified problem behavior, covert speech can be an antecedent to the problem behavior, or something that follows a behavior and serves as a reward or punishment (**BL1**). Mahoney (1974) and Meichenbaum (1977) developed a focus on the cognitions as behaviors, which was originally called cognitive behavior modification, now known as CBT. Meichenbaum used the term *self-statements* and developed a self-instructional approach that teaches clients how to become aware of and modify their own self-talk. Thus, the modification of internal speech is viewed as a coping skill (**BL3**). He used the term *stress-inoculation* for a strategy of having clients practice four stages of positive self-statements with minor stressors to be prepared for dealing with more severe real-world stressors. Novaco (1986) developed a similar approach for anger management.

WHEN IS THIS HYPOTHESIS A GOOD MATCH?

Table 6.10 gives examples of when dysfunctional self-talk is likely to be an important contributor to the problem.

TREATMENT PLANNING

Table 6.11 shows the different phases in a therapy plan to modify dysfunctional self-talk.

Three Techniques to Modify Self-Talk

The three options on page 224 allow the therapist to help the client modify self-talk.

Table 6.10   Applying the C4 Dysfunctional Self-Talk Hypothesis

Depression

Beck's *cognitive triad*—negative thoughts about self, ongoing experience, and the future—is manifested as automatic thoughts: *I never do anything right; nobody cares about me; things will never get any better.*

Suicidal Risk

Suicidal ideation is experienced as self-talk: *Life isn't worth living; I'd be better off dead; he'll be sorry when I'm dead.*

Problems of Impulsive Behavior

There is a lack of constructive self-talk mediating between the trigger event and the behavior. The therapist helps the client build intervening self-messages: *Slow down, think it over; think about the consequences.* This strategy is very useful with children.

Low Self-Esteem and Feelings of Worthlessness

Negative messages about the self contribute to depression, impaired coping, and social withdrawal. The self-talk can be expressed with either "I" or "You": *I'm no good; I'll never succeed at anything. You're a worthless, no-good loser.*

Anxiety

Negative self-talk can usually be identified when there is anxiety. Especially with social anxiety, it is probable that the person is increasing social fears and predicting rejection and failure. However, not all anxiety problems have cognitive mediation.

Phobias

When working with a client with a phobia, it is important to distinguish between cognitive-based fears and emotionally conditioned fears (**B2**). For cognitive-based fears, you can identify the self-talk. With emotionally conditioned fears, the person already knows it is irrational and the fear happens independently of how the person talks to herself. This differentiation is an extremely important part of the formulation, as it leads to very different treatment strategies (i.e., CBT versus systematic desensitization).

Anger Problems

Anger management programs often incorporate modification of self-talk. When a person faces a provocation, negative self-talk raises the "anger thermometer" from mild irritation to rage.

Stress and Crisis

The client needs to be able to calm himself down and use adaptive self-talk in response to the stressors and the demands of the situation.

Health, Eating and Substance Abuse Problems

Modification of self-talk is an important coping strategy in dealing with illness, behaviors that put health at risk, overeating and Anorexia or Bulimia, overcoming addictions, and avoiding relapse.

Table 6.11   Modification of Self-Talk

1. Awareness of Self-Talk

The client must develop awareness of self-talk at critical points in time, particularly before, during, and after stressful situations. The therapist asks specific questions to get at the internal speech.

> *What did you think when he told you he didn't love you anymore?*
>
> *What did you say to yourself after you saw that grade on your paper?*
>
> *What words go through your head while you are sitting in traffic?*
>
> *What are you saying to yourself right now?*

2. Recognition of the Effect of Self-Talk

The client is taught the ABC model: **Event** → **Self-Talk** → **Feelings**

Events do not cause feelings; rather, the self-talk in response to the event causes excessive emotional reactions. The client needs the awareness that he causes his own misery, and that he perpetuates the problem as long as he continues talking to himself that way.

3. Development of Belief That a Person *Can* Control Self-Talk

This is a major step: The client realizes that the messages are not "truth" but are auditory stimuli that he can control. By using the metaphor of a radio tuner, the client realizes that he can change the channel or use the mute button.

4. Deciding to Change

Once the client believes that change is possible, he must make a decision to change the problematic self-talk to more adaptive self-talk. The therapist should not begin a treatment intervention until the client makes this decision.

5. Planning a Self-Managed Program

The client is involved in planning and implementing a program to recognize and change self-talk. The client learns to evaluate his self-messages: Are they true? Are they rational? Are they helpful? More adaptive alternatives can be taught and must be rehearsed and practiced.

6. Practice and Self-Reward

The client becomes aware that it is difficult to change long-standing habits of internal speech, and it takes time, persistence, and practice. Change is expected to be gradual and there must be reasonable expectations about the pace of change. The client must practice the new way of thinking and reward himself for small steps on the way to the desired outcome. The client comes to realize that the positive self-talk causes him to feel and behave differently, and the new behavior elicits better responses from other people.

1. *Thought-Stopping:* The client learns to terminate the troublesome thought, perhaps by saying "stop" when the thought begins.

2. *Aversive methods:* The client inflicts a painful stimulus on himself when he begins to think the thought he wants to eliminate. Snapping a rubber band against the wrist can be sufficient.

3. *Reinforcing positive alternative:* The person chooses an alternate sentence to substitute for the dysfunctional self-talk, practices it, and rewards herself for using it.

Stress Inoculation

A stressful situation—one that triggers anxiety, anger, or depression—is broken into four stages, and the client is taught to identify dysfunctional thought at each stage and then to create and practice more adaptive alternatives. Here are examples of positive self-talk at each stage:

1. *Preparing for the stressor or provocation:* I can handle it. Just take it one step at a time. Remember to breathe deeply. I'm prepared.
2. *Confronting and handling the stressor or provocation:* Find a friendly face in the audience. He's trying to get your goat, don't give him the satisfaction of losing control. Count to 10. Use that "broken record technique."
3. *Coping with arousal and feeling overwhelmed:* Take a few deep breaths. It's okay to tell them you need a little time to collect your thoughts. Take a time-out. you don't have to stay in the room. It's okay not to be perfect the first time you try something new.
4. *Reflecting on the situation and reinforcing positive change:* I handled that really well. It's a small step, but it's important progress. It was a setback, but I won't brood about it; next time, I'll handle it better.

Homework Assignment

Homework is an essential part of a program to modify self-talk. Between sessions, the client keeps a chart, writing down self-talk in response to specific situations, and showing the corresponding feelings and behaviors. Then the client creates "alternate self-talk" that will lead to more adaptive feelings and behavior. The information from this chart is also helpful for **C3** and **C4.** Table 6.12 shows a sample homework chart for the problem behavior: *Difficulty controlling intake of food and drink.*

Role-Play Activities

If the self-statements say negative things about the self, it is useful to externalize the voice and then challenge it. If the message is not already in a "you" form (You're no good), then suggest the person change "I'm no good" to "You're no good." Ask the client to move to another chair and talk to "herself" from that voice. The client switches back to the original chair and disputes the message. Another activity is to ask the client to imagine that she is talking to another person, perhaps a young child, and to say the internal message to that person: "You're no good. You're a hopeless loser." This helps the client see how destructive the inner voice is; he can then develop more constructive and caring self-messages.

Table 6.12   Self-Talk Monitoring Chart

Situation	Self-Talk	Feelings	Behavior	Alternate Self-Talk
Working on a project for my job that is taking much longer than I expected.	I'll never get this done! I hate this job! Nothing I do is good enough!	Anxious, angry.	Went to vending machine and bought junk food.	I'll break it down into small subtasks; It just has to be good enough, not perfect; I can ask for help.
Sitting home on Saturday night.	I'll never find anyone who will love me. I'll be lonely and miserable for the rest of my life.	Sad, depressed, desperate.	Cried. Drank several glasses of vodka.	I'm feeling lonely; I'll call a friend. I'll make plans for next weekend.
At a restaurant, reading the menu.	I can order whatever I want. I don't care about losing weight.	Happy, liberated, elated.	Ate the calorie allotment for 4 days.	I'll feel bad tomorrow if I overeat. This is not my last chance to eat.

INTEGRATION OF HYPOTHESES

Be sure to examine internal speech when using the following two hypotheses.

P1 Internal Parts and Subpersonalities

There is a very natural integration of **P1** and **C4.** As you identify different internal messages, you often notice that they are spoken in different voices and actually represent different subpersonalities or inner parts. It becomes more appropriate to talk about an internal dialogue or group discussion rather than just a monologue.

ES2 Avoiding Freedom and Responsibility

Often, people argue that external events *do* cause their responses, claiming, "I can't help the way I think." But they can be persuaded that, even in uncontrollable external circumstances, they have a choice regarding the activity in their own minds: The example of Victor Frankl, a survivor of the Nazi concentration camps, provides compelling illustrations of how people could exercise the freedom to create their own thoughts.

SUGGESTED READINGS

These suggestions are for all cognitive hypotheses.

Cognitive Behavior Therapy

Bandura, A. (1977). *Social learning theory.* Englewood Cliffs, NJ: Prentice Hall.

Barlow, D. (2004). *Anxiety and its disorders: The nature and treatment of anxiety and panic* (2nd ed.). New York: Guilford Press.

Beck, A. T. (2000). *Prisoners of hate: The cognitive basis of anger, hostility, and violence.* New York: Perennial.

Beck, A. T., Emery, G, & Greenberg, R. L. (1985). *Anxiety disorders and phobias: A cognitive perspective.* New York: Basic Books.

Beck, A. T., Freeman, A., & Davis, D. D. (2003). *Cognitive therapy of personality disorders* (2nd ed.). New York: Guilford Press.

Beck, A. T., Rush, A. J., Shaw, B. F., & Emery, G. (1979). *Cognitive therapy of depression.* New York: Guilford Press.

Burns, D. D. (1999). *Feeling good: The new mood therapy.* New York: HarperCollins.

Burns, D. D. (2005). *Scared stiff: Fast effective treatment for anxiety disorders.* Portola Valley, CA: Institute for the Advancement of Human Behavior.

Ellis, A. (1998). *A guide to rational living* (3rd Rev. ed.). Los Angeles: Wilshire Book.

Ellis, A. (2001). *Overcoming destructive beliefs, feelings, and behaviors: New directions for rational emotive behavior therapy.* New York: Prometheus Books.

Greenberger, D., & Padesky, C. (1995). *Mind over mood: Change how you feel by changing the way you think.* New York: Guilford Press.

Lam, D. H., Jones, S. H., Hayward, P., & Bright, J. A. (1999). *Cognitive therapy for bipolar disorder: A therapist's guide to concepts, methods, and practice.* West Sussex, England: Wiley.

Segal, A., Teasdale, J., & Williams, J. M. G. (2002). *Mindfulness-based cognitive therapy for depression.* New York: Guilford Press.

Young, J. (1999). *Cognitive therapy for personality disorders: A schema-focused approach* (3rd ed.). Sarasota, FL: Professional Resource Press.

Young, J. E., Weishar, M. E., & Klosko, J. S. (2003). *Schema therapy: A practitioner's guide.* New York: Guilford Press.

Psychodynamic Theory with Cognitive Concepts

Horney, K. (1994). *The neurotic personality of our time* (Reissue ed.). New York: W. W. Norton.

Mosak, H. H., & Maniacci, M. (1999). *A primer of Adlerian psychology: The analytic-behavioral-cognitive psychology of Alfred Adler.* New York: Brunner/Mazel.

Sullivan, H. S. (1968). *The interpersonal theory of psychiatry.* New York: W. W. Norton.

Narrative Therapy

Friedman, S. (1993). *The new language of change.* New York: Guilford Press.

Parry, A., & Doan, R. (1994). *Story revisions: Narrative therapy in the postmodern world.* New York: W. W. Norton.

White, M. (1995). *Re-authoring lives: Interviews & essays.* Adelaide, Australia: Dulwich Center Publications.

White, M., & Epston, D. (1990). *Narrative means to therapeutic ends.* New York: Norton.

Family and Couples Therapy

Baucom, D. H., & Epstein, N. (1990). *Cognitive-behavioral marital therapy.* New York: Brunner-Routledge.

Christensen, A., & Jacobson, N. (2000). *Reconcilable differences.* New York: Guilford Press.

Datillio, F. M. (Ed.). (1998). *Case studies in couple and family therapy: Systemic and cognitive perspectives*. New York: Guilford Press.

Gottman, J. (1994). *Why marriages succeed or fail*. New York: Simon & Schuster.

Schwebel, A. I., & Fine, M. A. (1994). *Understanding and helping families: A cognitive-behavioral approach*. Hillsdale, NJ: Lawrence Erlbaum Association.

Other Books That Teach a Cognitive Focus

Aurelius, M. (1989). *The meditations of Marcus Aurelius Antoninus*. New York: Oxford University Press.

Bandler, R., & Grinder, J. (1990). *The structure of magic: A book about language and therapy*. Palo Alto, CA: Science and Behavior Books.

Cameron-Bandler, L. (1985). *Solutions*. Moab, UT: Real People Press.

Firestone, R. (1988). *Voice therapy: A psychotherapeutic approach to self-destructive behavior*. New York: Human Sciences Press.

Frankl, V. E. (1997). *Man's search for meaning* (Rev. ed.). New York: Pocket Books.

Graber, A. V. (2003). *Viktor Frankl's logotherapy*. Bristol, IN: Wyndham Hall Press.

Kelly, G. (1955). *The psychology of personal constructs*. New York: W. W. Norton.

Laborde, G. (1987). *Influencing with integrity*. Palo Alto, CA: Syntony Publishers.

Peale, N. V. (1996). *The power of positive thinking*. New York: Ballantine Books.

Serban, G. (1982). *The tyranny of magical thinking*. New York: E. P. Dutton.

Wadsworth, B. J. (1989). *Piaget's theory of cognitive and affective development* (4th ed.). New York: Longman.

Watzlawick, P., Weakland, J., & Fisch, R. (1974). *Change: Principles of problem formation and problem resolution*. New York: W. W. Norton.

Chapter 7

EXISTENTIAL AND SPIRITUAL MODELS

In applying the three hypotheses in this category, the therapist refuses to pathologize, medicalize, or objectify the client. Clients do not have a "disorder" but rather are struggling with the inevitable problems of human existence in the present moment of history. They search for a deeper understanding of themselves and seek meaning, self-actualization, inner peace, a sense of connection, and a path with heart rather than relief from symptoms. People often find the help they need from solitary self-reflection, healing relationships with family and friends, involvement in creative arts or service organizations, and mentorship by a wise member of the community. When they show up in the health care system, it is usually because of symptoms of anxiety, guilt, or depression. If clinicians' only goal is the relief of these symptoms, they fail to meet the deeper needs of their clients. With humility, we should wonder how graduate training and clinical licensure as a psychotherapist assure the necessary competence to provide help to these searchers. The "personhood" of the therapist and the quality of the relationship with the client are more important than other therapeutic ingredients. Therapists can often be most effective if they view themselves as fellow pilgrims, having struggled with the same issues. The help you give in applying these hypotheses must come not only from professional expertise but also from being fully engaged in the relationship, disclosing your own life experiences, and expressing genuine respect and care for the client.

The three hypotheses in this category, listed in Table 7.1, are frequently combined with each other. Because of the complexity of their philosophical underpinnings and their relative neglect in training programs, these hypotheses are discussed at greater length than most of the others.

Table 7.1 Existential and Spiritual Hypotheses

ES1 Existential Issues	The client is struggling with **Existential Issues,** including the fundamental philosophical search for the purpose and meaning of life.
ES2 Avoiding Freedom and Responsibility	The client is **Avoiding** the **Freedom and** autonomy that come with adulthood and/or does not accept **Responsibility** for present and past choices.
ES3 Spiritual Dimension	The core of the problem and/or the resources needed for resolving the problem are found in the **Spiritual Dimension** of life, which may or may not include religion.

ES1 EXISTENTIAL ISSUES

Definition

The client is struggling with **Existential Issues,** including the fundamental philosophical search for the purpose and meaning of life.

Explanation

Examples of existential issues include the purpose and meaning of life, mortality and death, and basic human isolation. Using the **ES1** hypothesis, you recognize that each person must find his or her own answers. Anxiety is a normal part of living and the pain from dealing with these issues cannot be eliminated. The therapist must abstain from taking the role of a guru or expert; instead, you are a fellow pilgrim who has struggled and continues to struggle with the same issues. (Decision making, which involves freedom, responsibility, choice, courage and commitment, is addressed in **ES2.**)

Examples

Claire reports feeling a total loss of meaning: Now that she has stopped trying to please others and is no longer living by her parents' rules, she is experiencing a void. "Even though I have lots of friends, I feel basically alone; no one else can make my decisions, and I, alone, am responsible for how my life turns out. I can't blame my parents any more."	Jake just turned 90. He wants to talk about his feelings about death. "We all die, and now that I realize my time is limited, I want to make the best choices for my remaining years or months." He complains that when he tries to talk about these topics in the retirement community where he lives, people avoid him or tell him not to be so morbid.	Steven, a 34-year-old salesman, has sought out therapy after feeling depressed for several months. He reports switching jobs about every 6 months, because "everything starts to bore me after a while." Steven is now in search of some meaning, something to help him "feel whole" for the first time in his life.

KEY IDEAS FOR ES1 EXISTENTIAL ISSUES

Psychotherapy textbooks usually cover existential, person-centered, and experiential therapies. However, if forced to make a commitment to a single orientation, trainees are often attracted to the more popular psychodynamic and cognitive-behavioral therapy (CBT) frameworks. It would be unfortunate to overlook the Existential Issues hypothesis not only because it is such a good fit for many clients, but also because it integrates very easily with other approaches. There is a rich philosophical heritage, a wide variety of therapeutic approaches, and fascinating case studies from which to learn.

Fulfillment of Potential

People often come to therapy wanting more than relief from symptoms or restoration of how they were before the current crisis. There is a yearning for a higher quality of living or the need to wrestle with deep questions and find a new orientation to life. These clients want to be responsible adults without sacrificing the vitality and sense of play of childhood. They want challenge and excitement in their daily lives, instead of stagnation and boredom. Typical goals might include meaning and purpose in their lives; fulfillment of their highest potential; a sense of control over their future paths; becoming more spontaneous and creative; feeling more alive, real, and whole; and achieving authentic contact with their inner being as well as with other humans. Mere conformity to society's definition of *normal* is not enough: Therapists will have an inadequate grasp of their clients' needs if they restrict themselves to goals endorsed by health care case managers. Many of these people do not suffer from *DSM-IV-TR* pathology but instead are experiencing what Maslow called the *psychopathology of the average*.

This hypothesis offers a philosophical perspective on what it means to live up to our potential as a human being. You are right if you recognize that there must be a cultural bias in this model. That doesn't mean that you can't "try it on" with members of any culture; there are people who feel trapped by the rules of their cultures and will welcome a liberating philosophical perspective. However, as you read the following sections, imagine how many of the premises would elicit a heated debate.

Emotional Suffering

Suffering cannot be eliminated from life. Although we cannot always control or prevent events that cause suffering, existential theorists believe that we have the freedom to choose how we react to those events. Imagine three people whose houses were demolished by a disaster such as a fire, hurricane, or mudslide. After an initial period of shock and disorientation, they demonstrate completely different responses:

- One collapses in despair and believes that there is no point starting over.
- The second is not only optimistic about rebuilding but also rallies neighbors to demand fair payment from the insurance companies.
- The third decides this is an opportunity to simplify life and gives up the stressful corporate career that supported the lifestyle that the house represented.

Whereas many therapists aim to eliminate symptoms of emotional distress, existentialists view the painful emotions as useful signals that can help a person live more effectively. They view anxiety as a natural part of life and an unavoidable consequence of taking risks and experiencing growth and change. Normal anxiety needs to be contrasted with "neurotic anxiety," which constricts rather than contributes to the self-actualizing process of people. Guilt is another emotion that can carry different messages. Ordinarily, a person feels guilty because of violating an internal rule regarding right and wrong behavior. Existential guilt, alternatively, comes from the awareness that one is not living an authentic existence and is refusing to grow. Clinical issues can stem from an avoidance and denial of these normal emotional experiences as when people numb themselves or engage in self-deception. In this framework, the goal of therapy is to enhance, rather than reduce, a client's awareness of feelings, visceral sensations, and inner dialogue.

One of the must puzzling and frustrating aspects of human functioning is that people will stay in painful situations when it seems obvious to an outsider that the pain must be unbearable and that they are free to leave. We can speculate that some people have higher thresholds for pain, or imagine a cost-benefit analysis where the pain of the current situation is less than the feared pain of choosing an alternative path. The realization that the motivation for change sometimes requires an intense experience of pain means that sometimes a process goal is to make people feel worse instead of immediately better. Using the metaphor of someone sitting in a seat that is uncomfortably warm, and asking *What does it take for the client to stand up and walk away?* the answer is, *When the chair gets hot enough, a person will get off.*

Meaning and Purpose in Life

Existential philosophers describe the human condition as the dilemma of meaning-seeking creatures thrown into a universe that has no intrinsic meaning. When we are young, we derive meaning from the rules and examples of our parents, which derived from the customs and traditions of their cultures. Many people live contented lives continuing to accept that meaning. However, other people experience a crisis of meaning, perhaps following a major loss or when they reach the pinnacle of the road they were told would bring fulfillment.

When the meaning systems that people have taken for granted are no longer viable, there are many distressing emotional responses. The existential literature describes the experience of "the absurd" and the response of nausea to the realization that there is no intrinsic meaning in the external world or the course of our lives. Clients may describe feeling emptiness—a void.

Building on his personal experiences in concentration camps, Viktor Frankl (1997) posited a motivational force that he called the *will to meaning.* For each person, the meaning is unique and specific and can only be fulfilled by that person, alone. Therefore, to invest meaning in a path that will bring you fulfillment, it is necessary to increase awareness of your feelings, desires, talents, ideals, and goals. Existentialists believe that it is better to live authentically, to fulfill your highest potential, and to use inner values to shape your life, than to follow a path ordained by others.

Authenticity and Honesty

Existentialists also believe that it is essential to face, honestly, *what is,* instead of filtering experience through illusions, fantasies, and fictions. People, in creating their lives, have a choice between living authentically, or living lives of dishonesty and self-deception. Some of the illusions that must be discarded are the very ones that gave us comfort in childhood: *Life is fair. If I am really good, I will be taken care of. Things happen for a reason.*

When asked to look inward for our true values and feelings, there can be the sense that there is nothing there—I am nothing more than the social roles I live or the opinions that others have of me. When people let go of inauthentic ways of living, there may be confusion and disorientation similar to the experience of culture shock when people take up extended residence in a different culture: The familiar frameworks and rules no longer operate and we lose the certainty and confidence that has built up over a lifetime.

Authenticity in human relations is a standard that many people have trouble living up to, and therapists who are not capable of it in their own personal relationships will not be able to provide this needed ingredient of the therapeutic relationship. When you are engaged in an authentic encounter, you would be (a) present in the moment rather than adrift on a mental side trip; (b) genuine and not hiding behind masks; (c) honest and truthful about what you choose to express, reserving the right to decline to reveal what you hold private; (d) open and vulnerable, allowing yourself to be impacted and changed by the other; and (e) willing to take the risk of being spontaneous. Spontaneity does not mean saying whatever comes into your head because you experience the vulnerability of the other person and want to be helpful. A precondition for authenticity with others is that you are vigilant against self-deception and have learned to hold yourself accountable for your own dishonesties.

The Question of Suicide

In his essay, *The Myth of Sisyphus,* Albert Camus (1991) uses a Greek myth to explore both the loss and the creation of meaning. As a punishment from the gods, Sisyphus spends his life pushing a heavy boulder to the top of a mountain. When it reaches the top, it rolls to the bottom, and he follows it down to put his shoulder to it, again, and start pushing uphill. Camus focuses on that moment at the bottom: The task is obviously meaningless, boring, painful, and there is no intrinsic purpose in continuing it—so why continue, if the choice of suicide is available? Camus wrote, "Dying voluntarily implies that you have recognized . . . the absence of any profound reason for living, the insane character of that daily agitation, and the uselessness of suffering" (p. 6). When a person seriously ponders the question of suicide, and decides not to carry through with it, he is positively affirming his life and making a freely chosen commitment. The project he is engaged in is no longer just a meaningless punishment, it is a voluntary undertaking and carries whatever meaning he invests in it, including one that can result in joy.

When therapists face people who are contemplating suicide, they frequently panic. They focus on assessing risk, taking emergency measures, getting medication evaluation, and doing whatever possible to get rid of the suicidal thoughts. Although all of these actions are essential, they are insufficient: The client needs someone to listen calmly and patiently and help her explore the crisis of meaning and the issues that have made life unbearable. When people have terminal illnesses, we consider it reasonable for them to contemplate how sui-cide will allow them to die with dignity and relieve their loved ones of burdens. However, when someone, by our standards, has sufficient reasons to find satis-faction in life, we are apt to label his or her wishes as abnormal, irrational, self-ish, or transient symptoms of depression.

> *The Sea Inside,* a 2004 Spanish film, told the story of Ramon Sampedro, who had become a complete quadriplegic at about the age of 20. For the following 26 years, because his condition prevented him from taking his own life, he fought through the courts for the right to have someone legally assist his suicide. Al-though his physical condition presented tremendous difficulties, he had many reasons to enjoy living: He was not clinically depressed. He had an intelligent mind, the capacity to enjoy TV and reading, the ability to write with an instru-ment held in his mouth, a family who loved him and catered to his needs, and women who fell in love with him and wanted to marry him. Furthermore, he stayed in bed by his own choosing, because it was possible to use a chair to get around. He eventually found a woman who loved him, and who truly took into her heart his implied message: Someone who really loves me will respect that I am the best judge of what I want and will help me terminate this life that I do not want to live.

Therapists who do not grasp the existential hypothesis might view his death as the failure of the mental health system to successfully change his way of think-ing. Others realize that he made a lucid choice based on the meaning that he had created for life and death.

Death and Dying

The theme of death enters therapeutic discourse in many forms, besides the question of suicide. People need support when they are coping with the death of a loved one or when they are dealing with their own impending death. Fre-quently, near-death experiences, like a car accident, or exposure to major cata-strophes, like an earthquake or terrorist attack, can make people ponder the significance of their lives. For people who are young and in good health, con-templating the inevitability and unpredictability of death puts a spotlight on the choices they make and forces them to look at how those choices will affect the course of their lives. In HIV prevention programs for teens, one strategy is to in-crease their awareness of their vulnerability to dying from AIDS. When the pos-sibility of death becomes personal, they are more likely to change their current high-risk behaviors.

Some existentialists also believe that *death anxiety* is a force in people's lives, even though it is deeply repressed and there are many defenses erected against awareness of it. It shows up in dreams, activities in the pursuit of im-mortality, and submersion in groups and ideologies that overcome feelings of personal vulnerability.

Aloneness and Isolation

Therapeutic strategies that increase interpersonal skills and reduce social anxiety can help lonely and isolated people have more fulfilling social relationships. However, there is no way of eliminating basic existential isolation, which is a given of the human condition. The phrase "we are born alone and we die alone" reminds us that no matter how close we feel with our loved ones, there are limits to what we can share. Although deep empathic attunement helps bridge the gap between people, people are justified in reminding each other, "you don't know how I feel, you're not inside my skin." Fortunately, the full experience of our separateness is not just a source of unpleasant feelings; it also opens the door to many positive experiences such as the enjoyment of solitude, a sense of independence and self-support, and realistic expectations of other people. Relationships built on a denial of the basic separateness between people show many destructive patterns. People try to control others as if they were possessions, treat conflicting opinions as if a separate point of view were a dire threat, and live vicariously through the other person instead of pursuing their own goals.

When people do not experience themselves as strong and worthwhile enough to survive alone, they will make unreasonable demands, have excessive needs and fears, and be unable to truly appreciate their partners as separate humans who do not revolve around them. Although the feelings of merger and perfect harmony are part of the joy of falling in love, they eventually yield to discovery of each other as separate individuals with different needs, opinions, reactions, and sensitivities. Couples who maintain the illusion that they are two halves of one whole are unable to tolerate signs of separateness without attacking the other, learning to live dishonestly, or withdrawing from the relationship. Many people jump immediately into a new relationship following the termination of the prior relationship because it is unbearable to them to be alone.

WHEN IS THIS HYPOTHESIS A GOOD MATCH?

Because this hypothesis embraces many aspects of the human condition, it can be used as a lens with all clients, and serves as an invaluable counterweight to the tendency to rely too much on *DSM* diagnostic categories. It should definitely be considered for the following types of clients.

Anxiety and Constriction

When clients present with anxiety problems, consider the meaning of the anxiety in the context of their entire lives. For some clients, anxiety is a healthy accompaniment to their courageous approach to life in which they take risks, seek growth, and accept challenges. For others, anxiety accompanies a constricted life in which minor deviations from routine are threatening. Some clients do not present with anxiety, but instead show the limitations they have created to suppress anxiety in opting for security rather than growth: They are constricted and rigid, out of touch with their wants and feelings, resistant to change, avoidant of risks, and utterly lacking in spontaneity and creativity.

Crisis of Meaning

There are many milestones and transition points when the meaning systems of the past are overthrown: One such point is the classic midlife crisis; others include adolescence, leaving college and searching for a meaningful career, retirement, and old age. Sometimes the trigger to the search for meaning is a major loss, such as the death of a spouse or child, the loss of the dream for success in your chosen career, or illness or disability representing loss of your healthy self. Clients also need new meaning systems when the old ones fail them, as when they discover that others cannot truly share their pain, bad things happen to good people, or hard work does not guarantee success. Sometimes the search for meaning comes after a big success, such as achievement of a long awaited promotion, when the unexpected reaction, instead of joy, is the feeling of "Is that all there is?" The crisis of meaning, regardless of cause, is usually accompanied by painful emotional states, including disillusionment, emptiness, grief, and confusion.

Lack of Awareness of True Desires

Those people who have always looked outside themselves to find meaning, identity, and direction are unprepared for the challenge of finding their own inner truths. They present with some of these characteristics: ignorance of what they feel or wish, dependence on the approval of others, and expectations that the therapist will provide magic solutions. Others may be super-responsible, over-burdened, or perfectionistic people who have the project in life of making others happy or being the best at something. They live according to rules and decisions they made when they were young, and are out of touch with what will make them happy.

Depression and Dysphoria

Emotional suffering can serve as a signal that the individual needs to address existential issues. Clients complain "life has no meaning," and describe how they feel empty, alone, and insignificant. A deep level of emotional pain usually follows major losses and catastrophes. The **ES1** hypothesis is a good match for depressed clients who seem to have enviable lives: financial success, nice homes, good careers, and the trappings of a happy family life.

Death and Dying

The **ES1** hypothesis is always relevant when death and dying are involved, including the following examples:

- Clients who raise the question of suicide, whether or not it is associated with depression.
- Aging clients who still have good health but who want to talk about fears of death.
- People with terminal illnesses facing their own deaths.
- People dealing with the impending deaths of loved ones.
- Those who are coping with deaths of others, which triggers their own concerns about mortality.

Intimacy and Isolation

A huge percentage of clients in therapy are there because of difficulties establishing healthy, lasting relationships. Here are examples of some of the problem titles for which the **ES1** hypothesis is a good match: *Unable to tolerate aloneness; failure to connect with others in a spontaneous, authentic, intimate way; difficulty tolerating the separateness of their partner (excessive jealousy, possessiveness, efforts to control).*

Growth, Fulfillment, and Actualization

The **ES1** hypothesis is the best match for clients who express the reasons for coming to therapy in the language of personal growth. Here are some examples of client complaints: "I'm bored with my job, which offers security and material rewards, but doesn't bring fulfillment"; "I'm not living up to my full potential"; "As a child I was very creative, but I lost that because I focused on grades and getting into the best possible college."

TREATMENT PLANNING

The therapist's stance is that the client already has the wisdom to find his or her own answers. The therapist's task is to facilitate the client's self-understanding, help remove obstacles to change and growth, shine a light on blind spots, and provide an authentic human encounter—but not to tell the client how to live. The therapist shows clients how to access inner sources of wisdom and overcome the tendency to devalue their own experiences. Although the therapist probably *does* have wisdom about how to live an authentic life, he or she knows that lecturing will undermine rather than enhance the client's personal quest. Moreover, the therapist definitely does *not* have wisdom about what would be an authentic life for the client. To say that the wisdom comes from within the client does not mean that the client is always right or that the therapist must withhold reactions and opinions and walk on eggshells. However, in offering a personal point of view, the therapist "owns" it as an opinion, not an absolute truth, and seeks a dialogue between equals rather than a position of authority.

The Role of the Therapist

Therapists who apply the existential hypothesis behave very differently from therapists who use CBT or psychodynamic approaches.

Phenomenological Approach

The therapist keeps the focus on the client's subjective point of view. The therapist puts aside preconceptions and strives to grasp the client's internal frame of reference. In offering verbal statements of understanding (empathy), the therapist knows that the client is the sole judge of the accuracy of these words.

Authentic Encounter

The therapist-client relationship is viewed as the medium for growth, a point that is often emphasized by the expression, *the relationship heals.* The "encounter" provides an opportunity to experience an authentic relationship and to overcome blocks to that kind of contact. The quality of *presence* is essential: Thus, the therapist must be fully attentive and attuned, be in contact with the client in the present moment, be open and vulnerable enough to be impacted by the client, and have emotional reactions. The therapist conveys to the client "I am here for you" and is experienced by the client as an authentic, genuine human being, not a detached expert hiding behind a professional role. Sheldon Kopp (1976) used these words:

> The therapist can interpret, advise, provide the emotional acceptance and support that nurtures personal growth, and above all, he can listen. I do not mean that he can simply hear the other, but that he will listen actively and purposefully, responding with the instrument of his trade, that is, with the personal vulnerability of his own trembling self. (p. 5)

The experience of this kind of relationship gives the client the sense of being genuinely cared for and valued.

Fellow Pilgrim

You are a companion on a journey. You have personally struggled with these issues and are willing to self-disclose, when it is appropriate to advance the client's self-discovery. Your goal in self-disclosing is not to give answers, and you must resist the pressure from some clients to be their guru and tell them what to do. You do not have an agenda to change the client in any specific direction, a point that Kopp (1976) made in describing his stance with a client:

> I let her know in many ways that I didn't care at all whether she stayed on with the government to make a great success of the project she was running, or if instead she chose to run off to the mischievously mindless fun of being a go-go dancer. My only interest was in helping her to find some happiness that would be just for herself, regardless of whether or not her friends and family were pleased or upset by how she ran her life. (pp. 82–83)

The client will use a position of powerlessness to put the therapist in the role of rescuer. For instance, when the client complains about getting nowhere, therapists often try harder to help when, instead, they need to redirect the power back to the client.

Accepting "No Change" as a Positive Outcome

The impetus for change must come from the client, not from the therapist. The therapist must notice when most of the energy comes from you, while the client seems very complacent, and realize you must reverse that imbalance. Remember that you are available to provide help, but should have no personal need to see the client change. It is often very helpful for therapists to try a "reverse format" and suggest that they see no particular reason why the client needs to change at all. Although often used as a paradoxical intervention, where the therapist really wants the client to change but attempts to outmaneuver the client's rebellious tendencies, a reverse format is also a very sincere stance of a therapist who really believes that the client must create her own meaning. When a client affirms a desire to keep things the same instead of striving for something different, it cannot be called "no change": A huge change has occurred. Instead of feeling like Sisyphus, forced to push the rock, she is now freely choosing her current project and may move from dissatisfaction to a more positive emotional and motivational state.

Using the Here and Now

The therapist seeks opportunities to explore the ways in which the client's problem manifests itself in the therapist-client relationship. A focus on process, rather than on content, will often yield the most powerful benefits.

Tolerating Negative Feelings

The therapist avoids the natural human tendency to rush in and try to make the client feel better. As discussed previously, the therapist sees the importance of deep emotional experience and fully exploring the messages that negative feelings bring.

Variety of Strategies

The therapist must not apply techniques from a formula or a manual, but must interact in a genuine way, permitting spontaneity and even normal human fallibility.

Philosophical Discussion

When the focus of therapy is the client's search for meaning, the dialogue between therapist and client can take the form of philosophical discussion—about both abstract theory and the client's specific philosophy of life. Sheldon Kopp (1976) challenged clients to examine some of the assumptions about life that they developed in childhood and proposed a set of his own philosophical truths, which include the following:

- Nothing lasts.
- There is no way of getting all you want.
- The world is not necessarily just.
- You don't really control anything.
- You can't make anyone love you.

Viktor Frankl's *Logotherapy* offers to the client three ways of satisfying the search for meaning:

1. Creating a work or doing a deed (e.g., achievement and accomplishment)
2. Experiencing a value such as goodness, truth, beauty, or love
3. Finding meaning in unavoidable suffering

A recent development in psychology is the career of "philosophical counselor." These counselors—who have an organization, American Society of Philosophy, Counseling, and Psychotherapy (ASPCP), and are part of APA's Division 24, Theoretical and Philosophical Psychology—do not describe what they do as therapy and do not view themselves as eligible for third-party payments in the health care system.

Persuasion and Teaching

Although therapists do not provide the meaning nor pick the path for the client, they *do* take an active role in convincing the client that he or she must create meaning, make choices, and take responsibility. Yalom (1990) expressed the following thoughts when his client explained why she wasn't making friends during a temporary job transfer:

> The problem with that attitude is you end up with an unpeopled life. Maybe that's part of the reason you feel empty inside. One way or another, every relationship must end. There's no such thing as a lifetime guarantee. It's like refusing to enjoy watching the sun rise because you hate to see it set. (p. 100)

Confrontation

Because this term has negative connotations of hostility or attack, the term *challenge* is often substituted. The therapist presents the client with data that expose contradictions and illuminate blind spots. For instance, the therapist can point out a contradiction between what the client says and what she expresses nonverbally or through her actions.

Honest Feedback

Sometimes confrontation takes the form of therapist self-disclosure. The therapist shares genuine reactions to the client in the here and now. This honest feedback, if negative, can be worded in ways that are constructive and not rejecting.

Yalom (1990) gives an example of how he dealt with a client whom he found very boring. He decided that he had to be precise about the behaviors that bothered him, so he explained to her "that I wanted to get closer to her but that her behavioral trait got in the way" (p. 95). Then he asked the client's permission to give instantaneous feedback and to interrupt to point out the behavior the moment it occurred. Feedback can also be positive. Many months later in therapy, Yalom told the client: "You are so much more available for love now than you were a few months ago. I can see, I can feel the difference. You look better, you relate better, you are so much more approachable and available now" (p. 112).

Giving Voice to Buried Feelings

Rollo May (1995) describes how his client was unable to experience or express anger, and he felt that it was essential for her to express her rage. He trusted his instincts, and, going against everything that analysts are taught, decided to express his own rage toward the people who had victimized his client. He explained, "I was giving vent to the rage the girl had never dared express herself. I was allying myself with that faint autonomous element which we must assume is in every human being, although in Mercedes it was practically nonexistent to begin with" (p. 141).

Experiential Therapy Techniques

There are many techniques that help the client tune into his or her own experience. The therapist might invite the client to notice a particular body movement or to exaggerate a gesture or facial expression. Therapists frequently direct an activity such as Gestalt therapy's empty chair exercise or Eugene Gendlin's (1982) *focusing* method.

INTEGRATION OF HYPOTHESES

The three hypotheses in the Existential and Spiritual category easily blend and overlap. The issues of freedom, responsibility, and commitment, addressed in **ES2,** are usually part of an exploration of the search for meaning, self-actualization, and connection. Meaning for many people is found in the spiritual realm (**ES3**), through connection to a higher power, adherence to a code of moral values, or participation in a faith community.

CS3 Developmental Transition

At each transition point in the life span, people inevitably find that there is a disruption in the system of meaning on which they were relying. For instance, at the "empty nest" stage, a woman no longer finds meaning in focusing on the needs of minor children, hopes for a new path that will bring satisfaction, and may suffer from feeling separate and alone.

CS4 Loss and Bereavement

Losses are associated with many of the existential issues addressed in **ES1:** suffering that is unfair and undeserved, the need to find meaning in life after the loss, and awareness of our aloneness in the universe.

C1 Utopian Expectations

This hypothesis addresses a philosophical question: What are realistic expectations for life? How do you distinguish between the average frustrations and distress of being human and a level of suffering that constitutes a reason for therapy?

C2 Faulty Cognitive Map

This hypothesis integrates seamlessly with **ES1:** The exploration of a personal philosophy is part of examining the client's existing map of the world and the search for meaning involves creating a new map.

SCE2 Cultural Context

Complaints of meaninglessness must always be understood in their cultural context as each culture offers different values (e.g., community versus individualism) and views on issues such as aging, material success, the status of unmarried women, and the importance of leisure. The *content* of existentialism—the specific set of beliefs and values—originated in Western Europe. The *process* of searching for meaning in times of crisis, dealing with suffering, and exploring one's connection to other humans is universal.

SCE5 Social Problem Is a Cause

If the form of government is oppressive or if there is discrimination, it is important that these external factors be addressed. Philosophical discussion and a focus on personal meaning can distract a client from involving herself in social action. Activism for social change, as with the feminist and gay rights movements, is a path for not only changing society but also creating new meaning systems.

SCE4 Social Role Performance

Social roles provide preestablished meaning systems and structures that make their occupants feel very embedded in a social system. As people transfer from one role to another, existential issues may arise surrounding meaning and isolation. For instance, when a worker in a factory is promoted to a supervisory position, the meaning of being rank-and-file conflicts with the meaning of being part of management, and if he finds himself excluded from social activities, interpersonal and existential forms of aloneness intermingle.

ES2 AVOIDING FREEDOM AND RESPONSIBILITY

Definition

The client is **Avoiding** the **Freedom** and autonomy that come with adulthood and/or does not accept **Responsibility** for present and past choices.

Explanation

Clients need help in making good choices to move toward positive goals and make commitments. They need to distinguish between limitations that are real and those that are self-imposed. Some people deny responsibility for past actions and others blame themselves for events for which they were not responsible. The avoidance of freedom takes many forms: maintenance of childhood illusions, blaming others, and depending on others to provide rescue. When clients are ready to take responsible action, they may need help in values clarification, decision making, planning, and implementation of plans.

Examples

Larry is living in the past, lamenting "If only I had finished college everything would have been different." He wallows in self-pity, feels hopeless, and has no future orientation. He spoils his friendships with his envy of his friends' professional and material success. Instead of recognizing their hard work and perseverance, he thinks, "it's unfair that they have been so lucky."	Julie is an attractive woman who "falls in love easily" but, she admits, is "afraid of making a commitment." She has repeatedly broken off engagements as the wedding day approaches. She claims that she is "terrified of growing up" and is tormented about "giving up my freedom." She sees her friends enjoy marriage, but wonders, "How did they know that someone better wouldn't come along?"	James, a 58-year-old successful corporate executive, has lost interest in his job. He has all the money he needs and could afford to retire, but he admits he has no interests or hobbies and has no idea how he would spend his time. Besides, he says, "people in my family have always worked until the age of 65." His wife is discovering new friends and activities, while he is just feeling bored and empty.

KEY IDEAS FOR ES2 AVOIDING FREEDOM AND RESPONSIBILITY

Therapists frequently face clients who feel trapped, immobilized, powerless, and out of control of their own lives. Although an outside observer thinks that they could easily make new choices to create a happier life, they do not experience themselves as free: These people seem, stubbornly, to resist awareness of their freedom, often to the frustration of exhausted friends who have tried to give them wise advice or a helpful kick in the pants. At other times, clients are convinced that they have unlimited possibilities and that the limitations that constrain others do not apply to them. They act impulsively, letting chips fall where they may, and move from one path to another without ever making successful, lasting commitments. Therapists must understand the concepts "freedom" and "limitations" and be able to help clients examine these two domains of their lives. The book *How People Change* (Wheelis, 1975) illuminates these complex issues.

Freedom and Limitations

The domain of freedom is not absolute. Forces outside us determine many actions and events. We are faced with *limitations, constraints,* and *necessity* and must make the best of what has been *given* or *imposed.* Each person has a subjective view about which areas of his or her life have the potential for free choice, in contrast to areas in which there are no possibilities, no freedom, and no room for choice. Alcoholics Anonymous and other Twelve Step programs have a prayer that helps members understand that they need courage to change the things that they can change and serenity to accept what they cannot. The most important thing to seek is the *wisdom to know the difference* between those two categories. Without that wisdom, people are at risk for two kinds of errors: (1) the illusion of freedom, when there are objective constraints, which leads to efforts to change things over which we have no control; and (2) the illusion of limitations, when they don't exist in reality, which leads to passivity in areas in which change is possible.

Therapists can help their clients to categorize their limitations as either reality-based or self-imposed.

Reality-Based Limitations

Reality-based limitations including geography, natural laws, and the will of another person, cannot be changed by choice, will, or effort. Facing such limitations means accepting the lack of possibilities and alternatives, and reconciling yourself to a narrower range of freedom than you would hope for, but, at the same time, it relieves you of the frustration of repeated unsuccessful efforts. Sometimes these limitations seem so overwhelming that there appears to be no space for free choice. However, Viktor Frankl (1997), a concentration camp survivor, reminds us that there is always room for freedom: "Everything can be taken from a man but one thing: the last of the human freedoms—to choose one's attitude in any given set of circumstances, to choose one's own way" (p. 86). The judgment that a limitation exists in reality will vary in different places and times in history. For instance, we generally conclude that our genetic makeup is a "given" of our condition. However, nowadays there are surgeries that make the consequences of genes, if not the genes themselves, fall within the domain of freedom. Progress in gene therapy will definitely affect the view of an unchangeable limitation.

Self-Imposed Limitations

Self-imposed limitations can be changed by the exercise of choice, will, and effort, but the person sees himself as yielding to some external necessity, and experiences the situation as one in which he has no choice. If you correctly identify the illusory nature of this type of limitation, you will expand the range of possibilities in your life. An example of an internal constraint, which can be suspended or disobeyed, is the statement, "I can't quit college and earn my living as a carpenter." It would be more accurate for the person to say, "I choose not to quit college because I'm not willing to endure the anxiety of taking a risk in life, and I'm afraid of my mother's displeasure." Another self-imposed limitation is using our childhood or physical disability as a reason to remain unhappy, instead of making positive choices from the alternatives available in the present. A metaphor of self-imposed limitations is the picture of someone in a prison cell, looking out the barred windows, wishing for freedom, and never noticing that the door to the cell is wide open.

An objective appraisal of the nature of limitations in an individual's life cannot produce a valid prediction of the amount of freedom a person will use. Someone who is behind bars but lets his mind travel freely has more real freedom than the guard who follows orders and never brings a higher human capacity to the moral issues of using freedom well.

Anxiety and Dread

You might think that a new awareness of freedom would bring optimism, exhilaration, and a sense of empowerment but, instead, it often triggers the pain of being "condemned to freedom"—on a lonely journey without a guide, landmarks, or road maps. Two interpretations of freedom were described by Erich Fromm in *Escape from Freedom* (1941): (1) the ability to develop individual potentialities and to live actively and spontaneously; and (2) a frightened, alienated state that makes people eager to submerge their individuality in something bigger than themselves, such as religious extremism or fanatical patriotism. Yalom (1980) makes the point that the dread of either freedom or limitation promotes extreme counter reactions to that dread. Dread of limits can lead to grandiose overextension of resources, whereas dread of freedom can result in a constricted life, with excessive structure and rituals, making each day exactly like the last.

Preconditions for Effective Exercise of Freedom

Free choice does not refer to emitting automatic, impulsive behaviors, but requires a set of preconditions. In his book *How People Change,* Wheelis (1975) writes:

> Nothing guarantees freedom. It may never be achieved, or having been achieved may be lost. Alternatives go unnoticed; foreseeable consequences are not foreseen; we may not know what we have been, what we are, or what we are becoming. . . . Freedom is . . . contingent upon consciousness, and so may be gained or lost, extended or diminished. (pp. 14–15)

Available Alternatives

Freedom remains a philosophical abstraction unless it becomes manifest, concretely, in a form that can be utilized. Without viable alternatives, there is no opportunity for choice. It is not enough that alternatives exist—the person must be aware of them. Wheelis (1975) describes an ant who is suffering in a concrete parking lot. If it knew that a certain car was about to drive to the country, it could jump on its wheel and soon be enjoying a wonderful picnic in a grassy paradise. However, without awareness of that alternative, the ant has no freedom to choose. One of the primary goals of therapy is to help clients discover and evaluate alternatives.

Ability to Contemplate Consequences

To choose wisely among alternatives, it is necessary to be able to imagine the probable and the possible consequences of each alternative. This condition requires a reasonable amount of time and life experience. Because it is impossible to predict the future, we need to accept that all major choices will be made with insufficient information and require, to some degree, a leap into the unknown.

Capacity to Postpone Action

If a person lacks the capacity to postpone an action, the choice cannot be considered free, even if he or she feels subjectively free at the time. Rather than freely chosen, the action is considered impulsive or is attributed to what the legal system calls an irresistible impulse. In using terms like *delay of gratification* and *frustration tolerance,* we address an individual's capacity to forego current pleasure and to endure unpleasant emotions, because of the prediction that present sacrifice will be rewarded by long-term positive consequences of alternative choices. When an action is involuntary and automatic, the causation is attributed to external factors or the givens of biology rather than free choice.

Choices Stem from Our True Desire

Choices would not be considered free and voluntary if they were coerced. What makes this condition more complicated than the others is that humans have the capacity to deceive themselves into believing that they have freely chosen a path, when they are operating from past conditioning, based on rewards and punishments from parents, or from beliefs and values that were accepted from authorities and never critically examined. For instance, a "workaholic" believes that he freely chooses to place work above other activities in life, although his choices were shaped by the fact that working hard and getting academic awards was compensation for being rejected by his peers. A "college dropout" believes that her choice was motivated by love of freedom and might not recognize that her dislike of school flowed directly from her parents' messages that she was not as smart as her siblings.

Structure and Self-Discipline

Although too much structure prevents the exercise of freedom, too little structure interferes with the ability to make choices that lead to highly valued future benefits—such as a loving marriage, productive work, and financial security in retirement. The meaning of freedom in adulthood is different from the adolescent view that *freedom means I can do whatever I want.* People who work out of home offices discover that unless they create a structure—a schedule for their day and a place dedicated to their work tasks—they feel overwhelmed and out of control. Retired people find that if they give themselves the freedom to stay at home all day in their nightclothes, they end up less satisfied with their lives than if they create a schedule to attend enjoyable activities. Houses that are full of clutter and disorder make people feel burdened and restricted, instead of free. Freedom does not mean the absence of rules; people who refuse to follow rules as a general principle create tremendous limits to their freedom to succeed at school, find good jobs, experience the benefits of marital fidelity—not to mention drive safely without traffic tickets or accidents waiting at every turn.

Skills and Resources

It is not easy to embrace freedom: We need not only awareness and courage, but also specific resources and skills, depending on the goals and available alternatives. Imagine someone who has been given a large plot of land but who lacks tools, seeds, and water. How free is he to be a farmer? How free are you to enjoy a can of soup on your camping trip, if you forgot to bring a can opener? It is very frustrating for people to have others preach that they should use their freedom, and be accused of being resistant or manipulative, when they are highly motivated to achieve their goals, but need help in acquiring information, skills, and other resources.

Maturity

From the prior list, it is clear that young children are not capable of free choice. First, they need help in identifying their own true feelings and desires. Second, they need to develop the mental capacity to anticipate consequences and delay gratification. Third, they need to have practice in making choices and experiencing the consequences that flow from their choices to develop competencies. In addition, until a person attains the legal age that marks her emancipation from her parents, freedom is limited by the legitimate power of guardians. Many people pass that age without having developed the attitudes and skills that are needed to use freedom effectively. In fact, many never attain the requisite maturity: Despite their chronological age, they function at the same level as very young children. The authority of their parents lives on in their minds, frequently continuing after their parents' death.

Evasion of Freedom

Often people are ignorant of the fact that constraints to their freedom are self-imposed. One important task of a therapist is to educate clients that many of the limitations they believe are real are, in fact, products of their own creation. Many people reorient their perspective on freedom and limitations when their errors are explained; others will go to extremes of illogic and stubbornness to continue to deny their freedom. Following are eight examples of ways in which people evade freedom.

I Need a Guarantee

In contrast to people who act without thinking about consequences, there are those who are reluctant to act unless they achieve 100% certainty that their choice will have a successful outcome. Their illusions that the future can be predicted with certainty and that they can obtain some kind of guarantee are huge barriers to using freedom, and often are clever disguises for the underlying fear of taking a risk.

This Is My Nature

A great deal of existential literature addresses the difference between the fixed essence of a nonhuman object and the dynamic existence of a human who is in an ever-unfolding process of becoming and changing. People deny their freedom when they fix a label on themselves and use the excuse that they can't be any different because this is their true nature.

> A 95-year-old woman with many physical disabilities but a clear, sharp mind, was losing vision in one eye from a cataract, a condition that was limiting one of the few remaining pleasures in her life, reading. Her daughter, with whom she lived, offered every possible logical argument to persuade her to have surgery, as did her physician and social worker. When she was asked why she refused, her answer was, "I'm a stubborn person. I never change my mind once I've made it up."

Parents contribute to the labeling process when they use language in a way that defines their child's essence: "My daughter is shy" instead of "She prefers to read in her room rather than mingle with guests." Mental health professionals also use labels in a way that diminishes the client's awareness of freedom of choice. Terms such as *agoraphobic, antisocial personality* or *bulimic* imply that the person has a disorder and cannot wake up the next morning and choose to be different. Naturally, there is a self-fulfilling prophecy that operates when people believe that a human's nature is fixed. Existentialists often disapprove of theories that use the concept of *self* as if there were a preexisting "true self" waiting to be discovered. Instead, they believe in an ongoing process of freely developing and creating one's self.

I Can't or I Couldn't

The person constricts the realm of possibility and avoids the anxiety associated with risk. "I can't help it" allows the person to deny having made a choice, while claiming to have good intentions. The words "I would if I could" is often a form of deception—to both the self and the other person. It is more honest and courageous to admit free choice and say, "I don't want to" or "I refuse to," thus risking negative consequences or earning respect from others. Many children learn that it is safer to plead stupidity and disability than to assert their will and risk a punishment. People are often very skilled at denying choices they have made: "I would have called you to tell you that I was going to be late, but my cell phone battery was dead" is a statement that ignores the choice not to borrow a phone or use a pay phone. Before rushing to judgment that "can't" is a copout, as Perls would have called it, it is important to explore the person's thought processes and ask about the perceived obstacles, in case it is a lack of awareness, skills, or resources.

I Don't Want To

If a person really does not want to do something, and does not do it, she exercises freedom of choice. However, the illusion of free choice is sometimes expressed as "I could do it if I wanted, but I don't want to" when the person has never viewed the rejected alternative as a legitimate possibility nor sampled it to see if it brought satisfaction. Often, the words "I don't want to" translate as "I'm afraid to."

I Have to or Had To

"I have to" or "I must"—along with phrases like "I shouldn't" and "I ought not"—create necessity where there could be freedom. The limitation is viewed as external and mandatory. A person who experiences himself as free would say, "I choose to do this because I have created this moral code for myself," or "I have evaluated the probable consequences of doing it, and I choose to take that risk."

You Can Do It for Me

People evade freedom by handing the power over to someone else. Often they don't experience this as a conscious manipulation: Their subjective perspective is that they are weak, helpless, incompetent, or entitled and that they need the other person to serve functions for them. Therapists can end up in the role of rescuer when people "play stupid" or "play helpless" to deny their own competence and get another person to provide answers and make decisions.

Habits

What once was a choice gets repeated over and over again until we do it on automatic pilot. Then it feels as if that is the only way we can be. We view it as our character. We always do things the same way, buy the same kinds of clothes, go to the same two or three restaurants, and travel to the same vacation spot. We also have habits of awareness, attending to certain aspects of experience and ignoring others. For instance, a person listens to every thought in his head but completely tunes out the information coming from bodily sensations and emotional reactions. A person attends to what others want and has no clue about her own needs and preferences. Another person is finely attuned to his own feelings but does not attend to the other person's words and reactions. People who exercise freedom understand that breaking old habits and forming new habits can be extremely difficult, but it is possible and under their control.

Conformity and Obedience

A certain degree of opposition to social norms is necessary for people to freely develop their unique potential and choose the path that has heart for them. Doing what is expected, being a good child, and being part of the crowd are paths that allow one to safely avoid a sense of freedom. People also look to a group larger than themselves—teenagers look to their peer group—to decide what is fashionable and appropriate. Choices are based on what everyone else is doing, and possibilities are ignored if they bring ridicule or shame. Acceptance and approval from others become more important than discovering your own needs, talents, and desires. Ways in which people submerge their individuality in larger groups are apparent in religious extremism, fanatical patriotism, teenage gangs, and exclusive ethnic and cultural communities. Becker, in his book *The Denial of Death* (1973), explained how people seek a sense of enduring, absolute truth through such *immortality systems* as religious groups, political philosophies, or cultural activities. Because they need to hold on to the righteous feeling that they have found absolute truth, they tend to be aggressively intolerant of people who have different truths. A component of real freedom is having an open mind to let new and disturbing ideas enter for your own independent evaluation, rather than having a rigid mental gatekeeper to screen out anything that does not fit what you already have decided to believe.

Responsibility

It is not enough for us to mobilize a sense of freedom in clients: We need to help them use their freedom in ways that make positive changes in their lives, without causing harm to others. Freedom and responsibility go hand and hand. *You are free to do whatever you want, but you are responsible for the consequences of everything that you do.* Responsibility is a complex topic with many definitions and applications, which students of law or philosophy struggle to grasp. It is not an all-or-nothing concept: We need to analyze every human situation on a case-by-case basis to apply it wisely.

Identifying the Cause or Creator of Actions and Consequences

Responsibility is sometimes equivalent to accountability. When there are consequences, good or bad, for choices made in the past, who should appropriately receive the praise or blame, rewards or punishment, forgiveness or moral judgment? If the present suffering of an individual is a direct consequence of her own past choices, the sufferer bears at least some responsibility for her own pain. Sometimes no one is responsible because it was not under human control—when a car accident is caused by weather or a well-maintained airplane develops a malfunction. Figuring out causation is complicated because there are usually multiple causes for a single event and often responsibility needs to be apportioned among several individuals. In some situations, a person is responsible for the behavior of someone else. For example, if a child breaks a window, the parents are obligated to pay for it. Likewise, if one is a member of a criminal conspiracy, he is punishable for the crime that was physically committed by a fellow conspirator.

Legal Concepts of Responsibility

There are many circumstances under which people are not held fully responsible for acts they commit: Legal terms like *diminished capacity, insanity,* and *duress* are used for reduced responsibility. People cannot control impulses because of brain damage. They are unable to distinguish between right and wrong because of severe mental retardation. Or they are coerced by someone else who held them at gunpoint. When the consequences of an action could not have reasonably been predicted, it is unreasonable to assign responsibility; it is fair to use terms like *accident* or *misadventure*. Alternatively, when the consequences of an action were foreseeable, to a reasonable person, and steps could have been taken to prevent harm, the term *negligence* is appropriate, and courts award damages—compensatory as well as punitive—to the person who suffered harm.

Clarifying Duties and Obligations in a Specific Situation

Without agreement about expectations, rules, moral codes, ethical principles, and social customs, we have conflicts when we say such things as "it's your responsibility," or "you were responsible, but you failed to do it," or "you are assuming responsibility that isn't yours." Duties and obligations can be determined in three ways: (1) free negotiation by equal parties, (2) the power of an authority, like a parent or teacher, or (3) the mores of a particular culture. In close relationships, it is natural for someone to feel disappointment when someone does not live up to our expectations. Frequently, people turn their often unspoken expectations into obligations that should be binding on the other person, even when that person did not sign up for them. The phrase "laying a guilt trip" is a colloquial expression for this process of first, imposing one's own wishes as a responsibility, and then trying to manipulate guilty feelings that, it is hoped, will lead to behavior that fulfills the wish.

Ways of Avoiding Responsibility

People are as clever about disclaiming responsibility as they are about escaping freedom. Blaming others, such as parents, past lovers, and coworkers, or claiming incompetence or powerlessness are convenient tactics to evade responsibility: "I was following orders." "He made me do it." "I couldn't help myself." Instead of taking ownership of one's own thoughts, feelings, and intentions, the cause is viewed as external, as when the person says, "He makes me feel (a certain way)"; "The idea came to me"; or "I did it because everyone else was." Mental health concepts and diagnoses can help people evade responsibility: "I do that because of my addiction, my dysfunctional family, my personality disorder." "My *fear of commitment* keeps me from moving our relationship to the next stage." "I don't have the *willpower:* It's not that I'm freely choosing to eat that piece of cake, it's that I can't control myself—and therefore should not be held responsible for being overweight." Symptoms and disorders can be described as entities that visit us and take over control, rather than as expressions of our own free choice: "It's not really me who is doing this, it's my compulsion. I have depression" is a way of disavowing that *I depress myself.*

Evaluating the Appropriateness of Guilt Feelings

Evaluation of guilt feelings—as excessive, insufficient, or appropriate—depends on the person's degree of responsibility for an action and the severity of the harm done. Guilt is the appropriate emotion when we realize that we have violated our own code of behavior, especially when harm has been done to others.

Therapists may be predisposed to think of guilt as a negative emotion that should be reduced rather than one that should be heeded. When we are clear about when guilt is appropriate, we will recognize three problematic conditions in clients:

1. *Inappropriate guilt:* The client suffers from undeserved guilt and self-blame, when the bad thing that happened was not the client's fault, or when the necessary thing that did not happen was not her responsibility.
2. *Excessive guilt:* The client bears all or some responsibility for a bad thing, but even after taking proper steps to atone and make amends, the guilt is preserved as a form of self-torture.
3. *Lack of guilt:* Bad things that happened were the client's fault and/or omissions of necessary behaviors were her responsibility, but she feels no guilt, contrition, or remorse.

Self-Blame

While it is appropriate to blame yourself for actions that cause harm, the next steps should be making amends, reparations, or restitution; seeking forgiveness and reconciliation; and committing to better behavior in the future. If a person assigns self-blame, sinks into depression, labels herself as bad, takes no actions to repair the situation, and continues to repeat the harmful act, the self-blame can be viewed as an avoidance of responsibility.

The Concept of Victim

The term *victim* is appropriately used when someone suffers from events or actions for which he or she does not bear responsibility. A child is a victim of physical, emotional, or sexual abuse inflicted by an adult: It was 100% the responsibility of the adult not to harm the child. If my car skids in the rain when I was driving a safe speed, I was the victim of an accident. If a person is not hired for a job because of the color of her skin, then she is a victim of racial discrimination. There are two errors in applying the concept of victim: (1) blaming yourself when you actually are an innocent victim, as when you are a victim of rape; and (2) presenting yourself to others in the role of victim when you bear responsibility for choices that contributed to your suffering or for failure to make choices to reduce your suffering. Victimhood, like responsibility, is not all or nothing. When a person is victimized while under the influence of alcohol, the decision to imbibe alcohol and put himself in a risky situation falls in the domain of his responsibility; the responsibility of the perpetrator, however, is not diminished by the victim's alcohol-induced impairments.

While the term *victim* is appropriately applied to children, it is questionable how well it fits adults who are now emancipated and free to make their own choices. Some adults continue using their status as a victim as a causal explanation for their current difficulties, without taking responsibility for needed changes in their lives. The belief that having been a victim in the past prevents positive actions in the present and destroys hope for happiness in the future, can be challenged by the fact that many people with horrendous stories of cruel mistreatment in childhood have managed to become successful, optimistic, and thriving adults.

Commitment

When you make a commitment, you freely decide to limit your own freedom. You turn your back on available possibilities. The capacity to make a major life commitment comes with knowledge of your own needs, talents, limitations, and values; experimentation with different temporary paths; and a realistic, nonutopian appraisal of what life has to offer. You agree to accept minor negative consequences because they are outweighed by the benefits that come from choosing a certain path. However, if, at a future time, you discover that prolonged pain and misery have replaced the benefits you anticipated, you are free to make new choices. Making a commitment sets limits on freedom but does not destroy it.

Clients bring problems at two extremes: (1) the inability to make and keep a commitment (often labeled "irresponsibility" by others), and (2) the inability to terminate an old commitment based on an updated cost-benefit analysis. People who avoid commitment sometimes fit the Jungian archetype of *puer aeturnus* (*puella* for females), meaning "eternal youth." They hold on to these attitudes: "I want it all—I want to have my cake and eat it too; I want to keep all my options open." Sometimes they have fears that have never been concretely identified, so it is important to ask questions like, *What are the consequences that you are afraid of? What will you be losing?* and *How will your life be 10 years from now if you never make this kind of commitment?* People who easily and frequently break commitments often have unrealistic expectations, imagining that life can be free of problems, stress, and negative emotions, or that another person can be free of flaws, perfectly attentive and devoted, and never grow older, fatter, or less sexually desirable. There are also many signs of childlike thinking in people who refuse to quit something that has not yielded success: "If I want it enough, it's got to work out." "I've got to show *them* that I'm not a quitter." "If I fail at this, I'm worthless and I'll never be happy." "I am afraid that without this I have nothing." In Los Angeles, many unhappy restaurant servers are committed to making it in the movie business and refuse to explore a different career possibility. There needs to be a middle road between never making a commitment because your desires seem to change constantly and making a commitment that is so set in concrete that you sacrifice future freedom.

WHEN IS THIS HYPOTHESIS A GOOD MATCH?

The **ES2** hypothesis (**Avoiding Freedom and Responsibility**) provides a useful lens for understanding a wide variety of clients. Many therapists use it without ever articulating the philosophical bases of freedom and responsibility as they guide their clients through a process of identifying their wants, evaluating their current behavior, clarifying alternatives, making choices, mustering their will, creating plans, and engaging in productive action.

Table 7.2 lists descriptions of clients who would benefit from application of this hypothesis: The first set of examples gives specific problem titles, whereas the second set provides illustrations of client's thinking and behavior.

TREATMENT PLANNING

When the goal of therapy is to enhance the client's autonomy, freedom, and sense of responsibility, the therapist has to be careful to maintain equality in the relationship and avoid attitudes that undermine the client's independence and competence. Self-disclosure is often useful, not only for the content, but for the process of making yourself an equal rather than an all-knowing expert.

Some clients are determined to find an authority who will tell them what to do and will find opportunities to interpret neutral comments as advice. The therapist needs to avoid slipping into the role of a nagging parent with clients who are not ready to make changes. The therapist may find opportunities to use the relationship between client and therapist to illustrate how the client avoids responsibility for change and hopes for someone to function as a rescuer.

Stages of Autonomous Decision Making

The process of autonomous decision making can be conceptualized into these stages:

Identify Wants → Evaluate Behavior → Choose → Will → Plan → Act → Evaluate

The process for a specific client can be easy or complicated. The best-case scenario is a motivated client who wants change, has expectations of success, is willing to expend effort and practice self-discipline, and has basic tools and competencies for achieving the goals. When there are blocks to the smooth unfolding of this process, the therapist needs to make an assessment and choose appropriate strategies, frequently integrating other hypotheses. Sometimes a client will need help at every stage. Other times, the therapy plan will focus on only a piece of the process. For instance, a client might be quite clear about what she wants and chooses, know exactly which plan is best, but feel incapable of developing the will and determination to persist and turn wishes into action. Another client might be stuck in a quagmire of confusion and ambivalence about what she feels and wants, but once there is clarity about the desired goal, the implementation of appropriate action is effortless. The following outline suggests the therapeutic issues for each stage. Understanding the issues leads to clearly stated process goals to guide selection of specific techniques, as shown in the following steps.

Table 7.2 Applying the ES2 Avoiding Freedom and Responsibility Hypothesis

PROBLEM TITLES

Struggling with making a choice:

Indecision about a job offer

Ambivalence over whether to make a marital commitment

Dilemma over choice of educational paths

Uncertainty over choosing timing of retirement

Stuck in an unhappy situation:

Victim of spousal abuse

Dissatisfaction with boring job

Feels incapable of living as an independent adult separate from parents

Difficulty setting realistic goals and developing constructive plans for future

Frustration with inability to behave in accordance with intentions (lack of self-control):

Difficulty adhering to weight loss plan

Excessive angry outbursts at children

Starts new sexual relationship despite intention to experience a period of celibacy

Inability to maintain sobriety

Engaging in behavior that brings negative consequences for self or others:

Engages in unprotected sex with multiple partners

Difficulty maintaining employment

At risk for flunking out of college because of poor grades

Exercises poor judgment in choice of partners

Emotional distress related to guilt, anxiety, or lack of confidence:

Anxiety over making major decisions

Inability to overcome guilt for past mistake

Excessive fear over taking risks and trying new experiences

ILLUSTRATIONS OF CLIENT'S THINKING AND BEHAVIOR

Self-imposed limitations (avoidance of freedom):

- Client believes that past misfortunes, such as inadequate parenting, permanently limit her possibilities for a happy future.
- Client is overly conforming and rule-ridden, talking in terms of "shoulds" and "can'ts" and doing exactly what her parents expected, despite being unhappy with some of these choices.

Failure to recognize real-world limits:

- Client describes grandiose fantasies for future projects without any realistic sense of the skills, resources, and self-discipline required to achieve these goals.
- Client persists in pursuing a career for which he lacks talent.
- Client copes poorly with the natural changes of aging and pursues surgeries in an attempt to pass for someone 20 years younger.

(continued)

Table 7.2   *(Continued)*

Avoidance of responsibility:

- Client's interpretation of painful experiences involves blaming others and taking the role of victim or martyr.
- Client reports guilt and shame over past behavior but does not take any action to make amends or to refrain from similar action in the present and future.
- Client refuses to accept obligations in life, insisting on doing whatever she wants, regardless of the consequences.

Lack of self-control and self-discipline:

- Client uses many words that show feelings of passivity and difficulty taking action toward goals: "I'm trying." "I'm working on it." "It's hopeless."
- Client states values and moral code, but then claims "I can't help it" for engaging in morally wrong behavior (e.g., having an affair).
- Client expects good things to come to him without needing to expend effort.

Identify Wants

Free choice requires awareness of your own desires, tastes, talents, interests, passions, and values. Sometimes people feel very vague and confused about what they want, because they have based all of their choices on the demands, desires, rules, and tastes of other people or on doing what's expected, being a good child, winning acceptance and approval, and being part of the crowd. Using the well-known methods of Carl Rogers (e.g., empathic restatements, a nonjudgmental acceptance of everything the client expresses, and a warm, caring presence) will facilitate the client's involvement in a process of self-discovery.

Evaluate Behavior

Reality therapy (Glasser, 1965) provides an important step: Focus on the client's current behaviors and actions and help the client evaluate her choices: *Is what you are doing getting you what you want? Does your behavior help you or hurt you?* She decides that her behavior needs to change not because a parental authority tells her so, but because she sees that she is defeating her own goals and is contributing to her own unhappiness. For instance, in trying to help an alcoholic give up drinking, it is important to have the client see how drinking behavior is wrong, not because others complain about it, but because it interferes with achievement of his valued goals. It is important that clients make the evaluation for themselves.

Choose

One possibility is that the client will choose to remain exactly the same. If the client is dissatisfied with the status quo, the choosing stage usually involves a process of exploring and weighing alternatives. The client may plead, "Tell me what to do," and the therapist can respond, *Let's look together at your alternatives.* It is important to generate a list of more than two alternatives. Egan (2002) recommends brainstorming a comprehensive list of possible alternatives, which includes ridiculous and humorous choices. The discussion of alternatives includes a cost-benefit analysis that incorporates values, priorities, and predictions of consequences to self and others. It can be very helpful to write down a chart to capture all the relevant information.

Sometimes the choice leads to a specific action plan such as "apply to med school," "take a yoga class," or "return to my home state." Other times, the client expresses the choice in vaguer terms such as "find a career that interests me," "take steps to become healthier," or "find a community where I feel a sense of connection." The therapist helps the client make goals more specific, making sure that they are realistic and under the client's control. Often there are multiple goals or competing goals. This is where the client needs help in resolving ambivalence or in setting priorities. The therapist shares hunches, confronts discrepancies and inconsistencies, and helps examine external pressures and real-world limitations. At this stage, the therapist identifies barriers to using freedom and taking responsibility.

Will

This is the most challenging of all the stages, and if there weren't so much pain involved, it would be humorous: How is it that a person cannot control her own arm? Yet, it is the arm that lifts the glass or the fork, and places it against the lips, even when it seems against the person's will. "I can't get myself to do what I intend to do" is the lament of people who have trouble implementing their positive choices. The client's commitment to work toward goals involves mobilization of a sense of power and optimism. "I choose that goal" evolves to "I *will* achieve that goal." The term *will* refers to an internal locus of choice and power. Think of the different meanings of *I may do it* and *I will do it.* The second phrase conveys an intention, a sense of purpose, and belief in your potency and competence. It is the bridge between thinking and behavior. The term *willpower,* not as common today as it was in prior generations, conveys that you are capable of conforming your behavior to your intentions. Without the capacity for self-control, the promise of *I will* is hollow. The term *commitment* fits here: You choose a specific course and renounce alternatives. The *stages of change* construct developed by Prochaska, Norcross, and DiClemente (1994) can be a useful framework. If the client is still at the *precontemplation* or *contemplation* phase, rather than an action phase, the therapist needs to help move the client to the *preparation* phase, instead of pushing prematurely for action. People who work in battered women's shelters are aware of how often clients change their minds before they muster the will to take action. The concept of *courage* is often relevant, when action involves feared consequences, and therapists therefore need to be aware of the need for *encouragement.*

Plan

If the only choices we make are those that can be implemented immediately, planning would be unnecessary. However, major decisions in life require commitment to a project for the future, which requires many stages, extended over a long stretch of time. For some clients, clarity about goals combined with an internal sense of purpose is sufficient, and they don't need the therapist's help any more. For others, a planning stage is necessary to move them toward action. Long-term goals may be broken into subgoals that create a step-by-step ladder to the desired outcome. Designing strategies to achieve goals requires creativity and flexibility. The client must evaluate, realistically, any available resources and predicted obstacles. The best tools for planning are found in the business section of a bookstore, in books written for managers that include topics on time management, delegation, breaking tasks into steps, and creating schedules.

Act

Without action, we stay in the restricted domain of our minds. With action, we begin to make an impact on others and the environment. Many small steps taken by the client can symbolize the move from preparation to action. If someone wants to get a college degree, he can read college catalogues or visit campuses. Some clients will be ready to terminate when they are clear about the path that they have chosen to follow. The therapist can help them harness the social support in their natural environment or find relevant community resources. Other clients might need the therapist's support and assistance in the action stage. In Reality therapy when a client fails to follow through on a plan, the therapist does not accept excuses nor does she criticize, but instead focuses on consequences of behavior and on making new plans.

Evaluate

It is essential to monitor the impact of actions, evaluating consequences and revising plans as necessary. Action usually begins before the plans are completed: Small steps toward goals can give feedback that will lead to improved plans. Clients must understand that they are free to reexamine their wants and to make new choices. A fear of action arises if people feel that, if things don't turn out the way they hoped, they are condemned to suffer without recourse. This constraint on freedom may stem from such parental warnings as *You made your bed, now you have to lie in it.*

Transactional Analysis

Bob and Mary Goulding (1979), authors of *Changing Lives through Redecision Therapy,* suggest that you ask clients to make two basic choices:

1. *Do you choose to live or die?* It is very effective to start with this basic existential choice. When the client affirms that he has chosen to live, the next choice is required.

2. *Do you choose to be happy or unhappy?* Clients are forced to face the fact that in many ways they have been choosing their own unhappiness.

Two very powerful TA concepts are the "early childhood decision" and the "script." Clients learn that when they were little they made choices based on limited information and restricted alternatives and that now they are free to "re-decide." They often discover that they have been operating on a programmed life script such as "I'll show them, even if it kills me."

Another suggestion from the Gouldings is that therapists should not offer any efforts to help the client change without establishing a contract for the session, asking the client *What do you want to change about yourself today?* With this approach, responsibility is constantly being placed on the client and the therapist refrains from undermining freedom.

Clients can learn about how they restrict the freedom and responsibility of themselves and others through a TA tool called the Karpman Triangle, which defines three roles that people play in relationships: Victim, Persecutor, and Rescuer. Clients recognize that they either take a fixed role, or switch between different roles. For instance, they can start as a victim, pleading, "Help Me," and then switch to persecutor, "You're no use, you're no better than anyone else." Deeper study of TA will lead to many useful concepts and techniques, particularly the analysis of interpersonal games, the topic of Eric Berne's (1996) famous book, *Games People Play.*

Existential Group Therapy

Yalom's (1995) group therapy text describes how individuals in groups get feedback, in the here and now, of the impact that they have on other people. In individual therapy, when the therapist gives feedback, the client can discount it as only one person's reaction. But in group therapy, when there is agreement among different members (*consensual validation*) that the client has elicited negative reactions, it is harder for the client to evade the truth. The following sequence leads the client to commit to new choices:

- Here is what your behavior is like.
- Here is the impact of your behavior on other people's feelings and opinions of you.
- How does this information influence your opinion of yourself?
- Are you satisfied with the world you have created?

Yalom describes how the therapist's task is "to help remove encumbrances from the bound or stifled will of the patient" (p. 175). He suggests that you find methods to guide the client to accept the following premises:

- Only I can change the world I have created for myself.
- There is no danger in change.
- To attain what I really want, I must change.
- I can change, I am potent.

Methods can include the following:

- Exhortation and teaching.
- Questions such as *Why do you continue to act counter to your interests? What stops you? What do you fear would happen if you did change?*
- Invitations to do experiments and try the new behavior, in small doses, to discover that a feared calamity doesn't happen.
- Examination of payoffs for staying the same.
- Hunches and interpretations about deeper reasons the client has for staying the same, often drawing on knowledge of the client's past relationships.

Persuasion and Confrontation

Therapists can challenge clients to confront freedom and responsibility in a variety of ways. For instance, there are useful slogans that can remind a client who is not making choices that it is impossible to avoid the burden of freedom: *You cannot choose not to choose* because *no decision is a decision.* Therapists urge clients to face *what is* rather than the fantasies and illusions in their heads. They help their clients to assess the degree of responsibility they should take for events that have happened in the past, to recognize their duties and obligations in current situations, and to view themselves as authors of the story of their future. Clients who see the advantages of evading responsibility may need to be persuaded that there are disadvantages to this approach to life—that they will go through life feeling as though unfortunate events are happening to them, rather than believing that they are in control of their own lives. They will endure repeated experiences of victimization and blame and will fail to learn lessons about how to live more effectively. Energy spent on searching for a guilty party could be spent on learning how to make better choices and plans that are more effective.

Therapists often need to challenge the limits the client creates with language, as follows:

- **Can't:** *What stops you? What's the obstacle? What do you fear would happen if you did?*
- **Have to:** *According to whom? What would happen if you didn't?*
- **Try:** *Are you going to "try" to do it, or are you going to do it?*
- **Work on:** *Do you want to "work on" that, or do you want to achieve it?*

Telling and Retelling of the Life Story

Examining a client's personal history will show what was imposed, and will also illuminate ways in which the child exercised her limited freedom. The purpose of telling and retelling stories about the past is not to discover an objective reality but rather to help the client discover ways to mobilize a sense of freedom and empowerment. Narrative therapists know that when clients tell you about key events in their past, they are not telling you about historical truth but instead are sharing the story that they have constructed of their lives. Often when the client starts therapy, this story emphasizes negative things that were imposed; ways in which the person was victimized; barriers and obstacles to getting what she wanted; and many other factors that contribute to the identity of someone who feels weak, powerless, controlled by external forces, and incapable of taking charge of her life or making choices that will lead to a happier future. The therapist listens and understands, and then helps the client reinterpret the past, find strengths and assets that weren't recognized, and reconnect to the power and vigor he had as a child. Therapists need to challenge a client's implicit philosophy of determinism and strengthen a sense of free will: "When you were little, you were a captive in that family and had few tools or resources for exercising freedom for your own benefit. Now, as an adult, you have choices." The client learns that, no matter how bad the childhood, how dysfunctional the parents, and how lousy the prior choices, he or she is now free to behave differently.

Relinquishing Childhood Illusions

Barriers to adult responsibility and constructive use of freedom often come from the illusions of childhood. In early childhood, it is natural to have magical fantasies and to have illusions of a fair and just world. Here are examples of childhood illusions that need to be uncovered and challenged:

- A prince will come along and find me and, without any effort on my part, we will live happily ever after.
- If I am good and do what I am told, then bad things won't happen to me.
- I am responsible for my mommy's happiness; if she isn't happy, then I have done something wrong.
- If I show that I am weak and helpless, someone will take care of me.
- If I show that I am vulnerable, people will take advantage of me and hurt me.

Sheldon Kopp (1976) describes how treatment affected a client:

> Her magical fantasy died hard, because she got so much satisfaction out of the mirage of being in charge of everyone else's well-being. But after a while, she began to experience the new reality of each person as being as strong and as weak as anyone else. Slowly, she learned that each of us grown-ups had as much and as little power as the other, and that we had better learn to take care of ourselves. (p. 83)

Paradox and Reframing: The "Don't Change" Position

There are certain therapeutic approaches that are called paradoxical because instead of pushing for change, they urge the client to accept the status quo and to agree that change is not necessary. The therapist can take one of three paradoxical positions:

1. *Where you are is exactly where you want to be; If you wanted things to be different, you would have changed already.*
2. *There is absolutely nothing wrong with staying exactly as you are now, so convince me why you should try to be any different.*
3. *Don't try to change, do more of the same.* (This tactic was called paradoxical intention by Frankl and is also referred to as *prescribing the symptom.*)

These approaches can lead to one of the following outcomes, all of which are positive:

- The client wants to prove you wrong and therefore needs to intensify her determination to change. This mobilizes the will to change and stimulates action.
- The client gets permission to stay the same and experiences your acceptance. You are not like all the other people who tried to change her, so she can relax and stop resisting you. This creates a space where she can experience her deepest feelings about the status quo. If the feelings turn out to be intensely negative, this pain can fuel some steps toward change.
- The client may discover that the status quo really is what she wants, and all the pressure to change was really coming from external sources, or from the messages she internalized from others. This means that now the client isn't stuck in a bad place, which she feels helpless to leave; instead, she is freely choosing this place.
- When a client stops trying to decrease a problem behavior, but instead increases it, he develops a sense of control over something that seemed out of control.

A paradoxical approach seems similar to what is sometimes called reverse psychology, getting someone to do what you want by ordering them to do the opposite. There is an important difference: With reverse psychology, the one who gives the instruction is trying to control the other person's behavior. With these paradoxical techniques, the therapist must truly feel that it is okay for the client not to change. The goal is not getting a specific change, but rather (a) to get the client to make free choices and take responsibility and (b) for the client to move from suffering to satisfaction.

A man in his mid-40s had been to many therapists. He began therapy with an inexperienced intern, and in the first session, he barraged her with a detailed summary of all his failures in life: he was unable to hold a job, had no close friends, had never had a successful relationship with a woman, was lonely, unmotivated, overweight, and was deeply depressed. His stance toward the therapist seemed to be "Fix all my problems for me, I bet you can't." As final proof of his desperation and misery, he threw out his last-resort solution, as if it were a threat: He would move back home and let his mother take care of him. The intern, a high achiever who valued independence and had ingrained values about "manhood" and "growing up," was getting geared up to work really hard with this client. In supervision, she was shocked when her existential supervisor made this suggestion: "Take the position that there is absolutely nothing wrong with letting his mother take care of him, if that's what he wants. Ask him what stops him?"

Neurolinguistic Programming

This system was named by Bandler and Grinder (1990) and its concepts and tools have been used by therapists, in business school, in organizational consultation, in popular motivational seminars, and in the Weight Watchers program. Its creators studied the contributions of famous therapists, such as Fritz Perls, Milton Ericson, and Virginia Satir, and so it already integrates many different therapeutic approaches. Neurolinguistic Programming (NLP) teaches a set of strategies for helping people expand their choices in life and get more control over their own thoughts, emotions, and behaviors. Neurolinguistic Programming teachers often use the metaphor of a computer: People internally process information, using different sensory modalities—visual, auditory, and kinesthetic. They often operate on "programs" that were developed without their conscious choice. By increasing awareness and learning specific tools, people can learn how to change this programming (the software in their brains) and create new programs that allow them to achieve their chosen outcome goals.

The tools from NLP have tremendous potential in helping people make choices and engage in effective action plans. This treatment approach would be very effective when clients have chosen a specific course of action, but complain that they are not able to motivate themselves—they feel incapable of getting themselves to do what they want to do. One NLP technique helps people to create an *effective internal strategy:* The first step is to educate the client on the three different sensory modalities (previously discussed in Chapter 2):

1. *Visual:* The client sees things currently in the environment (the view from the window) as well as two kinds of internal visual images: things that happened in the past (my bedroom when I was a child) and things that have never occurred that the client invents and imagines (a pink elephant). Visual images can vary in brightness, hue, and intensity.

2. *Auditory:* The client can hear external sounds (music on the radio) as well as recall sounds (her grandmother's voice) or invent sounds (imagining what someone will say when she brings her a gift). A special kind of internal sound is inner speech: the words that the client hears in her head. When

people refer to *thinking, ruminating* or *rehearsing,* they are attending to their inner voices.

3. *Kinesthetic:* The client can access messages that come from the body. These include emotions as well as somatic sensations. Physical movement falls into this category.

Clients can learn to develop effective internal strategies for meeting their goals by contrasting situations where they are successful and unsuccessful in motivating themselves. Here is an example of a client telling about an unsuccessful strategy to motivate herself to complete her dissertation:

> I decide that I am going to work for 4 hours (*internal speech*). I go to the kitchen, get some coffee, and turn the TV on (*action*) to watch the news. I tell myself I deserve this bit of relaxation before I start to work (*internal speech*). Suddenly I look at the clock (*external visual*) and I realize I've lost an hour (*internal speech*). I feel guilty (*emotion*). I tell myself to get started (*internal speech*), but then I start feeling angry (*emotion*). I start imagining the great vacation I will take when it is over, I see myself on the beach in Hawaii (*imaginary visual*). When I go into my home office (*doing*), I see the mess and clutter that I didn't clean up last night (*visual from environment*). I start feeling panicky (*feeling*).

By examining the details of the sequence, the client identified three choices that would facilitate effective on-task behavior:

1. End a workday by cleaning up the workspace and preparing a note regarding how to begin the next day (*visual from environment*).
2. Take her coffee and immediately go to the work space, sit down, and open a file called "free ideas" and start tapping out thoughts, just to get started (*action; elimination of internal speech*).
3. Wear headphones and play pleasant music while working (*auditory from environment*). This tactic served to override the self-defeating messages from internal speech and emotions.

If the client is occasionally but not always successful, it is very useful to contrast the successful and unsuccessful strategies. Here is an example of a client whose goal is to exercise more:

- *Unsuccessful strategy:* I open my eyes, tell myself I should get up, feel the warmth and softness of the bed, hear an internal voice saying "you can't make me," tell myself I can do it later, close my eyes.
- *Successful strategy:* I open my eyes, see my exercise clothes and shoes laid out from the night before, and get dressed. I remind myself of how good I feel after I exercise, and I walk out of the house.

We all have successful strategies. The information is inside us, but we need prompts to bring it to awareness. Sometimes there are successful strategies in different contexts that can be transferred to the current problem situation.

Another tactic is to ask the client to identify someone who is successful at the option with which she is struggling: A person who maintains weight loss, studies effectively, or can resist falling back into a bad relationship after breaking up. Then the client can go and interview this person, taking notes on that person's "winning strategy" to find tools to adapt for his or her own use.

Exploring Freedom and Responsibility through the Arts

There are many poems, stories, novels, songs, and films that illustrate issues of freedom and responsibility and how they are evaded.

- *Peter Pan:* A song in the musical version is *I Won't Grow Up.* This story illustrates the fantasy of staying a child and never having to face responsibilities.
- *The Road Not Taken:* Robert Frost's poem evokes the awareness that choosing one path means not knowing or having what lies on other paths. A song by Peter Allen *I Could Have Been a Sailor* describes two possible paths: taking *pleasure in my quiet hearth and happy home* versus giving *my heart its chance to roam.*
- *Commitment:* The movie *Metroland* shows a new father torn between freedom with his single friends and making a mature commitment to his wife and child. Two movies with Jack Nicholson, *Carnal Knowledge* and *Five Easy Pieces,* examine middle-aged unmarried men who stay stuck in adolescence:

INTEGRATION OF HYPOTHESES

The **ES2** hypothesis can be applied with any client and is compatible with all theories. Regardless of chosen treatment, you need the client to take responsibility for personal change. Assuring that the client freely affirms goals and commits to the therapeutic process is one of your mandatory tasks.

CS3 Developmental Transition

Issues of choice, freedom, and responsibility come up at developmental transitions, especially adolescence and middle age. This hypothesis is especially useful working with adolescents, as reality therapists have found. Parents, at this stage, need to give up the fantasy that they can control their teenager, and instead, adopt a parenting style that helps the child learn to make good choices, consider consequences, and learn how to balance freedom and responsibility. In middle age, people often begin to access their true wants and desires and discover that the path that they have been on for the past 30 years was not really freely chosen. At retirement, people face new freedoms and greater constraints.

BL1 Antecedents and Consequences

When people have trouble mobilizing their will to engage in desired behaviors and move toward goals, the tools of behavior therapy offer powerful assistance. Instead of relying on sheer willpower, people can use their will wisely to put themselves in situations that trigger desired behaviors and apply reinforcers appropriately.

BL2 Conditioned Emotional Response

The barriers to exercising freedom are often emotional—excessive anxiety and fear and inappropriate guilt. By deconditioning those emotions, therapists empower clients to take risks and engage more confidently in desired behavior. The technique of anchoring (p. 177) teaches clients how to condition a desired emotional state (e.g., "resourcefulness") to a tactile or auditory cue.

BL3 Skill Deficits or Lack of Competence

There are many skills that contribute to effective decision making and life planning. An autonomous adult needs the following skills: the ability to identify one's own wants, feelings, and values; the ability to weigh costs and benefits in making decisions; skills for planning, which include time management skills; and the ability to access resources in the community. Certain specific skills are needed for carrying out projects and attaining goals, such as skills of public speaking, writing, performance of a sport or performing art.

C1 Utopian Expectations

Utopian fantasies about life need to be challenged to help people stay in the realm of possibility.

C2 Faulty Cognitive Map

The topics of freedom, constraint, and responsibility all involve beliefs, assumptions, attribution of causation, and core schemas about a person's dependence and independence. Exploring and changing the narrative of a person's life involves major cognitive change.

C3 Faulty Information Processing

To accurately describe consequences from behavior or to evaluate whether a constraint is real or self-imposed, a person needs good information-processing skills.

C4 Dysfunctional Self-Talk

It is essential to examine the client's self-talk to discover both barriers and facilitators of effective and responsible exercise of freedom.

P1 Internal Parts and Subpersonalities

It is absolutely essential to consider this hypothesis when the client reveals conflict and ambivalence. A major reason people don't easily make choices is that they are pulled in different directions. One part of them would make one choice while another part wants the opposite. For instance, one part wants to lose weight and fit into smaller clothing, while the other part wants to eat whatever it wants, whenever it wants it. Often a "lack of willpower" means that a very powerful internal part is in conflict with the goal-setting part, and operates as a saboteur.

Using TA terms, a Parent or Adapted Child state sets the goals and a Free or Rebellious Child has a contrary agenda. The Adult as the executive of the personality needs to be in charge of decision making.

The contract is made with the Adult state of the personality, and therapy proceeds with Adult-Adult transactions between therapist and client. Therapists need to avoid slipping into the Parent state, which the client's Adapted Child is trying to elicit. The therapist also must resist being a Rescuer, keeping the responsibility for the client's life in the hands of the client.

SCE1 Family System

Often the greatest source of sabotage for growth and change is the client's family members. For instance, when a young adult is struggling to launch himself on the path of freedom and responsibility, parents may be reluctant to let go. Family systems theory helps to explain how the impairments of one family member serve a function for the entire family. Thus, the irresponsible person is the identified patient, or symptom bearer for the family system. Sometimes involving the whole family in therapy will be the most appropriate treatment plan; at other times, the autonomy of the client is best served by helping him separate from the family and teaching him how to minimize their effect on him.

SCE3 Social Support

Especially when people are trying to maintain a very difficult behavior change, such as abstinence from alcohol or reduced consumption of food, it is beneficial to be part of a support group. When people begin to make free choices, they may alienate those in their social network who are comfortable with them the way they always have been. The therapist can make the client aware of how to elicit support instead of sabotage from these people and how to find new sources of social support from like-minded people.

ES3 SPIRITUAL DIMENSION

Definition

The core of the problem and/or the resources needed for resolving the problem are found in the **Spiritual Dimension** of life, which may or may not include religion.

Explanation

An important application of the **ES3** hypothesis is when the client is dealing with religious issues, including his or her relationship to God. The term *spiritual* applies to a wide variety of experiences, beliefs and activities. Clients who are coping with death, moral dilemmas, and blocks to creativity often benefit from a spiritual focus. Tools from Eastern religions (e.g., meditation and mindfulness) and Western religions (e.g., prayer and Bible reading) can be integrated into therapy. Referral to or collaboration with clergypersons and other spiritual practitioners may be appropriate.

Examples

Charlene, with a great deal of embarrassment, begins to talk about some unusual experiences that seem to be altered states of consciousness, close to mystical experiences. She has profoundly moving dreams and says, "I feel as if a precious part of me that I have neglected is beginning to awaken." She is worried that you will think she's crazy.	Javier has feelings of guilt over his past behavior, which caused great pain to people who loved him. He has a need for some form of atonement and self-forgiveness but does not know what to do because the people he hurt are dead. He is aware that he punishes himself all the time and that because he is always morose his wife and children suffer.	Violet describes feelings of emptiness, meaningless, and stagnation. However, she discovers that when she looks at beautiful scenery she feels awe and a sense of reverence. She starts going to an art class and discovers that she has "come alive." During those 3 hours each week, she feels like she has rediscovered the spontaneity and joy that were lost in childhood.

SCE5 Social Problem Is a Cause

When a social problem such as racial discrimination is the root cause of a person's difficulties, the individual's fatalism and pessimism can make problems worse. The client may sink into an attitude of victimhood and not recognize those arenas in which she does have power and can take action. Self-imposed constraints compound the effects of the social injustice: "The last time I tried to look for another job, I got so many doors slammed in my face, I swore to never put myself through that again." "I've never been given a break, so what's the point of trying to get ahead?"

SCE7 Environmental Factors

Environmental limitations must be recognized. In discussing responsibility, it is important to recognize the role of environment. For instance, in a car accident, a manufacturer's defect in the car, heavy fog, and broken streetlights all have causal influence. In brainstorming for alternatives, ideas of changing or leaving the environment should not be overlooked. The idea of a person making choices to find the best "environmental niche," given her talents, interests, feelings, weaknesses, limitations, and fears, is very useful.

KEY IDEAS FOR ES3 SPIRITUAL DIMENSION

It is only in recent years that psychotherapists other than pastoral counselors have been encouraged to explore client problems and assets through the filter of spiritual and religious functioning. *Spirituality* is generally defined as a subjective, individual experience, whereas *religion* involves an institutional framework; a prescribed set of beliefs, practices, and rituals; and a community of people who participate together.

A useful web site for learning about major and minor world religions is http://www.religioustolerance.org, which uses a very inclusive definition for religion: "Any specific system of belief about deity, often involving rituals, a code of ethics, a philosophy of life, and a world view" (www.religioustolerance .org/rel_defn.htm, accessed February 17, 1006). In addition to the three largest religions in North America (Christianity, Islam, and Judaism) and the third and fourth largest religions in the world (Hinduism and Buddhism), the web site describes seven other major world religions, 21 smaller organized religions, and five Neopagan religious faiths. The term *theism* refers to a worldview that includes the following beliefs: God exists, humans are created by God, and divine influence operates in human affairs. The term *atheism* is used for the absence of that worldview.

Spirituality can be theistic or atheistic. Table 7.3 illustrates a sampling of spiritual values, goals, experiences, beliefs, and behaviors that illustrate the breadth of the concept of spirituality. All of the examples share the common denominator of acknowledging something higher or greater than the self.

Psychotherapy and Spiritual/Religious Issues

In the study of intellectual history of the twentieth century, it is often asserted that psychotherapy filled a void left by the decline of religion as a major influence in everyone's life. For a large part of that century, many organized religions were hostile toward psychotherapy, whereas clergy and psychotherapists are now building communication bridges and recognizing common concerns. Seminaries incorporate courses in psychology and training in empathy, pastoral counselors obtain secular licenses as psychotherapists, and clergypersons may refer members of their congregations to therapists.

At the same time, psychotherapists have shown an increased interest in integrating spiritual and religious issues into the practice of psychotherapy. There are two risks when therapy enters the spiritual domain: (1) The therapist will impose values and steer clients in a direction that is counter to the client's preferences, and (2) the therapist will be too timid to probe and challenge, as if the

Table 7.3   Concepts of Spirituality

Connection with the Sacred or Divine

Search for the sacred or divine

Transcending the self and connecting to a higher power

Feelings of harmony and oneness with truth, humanity, or God

Feeling uplifted and recharged by connection to a nonhuman source of energy and enlightenment

Experiencing one's own inner goodness and value as stemming from a higher power

Contacting an Inner Guide

Goals to Be a Better Person and Have a More Meaningful Life

Development of a personal moral code and the desire to live a virtuous, ethical life

Striving to be the best possible human being one can be

Seeking personal transformation, wholeness, or integration

Seeking to replace negative emotions such as anger, envy, and fear with positive emotions such as love, compassion, and forgiveness

The desire to be less selfish and self-oriented and become more altruistic, generous, and engaged in service to others

The search for meaning and purpose in life that is higher than one's usual material, superficial concerns

On a quest for some higher goal, such as one's "true (or higher, deeper) self" or a "path with heart"

Psychological Experiences

The capacity to enter into heightened states of consciousness that erase the boundary of the self

Having a specific mystical experience that cannot adequately be described in words, which involves contact with the divine and intense emotions such as awe, wonder, and bliss

Experiencing a sense of creativity and flow, which includes intense concentration, self-forgetfulness, and clarity

Experiencing a sense of unity, wholeness, and timelessness

Achieving a sense of inner peace and detachment

Beliefs

Believing in a divine purpose that permeates the universe

Believing that there is an alternate reality that is invisible but more real than the reality we experience with our senses

Believing that overinvestment in one's separate ego is a source of suffering instead of strength

Believing in the continuation of spiritual existence after the physical body has died

Believing that the spirits of our ancestors make demands on us that we are obligated to obey

Believing that one's work is a spiritual vocation to which one was called and chosen

Activities and Behaviors

Prayer; meditation; communing with nature

Reading tarot cards, using crystals for their healing energy, or communicating with spirits who have passed to the other side

Engagement in efforts to make the world a better place and stamp out problems such as hunger, social injustice, and racism

Singing or playing sacred music

Nourishing the soul through activities such as reading, viewing great art, listening to classical music, enjoying aromas, and creating art client's spirituality is too fragile to withstand a thorough exploration. Therapists may need to open the door to spiritual issues for clients who would not use that term. Some clients (particularly those with a strict, rigid religious upbringing) may be resistant to any discussion of spiritual issues because they have not learned that such thirsts can be quenched at nonreligious fountains.

Therapists may welcome the topic of secular spirituality but, especially if they are not themselves religious, may treat religious issues as taboo. The culturally competent therapist needs to understand and respect the client's religious identity, along with other sources of cultural diversity. We must understand that it is as inappropriate to ignore the religious dimensions of life as it is to impose prayer and Bible passages on a nonreligious client. As therapists, we need to develop the competencies taught in the diversity portion of the curriculum and to explore our own religious and spiritual beliefs, our intolerance of other beliefs, and our moral codes. We also must recognize the limits of our capacity to respond to clients' religious and spiritual goals and know when referral is necessary. Therapists who wish to work exclusively in a religious framework—with clients of their own religion in a clinical setting under the auspices of a religious institution—should receive specialized training, perhaps in a doctoral program that integrates psychology and religion.

The Client's Religious and Spiritual Background

The client's current and past involvement in organized religion should be part of the database. What was the religious context in early childhood? Were there stages of development of the concept of God, expressions of faith, and spiritual experiences? How does the client describe his or her current religious affiliation and beliefs? What are his or her current religious or spiritual practices? How often does the client attend a religious service? What kind of relationships does the client have with clergy and fellow congregation members? Is the client struggling in his or her private devotional life? How does the client experience his or her relationship to God? How has the client used religion in handling stress in the past and present?

Only by listening to the explanations of your clients will you discover their religious identities and affiliations, and the nature of their spiritual lives. Clinicians must be careful not to form preconceptions about a client's beliefs and practices based on textbook descriptions of a religion or its members. For instance, we might assume that a Native American believes in the sacredness of all of nature only to discover that the only religion she has ever known is Christianity. A client may tell you, "I am deeply religious" without being involved in formal religious practices, or say "I am not religious, but I consider myself a very spiritual person," while believing in God, praying regularly, and reading the Bible for inspiration. Because Judaism is treated as a religious category, Christian therapists may be surprised when their Jewish client explains that she is an atheist but celebrates Jewish holidays, intends to raise her children as Jews, and believes her Jewishness to be the most important aspect of her cultural identity.

A client might surprise you by saying that he didn't become Christian until a conversion experience in his early 20s when you know from his history that he was born into a Protestant family and attended church regularly as a child. Many adults feel justified in taking a "pick and choose" approach to their religion. As an example, a woman defines herself as a "devout Catholic," vehemently opposes abortion and homosexuality, yet feels comfortable using birth control and moving in with her boyfriend without marriage.

Another error to avoid is to make assumptions about religious background based on a few facts about the family. For instance, one trainee assumed that because her client had an Irish surname and came from a family with a large number of children, the family size was based on Catholic attitudes toward birth control. When she asked questions about the family size, she discovered that the oldest two siblings were from the divorced father's prior marriage and that her four youngest siblings were two sets of twins. It is also essential not to make assumptions about the spiritual life of individuals based on their overt behaviors.

> A man who had been a priest for 11 years gave up the priesthood and stopped attending church services. The therapist assumed that he was having a spiritual crisis and was feeling cut off from God. The client explained that his reason for leaving was that he wanted to marry and have a family. He admitted that his reason for not going to church was that he liked "running the show" and was irritated at being just a member of the congregation. He was finding spiritual fulfillment in solitary prayer and reading spiritual texts.

Resource for Health and Coping

Research with medical patients has found benefits of religiosity and spirituality in terms of reduced morbidity and mortality, healthier lifestyles, and fewer required health services. Religious faith, membership in religious communities, and spirituality provide resources for coping with stress, loss, and traumas. Here is a description of Lisa Beamer, the pregnant widow of one of the heroes who died in Flight 93 on September 11, 2001: ". . . her faith is a faith that sustains her—it's her crutch, her emotional stability, and she calls on her faith to help her through these times." (Retrieved from http://transcripts.cnn.com/TRANSCRIPTS/0201/11/lt.06.html.)

Negative Impact of Religion

Religion is not always a beneficial force in people's lives: It can also cause or exacerbate mental health difficulties. Some religions provide very punitive images of God and use fear-arousing images of hell and damnation to enforce good behavior. Carlson's (1994) book, *Why Do Christians Shoot Their Wounded?* described the cruel, blaming, detrimental exhortations that many evangelical religions provide to people suffering from severe depression. Destructive childhood contacts with religion—sexual molestation by priests, and experiences with dogmatic and punitive religious teachers—damage clients' self-esteem, ability to handle angry feelings, capacity for tolerance and open-mindedness, and appreciation of healthy sexuality. Many religions institutionalize inequities between the genders. For example, it is only in recent decades that women have been allowed to enter the clergy in Protestant and Jewish denominations. The rejection of gays and lesbians by most religious denominations is another example of how religion can hurt rather than help individuals.

Victims of Religious Prejudice and Persecution

Religious affiliation can result in discrimination and social rejection, especially in small communities where the majority of people share membership in one religious denomination. Following the terrorist attack on the World Trade Center, members of the Muslim faith experienced hostility ranging from rude suspiciousness to hate crimes. Genocide targeting members of specific religions leaves inexpressible psychological scars not only on immediate survivors but also on their descendents.

Morality

When clients are struggling with indecision, ambivalence, and inner conflict, elements of a *moral dilemma* often need to be addressed. The choice about what to do may require examination of the moral issues that are involved, as well as personal and religious values. Behavior that has consequences for the well-being of others is automatically part of the moral domain (Doherty, 1996). As part of the process of evaluating alternatives, it is important to examine the consequences for other people and, at the very least, to test the alternative against the standard of the Golden Rule.

Clients differ in their awareness of and concern for the moral dimension. Sometimes clients show a very strong sense of moral responsibility. A client poses the conflict in these words: "I agreed when I was hired to work for at least a year and I feel that keeping that promise is the moral thing to do, but the job is causing so much stress, I don't want to stay there." Another client struggles with indecision: "I found out that my friend's husband is cheating on her, and I can't decide if I should spare her the pain of finding out or if I have a moral obligation to tell her."

Other clients have no qualms about making choices that negatively influence the welfare of others. Therapists should not shy away from responses that invite clients to examine the moral implications of their behavior. For instance, a parent chooses to move away and cut off ties with her children, a college student is plagiarizing papers from the Internet to "save time," a spouse conducts an extramarital affair, or a person who tests positive for HIV refuses to wear a condom or tell his partner. Therapists have often been criticized for ignoring moral issues and taking a *let the chips fall where they may* attitude, instead of challenging the lack of social responsibility.

The training of therapists steers them away from the topic of morality, a problem that Menninger (1973) addressed in his book *Whatever Became of Sin?* Therapists search for symptoms of mental illness rather than moral wrongdoing;

they value tolerance and cultural relativism, and learn a style of interviewing that emphasizes empathy and nonjudgmental acceptance. When the therapist helps a client examine the topic of moral transgression, the therapeutic dialogue embraces a wide array of useful concepts: guilt, contrition, confession, repentance, atonement, expiation, penance, amends, reparations, restitution, seeking forgiveness, and forgiving oneself. Engaging in moral discourse is very challenging because it is easy for the therapist to fall into a style of moralizing, which risks driving the client away.

Love

The topic of love belongs in a discussion of spirituality and psychotherapy for several reasons. First, the core message of many religions involves love: love of God, love of fellow humans, and love of nature. Second, an effective component of the therapeutic relationship is often described as a form of nonpossessive love, using the Greek term *agape,* where the therapist prizes the client and accepts him for who he is, resulting in the client's beginning to love and value himself. Third, one of the most common topics of therapeutic conversations is the client's search for satisfying, committed, loving relationships. Therapists who are open to exploring spiritual issues can help clients to deepen their understanding of love, increase their capacity for loving, and make better choices in their relationships. Clients who feel empty inside, or incomplete and worthless unless they are involved in a romantic relationship, may benefit from understanding that they may be trying to fulfill spiritual needs through another human.

An example of how spirituality and love enter the discourse of therapy is through the concept of *soul mate.*

A group discussion focused on the topic of "soul mates." Half of the participants thought that the concept was ridiculous and that there were many possible partners with whom a person could create a lasting, fulfilling relationship. The other half of the group believed wholeheartedly in the concept. Two members, happily married, claimed that they had felt at an early stage in their relationships that they had found the partner who was "meant to be" their mate. One unmarried member, currently not dating anyone, believed that she would ultimately find her soul mate. One man admitted that he had not dated for 5 years after a 4-year relationship was terminated by the woman he believed to be his soul mate, admitting that he sometimes felt suicidal because his "one and only had come and gone." A woman, laughing sheepishly, said that she had the problem of jumping immediately into sexual relationships with poor choices of men because in the initial stage of attraction, she experienced a deep soul connection, which compelled her to use sexual union to bring a peak experience of merger. When the relationship failed, she concluded that she had been in error, and her true soul mate was yet to be found.

In contrast to people who believe that finding the right person ensures a spiritual bond, Martin Buber (1970), author of *I and Thou,* believes that it is the quality of the process between two people that determines the level of spirituality in the relationship. There are two basic ways of experiencing the significant other:

1. *As an object:* This means that no matter how much love you profess for the person, you view the other as a "thing" rather than a separate being with as much freedom, complexity, and unpredictability as you have. Buber used the phrase "I-it" for this kind of relationship, which occurs when the lover is incapable of empathizing, is possessive, wants to control not only behaviors but thoughts and feelings, and values the other as a trophy or as a tool for meeting needs. You can recognize this type of love by answers to the question, What do you love about him? "He makes me feel desirable," "She will make a wonderful mother." Parents will say, "Of course I love her, I would die for her," and yet they are angry when the daughter does not live up to a predetermined image of how she should be. The following is an example of "I-it" love:

   > A classic movie, *Rebel Without a Cause,* shows two parents who love their teenage son, as an object. They refuse to listen to him when he tries to tell them about a tragic death for which he was partly responsible. His mother's first response is "How can you do this to me?" and the father's advice for dealing with a complex moral dilemma is "Don't get involved."

2. *As a subject:* You seek to enter the other person's subjective perspective and understand, with empathy, how that person experiences the world. You want the loved one to exercise freedom. You know that the other person is separate and that you cannot expect to be the center of that person's experience or to control his or her life. The fact that the other person has friendships, work, and hobbies that do not include you is not a threat, because you want the other person to be happy. A dying spouse who wants the partner to find a new loving relationship in the future, instead of grieving forever, is showing this kind of love. In the movie *The Sea Inside,* described under **ES1,** the woman who, despite her desire to have a loving relationship, helps Ramon commit suicide, is perceived as having a more spiritual love than the family members who cannot bear to let him go and become angry at him for having those wishes. The following shows another example:

   > In the 1999 movie *Anywhere but Here,* a very needy and insecure mother becomes furious to discover that her daughter wants to go to a college on the opposite side of the country. When her daughter has to turn the school down because she didn't get a full scholarship, the mother is relieved, despite her daughter's misery. At the end of the movie, the shift in the quality of the mother's love is demonstrated when she sells her Mercedes to get the money to help her daughter leave home.

Relationships with pets offer insight into different styles of loving. Many people experience deeply loving, spiritual connections to their nonhuman companions. The relationship with their animal is I-thou, whereas to other people, the animal is an "it." With this understanding, it becomes clear why grief following the death of a pet can be so intense and why there is so much benefit from the use of pets in therapy with isolated individuals.

WHEN IS THIS HYPOTHESIS A GOOD MATCH?

This hypothesis obviously fits when the client presents with a problem that un-ambiguously has a religious or spiritual component. For instance, a religious client asks, "How can God do this?" and no longer finds solace in prayer and church attendance. A spiritual, nonreligious client no longer derives nourishment from activities that provided it in the past (e.g., solitude, appreciating nature, or creative activity).

The *DSM-IV-TR* diagnosis of V62.89 Religious or Spiritual Problem includes the following examples: *Loss of or questioning of faith, problems associated with conversion to a new faith,* and *questioning of spiritual values.* Other examples of problem titles that warrant the **ES2** hypothesis include:

- *Difficulties associated with interfaith marriage* (ambivalence over whether to sacrifice parental support and approval by marrying outside of faith; conflict with spouse over religious education of children).
- *Distress over perceived rejection and isolation by clergyman* (or congregation).
- *Ambivalence over specific rules and practices of religious faith group.*
- *Confusion and anxiety following mystical experience.*

Need for Spiritual Resources

Therapists will be in a position to recognize that the client would benefit from spiritual resources when the client does not conceptualize her needs in these terms. For instance, a client may express pain over "life's chaos" and long for connection to a "universal flow." The following categories are useful for recognizing when spiritual resources are beneficial.

Addictions

Alcoholics Anonymous and other Twelve Step programs have demonstrated effectiveness in helping addicts become sober and maintain sobriety. An essential ingredient in these programs is acknowledging that one cannot conquer the addiction without turning to a "higher power" for help. The organization permits the broadest possible definition of a higher power. For many members, the group they attend and the larger community to which they belong, as well as the commitment to sponsoring newcomers and helping them in their struggle, provide spiritual connection and nourishment.

Coping with Death and Trauma

When the client is dealing with terminal illness, religion and spirituality are usually addressed. Most physicians are ill equipped to deal with terminal patients because their job is to seek interventions that will promote a cure and they feel helpless and perhaps self-blaming when they have nothing further to offer the patient. At such a time, the patient and family need the services of spiritual counselors. Many end-of-life feelings and decisions have spiritual components. Decisions about life support and the wish to have control over the end of life involve examination of religious beliefs. Spiritual resources are also needed when coping with the death of someone else or any other major trauma. While the death of any loved one is difficult, perhaps there is no death more likely to savage a person's spiritual resources than the death of a child. Although spiritual resources serve as a buffer against mental health problems, severely traumatic events can overwhelm them. The client may develop spiritual symptoms such as anger at God, loss of faith and meaning, inability to derive comfort from prayer, disruption of a sense of safety in the world, and feelings of disconnection from fellow humans. Restoring and strengthening the comfort and meaning from spirituality can be a very effective strategy for these trauma victims. If another person has deliberately caused someone's suffering (e.g., rape, murder of a child, or fraudulent financial dealings), the victim is faced with a particular set of spiritual issues. That person must deal with the existence of evil, the question of "How could God let this happen to me, if he is good and all-powerful?" and the desire for vengeance.

Forgiveness Issues

Clients often believe that it is impossible to forgive the perpetrator of a wrong against them, whether it is a stranger who has committed a crime of violence, the parent who committed incest in childhood, or the spouse who has committed acts of infidelity. They need to understand that forgiveness is not the same as condoning, pardoning, or forgetting the wrongful act. What forgiveness can offer is a release from their anger and bitterness. In contrast to unforgiving clients, others are too quick to forgive: They deny their justified feelings, they accept an apology that does not include amends and penance, and they achieve a reconciliation with someone who is going to continue to do them harm.

Depression

The syndrome of depression is a common pathway for which many hypotheses should be tested. Here are some questions to steer you toward a spiritual formulation: Is the soul starving for nourishment? Would the client's self-love increase if she understood that her core worth as a human being had nothing to do with external appearances and approval of others? Is there a feeling of emptiness and isolation that could be healed with connection to something larger than the self? Have punitive self-messages been internalized from a harsh religion? Is some buried, spiritual part of the personality struggling to come out and be heard, but is being suppressed by more materialistic, achievement-oriented parts? Has the client who once found comfort and inner peace from religious faith now lost a sense of connection to God?

Dealing with Negative Effects of Religion

Clients may describe many negative effects of their childhood contacts with religion: deep feelings of shame and guilt, suppression of normal feelings of anger, difficulty making independent decisions, judgmental and intolerant attitudes, and negative feelings about sexuality. Victims of ritual child abuse and members of religious cults suffer deep psychological traumas. The recently highly publicized evidence of widespread sexual molestation of children and adolescents by priests demonstrates the damage done by both trusted religious authorities and parents who failed to believe and support their children.

Guilt-Free Doers of Evil

The *DSM* describes "disregard for and violation of rights of others" as one of the criteria for 301.7 Antisocial Personality Disorder. These people rarely believe that they need psychotherapy. However, people who feel no guilt for their wrongdoing may arrive in a therapist's office because others referred them, perhaps as a condition of probation. These clients may try to reduce punishment by insincere expressions of remorse, but when their court-ordered therapy is over, they have no motivation to change. Mental health professionals have a tendency to search for psychological explanations for the paths these people take; in contrast, other people may argue that the perpetrators are choosing evil and deserve punishment rather than mental health treatment. Sometimes it is possible to stimulate empathy in perpetrators for victims through special interventions. For instance, some prisons have programs where rape victims confront rapists. For these types of people, a sense of sin—the experience of moral pain—would be a positive treatment outcome.

Spiritual Emergencies

Grof and Grof (1990) coined the term *spiritual emergencies* for psychological difficulties stemming from spiritual practices and spontaneous spiritual experiences. An example would be a psychotic episode following intense immersion in spiritual practice (yoga and meditation). Rather than viewing the symptoms as part of a mental disorder, clinicians should appreciate them as offering an opportunity for spiritual and psychological growth. Because delusions with religious content could be associated with Schizophrenia as well as a transient spiritual emergency, diagnostic skills are essential.

TREATMENT PLANNING

There is a growing body of literature about how therapists from different orientations integrate spirituality into their work with clients (Shafranske, 1996; Sperry, 2001; Sperry & Shafranske, 2004). The field of marital therapy has developed many approaches that bring a spiritual focus to work with couples: combining acceptance with cognitive therapy, helping each partner to achieve an emotional understanding of the partner's pain to increase empathy and connection, and a focus on the healing power of forgiveness.

Therapeutic Competence

The American Counseling Association lists competencies for integrating spirituality into counseling, including the following six abilities. The professional counselor should be able to:

1. Demonstrate sensitivity and acceptance of a variety of religious and/or spiritual expressions in client communication.
2. Identify limits of her or his understanding of a client's religious or spiritual expression.
3. Demonstrate appropriate referral skills and generate possible referral sources.
4. Assess the relevance of the religious and/or spiritual domains in the client's therapeutic issues.
5. Be sensitive to and receptive of religious and/or spiritual themes in the counseling process as befits the expressed preference of each client.
6. Use a client's religious and/or spiritual beliefs in the pursuit of the client's therapeutic goals as befits the client's expressed preference.

The therapist needs to enter the client's inner world and understand his or her unique point of view. Qualities such as empathy, respect, tolerance of differences, and nonjudgmental acceptance are essential. The therapeutic relationship can involve spiritual healing components: Therapists need to develop healthy "I-thou" relationships with clients, rather than to treat the client as an "it."

Theories with a Strong Spiritual Component

Therapists who use the following three approaches are already attending to spiritual functioning of clients.

Victor Frankl's Logotherapy

The term *logotherapy* comes from the Greek word "logo," a word that denotes "meaning" as well as "spirit." In his 1948 book, *The Unconscious God: Psychotherapy and Theology,* Frankl speculated on "the transcendent unconscious" and suggests that man's relation to God may be unconscious. *Transcendence* refers to forgetting yourself because of the importance of a higher cause or value, rather than just pursuing your own personal needs and pleasures. He expressed the belief that self-transcendence is the route to the highest sense of meaning.

Jungian Psychology

Jung felt that dreams are not only about the dreamer but also about God, and that there is a divine presence, an archetype of wholeness, which operates autonomously in dream states or at moments of deep reverie. His term *individuation* denotes a process, seen throughout the life span, toward unity and self-realization as a whole person. Jung saw a connection between the Christian virtue of forgiveness and the healing of inner splits and struggles. Religious experience, for Jung, is the union of opposites—an encounter with the self that overcomes the split.

Transpersonal Psychotherapy

Transpersonal psychology was launched in 1969 with the first issue of the *Journal of Transpersonal Psychology*. Initially, it was interested in transcendent experiences such as peak, mystical, and near-death experiences. As a field of psychotherapy, it embraced Jungian theory and other Eastern and Western approaches to mysticism and spirituality. Transpersonal psychotherapists use techniques such as meditation, chanting, ritual, visualization, dream work, and art and music therapy. Goals of therapy may include a greater awareness of one's connection to the universe, a sense of one's intrinsic value, and an unconditional appreciation for one's life.

Integrating Practices from Eastern Religions

The Buddhist practice of bare attention means moment-to-moment awareness of changing objects of perception such as mind, body, and emotions, without trying to change anything. This practice requires the experiencing of raw sensory events, as if seen for the first time. Epstein (1995) describes its therapeutic benefit:

> With bare attention, we move from this automatic identification with our fear or frustration to a vantage point from which the fear or frustration is attended to with the same dispassionate interest as anything else. There is enormous freedom to be gained from such a shift. Instead of running from difficult emotions (or hanging on to enticing ones), the practitioner of bare attention becomes able to contain any reaction: making space for it, but not completely identifying with it because of the concomitant presence of nonjudgmental awareness. (p. 11)

This practice may be especially beneficial for people in recovery from drug or alcohol abuse, because they need to be able to be with their emotional pain without rushing to drown it out.

Cope (1999) discusses the benefits of yoga practice in terms of transformation of the sense of self, including genuine caring and love of self, pleasure in self-care, and the emergence of real interests and new energy.

Theistic Psychotherapy

Richards and Bergin (2000) provide description and case examples of interventions that stem from their theistic framework, including prayer, reading sacred texts, forgiveness and repentance activities, worship and ritual, fellowship and service, and seeking moral direction. Therapists working with religious clients can use biblical texts to promote mental and emotional health. Many clients bring very punitive images of God to therapy and benefit from discussions that help them to create an image of God consistent with self-love and love of others.

The following example shows how religious clients were able to use prayer effectively with a therapist who was not religious:

> The male therapist, who had been raised Protestant but had not practiced prayer since early childhood, was invited by a deeply religious couple to join them in prayer at the beginning of the session. The therapist immediately decided that by joining them he would not only harness their religious faith to the power of therapy but also create a good alliance with the somewhat oppositional husband. He bowed his head and joined hands with them, meditating in a manner that fit his own spiritual beliefs. This illustrates that therapist and client do not need to share the same beliefs or approach to spirituality. Therapy proceeded effectively with this couple, with an opening prayer becoming a ritual. Had the couple wanted a deeper focus on religious issues, the therapist would have referred them to a pastoral counselor.

Many nonreligious therapists have found that it is very powerful to bring biblical parables and tales into therapy with religious clients. Although metaphors and storytelling are always useful techniques, when the source is the Bible or another religious text, the client often perceives added authority.

Diagnosing and Treating Spiritual Emergencies

There are useful guidelines available from the Spiritual Competency Resource Center at http://www.spiritualcompetency.com/blackboard/lessons/lesson1.html. Nine interventions for spiritual emergency patients follow:

1. Normalize.
2. Create a therapeutic container.
3. Help the patient to reduce environmental and interpersonal stimulation.
4. Have the patient temporarily discontinue spiritual practices.
5. Use the therapy session to help ground the patient.
6. Suggest the patient eat a diet of "heavy" foods and avoid fasting.
7. Encourage the patient to become involved in simple, grounding, calming activities.
8. Encourage the patient to draw, paint, mold clay, make music, journal, write poetry, or dance.
9. Evaluate for medication.

After the emergency is over, psychotherapy helps the patient integrate the spiritual emergency into his or her life through a three-phase approach:

1. Telling the story of the spiritual emergency.
2. Tracing its symbolic/spiritual heritage.
3. Creating a new personal mythology, incorporating the spiritual emergency.

The Therapist as Moral Consultant

Doherty (1996) created a framework of moral consultation, offering a list of eight therapist actions, in order of increasing intensity:

1. Validate the language of moral concern when clients use it spontaneously.
2. Introduce language to make more explicit the moral horizon of the client's concerns.
3. Ask questions about the client's perceptions of the consequences of actions on others, and explore the personal, familial, religious, and cultural sources of these moral sensibilities.
4. Articulate the moral dilemma without giving your position.
5. Bring research knowledge and clinical insight to bear on the consequences of certain actions, particularly for vulnerable individuals.
6. Describe how you generally see the issue and how you tend to weigh the moral options, emphasizing that every situation is unique and that the client will, of course, make his or her own decision.
7. Say directly how concerned you are about the moral consequences of the client's actions.
8. Clearly state when you cannot support a client's decision or behavior, explaining your decision on moral grounds and, if necessary, withdraw from the case.

The Therapeutic Use of Art

Therapists should understand the benefits of art therapy, as well as the use of art classes as an adjunct to therapy. When people are given a chance to express themselves through an artistic modality, for instance painting or sculpture, significant changes occur that seem to have a spiritual dimension. Jung believed that the transition from talking to painting created a therapeutic step for patients to understand their own symbols. Art activities are beneficial when the client has the sense that something is happening inside that needs to be paid attention to, but for which there are not yet words: Using art can help the inner struggle emerge. Bavarsky (2000) described the spiritual and personal growth of members of an art class, providing samples of work at early and late stages of the group. A book that can be used as a self-help course as well as an adjunct to therapy is *The Artist's Way: A Spiritual Path to Higher Creativity* (Cameron, 2002), which provides a structure of daily journaling and a weekly commitment to have a "date" with your inner artist that does not include any other people. In a book written for blocked artists, London (1989) describes the experience of exploration, wonder, and discovery from seeing something firsthand:

> The challenge of art is the same challenge that life presents us with moment by moment: Can we awaken from our casual viewing of a stupendous world? Can we free up some of our mind from memory and give some over to perception and

some to imagination and be present and available to life as it streams over us? (p. 54)

Other Sources of Spiritual Nourishment

There are many activities besides art that provide spiritual nourishment, and therapists can help clients to identify and engage in them. Retreats are available that offer silence, solitude, beauties of nature, training in meditation, and many other experiences, which encourage spiritual experiences. Volunteer work that provides direct service to people in need can fill important spiritual and emotional needs. Married couples can go to marital enrichment retreats with a spiritual/religious component, such as Marriage Encounter®, at http://www.wwme.org.

Bibliotherapy

Recommending books may be appropriate for certain clients and issues. For instance, Kushner's (1981) book *When Bad Things Happen to Good People* provides comfort in times of suffering when people's faith in God is tested. Many self-help books focus on the soul, spirituality, and the quest for wholeness, such as Peck's (2003) best seller, *The Road Less Traveled.* Clients may be inspired by books that teach the spiritual wisdom from other cultures, such as Carlos Castaneda's (1985) reports of a guru's guidance in the *Teachings of Don Juan.*

Referral

Therapists may decide that they do not have the competence to work with the client's issues and that referral to a more qualified therapist is appropriate. It may also be beneficial to refer the client to a pastoral counselor from his or her own denomination or to a member of the clergy.

INTEGRATION OF HYPOTHESES

The **ES3** hypothesis is very compatible with the following hypotheses.

CS3 Developmental Transition

Jung's developmental model views midlife as a crucial period because after achieving the goals that had an external focus, people begin to feel empty and suffer from a loss of meaning. According to Jung, after midlife, the search for meaning must be inward and spiritual.

CS4 Loss and Bereavement

Dealing with loss is a time for spiritual resources. Beliefs about the afterlife are important factors in the grieving process. Many therapists assume that a healthy resolution to the loss of a spouse is for the client to disconnect from the deceased spouse. Such therapists may pathologize the process of a client who believes that the spouse continues to be present in a spiritual form, available to talk to, and that they will be rejoined in the afterlife for eternity.

C2 Faulty Cognitive Map

Religion provides clients with a cognitive map. If that map contains a punitive, unforgiving representation of God, it will produce suffering.

BL3 Skill Deficits or Lack of Competence

Meditation involves skills that develop with practice. Marsha Linehan (1993a, 1993b), who works with borderline patients from a behavioral, skills training perspective, found that the principles of bare attention can be distilled and taught to these patients to desensitize them to their own emotions. Christensen and Jacobson (2000) integrated a spiritual concept of "acceptance" in their cognitive-behavioral approach to marital counseling.

SCE2 Cultural Context

Religion is part of the client's cultural identity and is included under the umbrella of diversity. Frequently, the same religion is practiced differently in different cultures, for instance, Catholicism in Latin America and Ireland or Islam in Iran and Syria. Cultures with a heavy emphasis on materialistic, competitive, individualistic values may have the effect of diminishing people's contact with the spiritual dimension.

SUGGESTED READINGS

Recommended reading is listed separately for each hypothesis in this chapter.

ES1 Existential Issues

Barnes, H. E. (1962). *Humanistic existentialism: The literature of possibility.* Lincoln: University of Nebraska Press.

Barrett, W. (1962). *Irrational man: A study in existential philosophy.* New York: Anchor Books.

Camus, A. (1991). *The myth of Sisyphus and other essays* (Reissue ed.). New York: Vintage Books.

Frankl, V. E. (1997). *Man's search for meaning* (Rev. ed.). New York: Pocket Books.

Kaufmann, W. A. (1988). *Existentialism: From Dostoevsky to Sartre* (Rev. ed.). New York: Meridian Books.

Kopp, S. (1976). *If you meet the Buddha on the road, kill him* (Reissue ed.). New York: Bantam Books.

May, R., Angel, E., & Ellenberger, H. (Eds.). (1958). *Existence: A new dimension in psychology and psychiatry.* New York: Basic Books.

Sartre, J. P. (1956). *Being and nothingness.* New York: Philosophical Library.

Van Deurzen, E. (2002). *Existential counseling in practice* (2nd ed.). Thousand Oaks, CA: Sage.

Van Deurzen, E., & Arnold-Baker, C. (Eds.). (2005). *Existential perspectives on human issues: A handbook for therapeutic practice.* London: Palgrave Macmillan.

Yalom, I. (1990). *Love's executioner, and other tales of psychotherapy.* New York: Perennial.

Yalom, I. D. (1980). *Existential psychotherapy.* New York: Basic Books.

Journals

International Forum for Logotherapy

Journal for the Society for Existential Analysis

Journal of Humanistic Psychology

Journal of Phenomenological Psychology

Review of Existential Psychology and Psychiatry

ES2 Avoiding Freedom and Responsibility

Glasser, N. (Ed.). (1980). *What are you doing? How people are helped through reality therapy.* New York: Harper & Row.

Glasser, N. (Ed.). (1989). *Control theory in the practice of reality therapy: Case studies.* New York: Harper & Row.

Glasser, W. (1998) *Choice theory: A new psychology of personal freedom.* New York: HarperCollins.

Lakein, A. (1996). *How to get control of your time and your life* (Reissue ed.). New York: New American Library.

Pittman, F. (1999). *Grow up!* New York: Golden Books.

Von Franz, M. (2000). *The problem of the Puer Aeternus.* Bronx, NY: Inner City Press.

Wheelis, A. (1975). *How people change.* New York: Harper Colophon.

Wubbolding, R. E. (1988). *Using reality therapy.* New York: Harper & Row.

Yeoman, A. (1999). *Now or Neverland: Peter Pan and the myth of eternal youth.* Bronx, NY: Inner City Press.

ES3 Spiritual Dimension

Callahan, R., & McDonnell, R. (1996). *God is close to the brokenhearted: Good news for those who are depressed.* Cincinnati, OH: St. Anthony Messenger Press.

Cameron, J. (2002). *The artist's way: A spiritual path to higher creativity.* New York: J. P. Tarcher.

Carlson, D. L. (1994). *Why do Christians shoot their wounded? Helping (not hurting) those with emotional difficulties.* Downers Grove, IL: InterVarsity Press.

Cope, S. (1999). *Yoga and the quest for the true self.* New York: Bantam Books.

Cornett, C. (1998). *The soul of psychotherapy: Recapturing the spiritual dimension in the therapeutic encounter.* New York: Free Press.

Deikman, A. J. (1992). *The observing self: Mysticism and psychotherapy.* Boston: Beacon Press.

Epstein, M. (1995). *Thoughts without a thinker: Psychotherapy from a Buddhist perspective.* New York: Basic Books.

Goldstein, J., & Kornfield, J. (1987). *Seeking the heart of wisdom: The path of insight meditation.* Boston: Shambala.

Koenig, H. G. (Ed.). (1998). *Handbook of religion and mental health.* New York: Academic Press.

Miller, W. R. (1999). *Integrating spirituality into treatment: Resources for practitioners.* Washington, DC: American Psychological Association.

Pargament, K. I. (2001). *The psychology of religion and coping: Theory, research, and practice.* New York: Guilford Press.

Richards, P. S., & Bergin, A. E. (1997). *A spiritual strategy for counseling and psychotherapy.* Washington, DC: American Psychological Association.

Richards, P. S., & Bergin, A. E. (2000). *Handbook of psychotherapy and religious diversity.* Washington, DC: American Psychological Association.

Roukema, R. W. (1997). *The soul in distress: What every pastoral counselor should know about emotional and mental illness.* New York: Hawarth Pastoral Press.

Shafranske, E. P. (Ed.). (1996). *Religion and the clinical practice of psychology.* Washington, DC: American Psychological Association.

Sperry, L. (2001). *Spirituality in clinical practice: Incorporating the spiritual dimension in psychotherapy and counseling.* New York: Brunner-Routledge.

Sperry, L., & Shafranske, E. (2004). *Spiritually oriented psychotherapy.* Washington, DC: American Psychological Association.

Walsh, R., & Vaugh, R. (Eds.). (1993). *Paths beyond ego: The transpersonal vision.* New York: P. Tarcher.

Inspirational Self-Help Books

Beattie, M. (1990). *The language of letting go.* Center City, MN: Hazelden Foundation.

Cameron, J. (2002). *The artist's way: A spiritual path to higher creativity.* New York: J. P. Tarcher.

Hay, L. (1999). *You can heal your life.* Carlsbad, CA: Hay House.

Jampolsky, G. G. (1988). *Love is letting go of fear* (Rev. ed.). Berkeley, CA: Celestial Arts.

Roman, S. (1989). *Spiritual growth: Being your higher self.* Tiburon, CA: H. J. Kramer.

Chapter 8

PSYCHODYNAMIC MODELS

The term *psychodynamic* is an umbrella for theories that trace their roots to the work of Freud, Jung, and Adler. Psychodynamic models have three major emphases: (1) conflicts, mechanisms, and processes in the mind, which may include the concept of the unconscious; (2) different structures and stages of personality development; and (3) the causal significance of early childhood experiences on adult behavior. Table 8.1 lists the four psychodynamic hypotheses.

KEY IDEAS FOR P1 INTERNAL PARTS AND SUBPERSONALITIES

The construct of "the self" varies enormously among cultures, as do the values for what constitutes a "healthy self" or a "normal self." The idea of a "unified self" is a social construction. If people are taught to believe that inner unity is "normal," they may be reluctant to reveal the multiplicity of their inner parts, fearing that they will be diagnosed with the multiple personality disorder they have seen dramatized in films such as *Three Faces of Eve* and *Sybil*.

Table 8.1   Psychodynamic Models

P1 Internal Parts and Subpersonalities	The problem is explained in terms of **Internal Parts and Subpersonalities** that need to be heard, understood, and coordinated.
P2 Reenactment of Early Childhood Experiences	The problem is a **Reenactment of Early Childhood Experiences:** Feelings and needs from early childhood are reactivated and patterns from the family of origin are repeated.
P3 Immature Sense of Self and Conception of Others	Difficulties stem from the client's failure to progress beyond the **Immature Sense of Self and Conception of Others** that is normal for very young children.
P4 Unconscious Dynamics	The symptom or problem is explained in terms of **Unconscious Dynamics.** Defense mechanisms keep thoughts and emotions out of awareness.

P1 INTERNAL PARTS AND SUBPERSONALITIES

Definition

The problem is explained in terms of **Internal Parts** and **Subpersonalities** that need to be heard, understood, and coordinated.

Explanation

It is natural, not pathological, to be aware of diverse inner parts and subpersonalities. Problems stem from lack of awareness of and communication among internal parts, conflict among different parts, suppression of a part, and dominance by a particular part. Problems can be resolved by increasing awareness of parts and their dynamics, encouraging a healthy internal group process, and setting specific outcome goals for particular parts.

Examples

Sally says that there is a part of her that wants to marry Harry and a part of her that is unsure. She recently discovered that he is continuing to exchange occasional e-mail messages with an ex-girlfriend. She wants to believe him when he says that they are just friends, but a side of her is nagging at her that maybe he is not trustworthy. She says that it is very difficult to sort out logic from feelings and that the "little kid" in her is scared.	Dan is having a great deal of difficulty making decisions about his career. He explains his conflict in these words: "My Achiever wants to get a PhD, but my Beach Bum is sick to death of school and just wants to run off and live in Europe for a year." He read a book about Transactional Analysis and had some important insights. "My Critical Parent is driving me to be perfect. My Rebellious Child takes over when the pressure gets too great."	Suzy is a woman in her 30s who has been divorced twice and is frustrated that she cannot maintain a committed relationship. She admits that when she first starts dating a man, she suppresses her reservations and doubts about him. Then after she feels secure, she begins to focus on his faults. She explains that it is as if the "Adoring Lover" disappears and the "Critical Shrew" takes over. "I wish I had a 'Tolerant' part," she said.

Criteria for Healthy Internal Dynamics

The internal parts of an individual function together like members of a family (Schwartz, 1995). To recognize when there are dysfunctional parts or relationships among parts, we need to have an understanding of what healthy, functional internal dynamics are like. The criteria in Table 8.2 are the same as those for a functional task group or a healthy family.

Transactional Analysis

Eric Berne (1996), the originator of Transactional Analysis (TA), described three *ego states* that are accessible to consciousness: Child, Adult, and Parent. The capitals distinguish the internal ego state from the ordinary usage of these words. The popular use of these concepts is demonstrated when someone talks about "my inner child" or "being a better parent to myself."

Child

Child states include the Free or Natural Child, and the Adapted Child, which can either be conforming or rebellious. The Little Professor is the Adult-in-the-Child,

Table 8.2   Criteria for Healthy Internal Dynamics

Harmony, Cohesiveness, and Impulse Control

All parts, even unpleasant ones, are accepted and owned. They are not attacked, suppressed, or distorted but are allowed to be heard. The dynamics of the *internal group* are harmonious and free from coercion and abuse. As in a functional family, a hierarchy is maintained and the leadership comes from mature, responsible parts rather than from impulsive, Child parts. When a decision is made and an action agreed on, the inner selves cooperate and function as a cohesive, unified entity, without the presence of secret saboteurs. Child parts who usually want instant pleasure are able to tolerate frustration and delay gratification.

Good Morale and Optimism

There are internal sources of esteem: Parent parts are supportive, nurturing, and encouraging and when they evaluate and criticize, they are constructive, rational, and fair. Inner parts all feel and believe that the person has a right to happiness, pleasure, and success. There are sources of higher ideals and a sense of purpose. The internal parts can maintain morale in face of frustration and disappointments.

Ability to Set Goals and Engage in Goal-Directed Behavior

An executive (Adult) part is able to mediate among conflicting parts, create compromises, and assure unified cooperation toward a goal. Goals are based on values (Parent), reality testing (Adult), and respect for the rights of the Child to have pleasure, creativity, and a rich emotional life.

attempting to solve problems but lacking the logic and rational thinking of a mature adult. Child states are magical, creative, playful, curious, vulnerable, manipulative, grandiose, and needy. The Victim role is played from a Child state.

Parent

The Nurturing Parent is a source of soothing, comfort, and encouragement, whereas the Critical Parent nags, pushes, criticizes, and judges. The Parent carries ideals and morals and transmits rules and values from the culture and from prior generations. The Rescuer and Persecutor roles are played from the Parent.

Adult

The Adult part of the personality serves functions such as rational thinking, problem solving, reality testing, data gathering, and scientific reasoning. The Adult serves as the mediator between Parent and Child and functions as the executive of the personality, the one who creates plans to achieve goals.

An example of someone who is struggling to lose weight illustrates how these inner parts function in internal conflict:

- *Critical Parent:* You should take those pounds off, what's wrong with you, you're a self-indulgent, lazy loser—no I can't call you a loser, you're not losing but gaining. *Nurturing:* Don't worry, I know you're really stressed. Go ahead and have some ice cream, it will make you feel better.
- *Natural Child:* I love food! It tastes so good. It is so much fun! I feel so good when I eat an ice cream cone. *Adapted:* I know I'm bad, what's wrong with

me, I keep trying but I just can't do it. *Rebellious:* I'm going to eat whatever I want and you can't stop me. I don't care about your stupid rules; you just don't want me to be happy.

- *Adult:* Let's come up with a plan where I can maintain a steady weight loss of one pound a week yet still eat foods I enjoy and have certain meals where I can disregard the rules.

The same message can be delivered from different ego states with very different results, as illustrated by the example of a boss's reaction to her secretary on receiving a report with many typographical errors.

- *Critical Parent:* You can't do anything right! What's wrong with you?

- *Child in Victim role:* Why does this have to happen to me? Just when I think I'm finished, something always has to go wrong.

- *Adult:* We need to have a perfect draft by nine tomorrow morning. I need you to stay late tonight to correct these errors.

Subpersonalities and Inner Selves

Many theorists have contributed to an understanding of the multiple parts within the "self."

Gestalt Therapy

Gestalt therapists identify *polarities*—inner parts in opposition to each other, such as top dog and underdog—and assume that if opposing parts dialogue freely, the goal of integration will be attained. Recently, Polster (1995) described working with multiple inner selves, instead of focusing on two-sided polarities.

Psychosynthesis

Assagioli (1971) defined a *subpersonality* as a constellation of behaviors, feelings, and thoughts that originate to meet certain needs such as safety, belonging, and self-esteem. As the individual moves to adulthood, the function of that subpersonality is still important, but the methods it employs may be inappropriate and inflexible. For example, a woman, who as a child had tantrums to get attention from her mother, might find that this method of eliciting caretaking behavior from her husband actually has the opposite effect. When a person overidentifies with a particular subpersonality, she becomes trapped by a single worldview and self-image. The process of psychosynthesis involves "disidentification" from the subpersonalities, replaced by identification with the higher self. From a disidentified perspective, the individual can perceive both the valid purpose of the subpersonality and its ineffective or destructive pattern.

Voice Dialogue

Hal Stone and Sidra Stone (1993) created a typology of subselves, including Rulemaker, Pusher, Inner Critic, Perfectionist, Power Broker, Judge, Playful Child, and Magical Child, which are comparable to Berne's Parent and Child states. The two most important are the Protector/Controller and the Vulnerable Child.

1. *Protector/Controller:* Nicknamed the "boss," this self decides what is socially acceptable and assures that we act appropriately. It needs to maintain control over confusion, lack of direction, anger, sexuality, fear, and any subselves that are viewed as potentially dangerous. It buries the Vulnerable Child part to protect it. Therapists should contact this part to get permission to proceed with a therapeutic activity because it makes the decision about whether it is safe or dangerous.

2. *Vulnerable Child:* This part is usually disowned—protected and kept under cover so that it won't be hurt. Its feelings are easily hurt, and it fears abandonment. This subpersonality enables intimacy. It is exquisitely sensitive to nonverbal messages, especially those indicating rejection or withdrawal. It will only appear if it trusts the facilitator/therapist.

Voice Therapy

Although the name is similar to voice dialogue, voice therapy was developed by Robert Firestone (1997) to focus on a specific internal, self-hating part that creates "microsuicidal states" because it wants to thoroughly undermine and destroy the individual. In contrast to the intention of the Stones' "inner critic," which is usually "I want the best for her, I'm trying to help her improve herself," Firestone's negative voice believes, "She's no good, she's disgusting, and doesn't deserve to be alive." The inner critic can be persuaded to find different methods for getting her good intentions met, whereas Firestone's internal voice needs to be externalized and defeated by a healthy, self-affirming part.

The Concept of Resistance

Resistance is often explained as a battle between inner parts: one part wants to change, while the other doesn't—out of fear of the risks, or enjoyment of the benefits of staying the same (secondary gains). Another interpretation of resistance is that the person has different, conflicting needs or goals such as security versus adventure, material success versus spending time with family, or dependence versus independence. If progress is made toward one goal, the part that represents the other goal begins to feel threatened.

If therapists spend time exploring the viewpoints of different inner parts before creating the therapeutic contract, they can often promote a more constructive, cooperative alliance and circumvent resistance. Using the terms from TA, therapists need to make the contract for change with the Adult, the executive part of the personality, making sure that the Natural Child is going to get its needs met and "sign on" to the agreement. If the contract is made only with a Parent ("should") part, resistance is almost guaranteed. It is wise practice, whenever setting goals, to ask,

Imagine that you have just achieved the change (goal) you want. What part of you would be unhappy about that?

How Internal Parts Function in Relationships

Two people, each interacting from Parent, Adult, and Child states, can interact in very confusing and frustrating ways, unless they have tools for discussing internal parts and making autonomous choices about which subself should be dominant at a given time. Using the terminology of TA, clients learn to recognize when someone is "hooking" their child—triggering an emotional, inappropriate reaction from one of their Child states—and they develop skills of consciously switching into the Adult. Through TA, clients can understand the dysfunctional patterns, which Eric Berne (1996) called "rackets" and "games," recognizing how people avoid intimacy and reap "payoffs" of unhappy feelings.

Therapists can discuss client's real-world relationships, teach tools of analysis, and address how the client's internal parts are operating in the therapy session. For instance, many destructive patterns in relationships revolve around roles (e.g., Persecutor, Rescuer, and Victim), which can be viewed as subpersonalities. A client who initially presents as a needy Victim ("Help me!") can hook you into the Rescuer role. If you are unsuccessful in your efforts to help, the client can switch into the Persecutor role ("You can't help me; you're no good like everyone else.")

Summary of Goals

The various approaches to working with inner parts and subpersonalities share these goals:

- *Embracing all the selves:* Helping the client to achieve awareness of each part, reclaiming "disowned parts," and permitting verbal expression from each part without fearing it will take over the personality.

- *Strengthening the awareness and executive parts of the personality:* A strong, competent Adult needs to be behind the steering wheel, assuring that no single subpersonality dominates or acts out independently. The executive part examines the messages from different parts, describes and analyzes internal and interpersonal process, and communicates to others to resolve conflict. The client experiences increased choice, self-control, and autonomy.

- *Modifying parts:* Goals will include toning down a part that is too dominant, supporting and strengthening weak parts that need to be heard, updating the rules and methods of powerful Parent parts, creating new parts to serve important functions such as boosting self-esteem and soothing painful affects, and developing a strategy to deal with self-destructive parts.

- *Learning to tolerate vulnerability in the self and in others:* This opens up the opportunity for intimacy and the development of mature ways of taking care of one's need for safety and trusting relationships.

WHEN IS THIS HYPOTHESIS A GOOD MATCH?

What most people continue to call multiple personality disorder was renamed Dissociative Identity Disorder (300.14) in *DSM-IV*. A person with this disorder shifts identities as each struggles to take over the personality. Alternate identities take control in sequence and deny knowledge of one another, resulting in gaps in memory for personal history that far exceed ordinary forgetfulness. This disorder fits **P4 (Unconscious Dynamics)** because of the unconscious components. It is essential for therapists to rule this diagnosis out if they want to use the techniques appropriate for **P1 (Internal Parts and Subpersonalities)**.

Gathering Client Data to Support the P1 Hypothesis

To assess the fit of this hypothesis, you must gather data about the client's inner dynamics. The empathic, nonjudgmental therapist is able to contact and understand the various subpersonalities of the client, some of whom are inarticulate and emotional. Clients can have a great deal of shame and embarrassment about certain inner voices and may be reluctant to reveal socially undesirable parts. In exploring inner parts, you send the message that the client is not defined by any one part—that we all have inner parts that we would not ordinarily reveal. To help the client understand the concept, use a common, everyday experience as an example, for instance, a conflict over making an expensive purchase or ordering a fattening desert.

Client Content

Clients are often already aware of the multiplicity of their inner selves and say things like "A part of me wants to be thin, but another part just wants to enjoy food and eat whatever I want, whenever I want it."

Client Process

Different inner parts or subpersonalities are revealed by nonverbal behavior such as shifting body posture, different mannerisms, and variable styles of speaking, such as a scolding tone with lots of "shoulds." When the client is in a Child state, the therapist can pinpoint a specific age from the tone of voice, facial expression, choice of vocabulary, and posture. These observations provide objective data for the **P1** formulation:

> As the client talks, the nonverbal messages—body posture, tone of voice, facial expression—shift from an angry, dominating person (Critical Parent) to a weak, passive, obedient one (Adapted Child).

Problems That Fit this Hypothesis

Table 8.3 provides example of problems for which hypothesis **P1** was effectively applied.

Table 8.3   Problems Explained by P1 Internal Parts and Subpersonalities Hypothesis

Difficulty Making a Decision and Selecting a Course of Action

Inner conflict: Any problem title that contains words like *indecision, ambivalence, confusion, dilemma,* which could be expressed as "torn between two lovers," or "to stay or to break up."

Problems of fear and avoidance: A part of the client wants to do something, another part holds back, is afraid, thinks "I can't," or feels fear.

Indecision, with immobilization and inner torment: As an example, Hamlet's famous soliloquy, "to be or not to be," deals with the conflict between a passive part and a part that wants to *"take arms against a sea of troubles and by opposing end them."*

Difficulties Sticking to a Chosen Course of Action

Internal opposition:

Difficulty breaking bad habits: "A part of me says I should stop smoking, another part just loves cigarettes."

Procrastination: "I should do something, but I just can't get myself to start it."

Lack of persistence: "It's not worth it." "It's too much trouble." "I didn't want it anyway."

Impulsivity: Restraining parts (e.g., voice of reason, reminders about consequences, self-control, or responsibility to others) are either silent or too weak to exert any influence on the impulsive parts.

Poor frustration tolerance: An impatient Child part wants exactly what it wants, immediately. There is a lack of a good planner part who knows how to break the task into small bits and reward small accomplishments.

Suppression of Feelings and Spontaneity

Rigidity: Goals are based entirely on "shoulds," obligation, duty, or concern for the reaction of others. The parts that represent passion, play, pleasure, and spontaneity are completely ignored and may act as saboteurs.

Blocks to creativity: Overly perfectionistic and critical parts interfere with immersion in creative process; there is suppression of a creative, grandiose part.

Problems Related to Depression

Suicidal risk: There are parts that want to die versus parts that want to live. It is crucial for therapists to search for, find, and strengthen the parts that want to live.

Self-hatred: The hypothesis of anger turned inward can be explored by identifying a self-critical—perhaps self-loathing and self-destructive—inner part.

Excessive guilt: There is the presence of a punitive, internal voice, combined with the lack of a part that is nurturing, tolerant, and forgiving.

Low self-esteem: An inner part that attacks the self, combined with the lack of inner parts that soothe and offer self-praise.

Problems of Stress, Exhaustion, and Overwork

Excessive commitments and obligations: Multiple parts make commitments without regard to reasonable limits set by time and health. A pleaser part that can't say no to the demands and requests of others.

Lack of relaxation and pleasure: There is a lack of a strong advocate for the inner parts that demand relaxation and pleasure; There is a moralistic, demanding Parent part ("can't play until all the work is done") and a worthless part, which only feels good when it is busy and productive and thus comes out when there are no obligations to fulfill.

Table 8.3   *(Continued)*

Perfectionism: There is a perfectionist part or a relentless pusher with unrealistic demands and standards. An Adapted Child part feels like a failure unless he gets straight As.

Instability in Emotions and Relationships

Dramatic alternation of moods: Alternation between grandiose self and weak, empty self, and a lack of inner parts that maintain self-esteem and soothe moods. If the Vulnerable Self makes appearances and gets hurt, the powerful parts rush in to protect it.

Unstable relationships: The person switches among different roles in relationships, such as Victim, Persecutor, or Rescuer, or shifts from a part that idealizes another to a part that devalues the other person.

TREATMENT PLANNING

Listen to what the client says and respond by identifying different inner parts or voices, using a tentative tone that shows you are open to being corrected:

> It sounds like a part of you really wants to succeed, but another part is ready to give up.
> What exactly does that inner voice say to you?
> I get the impression that there's a Parent voice telling you to study hard, but the Child part just wants to have fun.

You can focus on the process and comment on the client's body language and tone of voice.

Naming the Parts

Inner parts work is enhanced when the subpersonalities are given nicknames. It is best to let the client choose the name, but the therapist can make suggestions: *It sounds like you have a real Perfectionist operating. . . . Let's hear from the Critic. Is there a Free Spirit part that wants to respond?* The client might recognize inner personalities and give them names such as Achiever, Caretaker, or Pleaser. Polster (1995) gives an explanation of the benefit of naming inner selves:

> To talk about selves seems a strange way to talk about a person, as though these selves were his tenants or employees or internal sprites. . . . With the naming of each self, the self becomes an agent of the person. . . . Just as the novel creates human images that echo in the minds of its readers, the image of selves also comes alive, giving membership and coherence to otherwise disconnected parts of the person. (pp. 58–59)

Psychoeducation

The concept of internal parts and subpersonalities can be directly taught, using diagrams on a white board or paper if this helps the client to visualize what you are explaining. With this approach, the client is encouraged to practice identifying inner parts and recognizing which part is speaking at any given time. There are many books that clients can read, such as *Born to Win* (M. James & Jongeward, 1996) or *Embracing Our Selves* (Stone & Stone, 1993); you can suggest homework to practice identifying internal parts. Through these experiences, the client strengthens the executive part of the personality—known by names such as Aware Ego, Adult, or Higher Self—that has awareness of all the inner parts and can analyze their dynamics.

Communicating with Child Parts

If you want to access a Child state of the client, you must adjust your voice and language and watch for nonverbal clues (e.g., timid or vulnerable body language) that the client has moved out of the Adult or Parent state. It is important to be able to talk in language that children understand. This does not mean talking down to the client, but it requires the ability to ask questions and make statements with simple sentence structure. The Vulnerable Child will not make an appearance unless it feels secure that the therapist can provide protection. It is extremely important to stay empathically attuned and not express judgment. You need to be clear on process goals. If your goal is to welcome the Vulnerable Child into the room, you must refrain from pointing out irrational thinking or giving advice. Use feeling words and be sure that they are words in a child's vocabulary.

Bring your own natural spontaneity, playfulness, and creativity to the session if you want to access the Child. You can use colored markers on big white pads, sit cross-legged, and use props such as teddy bears. Asking the client to write with the nondominant hand can help access the Child parts. One useful strategy, when asking about early childhood experiences, is to ask the client to talk in the present tense.

Experiential Techniques

Although experiential techniques differ, they share a common feature: The client does not talk *about* the parts, but talks *from* each part. A separate location (e.g., position of a chair or a different chair) is designated for each separate part, and the client must switch positions to talk from a different part. If, in the course of the interview, the client and therapist have identified and discussed different parts or voices, it can be a very natural next step to invite the client to let each part "speak for itself." This can be by simple invitation (*Let's hear directly from that judging part*). The therapist must feel comfortable saying things like *I'd like to hear from a different part now. Are you the part that is afraid?* and *I'm hearing a different part creep in, let's hear from her later.* You will gather important data just by seeing if accessing different parts comes naturally. For clients who are unclear about the instructions or are self-conscious and afraid of appearing ridiculous, give clear directives and a bit of reassurance and coaching. You may also use yourself as a model and dramatize your own inner parts, picking a common, nonthreatening situation such as deciding on where to go for vacation. You must be willing to drop the suggestion if it seems inappropriate to or uncomfortable for the client.

Having the Client Dispute a Negative Part

In voice therapy (Firestone, 1997), the client first plays the negative, critical part, sitting in a different chair and speaking harshly to the seat she usually sits in: "You jerk, can't you get anything right? You're a total loser, nobody will ever love you." Then, back in the original seat, the client disputes the message, bringing power and certainty into her voice: "You're wrong! I *am* competent. You only have destructive things to say. I'm not going to listen to you anymore." The therapist wants to empower the client and to help her externalize a very destructive introject.

Dialogue between Two Parts

In most cases, different parts will all have something valid to offer, and share a common goal of wanting the best for the client's life. In the Gestalt two-chair technique, the therapist guides the client back and forth between two parts, each spatially linked to a different chair. The therapist's role is to clarify which part is speaking and to make sure that the client is talking to the other chair and staying in role. The timing of the shift can come from the therapist's instruction (*Now switch!*) or from the client's own sense of when the other part should respond. Through this activity, the client comes to understand each part and what it wants and fears. However, the dialogue can become very emotional and the spontaneity and intensity of the experience can overcome the client's defenses, with possible ill effects, as well as overwhelm an inexperienced therapist. This method is not appropriate for making major life decisions because there can be a total absence in the dialogue of Adult parts who need to rationally evaluate consequences.

Voice Dialogue

A technique that is much safer and has the advantage of incorporating the executive of the personality is voice dialogue: The separate parts never dialogue with each other, but instead take turns talking to the facilitator. Table 8.4 gives instructions adapted from the books by the Stones (1989, 1993). You will see that by always having the client return "to the center," you promote the client's self-reflection and protect the client from experiencing any one part as overwhelmingly powerful. The skills needed by the facilitator are basic listening skills, and so this technique is easy to master.

Group Techniques

A group provides an extremely effective format for enacting different parts of an internal conflict.

Table 8.4   Voice Dialogue Instructions

Physically Separate the Subpersonalities

Either the therapist or the client can pick a subpersonality to hear from first. An easy method is to have a wheeled chair and let the client choose whether to roll the chair right or left.

Talk to the Subpersonality

Talk to the subpersonality as you would talk to a real person. Begin the conversation by asking *Who are you?* or *Which part of Alice am I speaking to?* Ask open-ended questions and paraphrase back what you hear, being empathic and nonjudgmental: *Tell me about yourself. What about that bothers you? Sounds like you get very frustrated when she ignores you. What do you want for yourself? How do you feel about her?* The therapist must not take sides or reject any parts. Your goal is to facilitate the self-expression of the subpersonality, not to try to change it in any way.

Coach the Subpersonality to Stay in Character

Guide the subpersonality to speak of the whole person as a separate entity. You might paraphrase what the subpersonality says, changing pronouns, *"You mean she (referring to the position where the client sits during the session) wants to finish the dissertation but you want to quit and just stay home with your children."* If it sounds like a separate subpersonality is beginning to speak, you can say, *"I hear that the part who feels guilty is coming in. We can hear from him later, but now let's stay with what you have to say."*

Learn about the History of the Subpersonality

Often the subpersonality is focused on the current issue. It is important to move from talking to a part in a specific conflict to a subpersonality who has been around for a long time. Ask the subpersonality: *When did you first join her personality? Can you think of a time in childhood when you had a big part to play in her life?*

Invite the Client to Return to "the Center"

Before ending the conversation with the subpersonality, ask *Do you have anything further to say before you return to the center position?* Then when the client is back in the original position, allow her to settle in and return to her normal state of consciousness. Ask for reactions to the subpersonality: *What is your reaction to what she said?*

Consider Hearing from Another Subpersonality

If it seems appropriate to hear from a different subpersonality, ask the client to move to a different position. Again, the choice of which part to hear from can come from the client or the therapist.

Assure Closure to the Exercise

The exercise ends with the client back in the center position, given time to reflect on the activity. Never end the activity with the client in a subpersonality. Be sure to allow time for the client to get back to normal consciousness before leaving the session. At the very end of the exercise, if you want, you can ask the client to stand behind you and look at the chair as you summarize the different phases of the activity. This gives the higher, "aware self," a chance to process the experience and possibly have new insights.

Psychodrama

Developed by Jacob Moreno, psychodrama involves members of a group of unrelated people (in contrast to family therapy) playing roles in a dramatization of the issues of the *protagonist*—the person who has volunteered for the psychodrama. Under the direction of the facilitator, group members are given parts in the drama and their participation can be verbal or physical. The protagonist also participates in the drama, unless a designated *double* is asked to fill in for her. The psychodrama involves a variety of scenarios: present life situations, family of origin scenes, and dramas of subpersonalities. For instance, if the protagonist is dealing with depression, one of the parts may represent violent angry feelings that have been suppressed. Another part can be a very negative, hostile voice. Characters might represent the client as a child in different developmental stages. Blatner (2000) provides concise summaries of over 70 techniques.

Parts Party

In contrast to psychodrama, the volunteer does not participate in this activity. He explains the issue and everyone listens and tries to identify specific internal parts. Each member of the group chooses a part to play, usually selecting one that is related to his or her internal dynamics. After some preliminary coaching by the volunteer, the "parts" dramatize the conflict, sitting in a tight circle, while the client stays with the therapist outside of the group circle and observes. As the client watches other people reproducing his internal drama, there are opportunities for awareness, new insights, and clarity about what needs to change. At the end of the dramatization, the client expresses his reactions. The different group members can share how they felt playing their roles. The therapist can make interpretations about some of the observed dynamics such as the lack of any internal mediator, the suppression of certain emotional parts, or the excessive power of one particular part.

Creative Activities

Either directly or indirectly, you want to engage the client's "Creative Part" in the therapeutic work, both during the session and in homework assignments.

Writing

Use one of these assignments or create your own.

- Imagine a bus that contains all of your subpersonalities. Watch it come toward you down the road, draw up, and stop. Describe these personalities, one by one, as they get off the bus. Give each one a nickname (Snow, 1992).
- Write a dialogue between two different parts that are involved in a specific conflict.
- Write a scene in a drama that includes several of your subpersonalities. First, list the cast of characters, describing each one briefly.

- Write a letter from a subpersonality to the whole personality, describing its feelings and needs.
- Have a specific subpersonality answer a list of questions such as the following, taken from Rowan (1990): What do you look like? How old are you? What situations bring you out? What is your approach to the world? What do you want? What do you need? What do you have to offer? Where did you come from? Where did you first meet (name of person)? What would happen if you took over permanently?

Art

These activities are useful for exploring emotional aspects of internal dynamics. They also help strengthen creative and nonverbal subpersonalities.

- Using different colored markers, draw all the different inner personalities that you are aware of now, showing their relationships to each other, and giving them names. Draw bubbles over their heads to show what they think and feel.
- Have the client create drawings or paintings from separate subpersonalities.

INTEGRATION OF HYPOTHESES

Inner-parts work frequently leads to the use of one or more of the following hypotheses.

BL3 Skill Deficits or Lack of Competence

If an inner part is afraid to do something because the person lacks adequate skills, skill building will be a part of therapy. For instance, the inner part that wants closeness needs skills in spontaneous self-disclosure and empathic listening. A client can appear resistant in therapy when there is not only internal conflict but also lack of particular skills.

C4 Dysfunctional Self-Talk

Each of the different subselves provides its own stream of internal talk; goals for modification of self-talk can be set for each part. For instance, a Critical Parent can develop a more positive, constructive way of speaking: Instead of saying, "You messed up! You're stupid, you can't get anything right," it could say "Let's learn from this mistake, You'll do better next time. Don't give up!" If there is a lack of self-nurturing, the person can agree to build habits of positive self-talk and practice this new part until it feels natural. For example, the person with a strong Workaholic part can build an Advocate for Relaxation who says things like "Take the weekend off and you'll be more productive next week."

ES2 Avoiding Freedom and Responsibility

When people are struggling with making responsible choices, it can help to examine internal parts and the sources of ambivalence. Many of the problems in Table 8.3 were examples of difficulties in making choices and following through. Common conflicts are between the following pairs of parts: Spontaneous Free Spirit versus Responsible Controller, Courageous Risk-Taker versus Security-at-any-cost, and Head versus Heart.

By exploring internal parts, the client gets clarity about true feelings and desired goals. An assessment can be made about whether the client currently has internal parts that sabotage autonomy, such as Blamer or Victim.

ES3 Spiritual Dimension

The idea of disidentifying from certain aspects of the personality is compatible with many religious and spiritual practices. Some of the theories of subpersonalities subscribe to the idea of a "higher" awareness, who is separate from the personality and can examine the workings of inner parts from a higher point of awareness. A "higher guide" can be experienced as a subpersonality.

P2 Reenactment of Early Childhood Experiences

The two-chair technique that starts with the client dialoguing with an internal part may lead to recognition that the internal voice is an exact replica of a parent's voice. At that point, the client can be asked to play the role of that parent rather than an inner part. When the client switches to the other chair and confronts the parent, it presents a chance to resolve "unfinished business" from childhood.

SCE2 Cultural Context

Cultures differ in their view of "the self," judgments about what constitutes a "healthy" or "normal" self, and acceptance of the multiplicity of internal parts. As people go through the acculturation process, they may be aware that the old culture and the new culture are represented internally by different subpersonalities. By dialoguing with each part separately, the client can create a new, integrated bicultural identity without feeling torn in two directions.

KEY IDEAS FOR P2 REENACTMENT OF EARLY CHILDHOOD EXPERIENCES

Events in early childhood affect relationships later in life. In some way, all adults reenact the patterns that were laid down when they were young. When early childhood experiences were positive, the reenactments in adulthood create healthy relationships and happy experiences. However, unsatisfactory experiences in the family of origin can create many difficulties in adult life. For better or worse, we create templates from early relationships and tend to fit subsequent relationships into those patterns (Kahn, 1997).

P2 REENACTMENT OF EARLY CHILDHOOD EXPERIENCES

Definition

The problem is a **Reenactment of Early Childhood Experiences:** Feelings and needs from early childhood are reactivated and patterns from the family of origin are repeated.

Explanation

Early childhood experiences can have profound influences on adult functioning. Many adult problems can be understood as efforts to resolve conflicts and satisfy unmet needs of childhood. Relationships with parents and other significant family members function as templates for adult relationships. Insight into the recurring pattern may not be enough; the client may need to experience and learn to tolerate painful emotions and change self-protective styles of relating.

Examples

Tanya repeatedly chooses men who are aloof and unavailable; if they become more affectionate, she loses interest. She realizes that her father was cold and that she is choosing men exactly like him. She's trying to win her father's love, but when the man treats her nicely, he no longer reminds her of her father.	Carlos's gastrointestinal symptoms were related to anger that he couldn't express to his wife. He was assuming she would treat him just as his mother did, and that she wouldn't care about his problems or feelings. His wife, he admitted, had never treated him that way and was, in fact, a very caring, concerned person.	Henry was always envious of his older brother and competed with him as a child, always falling short in his father's eyes. Now as an adult, he is focused on being number one in everything he tries and has no male friends because he views all men as hostile competitors. His doctor has told him to slow down but he refuses.

The concept of reenactment appears in many theories under different names. Freud used the terms *transferences* and *repetition compulsion,* Gestalt Therapy used *unfinished business,* and TA used *scripts* and *early childhood decisions.* Although reenactment patterns can be self-defeating, maladaptive, and painful, they are also attempts at healing old wounds and solving difficult problems. Freud believed that *repetition compulsion*—the term he used for the tendency of trauma victims to mentally reexperience traumatic experiences—was the mind's attempt to achieve mastery and control.

Attachment Theory

The attachment of the child to the original caregiver functions as a template for adult intimate relationships (Ainsworth, 1982; Bowlby, 1988; Bretherton, 1992). Children build important belief systems (*internal working models*) regarding the reliability of attachment figures, and their own lovability, worthiness, and competence. Three types of attachment styles were originally identified, but a fourth one has been added in recent years (Cassidy & Shaver, 1999).

1. *Secure:* The child develops faith in herself and her attachment figures, and feels free to explore the environment because she can count on the other to

be available for comfort and reassurance. This is the most adaptive style in adulthood.

2. *Anxious-ambivalent insecure (also called anxious-resistant):* The attachment figure is inconsistent and unreliable, and the child grows up to have low self-esteem, and is often clingy and insecure in adult relationships.

3. *Anxious-avoidant insecure:* The child was rebuffed, rejected, and ignored, and so develops a cold, distant attitude; in adulthood, a person with this style rejects others and treats relationships as if they do not matter.

4. *Disorganized:* In contrast to the prior two styles, which have coherent patterns and are sometimes effective, this style refers to the lack of a coherent template for interacting.

At the beginning of an adult romantic relationship, partners often feel secure because they are totally focused on each other. In later stages, as each person deals with physical separations and emotional unavailability, deep-rooted attachment styles learned in childhood become recognizable. Attachment theory is also a useful model for understanding the difficulties that parents may have in dealing with their children's needs for separateness and autonomy. Parents who never developed secure attachments as children may either cling to their own children or withdraw emotionally from them when they move off to explore the world.

Birth Order Position

Adler stressed the importance of birth order and the interpretation of one's position in the family. An only child may not learn to share or cooperate and may want to be center stage in all relationships. Older siblings are often trailblazers, setting down patterns that will either be followed or avoided. Middle children can feel angry and cheated, or they can develop as mediators and peacemakers. Birth order can also affect the harmony in a marriage. For instance, when two last-born "babies" marry each other, neither thinks his or her needs are adequately met and each may experience the other as the belittling, teasing older sibling.

Family Rules

One explanation for reenactments is that the adult is following either explicit or covert rules from the family of origin. Some covert rules could be *Don't show your weak, vulnerable side, Keep it a secret that your father is a drunk,* and *Don't express anger.* Transactional analysis (TA) theory describes parental messages that are internalized and persist into adulthood as "drivers" of the personality, such as *Be Perfect, Be Strong,* or *Please Them.* The absence of rules is also influential: *It's okay not to come to the dinner table if you're not in the mood. You don't need to tell me where you are going or when you'll be back.*

Unfinished Business

Gestalt therapy coined the term *unfinished business* (a concept developed from experiments on perception) for explaining why people show a drive toward completion and wholeness. Polster (1995) explained this concept using the metaphor of a vinyl record with a needle stuck in a groove, repeating the same sound over and over. Gestalt therapists believe that clients need an intense experience of the emotions that were frozen, and a visit back to the event in the past where the "stuckness" occurred. Fritz Perls (1973), one of the founders of Gestalt therapy, provides a case example of a man who has never finished the labor of mourning a dead parent and who continues to base his life on that parent's directions:

> To become self-supportive and to participate fully in the present as it is, he has to give up this guidance; he has to part, to say a final goodbye to his progenitor. And to do this successfully, he has to go to the deathbed and face the departure. He has to transform his thoughts about the past into actions in the present which he experiences as if the now were the then. He cannot do it merely by re-recounting the scene, he must re-live it. He must go through and assimilate the interrupted feelings which are mostly of intense grief, but which may have in them elements of triumph or guilt or any number of other things. It is insufficient merely to recall a past incident, one has to psychodramatically return to it. (p. 65)

The technique proposed by Perls is to have the patient face his father in vivid fantasy, in the present, and express his thoughts and feelings. When the energy bound to the past is freed up, the patient can live life as an adult who sets his own course rather than a child still ruled by parental rewards and punishments.

Solutions to Early Childhood Problems

Reenactments can be viewed as the solutions that the little child created when faced with the problem of getting her needs met without causing major catastrophes of abandonment, loss of love, and punishment. The child faced these problems with major disadvantages: Her cognitive skills were very immature and she was completely dependent on others to meet all her needs. Given these limits, the solutions made sense at the time but are poor choices for adult life outside that family.

Transactional analysis explains the persistence of "early childhood decisions" into adulthood (Goulding & Goulding, 1979). Faced with contradictory messages from the Parent and Child ego states of both parents, the child's Little Professor (the Adult-in-the-Child state) comes up with decisions that cover the continuum from constructive ("I'll do great in school and they'll be proud of me") to destructive ("I'll never amount to anything so I won't bother trying"). Children in extremely abusive and cruel families can make healthy decisions ("My parents are sick and crazy, I'll listen to my friend's parents instead") and children with very loving and well-intentioned parents can make decisions that have harmful consequences ("No one understands me, I'll never be close to anyone"). Because decisions are based on the logic of a little child, they represent magical and distorted thinking. For instance, if a child one day wishes that a brother were dead, and the next day the brother dies in a car accident, the child can then decide, "I'm bad and deserve to be punished because I caused my brother's death." Early childhood decisions are under the surface, usually not put into words, and have profound influence on emotions, thoughts, choices, and behavior. Decisions like "I will be good and obedient and win my parent's love" or "I am helpless and incompetent so if I cry and show how weak I am, I can get someone to take care of me" can influence occupational performance, courtship, illness behavior, and parenting styles. Often the solution functions as an agenda or mission:

- *I will try to get unavailable men to love me* (*like I tried with daddy*): The adult enacts her own childhood role and tries to find a father substitute.

- *I will push anyone away who tries to get close and make him feel worthless* (*like my father did to me*): The adult identifies with the parent and induces in others the pain that she felt when she was little.

- *I will try over and over again, until I get it right:* A script is installed that requires repetition without permission to discontinue when success is clearly impossible.

Adults, possessing mature cognitive skills and the ability to function independently of the parents, should easily be able to create better solutions. One reason they do not is that they are trying to change something in the past through symbolic means, instead of trying to become happy in the present. The self-defeating pattern is also comfortable because it is familiar, habitual, and automatic, whereas change, because it opens the door to the unknown, is scary. Furthermore, reenactment patterns are resistant to change when the person is in a relationship that supports and maintains the view that the person already has of herself.

Defense and Self-Protection

The major problem that the child has to solve is how to deal with intense emotional pain from feelings of abandonment, vulnerability, aloneness, rejection, and loss, as well as cope with fears of being hurt, or hurting others, and being punished. Emotional pain and childhood wounds are caused by extreme mistreatment, neglect, or abuse, as well as more subtle injuries such as insensitivity to needs and feelings, painful losses and separations, and the cruelty of siblings. Many children grow up with deep feelings of shame—that they are defective and inadequate to the core and, if others find out that secret, they will be rejected, humiliated, and abandoned.

The childhood solutions serve to keep painful emotions out of awareness, and for that reason they are very resistant to change, because any attempt at change causes pain to resurface. To protect against pain, the person will only pursue paths that are designated as safe and will distort reality and avoid opportunities to test reality. In addition, adults create self-fulfilling prophecies, exerting pressure on other people to get them to fill their designated role.

Protecting the Parents

Children who have been mistreated and even severely abused by their parents will continue to protect their parents. The belief that "they are good parents, I get this treatment because I'm bad," is easier to tolerate than "My parents are not good, and therefore I am completely helpless and unprotected." Sometimes the client will be unable to change maladaptive adult patterns until she can face the truth about her parents: "I never was adequately loved by my parents. They were not good people; they were not capable of love." Given the pain and grief this realization would cause, it is not surprising that there is resistance to facing these emotions.

The client must discover that now that he is an adult and not a helpless child, the pain is tolerable, and he has the resources to cope with it.

> A 42-year-old unmarried man recognized his maladaptive reenactments: He was trying to make his parents love him by pursuing material success, although paying the price in shallow relationships. "My parents never gave me adequate love, never will view me as *good enough* and, even if they do now come to show love the way I want, can never change the way they were when I was little." This process involved expression of deep pain and an extended grieving process, resulting in changes in thinking followed by new life priorities: "I can tolerate pain, I can get the love I need from other people besides my parents, and I am good enough in my own eyes."

Mate Selection

The selection of a mate often demonstrates a reenactment process: "This man is equivalent to my father: If I can get him to love me, I can (magically) undo the pain of my childhood rejection and prove that I am a worthwhile person deserving of love." This plan becomes a repetitious pattern with different partners, and the person enters each new relationship believing, "This time I'll get it right, this time I'll make him love me, appreciate me, and listen to me."

A reenactment requires the person to find a partner who can function as a symbolic substitute for the parent. If a person struggles with unmet childhood needs, the selected partner must be someone who is also not going to meet those basic needs. The client can then struggle, be good, punish, and use different strategies to try to get this person to change—as she wanted her parents to change when she was a child. This symbolic agenda to change the past is clearly an impossible goal, resulting in unfulfilling adult relationships.

This theoretical model explains why individuals who say they want closeness will discard a partner who starts to behave the way they claim they wanted. Because only the current partner has changed—not the parents in the past—the new positive behaviors bring not contentment but rather a need to continue the reenactment and find a new person to serve as a parent fill-in.

Table 8.5   Reenactment Patterns in Marriage

Projection Processes

Framo (1972) explained that the child handles the frustration and disappointment with his parents by internalizing the emotional relationship; then "active, unconscious attempts are made to force and change close relationships into fitting the internal role models" (p. 275). The chosen mate is cherished or persecuted, depending on the nature of the projection process. Stone and Stone (1989) describe a system of disowned selves: "those things that we resent, reject, despise, and judge in other people are direct representations of our disowned selves" (pp. 73–74).

Negative Bonding Patterns

The Stones propose that, initially, a stable, harmonious relationship can be established between two subselves, perhaps a dominating Parent subself in the man and a flighty, insecure Child part in the woman. However, over time, one partner will make a dramatic shift into a different subself, typically when the Vulnerable Child has been threatened. Perhaps the woman shifts into a disapproving critical Mother subself and this pulls from the husband his rebellious Son response. A negative bonding pattern occurs when the negative Child selves of one are locked into the Parental selves in the other.

Imago Matching

Hendrix (1988), creator of imago relationship therapy (IRT), believes that a person who was deeply wounded in childhood will select a mate who carries the "imago" of the key negative traits of the parents. The painful part of this kind of marriage is that each spouse wants the other one to provide exactly what it is most difficult for that person to give. The struggle to change the other person, however, offers the potential of mutual growth and deepening love: If each partner chooses to give what the other one needs to feel loved, each will reclaim lost parts of the self and achieve a healing sense of interconnectedness.

When this process of mate selection does result in marriage, the odds seem to favor a destructive relationship that will probably end in divorce or a lifetime of misery. However, Hendrix (1988) proposes that people intuitively choose partners who represent qualities in their parents—called *imagos*—so that they can work out a way to heal their old wounds and create safe and loving relationships.

Table 8.5 illustrates several theoretical models for understanding reenactment patterns in marriage.

Parenting

Parents can reenact their childhoods by responding to their child according to fantasies and projections, instead of discovering who their children are as separate, unique emerging individuals. They can project characteristics, expect the child to fulfill unmet needs, assign the child to a role, or treat the child as a target for revenge or a trophy proving their worth. Framo (1972) described the function of the family projection process as "recapturing the symbolically retained old love objects who have their representation in current real family members, thus delaying the pain of loss and mourning" (p. 279). When the child grows up and starts a family, his reenactments carry bits of his parents' and grandparents' lives—a phenomenon called the *multigenerational transmission process* (Bowen, 1994).

At a conscious level, people can describe how their parenting styles are shaped by their own early childhood experiences. Using their own parents as templates, they either repeat the treatment they received or show determination to do the opposite. Parents make choices to provide children with what they did not adequately receive. At worst, these reenactments create problems for children that will be passed down to future generations; at best, they provide parents with an opportunity to heal old wounds as they provide better parenting for their children than they received.

WHEN IS THIS HYPOTHESIS A GOOD MATCH?

Two kinds of data reveal the relevance of this reenactment hypothesis: (1) the stories the client tells about present and past relationships and (2) the type of relationship the client forms with the therapist.

Table 8.6 lists common problems that benefit from recognizing the reenactment of early experiences.

TREATMENT PLANNING

In developing a good case formulation using the **P2** hypothesis, it is not sufficient to make a vague statement: *The client is reenacting something from the family of origin.* You need to be specific about *what* from the early family is being reenacted and offer your hypothesis about *how* and *why* the reenactment is occurring.

Psychoeducation

The therapist can explain the concept of reenactment from selected theories and teach tools for the client to use, as well as assign books to read (e.g., Hendrix, 1988, *Getting the Love You Want.*) Alice Miller's (1981) book, *The Drama of the Gifted Child* is a good choice for clients who were extremely talented and gifted and who suffered from narcissistic mothers who could not empathize or allow them to be children.

Exploring the Past

The historical accuracy of the story the client tells is not as important as how the client interpreted the events. In discussing the client's history of relationships, the therapist and client engage in a search for repeating patterns. Therapists can help clients reach their own insights into how the past is being replayed, or they can offer interpretations of the dynamics, phrased as hunches rather than absolute truths.

Table 8.6   Problems Explained by the P2 Reenactment of Early Childhood Experiences Hypothesis

Problems with Authority Figures

Authority figures in the client's life are targets for feelings toward parents. The client's responses reflect negative feelings of being dominated, controlled, and disrespected, as well as inappropriate positive expectations to be indulged and rescued. These emotional responses are excessive to the real stimulus: The client will interpret behavior from the boss as outrageous and intolerable, whereas the therapist will think that it is, at worst, typical insensitivity of someone with poor managerial skills. Some of the problematic reactions are helpless dependence, blind defiance, misperceptions of favoritism, and irrational fears of expressing independent thought.

Difficulty Establishing and Maintaining Satisfying Intimate Relationships

Perhaps the most common reasons people seek therapy include (a) difficulty finding an appropriate partner; (b) maintenance of frustrating and painful relationships; (c) repetitious patterns (e.g., falling in love with the "perfect person" and then discarding her; pursuing relationships with unavailable or rejecting people); (d) marital problems (e.g., excessive conflict, inability to tolerate separateness in their partner, and withdrawing and distancing behaviors).

Inappropriate Emotional Reactions

When the presenting problem is excessive anxiety or anger, the roots of these reactions often lie in early childhood experiences. For instance, overreactions to separations can reflect an insecure attachment. When the client becomes enraged at the therapist's minor lapses in empathy, the client may be reacting as she did when she was a child with a self-absorbed mother.

Difficulty Maintaining Equal and Cooperative Peer Relationships

The client may relate from either a position of superiority or inferiority, may be unable to quell competitive feelings, could take a role of self-sacrifice and put others' needs ahead of her own, have inappropriate expectations of being spoiled and catered to, and experience jealousy and hostility over the achievements of others.

Difficulties with Parenting

Parenting styles can either replicate or completely reverse what one experienced in childhood. As children reach successive birthdays, new childhood issues are reactivated for parents.

Problems in Relationships between Adult Children and Their Parents

Problems can include excessive emotional reactivity when relating to parents, difficulties dealing with parents in grandparent role, and continuing to respond to the mother-of-today as if she were the mother-of-childhood. Another problem that is becoming more common as the life span gets longer is the difficulty of coping with aging parents. When adult children are put in caregiver roles for their elderly parents, the roles are reversed from childhood and the child has the power while the parent is helpless and dependent. This can provide healing opportunities, as the child sees the parent in a new light, or it could be the recipe for elder abuse.

When the client is talking about present difficulties, the therapist can guide her back in time to early childhood experiences. Therapists can use questions (*Did anything like this happen when you were little?* or *When have you felt this before?*) and interpretive hunches (*When you were describing the conflict with your roommate, I was remembering what you told me about the fights you had with your sister when she took your things*). One particularly effective technique is to find an *affect bridge* between the present and the past. The therapist guides the client:

> Close your eyes and let yourself experience what you are feeling right now. (Pause) Focus on the feelings . . . and now go back in time, go back to a time when you were young, and you felt those very same feelings.

Sometimes clients go right to an early childhood scene. Other times they recall an event from adolescence or young adulthood. After exploring that experience, the therapist can repeat the instruction, asking for an earlier experience. A similar technique using imagery is to ask the client to imagine a clothesline that represents her life, from birth to now. Ask the client to clip the current situation to the right and then go back to a recent situation with the same feelings, and to clip that one to the line, a little to the left of the first one.

> Continue going back over your life and find other experiences to put on the clothesline until you get back to your early childhood.

The client does this activity, silently in imagination, and when she is ready to report what she found, the therapist can write down the list. Another possibility is to ask the client to draw a clothesline on paper, and write down the events.

Cognitive Insight

Cognitive insight and a revised narrative of the life story can come from the client's sharing of stories about her early life experiences. Through self-reflection as well as the therapist's interpretation, the client reaches a realization: *I married my father. I am sabotaging my relationships because I'm operating from the needs of a child instead of an adult. I have most of the qualities that were in the book on codependency.* Instead of being in the drama, the client is now an observer. Using TA, the therapist can help the client examine the way his Child is triggered in adult relationships and the way he reenacts the behavior of his parents, now operating through his own internal Parent.

Validating the Child

When the adult client becomes aware of early decisions and solutions, and how destructive they have been, it is natural to feel shame, anger, and grief. The therapist must believe and convey to the client that the little child who created the solution *did the best she could, had good reasons, needed that to survive,* or *couldn't have dealt with the pain of childhood without that strategy.*

Emotional Reexperiencing

Insight is not enough; it is usually necessary for clients to experience the emotions from their childhood—both those they remember and those that were repressed or disowned. To relinquish self-protective childhood beliefs and decisions, the client has to be able to tolerate the emotional pain that was pushed out of awareness. The child was not able to handle those feelings, but now, the adult can.

Kahn (1997) describes four process goals of therapy, citing the work of Gill:

1. Feelings, impulses, and expectations are experienced in the presence of the person to whom they are now directed. (In individual therapy, this presupposes a transference reaction to the therapist; in couple therapy, it involves the presence of the spouse or partner.)
2. These feelings are expressed toward the person, not experienced silently.
3. The current target of the old feelings and expectations (therapist or partner) must be willing and able to accept these feelings and impulses, without defensiveness, and to discuss them with interest and objectivity.
4. The client is helped to learn the early childhood source of the reexperienced feelings and impulses.

Gestalt Therapy and TA provide other methods for creating emotional reexperiencing. The *empty-chair technique,* described under **P1** as a method for dialoguing with an internal part, is also a technique for experiencing and expressing feelings toward key figures from the past. *Put your father in the chair and tell him how you feel* is a simple way to switch from talking about the past to making the unfinished business from the past come alive and be completed in the present.

Redecision therapy, developed by Bob and Mary Goulding (1979), is an offshoot of TA that integrates Gestalt experiential activities. The client revisits an event in childhood when the faulty *early childhood decision* was made. After the Child has fully expressed her feelings and thoughts to the imagined parent, it is as if the Adult-of-the-present comes back to the scene to help create a "redecision," and the therapist is providing protection and permission to speak up in a powerful way to the people with whom she used to feel very weak and helpless. The redecision can now be dramatized. For instance, if the little girl decided, "I'll never let anyone get close," the adult redecision could be "I couldn't get close to you because you were so mean, but I'm going to let myself get close to safe, caring people."

Utilization of Transference

Basch (1980) described transference as the "remobilization of the parent-child relationship in all its possible forms" (p. 40) and provides clear discussions and case examples of how therapists use transference with a variety of clients. Many therapists believe that the most effective way to work with reenactments is to have them appear as transference—the client reacts to the therapist in a way that originated with the parents, using coping strategies that were used in early childhood. As Freud discovered in his treatment of obsessional neurosis (discussed in **P4**), transference can be a royal road to discovering how current problems are representations and reenactments of early conflicts and relationships.

You need advanced training in a psychoanalytic institute to use transference as your primary intervention. However, you can find opportunities to recognize and utilize transference when your client treats you as if you were someone else, or wants you to gratify early childhood needs that are being activated in the therapy relationship. Ask yourself these questions: *How does my client see me? How does the client see me seeing him? How does the client construe my intentions? What kind of impression might the client be seeking to make on me? What role does the client put me in?* The therapist needs to have patience and wait for several pieces of data that will document the existence of a reenactment. When the timing is right, you can point out what you have experienced: *You seem to be waiting for me to tell you what to do,* or *I think because you've noticed I have a cold, you're more concerned about taking care of me than you are about using this time for your own need.* With what is called an *intersubjective* stance (Orange, Atwood, & Stolorow, 1998), the therapist abstains from implying that the client's experience is immature and irrational; instead, the therapist seeks to understand how the client's viewpoint makes sense in terms of her life experiences.

Countertransference Avoidance of Pain

Therapists usually feel good when they are helping clients feel better but may have difficulty sitting and tolerating the client's pain. When the logical treatment strategy is to permit the client to access and express buried pain and anger, it means that you must allow the pain level in the room to increase rather than decrease. Countertransference responses to those emotions may lead you to shut them off prematurely. A. Miller (1981) proposes that we are unconsciously motivated to protect our own parents and avoid our own childhood pain, claiming that we rush too quickly to encourage clients to take an adult perspective—to have empathy for their parents or to forgive them. Although these are appropriate long-term goals, they need to be pursued after the client has had the chance to access buried feelings and grieve painful losses.

Utilizing Countertransference Responses

Countertransference can be an invaluable therapeutic tool because your reactions to a client give you information about how that client relates to people in the outside world. When you identify reactions triggered by a client, you can decide what those reactions mean:

- I am experiencing the "pull" of the client's behavior. He is casting me in a specific role. This is how he treats other people and now I am experiencing how others feel with him and how they want to react.
- I am experiencing something about the client's childhood experiences.
  —How the client was treated as a child (*the client treats me as he was treated*).
  —What the parent was like (*the client portrays that part or casts me in that role*).
  —What experiences and emotions the client is feeling and not expressing, or not even feeling, because they are disowned (*I'm feeling them;* this phenomenon is known as "projective identification").

By understanding these reactions, you will be able to interact with the client in a way that either highlights or corrects the pattern of behavior in which the client is attempting to engage. In this way, you are interrupting the client's reenactment—preventing it from being a self-fulfilling prophecy—and helping the client have a more spontaneous, authentic connection with another person.

Should Clients Confront their Parents?

When a client wants to confront a parent, it is important to help the client admit when he has the fantasy of changing the parents and somehow repairing the pain and losses of childhood. If the agenda with the parent has to do with the "parent of the past," the client must understand that these feelings and goals are what keep him stuck in reenactments. The "parents of the present" may already be very different people. If a client is able to work through resentments and unmet needs by addressing the past, the urgent desire to confront and punish parents usually dissipates.

When the client has removed the burden of unfinished business, there may be current issues with the parents that need to be confronted, as happens in all close relationships. The client can be encouraged to use effective communication skills to seek behavior change, more closeness, or any other reasonable goal. In some cases, the client may need to limit contact, especially if the parent is abusive.

Conjoint Couple Therapy

When both partners come to therapy, there are effective ways of modifying destructive projections and reenactments that have hardened into repetitious conflicts and a painful loss of intimacy. The key to therapeutic change is for clients to tolerate feelings of vulnerability, trust the partner enough to expose them, and develop more mature and conscious strategies of self-protection. These methods do not treat the emotional needs as inappropriate or immature but instead help the partners develop emotional safety where their needs can be met. Table 8.7 illustrates three strategies for working with couples.

Group Therapy

Groups offer the opportunity for the client to reenact many past relationships with different members of the group. Yalom (1995) explains how each member of the group creates his or her social microcosm in the group, bringing faulty patterns of relating into the group experience. Through *corrective recapitulation of the family,* which he lists as 1 of 11 therapeutic factors, clients have the opportunity to alter their reenactment patterns. In psychodrama, the protagonist enacts early family dramas with members of the group and through powerful emotional experiences can understand and change recurring patterns in relationships.

Self-Help Groups

In groups such as Adult Children of Alcoholics (ACA) and Codependents Anonymous (CoDA), participants learn how they are reenacting their role in

Table 8.7 Strategies for Helping Couples

Facilitate Insight

The therapist helps the clients recognize patterns: What triggers an emotional response? What are the origins in childhood? Having each partner listen while the therapist interviews the other about his or her family of origin creates insight into how each is bringing old patterns into the relationship. The therapist can explain concepts from Table 8.5, such as bonding patterns or projective processes.

Make It Safe to Be Vulnerable

Johnson (2004) talks separately to each partner while the other listens, using a very slow and rhythmic voice that captures deep feelings of hurt and pain that lie under angry and distancing behaviors. Imago relationship therapy (Hendrix, 1988) uses "parent-child dialogue": Playing herself as a child, the wife expresses pain from a childhood incident and forms a request: "What I need from you most is _____" to her husband, who is playing the role of her parent. He responds by saying: "You deserve to have all that. I wish I could have given it to you."

Give Directions to Change Communication Patterns

During the session, the therapist can give a directive: *Can you turn to your husband and tell him how deeply, painfully alone you feel?* Hendrix (1988) provides a structure for couples to practice listening, empathically, adding a step called validation, where they say, "your view makes sense."

---

their family and continuing to use the same strategies to numb feelings, try to meet the needs of others, and neglect their own true needs. The participant can relieve buried feelings of shame when she tells a deeply personal story to the group and receives support without criticism or invalidation.

INTEGRATION OF HYPOTHESES

It is a faulty assumption that early childhood origins of problems require long-term psychoanalytic therapy. The **P2** hypothesis adds depth to problem-focused approaches like crisis intervention and cognitive-behavioral therapy (CBT).

CS2 Situational Stressors

Excessive emotional reactions to mild and moderate stressors suggest that there are vulnerabilities rooted in early childhood experiences.

BL2 Conditioned Emotional Response

The extinction of childhood pain is a major component of the change process. The present emotional fears were generalized from the original people and events where the fear was first experienced to new situations and people where there is no longer a threat. An approach such as desensitization would provide the ability to maintain calm instead of repeating old patterns of reaction. Psychodynamic therapy provides desensitization by allowing the client to slowly and gradually experience the painful emotions in the presence of a safe person, substituting feelings of trust for fear and anger.

BL3 Skill Deficits or Lack of Competence

Insight into how a person is repeating maladaptive patterns may not be enough to ensure positive change. The client may need to learn the skills for healthy relating that were not taught in the family of origin. Many therapists decide that it is not necessary to understand the origins of the deficient interpersonal skills; it is sufficient to provide learning experiences to create more adaptive behaviors.

C2 Faulty Cognitive Map

All reenactments include cognitive elements: beliefs, expectations, predictions, assumptions, and rules. The reenactment hypothesis can be expressed in terms of specific underlying schemas such as: "I am basically unlovable. This man is equivalent to my father: If I can get him to love me, I can (magically) undo the pain of my childhood rejection and prove that I am a worthwhile person deserving of love." Young's list of early maladaptive schemas, presented in Table 6.6 under **C2**, is a useful tool to help clients see the early childhood roots of their current functioning.

Cognitive techniques use an Adult-Adult dialogue and are based on the assumption that the mature adult can make changes using reason, logic, and scientific methods. This is true in many cases. However, when cognitive therapy is not effective in changing maladaptive patterns, the therapist can integrate hypothesis **P2**, recognizing that it is necessary for the client to experience the early childhood pain: The Child needs to be brought into therapy and allowed to express feelings and access the early decisions that were made with the logic of a child's thinking.

C3 Faulty Information Processing

The pattern of reenacting early childhood experiences in adulthood is maintained by faulty information processing (**C3**): The client's basic distortion and overgeneralization is demonstrated when she treats a person she has recently met as if he were someone from the past.

ES2 Avoiding Freedom and Responsibility

The client needs to be made aware that the responsibility for changing reenactment patterns lies with her. Once she recognizes the repetitious pattern and realizes how it sabotages getting what she wants, she can no longer blame her parents for her current choices to maintain the pattern. When deeply attracted to a man that she knows "hooks" her Child and may cause her to once again reenact the drama with her father, she has the choice to walk away.

Therapists with an existential orientation find opportunities to confront the client's behavior in the here and now when the client is reenacting a pattern from childhood with the therapist. For instance, when Fritz Perls felt that a client was "playing helpless" to get her needs met, he pointed it out to her and deliberately frustrated the manipulative maneuvers. This encourages her to see that she can choose how to relate and that she is capable of a more mature, empowered, competent way of presenting herself.

SCE1 Family System

Using a family therapy modality can bring in multiple reenactments, and an important tool of marital therapy is helping each partner understand the spouse's family of origin and the *multigenerational transmission process.*

P3 IMMATURE SENSE OF SELF AND CONCEPTION OF OTHERS

Definition

Difficulties stem from the client's failure to progress beyond the **Immature Sense of Self and Conception of Others** that is normal for very young children.

Explanation

Other people are not appreciated as unique individuals with distinct needs, feelings, and perspectives but rather are experienced as extensions of the self and valued for the functions they serve. The client needs others to shore up her self-esteem and to soothe painful emotions, lacking the capacity to provide these functions for herself. Based on assessment of the capacities and deficits of the adult, we can pinpoint the stage in early childhood when healthy maturation was disrupted.

Examples

In her 6-month relationship with Sam, Jenny was clinging, possessive, and devoted. She bragged to her friends that Sam treated her "like a princess" and was the love of her life. Then Sam's mother died unexpectedly, and he became sad, preoccupied, and inattentive. One month later, when Sam was away on a business trip, Jenny went to a party and fell in love with another man.

Trisha came to therapy to work through her latest in a series of romantic breakups. In every session, Trisha speaks for the entire session, leaving little space for any participation from the therapist. She only wants attention, confirmation, and agreement. When the therapist broke her leg and came to sessions with a cast and crutches, Trisha seemed not to notice.

Joe is a successful editor for a major publishing company. He has been working on a novel for 15 years, and keeps revising it, but can never finish it. On some days, he has the fantasy of making the New York Times bestseller list; on other days, he knows "it is worthless trash." It was only when he was getting As and praise from teachers that he felt good about his talents.

KEY IDEAS FOR P3 IMMATURE SENSE OF SELF AND CONCEPTION OF OTHERS

At a very early age, a child uses the words *I, me,* and *myself,* showing awareness that he is separate from other people. The "self" is the subjective experience of one's separate personhood, unlike *ego,* which is an abstract term that refers to a domain of personality functioning. Many texts (e.g., McWilliams, 1999; S. A. Mitchell, 1996; Pines, 1990) employ both concepts, but it is easy to remain confused; the best way to understand what is meant by "self" is to review the specific capacities that it embraces. Table 8.8 presents items from Masterson's (1990) list of eight capacities of a "healthy self."

Narcissistic Needs

The term *narcissistic* is generally associated with unpleasant characteristics of adults—grandiosity, self-centeredness, bragging, an inflated sense of entitlement. However, healthy narcissism is a precondition for many of the capacities listed in Table 8.8. A child has normal, healthy narcissistic needs for appreciation, understanding, and recognition as a unique and separate individual, as well as for joyful participation by others in her existence. When these needs are adequately met, the positive responses of the significant others become internalized. When the needs are not met, the core of the self can be experienced as

Table 8.8   Examples of Capacities of a Healthy Self

Spontaneity and aliveness of affect	You can experience emotion deeply and have a capacity for aliveness, joy, vitality, excitement, and spontaneity.
Self-entitlement	You feel entitled to appropriate experiences of mastery and pleasure and to the environmental input necessary to achieve these objectives. This sense is neither deficient nor inflated.
Self-activation, self-assertion, and self-support	You are able to identify your unique wishes and to use autonomous initiative and assertion to express them in reality and to support and defend them when under attack. Direction comes from internal ideals, values, and ambitions.
Maintenance of self-esteem	You can fuel adequate self-esteem, on your own, by giving positive acknowledgment to yourself.
Soothing of painful affects	You are able, on your own, to devise means to limit, minimize, and soothe painful affects.
Continuity of self	You recognize and acknowledge that the "I" of one experience is continuous over time and related to the "I" of another experience.
Commitment	You can commit to an objective or a relationship and persevere, despite obstacles, to attain that goal or maintain that relationship.

empty or bad, and defensive layers can be built to protect the weak, vulnerable self from shame and deflation.

Object Relations

Object relations is the psychoanalytic jargon for "relationships with other human beings" and the name of a complex theory that has been explained with clarity by various authors (e.g., Scharff & Scharff, 1995; St. Clair, 1996). Table 8.9 lists the characteristics of *mature object relations*.

Table 8.9   Mature Object Relations

Other People Are Real and Separate and Do Not Revolve around You

You experience others as free, separate selves with their own feelings and experiences. The other person has his or her own center of initiative, exists without you, is not an extension of you, does not revolve around you and your needs, nor can be controlled by you. You deal with the reality of the other person, not your fantasy of who the other person is.

Other People Are Unique and Different from You

Others are not just interchangeable, replaceable "things" who serve functions for the self, but you appreciate them as separate, unique persons with their own needs, feelings, and talents. Another human will never be your perfect clone. Although we may often have similar feelings and opinions, it is impossible to always feel the same or to agree on everything. Because this is understood, disagreements are expected and are not experienced as threats to your sense of self or the relationship.

There Are Multiple Valid Perspectives

Because you can shift perspectives, you realize that you are not the center of every event and interaction. You can think in terms of multiple perspectives, instead of one absolute truth. You can observe yourself from the perspective of another person and accept negative feedback without viewing it as an attack on yourself. You can imagine how you appear to others and the impact that your behavior has on them.

You Can Tolerate Ambivalent Feelings toward Someone You Love

People are not all good or all bad. Only in fantasy is someone perfect, so you know that idealization of another person can't last. When flaws appear, you do not flip into devaluation of the person. You can express anger and receive anger in the relationship without it destroying the bond.

You Can Experience Interdependence in Relationships

It is normal in times of stress to turn to others to have them serve functions such as shoring up self-esteem and soothing painful emotions. However, the roles can be reversed: You can do the same for another person in need. When you set goals, you can consider the impact on the other person. You can put another's needs ahead of yours.

You Are Capable of Committed Intimate Relationships

You are able to sustain trust, develop secure attachments, and tolerate separation, believing in the constancy of another even when that person is not physically present. Because you love a real person, you do not fluctuate between idealization and devaluation, but rather can tolerate periods when needs are not met.

The Selfobject Concept

Heinz Kohut (Kohut & Wolf, 1978) invented the word *selfobject* (sometimes written as two words) to describe the immature level of object relations that is transitional between the symbiosis of infancy and the mature object relations described in Table 8.9:

> *Selfobjects* are objects which we experience as part of our self; the expected control over them is, therefore, closer to the concept of the control which a grown-up expects to have over his own body and mind than to the concept of the control which he expects to have over others. There are two kinds of selfobjects: those who respond to and confirm the child's innate sense of vigor, greatness, and perfection; and those to whom the child can look up and with whom he can merge as an image of calmness, infallibility and omnipotence. (p. 414)

Baker and Baker (1987) clarify that selfobject relations continue to be important in adulthood:

> An old slogan of the American Dairy Association proclaims: "You never outgrow your need for milk." The same is true of empathically accurate self-objects. We always need them, although they undergo developmental maturing. . . . During adolescence, the peer group is a crucial self-object. In adulthood, the spouse, friends, and careers may be self-objects. . . . The person becomes more internally competent, less externally needy, and more flexible in meeting the remaining self-object needs. (pp. 2–3)

The idea of a separate, completely independent self, is a fiction. Each individual is embedded in a matrix of selfobject relations, so that interdependence is a normal state and healthy functioning is a balance of independence and dependence. Often it is only after losses—death of a loved one, termination of employment, or geographic relocation—that the dependence on selfobjects is discovered. When we talk about cultural differences, contrasting "individualistic" and "collectivistic" cultures, we are addressing different value systems regarding the desirable dependence on selfobject relations.

Adult pathology may stem from inadequate selfobject relationships and unmet needs in childhood: The adult maintains the belief that his needs will never be met, uses maladaptive strategies to protect against emotional pain, and alternates between hopelessness and outbursts of what we call "narcissistic rage."

Developmental Diagnosis

A *developmental diagnosis* involves pinpointing the stage of early childhood development beyond which the person has failed to progress. As you listen to the client's stories and notice the exact type of transference relationship that the client is creating, you form a hypothesis about the level of development at which the client is functioning. Mature clients may or may not manifest strong transference reactions: If transference develops, it will be one in which the client experiences you as a *real object* but not who you really are. However, clients who function at immature levels inevitably will distort the relationship, and it is important to distinguish whether the transference they create is a *merger* or *selfobject* relationship. Be aware that a person who is severely impaired in emotional and interpersonal functioning may be very talented and successful in educational, occupational, and recreational domains.

Table 8.10 gives an overview of three stages of child development and their parallels in adulthood, based on research in child development (Mahler et al., 1975; Stern, 1985) as well as the self-psychology and object relations theory described previously.

Conditions for Healthy Development

The following are considered desired qualities and functions of *good-enough* parents—a term coined by Winnicott (1965)—and are the same conditions that therapists provide to help the client progress to a more mature level of functioning:

- Empathically in tune with the child (nonnarcissistic), experiencing the child as separate, accepting and helping to label feelings, and not trying to shape the child into something she is not. The parent can tolerate negative feelings directed toward himself.

- Able to adequately fill selfobject functions and not expect a reciprocal relationship from a very young child; the parent looks to a spouse or friends to meet her selfobject needs, not to the child.

- Able to adapt to the developing child's changing needs and to raise standards for reciprocity as the child gets older. The parent enjoys both dependence and independence in the child and does not feel rejected by the child's separateness and autonomy.

- Able to provide *optimum frustration* (frustrations that are tolerable and challenging rather than overwhelming and traumatic) by not being perfectly attuned or always ready to meet selfobject needs, as the child's capacity for independence and self-soothing increases; without frustration, the child would not internalize selfobject functions and learn how to maintain her own self-esteem and regulate her own emotions.

Kohut and Wolf (1978) explain: "It is not so much what the parents do that will influence the character of the child's self, but what the parents are" (p. 417). When parents have not progressed beyond an immature level of development (probably because their parents were immature and failed to meet selfobject needs), there is tremendous risk that the child will be used as a selfobject, and later pass this legacy of poor parenting on to her own children. Alice Miller (1981) describes the attitude of the narcissistically damaged mother:

Table 8.10 Model of Developmental Diagnosis

Childhood	Adulthood Parallels
MOST IMMATURE STAGE: SYMBIOTIC MERGER	
First Months of Life	**Borderline Personality Features**
The infant experiences the mother and self as one. There is no experience of an "I" separate from not-I. The foundation of basic trust is being laid.	The person creates fused relationships, lacks ability to regulate emotions, and has severe impairments in reality testing.
Feared catastrophe: annihilation	**Type of transference: merger**
INTERMEDIATE STAGE: NARCISSISTIC SELFOBJECT RELATIONS	
About 9 Months to 3 Years of Age	**Narcissistic Disorder of the Self**
The child experiences self as separate from mother. Feelings of omnipotence and grandiosity alternate with inadequacy and anxiety. The child explores the world but needs to return to mother for refueling. The child needs others for selfobject functions: *mirroring* (prizing the separate self of the child), *soothing* (reducing painful affects and restoring calmness), and *being idealizable* (providing someone to look up to and aspire to be like). The child engages in *splitting*— viewing the self or other as all good or all bad.	The person uses others as selfobjects to maintain self-esteem and achieve emotional regulation. He cannot meet the selfobject needs of others and lacks the capacity to take their point of view and empathize with them. There are swings between idealization and devaluation of others.
Feared catastrophe: abandonment	**Type of transference: selfobject**
MATURE STAGE: COHESIVE SELF AND REAL OBJECT RELATIONS	
Above 3 Years of Age	**Mature Relationships and Cohesive Self (See Tables 8.8 and 8.9)**
The child can tolerate good and bad feelings towards the same object *(ambivalence)* and will not reject or replace the love object if it is absent or frustrating. Gradually overcoming egocentric thinking, he begins to develop the capacity for empathy and altruism. The child internalizes selfobject functions and is becoming able to soothe himself. Other people are related to as real people, not just mother substitutes. The child develops awareness of triadic relationships and begins to experience jealousy and rivalry.	The person views others as separate and unique, and demonstrates empathy. The person shows capacities of an *observing ego* and can accept feedback and interpretation without needing to protect self-esteem.
Feared catastrophes: loss of love, rejection, or punishment	**Type of transference: neurotic (real object)**

A child cannot run away from her as her own mother once did. A child can be so brought up that it becomes what she wants it to be. A child can be made to show respect, she can impose her own feelings on him, see herself mirrored in his love and admiration, and feel strong in his presence, but when he becomes too much she can abandon that child to a stranger. (p. 11)

The key quality in good-enough parents is the capacity to conceive of their child as a separate human being, with feelings and thoughts that they cannot always know, and definitely cannot control. Good-enough empathy is the sincere effort to understand by asking questions and offering hunches, without trying to be a mind reader. Parents (or therapists) who always are accurate in their empathic hunches will be, in a sense, violating the child's (or client's) boundaries around her inner experience, and will interfere with the other person's development of skills of self-expression and tolerance of being misunderstood.

WHEN IS THIS HYPOTHESIS A GOOD MATCH?

A wide range of problems result from weak, defective selves and immaturity in object relations. Tables 8.8 and 8.9 should be reviewed to identify specific deficits that might serve as problem titles, such as *Inability to maintain self-esteem without external support* or *Excessive reactions of hurt and anger to normal separations and misunderstandings in relationships*. Table 8.11 lists the most common problem titles for which hypothesis **P3** is a good match.

DSM-IV-TR Diagnoses

Three personality disorders include criteria that refer to an immature sense of self and conception of others. *DSM* diagnoses are based on behavioral descriptions, whereas developmental diagnoses are based on the clinician's evaluation of the client's level of psychological development.

Table 8.11 Problems Explained by P3 Immature Sense of Self and Conception of Others Hypothesis

Emotional Symptoms

Depression, often with feelings of emptiness and shame; Low self-esteem; Poor emotional regulation

Relationship Dysfunction

Excessive dependence; Difficulty sustaining intimate relationships in the face of conflict; Inability to tolerate aloneness; Inappropriate efforts to control other people; Difficulty coping with independence of children; Lack of empathy; Indifference to the needs of others

Struggles with Autonomy

Difficulty separating from family of origin; Lack of awareness of own true feelings and desires; Reliance on external direction

Problems with Work and Creativity

Difficulty accessing creativity; Excessive grandiosity in self-appraisal and ambitions; Inability to tolerate frustration in work environment

Substance Abuse

Dependence on alcohol or drugs to soothe painful emotions

Borderline Personality Disorder

The criteria for Borderline Personality Disorder include the following: frantic efforts to avoid real or imagined abandonment; relationships characterized by alternation between idealization and devaluation; unstable sense of self; chronic feelings of emptiness; and inappropriate, intense displays of anger. People diagnosed as borderline do best when they are in a nurturing supportive relationship and have adequate structure in work. Intense anger is often triggered when a friend or partner is seen as abandoning or neglectful. The description of this disorder suggests a "narcissistic disturbance," as does the following one.

Narcissistic Personality Disorder

Narcissistic Personality Disorder involves a pervasive pattern of grandiosity that includes devaluing others; the need for excessive admiration and attention; a sense of entitlement with expectations of favored treatment; and a lack of empathy for others. People who meet criteria for this disorder fail to recognize the desires, subjective experiences, and feelings of others, and expect to have their own needs met, regardless of the impact on others. These people are assumed to have very vulnerable self-esteem, and they are very sensitive to injury from criticism or defeat, after which they experience anger, shame, emptiness, and humiliation.

Dependent Personality Disorder

The criteria for Dependent Personality Disorder relate to deficiencies in the self and reliance on others to fill functions for the self, such as making small decisions, initiating projects, and taking responsibility. People who meet criteria for this disorder deal with the need to be taken care of and the fear of abandonment through appeasement, clinging behaviors, submissiveness, and withholding any expression of disagreement. When the relationship that provides support ends, the person urgently seeks a replacement.

Kohut's Personality Types

Kohut described two pathological types and three variants on normal personality. The relevance of hypothesis **P3** is recognized when the client fits into one of these categories, based on both stories of outside relationships and the type of transference that is formed.

Pathological Types

- *Merger-hungry:* The self lacks internal structures and therefore the person depends on selfobjects, having difficulty discriminating her own thoughts, wishes, and intentions from those of the selfobject.
- *Contact-shunning:* The person has intense needs for selfobjects, but avoids them because of fear that the yearned-for union will destroy the self and lead to the unbearable pain of rejection.

Variants of Normal Personality

- *Mirror-hungry:* The person feels worthless without continual confirming and admiring responses; if a relationship with a reliable mirroring partner is established, there may be an absence of symptoms.

- *Ideal-hungry:* To feel worthwhile, the person must be connected to selfobjects who are admired for prestige, power, beauty, or other ideal qualities. When flaws are found in the selfobject, the person seeks someone new.

- *Alter-ego hungry:* This person is looking for a twin—someone with identical feelings, values, and opinions. Although normal in adolescence, adults who seek this kind of selfobject feel estranged when normal differences appear, and are likely to seek one replacement after another.

TREATMENT PLANNING

In early sessions, the client may seem to function at a high level of maturity, so it is important to hold off on your developmental diagnosis until the client-therapist relationship has had time to develop. Many therapists believe that the type of transference the client develops—merger, selfobject, or real-object transference—is the major key to making the correct developmental diagnosis, which, in turn, is crucial for making decisions about treatment.

Trial Interpretation

The client's response to a gentle interpretation in the early sessions can help the therapist determine whether the client has developed an "observing ego"—a capacity which distinguishes between people at selfobject and real-object levels of functioning. (An interpretation is an idea that comes from the therapist's perspective, and it represents a break in the empathic connection.) For instance, the therapist might say, *Perhaps he thinks you are making unreasonable demands.* The mature client, who is not dependent on constant positive connection to a selfobject, may be resentful of this suggestion but has the capacity to ponder the idea; she can indeed shift perspectives and sustain positive feelings about herself in the absence of external validation. A client whose self-worth depends on the selfobject connection will either ignore the comment or treat it as an insult or an attack.

The Point-of-View Exercise

Another method for evaluating the client's level of object relations is an activity used by Neurolinguistic Programming (NLP) practitioners called "Shifting Perspectives" or, simply, "The POV Exercise" (Linden, 1998). The acronym POV (for point of view) is used in filmmaking for each of three perspectives that the camera can take for any situation: that of the Self (the main character), that of the Observer (the audience), and that of the Other. Once you and the client have

Table 8.12   Demonstration of Point-of-View Exercise

Instructions	Client Response
First POV: Yourself	
This is the way you ordinarily experience the situation. You are inside your own self, seeing, hearing, and feeling your own experiences. When you use the pronoun "I," you are referring to yourself.	I see my wife looks very sad. She is talking in a slow voice. I hear an anxious voice in my head criticizing my performance; I feel frustrated. I want to leave the room and get back to my computer.
Second POV: Observer	
Now pretend you are an objective observer. You are not in the situation, you are seeing and hearing the interaction between (client's name) and (other person's name) with impartiality and compassion. Refer to the two people in the situation as "he" and "she." When you use "I" you are speaking as this observer.	The relationship between the two isn't very connected or warm. They're each in a cocoon. She seems sad and needy, and he seems detached and worried. She's in a lot of pain and he doesn't want to help. I also think that she sounds judgmental and doesn't sympathize with his level of work pressure.
Third POV: Other	
Now you are (other person's name). You see through her eyes and try to feel like you are inside her skin. You describe her feelings, thoughts, sensations, memories. In this position, "I" refers to the other person and "you" refers to you.	I feel overwhelmed with pain and hopelessness. You look bored and impatient. You always put your work first. I need you to help me, and you just don't care.
	(The client should be assuming the posture, gestures, and tone of voice of his wife.)

identified an interpersonal situation that needs to be explored, and you have explained the three POVs, you invite the client to tell the story from three different positions, either using three chairs or having the client move a chair to three different places in the room. Table 8.12 gives a demonstration of this activity.

Here are examples of how different clients may react to this exercise:

- The client described in Table 8.12 shifts POV easily and shows an empathic understanding of the other, as well as the ability to be objective and let go of righteous and blaming attitudes. In this case, you conclude that the client has a mature level of object relations.

- The client is challenged because this is a brand-new experience. Although the client has never thought of doing this before, she shows the ability to take another POV. She gets new ideas and information or realizes that she has no idea what the other person would say but that this is important to know. In this case, you have data that your trial intervention is effective; you can continue to use it as a therapeutic strategy.

- The client is either incapable of shifting from her own POV, or if she does actually speak from other voices, she lacks imagination and objectivity. While complying with the instructions, she will give answers that are indistinguishable from her own POV. This confirms that the client functions at an immature level of object relations.

Psychoanalytic Strategies

One treatment approach for clients who function at immature levels is to use the selfobject transference for the purpose of character change. Competence to work with clients with severe pathology requires years of advanced postdegree training. However, treatment ideas explained in good texts (e.g., Basch, 1980; Wolf, 1988) can be applied to higher functioning clients. The therapist needs to be "good enough" in the same way that parents are—provide a good selfobject relationship, while helping the client build internal capacities, which lead to more mature styles of relating. Table 8.13 summarizes components necessary for implementing this model of therapy.

Table 8.13   Using the Selfobject Transference

Selfobject Transference

The client's "archaic needs" are activated in therapy. The therapist allows herself to be "used" as a selfobject—as a parent does with a child—and needs to cope with countertransference reactions from the client's lack of appreciation of her as a separate person.

Empathic Attunement

The key tool in the therapist's repertoire is remaining empathically attuned to the client and attempting, through "vicarious introspection," to enter the client's subjective world.

Effective Management of Empathic Failures

Because no one can be perfectly attuned to another human being, and because the narcissistically wounded client is exquisitely sensitive to small lapses in empathy, there will be occasions when there are ruptures in the therapeutic alliance and the client overreacts to "empathic failures" on the therapist's part. When properly handled, these incidents provide the *optimum frustration* that helps the client internalize the selfobject functions and build new structures in the personality.

Appreciation of Intersubjectivity

Although the concepts of "transference" and "countertransference" are important for understanding the dynamics of therapy sessions, it is a mistake to assume that these processes are really separate or that you, as the therapist, are not bringing your own distortions into the session. In what is called an "intersubjective" awareness, you realize that you contribute to the emotions the client feels toward you and that you and the client are "co-creating" what happens in the relationship.

Accessing Early Emotional Experience

In therapy, the client experiences the breakthrough of intense early childhood feelings. When "narcissistic rage" erupts, the client is reacting to the current "insult" as well as spilling out the pain, hopelessness, and fury of being a child with parents who were unable to meet his selfobject needs. If the therapist does not shut off feelings or leap to the defense of the parents, the client learns that he can tolerate the experience of pain and face the truth of his childhood.

Explanations

The therapist helps the client understand how she copes with disruptions of selfobject ties and frustrations of her needs, without invalidating the "rightness" of her emotions in view of her past experiences.

Humanistic and Existential Psychotherapies

The humanistic therapies (Cain & Seeman, 2001) make an important contribution to treatment of people who have failed to develop a healthy self. They provide experiences that enable the client to access feelings, strengthen reliance on inner resources, develop self-esteem, and become less dependent on the approval of others. Bohart and Greenberg (1997) edited a volume with multiple perspectives on the importance of empathy, and S. M. Johnson (2004) describes an approach to couples therapy that relies heavily on empathic attunement. Kahn (1997) compares the contributions of Carl Rogers and Heinz Kohut—both of whom put primary emphasis on empathy—and finds many similarities in the desired behavior of the therapist, despite different theoretical underpinnings.

Existential therapists have always emphasized the creation of a "real" relationship in which the therapist self-discloses, offers honest feedback, and presents a model of healthy interpersonal functioning. Conditions of therapy include a therapist who does not assume the role of expert; appreciation of the relativity of truth in interpersonal relations; and a willingness to explore in a collaborative way, in the "here and now," the complex distortions and misunderstandings that arise in relationships. This kind of relationship offers the client opportunities to develop a more mature style of relating.

INTEGRATION OF HYPOTHESES

The following hypotheses make good partners for **P3.**

B3 Mind-Body Connections

Future brain research will probably add support to the beliefs of Schore (2003), Siegel (2001), and others, who state that difficulties with emotional regulation and the development of a healthy self have their roots in neurophysiology.

CS4 Loss and Bereavement

With clients who are suffering from a recent loss, it is useful to use the **P3** hypothesis to understand if the relationship to the deceased was a selfobject or real-object relationship.

BL2 Conditioned Emotional Response

The person who is dependent on support from selfobjects is someone who has intensely painful emotional reactions conditioned to separations. A counterconditioning approach, using a hierarchy of difficulty, could help the client substitute responses of relaxation, peace, and comfort for emotional distress.

BL3 Skill Deficits or Lack of Competence

Therapists can focus on three major skills deficits:(1) poor empathy skills, (2) inability to take the POV of others, and (3) poor emotional regulation skills. Marsha Linehan (1993a, 1993b) provides treatment plans for working with these deficits.

C2 Faulty Cognitive Map

Jeffrey Young's list of early maladaptive schemas (see Table 6.6) offers examples of faulty schemas that will fit clients who behave in immature, narcissistic ways. With a modified, more adaptive model of the world, the client will realize that other people do not exist just to serve his needs, but instead are separate individuals with their own needs, feelings, and point of view. Beliefs about the self as empty, weak, and incapable of self-support can be challenged and modified.

C4 Dysfunctional Self-Talk

When psychoanalytic therapists talk about the "internalization of a soothing selfobject," this goal can be redefined as the development of soothing self-talk.

ES3 Spiritual Dimension

The *I-thou* relationship creates a spiritual connection between two people, whereas in the *I-it* relationship, the other person is treated as a thing, used and exploited, and often discarded when he fails to meet needs or when a better trophy comes along. Teachings of major religions will move people to higher levels of maturity, encouraging people to not treat others as they do not want to be treated, or to appreciate the presence of God in every human being.

P1 Internal Parts and Subpersonalities

Deficiencies in the self can be framed as the lack of functional internal parts such as Self-Soother (Nurturing Parent) or Inner Cheerleader, as well as the presence of an overly powerful Inadequate, Needy Child.

SCE Family System

Bowen's (1994) theory about differentiation of self expresses the same hypothesis as **P3,** putting the focus on the entire family system. In enmeshed families, most of the members have very immature object relations, and react to rupture in the selfobject bonds with intense emotions. Therapists who work with children need to evaluate the level of differentiation of the parents and recognize when family systems are fused and intolerant of expressions of separate identities.

SCE2 Cultural Context

In reading the key ideas in the **P3** hypothesis, you probably recognize the Western cultural bias, favoring individualism over collectivism. T. B. Smith (2004) advises that in many cultures the "lack of individuation should not be considered as abnormal, primitive, or pathological, but rather as a cultural style of family relationships" (p. 242). The construct of "healthy, separate self" does not exist in many cultures.

SCE3 Social Support

All people, regardless of their psychological maturation or cultural context, require connection to other humans to function effectively. Individuals differ in their needs for social support; those who fit the description of immaturity described in **P3** will benefit from being embedded in a social or family context where the very strong selfobject needs are adequately met.

KEY IDEAS FOR P4 UNCONSCIOUS DYNAMICS

Freud's model of personality is often represented as an iceberg: The conscious realm is above water, the subconscious (or preconscious) is underwater but near the surface, and the unconscious is at the deepest, unreachable level. We use the term *unconscious* when something that was experienced by a person cannot be brought into awareness by ordinary efforts to retrieve memories.

P4 UNCONSCIOUS DYNAMICS

Definition

The symptom or problem is explained in terms of **Unconscious Dynamics.** Defense mechanisms may be keeping thoughts and emotions out of awareness.

Explanation

The client suffers from irrational, self-defeating behaviors or distressing symptoms that do not respond to ordinary interventions, and which may stem from unconscious conflict or self-protective responses to traumatic events. Defense mechanisms function to keep the conflict and unpleasant affects out of awareness.

Examples

Roger suffered from depression, avoided social contact, and had many anxiety symptoms. His symptoms improved only after he remembered a traumatic childhood event, and experienced the emotions he had repressed.	Elizabeth is a high-functioning client with mature relationships. Her problem is that as a relationship moves toward sexual intimacy, she becomes extremely anxious, with nausea and somatic symptoms, and breaks it off.	Frank went to therapy at his wife's insistence because of his rejection of their gay son. A Jungian therapist helped him accept his "anima," his disowned "feminine" side, which his father had forced him to suppress.

Explanations for the lack of recall include defense mechanisms, memories have not been encoded in verbal memory, and simple forgetting.

Explaining Irrationality and Resistance

When people act counter to their own interests, show disregard for the perception of reality that is shared by others, and increase rather than decrease the pain and punishment in their lives, we hypothesize the operation of factors that are outside of conscious awareness.

Speculation about the unconscious origins of problems is warranted when the problems do not respond to treatment methods that rely on conscious cooperation, therapeutic conversation and activities, or compliance with homework assignments. The premise of this hypothesis is that by recovering the unconscious elements, the problem will be resolved.

No matter how maladaptive or bizarre a person's behavior, it would make sense if we understood what was happening at the unconscious level. A woman repeatedly gets involved with the same kind of lover, despite the fact that the outcome invariably involves suffering; a man with a serious heart condition continues the same stressful, overburdened, unhealthy lifestyle that his doctor told him was harmful to his health. There must be rewards and benefits for the seemingly irrational behavior, as well as punishments and costs for what would be a more rational, healthier, adaptive alternative. The woman's poor choice of a romantic partner could mean keeping alive the hope of receiving a father's love and the workaholism of the man with serious health problems could be a triumph over the younger brother who displaced him in his mother's heart. In both cases, changing the pattern of behavior would result in confronting emotional pain.

Validation through Treatment Success

Because we cannot see or measure these hypothetical unconscious elements, the only way to validate this theory is by a positive therapeutic outcome resulting from the client's demonstrated retrieval of forgotten experiences or emotions.

Freud's description (S. Freud, 1996) of his treatment of a man with Obsessive-Compulsive Disorder (OCD) (nick-named the "Rat Man") demonstrates how an intense transference reaction was the means to recovery of unconscious memories. According to Freud's theory, when the painful memories and feelings from childhood are made conscious, the patient would no longer need neurotic defenses to keep this material out of awareness, and therefore the neurotic symptoms would no longer be necessary. Freud discovered in this case that offering an interpretation of the unconscious roots of the symptoms was not successful in removing the symptoms. However, when a negative transference developed, and the patient "began heaping the grossest and filthiest abuse" on Freud and his family, and "behaved like someone in desperate terror trying to save himself from castigations of terrific violence," the patient understood that Freud did not deserve these feelings and that they must be coming from his childhood. By experiencing repressed emotions in the transference, he was able to recall incidents of his father's abuse. The emotional experiencing of early childhood rage and fear was pivotal to the successful outcome: cessation of symptoms and improved functioning in work and intimacy.

Unconscious Conflict and Compromise Formations

The explanation for neurotic symptoms such as the Rat Man's obsessions and compulsions is *unconscious conflict:* the clash between a wish for something forbidden or dangerous and the fear of a calamity such as abandonment, punishment, or loss of love. The concept of *compromise formation* as a solution to the unconscious conflict is explained very clearly by Brenner (1982) in *The Mind in Conflict.* A compromise formation is a conscious wish, belief, plan, behavior, fantasy, or symptom that accomplishes two aims:

1. Provides some expression and gratification for the unconscious (buried) wish.
2. Keeps the unpleasant emotions (e.g., anxiety, depressive affect) that are associated with gratification of the wish within tolerable limits.

Compromise formations are not only problematic aspects of functioning, such as irrational behavior and neurotic symptoms, but also positive adaptations such as career choice and philanthropic activities.

Defense Mechanisms

Symptoms and maladaptive behavior patterns are outcomes of defensive strategies to keep painful affects out of awareness. A list of defense mechanisms (A. Freud, 1967) usually includes repression, denial, reaction formation, projection, displacement, rationalization, sublimation, regression, introjection, identification, and compensation. With mature defenses, such as repression and sublimation, the person avoids painful affects and is able to function effectively in work and relationships. In contrast, primitive defenses such as projection and denial result in distorted perceptions of self and external reality. The concept of defense extends beyond the list of mechanisms: Any aspect of functioning can serve a self-protective function. Defenses function unconsciously and work for protection, even when the individual claims to want to recover the feelings. When defenses are weakened, painful emotions move into conscious awareness. If the person experiences the feelings and discovers that they are tolerable, there will no longer be a need for defenses.

Dissociative Reactions

Dissociation is recognized when the lack of memory for information and events is more extensive than can be explained by normal forgetting and is assumed to stem from trauma. Amnesia refers to the loss of memory about personal information, leaving gaps in personal history. A fugue state involves traveling away from home and being unable to remember one's personal past upon arrival in the new location. After the fugue, the person is usually unable to remember what happened during the fugue state. In Dissociative Identity Disorder, formerly called "multiple personality disorder," the person has separate identities that have amnesia for experiences that occurred when the person was operating from another identity.

Disowned Selves

While hypothesis **P1** involves internal selves that are available to consciousness, hypothesis **P4** addresses selves that are unconscious and often projected onto other people. Jung's theory provides examples of unconscious parts of the personality:

- *Shadow:* An inner figure that embodies those attributes that the ego disowns and rejects (e.g., rage, sexuality, or fragility.) The Shadow appears in dreams and in highly charged reactions to others.
- *Anima/animus:* An inner figure of the opposite gender. Men try to disown tender, receptive nurturing qualities, whereas women disown their powerful, aggressive side.

It is often through our intense reactions to others—irritation, revulsion, erotic pull—that we get clues to our disowned inner parts. In intimate relationships, disowned parts of the self are "carried" by the other person, where they can be cherished and persecuted (see **P2** for more discussion of mate selection).

Projective Identification

The term *projective identification* is used when the person who is the target for projections identifies with whatever is being projected and experiences those thoughts and feelings as if they originated from within. If person A projects hostility onto person B who just feels puzzled by why he is being treated like an enemy, there is no identification. However, if person B starts feeling annoyed, then angry, and then begins to dislike person A, the process of projective identification has occurred. When therapists experience projective identification they are gaining access to unconscious processes in their clients.

WHEN IS THIS HYPOTHESIS A GOOD MATCH?

In comparing this hypothesis with the prior one, the tools of developmental diagnosis, explained under hypothesis **P3** in Table 8.10, are important. Hypothesis **P3** specifies an immature level of personality development that is commonly called narcissistic or borderline. The current hypothesis, **P4,** is a fit for clients who function at a more mature level. Freud's Rat Man patient, described previously, was aware that his transference reactions were inappropriate—that is, he had an *observing ego* and was able to understand that Freud did not deserve this treatment and that his reactions were being displaced from another person, his father.

"Neurotic" Symptoms

The term *neurosis* was used by Freud for disorders (e.g., hysteria, phobias, and obsessional states) without an organic cause, which represented disguised expression of repressed material. A person who had an unconscious urge to aggressively kick someone would get hysterical paralysis of the leg and someone who had unconscious guilt for visual sexual fantasies would get hysterical blindness. *DSM-III* substituted the category of anxiety disorders for neuroses in *DSM-II* to eliminate definitions based on theory in favor of behavioral inclusion criteria.

We can still use the hypothesis of unconscious causation for anxiety disorders when cognitive-behavioral interventions are not effective. The **P4** hypothesis would predict *symptom substitution* if a behavior therapist successfully treated a phobia: Other symptoms would soon arise to prevent the emergence of unconscious material. In research on behavior therapy, there was no empirical evidence for symptom substitution, but instead strong empirical support for treatment effectiveness. Although behavior therapy should be considered the treatment of choice for phobias, the **P4** hypothesis can be considered as a backup in case a phobia does not respond to treatment, or if, in an unusual case, some kind of new symptom did develop after the successful completion of treatment.

Trauma, Posttraumatic Stress Disorder, and Dissociative Disorders

The origin of dissociation is presumably a trauma that was too overwhelming for the person to cope with and integrate. When treating a client who has experienced trauma, the **P4** hypothesis should be considered. A strategy of prevention is to help trauma victims put the facts and events into verbal memory and express the emotions in the presence of safe, supportive people, thereby preventing dissociative symptoms from developing.

Maladaptive, Irrational Behaviors

When adults do not alter their behaviors when they are faced with evidence of negative consequences, self-defeating ramifications, and faulty reasoning, it is useful to speculate about unconscious processes.

When Other Hypotheses Do Not Lead to Therapeutic Change

Many therapists function without including this hypothesis in their repertoire. However, it serves as a useful backup hypothesis when other approaches fail to produce the desired change in the client.

TREATMENT PLANNING

A wide variety of therapeutic activities can lead to the discovery of feelings, experiences, and memories that were previously inaccessible. The safety of the relationship, the permission to respond spontaneously, and a focused exploration that disrupts usual strategies of evasion all contribute to surprising insights and intense emotional upsurges. Examples of therapy processes that help people access buried material include:

- Telling and retelling life stories with an empathic listener.
- Participating in dramatizations such as Gestalt empty chair or psychodrama.
- Focused questions exploring fears.
- Guided imagery.
- Ask the client to bring music from an early period of life, close her eyes, and let feelings emerge.
- Have the client bring photos and mementos.

Using Neurotic Transference

A major goal of therapy using **P4** is to make "the unconscious conscious." Remember that cognitive insight is not enough; it is the emotional experience buried in the unconscious that needs to be experienced and integrated. Freud's Rat Man case shows that the emotional reexperiencing of unconscious feelings by a client who has sufficient observing ego to recognize distortions is the route to positive therapeutic outcome.

Refer back to Table 8.10 to see in the right column how types of transference correspond to levels of development. With selfobject transference, described under **P3,** the clinical formulation stresses unmet childhood needs as the root of the problem. At the higher level of development, the more mature defense mechanism of repression is used, whereas in early stages, primitive defenses such as denial, projection, and splitting are relied on. The procedures of traditional psychoanalysis—using a couch, multiple sessions per week, and a nondisclosing therapist—were designed to maximize the intensity of transference and to permit repressed material to come into consciousness.

The development of transference is both a diagnostic tool and the medium for therapeutic change. With a neurotic transference, the hypothesis is that there are unconscious feelings and feared calamities that need to be accessed and experienced. When a selfobject transference develops, the therapist seeks to provide a good selfobject relationship. The methods that increase a neurotic transference are very inappropriate for clients who create selfobject transferences and need support, encouragement, and empathic attunement.

Free Association and Interpretation

In free association exercises, the client is instructed to say whatever comes to mind, without censorship. This is requesting the impossible. The mind is always filtering, and the therapist can gather clues about what is hidden from awareness by attending to nonverbal behavior, noting what is omitted as well as what is repeated, speculating about the sequence of ideas, and tuning into the responses the patient evokes. The minimal responsiveness of the therapist, and the lack of approval and disapproval, challenges the client to find direction from inside—from conscious and unconscious sources. As stated previously, interpretation is usually not sufficient in the absence of emotional reexperiencing; however, in some cases an accurate, well-timed interpretation will trigger recollections and reduce the need for defenses.

Using Countertransference

The countertransference reactions of the therapist have the potential to illuminate the unconscious dynamics of the client. To use countertransference, you must be able to sort out what is coming from the client and what is coming from your own internal world. Think to yourself, *Is what I am currently experiencing something that my client is not able to experience on a conscious level?* Through awareness of your own inner reactions, you will recognize the "pull" of the client's projection or discover the emotions that the client is warding off. By being aware of the earliest tendency to identify, while resisting the pull, the therapist can use these processes to understand the unconscious experiences that the client cannot handle. The therapist can serve as a container for the projected feelings and gradually help the client integrate them into his awareness.

Dream Analysis

Freud called dreams "the royal road to the unconscious." Unconscious material that is kept out of awareness by defense mechanisms can bypass the censor when the person is sleeping and appear in disguised forms in dreams. Jung similarly valued dreams as a source of encounter with inner selves that are outside of conscious awareness. Therapists can encourage clients to talk about their dreams and suggest methods to facilitate recall, such as keeping paper and pen or a tape recorder by the bedside. When clients know that dreams are an important part of therapy, they tend to dream more frequently.

You should not impose preconceived dream interpretations from a codebook of symbols but rather help the client to decipher the messages coming from the dream. Strategies for working with dreams include free association to the content of the dream, creative storytelling about the dream elements, drawing pictures of the dream, or the Gestalt strategy of having the person role-play the part of every person and object in the dream.

Projective Tests

The best-known projective tests are the Thematic Apperception Test (TAT), a set of ambiguous photos and drawings, and the Rorschach Inkblot test. The premise of this kind of testing is that the client projects unconscious needs, fears, feelings, and conflicts into the stimuli, and reveals them in his verbal responses.

Therapeutic Use of Art

Jung, in particular, valued the use of art activities as a means of accessing the unconscious. What we call "unconscious" can mean "not having been encoded in words," but possibly encoded in visual memory. Through use of the visual arts, clients may be able to access these experiences. For instance, a child who is unable to talk about sexual abuse may be able to draw pictures about the place where it happened and begin to talk about it as she looks at the picture. There are several art therapy journals that illustrate the variety of ways that art therapy is used: *Art Therapy: Journal of the American Art Therapy Association; The Arts in Psychotherapy;* and *American Journal of Art Therapy.* In addition, a web site, www.drawntogether.com is a useful resource.

There are two phases of art therapy: (1) the production of art and (2) the interpretation of its meaning. The process of creating art, without any interpretation, is often viewed as therapeutic in itself. The act of making art allows for expression of unconscious feelings and symbolic representation of internal conflict and, at the end of the experience, the client has less need for defensive processes. The creation of the art can be a healthy form of sublimation. When the client's problem stems from hidden emotions, the art making can lead to accessing those feelings and give the client a sense of confidence in being able to contain and express them. If the "disowned creative part" is a clinical issue, the task of producing an art product will activate the struggle to access that part. When there is a stage of interpretive discussion, therapists are careful to let the client direct the interpretation and not impose their preconceived ideas. Often insight can come from having the client free associate to the completed work.

Other forms of art such as dance and music may also be used for work with unconscious processes.

Hypnotherapy

The use of hypnosis in therapy has the potential to help clients to access memories that are not recalled in their ordinary state of consciousness. In the relaxed, focused state of hypnotic trance, characterized by increased suggestibility and a willingness to follow the therapist's directions, the client's defenses are lowered. Therapists have used hypnotic suggestions to ask the subconscious part of the personality to create a dream, using whatever symbols it wants, which will help shed light on the problem. Milton Erickson wove hypnotic suggestions through regular conversation and was able to bypass the client's resistances to change as well as activate beneficial processes outside of awareness. Hypnosis is one of the treatments recommended for dissociative disorders.

INTEGRATION OF HYPOTHESES

Three hypotheses have links to the concept of unconscious dynamics.

B3 Mind-Body Connections

Neuroscientists distinguish between two types of memories: (1) explicit memories, which are available for conscious recall, and (2) implicit memories, which are not voluntarily retrieved, although they can pop up into consciousness, as with flashbacks in PTSD. Future brain research may lead to new understanding of what we now refer to as unconscious.

BL1 Antecedents and Consequences

Behavioral concepts can be used to understand the persistence of maladaptive neurotic behavior. The neurotic symptom is maintained by its consequences: (a) it eliminates or avoids painful affect; and (b) there are rewards and payoffs for having the symptoms, such as avoiding work or getting other family members to be helpful (secondary gains). A behavioral plan could change the reinforcement contingencies: remove rewards from the maladaptive behaviors and produce rewards for the desired, new behaviors.

BL2 Conditioned Emotional Response

By keeping material in the unconscious, the person is avoiding intense anxiety. Therefore, the technique of systematic desensitization can be used. The hierarchy can be constructed along symbolic, psychodynamic concepts, such as "similarity to father," or "gradations of abandonment feelings." Similarly, flooding techniques can be used: The person can be presented with imagery of the most exaggerated form of the feared calamity, so that the intense emotional response is experienced in the session and then begins to be extinguished.

SUGGESTED READINGS

Recommended reading is listed separately for each hypotheses although many books are relevant for all four hypotheses in this chapter.

P1 Internal Parts and Subpersonalities

Berne, E. (1996). *Games people play: The psychology of human relationships.* New York: Ballantine Books.

Blatner, A. (2000). *Foundations of psychodrama: History, theory, and practice* (4th ed.). New York: Springer.

Fagan, J., & Shepherd, I. L. (1970). *Gestalt therapy now.* New York: Harper Colophon Books.

Humber, E. (1983). *C. G. Jung: The fundamentals of theory and practice.* Wilmette, IL: Chiron.

Johnson, R. A. (1989). *Inner work: Using dreams and creative imagination for personal growth and integration.* New York: Harper & Row.

James, M., & Jongeward, D. (1996). *Born to win: Transactional analysis with Gestalt experiments.* New York: Addison-Wesley.

Leveton, E. (2001). *A clinician's guide to psychodrama* (3rd ed.). New York: Springer.

Midgley, D. (1999). *New directions in transactional analysis counseling: An explorer's handbook*. London: Free Association Books.

Perls, F. (1992). *Gestalt therapy verbatim* (Rev. ed.). Gouldsboro, ME: Gestalt Journal Press.

Polster, E., & Polster, M. (1974). *Gestalt therapy integrated: Contours of theory and practice*. New York: Vintage Books.

Rowan, J. (1990). *Subpersonalities: The people inside us*. London: Routledge.

Stone, H., & Stone, S. W. (1989). *Embracing each other*. Navato, CA: Nataraj Publishing.

Stone, H., & Stone, S. L. (1989). *Embracing our selves: The voice dialogue manual*. Novato, CA: New World Library.

Stone, H., & Stone, S. (1993). *Embracing your inner critic: Turning self-criticism into a creative asset*. San Francisco: Harper.

Zinker, J. (1978). *Creative process in Gestalt therapy*. New York: Vintage Books.

P2 Reenactment of Early Childhood Experiences

Basch, M. (1980). *Doing psychotherapy*. New York: Basic Books.

Berne, E. (1981). *What do you say after you say hello?* Toronto, Ontario, Canada: Bantam Books.

Bowlby, J. (1988). *A secure base: Parent-child attachment and healthy human development*. New York: Basic Books.

Brown, N. W. (2001). *Children of the self-absorbed*. Oakland, CA: New Harbinger.

Cassidy, J., & Shaver, P. R. (Eds.). (1999). *Handbook of attachment: Theory, research, and clinical applications*. New York: Guilford.

Clarkson, P. (1999). *Gestalt counseling in action* (2nd ed.). Thousand Oaks, CA: Sage.

Goulding, B., & Goulding, M. (1997). *Changing lives through redecision therapy*. New York: Grove Press.

Hendrix, H. (1988). *Getting the love you want: A guide for couples*. New York: Henry Holt.

Holmes, J. (2001). *The search for the secure base: Attachment theory and psychotherapy*. London: Brunner-Routledge.

Johnson, S. M., & Whiffen, V. E. (Eds.). (2003). *Attachment processes in couple and family therapy*. New York: Guilford Press.

Kahn, M. (1997). *Between therapist and client: The new relationship* (2nd ed.). New York: Freeman.

Lewis, J. M., & Gossett, J. T. (1999). *Disarming the past: How an intimate relationship can heal old wounds*. Phoenix, AZ: Zeig, Tucker & Co.

Natterson, J. M., & Friedman, R. J. (1995). *A primer of clinical intersubjectivity*. Northvale, NJ: Aronson.

Parkes, C. M., & Stevenson-Hinde, J. (Eds.). (1982). *The place of attachment in human behavior*. New York: Wiley.

Perls, F. (1973). *The Gestalt approach*. Palo Alto, CA: Science and Behavior Books.

Steiner, C. (1990). *Scripts people live: Transactional analysis of life scripts*. New York: Grove Press.

Whitfield, C. (1987). *Healing the child within*. Deerfield Beach, FL: Health Communications.

Woititz, J. (1990). *Adult children of alcoholics*(Expanded ed.). Deerfield Beach, FL: Health Communications.

P3 Immature Sense of Self and Conception of Others

Firestone, R. W., & Catlett, J. (2000). *Fear of intimacy.* Washington, DC: American Psychological Association.

Greenberg J. R., & Mitchell, S. A. (1983). *Object relations in psychoanalytic theory.* Cambridge, MA: Harvard University Press.

Horner, A. (1984). *Object relations and the developing ego in therapy* (2nd ed.). New York: Jason Aronson.

Kohut, H. (1976). *Restoration of the self.* Madison, CT: International Universities Press.

Kohut, H. (2000). *Analysis of the self.* Madison, CT: International Universities Press.

Mahler, M., Bergman, A., & Pine, F. (1975). *The psychological birth of the human infant.* New York: Basic Books.

Masterson, J. (1981). *The narcissistic and borderline disorders: An integrated developmental approach.* Philadelphia: Brunner-Routledge.

Masterson, J. (1990). *The search for the real self: Unmasking the personality disorders of our age.* New York: Touchstone Books.

Scharff, J. S., & Scharf, D. E. (1995). *The primer of object relations therapy.* Northvale, NJ: Aronson.

St. Clair, M. (2003). *Object relations and self-psychology: An introduction* (4th ed.). Belmont, CA: Wadsworth Publishing.

Stern, D. N. (1985). *The interpersonal world of the infant: A view from psychoanalysis and developmental psychology.* New York: Basic Books.

P4 Unconscious Dynamics

Brenner, C. (1982). *The mind in conflict.* Madison, CT: International Universities Press.

Ellenberger, H. F. (1970). *The discovery of the unconscious.* New York: Basic Books.

Freud, A. (1967). *Ego and the mechanisms of defense: Vol. 2. The writings of Anna Freud* (Rev. ed.). Guilford, CT: International Universities Press.

Freud, S. (1996). *Three case histories.* New York: Touchstone.

Gendlin, E. T. (1985). *Let your body interpret your dreams.* New York: Chiron.

Grotstein, J. S. (1981). *Splitting and projective identification.* Northvale, NJ: Aronson.

Hall, J. A. (1983). *Jungian dream interpretation: A handbook of theory and practice.* Toronto, Canada: Inner City Books.

Rubin, J. A. (2001). *Approaches to art therapy: Theory and technique.* New York: Brunner-Routledge.

Chapter 9

SOCIAL, CULTURAL, AND ENVIRONMENTAL FACTORS

The client is part of social units as small as the family and as broad as the socioeconomic system in a specific historical context. There are overlapping social subgroups with which the individual identifies, such as gender, race, occupation, sexual orientation, and ethnic or cultural groups. Table 9.1 lists the seven hypotheses that contrast with the traditional perspective that the problem lies in the individual, instead placing the client in a larger system.

KEY IDEAS FOR SCE1 FAMILY SYSTEM

Family systems theory originated in the 1950s and 1960s and represented a huge paradigm shift. Instead of locating the problem inside an individual—in biology,

Table 9.1   Social, Cultural, and Environmental Factors

SCE1 Family System	The problem must be understood in the context of the entire **Family System.**
SCE2 Cultural Context	Knowledge of the **Cultural Context** is necessary to understand the problem and/or to create a treatment plan that shows sensitivity to the norms, rules, and values of the client's cultural group.
SCE3 Social Support	The problem is either caused or maintained by deficiencies in **Social Support.**
SCE4 Social Role Performance	Difficulty meeting demands for **Social Role Performance** contributes to the client's distress and dysfunction.
SCE5 Social Problem is a Cause	A **Social Problem** (e.g., poverty, discrimination, or social oppression) **is a Cause** of the problem. Social problems can also exacerbate difficulties stemming from other causes. You must avoid *blaming the victim.*
SCE6 Social Role of Mental Patient	The problem is causally related to disadvantages or advantages to the **Social Role of Mental Patient.**
SCE7 Environmental Factors	The problem is explained in terms of **Environmental Factors.** Solutions can involve modifying the environment, leaving the environment, obtaining material resources, or accepting what can't be changed.

SCE1 FAMILY SYSTEM

Definition

The problem must be understood in the context of the entire **Family System.**

Explanation

The symptoms of the identified patient can serve a function for the family or stem from deficiencies in the family's structure, rules, level of emotional differentiation, or communication patterns. When symptoms serve to stabilize the homeostasis of a family, improvement in the client can result in symptoms in another member. It is therefore useful to treat family members together so that changes can be made in the entire system.

Examples

Mollie is a 25-year-old woman who wants to move out of her parents' home and begin to "feel like a real adult." She is an only child and believes that her mother totally depends on her for emotional support. "If I leave, I'm afraid that she will be very depressed, and I will end up feeling guilty." She also worries that she won't be able to cope on her own because her mother has always made decisions for her.

Ruth, a married woman, was 50 pounds overweight, depressed, and socially isolated. She entered therapy and a weight-loss support group. She is now five pounds away from her desired weight and has begun to feel good about herself. At the point when she began to feel confident enough to find new social activities and start making friends, her husband developed panic attacks.

Johnny, a 10-year-old child, experienced severe anxiety problems. Whenever his condition improved, his parents would engage in bitter conflict with each other, leading to threats of divorce. At that point, Johnny's symptoms would recur, at even greater intensity than before. The parents would agree to stay together to help him. At the urging of their son's therapist, they went to marital therapy.

cognitive maps, personality, intrapsychic conflict, skill deficits, or free will—we can understand the problem as stemming from processes and structures of the entire family system. Systems are composed of elements and units that are interrelated in such a way that change in one part causes change in other parts. A system is more than the sum of its parts because of the regulatory mechanisms that operate to develop and maintain a stable way of functioning—equilibrium or homeostasis. When an event destabilizes the system, these mechanisms work to resist change and maintain the status quo. When it is not possible to restore the prior homeostasis, disequilibrium presents opportunities for either positive change, such as more flexible communication patterns, or negative change, such as the development of symptoms in a family member.

Goldenberg and Goldenberg (2000) provide an overview of the current field of family therapy. The individual and family perspectives are not mutually exclusive: As individuals, we internalize our families and carry them with us, and families, despite having properties of systems, are still composed of separate individuals. Most family and couple therapists pay attention to both individual and relationship variables in assessment, goal development, and treatment, although they believe that the best way to assess and treat relational dynamics is to see the people in the relationship together, in the format called "conjoint therapy."

There is often confusion about the way the term *family systems therapy* is used. It can have a broad definition—*any model of therapy that conceptualizes a person's symptoms as having origins in the functioning of a relationship*—or have a narrow meaning, such as a specific model of therapy associated with a specific theorist such as Murray Bowen. I am using the term in its broadest sense. The term *family* is not restricted to parents and children, but embraces couples, married and otherwise, with or without children; siblings; three-generation families and other extended families; and groups of interrelated friends or coworkers. Family systems concepts can be used in organizational settings to help enhance productivity and morale.

Symptoms from a Systems Perspective

Families are always changing: New children are added, older ones leave home, and each person progresses through developmental stages, which place new demands on the system. The equilibrium of a family can never stay the same and adaptation is a necessity. Symptoms can be a reaction to change, a way to try to get the system to change, or tactics to resist change; they can have a protective function or serve as a stabilizing device. One of the functions of the symptom is to attempt to solve a problem; for instance, the unmanageable symptoms of children can bring parents into therapy to resolve their relationship problems. Symptoms also develop as a method to coerce someone into staying the same and not disrupting the status quo. As an example, when a woman who has served in the roles of wife and mother begins to spend time away from home to pursue a career, the husband might get depressed or a child might start acting out in school—and if the worried mother gives up her career aspirations and stays home, the symptoms in her family members suddenly disappear.

Concept of an "Identified Patient"

The term *patient,* which implies that there is pathology solely in one individual, is no longer appropriate if the symptoms in one family member may represent dysfunction in the family as a unit. The term *identified patient* (IP) was coined to resolve this problem: The IP is viewed as the *symptom bearer,* but not as a person with pathology, and every member of the family is involved in the problem. For instance, when a child is brought into therapy with behavioral problems, the therapist realizes that the symptoms might serve the function of keeping a marriage together, and that, therefore, the whole family, or perhaps just the marital dyad, need the treatment. From this perspective, seeing the child alone in play therapy would not solve the problem, and might make things worse, because this strategy fails to address the real issue, and, moreover, detracts from the parents' feelings of competence.

Couples' Systems

In a romantic relationship, two people often get stuck at an equilibrium where neither is happy: Partner A complains that the relationship is too distant and that his or her needs for closeness are not met; Partner B complains about being suffocated and that Partner A's demands encroach on his or her independence. From an individual perspective, it looks like the first one has a higher need for intimacy, or perhaps greater dependency and insecurity. The other partner seems to be more self-sufficient and has a lower need for intimacy. From a systems perspective, however, they have achieved exactly the best balance to meet both of their dual sets of needs for closeness and separateness. Partner A, who overtly demonstrates the need for more closeness, gets to maintain the illusion of truly wanting closeness. However, if partner B changes and moves closer, Partner A dances away and now feels smothered. The two partners collude in carrying functions for each other, together making a "whole self."

Circular Causality

Cause-effect thinking is usually built on assumptions of linear causality: If A causes B and B causes C, C cannot cause A. However a study of systems shows that causality can be circular, and C *can* cause A. A common example of linear thinking is the pattern of mutual blaming in a marriage. Each partner thinks that the other person's behavior is the cause of the problem and that the solution lies in fixing that person.

- **Wife's point of view (POV):** *I nag because my husband withdraws*
- **Husband's POV:** *I withdraw because my wife nags.*

The consequences of each person's behavior is to increase the undesired behavior in the other person:

> Husband withdraws → Wife nags → Husband withdraws more
>
> Wife nags → Husband withdraws → Wife nags more

Putting those two patterns together, we can create a circular diagram (Figure 9.1) and recognize that causation cannot be placed in either individual but rather in the dynamic between them.

The two partners are in an interlocking pattern. Both spouses must look at how their behavior serves as a trigger for the other person's objectionable behavior. Figure 9.2 shows an example of circular causality that includes a child. Imagine that the child comes to therapy with problems of misbehavior in school. With an individual perspective, the problem is "in" the child, and causation stems from his lack of motivation, his depression, or perhaps a biologically based condition like Attention-Deficit/Hyperactivity Disorder (ADHD). However, to understand causation adequately, the entire system must be understood:

- The wife experiences her husband as too withdrawn, so she looks to a child to meet her emotional needs.
- The husband feels left out of these close mother-child interactions so he becomes more withdrawn and less responsive to his wife's needs.

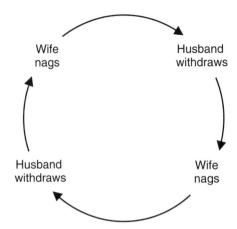

Figure 9.1 Circular causality in a couple's conflict.

Second-Order Change

For a social system to change, it has to create rules and processes that alter its structure, level of differentiation, and communication patterns. Those changes are called second-order changes; first-order change refers to changes that, from a systemic perspective, are really "more of the same." In the prior example, the father's withdrawing and the mother's increasing overinvolvement in the child were examples of first-order change—solutions that only increased the severity of the problems, instead of leading to constructive change. An example of second-order change would be for the two parents to work together on the marital relationship, learning to get their needs for closeness and separateness met in a mutually satisfying way, with each parent maintaining a close connection to the child, and the three of them engaging in enjoyable activities together.

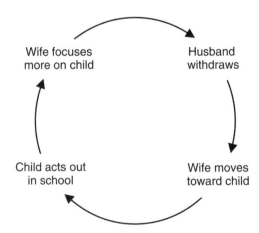

Figure 9.2 Circular causality in three-person family with child "IP."

Family Systems Concepts

Table 9.2 illustrates concepts related to family systems, all of which need to be understood in the client's specific cultural context.

Intergenerational Transmission Process

Patterns from the grandparent generation may show up in a family as rules, customs, and rituals. This principle is illustrated in the following story:

> A woman was asked by her husband, after many years of marriage, why she always cut off the ends of the ham when she made Easter dinner. Her answer was, "That's how my mother always did it." Curious, however, she asked her mother the same question and gets the same answer, "That's how my mother always did it." She then goes to her grandmother, who fortunately is still alive, and asks the same question. The answer was, "I only had one pan and had to cut it to make it fit."

Parents may project onto a child the image of someone from their family of origin and behave in a way to create a self-fulfilling prophecy. For instance, a father thinks about his first-born son, whom he names after his father, *Joey will carry on the family tradition of being a scholar,* but, annoyed at his youngest daughter, thinks, *Susie is a spoiled brat just like my younger sister.*

An example of intergenerational transmission, which was mentioned under **CS2,** is the symptoms of the second and third generation of Holocaust survivors.

Dysfunctional Communication Patterns

Communication patterns need to be examined not just in terms of skill deficits (discussed in **BL3**) but as processes through which systems maintain their equilibrium and resist change. It is important to focus on the process rather than just the content of communication: In a given sentence, multiple messages are being sent through verbal and nonverbal channels and communication can be analyzed in terms of the congruence among these messages. Furthermore, *behavior is communication:* Paying attention to what people do as well as what they say is an important rule for understanding interpersonal dynamics.

All communication contains a relationship component, attempting to define the relationship or accepting the other person's bid for a specific definition. The term *metacommunicate* means to communicate about communication—to discuss the process of the interaction and to comment on what is not said directly. Many dysfunctional patterns can be maintained only because of an unspoken rule such as "do not comment on the communication." Therefore, the ability to both recognize patterns as they occur and talk about them is an important therapeutic goal. Table 9.3 presents examples of dysfunctional patterns.

Table 9.2   Family Systems Concepts

Family Rules

An unspoken code of conduct dictates what is permissible and what will lead to negative sanctions. Family rules govern communication patterns—who talks to whom, when, how, and about what. One very powerful rule that prevents growth in families is "Don't talk about family problems outside of the family." At transition points in the family life cycle, families need to adapt to changes and modify outdated rules. Sometimes families suffer from a lack of clear, consistent rules and what is rewarded one day can be punished the next. The family rule regarding "how we deal with change" is an important focus at the beginning of therapy.

Roles

The most obvious role differentiation is between parents and children. Gender roles may be fixed and traditional (e.g. man as breadwinner and head of family, woman as homemaker and subordinate) or flexible and equal. Families can designate one of its members to be the *scapegoat*—the one to blame for everything that goes wrong in the family. Unfortunately, a child who is viewed this way often identifies with the role and fulfills the negative prophecy of being a destructive, incorrigible troublemaker. Another role is *parentified child*—the one who is responsible for taking care of the parents' emotional needs. Family members can take over-responsible and underresponsible roles. Satir described roles of Placator, Blamer, Super-Responsible, and Irrelevant (Distracter).

Hierarchy

Family members have power differences; in functional families, the parents are the leaders. A dysfunctional pattern occurs in families when a parent creates an alliance with one of the children and relegates the other spouse to a lower position of power.

Types of Boundaries

A boundary exists between the nuclear family and the extended family.

A boundary exists between the family unit and the outside community.

An intergenerational boundary exists when the parents function together as a separate system and the children have their own sibling subsystem.

A personal boundary exists around every separate individual, including infants: each individual is presumed to be the expert on his or her internal experiences.

Healthy Boundaries

Permeable boundaries: Allows close exchanges while maintaining individuality.

Respect for boundaries: Permission is needed to cross personal boundaries (e.g., both physical and psychological) and the individual's desire for separateness (e.g., solitude, privacy, and expression of discrepant opinions) is respected.

Boundary Problems

Rigid: Prevents contact.

Weak and damaged: Confusion about what is inside and what is out.

Boundary violations: For example, a father, in frustration, jams a spoon of food into the mouth of a protesting infant; a mother opens the door to the bathroom when her adolescent son is inside; or a husband opens his wife's mail without permission.

Table 9.2 *(Continued)*

Theory of Differentiation

In our close relationships, we all seek a balance between our need for togetherness and our need for individuality or "differentiation." Murray Bowen's (1994) theory of differentiation examines how the family can promote or impede the movement of a child from the dependence of infancy to a state of maturity where she can function competently as a separate person, while maintaining bonds to the family. A psychologically separate, or *differentiated,* person is aware of and takes responsibility for his own thoughts, feelings, and actions; can recognize that other people have different thoughts and feelings; and can tolerate these differences without feeling threatened or unloved. Bowen's concept of differentiation includes the separation of intellect and emotion as well as the independence from other people.

Enmeshment

When people function at a low level of differentiation, the boundaries between them are "fused." They answer for each other. Parents do not treat children as separate selves, but instead assume that they know what is in their child's mind (e.g., the mother who says to her child, "I'm cold, put your coat on"). Expressions of differences are experienced as a threat to the whole: There is pressure to agree, feel the same way, and suppress individuality for a sense of "we-ness." In an undifferentiated (enmeshed) system, any movement towards separateness increases anxiety and people respond in volatile ways to behavior of which they disapprove.

Emotional Reactivity

The term *emotional reactivity* refers to responses of undifferentiated people to a rupture in the togetherness in the relationship. To differentiate successfully from an enmeshed family, the individual must withstand negative emotional reactions intended to pull her back into the fusion of the family. Emotionally reactive people do not experience that they have a choice to be guided by reason instead of emotion. The thought pattern *"he made me angry when he did that,"* is experienced as a valid statement of causation and inevitability, in contrast to the thinking of a person who has achieved greater differentiation, who might respond: *"I didn't like it when he did that. I became angry, but I realize there were other ways I could respond."*

Disengagement

There are rigid boundaries between members, resulting in a degree of separateness that interferes with a sense of belonging, connection, and mutual responsibility. Low-cohesion families fail to develop interdependence and members' needs for support and closeness go unmet. Often in a family, one parent might be enmeshed with a child while the other parent, and perhaps another child as well, are disengaged from both of them (see Figure 9.2 for an example).

Emotional Cutoff

Emotional distance may involve a lack of contact and communication. While the person may imagine that this is a way to achieve differentiation, it is actually a sign of his fusion with the family, because it fails to change his own emotional reactivity and intolerance of differences.

Triangulation

When there is anxiety in a dyadic relationship, the two people recruit a third person to become part of the relationship, helping them to lower anxiety, avoid conflict about their relationship, and stabilize the relationship. The parents may project their issues onto a child and attempt to deal with them by fighting over how to treat the child's problems. In families where the children are grown, two family members may focus all of their communication on the behavior of a third. An elderly couple may feel incapable of making decisions unless one of their adult children is drawn into the process.

Table 9.3 Dysfunctional Communication Patterns

Symptom as Communication

Symptoms may be attempts to define and control a relationship. For instance, a symptom such as agoraphobia allows a person to control someone else's behavior while being able to say, "I can't help it."

Double-Bind

This term refers to a "damned if you do, damned if you don't" type of message, where the person gets contradictory messages from the same person. For instance, a child can be criticized for not showing affection, but then when she approaches for a hug, the parent stiffens and pushes her away because she is dirty. This pattern allows the parent to take a position, *See me as a person who wants to be close,* while at the same time, maintaining distance.

Mystification

This is a communication tactic where one person denies the validity of another person's experience. For instance, a wife accurately senses that her husband is having an affair and confronts him. He responds, "How can you think that? You are so insecure and jealous, maybe you need to go to therapy and get some help for yourself."

Pseudomutuality

This is a style of communication where only agreement is tolerated, creating a false sense of closeness and harmony, while suppressing and denying the existence of differences.

Pseudohostility

Based on the negative communication, it looks as if the people hate each other; however, they have developed a pattern of bickering and put-downs that is comfortable and predictable, protecting them from the vulnerability of real intimacy.

Hidden Agendas

When attention is paid to the process rather than content of communication, it is possible to identify the hidden agenda, such as being right, special, more powerful, or deserving of protection.

WHEN IS THIS HYPOTHESIS A GOOD MATCH?

When the client is a child or adolescent, it should be mandatory to consider family systems hypotheses. Unfortunately, many clinics continue the old-fashioned child guidance model of sending parents and children to different therapists instead of viewing problems in the context of the family system. If the child's symptom exists to protect the parents, the therapist will not have the data for that formulation if the parents are not included. Furthermore, intervening with the child alone may cause problems elsewhere in the system, deprive the parents of a chance to be coached to be more competent parents, and fail to address the factors that will cause relapse in the child.

Leaving Home

At the developmental transition when a young adult expects to leave home and parents are facing an empty nest, it is extremely beneficial to work from a family systems model. The parents may sabotage the separation process because as long as the child stays in the family, they do not have to deal with their relationship with each other. Haley (1997) advised therapists to tell parents that they are obligated to stay together until their young adult child is on her feet, knowing that if the parents separate, the child will feel obligated to stay home to keep them together.

Marital Dissatisfaction

If an unhappy married person goes into individual therapy with marital distress as the primary issue, the therapist should consider the advantages of having the client and spouse go together to conjoint couple therapy. If spouses attempt to deal with marital problems by going to separate individual therapists and no one is helping them change their marital system, the likelihood of a relationship breakup increases. Moreover, the therapist's source of data is limited: There is no opportunity to hear the spouse's side or to observe the two of them interacting together. Even if the client (or couple) is certain there is no hope for the marriage and divorce is inevitable, there is still benefit in using the systems hypothesis to achieve second-order change: They will say they have tried everything, but the therapist might note that they have tried one thing, and have done it over and over again. If divorce is the outcome, clients enter their next relationship with greater insight and differentiation and less reactivity and projection. If there are children, it is especially important to have the couple work out parenting issues together.

Psychiatric Symptoms

The lens of the family systems hypothesis can be used to view any symptom or psychiatric disorder, such as a phobia, compulsion, anxiety, depression, or anorexia. By wondering "why now?" and examining family systems factors at the time the symptom originated, you might find evidence that the symptom arose to stabilize the system, to express feelings that were otherwise suppressed, or as an indirect effort to meet some underlying need. Even when the cause of the disorder is biological or from other individual factors, addressing family systems factors can be a beneficial part of treatment.

Alcoholism and Addictions

Alcoholism, like any symptom, can stabilize a family. There is an implicit interpersonal bargain between the alcoholic spouse and the nurturing partner: The concept of *enabler* entered addiction theory when it became apparent that the family members of the addict, despite their outward objection to the problem, were covertly supporting it. When addicts succeed in a recovery program, other members of the family may develop symptoms or behave in ways to encourage relapse in the recovered addict. Adolescent drug abuse is a symptom that unites family members around one concern.

Battered Woman Syndrome

When "battered woman syndrome" is explained from an individual perspective, the causation is placed in the man: He has Borderline Personality Disorder; abuses drugs or alcohol; has anger management problems, low self-esteem, and poor impulse control; is a sadist; or is reflecting a culture that teaches men to dominate women. The explanations for why a woman does not leave an abusive spouse focus on her socialization to be a peacekeeper, her lack of self-esteem or psychological energy to leave, and the brainwashing she has endured, which convinced her that she is the cause of the violence.

By focusing on individuals, therapists fail to treat the relationship and intervene in the system. The opposition to conjoint therapy for domestic violence may have its basis in ideology rather than professional expertise because of the implication that both partners must change their behavior (Hoff, 1999). One family systems hypothesis is that the victim disowns the anger and carries traits of passivity and dependency, while the abuser carries the anger for both of them. The family systems approach sees anger and violence in the context of the relationship dynamics.

Using this model, the therapist would not condone violent behavior nor seek to relieve the batterer of legal consequences for criminal behavior, but would want to provide conjoint treatment when the battered spouse is motivated to keep the relationship together. Most service providers have such a strong bias in favor of terminating the abusive relationship that battered women who choose to stay with the spouse tend to withdraw from treatment (Ben-Ari, Winstok, & Eisikovits, 2003). Busby (1996) and Roberts (1998) provide perspectives on family violence that include family systems factors.

Sabotage of an Individual's Improvement

Sometimes a client makes great strides in individual therapy but then, when back in the family system, there is relapse or the development of new problems, suggesting that family members are sabotaging the positive change. In setting goals with all clients, it is useful to address family systems factors: *If you achieved your goal, who would object? Who would try to pressure you to stay the same? What other problems might appear in other family members if you began to act in a healthier way?* (see Table 12.1 in Chapter 12). If you suspect that other family members will sabotage the client's improvement, it might be useful to see them together to help them adjust to your client's changes.

TREATMENT PLANNING

The treatment of choice when applying the **SCE1** hypothesis is conjoint therapy, which means meeting with multiple clients in the same room at the same time. Therapists who work with the individual client, alone, despite the belief that the family systems hypothesis is the best match, often lack conviction in the benefits of conjoint therapy or have self-doubts about their effectiveness with this very challenging modality. To become a competent conjoint therapist requires education and training so if this is not your area of competence, you will need to provide referral. Therapists who believe that conjoint therapy is the treatment of choice are usually able to overcome the obstacles that clients present:

- *Deceased parents:* Use siblings and other relatives.
- *Geographic distance:* Use conference calls; arrange for lengthy sessions when family members are in town for a visit.
- *Other members refuse to attend:* Call them yourself; find the family member who has the power to get them all to show up at least once.

Choosing to use a conjoint therapy treatment approach does not mean that every single therapy session includes the entire family. There will also be instances when it will be preferable to work with an individual or a part of the system, as when an older adolescent or young adult needs to develop a greater sense of psychological separateness from the family or when the parents are discussing their sexuality and children should not be included. For a young adult separating from the family of origin, it could be beneficial to meet with the mother and a grandmother together or meet with one or both of the parents to help them deal better with the family transition.

It is beyond the scope of this book to address techniques of family therapy, but the reading list at the end of the chapter will provide direction for further study.

Family Systems Concepts in Individual Therapy

Table 9.4 suggests ways in which family systems concepts can be integrated into individual therapy.

Couple Therapy

Working effectively with couples requires specialized training. When you see the two members of a relationship together, you need to be able to put yourself in the place of each one, even the one you may secretly think is at fault, and try to see how things look from that person's POV. Table 9.5 presents some strategies for working with couples.

Multifamily Group Therapy

Multifamily group therapy is a format where unrelated families meet together, and it may be preferable for some families who would otherwise not go to therapy. The families experience the benefit of meeting other people who are experiencing the same problems and emotions. Children can be paired with adults

Table 9.4   Using Family System Concepts in Individual Therapy

Psychoeducation

The therapist teaches family systems concepts such as the role of the identified patient in a family, how symptoms can be attempts to control behavior, and the process of differentiation of self. For instance, an adult who is dealing with elderly parents who are always arguing can recognize that she is being *triangulated* into their relationship and that she needs to set better *boundaries.*

Use of Genogram

The genogram is a technique developed by Murray Bowen (1994) and explained by McGoldrick, Gerson, and Shellenberger (1999) for mapping at least three generations of a family, using a diagram of a family tree, with designated symbols to illustrate boundaries, cutoffs, coalitions, and other structures and processes. It can be used as a data-gathering tool with any new client, and can provide information to show the relevance of the family systems hypothesis for a designated problem. When used as a technique in individual therapy, the client can develop insight into family patterns and recognize intergenerational transmission patterns.

Reframing

The therapist can provide new interpretations for the behaviors of family members, showing the client how to search for the underlying positive intentions. For instance, the nagging behavior of one spouse can be framed as an effort to get closer to the partner (rather than as hostile criticism) and the withdrawal behavior of the other spouse can be framed as protection against feelings of vulnerability (rather than as rejection of the partner).

Interpretation

The therapist can provide interpretive hunches about how the client's behavior is related to family systems factors. For instance, the therapist can suggest that the client's competitiveness with her daughter is related to the dynamics of her family of origin when she was 15, or that she is showing fused boundaries with her disabled mother by making decisions without asking for the mother's opinion.

Straightforward Directives

The therapist gives the client instructions and directions that will modify the family system or help him in the differentiation process. For instance, a client who is having a difficult time with his adolescent child could be instructed to work more cooperatively with his wife and present a united front, rather than taking turns siding with the daughter against the other parent.

Paradoxical Directive

The directive is designed so that whether the client obeys or disobeys, there will be a positive result. For example, referring to Figure 9.2, the therapist could ask the mother who is overinvolved in her child's life to increase her involvement. If she obeys, she may start resenting having her mothering take up so much of her time and decide to back off. If she resists the suggestion and becomes less involved, then the desired outcome is achieved in one step (the use of paradoxical directives is controversial and should be used with caution).

Assignment to Interact with Family of Origin

Murray Bowen would help individual clients differentiate from their family by giving them assignments to visit their family of origin and achieve two goals: control their usual emotional reactivity and get to know their family members as separate individuals. When adults return home to their parents, the pull to return to childhood behavior is so strong that success is sometimes measured as being able to tolerate a few hours. Therefore, the assignments can initially be for very small amounts of time, and then gradually increase. Therapists can also give specific assignments to change the communication patterns, roles, and rules.

Table 9.5   Working with Couples

Psychoeducation

You can teach the couple about their negative interaction patterns, emotional systems, and mutual projective processes, as well as how the family of origin of each partner has influenced their relationship patterns. One important lesson (Christensen & Jacobson, 2000) is the importance of accepting those characteristics of the partner that are not going to be changed.

Directives and Homework Tasks

You can instruct the partners to make unilateral changes and offer pleasurable behaviors to their partner, to pretend to have certain responses so that the partner is not sure what is real and what is feigned, or to use "I-messages" and avoid mind reading and invalidation in their arguments.

Enactment

You can give the partners a task in the session that will stimulate their usual pattern of interacting, for instance, deciding how to spend the weekend or discussing a controversial topic.

Coaching

You can instruct the couple to talk to each other using new communication skills and intervene, when necessary, to improve their performance. Hendrix (1988) teaches couples to follow a script in a structured dialogue. After one person expresses deepest feelings of hurt and pain, the partner must not only reflect back what he has heard but also provide validation through a statement of how the spouse's feelings make sense.

Talk to Each Person Separately

You can talk with one partner while the other is instructed to listen and not interrupt. This process lowers the emotionality in the room, and promotes differentiation because each person learns to maintain a calm, nonreactive state. The couple will use you as a role model of how to make the relationship safe when you respond with empathy and point out moments of vulnerability.

Affective Focus

You can uncover the deeper vulnerable emotions (hurt and fear) that lie under the secondary defensive emotions (anger and blaming) and help the partners reduce their anxieties around intimacy.

from different families to practice new ways of relating, thus developing competence when emotional reactivity is low.

INTEGRATION OF HYPOTHESES

Almost all hypotheses can be integrated with a focus on family systems. The following examples show the broad applicability of SCE1.

CS3 Developmental Transition

Families go through developmental transitions whenever a member moves to a new stage. For instance, when the last-born child is moving from adolescence to adulthood, the mother deals with the loss of her role as mother and can unknowingly sabotage the growing independence of the child.

BL1 Antecedents and Consequences

Behaviorists have traditionally used models of linear causation and can benefit from learning how circular causality works. A thorough behavioral analysis addresses social systems factors, including the family.

BL2 Conditioned Emotional Response

The concept of emotional reactivity in a family may be seen as the result of conditioning. Clients need to be able to substitute a response of serenity for the original intense emotional reaction. A desensitization hierarchy could help family members cope with challenging emotional triggers.

BL3 Skill Deficits or Lack of Competence

Many family therapists include training in communication skills in their treatment approaches. Highly differentiated people have the ability to think calmly and rationally about emotionally charged subjects. These emotional regulation skills can be built, as demonstrated by Linehan (1993a, 1993b) in her skills training program for Borderline Personality Disorder. Parents need a certain skill set to maintain a hierarchy and meet their children's needs for both closeness and autonomy.

C2 Faulty Cognitive Map

Narrative therapists work with families to change problem-saturated stories of their lives into more constructive alternatives. Couples need to understand how their cognitive maps differ because of experiences in different families of origin.

P2 Reenactment of Early Childhood Experiences

Introjects from parents get projected onto mates and children; the original family's rules, roles, and communication patterns are also replicated in adult relationships. From childhood experiences, we learn to disown a part of the self and then find it in another person. When working with couples, the material in the **P2** section is essential.

P3 Immature Sense of Self and Conception of Others

The tools of developmental diagnosis described in **P3** are useful for family therapists. The discussion of the maturity of the self under **P3** contains Bowen's ideas about differentiation. When examining the functioning of a family, it is important to assess the members' levels of object relations and decide whether they are able to take the POV of others and empathize.

SCE2 Cultural Context

Culture is transmitted to the child through the family. Most family rules are shared by members of the same culture or cultural subgroup. Some cultural groups have a very isolated nuclear family, whereas others encourage permeable boundaries with extended family members involved in each other's lives. The concept of family "enmeshment," which is used by family therapists as a sign of dysfunction, is Eurocentric in its bias against Asian, Latino, and the Middle-Eastern cultures. Immigrant families suffer a specific set of problems when the parents, who are supposed to be higher in the family hierarchy, are less acculturated than their children.

SCE3 Social Support

At times of crisis and change, when individuals most need the support of families, family systems factors may cause an increase rather than a decrease in its members' stress. For instance, when a man who has always been strong and protective discovers that he has a terminal illness, he refuses to burden his family and show weakness. The family rule, "don't talk about bad things," means that the family visits him in the hospital and instead of responding to his obvious decline, they talk cheerfully about how his golf clubs are waiting for him. His undifferentiated wife, who believes she can't survive as a separate person, becomes increasingly depressed.

SCE2 CULTURAL CONTEXT

Definition

Knowledge of the **Cultural Context.** is necessary to understand the problem and/or to create a treatment plan that shows sensitivity to the norms, rules, and values of the client's cultural group.

Explanation

The client's cultural identity and life experiences in a specific culture must be addressed. The stage of acculturation of the individual, as well as all members of the family, will be an important factor. Therapists must understand their own biases and understand how their culture influences the therapeutic relationship.

Examples

Clara just moved to this country with her husband, an American citizen, whom she had married in her own country. At first she experienced a period of euphoria and well-being. Then suddenly she "crashed" and has been feeling confused, homesick, depressed, and apathetic. You explain to her the concept of "culture shock" and help her recognize the normality of her symptoms.	Ari is a 28-year-old Armenian high school teacher who lives with her parents and older brother. She has been going out to dinner frequently with a handsome colleague but is lying to her family, saying that she is staying late to prepare her classes. She cries in the session, saying that if her parents knew she was dating a man who wasn't Armenian, they would probably disown her.	Peter, a 45-year-old university professor, spent a sabbatical year in Spain. He enjoyed the leisurely midday meals and sitting in a central plaza with his wife and children until late in the evening. He discovered a very different value system from the competitive, "workaholic" one he had grown up with and understood, for the first time, the cultural causes of his chronic state of stress.

SCE6 Social Role of Mental Patient

Mystification, the tactic of contradicting a person's perception of reality, in extreme forms can induce a person to doubt her mental stability and wonder, "am I going crazy?" Clinicians need to understand these dynamics and the concept of IP, and avoid confirming a person in the status of "mentally ill" without a thorough, unbiased diagnostic assessment.

KEY IDEAS FOR SCE2 CULTURAL CONTEXT

In recent years, multicultural competence has been recognized as a requirement for ethical practice and therefore an important goal of training programs.

Multicultural Competence

Three major domains of competence are (1) knowledge of culture and diversity, (2) therapeutic skills for working with clients of different cultures, and (3) therapist self-awareness (T. B. Smith, 2004). Many useful books are available, with chapters organized in different ways: by ethnic groups (e.g., Vace, DeVaney, & Brendel, 2003), by settings and populations (e.g., Tseng & Streltzer, 2004), or by case studies (e.g., Ancis, 2004). Journals such as *Cultural Diversity and Ethnic Minority Psychology, Journal of Multicultural Counseling and Development, Journal of Cross-Cultural Psychology,* and *Journal of Multicultural Social Work,* are sources of articles on theory, research, and clinical applications. The clinical literature should be supplemented with books on cross-cultural psychology that incorporate perspectives and knowledge from sociology and anthropology (e.g., Shiraev & Levy, 2004), including:

- The influence of culture and social context on manifestation of distress and help seeking behavior.
- Cultural values, beliefs, and customs.
- Classification of cultures as individualistic versus communal/traditional.
- Family structure, kinship networks, and community bonds.
- Culture-bound syndromes.
- Indigenous healing practices.
- History of oppression and racism.
- Role of spirituality and religion.

Knowledge is gained not only by reading, academic courses, and supervised clinical experience but also through interaction with informants from different cultures and reading fiction and memoirs written by members of other cultural groups.

The literature on cultural competence for therapists focuses primarily on the minority groups that have been oppressed and whose identity is recognized by physical appearance: African American, Latino/as, Native Americans, and Asians. In each of these groups, there is considerable diversity based on differences in place of birth, country of origin, religion, tribal affiliation, and level of acculturation. Depending on where you practice, other cultural groups may have large populations. For instance, in Los Angeles County, there are large groups of Armenians, Israelis, and Persians. Moreover, there is a tendency to view Caucasians as a homogeneous group not requiring cultural sensitivity; however, religion, national origin of grandparents, and geographic region of birth all exert profound influences.

Cultural competence requires intense self-examination so that you understand your biases and prejudices. As therapists, we must be able to recognize the lens of our culture and how it influences our worldview, values, and expectations. We need to understand attitudes and beliefs that might negatively influence work with clients from diverse cultures and sexual orientations. Tinsley-Jones (2003) cites research studies that demonstrate the subtle forms that racism takes in individuals who regard themselves as unprejudiced. Ideally, training of clinicians includes culturally diverse experiential groups where members are challenged to explore their unconscious prejudices and learn about each other's life experiences. This goal requires sensitive facilitation to avoid the risk of triggering hostile, defensive reactions rather than curious self-exploration.

Cultural Dominance and Subjugation

Freedman and Combs (1996) use a quotation from Martin Luther King Jr. to remind us that the dominant stories of a culture can be subjugating, particularly in the areas of race, gender, class, age, sexual orientation, and religion:

> Today psychologists have a favorite word, and that word is maladjusted. I tell you today that there are some things in our social system to which I am proud to be maladjusted. I shall never be adjusted to lynch mobs, segregation, economic inequalities, the madness of militarism, and self-defeating physical violence. (p. 42)

Racial discrimination is an important factor in many people's lives, and the most serious consequence is the internalized devaluation of self that occurs. Racism is a mental health risk factor in the same way as physical and child abuse; it also creates a chronic state of vigilance and anxiety (Tinsley-Jones, 2003). In seeking to understand an individual's ethnic identity, we must never ignore the effects of oppression. Caucasian therapists must be aware that minority clients may view them as beneficiaries of "White privilege," even if their own life narratives have stories of hardship and struggle. All therapists need to study feminist theory to understand the negative consequence's of society's unequal distribution of power and status between the sexes.

Biases in Traditional Psychotherapy

Therapists need to understand the assumptions and cultural biases in the models of diagnosis and treatment that they have been taught (Thompson, 2004). T. B. Smith (2004) gives many examples of the cultural encapsulation of our profession:

- Preference for values of individualism, including freedom, responsibility, and achievement.
- Devaluation of collectivist values such as interdependence, conformity, and placing the family's needs ahead of the individual's.
- Ignorance of support systems.
- Perpetuation of racism by protecting the status quo.
- Neglect of the spiritual dimension.

Diversity and Uniqueness

Each new client must be respected as a unique individual who needs to be located in a sociocultural-historical context. Complicating this task is the fact that each person has multiple identity dimensions—gender, race, ethnicity, religion, social class, and sexual orientation, to name a few. Furthermore, in a specific ethnic group, many variables contribute to diversity, including cultural attitudes and values, racial/ethnic self-identification, level of identification with the majority culture; social class, cultural commitment, and level of acculturation (Karlsson, 2005; Wong, Kim, Zane, Kim, & Huang, 2003). Biracial individuals (Root, 1996) and women of color (Comas-Diaz & Greene, 1994) have special challenges in the way they view their identity and experience racism and prejudice. Each family provides a unique cultural experience, and even then, different children in the same family develop different values, beliefs, and identities.

Biculturalism refers to the experience of membership in two different cultural groups. Although *bicultural* is a term commonly used for immigrants who are going through an acculturation process, it also applies to third- or fourth-generation Americans.

People belong to many groups that function as cultures. The culture of a corporation has a tremendous influence on the functioning and satisfaction of its members. Geographic regions in the United States have distinct cultures: Following the 2004 presidential election, "blue" and "red" states appear to be distinct cultural groups. Categories like "the elderly" and "teenagers" are useful for understanding beliefs, values, stresses, customs, and rituals; relations between different generations in the same family can have characteristics of intercultural communication. In the mental health field, different professions—psychiatry, psychology, social work, marriage and family therapy—often function as cultures, providing different lenses for viewing the world.

Ethnic/Racial Identity

Ethnic identity involves a sense of membership in our own ethnic group and the degree of identification with the majority culture. Kwan and Sodowsky (1997) describe two different aspects of ethnic identity:

1. *Internal:* knowledge, self-images, sense of obligation, feelings of attachment and solidarity, sense of comfort and security with same-ethnic-group people and customs.
2. *External:* observable social and cultural behavior such as use of language, friendships, participation in activities, maintaining traditions, media preferences.

It is important not to make assumptions about cultural or racial identity based solely on physical characteristics. Asian Americans who view their major identity as "American" must deal with the frequent unpleasant experience of having people ask, "Where are you from?" The following example of two siblings shows the importance of taking the time to learn about how individuals construe their ethnicity:

> A woman was adopted at birth from an Asian country and raised by Caucasian American parents. She is annoyed at people assuming they know her ethnic identity from looking at her. Furthermore, she frequently gets the message that she needs to go to Asia and discover her roots, as if there is something wrong with her for not feeling Asian. She insists that her "problem" is not the lack of an Asian ethnic identity but rather the effects of stereotyping. In contrast, her brother, adopted from the same place, is passionately interested in learning about his heritage and has made several trips to the country where he was born.

Some approaches to the development of ethnic/racial identity describe progression through stages, for instance, Cross's (1971) five-stage theory for the development of racial identity in African Americans, which may have been more accurate in the post-Civil Rights era of "Black Power" than with the cohort of African Americans now in their twenties:

1. *Pre-Encounter:* The period before the individual is aware of race and skin color differences.
2. *Encounter:* The individual experiences the consequences of racial group membership through entering an integrated school or encountering discrimination.
3. *Immersion/Emersion:* Idealization of one's own racial group with devaluation of the dominant group, followed by emergence of a Black identity that is not based so much on anti-White sentiments.
4. *Internalization:* Establishment of a stable and internalized Black identity that is accepting of Whites and other worldviews, while maintaining a

realistic appreciation of differences in racial status and racial group membership.

5. *Internalization-Commitment:* If the individual progresses to this stage, she engages in activities to help others develop a positive identity or to fight racial injustice.

Narrative therapists (Howard, 1991; Yi & Shorter-Gooden, 1999) prefer a constructivist narrative model of ethnic identity because it views the development of identity as more fluid and dynamic. The therapist helps the client develop an ethnic self-story that enhances dignity and promotes growth and flexible adaptation.

Lesbian, Gay, and Bisexual Clients

The terms *lesbian, gay* and *bisexual* (LGB) refer to sexual identity and lifestyle choices; the term *homosexual* is used as an adjective—*he had his first homosexual experience, or she became aware of homosexual feelings*—but is not currently used as a noun to refer to a person. The acronym LGBT embraces transgender individuals because of common causes as sexual minorities. To develop competence in working with this population, the American Psychological Association guidelines (2000) recommend education in the following areas: human sexuality, identity development, the "coming out" process, the effects of stigmatization, same-sex relationship dynamics, family of origin relationships, parenting issues, workplace issues, and struggles with spirituality and religious group membership. Table 9.6 summarizes important issues of lesbian, gay, and bisexual (LGB) clients.

Acculturation Issues

The experience of relocating to a different culture brings many stressors, problems, and challenges. The process is more difficult for refugees than for immigrants who have made a thoughtful choice, had time to prepare, and bring their possessions with them. It is quite common that there are generational differences in acculturation in a family, with children proceeding at a much more rapid pace. There are various models of adjustment to a new culture and individuals within the same family may choose different paths:

- *Assimilation:* Identification with host culture and majority group, with minimal attachment and loyalty to the original culture.
- *Biculturalism:* Integration into the new culture while remaining part of the ethnic community of their place of origin.
- *Maintenance of original identity:* Living in neighborhoods where the original language is dominant, keeping contacts with the host culture to a minimum. Adult immigrants may choose this option, but by sending their children to public schools, they are assuring that the child chooses one of the other alternatives.

Table 9.6   Issues of Lesbian, Gay, and Bisexual Clients

Stigma and Discrimination

The term *homophobia* is used in the same way as racism or sexism, and like racism, homophobia may be latent as well as overt. Other terms for this bias are *heterosexism* and *heterocentrism* (Pachankis & Goldfried, 2004).

Internalized Homophobia

The internalization of the devaluation of society can be the underlying cause of many presenting problems, including anxiety, depression, substance abuse, and relationship difficulties.

Coming Out

Coming out is the term for developing an openly lesbian, gay, and bisexual (LGB) identity and no longer choosing to "pass" as heterosexual. Ritter and Terndrup (2002) summarize the stages of identity development that are found in the literature:

Pre-Coming Out: Pre-adolescent feelings of being different from same-sex peers.

Perception of Self as Sexually Different: Occurs after puberty; difficulties are exacerbated if the individual has no one to talk to and there are no role models of positive identity.

Toleration of LGB Identity: Individuals may lead a double life, seeking out LGB individuals and communities while concealing this facet of life from family and friends.

Acceptance: The individual demonstrates pride in identity, becomes open about identity in more situations, and may overidentify with sexual identity.

Integration: Successful outcome of coming-out process is integration of LGB identity into overall sense of self.

Issues of Family Acceptance

Unlike with other minority groups, the family may be a source of rejection rather than support. Savin-Williams (2001) describes that families go through their own gradual coming-out process.

AIDS Issues

Homophobia is increased for people who associate the AIDS crisis with homosexuality, therefore putting LGB clients at greater risk for violence and discrimination. Gay men are often coping with the fear of testing HIV positive in the future because of behaviors in the past, dealing with grief, and facing their mortality because of the frequent deaths in friendship networks.

Unique Issues of Bisexuals

The sexual orientation of bisexual individuals is often inaccurately perceived as a transitional rather than a valid choice. Bisexuals are the targets of negative judgments from both heterosexual and homosexual communities. When a bisexual person is married to a heterosexual spouse, he or she faces issues of coming out to both spouse and children. Hutchins and Kaahumanu (1991) provide a collection of articles from bisexual authors.

Acculturative stress is a recent name for what has been known as "culture shock." Shiraev and Levy (2004) list sources of distress:

- *Nostalgia:* Longing for relatives and friends and familiar experiences.
- *Disorientation and loss of control:* The competence built in the native culture is often useless and there are no familiar cues as to how to behave.
- *Language barriers:* Difficulties in communication create frustration and feelings of isolation.

- *Loss of habits and lifestyle:* Previously enjoyed activities are unavailable.
- *Exaggeration of differences and values:* The person has difficulties accepting the host culture and idealizes aspects of the home culture.

Other stressors include:

- Loss of occupational status for professionals.
- Isolation at work by members of host country who find interaction to be tiring and troublesome.
- Discrepancy between expectations and reality.

In a review of the literature and interviews with new immigrants in Israel (Ingram, 1990), I found that the following factors facilitate adjustment and serve as buffers against negative psychological consequences:

- Playing a part in the decision to migrate.
- Amount of preparation, including knowledge of new culture and language learning, and involvement in a predeparture preparation program if available.
- Similarity between original and host cultures.
- The positive feelings about the new culture—either hopefulness about economic opportunity or idealism about the values of the new home.
- Migration occurs with a piece of the social support network intact.
- Tolerance for being a beginner who makes mistakes, and willingness to seek and utilize help.

Acculturation issues are relevant in two other situations:

1. *Reverse immigration:* Returning to your original culture after an extended stay in another culture.
2. *"Global nomads":* Children of American parents who were raised in foreign countries and are living in the United States for the first time, perhaps when they enter college.

WHEN IS THIS HYPOTHESIS A GOOD MATCH?

All clients come from a specific culture and information about cultural background is important with every client. This hypothesis is reserved for use when factors in the culture help explain a problem or influence the design of a treatment plan.

Culture-Bound Syndromes

Appendix I of *DSM-IV-TR* provides a glossary of 24 culture-bound syndromes. Some of these syndromes are recognized as illness in the cultural group (e.g., *amok*), others are explanatory mechanisms (e.g., the *evil eye*), and some are not seen as pathological in the culture (e.g., communicating with spirits). Some disorders, like depression, are viewed as universal, but the way the symptoms are expressed will vary from culture to culture.

Cultural Identity Issues

Therapists need to recognize when ethnic, racial, or sexual orientation identity issues are an important factor in problems such as low self-esteem, difficulty forming intimate relationships, family conflicts, and struggles achieving occupational success. For instance, if a client has divorced parents of two different cultures and the custodial parent pressured him to reject completely the other parent's culture, there may be psychological consequences. Therapists need to be alert to the impact of discrimination, marginalization, and oppression, which includes loss of opportunity, internalization of negative messages, and attitudes of distrust that will influence the formation of a therapeutic relationship.

Difficulties Associated with Acculturation and Immigration

The *DSM-IV-TR* lists Acculturation (V62.4) as a focus of therapy, including in this category language difficulties, employment problems, loss of social ties, and "acculturative stress." Clients may experience stress from different levels of acculturation in the family and struggle with conflicts over assimilation versus biculturalism.

Sources of Stress in the Culture

The client may be dealing with stress that comes from the values and rules of a particular cultural group, such as pressure to accept an arranged marriage, demands to take over the family business, and "guilt trips" for choosing to remain childless and not provide grandchildren. American culture is a source of stress that an outsider can recognize better than we can: paid vacations usually limited to 2 weeks instead of the month minimum in many European countries, lack of a social safety net, and (what is usually considered an advantage) the demand to make independent choices about a career instead of following a predetermined path. Although cultural similarity between therapist and client is often viewed as an advantage, it has one major shortcoming: The therapist may accept as "givens" some of the arbitrary rules and restrictions from which the client suffers.

TREATMENT PLANNING

Because the treatment plan must be individualized for each client, there is a risk that when you apply this hypothesis you will rely on simplistic generalizations based on cultural group membership. Guidelines on how to work with members of different cultures may be helpful, but must never supplant your own clinical judgment. With that caveat in mind, knowledge of the following ideas may be helpful.

Rapport and Credibility

Ways of creating rapport with a client of a different culture include the use of appropriate metaphors and symbols, matching client's rhythm and pace of speech, awareness of comfort level with eye contact and physical distance, and respect for hierarchy in the family and extended family. Credibility of the therapist is very important and comes from cultural knowledge and clinical competence. With Asian clients, it is important to maintain formality, whereas Dana (2002) suggests that African Americans look for signs of genuineness, authenticity, and approachability. Cultural mistrust is a very appropriate response for many clients (Stevenson & Renard, 1993). Sometimes therapists may be trying to show cultural sensitivity but inadvertently strengthen mistrust, for instance, by asking in the first session, before getting to know the client, "How do you feel about having a White therapist?" (Tinsley-Jones, 2003) or making assumptions that a client is less acculturated than she is.

Should Clients Be Matched with Someone of Their Own Cultural Group?

Stanley Sue (1998) found evidence that there were fewer dropouts and more sessions with a same-ethnicity match between client and therapist; however, there were no findings that outcome was better in that condition. Karlsson's (2005) extensive review found that ethnic matching did not affect the outcome of therapy. Some clients may prefer someone of the same group so it is important for clinics to hire staff members who represent a variety of cultural groups.

Learn about Your Client's Culture

It is appropriate to let your client teach you about his cultural background, particularly the factors that he believes are most relevant to his problems. However, it is also important that you have people with whom you can consult when you are unfamiliar with a culture and that you are willing to consult books and articles. An innovative tool called the *community genogram* (Rigazio-DiGilio, Ivey, Kunkler-Peck, & Grady, 2005) can be used with the client to gather cultural as well as personal information.

Ethnic Specific Therapy

Therapists need to be knowledgeable about indigenous healing practices, such as the use of *curanderos* and *espiritistas* for Latinos, and be able to utilize them when appropriate. Lam and Sue (2001) describe the successful use of sweat lodges and talking circles with Native Americans and the use of folk tales (*cuento* therapy) with Puerto Rican children. Religion and spirituality are very important for some cultural groups and should either be integrated into therapy or encouraged as additional resources.

Modifications in Therapist-Client Relationship

Therapists should be flexible enough to make modifications in the treatment and therapeutic relationship based on the client's culture. For instance, there can be adjustment in boundaries, such as seeing the client outside of the office and sharing personal stories. The client's culture may have models of effective helper-helpee relationships on which you can pattern therapy, taking a role such as teacher, expert, partner, or guide. An exclusive focus on the individual is often viewed as culturally inappropriate. In addition to including family members, consider the following guidelines:

- Understand the role of extended family and community.
- Pay attention to the family hierarchy and traditional patterns of power differences.
- Consider the use of existing helping networks.
- Recognize respected change agents in the community.

Best Treatment Models

No therapeutic approach should be ruled out just because a client is a member of a different cultural group. However, the following approaches are particularly relevant when cultural factors are important.

Directive, Problem Focused

Cultures such as Asian (Zane, Morton, Chu, & Lin, 2004) and Arab-American (Erickson & Al-Timimi, 2004) expect the therapist to be in the role of an expert and give the client specific assignments, advice, and education. Cognitive-behavioral therapy (CBT) and other directive approaches are effective matches.

Narrative Therapy

Witztum and Goodman (2004) describe complex cases that show the effectiveness of a narrative approach. Three tasks are essential: (1) understand the social construction of meaning, (2) join the client's narratives and use cultural metaphors, and (3) find in the culture a narrative that resolves the problem.

Family Systems

Therapists need to understand the importance of families in the lives of clients from cultures where individualism is discouraged, and include the family in therapy. This is especially important when there are rules against discussing problems outside the family.

Empowerment Focused

A core goal of feminist therapy is empowerment, and therefore it is suitable not only for women but also for members of oppressed minorities. McWhirter (1994) listed goals for people who are powerless or marginalized:

- Become aware of the power dynamics at work in their life context.
- Develop skills and capacities for gaining reasonable control over their lives.
- Exercise these skills without infringing on the rights of others.
- Actively support the empowerment of others in the community (p. 12).

Strength-Based Approach

Stevenson and Renard (1993) argue for the importance of emphasizing strengths when conducting therapy with an African American family: strong kinship bonds; religious orientation; community support; valuing of education, achievement, and stability; and love of children regardless of circumstances of their birth. When working with Asian clients, who are sensitive to losing face, it is important for the therapist to focus on strengths and find ways of reframing weaknesses to protect the client from shame.

Therapy with Lesbians, Gays, and Bisexuals

The approach to therapy called "affirmative therapy" views both homosexuality and heterosexuality as "natural or normal attributes" (Krajeski, 1986, p. 16) and has the goal of building a positive identity. Psychological adjustment is aided by several factors: commitment to the sexual identity, involvement with other LGB individuals, family support, and openness about sexual identity (Pachankis & Goldfried, 2004). Therapy will include some or all of these goals and tasks:

- Encourage building of support system (e.g., explain that it helps to interact with LGB people with positive identities).
- Help clients develop awareness of how oppression has affected them and allow their expression of anger.
- Help clients deal with internalized homophobia (e.g., desensitize shame or challenge beliefs).
- Act as an advocate in helping them face societal issues.
- Share knowledge of resources and community groups. For instance, Parents, Families, and Friends of Lesbians and Gays (PFLAG) has local chapters as well as a web site (www.pflag.org).
- Help clients progress through the coming-out process at his or her own pace.
- Help clients deal with fears of coming out, both fears that can be dispelled and those that have a basis in reality.

- Encourage clients to test the waters and weigh costs and benefits of coming out at this time to particular others, instead of rushing too quickly.
- Help clients cope with the reactions of family members to their disclosures about sexual orientation, explaining that the immediate reaction does not mean that the family will not eventually achieve acceptance.

Pachankis and Goldfried (2004) give examples of ways that therapists mistreat LGB clients:

- Trying to change the orientation.
- Assuming that a client is heterosexual (e.g., in the choice of a pronoun for referring to a romantic partner).
- Focusing on sexual orientation when it is not relevant to the issue for which the client is seeking help.
- Showing ignorance about important aspects of LGB experience (e.g., the development of alternate family structures and lack of legal rights and protections).
- Using the client to deal with your own sexual-identity issues (e.g., if you are an LGB therapist who has recently come out).

INTEGRATION OF HYPOTHESES

Be sure to consider the cultural background of the client when using the following hypotheses.

B1 Biological Cause

Cultural factors can explain the low-utilization of medical services, poor medication compliance, and similar obstacles to effective health care. An example of culture clash with Western medicine is the case of a Southeast Asian girl who is diagnosed with epilepsy but whose parents explain her symptoms as "The spirit catches you and you fall down" (Fadiman, 1998).

B3 Mind-Body Connections

In certain cultures, the idiom of distress is somatic rather than emotional or mental. Health may be defined as mind-body balance. "Culture shock" is a stress syndrome with somatic symptoms.

CS2 Situational Stressors

Acculturation brings a variety of situational stressors, and responses to situational stress can vary greatly in different cultures. For instance, *ataque de nervios* is a culture-bound syndrome among certain Latino cultures. Racism functions as both an acute stressor and an experience of chronic stress.

C2 Faulty Cognitive Map

Every culture offers and perpetuates a socially constructed model of the world. Freedman and Combs (1996) explain that "societies construct the lenses through which their members interpret the world. The realities that each of us takes for granted are the realities that our societies have surrounded us with since birth" (p. 16).

In deciding what elements of the cognitive map are faulty or maladaptive, we must be careful not to impose our biases inappropriately. At the same time, an attitude of cultural relativism is inappropriate when faced with human rights abuses in different cultures (e.g., genital mutilation, selling children, and beating wives).

ES3 Spiritual Dimension

Religion and spiritual practices are components of culture. Some cultures have spiritual explanations and treatments for what we consider mental problems.

P1 Internal Parts and Subpersonalities

Conflict among different cultural identities may be a focus of treatment. For instance, a person going through the process of acculturation could be asked to dialogue with the "Native Land Self" and the "New Home Self."

SCE1 Family System

An understanding of the family and its relation to the wider community is an essential part of cultural competence. Working with the family is often recommended. When children are more acculturated than their parents, it upsets the family hierarchy, and structural family therapy can be effective. What we, in our individualistic culture, view as an unhealthy "enmeshment" in a family may be viewed as healthy interdependence in a collectivistic culture.

KEY IDEAS FOR SCE3 SOCIAL SUPPORT

Social support is a buffer (protective factor) against the negative effects of stress and trauma, for instance for abused children, immigrants, disaster victims, and people with life-threatening illnesses. Social support also reduces the risk of relapse for people who have been diagnosed with and treated for mental disorders. The beneficial components of social support were described by House (1981):

- *Social support:* esteem, affection, trust, concern, and listening.
- *Appraisal support:* affirmation, feedback, and social comparison.

SCE3 SOCIAL SUPPORT

Definition

The problem is either caused or maintained by deficiencies in **Social Support**.

Explanation

Social support plays an important role in prevention of mental health problems such as depression. The quality of the individual's social network will greatly affect coping with stress and resilience following trauma. Social isolation can be both the cause and the effect of problems. Individuals differ in their need for social support versus solitude.

Examples

Lisa developed depression after being transferred to a job in a new city. She is extremely shy, and she has not made any new friends. She doesn't call her old friends because she feels ashamed that she is not coping better. The counselor she saw through the Employee Assistance Program helped her understand the need to take action to overcome social isolation.	When John's wife died of cancer, he had a very supportive social network. However, he has been turning down invitations because he doesn't want to "inflict my mood on people." At the recommendation of his doctor, he joined a bereavement support group. Although he did not choose to share his experiences, he found listening to the others very helpful.	Gail was extremely frustrated with the failure of her efforts to lose weight. Her family had always emphasized "willpower" and not sharing your problems with others. After she joined Weight Watchers and attended aerobic classes, she found that the support of other people helped her to stay motivated. She also appreciated the advice and suggestions from others.

- *Informational support:* advice, suggestion, directives, and information.
- *Instrumental support:* supplies, tools, and money.

Individual Differences in Desired Social Support

The database for every client should include information about the client's social network and sources of both social support and social stress. In exploring the client's cognitive map, it is important to discover, concretely, what kind of behaviors the client defines as supportive. Imagine three clients all experiencing the stress of finishing their dissertations (or any other major work product): One might want a friend to take her out for dinner after a hard day's work, the second might want a friend to help by proofreading the references, and the third might want to be left alone and be relieved of any guilt for neglecting social obligations. Studies of grieving and trauma show that people differ in the benefits they derive from sharing feelings in a group. Furthermore, the level of differentiation and emotional maturity (see **P3** and **SCE1**) will determine the degree to which a person needs another person to shore up self-esteem and soothe troubled emotions.

Social Competence

Alvord and Grados (2005) provide this quotation from Bandura: "Social support is not a self-forming entity waiting around to buffer harried people against stressors." Rather, the individual determines the type of social support network that is available. The process of creating and maintaining supportive relationships has many components, including how a person responds to others, for example, giving positive responses and affection, and how easy a person is for others to relate to. The qualities of *social competence*—getting along with others and forming friendships—may end up being goals for people who lack adequate social support.

WHEN IS THIS HYPOTHESIS A GOOD MATCH?

Lack of social support can be both a cause and consequence of a specific symptom or impairment. It will help you if you draw a circular diagram to get a picture of the interaction of individual and social variables, such as that depicted in Figure 9.3.

If *lack of social support* is defined as a problem, the client's mood disorder and avoidance of people are the explanatory variables: Remediate the depression and reinforce social activity, and the client will have a more satisfying social network. If depression is the problem, then increase social support, perhaps by recommending a support group or working with the family system, and the depression should be alleviated. These frameworks can be combined, and multiple interventions can be implemented. This hypothesis is useful when the lack of social support contributes to the problem or when the mobilization of a good support system should be part of treatment.

TREATMENT PLANNING AND INTEGRATION OF HYPOTHESES

Throughout the prior sections in Part II, there have been numerous references to the use of social support as part of the treatment, including the following problems: medical illness in self or loved one and substance abuse (**B1**); disasters,

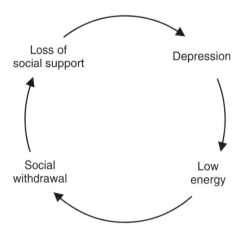

Figure 9.3   Loss of social support as both cause and effect of depression.

traumas, and other situational crises (**CS2**); bereavement (**CS4**); parenting difficulties (e.g., dealing with autism or conduct disorder in children; **CS3, BL3**); learning new skills (**BL3**); and spiritual quests (**ES3**). Social support issues should be addressed when an individual is adjusting to a new situation (e.g., geographic location, job, or school; **SCE4**).

Given the diversity in individual needs, the therapist needs to help each client set his or her own goals, if social support is found to be insufficient. Sources of social support include the following:

- The therapist provides support for the client and may consider increasing the frequency of sessions during a crisis.
- Group therapy.
- Support groups, including self-help groups in the Twelve-Step movement.
- Existing friendships.
- Making new friends.
- Involving the family.
- Religious and community organizations.
- Internet groups, chat rooms, and Listservs.

SCE4 SOCIAL ROLE PERFORMANCE

Definition

Difficulty meeting demands for **Social Role Performance** contributes to the client's distress and dysfunction.

Explanation

The concept of *social role* requires attention to fields other than clinical psychology (e.g., sociology, social psychology, organizational psychology, and anthropology). It is important to understand how an individual fits into social systems, apart from the immediate family. Social role requirements change when people enter new roles and when there are other changes in the social system. Role overload, role strain, and role conflict function as stressors. Role models and mentors may be more helpful than therapists.

Examples

Penelope, who recently received her license as a psychologist, accepted a position in a major health-care corporation. After five weeks, she began to develop headaches and was "angry all the time." She decided to quit: "I have to be my own boss, I refuse to take orders from people who only care about 'the bottom line,' and I want to have control over my time schedule."	Shelley is struggling to be a good wife and a successful attorney. Her mother, whom she describes as a "typical housewife," never worked outside the home. Her husband, like her father, does not participate in household chores, so she is exhausted every night. Her therapist helped her understand that she never had a role model to show her how to balance the roles of wife and career woman.	Enrique was elated when he received a promotion at work and became a supervisor. The new position meant he earned more money and had more free time in the evening. Despite all these happy feelings, he finds himself anxious, irritable, and dreading getting up in the morning. He admits that the people he considered close friends at work are treating him differently and do not invite him to lunch.

KEY IDEAS FOR SCE4 SOCIAL ROLE PERFORMANCE

The fields of social psychology, sociology, and anthropology offer concepts that help in formulating the stresses and challenges that people face because of their position in a social structure, such as the following:

- People can be *members of multiple groups* with conflicting expectations.
- Changes in *social status* have effects on how a person is treated and how a person views the self.
- *Norms*—the rules for how members of a group should behave—may conflict with personal values.
- *Social roles* carry sets of behaviors that people are expected to perform.
- Groups have *sanctions*—actions from the group that reward or punish adherence to norms.
- Concepts such as *role overload, role strain,* and *role conflict* can be useful in framing causes of distress.

Stress at Work

There are many sources of stress at work, which may interfere with successful performance of the role for which one is being paid. The National Institute for Occupational Safety and Health (NIOSH), part of the Department of Health and Human Services, can be accessed at www.cdc.gov/niosh/stresswk.html for descriptions of and research on job stress, the condition that results "when the requirements of the job do not match the capabilities, resources or needs of the worker." Examples of sources of job stress include the following:

- *The design of tasks* (e.g., heavy workload, infrequent rest breaks, long hours, and routine tasks with little meaning).
- *Management style* (e.g., lack of participation by workers in decision making, poor communication, lack of family friendly policies, or unreasonable performance demands).
- *Interpersonal relationships* (e.g., bullying or harassment, lack of effective communication, office politics and conflict with coworkers, lack of support or help from coworkers and supervisors, and unmet needs for recognition and appreciation).
- *Work roles* (e.g., conflicting or uncertain job expectations, too much responsibility, or too many "hats to wear"). The Peter Principle (Peter, 1969) refers to the belief that people in an organization rise to the level of their incompetence. People are often promoted to supervisory and managerial positions without being taught skills for handling the new responsibilities.
- *Career concerns* (e.g., job insecurity, lack of opportunity for advancement, or rapid changes for which workers are unprepared).

WHEN IS THIS HYPOTHESIS A GOOD MATCH?

It is helpful to bring sociological concepts to your understanding of the following problems.

Difficulty Adjusting to Major Life Change

- Parenthood or stepparenthood.
- Promotion.
- Job change.
- Retirement.

Difficulty Coping with Stress

- Committed to too many roles.
- Lack of support in work environment.

Conflict between Competing Roles and Obligations

- Multiple family roles (e.g., caretaker of elderly parent and parent of young children).
- Overload from multiple roles (e.g., wife, mother, graduate student, and working person).
- Conflicting demands from different bosses at work.

Dissatisfaction with Current Role

- "Stuck" in dead-end job.
- Frustration as caregiver of disabled child or aging parent.
- Promoted to a position past the point of one's competence (the "Peter Principle"; Peter, 1969).

TREATMENT PLANNING

Discussing these concepts with the client can provide many benefits: a framework of meaning, awareness of choices, and understanding of the gradual nature of many transitions. In addition, clients can be directed to find a mentor, someone who is knowledgeable about the social system and who will provide information, support, and perhaps clear the path of some of its obstructions. Clients can be advised to read about the specific role they are entering.

INTEGRATION OF HYPOTHESES

This hypothesis overlaps with both **C2** and **C3** because situational stressors and developmental transitions are also occurring when an individual enters a new social role.

SCE5 SOCIAL PROBLEM IS A CAUSE

Definition

A **Social Problem** (e.g., poverty, discrimination, social oppression) **is a Cause** of the problem. Social problems can also exacerbate difficulties stemming from other causes. You must avoid *blaming the victim*.

Explanation

Discrimination, economic injustice, and social or political oppression have been part of the client's experience. Certain problem behavior can be understood as an adaptive, if undesirable, response to a social problem. One implication of this hypothesis is that social activism may be a more appropriate activity than therapy. Regardless of the severity of the problem and the reality of victimization, clients must make choices that increase their sense of control and level of achievement.

Examples

The other members of the case conference are discussing DSM criteria, and considering a diagnosis of Antisocial Personality Disorder because Luis has broken certain laws and has no guilt or remorse. But you suggest that this client has not been able to feed and clothe his children on the minimum wage he earns for unskilled labor. You argue that giving a psychiatric diagnosis would be an example of "blaming the victim."

Jennifer's depression and anxiety began when, after working at the same job for 20 years, she was laid off because her company merged with another one. Then she discovered that the company had engaged in illegal practices, and her retirement fund was now worthless. She began looking for a new job, but the whole industry has cut back and she will have to consider retraining for a different field.

Working with a therapist who practiced feminist therapy, Betty began to understand some of the root causes of her depression and stagnating career. She had been raised to be sweet and conciliatory and to hide her competitiveness. She had been a victim of blatant sexual discrimination in her workplace: When she had a child, she was not chosen for important assignments that involved traveling.

CS4 Loss and Bereavement

No matter how desired the role change might be, it still represents losses. In corporations, when people move up the ladder, they lose the close relationships they might have had with their former peers.

BL3 Skill Deficits or Lack of Competence

New skills are needed for the new role. People need time and experience to develop competence.

ES2 Avoiding Freedom and Responsibility

A highly desired new social role (e.g., marriage, parenthood, a promotion at work) may bring with it unanticipated negative consequences in the form of restricted freedom and increased responsibilities. An analysis of advantages and disadvantages of a new role that has been either chosen or imposed, such as a promotion at work, can result in making a choice to leave the role (e.g., to ask for a transfer or quit) or to assertively pursue modification in role expectations.

KEY IDEAS FOR SCE5 SOCIAL PROBLEM IS A CAUSE

The principles of this hypothesis are best conveyed in Ryan's (1976) *Blaming the Victim,* an important contribution to the community psychology movement. Society's social arrangements and institutions favor some people more than others; those who "have" look at the "have-nots" and assume that their lack of success can be traced to their own defects. The position that the poor are held back by their lack of work ethic, poor family values, or laziness is an example of "blaming the victim." If the root cause of a problem is the social structure, and "helping professionals" try to solve it by rehabilitation or psychotherapy, the social problem remains unsolved and the client internalizes the devaluation of the people who have been favored by the social system.

> Therapists must not pathologize people whose problems are products of social injustice.

By engaging in individual therapy and ignoring the social problem, therapists function as agents of society and, possibly, suppress the distress that leads to radical social change. Therapists need to educate themselves before they can help clients. Until the therapist understands the concept of *blaming the victim,* in its subtle as well as overt forms, he or she will continue to perpetuate the abuse.

Social Change

Change the social system will come to mind as a logical prescription when this hypothesis is applied. This may seem like a hopelessly idealistic solution for an individual's emotional distress. Therefore, you need to imagine how the country would be today if all the people who marched for civil rights had instead gone into individual therapy for "feelings of demoralization" and "anger problems." Many of the strongest supporters of programs to help the "disadvantaged" may be people who would vehemently oppose social change because it would result in a reduction in their own amount of privilege. Change at the social and economic levels, such as the creation of jobs for unskilled people that pay an adequate living wage, would be more beneficial than psychotherapy for victims of poverty. Our society fails to provide adequate cheap housing and a safety net for people who are starting on the downward spiral that leads to homelessness.

We can look back over the past 50 years and find several examples of social changes that have had profound effects on mental health problems and treatments: The court system protects rape victims from having their past sexual history used against them; police now respond to domestic violence and can take action against perpetrators without actually witnessing the violent action; and people with disabilities have the right to reasonable accommodations. These changes would not have occurred without advocacy and political action.

Damaging Effects of Service Delivery Systems

It is unfortunate that very often the social services that are supposed to help people instead inflict harm. People in need "fall through the cracks," they are frustrated and confused by the lack of coordination of services from multiple agencies, and they may also find the actions of bureaucrats or overworked case managers to be against their best interests. Another problem with service delivery is that comprehensive "wraparound" programs may be *too* helpful; there is a risk of clients becoming dependent and abdicating responsibility.

WHEN IS THIS HYPOTHESIS A GOOD MATCH?

Several examples are selected to illustrate how social problems affect client's lives.

Racism and Other Forms of Prejudice

Racism and other forms of prejudice are chronic stressors. The attitudes and behaviors that make people feel "less than" and marginalized because of skin color, accented speech, dress, and other signs of minority status are embedded in social institutions and the cultural heritage of the majority culture. Therapists need to bring the hypothesis of racism to the client, not wait for the client to bring up the topic:

> An African American woman in her early 20s came to therapy because she was frequently depressed and was generally unhappy with her work and relationships. She expected to focus on her low self-esteem, her rivalry with her older sister, and her discomfort in social situations. However, her therapist, also an African American woman, insisted that she discuss her life experiences related to race. She recalled that in college when she tried to fit in with her White sorority sisters, her Black friends called her an "Oreo." When she began to show her ethnic pride through her hairstyle and dress, her boss switched her from the front desk to a back office.

Poverty

Growing up in poverty is especially damaging when the child lives in a high-poverty community, which brings increased exposure to street violence, illegal drugs, negative role models, reduced accessibility to jobs, and lower expectancies from teachers (McLoyd, 1998). McLoyd cites studies that show that poverty status is a more powerful predictor of lower IQ scores in children than is maternal education. The 1996 welfare reform law mandated a 5-year lifetime limit on welfare assistance, a public policy that may put children at risk for detrimental effects.

Societal Prejudice against Lesbians, Gays, and Bisexuals

When the American Psychiatric Association revised its diagnostic manual in 1980, it removed homosexuality as a category of pathology. Nevertheless, there are still therapists who believe that gay clients should try to change their sexual orientation. Causes of distress in LGB clients stem from such factors as social stigma, discrimination, and intolerance. Lesbian, gay, and bisexual clients may have more to gain from social equality (e.g., the legalization of marriage) than from individual psychotherapy to work on their self-esteem issues.

Gender Bias

The feminist movement arose in protest of the disadvantages women experienced in every aspect of their lives: career aspirations as children, power differences in marriage, unequal wages and job opportunities, and the glass ceiling in the corporate environment. In its early stages, psychoanalysis perpetuated a disservice to women clients, encouraging their acceptance of the passive, female role dictated by a patriarchal society. We also must be aware that men suffer from the biases in our sociocultural system when they make "unmasculine" choices such as staying home and raising children or pursuing careers in female-dominated professions such as nursing.

TREATMENT PLANNING

Although the explanation of this hypothesis stresses social change as the cure, the reality of effective treatment planning is that you need to help the individual client deal with the problems on a personal level.

Pretherapy Orientation

When working with poor and minority clients, therapists cannot risk assuming that their clients know what psychotherapy is and why and how it should help. An extra step of orientation, where there is an explanation of the process of seeing a therapist, may increase utilization of service and prevent premature termination. In the culture of psychotherapists it makes sense for people to come weekly, at the same time, for a standard length of time, whether they are concerned about their problems that day, or not, but for clients this may seem like a waste of time and money—they'd prefer to call when they need it. Therapists need to give a rationale that clients can understand or be flexible enough to provide "as needed" services.

Normalizing

The term *normalizing* is used to convey that a client's reactions and symptoms, no matter how severe and dysfunctional, are normal responses and that anyone, in the same situation, would feel the same way.

Education

The therapist can explain and discuss the causal links between current suffering and limitations and the specific social problem.

Strengthen Protective Factors

Studies of *resilience* identify protective factors that you can deliberately plan to strengthen. Research on children shows the following protective factors: success at making friends, ability to regulate behavior, competent parents, support networks, and effective schools (Alvord & Grados, 2005).

Empowerment and Activism

Many social problems leave clients feeling weak, powerless, helpless, bitter, and victimized. No matter how justified such responses may be, they further compound the client's difficulties. The therapist must help clients distinguish between factors in their history and current situation where they have no control and were indeed victims, and those aspects of their lives where they have choice, alternatives, and positive possibilities. Clients who get involved in organizations and activities that work toward remedying a social problem not only find solutions for their own distress but also make a contribution that brings pride and meaning.

Group Formats

Groups are less stigmatizing than individual therapy: They help to universalize the problem and prevent individuals from feeling exceptional—and to blame—for their difficulties. Groups provide opportunities for joint problem solving and sharing of coping strategies and resources, as well as the healing power of social support.

INTEGRATION OF HYPOTHESES

The following hypotheses are recommended when working with clients who are victims of social problems.

CS2 Situational Stressors

The social problem brings acute and chronic stressors; treatments may include crisis intervention, support, and problem solving.

BL3 Skill Deficits or Lack of Competence

A skills-deficit formulation is less stigmatizing than a diagnosis of pathology. The therapist needs to emphasize the strengths and assets that already exist, and avoid *blaming the victim* for problems that were the result of bad schools, teachers with negative expectations, and lack of resources in the family. Clients can be referred to community resources to advance their education and develop job skills.

C2 Faulty Cognitive Map

Therapists from cultures of immigrants who "pulled themselves up by their own bootstraps" may need to examine their own schemas and learn how their generalization from their grandparents' experiences may be inappropriate.

ES2 Avoiding Freedom and Responsibility

Clients need to discover that they have freedom in their choice of how to respond to social injustice. The fact that they were victims in the past cannot be accepted as an excuse for not taking action to achieve desired goals.

SCE2 Cultural Context

It is important for therapists to understand the culture of poverty and the cultural groups who have faced severe discrimination and oppression.

SCE3 Social Support

When people are suffering from the same external stressors and have shared experiences as victims of the same social problems, they can provide each other with social support as they work to meet common goals, together.

KEY IDEAS FOR SCE6 SOCIAL ROLE OF MENTAL PATIENT

This hypothesis exists because our society provides a social role of mental patient, which is entered through the actions (diagnosis, hospitalization) of socially-designated experts.

Disadvantages of the Mental Patient Role

The term *stigma* refers to the adverse perceptions and social responses that are evoked by a trait of an individual or group. Goffman (1963) stressed that it was

SCE6 SOCIAL ROLE OF MENTAL PATIENT

Definition

The problem is causally related to disadvantages or advantages to the **Social Role of the Mental Patient.**

Explanation

The stigma of a diagnostic label causes problems independent from actual impairments. Clients can fake symptoms of mental illness for objective benefits (malingering) or for unknown psychological reasons (factitious disorder). In addition, family members can benefit or suffer from a family member being diagnosed, hospitalized, or ruled incompetent.

Examples

Igor continues to complain of pain and depression and doesn't seem motivated to implement the behavioral strategies to manage chronic pain. You entertain the hypothesis that he is faking and try to ascertain if there are identifiable reasons to explain malingering. You learn that he has a personal injury lawsuit in progress.	Phillip, an outpatient at a Veterans Administration hospital, participates in a group of men with PTSD. Phillip's descriptions of his combat experiences are always the most dramatic, and he frequently sobs uncontrollably. Reading through his records, the group leader discovers that he has never been overseas.	When Liz was a teenager, she was hospitalized and treated for severe depression and behavioral problems. Now she is 28 and a successful attorney. She has been dating a man who wants to get more serious, but she has been pushing him away. She is afraid that too much emotional involvement will trigger her "mental illness."

not the impairment that created the greatest problems but rather the negative perceptions of society. Lai, Hong, and Chee (2000) discuss both overt effects of stigma (e.g., social rejection and loss of employment opportunities) and more subtle forms, such as condescending attitudes. If people internalize the view of others—which they do not always do—the negative consequences include lowered self-esteem, social isolation, and reduced motivation. Awareness of the problem of stigma led to replacing the phrase "a schizophrenic" with "a person with Schizophrenia."

> Diagnostic labels can be erroneously applied and impossible to remove.

Rosenhan's (1973) study demonstrated that healthy people could go to psychiatric emergency rooms, state that they heard a voice that said "thud" and be diagnosed with Schizophrenia. Once admitted, when they said they no longer heard the voice, the diagnosis would not be removed. As long as therapists are required to put diagnostic labels on new clients after one or two sessions, because of clinic rules or to get payment from insurance and managed care companies, there will be bias and errors in the use of these labels. Sometimes a diagnostic label alone—even one from the distant past—is sufficient to maintain a person in that role, even in the absence of any current symptoms. The information that someone has been previously diagnosed with a certain disorder, or that a parent had that disorder, should lead to a reasoned consideration of that diagnosis, but in many cases, it causes the clinician to immediately select that diagnosis without going through an orderly process of differential diagnosis.

One of the factors that maintains a person in the social role of mental patient is the faulty belief that recovery from a certain mental illness is impossible—consider that the term *in remission* can follow a former patient for a lifetime. Mental health professionals create negative self-fulfilling prophecies when they assume that the prognosis for Schizophrenia and other severe mental illnesses is universally poor. A person who has recovered will continue to carry the self-identity of being mentally ill and possibly overreact to normal symptoms of stress as if they heralded a relapse.

Advantages of the Mental Patient Role

The opposite side of the coin is that there are significant advantages of the role of mental patient, either for the patient or the family:

Advantages for the Patient

Access to paid health care; avoidance of legal consequences for criminal actions; receipt of disability payments; escape from frontline military action; reduction in responsibilities; increase in social support; financial gain from lawsuits; prescriptions for desired medications.

Advantages for the Family Member

Advantages of legal guardianship if the mentally ill person is declared incompetent, including control over financial assets and decisions; benefits of scapegoating one member for the problems of other family members or the entire family unit; financial benefits from lawsuits; satisfaction of need to be a caretaker; sympathy and support from other people.

WHEN IS THIS HYPOTHESIS A GOOD MATCH?

The most frequent application of this hypothesis will refer to the disadvantages of the mental patient role:

- Lack of hope, self-esteem, and integration into the community.
- Discrimination and social rejection from the stigma of mental illness—in present or past.
- Lowered expectations for "stabilization" rather than "recovery" by mental health professionals as well as the client and family.

Malingering

The diagnosis of malingering is warranted when the person is feigning, fabricating, or exaggerating symptoms and impairments to get some kind of identifiable gain. The question of whether an individual is faking is often directed at forensic experts. However, all psychotherapists may encounter a client whom they suspect is malingering. You need to distinguish between "retrospective malingering" (exaggerating symptoms or diminished responsibility for a past event) and "current malingering" (presenting feigned symptoms at the present time). It is also important to realize that real impairment can be combined with malingering.

Factitious Disorder

The *DSM* diagnosis of Factitious Disorder is used when the person is intentionally feigning symptoms to assume a sick role without external incentives for the behavior. Munchausen syndrome and Munchausen by proxy fall into this category. "Factitious bereavement" refers to someone attributing his or her severe emotional distress to a major loss that did not happen, and "factitious PTSD" refers to someone alleging flashbacks and other symptoms for a traumatic event that he or she did not experience. Factitious Disorder with psychological symptoms is difficult to diagnose and needs to be distinguished from somatoform disorders (Phillips, 2003). Symptoms have the following characteristics:

- Change from day to day or from one hospitalization to the next.
- Changes in symptoms when patient feels observed.
- Unconventional and fantastic symptoms.
- Uncommon association of symptoms that belong to several different psychiatric disorders.

The history often has dramatic, exaggerated stories and vague details.

Unlike malingerers, who have a clear external gain for being judged mentally ill, people with Factitious Disorder are motivated by unknown, internal factors. Elwyn, Ahmed, and Burns (2002) list some possible explanations:

- Underlying masochistic tendencies.
- A need to be the center of attention and to feel important.
- A need to assume a dependent status and receive nurturance.
- A need to ease feelings of worthlessness or vulnerability.
- A need to feel superior to authority figures that is gratified by deceiving them.

With this diagnosis, we agree that the person does have a severe mental disorder, but not the one that is being simulated. The prognosis is very poor because of the unlikelihood that the person wants to give up the desired mental patient role.

Gaslighting

The 1944 movie *Gaslight* tells the story of a Victorian husband who systematically attempts to drive his fragile wife mad and is the origin of the phrase "to gaslight" someone—to deliberately cause someone to develop mental illness by manipulating his or her environment and using powers of persuasion. You need to be open to the possibility that family members are treating the person in a way that will induce symptoms or result in the person being labeled as mentally ill. These other people are the ones who gain from having an individual hospitalized or declared incompetent.

TREATMENT PLANNING

The key principle of treatment is to refrain from treating a nonexistent disorder.

Helping the Stigmatized

People who have internalized society's negative appraisals and who believe that recovery is impossible will benefit from reading memoirs of people who have been severely mentally ill and have recovered (Fisher & Ahern, 2005). The National Empowerment Center (www.power2u.org) provides access to stories of recovery and encourages advocacy for mental health reform. Therapists must recognize when the goals of stabilization and maintenance should be replaced by the goals of self-sufficiency, rehabilitation, and community integration. "Recovery" is the goal of multidisciplinary psychosocial rehabilitation programs, which set the following goals for clients: coping with symptoms, responsible management of one's own medication, accessing resources, learning skills, finding good housing, and developing social support (McGuire, 2000). People who have disabilities from mental illness need to develop self-definitions that "I am more than this disability." Involvement in organizations like NAMI (National Alliance on Mental Illness) can be beneficial, putting ex-patients into the role of consumers, advocates, and activists for social policy changes. Clients need to know their rights under the American with Disabilities Act (ADA) and understand how to protect themselves from unlawful discrimination.

Using Judgment

What do you do with a malingerer? Do you confront and say that you know he is lying? Do you continue seeing someone in therapy when you know that the only reason he is coming is to strengthen his claims of psychological disability? The problem of malingering comes up with people in the military, and there are clear guidelines in that setting. The treatment goal for malingerers in the military is to return the person to duty. The threat of court martial is usually sufficient for the person to drop the simulation. Clients who fit the profile of Factitious Disorder lead to frustration, anger, and bewilderment in therapists. When therapists suspect the client is lying (e.g., about a death in the family) they may want to seek corroboration, yet they are bound by rules of confidentiality. One of the benefits of a case formulation method, which requires you to monitor progress, is that you will begin to get suspicious when progress does not occur. People who want to stay in the sick role will defeat your efforts to help them. As with all challenging situations, you must seek consultation and document data, assessment, and actions in chart notes and memos.

INTEGRATION OF HYPOTHESES

The following hypotheses can help you when clients are erroneously being labeled "mentally ill."

CS1 Emergency

If someone is trying to get your client declared incompetent, you need to be directive and assure that the client gets good legal representation.

BL1 Antecedents and Consequences

In your behavioral analysis you may discover reinforcing consequences to the "illness behavior." The person may perform the sick role in the presence of certain stimuli (other people are watching) but not at other times. You need to identify the triggers to the individual's taking on a "mentally impaired" role. It could be that well-intentioned family members need to be educated.

ES2 Avoiding Freedom and Responsibility

The client can be confronted on the consequences of choices. Your goal might be to point out benefits that the client is missing by staying in the sick role.

SCE1 Family System

Family members, by treating someone as mentally ill or incompetent, can cause that person to live up to their expectations. When a family member is being induced into a sick role by family members, you need to switch to the family systems model, referring the client to a family therapist who will see the family as a group and assure that the problems in the family are correctly identified and that a single individual (the IP) is not scapegoated.

KEY IDEAS FOR SCE7 ENVIRONMENTAL FACTORS

Human behavior is influenced by such diverse environmental factors as geography, weather, architecture, and technology. The nonsocial environment is significant either as a cause of the problem or as the source of benefit. As an example, consider this problem: *Difficulty skiing* (nonskiers should apply this inventory to your preferred sport or hobby). Your level of skill, the physiological condition of your body, and your level of energy for that day are personal factors that account only partly for the quality of performance. Environmental factors include:

- *Weather:* If it is stormy, there is poor visibility, the wind pushes against you, and the cold creates discomfort. The gray and gloomy day, with low barometric pressure, creates a more negative mood than a blue sky on a sunny day.
- *Terrain:* Quality of skiing performance is influenced by the incline of the slope, the quality of the snow, whether it has been groomed, how cluttered it is with other people, and hazards created by exposed rocks.

SCE7 ENVIRONMENTAL FACTORS

Definition

The problem is explained in terms of **Environmental Factors.** Solutions can involve modifying the environment, leaving the environment, obtaining material resources, or accepting what can't be changed.

Explanation

Solutions can be found outside of the field of mental health intervention. The field of public health offers examples of risk factors that are present in the environment. The concept of "environmental niche" is useful for realizing that people do not have to change themselves to be happy.

Examples

In Austria in the 1930s, the 9-year-old son of a famous psychoanalyst had a phobic avoidance of specific streets in his neighborhood. His famous mother interpreted his fear in terms of his unconscious dynamics, especially related to "phallic-" shaped trees on the street. She ignored the fact that her son was being physically threatened by anti-Semitic bullies on those streets.

Samantha moved to Los Angeles from a small Midwestern town. She complains of depression, loneliness, and a series of unsatisfactory relationships. She wants to quit her job and go back home, but her therapist says that she shouldn't run away from her problems. She quits therapy without explanation, and 6 months later, she is back home and happy.

John is a 46-year-old single college professor who lives alone and works at home. He had multiple psychological and emotional complaints: headaches, backaches, inability to relax, writing blocks, and stress from missing deadlines. Instead of going to therapy, he buys a $1500 desk chair and hires a feng shui consultant to redesign his office. His problems disappear.

- *Clothing:* The way you dress affects comfort and mobility. Today's fabrics are technologically advanced, so if you wear older clothing, you are more likely to get wet and cold.
- *Tools and Equipment:* The technology of skis and ski boots changes every year. Getting new equipment can radically improve performance. The fit of boots affects the control you have over the skis. The amount of wax on the bottom of the skis and the sharpness of the edges affects speed and control.

With every client it is important to assess: To what degree is environment a barrier to or a facilitator of attaining your goals?

Desirable Environments

If geographic location—the city or neighborhood in which you live—were not an important factor in life satisfaction, there would be no magazine articles listing the "best places to live in America." One such list was created jointly by *Money* magazine and *CNN,* and is available at http://money.cnn.com/best/bplive, with encouragement to find a place "where you would want to raise children and celebrate life's milestones." However, they acknowledge that choices are influenced by factors such as marital status, presence of children, achieving retirement age, personal attitudes about cultural activities, and cold weather. The idea of "environmental niche" comes from ecology: An individual can thrive in one environment yet suffer in another. Therapists can help their clients develop enough self-knowledge that they can make wise choices about the living environment that best suits them.

Environmental Risk Factors

There are environmental causes for mental as well as physical health problems, and there are environmental barriers to as well as facilitators of healthy lifestyles. For instance, AIDS prevention programs with adolescents include not only information and skills development (e.g., saying no to unsafe sex) but also environmental interventions: increasing access to condoms.

The Fundamental Attribution Error

David Levy (1997), in his book *Tools of Critical Thinking,* provides a good discussion of the *fundamental attribution error,* explaining how, in assigning causes of other people's behavior, we tend to underestimate situational attributions (*causation attributed to circumstances, surroundings, environment, and other external influences*) and overestimate dispositional attribution (*causation attributed to internal influences such as personality trait or attitudes*). Most problems that clients bring to therapists will have both situational and dispositional causes. However, because psychotherapists tend to overemphasize the psychological, Levy's advice is invaluable for the case formulation process: "Never underestimate the power of the situation" (p. 89).

Knowledge of Other Fields Helps

Therapists who learn about economics, urban planning, environmental psychology, and even interior design will be able to apply concepts from those fields. For instance, when the economy is "sluggish" and unemployment is high, individuals suffer in the following ways: anxiety, physiological stress symptoms, and family conflict from prolonged unemployment; impaired self-esteem from not being able to achieve the standard of living of their parents; and the loss of potential satisfactions in the workplace from needing to place job security above personal happiness. The presence of safe neighborhood parks provides many psychological benefits to people in the area, such as companionship for the elderly and friendship networks for mothers of toddlers. Feng shui is a Chinese discipline that offers guidelines for interior design, landscaping, and even selecting a home's location. Many people report enhanced psychological functioning after following those principles. At a less esoteric level, people can consult books on how to reduce clutter and increase the order and organization in their lives. When a person lives in a soothing, serene environment, there are tremendous benefits of inner peace, productivity, and enjoyment of time at home.

WHEN IS THIS HYPOTHESIS A GOOD MATCH?

You need to view all clients through the lens of this hypothesis, just as you do with the biological hypotheses. As you gather data, you hold in mind the concept of "environmental niche": Is it possible that if my client were in a different environment—home, neighborhood, office building, or city—the emotional symptoms would disappear or the goals would be more easily achieved? Is there some tool or resource (think of the earlier condom example) that would help solve problems?

When the client verbalizes the belief, "If I moved away, things would be better," examine the validity of this idea, without assuming that there are deeper psychological issues that need to be addressed. Data about the client's history is extremely important: Is this a person who repeatedly moves and always has the same problems? The film, *Rebel Without a Cause* offers exactly that kind of clinical example: When the teenage son tries to tell his parents about the tragedy of another boy's death and express his sense of moral responsibility, the mother responds, *"It doesn't matter because we're moving!"* At the other extreme are people who are very resistant to the idea of moving: They may have no idea how the environment contributes to their difficulties, they may never have considered leaving the place where their ancestors settled, and they may find the idea of moving and adjusting to a new place completely overwhelming. In both cases, "leaving the environment" can remain as one of many possible alternatives in the search for solutions.

TREATMENT PLANNING AND INTEGRATION OF HYPOTHESES

If the only hypothesis that fits is environmental, there is no need for therapy: A single problem-solving session is sufficient. In most cases, there will be an integration of hypotheses, so treatment ideas are presented in this section.

B3 Mind-Body Connections

Environment has profound effect on health and stress level. The decision to change environments may stem from health concerns such as difficulty breathing in areas of high pollution.

CS2 Situational Stressors

Environmental factors such as disasters, unsafe neighborhoods, and overcrowded living spaces function as situational stressors. Often, a tremendous amount of stress is caused by the chronic, daily hassles in a particular environment. For instance, working in Los Angeles can mean that a person drives in heavy traffic for 2 hours a day to be able to live in a suburban home and work in a higher paying job. The crisis intervention model can guide the problem-solving process.

BL1 Antecedents and Consequences

Environmental variables are part of a complete behavioral analysis. The environment provides triggers and reinforcers. Behavior change programs can be based entirely or partly on changing the environment. For instance, relapse for substance abuse can be avoided if the individual stays away from environments where drugs are sold and used.

BL3 Skill Deficits or Lack of Competence

When the environment is blamed as the cause of a problem, it is important to examine whether the client might lack important skills. For instance, when someone says, "I'm lonely because this is a very unfriendly city," you need to explore what the person has done to make friends and what behaviors she has used to approach people, initiate social contacts, and move an acquaintanceship toward friendship.

C2 Faulty Cognitive Map

Cognitive factors can provide resistance to environmental change solutions. The person's cognitive map may contain rules about "sticking things out," and "not quitting."

ES2 Avoiding Freedom and Responsibility

The concepts from this hypothesis—such as the domains of freedom and limitations—are very important to use when evaluating the choice of leaving or changing an environment. Clients need to experience their freedom to move, even if they don't make that choice.

SCE2 Cultural Context

The norms and values of a culture will affect the types of environments that people live in, the availability of environmental solutions, and the acceptability of the environmental hypothesis. Consider how organizations in our culture create stressful environments and then limit the amount of vacation to 2 weeks. In many European countries, the typical vacation is 4 weeks. The way a culture treats its elderly citizens will have tremendous influence on their level of stress.

SUGGESTED READINGS

Recommendations are listed for each hypothesis in this chapter.

SCE1 Family System

Berg, I. K. (1994). *Family based services: A solution-focused approach.* New York: Norton.

Bowen, M. (1994). *Family therapy in clinical practice.* Lanham, MD: Aronson.

Brown, R. (1999). *Imago relationship therapy: An introduction to theory and practice.* New York: Wiley.

Connell, G., Mitten, T., & Blueberry, W. (1998). *Reshaping family relationships: The symbolic therapy of Carl Whitaker.* New York: Brunner-Routledge.

De Shazer, S. (1985). *Keys to solution in brief therapy.* New York: Norton.

Framo, J. (1992). *Family-of-origin therapy: An intergenerational approach.* New York: Brunner/Mazel.

Freedman, J., & Combs, G. (1996). *Narrative therapy.* New York: Norton.

Goldenberg, I., & Goldenberg, H. (2000). *Family therapy: An overview.* Belmont, CA: Brooks/Cole.

Gottman, J. (1994). *Why marriages succeed or fail.* New York: Simon & Schuster.

Gottman, J. (1999). *The marriage clinic: A scientifically based marital therapy.* New York: Norton.

Haley, J. (1987). *Problem-solving therapy* (2nd ed.). San Francisco: Jossey-Bass.

Luquet, W. (1996). *Short-term couples therapy: The Imago Model in action.* Bristol, PA: Brunner/Mazel.

Madanes, C. (1979). *Strategic family therapy.* San Francisco: Jossey-Bass.

McGoldrick, M., Gerson, R., & Shellenberger, S. (1999). *Genograms: Assessment and intervention* (2nd ed.). New York: Norton.

Minuchin, S. (1993). *Family healing.* New York: Simon & Schuster.

Minuchin, S., Simon, G., & Lee, W. (2006). *Mastering family therapy: Journeys of growth and transformation* (new ed.). Hoboken, NJ: Wiley.

Napier, A. Y., & Whitaker, C. (1988). *The family crucible: The intense experience of family* (Reissue ed.). New York: HarperCollins.

Pipher, M. (1996). *The shelter of each other: Rebuilding our families.* New York: Ballantine Books.

Satir, V. (1983). *Conjoint family therapy* (3rd ed.). Palo Alto, CA: Science and Behavior Books.

Satir, V. (1988). *New peoplemaking.* Palo Alto, CA: Science and Behavior Books.

Scharff, D., & Scharff, J. S. (1987). *Object relations family therapy.* Northvale, NJ: Aronson.

Scharff, D., & Scharff, J. S. (1991). *Object relations couple therapy.* Northvale, NJ: Aronson.

Titelman, P. (Ed.). (1998). *Clinical applications of Bowen family systems theory.* Binghamton, NY: Haworth Press.

Walter, J., & Peller, J. (1992). *Becoming solution-focused in brief therapy.* New York: Brunner/Mazel.

SCE2 Cultural Context

Atkinson, D. R., Morten, G., & Sue, D. W. (1998). *Counseling American minorities: A cross-cultural perspective* (5th ed.). Boston: McGraw Hill.

Baruth, L. G., & Manning, M. L. (1991). *Multicultural counseling and psychotherapy: A life span perspective.* New York: Merrill.

Chernin, J. N., & Johnson, M. R. (2002). *Affirmative psychotherapy and counseling for lesbians and gay men.* Thousand Oaks, CA: Sage.

Comas-Diaz, L., & Greene, B. (Eds.). (1994). *Women of color: Integrating ethnic and gender identities in psychotherapy.* New York: Guilford Press.

Comas-Diaz, L., & Griffith, E. H. (Eds.). (1988). *Clinical guidelines in cross-cultural mental health.* New York: Wiley.

Cramer Azima, F. J., & Grizenko, N. (Eds.). (2002). *Immigrant and refugee children and their families: Clinical, research and training issues.* New York: International Universities Press.

Cuellar, I., & Paniagua, F. A. (Eds.). (2000). *Multicultural mental health.* San Diego, CA: Academic Press.

Davis, L. E. (1998). *Working with African American males: A guide to practice.* Thousand Oaks, CA: Sage.

Davis-Russell, E. (Ed.). (2002). *Multicultural education, research, intervention, and training.* San Francisco: Jossey-Bass.

De Rios, M. D. (2001). *Brief psychotherapy with the Latino immigrant client.* Binghamton, NY: Haworth Press.

Dudley, G. R., & Rawlins, M. R. (Eds.). (1985). Psychotherapy with ethnic minorities [Special Issue]. *Psychotherapy, 22*(2s).

Falco, K. L. (1991). *Psychotherapy with lesbian clients: Theory into practice.* New York: Brunner/Mazel.

Herring, R. D. (1999). *Counseling with Native American Indians and Alaska Natives: Strategies for helping professionals.* Thousand Oaks, CA: Sage.

Hong, G. K., & Domokos-Cheng Ham, M. (2001). *Psychotherapy and counseling with Asian American clients: A practical guide.* Thousand Oaks, CA: Sage.

Ivey, A. E., Ivey, M. B., & Simek-Morgan, L. (Eds.). (1997). *Counseling and psychotherapy: A multicultural perspective.* Boston: Allyn & Bacon.

Jackson, L. C., & Greene, B. (Eds.). (2000). *Psychotherapy with African American women: Innovations in psychodynamic perspective and practice.* New York: Guilford Press.

Kobeisy, A. N. (2004). *Counseling American Muslims: Understanding the faith and helping the people.* Westport, CT: Praeger.

Lee, L. C., & Zane, N. W. S. (Eds.). (1998). *Handbook of Asian American psychology.* Thousand Oaks, CA: Sage.

McGoldrick, M. M., Giordano, J., & Pearce, J. K. (Eds.). (1996). *Ethnicity and family therapy* (2nd ed.). New York: Guilford Press.

Mezzich, J. E., Kleinman, A., Fabrego, H., & Parron, D. L. (Eds.). (1996). *Culture and psychiatric diagnosis: A DSM-IV perspective.* Washington, DC: American Psychiatric Press.

Pedersen, P. (Ed.). (1985). *Handbook of cross-cultural counseling and therapy.* Westport, CT: Greenwood.

Pedersen, P. B., Draguns, J. G., Lonner, W. J., & Trimble, J. E. (2002). *Counseling across cultures* (5th ed.). Thousand Oaks, CA: Sage.

Perez, R. M., Debord, K. A., & Bieschke, K. J. (Eds.). (1999). *Handbook of counseling and psychotherapy with lesbian, gay, and bisexual clients.* Washington, DC: American Psychological Association.

Ponterotto, J. G., Casas, J. M., Suzuki, L. A., & Alexander, C. M. (Eds.). (2001). *Handbook of multicultural counseling* (2nd ed.). Thousand Oaks, CA: Sage.

Richards, P. S., & Bergin, A. E. (Eds.). (2000). *Handbook of psychotherapy and religious diversity.* American Psychological Association.

Ritter, K. I., & Terndrup, A. I. (2002). *Handbook of affirmative psychotherapy with lesbians and gay men.* New York: Guilford Press.

Root, M. P. P. (2001). *Love's revolution: Interracial marriage.* Philadelphia: Temple University Press.

Savin-Williams, R. C. (2001). *Mom, Dad, I'm gay: How families negotiate coming out.* Washington, DC: American Psychological Association.

Shiraev, E., & Levy, D. (2003). *Cross-cultural psychology: Critical thinking and contemporary applications* (2nd ed.). Boston: Pearson.

Sue, D. W., Ivey, A., & Pederson, P. (1996). *A theory of multicultural counseling and therapy.* Pacific Grove, CA: Brooks/Cole.

Sue, D. W., & Sue, D. (2002). *Counseling the culturally diverse: Theory and practice* (4th ed.). Hoboken, NJ: Wiley.

Zane, N., Hall, G. C. N., Sue, S., Young, K., & Nunez, J. (2004). Research on psychotherapy with culturally diverse populations. In M. J. Lambert (Ed.), *Bergin and Garfield's handbook of psychotherapy and behavior change* (5th ed., pp. 767–804). Hoboken, NJ: Wiley.

SCE3 Social Support

Ackerman, R. J. (1983). *Children of alcoholics: A guidebook for educators, therapists, and parents.* Holmes Beach, FL: Learning Publications.

Brugha, T. S. (Ed.). (1995). *Social support and psychiatric disorder: Research findings and guidelines for clinical practice.* Cambridge, England: Cambridge University Press.

Kauth, B. (1992). *A circle of men: The original manual for men's support groups.* New York: St. Martin's Press.

Klein, L. L. (2000). *The support group sourcebook: Where they are, How you can find one, and how they can help you.* New York: Wiley.

Kurtz, L. F. (1997). *Self-help and support groups: A handbook for practitioners* (Sage Sourcebook for the Human Services, Vol. 34). Thousand Oaks, CA: Sage.

Milne, D. (1999). *Social therapy: A guide to social support interventions for mental health practitioners.* New York: Wiley.

Shaffer, C. R., Anundsen, K., Peck, M. C., & Backlar, P. (1993). *Creating community anywhere: Finding support and connection in a fragmented world.* Ontario, Canada: Perigee.

Weiss, R. S. (1973). *Loneliness: The experience of emotional and social isolation.* Cambridge, MA: MIT Press.

Wuthnow, R. (1996). *Sharing the journey: Support groups and America's new quest for community.* New York: Free Press.

SCE4 Social Role Performance

Brehm, S., Kassin, S., & Fein, S. (2005). *Social psychology* (6th ed.). Boston: Houghton Mifflin.

Goffman, E. (1959). *The presentation of self in everyday life.* New York: Anchor.

Harrigan, B. L. (1992). *Games mother never taught you* (Reissue ed.). New York: Warner Books.

Heim, P. (1993). *Hardball for women: Winning at the game of business.* New York: Plume.

Nelson, D. L., & Burke, R. J. (2002). *Gender, work stress, and health.* Washington, DC: American Psychological Association.

Palmer, S. H. (1981). *Role stress: How to handle everyday tension.* Englewood Cliffs, NJ: Prentice Hall.

Schein, E. H. (1999). *The corporate culture survival guide.* San Francisco: Jossey Bass.

SCE5 Social Problem Is a Cause

Brown, L. S., & Root, M. P. P. (1990). *Diversity and complexity in feminist therapy.* New York: Haworth.

Comez-Diaz, L., & Greene, B. (Eds.). (1994). *Women of color: Integrating ethnic and gender identities in psychotherapy.* New York: Guilford.

Rosewater, L. B., & Walker, L. E. A. (Eds.). (1985). *A handbook of feminist therapy: Women's issues in psychotherapy.* New York: Springer.

Ryan, W. (1976). *Blaming the victim* (Rev. ed.). New York: Vintage Books.

Worell, J., & Remer, P. (Eds.). (1992). *Feminist perspectives in therapy: An empowerment model for women.* New York: Wiley.

SCE6 Social Role of Mental Patient

Elizur, J., & Minuchin, S. (1989). *Institutionalizing madness.* New York: Basic Books.

Feldman, M. D. (2004). *Playing sick? Untangling the web of Munchausen syndrome, Munchausen by proxy, malingering, and factitious disorder.* New York: Brunner-Routledge.

Feldman, M. D., Ford, C. V., & Reinhold, T. (1995). *Patient or pretender: Inside the strange world of factitious disorders.* New York: Wiley.

Link, B. G., Cullen, F. T., Frank, J., & Wosniak, J. F. (1987). The social rejection of former mental patients: Understanding why labels matter. *American Journal of Sociology, 92,* 1461–1500.

Miller, A. G. (Ed.). (1982). *In the eye of the beholder: Contemporary issues in stereotyping.* New York: Praeger.

Rogers, R. (Ed.) (1997). *Clinical assessment of malingering and deception* (2nd ed.). New York: Guilford Press.

Szasz, T. (1974). *The myth of mental illness: Foundations of a theory of personal conduct* (Revised ed.). New York: Harper & Row.

Sales, B. D., Miller, M. O., & Hall, S. R. (2005). *Laws affecting clinical practice.* Washington, DC: American Psychological Association.

SCE7 Environmental Factors

Bell, P. A., Greene, T. C. & Fisher, J. D. (2000). *Environmental psychology.* Belmont: Wadsworth.

Gallagher, W. (1994). *The power of place: How our surroundings shape our thoughts, emotions, and actions.* New York: Harper Perennial.

Saari, C. (2000). *The environment: Its role in psychosocial functioning and psychotherapy.* New York: Columbia University Press.

Powell, M. (1980). *Environment and aging.* Belmont, CA: Brooks/Cole.

Chapter 10

USING CLINICAL HYPOTHESES

When you are ready to prepare an assessment section (discussed in Chapter 14), your task will be to select the hypotheses that best explain the problem and lead to good treatment plans. These hypotheses must be consistent with the database.

> By combining hypotheses from different theoretical models and levels of functioning (biological, psychological, and social), you create an integrative clinical case formulation.

This chapter will give you the opportunity to practice skills and to gain confidence and mastery in using the material from the previous seven chapters. The skills for using clinical hypotheses to develop case formulations are presented in Table 10.1. The first set of skills are practiced with case histories, clinical vignettes, data you have about yourself or close friends, as well as data that you have gathered from several sessions with a client. The second set of skills is learned by conducting clinical interviews with peers, before facing real clients.

BRAINSTORMING

ACTIVITY 10.1

Brainstorm Hypotheses

This activity in Appendix III asks you to (a) select a problem, (b) create timelines for life history and recent history, and (c) review the list of hypotheses, and then write down the ones that fit.

At the brainstorming stage, you want to include the hypotheses that make sense, without worrying about which ones you would find most useful for treatment planning. Here is a sample that a trainee wrote about her close friend.

Table 10.1   Skills for Using Hypotheses

SKILLS FOR USE ON COMPLETE DATABASE

Knowledge of Hypotheses

You need knowledge of the data that are consistent or inconsistent with each hypothesis. It takes time to build confidence with all 28 hypotheses. Your initial formulations should use hypotheses with which you are already familiar. Whenever you have case material, take the list of hypotheses (see Appendix II, Chart II.A) and mentally review what each hypothesis means and whether it fits.

Brainstorming

By reviewing the entire list and excluding those hypotheses that do not fit, you will be left with a long list of possibilities, more than you would actually use for your formulation. You want initially to be as inclusive as possible. Therapists tend to have tunnel vision and only look for what they want to find, so brainstorming helps keep an open mind.

Select "Best Fit" Hypotheses

Now you are ready to be selective and include only hypotheses that will lead to treatment plans that you think will be effective. You need to write a sentence or two to explain how the hypothesis provides an explanation. If you are a busy clinician, with a full practice, you might not get beyond this stage. However, to produce the best possible formulation, you must proceed to the next skill.

Write a Coherent Discussion

Your discussion must focus on the specific client and stay close to the data without branching off into an abstract discussion of theory or personality. You may wonder why you would bother to write formal essays if you are not studying this book as part of a course (there is enough paperwork in clinical practice to keep you busy). The main reason is that writing forces you to improve your thinking. The standards for this explanatory essay are explained in Chapter 14.

SKILLS FOR USE IN THE INTERVIEW

Readiness for Interview

First, you need to be able to listen to a client's words, pay attention to the process, and recognize the preliminary fit of the hypothesis. Second, you must know how to formulate a question or use a different strategy to direct the client to provide you with information you need to rule in or rule out the hypothesis. These skills can be learned by watching other people's counseling sessions, live or on video.

Interviewing

Your interview begins with open questions, so that data pour in without your using the hypotheses to structure the interview. Once you have recognized the preliminary fit of a specific hypothesis, you can gather more data in an unbiased way (without communicating your expectations) to test the goodness-of-fit of that hypothesis. You are able to pursue this line of inquiry, with both empathy and persistence, until you can judge whether the hypothesis should definitely be used, be ruled out as incompatible with the data, or be retained as one that needs future examination.

Patience

A common beginner error is to pursue every idea you think of the minute you think it. You need to be able to store up data in your mind, and sift through hypotheses, without channeling every idea into an immediate verbalization with the client. Often, when you postpone a direct question, the information you need will arrive, spontaneously.

Problem: *Difficulty Adjusting to Pregnancy*

Tania is a 32-year-old woman who has been married for 6 years and is now 6 months pregnant. She is feeling resentful, angry, and trapped by being in a situation that will totally disrupt her life.

Biological Hypotheses

- **B3 Mind-Body Connections:** Pregnancy is a physiological condition. Hormonal changes contribute to mood and sensitivity. Furthermore, her worrying and negative thinking is creating tension.

Crisis, Stressful Situations, and Transitions

- **CS3 Developmental Transition:** Tania is about to make a transition to parenthood, which is a developmental step for her as well as for her marriage. She is anxious about the changes the baby will cause to her marriage as she and her husband negotiate how to function together as parents.

Cognitive Models

- **C2 Faulty Cognitive Map:** Tania has negative schemas about the label and role of being a mother. She believes that by becoming a mother, she will be "giving up her sense of self."
- **C3 Faulty Information Processing:** Tania engages in mind reading, believing that others now see only the baby and not her.

Existential and Spiritual Models

- **ES2 Avoiding Freedom and Responsibility:** Tania's problem is a result of avoiding responsibility and feeling like a victim. She needs to face that it was her choice to become pregnant and that she has the ability to make decisions to take care of her emotional needs.

Psychodynamic Models

- **P1 Internal Parts and Subpersonalities:** The parts Tania has mentioned so far are: Mother, "Self-Actualizer," Wife, Guilty Person, Resentful Person, the Judge, and "Unhappy Pregnant Whale."

Social, Cultural, and Environmental Factors

- **SCE 2 Cultural Context:** She and her husband have planned for her to stop working for the first 2 years of the child's life. This represents a loss of status and power: Her culture values those who work and earn money and devalues those who are dependents. Furthermore, Tania's negative body image results from the culture's idealization of thinness in women.
- **SCE4 Social Role Performance:** Tania is uncomfortable in the transitional role of mother-to-be and is lamenting the loss of her "married without children" role.

APPLYING AND TESTING HYPOTHESES

The following activity is a very effective way to review all of the hypotheses and to practice the skills of applying hypotheses and recognizing the additional data you need to gather. Four additional practice vignettes are found in Appendix III, Activity 10.2. Completion of this activity should take less than 2 hours, and at the end, you will have a sense of mastery of the 28 hypotheses and confidence in your ability to integrate hypothesis testing into interviews.

ACTIVITY 10.2

Apply and Test Hypotheses with Case Vignettes

Four vignettes (Appendix III, Activity 10.2) each contain enough data so that you can apply several hypotheses. After each vignette, three different hypotheses are indicated. For each hypothesis, provide the following:

- **Explanation:** Write a sentence or two explaining the hypothesis and how it fits the data.
- **A probe to test the hypothesis:** Write, verbatim, a question or statement you would use to gather additional data (or describe another method for gathering data—e.g., homework, referral to an expert, or consulting other information source).
- **New invented data:** Use your imagination and invent new information that the client would give in response to your probe, supporting the usefulness of the hypothesis you are testing (do not repeat data that are in the vignette—you must add something to the story).
- **Add an additional hypothesis:** Write the code and name of a different hypothesis that also fits the data. Then complete the same instructions: provide an explanation, a probe to test the hypothesis, and new invented data.

The following case, with answers for three hypotheses, should be studied before you do Activity 10.2.

> ### Problem: *Bridge Phobia*
>
> Sharon is a 32-year-old married woman with a husband and a 5-year-old son. She was working as a realtor when she first married Jim, a college professor, 7 years ago, but, when Daniel was born, she became a stay-at-home mom. A few weeks ago, when she was driving to Manhattan to buy Christmas presents, she had a panic attack on a bridge. She made it across the bridge, but then immediately turned around and did her shopping at a local mall. Since then, she has avoided crossing bridges either by car or by foot. When she drives on the street that approaches the bridge, she describes intense anxiety symptoms: sweaty hands, rubbery legs, chest pains, fear of having a heart attack. She avoids activities of great importance to her (e.g., her only nephew's wedding) if they require crossing a bridge. She admits with embarrassment that she even gets anxious in movie theaters when a bridge appears onscreen.

BL1 Antecedents and Consequences

- **Explanation:** There are positive consequences for avoidance of bridges. Even though she says she wants to be able to drive on bridges again, there are payoffs for not being able to.
- **A probe to test the hypothesis:** Since you developed this problem, has there been any change in your husband's behavior?
- **New invented data:** The client describes her husband as a "control freak." She is always running errands for him, and he is very demanding and domineering. Now when he asks her to go to Manhattan, she can say, "I can't." With a big smile she says, "Now he has to do his own errands."

BL2 Conditioned Emotional Response

- **Explanation:** Somehow the bridge has become a conditioned stimulus for intense anxiety. Something that happened while she was crossing the bridge triggered anxiety, and the bridge was paired with that other stimulus.
- **A probe to test the hypothesis:** Pretend you are back on that day, driving on the bridge. Speak in the present tense, and tell me what you see, hear, and feel.
- **New invented data:** She recalled that the driver in front of her had stepped on his brakes unexpectedly, and she had almost crashed into him because she had been momentarily inattentive.

P4 Unconscious Dynamics

- **Explanation:** The bridge-related anxiety is really a displacement or disguise for another source of anxiety, which remains outside her awareness. It is "safer" to have the symptom than to have awareness of her hidden feelings or impulses.
- **A probe to test the hypothesis:** Let me explain a process called "free association," and I will ask you to do something new.
- **New invented data:** The client free associates to her memory of the bridge and reveals fantasies about leaving her husband and child.

Before going on to Activity 10.2, select an additional hypothesis for this vignette. If you are using this book with classmates or fellow trainees, you will be surprised when you share your choices at how differently people approach the same case. You discover the benefits of group discussions—either in supervision or with peers—to help you integrate different ideas.

SELECTING AND COMBINING BEST-FIT HYPOTHESES

The following samples are based on sessions conducted by graduate students with peer volunteers prior to meeting their first real client. Assume that for each sample, the database is complete and consistent with these hypotheses. The challenge at this stage of skill development is to "talk" the ideas in the hypotheses, using natural language instead of writing in sentences that have been borrowed from texts. Through practice in expressing the hypotheses in your own words, you accomplish two goals: (1) overcome the disconnect between learning the theory in the classroom and applying it as a useful tool, and (2) develop proficiency in explaining complicated ideas in the exact same language that you will use with your clients.

I. Problem: *Difficulty accepting the termination of a relationship*

> Becky is a 28-year-old African American graduate student living with two roommates.

CS4 Loss and Bereavement

Becky is going through a process of grieving, following the breakup, 7 months ago, of her 3-year relationship with R. For the first month after he left her for another woman, she continued to believe that he would return and that the relationship was still intact. Although this denial process is normal following the shock of the loss, my hunch is that she has not allowed herself to fully experience the anger, bargaining, and depression that naturally come with a loss of this magnitude. This hunch is supported by the fact that in the third session, she mentioned that there was new information about R., but she was unwilling to discuss it, because "the feelings were too difficult" for her to process.

P2 Reenactment of Early Childhood Experiences

Despite the pain that R. put her through, and the concrete evidence that he was not being honest with her, she was still willing to continue the relationship with him. Even now that the evidence of his infidelity is undeniable, Becky still holds R. in high regard and speaks of him with admiration. My hunch is that Becky's needs for love and affection were not adequately met as a child. As an adult, she chooses mates who cannot meet her needs, she is willing to take whatever love and affection she can get, and has difficulty "letting go" because R. represents the hope of attaining a parent's love.

II. Problem: *Frustration over not being in a romantic relationship*

> Max is a 29-year-old midwestern Protestant computer programmer who lives alone in the city where he completed college. He is experiencing the pain of not being in a meaningful relationship with a woman.

CS3 Developmental Transition

I believe that Max is at a developmental transition as he watches his friends marry and desires to do the same. He has difficulty relating to women as adults and seems more comfortable in relationships with "girls as friends." Perhaps he doesn't view himself as an adult yet.

P3 Immature Sense of Self and Conception of Others

Max's difficulty creating a significant relationship with a woman seems to have its roots in early childhood experience with a rejecting and emotionally cold mother. He continuously looks for women who will possess the characteristics of the "good mother" that he never had. He wishes to be understood, loved, and have his needs met. He doesn't address what his role would be in satisfying the needs of a woman. He only focuses on how a woman would meet his needs. He is able to initiate relationships and have a few dates with a woman but is unable to keep women interested after that. I suspect that women see him as immature and needy. He is successful in developing platonic friendships with women, possibly because he is more relaxed on that level and because women may feel sorry for him and take on the role of helper and nurturer.

BL3 Skill Deficits or Lack of Competence

Max's difficulty with creating successful adult relationships with women can be understood in terms of his skill deficits. He lacks the interpersonal skills for successful dating. He has never been successful in moving a casual dating relationship to a greater level of intimacy, so he needs to develop competence in that area and recognize the behaviors he uses that turn women into friends instead of lovers. His conversational skills need improvement, and he would benefit from practice in talking about personal issues and feelings. He needs to learn to focus on the woman, using empathy skills, instead of worrying about the impression he is making. He needs to find role models of successful relationships, because his parents' marriage lacked warmth and any kind of intimate communication.

III. Problem: *Excessive anxiety associated with school performance*

Sarah is a 24-year-old married Chinese American graduate student.

C4 Dysfunctional Self-Talk

There are many cognitive elements contributing to Sarah's high stress level. Whenever she is pressed for time, she starts to worry and maintains this self-talk: *I have so much work to do; I won't be able to manage all of it.*

C3 Faulty Information Processing

She demonstrates irrational, all-or-nothing thinking: *If I don't get an A on this paper, I will fail my classes.* This kind of thinking leads her to feel anxious, and it keeps her distracted from doing the work. Therefore, she might fall behind in her work and that could lead to further stress. Sarah also has a problem with using mind reading on her husband. She worries that, because she is so busy with school, *He probably thinks that I care more about my grades than about him, and that's not true.* This thought leaves her feeling more stressed, anxious, and guilty when she does focus successfully on her school work.

BL3 Skills Deficit and Lack of Competence

Sarah describes her mother as an extremely anxious and excitable person. When her mother was faced with a stressful situation, she would start to feel helpless and anxious instead of coming up with a solution. Her mother never provided a good role model for coping with stress, and she never learned any tools for calming herself down. She would definitely benefit from learning to use tools for lowering her own anxiety level, such as relaxation training or meditation. She needs to learn how to focus on her breathing and tune out the constant talk in her head, perhaps through mindfulness activities.

SCE2 Cultural Context

Growing up in a Chinese American family, Sarah had a lot of pressure directly from her parents and indirectly from her cultural community. She told me that in Asian culture it is expected for an individual to do well in school. She felt that if she did not excel in school she would shame her family. Her anxiety while she studied for exams was increased when she imagined how disappointed her parents would be if she did not get an A.

IV. Problem: *Poor grades in school*

> Tiffany is a 15-year-old ninth grader living with her parents and attending a large, suburban high school.

CS3 Developmental Transition

Tiffany is in the middle stage of adolescence and has changed from being the compliant child that used to get good grades and tried to win praise from her parents. If a course interests her, she pays attention and does the assignments, but if she finds it boring, her mind wanders. She admits that after school she prefers to talk on the phone or use the computer to contact friends rather than to study. Her new friends have similar attitudes toward school, placing higher value on clothes, music, and a social life. To some degree, her behavior is normal for her age.

ES1 Existential Issues

Tiffany recently attended the funeral of a friend she had known since elementary school who died in an automobile accident. This event stirred up feelings that she claims she has had for several years: *Life is such a waste* and *if I knew I was going to die, I would go places, eat anything, do whatever I want, rather than waste my life sitting in a boring classroom.* She is searching for meaning and purpose in life and has yet to find it in school. Although she does not meet criteria for depression, she has been feeling sad and lonely, and these feelings contribute to her difficulties focusing on schoolwork.

BL1 Antecedents and Consequences

A behavioral analysis yields several conclusions. The desired behavior, "focused study," occurs less than 2 hours a week. Her home environment triggers behaviors incompatible with study because she is expected to do homework in her bedroom where she has her computer, phone, and TV. There are many reinforcers in her life that she is receiving "free," without the necessity for her to earn them as rewards. (Expressed rewards: new clothes, new CD, favorite restaurant, and snowboarding trip; Observed reinforcers: phone time, mall time, computer, and use of cell phone.)

SCE1 Family System

Tiffany's mother seems to have always had difficulty allowing her to progress to the next developmental stage, as demonstrated by her breast feeding her until she was 2. The mother had Tiffany when her two children from her first marriage had already left home, and she seems to have formed an attachment that has impaired her daughter's ability to cope with stress and changes. The mother is aware of steps she could take to encourage more effort in school, for example, turn TV and telephone time into rewards following time spent studying, but she is unwilling to take these steps for fear of eliciting her daughter's anger. Tiffany noted that throughout elementary and middle school, her father always bragged about how "gifted" his daughter was. When she described how he would "lose his bragging rights" if she didn't get into an Ivy League school, I formed the hunch that she might want to sabotage her school success as a means of punishing her father for his overemphasis on school performance at the expense of a caring, warm relationship. It is very possible that her parents are avoiding the problems in their marriage by focusing on their daughter, and they should deal directly with their marital problems first, to be more effective parents during this transitional stage in her life.

V. Problem: *Difficulty managing feelings of guilt, frustration, and anger while caring for elderly mother*

Claudia is a 58-year-old married Latina mother of three grown children, living with her husband and her 90-year-old mother who requires extensive care.

CS2 Situational Stressors

Claudia described losing her temper and being too hard on her mother. However, when details were elicited, it became clear that there is no elder abuse or risk of elder abuse. She feels guilty over crying and raising her voice. Her description of her mother's uncooperative behavior, tantrums, hostile moods, and insulting speech confirms that she is dealing with a high level of external stress, and most women in her situation would feel angry and frustrated. As her mother's condition deteriorates, Claudia's stress level rises.

SCE2 Cultural Context

The guilt caused by her feelings of anger and resentment has roots in her culture's definition of a "good daughter." She believes that any negative thought negates the assistance she provides for her mother. *A good daughter should be happy to help her mother* is the cultural message that she has internalized. She also firmly believes that it is unacceptable in her culture to place her mother in an assisted-living facility, even though she and her siblings could afford it.

C2 Faulty Cognitive Map

As long as she believes that she is a bad daughter if she experiences anger, she will lack the ability to cope successfully with her normal emotional responses. The more she tries to suppress negative thoughts, the more likely it is that they erupt in screaming. She personalizes her mother's aggressive, ungrateful behavior as if it were proof that she is not doing enough. She needs to recognize the futility of trying to get appreciation and validation from her mother. Not only was her mother always cold and rejecting in her childhood, but elderly people with her mother's medical and mental problems rarely provide the kind of gratitude that she is seeking. She needs to develop cognitive strategies for lowering her level of anger and frustration. Another cognitive barrier to improved coping with her mother is that she believes that she "has no right" to take time for herself. When she is not caring for her mother or going to work, she feels obligated to put her husband's needs before her own.

SCE3 Social Support

A paid assistant comes several times a week to help with her mother; however, apart from this, the burden falls entirely on Claudia. Her siblings live in other states, and she doubts that they could provide the quality of care her mother requires. Although they have offered to help, Claudia insists that she feels better having her mother with her. Her husband, a Latino man, refuses to engage in what he sees as "woman's work." Because she believes her negative feelings are unacceptable, Claudia has never expressed her anger and frustration to anyone before her sessions with me. She would benefit enormously if she could turn to friends for support, or if she would be willing to join a support group for caretakers of elderly parents where she could not only experience the universality of her emotions but also receive concrete advice on how to cope better.

VI. Problem: *Fear and distrust of men*

> Ayesha is a 26-year-old Arab-American Muslim female living at home with her parents, grandmother, and younger brother.

BL2 Conditioned Emotional Responses

Ayesha's initiation into the world of adult intimacy occurred at age 12, when she was repeatedly raped by her 18-year-old neighbor. Any resistance was met with physical restraint or injury and the perpetrator convinced her that if she talked about it, everyone would blame her, not him.

Because of her emotional conditioning from the early abuse, she has responses of intense anxiety in situations where she is alone with a man. This anxiety interferes with her ability to have a comfortable conversation and is so intense that she prefers to avoid these situations completely.

C3 Faulty Information Processing

Because of this early experience, Ayesha overgeneralizes, and believes "all men are the same," and will hurt her, both physically and emotionally. She sees herself as damaged goods because of the abuse and rape, and believes that no decent, trustworthy man would ever want to be with her. Therefore, anyone who shows an interest in her is automatically dismissed as untrustworthy. When she goes on a date, she engages in mind reading and makes assumptions about the man's evil intentions before she has a chance to get to know him. As part of her faulty view of the world, she blames herself for the abuse she experienced.

SCE2 Cultural Context

She never talked about having been raped because she feared that she would be rejected, especially by her family, for not being a virgin. As she explained to me, in her culture, women who are not virgins are devalued, shamed by their family, and must lower their expectations of finding a good spouse. According to her beliefs, there is no distinction made between engaging in voluntary sexual activity and being a victim of rape. These beliefs have prevented her from talking about the sexual abuse; therefore, she has never been able to expose her faulty beliefs to helpful people, such as trained rape counselors or groups of survivors of childhood sexual abuse, who would help modify them.

BL3 Skill Deficits or Lack of Competence

She learned to survive by shutting down physically and emotionally, a coping strategy that helped her endure a very difficult and frightening time in her childhood. She carried these learned skills with her when she began to date and found that they no longer worked for her. These skills, which served her so well in childhood, are now a hindrance to what she wants for her life—an intimate, satisfying relationship. Because of her avoidance of men, she lacks social skills for meeting and establishing even friendships with men.

INTEGRATING HYPOTHESIS TESTING INTO THE CLINICAL INTERVIEW

A key requirement for hypothesis testing is to avoid biasing the client's responses.

> Because therapists have a natural tendency to want to confirm their hunches, and many clients have a tendency to want to please the therapist, you must be very careful not to reveal your expectations when you explore hypotheses.

Here are some of the ways that data can be gathered to explore and test specific hypotheses:

- *Open question:* Tell me more about your parents' marriage (testing to see if the client's problem could be a symptom of a dysfunctional family system, **SCE1**).
- *Closed question:* What was happening right before you did that (applying **BL1,** and doing a behavioral analysis to determine antecedents)?
- *Offer a hunch and seek confirmation or disconfirmation:* It sounds like you believe that there is no point in trying. Is that correct (confirming the relevance of **C2** by identifying faulty elements in the client's cognitive map)?

- *Direct an experiential activity:* Pretend that you are your husband and tell me what he would say (testing **P3** to determine if the client functions at an immature, narcissistic level and is not able to take the point of view of others; also exploring **SCE1,** to see if there are family systems factors such as circular causality in the marital interaction).

- *Homework assignment:* Keep a chart and every time you get angry, fill in where you were, who you were with, and what you were telling yourself (testing whether a focus on **Dysfunctional Self-Talk C4** would be useful).

Using Transcripts of Sessions to Practice Applying Hypotheses

Another way to develop skills of applying hypotheses is to read a transcript of a therapy session and put comments next to the content or behavior. These comments can reveal the hypotheses that the clinician was thinking of during the session and show recognition of ideas you hadn't thought of before and would like to pursue in a future session. Tables 10.2 and 10.3 show trainees writing commentary for their own transcribed sessions using two columns, one for the client's exact words and one for the therapist's postsession hypothesizing.

ACTIVITY 10.3 _____

Provide Commentary for a Transcript

In Appendix III, you find an excerpt from a therapy session in the left column, with the right column empty so you can write your thoughts about relevant hypotheses.

INTEGRATING PSYCHODYNAMIC HYPOTHESES

Psychodynamic hypotheses are the most difficult to master without extensive reading and training; the following two questions may help you in deciding which hypothesis is the best fit:

1. Are the inner parts conscious or disowned?

   Hypothesis **P1** is the only one of the four psychodynamic hypotheses that deals exclusively with the conscious level of experience. If you hypothesize that inner parts are disowned (out of awareness), and possibly projected into someone else, hypothesis **P2** or **P4** should be integrated.

2. Which stage of object relations does this person's functioning reflect: narcissistic or more mature?

   P3 is the hypothesis to use when the person relates to others as if they are extensions of the self or for the functions they fill. When the person is at a more mature level of object relations, capable of taking the point of view of other people, hypothesis **P3** is not an appropriate match.

Table 10.2   Problem: *Excessive Alcohol Use*

The client is a 31-year-old woman who is struggling with her excessive use of alcohol. She recently started dating a man who gave up drinking and leads a healthy lifestyle. She is describing a weekend without alcohol.

Transcript from Session	Therapist's Hypothesizing
Client: It felt so nice, so much more fun and easier with a companion. I don't feel as lost. Like what was so hard about being alone and fighting this battle was that no one knew that I was fighting it. And if no one knew that I was fighting it, and no one knew that I had a battle in the first place, I was able to conceal it so well. I could just get smashed at my house and, you know, go to work the next day. If I could do both and no one knows, why should I want to struggle? Why can't I just get smashed and then go to work if there's really no consequences and no one questions and no one knows? Now he knows. And it's like . . . I don't feel alone in the struggle. . . . But then what also makes me nervous is what happens if we stop hanging out. Will I go back into my old pattern?	Social support seems to help her control her drinking. I should explore why she resists going to AA and getting support from that program (**SCE3**). That question, *If I could do both and no one knows, why should I want to struggle?* shows an interesting schema (**C2**). We could explore her cognitive map. Are there benefits and advantages to staying sober, even if others don't know about her struggle? She sounds like she has not developed a mature sense of self. She is not guided by internal abstract moral principles but rather by whether there is external punishment. She seems to need the connection with another person to shore up her sense of self (**P3**).
Later in the Session	
Client: Last week when I was visiting my mom, I would take a bunch of alcohol and there would be a significant amount gone in the bottle and she wouldn't say anything. I kinda thought, if I am not getting the attention for the alcohol, why am I drinking it? It almost made me think, there's no fun in this. I don't even get any bad attention. It is kind of like a little kid, you know. Like trying to do something bad, but you are not caught. So should I even be doing this?	She is revealing data for a behavioral analysis, showing that drinking has been reinforced by attention (**BL1**). I wonder what the rewards are for staying sober. This sounds like there are different voices inside (**P1**): I could explore the different "parts"—First speak to the part that thinks "I'm going to drink, no matter what," and then hear from this part, "There's no point in drinking so much, if there's no payoff."

The following two examples may provide further assistance in understanding the distinctions:

DONNA

Donna, a 62-year-old retired school teacher, has enrolled in art school and wants to develop her creativity. The therapist applies **P1** and uses inner parts work with the Neglected Creative Child and the Rigid Over-Controller parts of her personality. The Neglected Creative Child recalled early memories of playing with crayons while her mother beamed adoringly at her. The therapist applied **P3**, hypothesizing that the creative, grandiose part of the self needed the affirmation of her mother and was unable to sustain itself without that external support. This

Table 10.3   Problem: *Concerns over Living apart from Parents*

The client is a 25-year-old man who lives with his parents. His parents announced that they are moving to another state to enjoy their retirement.

Transcript from Session	The Therapist's Hypothesizing
Client: I was thinking that maybe it wouldn't be so hard to live on my own. I mean I know it's expensive but I spend money on dumb stuff sometimes because I know that I don't have to pay rent to my parents. I think I could afford to live on my own, I don't think it would be that bad, plus it's not like I couldn't ask my parents for some help if I needed to. I mean if I was stuck in a tight squeeze they wouldn't just turn their backs you know. . . .	I definitely hear ambivalence: He's trying to convince himself. There's definitely a part that wants to stay with his parents (**P1**).
	In prior sessions, the client revealed the schema *If I'm not with my parents, I'm all alone, without support.* Here are data that he has successfully modified that schema to *Living apart from my parents does not mean that they are not still there to provide support if I need it.* (**C2**).
	His anxiety might respond to desensitization through imagery (**BL2**). He also lacks "living alone" skills (**BL3**), a normal condition for someone leaving his parents' home for the first time.

Later in the Session

Therapist: What are your thoughts now about relocating with your parents instead of staying here?	The question is intended to gather data about the "don't want to leave them" part of the conflict (**P1**).
Client: I guess I still wonder if I should, but I honestly think that I might just be keeping that in the back of my head because I'm scared about what I'm going to do. (Short pause).	I don't respond but allow him to think about it, testing whether he will take the initiative to explore the issue without prompting. By not jumping in as a "parent figure" to guide him, I am allowing him to take responsibility and look to himself for resources (**ES2**).
It's not like I have a lot of time to figure this all out, I mean they plan on moving pretty soon (pause). I mean, even if I made lots of money, it still would take some time to find a place. I do know that I don't want to move with them because I know nothing will change, everything will be the same, just in a different area. (pause)	I would like to gather data about the time frame: Is it possible that the parents can delay their move another month to give him a more gradual, less stressful transition period (**CS2**)?
I'm 25 and still live with my parents (laughs). I mean I think that it's time for that to change and I think this kind of kicks me in the ass to do something different. I know I just need to take control over my life. Things have been too easy for me . . . well not easy, but convenient I guess. They have helped me out so much, I think that's why I have stayed with my parents for as long as I have, I mean they don't bug me. I actually like hanging out with them every so often.	The client is making a developmental transition, and seems motivated to move to the next stage (**CS3**).
	There is definitely a cultural rule operating (**SCE2**): "Single men should not keep living with their parents after a certain age." In some cultures, this would be perfectly acceptable.

hypothesis was supported by new data: with a cold and critical art teacher, Donna froze up, but with the warm, caring teacher, she felt free and spontaneous. The process goals for treatment were to strengthen the Creative part and get the Rigid Over-Controller to relax, and to help Donna to internalize the mirroring, affirming functions that she looked for in others.

JOHN

John, a 48-year-old divorced father of grown children, was the child in his family who was responsible for making his mother happy. He was attuned to her moods and did whatever he could to put a smile on her face. Whenever she was unhappy, he felt inadequate and covered those feelings with anger. Now, he is in therapy because his fiancée thinks he has "anger problems." He, however, thinks that she is too critical and "can't ever be pleased." He has been through a cognitive-behavioral anger management program and has learned methods for controlling anger, but that doesn't seem to help him with his fiancée. The anger episodes are more intense whenever they are feeling closer and sit down to set a date for their wedding. The therapist develops a formulation using two psychodynamic hypotheses. First, John is reenacting his early childhood experiences (**P2**), having selected someone like his mother. When his fiancée doesn't show appreciation for him, it reactivates the feelings of inadequacy and anger he had as a child. Second, his anger serves a defensive function (**P4**): It keeps him from painful feelings. He has achieved a compromise: He maintains a close connection with a loyal woman so he doesn't feel lonely, and at the same time, he maintains the safety of a wall around his core vulnerable self.

PART III

Steps to a Complete Case Formulation

The chapters in Part III take you through five components of a complete case formulation report: *problems, outcomes, presentation of data, explanatory essays, and treatment plans.* Each chapter presents in sequence the standards for a case formulation report (see Chart II.B in Appendix II) with explanations and illustrations. You will get the most out of this section if you go through it twice: first, to get an understanding of the method and standards; second, with a complete case formulation in hand so that you can practice evaluating whether the standards are met.

By learning the standards, you develop the skill to evaluate and correct your own formulations. Mistakes are to be expected. The goal is for you to be able to recognize your own mistakes, not for you to attain perfection on the first try.

Why go to the effort of writing formal paragraphs and crafting complex sentences? Why not just present the data as a list of facts? Once you have mastered the skills of case formulation, and are using this method for yourself as a tool for guiding effective therapy, then any shortcut you want to use is fine. However, during the learning process, the effortful thinking that goes into writing a coherent essay contributes immeasurably to the quality of the formulation. By writing a narrative of a person's life and the development of problems, the therapist must envision a unique, complex, three-dimensional person; you see gaps in the database, you develop empathy for the person, and you can place the person in a sociocultural and historical context. Writing an analytic essay for the assessment section forces you to *integrate* the hypotheses and justify that your choices really are a good match for a unique individual.

When you finish Chapter 15, you will be ready to use this method with clients.

Chapter 11

PROBLEM IDENTIFICATION AND DEFINITION

Skills of problem definition involve two separate processes: (1) *identifying problems* by gathering data, leading to a preliminary problem list, and (2) *defining problems* by conceptualizing and giving titles to the problems that will be treatment targets.

PROBLEM IDENTIFICATION

HOW I WAS FIRST INTRODUCED TO THE PROBLEM-ORIENTED METHOD

In the 2nd year of my clinical psychology doctoral program, I was a trainee at a Veterans Administration hospital in Los Angeles. I was expected to meet with each of my assigned patients in an individual session and "do therapy." I had absolutely no idea what to do. My supervisors were not helpful: They told me I was doing fine, shared anecdotes from their own cases, or gave me reading assignments. In desperation, I pleaded for help from George Saslow, head of the psychiatry residents' educational program. He agreed to meet with me individually and suggested that we start right away. He sat me down in front of a videotape of a patient. He handed me a blank index card and a pencil and told me to *Write down every problem you hear or see.* Problem? What's a problem? I wanted a complex, technical definition. I received no further guidance. Tentatively, I jotted thoughts on the index card: *No job. Stops taking medication after a few months. Talks in boring, monotonous voice. Lonely. Angry at mother. Poor grooming.* I read my list aloud with embarrassment. Such simple ideas. Could this be what he wanted? It was. I had just taken the first step of the problem-oriented method.

Sit down after the first session and write a list of every single problem you can think of, from both the client's content (*subjective data*) and your observations of the client's process during the session (*objective data*). Here are examples of problems that bring clients to therapy:

- Complaints of emotional suffering and dissatisfaction.
- Needs that are not being met.
- Dilemmas where a decision or choice is required.
- Unhappiness in their interpersonal relationships.
- Specific symptoms.
- Impaired functioning in important domains of life.
- Behavior that is creating problems for others.
- Painful life circumstances, which require endurance rather than action.

Problem identification takes time and often feels like trial and error. As the client begins to speak, you tentatively identify problems. As the story unfolds, you hear other problems, and you begin to notice some problems in her style of interaction. Your preliminary comprehensive list includes everything that strikes you as a problem:

> With the attitude of someone who is brainstorming, write down every possible problem.

- What are the complaints and problems from the client's point of view?
- If you were to talk to family members (or close friends, teachers, and work associates), what would they see as problems?
- If you were able to videotape the client from morning until night (without being seen), what problems might be observed?
- What problems are you aware of in your interaction with this client (rapport, social skills, impairments in mental status, or inappropriate responses)?
- Is there a crisis that needs to be addressed?
- Will the failure to address a specific problem result in the development of other problems?

There are problems that the client brings you: The client complains that he is not productive enough at work and is suffering because he is not organized enough and wastes too much time.

There are problems that the therapist discovers: The client blames problem on other people's lack of understanding but the therapist finds that the client has poor communication skills.

Some problems are overt and troublesome to others: The classic problem child in elementary school who is disruptive, acts out, and is reprimanded the most will draw attention to himself and elicit intervention.

Some problems are internal and easily overlooked by others: The quiet child who suffers from equally serious problems such as depression or anxiety may not get needed help because the problems are internal and the child does not disturb the class.

A common question is *Should you just accept the client's stated problems or do you go further and find other problems?*

All therapists know that they need to screen for child abuse, a client's inability to take care of basic needs, and risks of danger to self or others, even if the client doesn't bring those topics up directly. When it comes to issues apart from those mandatory topics, there are three positions that a therapist can take, illustrating a continuum from a narrow to a broad approach to problem identification:

1. *Narrow position:* The client is a consumer: Accept the request as presented. Don't create awareness of needs that the client hasn't mentioned. Don't offer additional services.
2. *Intermediate position:* Focus on the client's request, but if another problem becomes obvious, invite the client to consider adding a new goal.
3. *Comprehensive position:* Be concerned about the whole person, examine all aspects of functioning, and seek to identify problems in the context of the person's whole life. Identifying a problem does not mean that it will necessarily be accepted as a target of treatment.

The therapist's values inevitably enter the problem identification process. The following questions may help clarify your own position:

- Is it wrong to inform a client who seeks help for public speaking anxiety at work that his social isolation and lack of intimate friendships may be something worth examining? Is it wrong *not* to?
- Can you ignore the unmentioned problem if it is something like alcohol abuse? If the person is making choices that will hurt another human being?
- If a divorced woman with a young child is talking about her frustration in her career and her workaholic tendencies, should you address how well she cares for her child, whether she takes care of her own health, and why she lacks intimate friendships?

The approach of this book is that you should aim to be comprehensive and to create the broadest possible problem lists. It is better to start by being too inclusive than to miss something important or to deprive the client of unnoticed opportunities.

If you write down every single problem that you identify in your first few sessions with a client, a huge list often results. The quantity of problems on the preliminary list might make a therapist start to feel as hopeless as the client does. Remember that through the problem definition process, you are going to combine and condense that list until it becomes a manageable size.

The BASIC SID acronym that was explained in Chapter 2, Tables 2.4 and 2.5, is an invaluable tool for assuring that your preliminary list is comprehensive. Table 11.1 shows examples of problems in the eight categories.

Table 11.1   Using the BASIC SID for Problem Identification

Category	Examples of Problems
B Behavior What the person is doing and not doing; what others can observe; the quality of skills	Lack of empathy skills Avoidance of dating opportunities Excessive out-of-seat activity in classroom Inability to take care of basic needs Suicidal risk Aggressive behavior Disregard of rules on inpatient ward Poor medication compliance
A Affect Internal experience of feelings and the overt expression of feelings	Lack of awareness of own feelings Inability to express feelings to intimate others Depressed mood Excessive anxiety in public speaking situations Lacks motivation for getting help
S Sensation Awareness of the body; use of senses; sensory data with minimal filtering through cognition	Auditory hallucinations Painful muscular tension Inability to focus on sexual sensations Overly sensitive to noise when studying
I Imagery Mental imagery about past, present, or future; fantasies and dreams	Obsessive mental images Disturbing nightmares Distorted body image Flashbacks of past trauma
C Cognitive Constructed meaning; self-talk; beliefs and schemas; information-processing skills and other mental abilities	Poor problem-solving skills Obsessions about contamination Delusions of grandeur Confusion Tangential thinking Poor school performance
S Spiritual Spirit or soul; religion; religious as well as non-religious aspects of spirituality; creativity; moral issues; and the lack of spirituality	Excessive guilt over minor moral transgressions Lack of meaning and purpose in life Distress over lack of creativity Difficulty accessing feelings of inner peace Ambivalence over religious faith

Table 11.1   *(Continued)*

Category	Examples of Problems
I **Interpersonal** Relationships with others; family interaction patterns; membership in social groups, cultural factors, and issues of social injustice	Social isolation Inability to resolve conflicts in close relationships Socially unacceptable behavior Difficulties with intercultural adjustment Difficulty getting along with others Avoidance of sexual relationships Marital conflict Poor parenting skills Victim of discrimination
D **Drug and Biological** Physiology, biology, genetics, medical issues; use of legal and illegal drugs, including alcohol	Alcohol/substance abuse Organic brain syndrome Overweight and physically unfit Acute (or chronic) physical illness (specify) Physical defect or injury (specify) Erectile dysfunction

The best way to develop problem identification skills is to have real case material with which to work. If you are already seeing clients, you have the data from your first few interviews. You can also use yourself, a friend, or relative, or a classmate to provide the thorough database needed for developing an initial list of preliminary problems.

ACTIVITY 11.1 _____

Using the BASIC SID for a Preliminary Problem List

In Appendix III, you will read a case history of a woman named Maria and write problems in each BASIC SID category.

Lists of Impairments

The importance of identifying a specific type of problem called an *impairment,* rather than using diagnostic labels, is explained by Goodman, Brown, and Deitz (1992):

Impairment describes a worsening, lessening, weakening, damaging, or reduction in ability to function and, in turn, anticipates a potential for repair, improvement, enhancement, and strengthening . . . impairments are the reasons why a patient requires treatment. They are not the reason for the presence of the disorder, nor are they the disorder itself. Rather, they are observable, objectifiable manifestations that necessitate and justify care. (p. 31)

These authors point out that the diagnostic label is not sufficient for clinical decision making and that clinicians must ask themselves: *What is treatment needed for?*

Although lists of impairments can be useful (see Appendix II, Charts II.E and II.F), they have drawbacks. The names of impairments are not specific enough to meet the standards for good problem titles, which are explained later in this chapter. Labels for impairments fit groups of patients who are presumed to be homogeneous. Problem titles, however, are individualized to describe the target of therapy for a unique individual. In addition, impairments are problems that meet the requirements of insurance and managed care companies and are thus narrowly limited to those for which the current health care system is willing to pay.

Furthermore, therapists need to balance the psychiatric model's emphasis on pathology and remediation with concerns for competence, personal growth, self-fulfillment, and development of potential. Martin Seligman (2002) named his approach *positive psychology,* asserting that therapists need to help their clients build a large variety of strengths rather than just deliver specific damage healing techniques.

> A label from a list of impairments is not a substitute for developing unique, specific problem titles for each client.

Domains of Functioning

Therapists need to evaluate the client's functioning in the tasks of daily living. In a medical examination, a physician evaluates physiological functioning in 10 systems, including cardiovascular, pulmonary, and gastrointestinal. Similarly, psychotherapists must review all systems of a person's psychological and social functioning. Freud presented an easy list to remember: *love and work.* At a minimum, we need a third domain, *play,* to represent the areas of leisure and pleasure in a well-balanced life. Chart II.G in Appendix II gives an expanded list, including *health maintenance, home management, financial status, academic, employment, legal status, leisure and recreation, friendship, family, intimacy, parenting, communication, cultural competence, and life planning.* Examples on that chart are provided for both strengths (skills, resources, and assets)—which will provide ideas for outcome goals—and difficulties (problems, weaknesses, and deficiencies).

Emotional Intelligence

Emotional intelligence is a framework for describing the competencies a person needs to face challenges of daily life. The term *emotional* is misleading because the lists of competencies developed by both Goleman (1995) and BarOn (1997) embrace cognitive, behavioral, and interpersonal skills, as well. Chart II.H in Appendix II contains BarOn's list of 15 competencies, including *self-regard, assertiveness, empathy, reality testing, stress tolerance,* and *optimism* and will be useful both for problem identification and setting outcome goals. Examination of the definition for each competency will give you ideas for describing the client's problems as well as strengths.

Psychological Needs

Once the basic survival needs are met—food, shelter, clothing—all other needs are psychological. Chart II.I in Appendix II presents a list of 38 needs in six categories (*Basic Needs, Freedom, Pleasure and Personal Comfort, Social Needs, Occupational Needs, and Aesthetic and Spiritual Needs*), with examples of problems that would indicate frustration of each need. Abraham Maslow's well-known hierarchy of needs gave a model of an invariant prioritizing of needs: The needs lower on the pyramid needed to be satisfied before the person focused on a higher need. However, it is currently accepted that the saliency of needs differ across cultures and individuals. For instance, people differ in their need for affiliation versus achievement or solitude versus intimacy. One important reason for evaluating need fulfillment and frustration is that it can help you understand the source of a person's pain and the potential for finding different means of satisfying needs when a pathway to one specific goal has been blocked. Psychological autopsies on suicide victims often reveal the frustration of a highly salient need, such as the need to be loved, to be free, or to belong, combined with the hopelessness of ever getting that need satisfied.

PROBLEM DEFINITION

Problem definition is the most important part of the case formulation process. The way the problem is defined will determine the goals of therapy and shape the entire therapeutic journey. Different problem definitions based on the same data can lead to solutions that differ enormously.

When you define a problem, you write a title that describes the target of your future therapeutic efforts. A *problem title* is a *brief, specific phrase*—neither a full sentence nor, except in rare cases, a single word. It often begins with words such as *difficulty, lack of,* or *excessive,* or uses terms that we recognize as problem states such as *stress, depression, conflict,* or *anxiety.* To make the title specific, you add details without jumping to an explanation. You are staying focused on the reason for being in therapy, not yet moving to your conceptualization of the problem. Here are examples of appropriate problem titles: *Stress following geographic relocation and a new job* and *Depression accompanied by social withdrawal and impaired work performance.* Notice that the words *following* and *accompanying* are descriptive, not explanatory. Avoid using phrases that propose an explanation, such as *because of, due to,* and *stemming from.*

Problem definition is a creative and sometimes frustrating activity. At times, good titles for problems may jump to mind very early in the first interview. At other times, the therapist has collected a hodgepodge of seemingly unrelated problems that are later bundled together under a single title.

There are always multiple ways of defining a problem and there is no single right way to create the formal problem list. All items on the preliminary list of problems must be included under one or more titles.

The development of the formal problem list is a collaborative process between the therapist and the client. Agreement on the treatment targets is part of the therapeutic contract and includes an agreement between therapist and client about which goals are going to be pursued through therapy. The concept of *informed consent* means that the client is fully informed about the problem definition and has the right to veto the therapist's proposals.

Does the Client's Presenting Problem Always End Up as a Formal Problem on the Final Problem List?

The client's presenting problem should never be ignored. However, the problem title may undergo considerable change from how the client first worded it. You need to be aware that the first problem that the client presents is often not the real problem, but a secondary issue that is used as a "ticket of admission" while the client evaluates you, develops trust, and works up his courage. It is also possible that the client might change his perception of his problems during the first few sessions. Additionally, during the intake, the problem might be redefined. For instance, an initial problem *Frustration over husband's lack of interest in social activities* can become *Difficulty accepting unchangeable aspects of husband's personality* or *Difficulty engaging in social activities on her own*.

An important resource for building problem definition skills is *Change* by Watzlawick et al. (1974). These authors explain that poor problem definitions can prevent the achievement of satisfactory outcomes. Problems are frequently defined in ways that make them unsolvable. An example adapted from their book will demonstrate the importance of good problem definitions:

A PROBLEM DEFINITION STORY

A very high office building was constructed with four elevators. After the building was fully leased, complaints were brought to management from many tenants about how long they had to wait for elevators when they were in a hurry to leave the building at the end of the day. A team met to discuss the problem. One person defined the problem as "too few elevators for a building this size." The implied solution: put in more elevators. This of course is an extremely costly solution. Someone else defined the problem as "too many people leaving at the same time," and suggested that companies in the building change to flextime so that people in the building would end their workdays at different times. But the team realized that they had no control over their tenant companies and did not have the ability to implement this solution. The solution that was eventually implemented was cheap and easy: They put mirrors next to the elevators on each floor. What problem definition guided this plan? *Complaints about long waits.* Someone had the creativity to realize that it wasn't the long wait that was the problem; the problem was the *dissatisfaction* with the wait. When the mirrors were in place, the complaints stopped.

There is an important lesson here for problem definition:

> The pain that the client brings to therapy must be addressed; however, the client's problem definition cannot automatically be accepted.

Faulty Problem Definition

Clients often come to therapy because their problem definitions are deficient. Watzlawick and his coauthors explained that clients often bring in their *attempted solutions* as the problem to be solved. The client's form of problem definition has *not* worked, and he or she is "doing more of the same" rather than going back to the data and creating a new problem definition. One clue that the client has not successfully defined his problem is when he says, "I've tried everything." In this case, it is likely that he has tried *one* thing, and then done it over and over and over.

Sometimes, all the client needs is help in defining the problem. When a brief therapy encounter gives a client a good problem definition, he or she may no longer need the therapist because the resources for the solution are already available.

Table 11.2 illustrates faulty problem definitions. In each case, the problem title was really a proposed solution.

STANDARDS FOR PROBLEM DEFINITION

Skills for problem definition can be developed by studying seven standards.

> **Standard 1.** Problems are defined so that they are solvable targets of treatment.

Watzlawick and his associates (1974) made an important distinction between a *problem* and a *normal life difficulty*. With a problem, there is a discrepancy between how things are and how they should be. With a normal difficulty, there is no such discrepancy: Life has normal, expected ups and downs; problems exist; things change; bad things happen; and unpleasant emotions, such as anger, fear, sadness, grief, are part of normal living. "Life is difficult" were the opening words of one of the best-selling self-help books of all time (Peck, 2003). Watzlawick uses the term *utopian syndrome,* which I list as a separate hypothesis (**C1**) so that therapists can recognize when unrealistic expectations about "how life should be" are causing a faulty problem definition.

Therapists need to be open to the possibility that you may be facing a person for whom there will be no definable problem. All people who show up in the office of a psychotherapist are not in need of therapy. There is a tremendous bias in mental health settings to find mental health problems in people who show up at their doors. It is simply assumed that every person who makes an initial appointment is a client-to-be. This important point is illustrated by a supposedly true story at the psychiatric emergency room where I did an internship rotation.

Table 11.2   Examples of Faulty Problem Definition

COMPLAINT: MY STEREO IS BROKEN: NO SOUND HEARD FROM THE LEFT SPEAKER

Faulty problem definition: Broken left speaker.

Assessment: Need new speaker.

Solution: Get new left speaker.

When the new speaker is installed, there still is no sound coming from the left speaker.

Before jumping to a solution, the owner should have gathered more data by switching the speakers. Because the left side lacks sound with a different speaker, the defect must be in the receiver.

Appropriate problem definition: No sound from left speaker.

Assessment: Broken receiver.

Solution: Repair the receiver.

COMPLAINT: MY ROOM IS TOO HOT

Faulty problem definition: Not enough cold air.

Assessment: Need more cold air in room.

Solution: Open window to let in cold air.

This solution fails to resolve the problem. In fact, the room gets hotter because of the way the thermostat works. The cold air sends the message to turn up the furnace.

Appropriate problem definition: Room too hot.

Assessment: Thermostat set too high.

Solution: Keep the window closed and lower the thermostat.

COMPLAINT: MY TEENAGER IS DEFIANT AND REBELLIOUS

Faulty problem definition: Not enough parental control.

Assessment: Need more control and discipline.

Solution: Parents become more restrictive and punitive.

This solution results in intensified family conflict and hostility and increased misbehavior from the teenager. Instead of needing to become stricter, the parents need to cope better with normal adolescent phase-appropriate rebellion. This entails learning about adolescent development and developing parenting skills appropriate to their child's new developmental stage.

Appropriate problem definition: Distress over teenager's lack of compliance and cooperation.

Assessment: Normal teenage development; poor parenting skills.

Solution: Education and skills training for parents, along with family sessions to improve communication and cooperation.

When asked the classic opening question by the therapist, *What brings you here today?* a patient answered, *My feet are hurting.* The inappropriateness of this statement created the expectation of severely disturbed thought processes. The end of the story is that the patient had been directed to the wrong room and was looking for Podiatry instead of Psychiatry.

When I was going through my psychology doctoral program, I made an appointment with a well-known therapist, and spilled out a description of all my stress and misery. At the session's end, he gave me this formulation: My suffering was a normal, predictable consequence of my decision to be a graduate student in the field of clinical psychology. He helped me realize that my distress was a normal response to some of the difficulties associated with my educational goals, rather than a serious problem requiring psychotherapy. I left his office in a much better mood, stayed in the doctoral program, and saved a large sum of money.

What if the client wants to talk to an objective, skilled professional about normal life difficulties? The title must be worded appropriately, for instance, *Difficulty tolerating normal amount of conflict in marital relationship.* In some cases, the therapist must make clear that in her professional judgment, therapy is optional. Be aware that in some cases, putting the individual into the role of "psychotherapy patient" will create more problems than it solves (see hypothesis **SCE6, Social Role of Mental Patient**).

The wording of the title must be closely scrutinized to be sure that you are really defining a target of treatment, rather than a normal life difficulty. *Grief over death of beloved pet* is an example of distress that is not a problem, but rather a normal, inevitable, human reaction. Here are acceptable problem titles: *Prolonged and excessive grief over death of pet* or *Feels ashamed over normal reactions to death of pet.*

When you read your problem title, you should ask yourself, *Is there something that can be done about this? Is this something that a therapist would work to change? Can I imagine a realistic, attainable outcome?* If your answer is no, perhaps you have identified a life difficulty. Try rewording the title so that it truly expresses a target of treatment. Instead of *Irreversible memory impairment,* try *Difficulty coping with irreversible memory impairment.*

An extremely common faulty problem definition occurs when the desired solution is under someone else's control. If you define a problem in such a way that the client cannot solve it unless another person changes, you have failed to meet the criterion of *solvable.* So instead of *Overly controlling husband,* make it *Dissatisfaction with overly controlling husband* or *Difficulty asserting her freedom for fear of negative reactions from husband.*

The skill of defining problems involves asking yourself, *Is this a solvable problem? Could I specify a desired outcome?* Therefore, problem definition must be integrated with setting outcome goals, which is addressed in Chapter 12.

Consider beginning the title with phrases such as these:

- Difficulty coping with/accepting/achieving
- Frustration with/Distress over/Fear of
- Excessive
- Lack of
- Inability to/Avoidance of
- Impaired performance in
- Conflict between/Indecision about/Ambivalence over

Sometimes when there are many problems in the client's life the therapist recognizes that they form a circular loop. Problem A increases Problem B, which then increases Problem A. As an example, suppose that a client's initial problems are *Difficulty maintaining good grades* and *Dissatisfaction with relationship with roommate.* After gathering data and discovering patterns, you recognize that the cycle illustrated in Figure 11.1 is occurring.

Beahrs (1986) advises the therapist to find the "focal point," which is a small part of the client's issues which, when modified, will lead to additional changes in many other problem areas.

For the circular loop in Figure 11.1, a good target of treatment would be *Lack of assertiveness in coping with conflict* or *Difficulty managing anger and anxiety.* Resolving either of those problems should result in improved grades, relief from uncomfortable emotions, and possibly a better relationship with the roommate. It could even be that the best way to define the problem is *Poor choice of roommate.* The decision about which problem to focus treatment on will depend on the constraints of the clinical situation, the client's assets and values, and also the therapist's skills and training. In this case, you would focus first on a problem that could be resolved before finals week because the poor grades was the greatest concern.

To check the quality of your problem definition, you need to review it after you have completed writing your treatment plan. You need to ask yourself, *What problem is this plan intended to resolve?* What looks like an excellent title might not really be correct, if your treatment plan is not addressing it. When there is a discrepancy between problem titles and treatment plans, the first few sentences

Figure 11.1   Circular loop of problems.

in the plan will often reveal an *implicit* problem title. If this is a better title than what you originally wrote, you need to change the title. However, if the original problem title is appropriate, the plan needs to be rewritten.

> **Standard 2.** Titles refer to the client's current, real-world functioning.

There are two key points in this standard: (1) the problem is in the present, not the past, and (2) the problem is described in terms of functioning, not vague abstractions.

Often when the client tells a story of a very difficult life, you will be tempted to select experiences from the past and use them as problem titles. Here are faulty titles that reflect that error: *Abandoned by father* and *History of drug abuse.* These phrases do not belong in problem titles for the obvious reason that they can't be changed. They belong in the assessment—and you can use them for the "title of the explanation" explained under Standard 4.

When you recognize that your initial attempt at a problem title contains a problem from the past, ask this question: *How does this affect functioning now, in the present?*

- *Abandoned by father:* What is the problem today that this has caused?
  —*Difficulty trusting men* or *Selects romantic partners who refuse to make a commitment.*
- *History of drug abuse:* What is the problem today that this has caused?
  —*Blames all current difficulties on drug use as a teenager* or *Difficulty maintaining steady employment.*

> **Standard 3.** Titles are descriptive, designed for a specific client, and are justified by the data.

Titles must be descriptive and avoid jargon. The title needs to be clear and specific enough to maintain a focus as you proceed with the complete case formulation and write the treatment plan. If your problem title contains a vague abstraction, try to define it in terms of functioning that can be observed, measured, or evaluated.

Replace the faulty problem title *Unresolved issues with dependency* with titles like *Excessively demanding and clingy in close relationships with women friends; Difficulty moving out of parents' home and becoming self-supporting.*

It is not uncommon to use the term *Low self-esteem* as a problem title. That problem should be explored further to discover how it is manifested. The resulting answers would become the problem titles:

- *Self-doubt regarding ability to succeed in graduate school.*
- *Lack of confidence in public speaking situations.*
- *Selects friends and romantic partners who ignore her needs.*

Sometimes clients bring the presenting problem, "I have low self-esteem," describing a painful subjective experience. *Distress over experience of low self-esteem* would then be an appropriate title.

If you rely on lists of impairments in treatment planning manuals, you will get into the habit of writing problem titles that are appropriate for groups of people but not individualized to fit a specific person:

- *Relationship problems:* Compare that broad, vague title to specific titles such as *Excessive conflict with roommates; Difficulty maintaining an intimate relationship; Difficulty making new friends following geographic relocation.*
- *Chronic pain:* The title could be expanded to convey more information, for example, *Chronic pain from arthritis preventing involvement in physically active hobbies; Chronic pain combined with depression and social withdrawal.*

The following example shows a continuum in problem titles from very broad and general to more specific and detailed:

- *Marital problems, Poor marital communication, Difficulties resolving disagreements without verbal abuse.*

> **Standard 4.** Problem titles do not contain theoretical, explanatory concepts.

In defining problems, it is essential to remember the distinction between data and formulation. Problem titles and outcome goals must be free of formulation ideas. The problem title, based on data about the client's current situation, must be acceptable to therapists of all theoretical orientations. Here are examples of faulty problem titles, which inappropriately reveal the therapist's preferred clinical hypothesis.

Behavioral
- *Faulty:* Binge eating as a maladaptive response to feelings of anger and frustration.
- *Corrected:* Binge eating associated with feelings of anger and frustration.

Psychodynamic
- *Faulty:* Fragmentation of the self under stress.
- *Corrected:* Confusion and intense anxiety when experiencing relatively mild stress.

Family Systems
- *Faulty:* Overly enmeshed family.
- *Corrected:* Lacks clear sense of own needs and feelings.

Humanistic-Existential

- *Faulty:* Living an inauthentic existence.
- *Corrected:* Ignores own feelings and values and turns to external sources of authority when making major decisions.

The explanatory titles that are incorrect for the problem title provide good topic sentences for the assessment discussion (see Standard 25), and therefore can be considered "titles for the explanation."

TITLE OF PROBLEM

The problem title (found at the top of the SOAP) indicates the target of your treatment efforts. Successful outcome is defined in terms of resolving this.

TITLE OF EXPLANATION (ASSESSMENT IDEA)

The explanation title (found in the assessment section of the SOAP) is a brief label for your own conceptualization, which could refer to an explanation of causes or a justification for the treatment plan you would recommend. Examples include *unresolved anger toward father, lack of insight into defense mechanisms, negative self-talk,* and *too enmeshed with mother.*

When you realize that the problem title you wrote is really the title for your explanation, you should move it to the assessment section, and come up with a new problem title. You need to ask yourself questions such as: *What is the problem that is explained by this hypothesis? What problem would be solved by resolving this issue?* For instance, "unresolved anger toward father" could explain the following problems:

- *Difficulty controlling temper when criticized.*
- *Reacts defensively to wife's opinions and suggestion.*
- *Inappropriate reactions to authority figures at work.*
- *Difficulty controlling temper in presence of father.*

Often a specific title could function either as a problem title or as an explanation title. For instance, in some cases "lack of assertive skills" might best be considered the explanation for problems such as *Frustration with lack of advancement at work* or *Difficulty asserting her needs with her husband.* However, in another case, the client could have come in complaining of lack of assertiveness and specifying situations where assertiveness is needed; in that case, "lack of assertive skills" serves very well as a problem title.

In the sentences after the problem title that provide a few details, be sure not to add your formulation ideas, as was done in this example: *Difficulty moving out of family home and setting up own residence:* She is unable to separate her needs from the needs of her mother. Here is what the therapist should have written: "She is clear about her desire to move out but feels guilty over leaving her mother." Here is a tip that bears repeating:

> Imagine a line between the O and A sections of the SOAP, and remind yourself that formulation ideas should not appear in any section prior to that line.

ACTIVITY 11.2

Is It a Problem Title or an Assessment Idea?

This activity in Appendix III is a self-test to check your understanding of the distinction between problem titles and explanation titles.

> **Standard 5.** The therapist is not imposing cultural or personal values in problem definitions.

Values and biases inevitably enter into the problem titles and therefore it is essential to be aware of them. Ideas of "unhealthy," "dysfunctional," "maladaptive," and "abnormal" imply values that could be universal, cultural, or personal. A title may reflect universal values, especially when the client harms other people, but is never value free. Because the definition of the problem guides the kind of influence that therapy will have on the client, it is essential that you guard against inappropriately making decisions in the realm of private, personal values. This standard requires high levels of personal awareness, tolerance for other value systems, and vigilance for subtle ways in which you can interfere with the independence of your clients.

Nowadays, all therapists in training are fortunately being encouraged to develop *cultural competence.* As part of increased emphasis on *cultural diversity* and *cultural sensitivity,* students are taught to understand the client's culture and to design treatment plans that take cultural values into account. This poses an interesting challenge at the problem identification stage. Do you just accept the values of the client's culture and agree immediately to help the person conform? Or do you identify the values involved and help the client explore them, deal with internal conflict and external conflict with parents, and make mature choices about the value system he or she wants to create, as an adult? (I am aware that my own biases and values are evident in the way I worded that choice.)

Cultures place different emphasis on the relative importance of the family and the individual and have contrasting value systems—individualistic versus collectivistic or communal. Especially when working with young adults, you need to be aware of how the client's developmental stage of "leaving home" is enormously influenced by the culture's views on independence, individuality, community, the correct ways of showing respect for parents and grandparents, and so on.

The question of whose needs are more important, the individual's or the family's, comes to life when a client bring problems related to choice of career, spouse, or sexual orientation. *Should I pursue the career that I love or work in the family business like my parents expect me to? My parents expect me to marry within my culture (which could be Jewish, Catholic, Armenian, or Pakistani) but I'm in love with someone from a different culture. I'm gay and have come out to all my friends and coworkers, but I can't tell my parents because they will disown me.* It could be very easy to slip into using a problem title that shows some kind of bias. Just as I might be tempted to write, *Difficulty choosing own life path and tolerating disapproval of parents,* someone else might argue that the title should be, *Difficulty making choices that serve the needs of the family and honor the authority of parents.*

Fortunately, the structure of the problem-oriented method (POM) provides a solution to this dilemma. The problem title must be worded in a way that does not impose a solution. The following titles capture the nature of the problem, while allowing for outcomes that can place either the individual or the family first:

- *Ambivalence over whether to choose a spouse without parents' approval.*
- *Indecision over whether to work in family business.*
- *Distress over parents' refusal to accept sexual orientation.*

In the assessment (A) section, you must discuss the hypothesis **SCE2,** Cultural Context, in your analysis of the client's problem.

> Become aware of your own values and avoid arbitrarily imposing them on the client.

The subtle ways that therapists impose values is especially evident when a married client seeks help to decide whether to get divorced. When I was a divorced woman in my 30s, I assumed that the problem title was *Difficulty deciding whether to get a divorce* and that the client needed individual therapy without the pressure of the spouse's presence. Now that I am a married woman in my 50s, I am much more likely to define the problem as *Painful marital interactions and unmet needs in marital relationship* and recommend conjoint couple's therapy so that the couple can try to resolve these problems together, before either spouse decides to terminate the relationship.

Therapists must be very cautious about defining problems in a way that imposes the values of the culture's majority. For instance, *Difficulty establishing marital commitment* or *Lack of readiness for parent role* are titles that imply that one *should* get married and be a parent. If the client holds those values, the problem titles are appropriate. But if, without further exploration, the therapist assumes that without marriage and children the client cannot have a satisfying life, the therapist is inappropriately limiting the client's freedom of choice.

Even when it seems that the client is clear about his values, I think that you should ask metamodel questions (see Chapter 2, Table 2.7) to see if the client has internalized, without conscious examination, the culture's messages. Some people argue that "cultural sensitivity" means accepting the client's values without question; however, a nonjudgmental exploration of the value will not shake a deeply entrenched value and will give "equal opportunity" to members of minority cultures to exercise freedom of choice (**ES2**). You can explore whether the client's other parts or subpersonalities (**P1**) disagree with the stated values. These techniques of exploration are essential when the client uses the word *should* instead of *I want to* in describing goals. One good way to make values explicit is to use this questioning strategy:

> After you think you have appropriately identified a problem, try challenging it with these two questions: So what? Why is that a problem?

Although a questioning strategy is part of the problem definition process, it is also a useful intervention. You don't buy into the client's belief that something is bad, deviant, deficient, and objectionable. Instead, you offer the client the possibility that everything is perfectly all right exactly the way it is. The client has to convince you that it is a problem, referring to goals, a description of impairment in functioning, or actual real-world negative consequences. For instance, if a college student's problem is poor grades in chemistry, it may indeed be a problem if his ambition is to go to a medical school but it may not be a problem if he is just in college to humor his parents and intends to be an artist.

> One of my earliest clients during my training was a man in his mid-40s who had moved to Los Angeles from the East Coast and was receiving financial support from his parents who were urging him to come back and live with them. The obvious problem title was *Difficulty establishing himself as an independent, self-supporting man,* with many subproblems, such as *Inability to maintain gainful employment* and *Excessive, age-inappropriate dependence on parents.* I had formulated the problem in existential terms (**ES2**, *Difficulty accepting responsibility for his own life*) and as a skills deficit (**BL3**), requiring a strategy of small steps toward competence. However, he refused to take the smallest step, while continuing to express shame and embarrassment about his situation. In frustration, I was beginning to label him a "resistant client" when my supervisor suggested that I play the devil's advocate and ask questions such as *Why is it a problem to accept money from your parents? Why is it important to have a job if your parents are willing to support you? What are the benefits of living here and struggling to succeed on your own when you have the opportunity to be taken care of in your parents' home?* Truthfully, I thought that by asking these questions I was

using a paradoxical technique and that he would start working harder toward the goal of financial independence. Instead, his eyes opened wide as if he'd just opened the best birthday present of his life. He terminated therapy and moved back east. In retrospect, I can see that the problem title for him was *Difficulty choosing a lifestyle that is negatively judged by the dominant cultural group.*

In his book *Solitude,* Anthony Storr (1989) notes a huge bias among most psychotherapists, claiming that they seem to believe "that health and happiness entirely depend upon the maintenance of intimate personal relationships . . . [and that] love is being idealized as the only path to salvation" (p. 8). We, as therapists, need to question whether we assume that if someone has no intimate attachments, there is something wrong with him or her, even if he or she enjoys solitude and finds deep satisfaction in work, creative activity, and hobbies.

By comparing different problem definitions for the same client, you will see the important role that values play.

CASE I: TWENTY-EIGHT-YEAR-OLD GRADUATE STUDENT

The client has been in an exclusive, sexual relationship for 3 years. The partner wants to get married, preferably in the next year. The client avoids these discussions and feels anxious and confused:

- **Problem:** *Difficulty moving committed relationship to the next level.*
- **Outcome goal:** The client will be comfortable moving the relationship to the engagement stage and ultimately to marriage, feeling satisfied about the choice of mate.
- **Problem:** *Ambivalence over relationship with partner who is pushing for engagement.*
- **Outcome goal:** The client will reach a decision over whether to move the relationship to the engagement stage, resolving conflict about this person as a life mate, and determining readiness for marriage without succumbing to external pressures.

It is my hunch that problem definitions for this particular vignette will vary based on the therapist's marital status, gender, and age. Furthermore, reactions to the vignette might differ if the client's gender, culture, or sexual orientation were varied. When the problem definition pertains to decisions about marriage and commitment, values and biases such as the following will exercise an enormous influence:

- A woman should put marriage ahead of her career. A man should take care of his career goals before getting married.
- Use your head in choosing a mate. Passion fades and you want someone who has good character traits and shares your interests.
- Follow your heart: If it doesn't feel right, don't do it.
- You unconsciously select a partner who offers the perfect opportunity to work out unresolved issues with your parents; therefore, even if it feels terrible, it is probably good for your personal growth.

CASE II: TWENTY-FIVE-YEAR-OLD WOMAN, LIVING WITH WIDOWED MOTHER

The client feels depressed, trapped, and hopeless. She is bitter over her mother's emotional neglect when she was a child. She only completed 1 year of college and works at a low-paying clerical job without any opportunities for advancement. She has no close friends, complaining that her high school friends are either married or have moved away to pursue careers. She feels obligated to provide companionship and financial support to her mother. One student defined the problem in this way:

- **Problem:** *Difficulty leaving mother's home, establishing her own residence, and pursuing a satisfying career.*
- **Outcome goal:** The client will be comfortable moving out on her own, perhaps finding a congenial roommate, and will discover her own interests to pursue a career that gives her satisfaction.

A second student used this definition:

- **Problem:** *Distressing relationship with mother.*
- **Outcome goal:** The client will reach her own decision about her relationship with her mother, including living arrangements, style of communicating, and how best to balance her sense of obligation with her own needs.

This second student then defined two additional problems:

1. **Problem 2:** *Lack of satisfying career.*
2. **Problem 3:** *Lack of close friendships.*

Abstract values that enter into problem definition for that case include:

- You should (should not) feel responsible for the happiness of your parent.
- You should put your own (other people's) needs first.
- Unmarried young adults should (should not) live on their own, apart from their family of origin.

Problem definition *must* reflect society's values when the client is at risk of causing harm to self or others, including the harm of being incarcerated, losing custody of children, or becoming homeless (e.g., *Perpetrator of child [spousal, elder] abuse, Vandalism leading to incarceration in youth facility, Inability to sustain gainful employment*).

A special challenge for therapists occurs when the client is not seeing you on a voluntary basis but rather is attending sessions of mandated therapy to meet the legal system's requirements. The system has defined a problem such as *Perpetrator of child abuse, User of illegal drugs,* or *Antisocial behavior.* In these situations, the *reluctant client,* as he is known, might benefit from therapy if the therapist can help define additional problems that fit his values and needs. For instance, the perpetrator of child abuse might want to find solutions for *Frustration over inability to get compliance and cooperation from child;* the person who is abusing illegal substances might agree that she wants help in reducing *Painful emotions of worthlessness and abandonment;* and the juvenile who is incarcerated in a youth facility might want to overcome *Lack of job skills necessary for earning money and leaving gang-ridden neighborhood.*

Standard 6. Lumping and splitting decisions are justified in that they lead to good treatment planning.

After the first session, you start writing down your preliminary list of problems—and this list can easily contain over 20 problems. What do you do with them? How can you possibly formulate a case with so many problems? You are faced with the task of organizing these preliminary problems in a coherent way; you are ready for the tasks of *lumping and splitting.*

Lumping: Combining Separate Problems into a Single Problem

Suppose your preliminary problem list contains *cries excessively, poor concentration, feels worthless, social withdrawal, poor appetite, very slow speech* and *slumped posture.* Looking at that list, you would recognize the signs and symptoms of a depressive syndrome, and you would be justified in lumping these problems under the title *Depression.*

Splitting: Dividing One Problem into Separate Problems

You recognized "social withdrawal" as a sign of depression and lumped it accordingly. As you learn more about the client, you realize that social withdrawal is a separate problem: The client stated she has always had trouble making friends. When the client's depression is resolved, this social difficulty would still be a problem. Another reason for splitting is that if you target "social withdrawal" as a separate problem, you are choosing a good focal point that will result in less depression.

The theoretical orientation in which you have received the most training will influence your leanings toward lumping or splitting. The skills of behavioral analysis teach clinicians to be very specific and concrete, leading to splitting. The use of personality theories, such as those of Freud, Jung, and Rogers, which use abstract constructs such as *character, individuation,* or *the self,* encourages lumping.

Furthermore, decisions to lump or split will depend on individual differences in the therapist's *cognitive style* (see hypothesis **C3**). Some of us think in global, abstract terms and are always looking for the big picture. Others of us just naturally break things down into components and like to deal with a piece at a time.

Although the decision to lump or split is usually at the clinician's discretion (see Table 11.3), *there are certain times when splitting is mandatory.* When a problem must be monitored for legal reasons and for the protection of people from harm, it must be split off from a larger problem, and you would use the hypothesis **CS1, Emergency.** For instance, an inappropriate example of lumping is a problem defined as *Depression with suicidal risk.* You must split suicide risk from depression so that you can monitor suicidality and intervene appropriately. It is possible that as the depression becomes less immobilizing, suicide risk will increase.

Table 11.3   Guidelines for Lumping and Splitting

When to Split	If a problem is associated with dangerous behavior or other reasons for urgent action (e.g., split *suicide risk* from *Depression*)
	If you are going to recommend treatments conducted by different people, using different modalities, or occurring in different places in the community (e.g., split *Poor money management skills* from *Difficulty coping with death of spouse*)
	If you want to demonstrate to others (e.g., because of legal issues or supervision) that you are monitoring a specific aspect of a problem
When to Lump	If you think the signs and symptoms covary—that is, if the frequency of one symptom increases, they all increase (e.g., poor concentration, low self-worth, and sadness are lumped as *Depression*)
	If you see different problems as stemming from a common cause (e.g., poor emotional regulation causes both *Inability to maintain a job* and *Inappropriate abusive outbursts with friends*)
	If you make the same treatment plans for several problems (e.g., communication skills training is the plan for *Marital conflict* and *Distress over failure to get promotion*)

Here is an example of two approaches to problem definition with the same client.

A client who is employed in the family business is extremely unhappy at work, but says he is obligated to stay there because his father counts on him. Whenever he talks about pursuing a career in graphic arts, his mother scolds him and accuses him of being a bad son.

One student used a single problem title:

- *Dilemma of pursuing own career interests versus yielding to parental demands.*

Another student defined three separate problems:

- *Conflict and indecision over future career goals.*
- *Dissatisfaction with current employment.*
- *Confusion over immediate relationship with parents.*

Sometimes when you lump problems together, you create a single problem title. Other times, you want to keep the original titles for *subproblems*. When you create a broader title that encompasses several subproblems, you can call it the *umbrella title*. With this approach, you only need to write one SOAP; however, you need to develop outcome goals for each of the subproblems. Table 11.4 provides examples of appropriate use of umbrella titles.

The process of lumping and splitting is the most creative part of problem definition. The "how to" of creating the problem list is learned through practice with case studies and clinical experience. You cannot learn it from reading; you need to experience a learning process that sometimes feels like trial and error. There is no "right" way of defining problems. A teacher cannot look at the problem list and evaluate it without reading the whole report. Often, only after you begin to implement some of your treatment plans do you begin to see new and better ways to lump and split your original problems.

Table 11.4   Examples of Umbrella Titles with Subproblems

Umbrella Title: *Difficulty initiating and maintaining social interactions*

Subproblem titles:

1. *Anxiety and shyness with strangers and in new social situations*
2. *Poor conversational skills*
3. *Avoids social gatherings*

Umbrella Title: *Difficulty dealing with the breakup of an intimate relationship*

Subproblem titles:

1. *Difficulty expressing anger about breakup*
2. *Difficulty engaging in dating*

Umbrella Title: *Difficulty setting limits for the treatment she will accept for herself in abusive relationships*

Subproblem titles:

1. *Difficulty setting limits for the treatment she will accept for herself at work.* (This was a temporary problem that was actually resolved between the second and third sessions when the client quit her job.)
2. *Difficulty setting limits for the treatment that she will accept for herself from her husband.* (This is the long-standing problem that will be the focus of treatment.)

You need to review the entire database to evaluate the final problem list. What matters most is whether the problem definition leads to successful therapeutic outcome. A benefit of discussing cases in groups is that the exchange of different ideas about the same client can improve decisions about problem definition by forcing you to explain your lumping and splitting decisions.

THE CREATIVE PROCESS OF PROBLEM DEFINITION

A trainee started with a preliminary problem list and then crafted these three problem titles:

Problem 1: *Frustration over lack of advancement at work.*

Problem 2: *Inhibited and shy in social situations.*

Problem 3: *Lack of social support.*

After SOAPing each problem separately, she found herself writing in all three assessment sections that the problem seemed to stem from a lack of assertiveness. In writing the plans, she stated that she would help the client build assertive skills. She then decided that a good umbrella title that would link the three separate problems was *Lack of assertive skills.* She kept the three original titles as subproblems. The outcome goals were worded to make clear that the problem would be resolved when:

1. The client asserted herself at work in ways that would contribute to favorable recommendations for promotion.
2. The client initiated contacts at social gatherings.
3. The client asserted herself with friends to elicit needed support.

One of the drawbacks of using diagnostic labels from *DSM-IV-TR* is that they force you to lump in a way that is not always effective for treatment planning. Once you have arrived at a diagnosis, the needs of your client are often best served if you go back to the items on the list of criteria that led you to choose the diagnosis. You cannot treat the abstraction called *Borderline Personality,* but you can treat the problems and impairments that led you to use that label.

Supposing that you decided that your client fit into the diagnostic category called Borderline Personality. I would immediately refer you to Marsha Linehan's (1993b) *Skills Training Manual for Treating Borderline Personality Disorders* so that you could see how to split this problem into titles that would lead to effective treatment planning. Table 11.5 shows examples of problem categories that serve as good umbrella titles, with specific subproblems listed for each category.

Table 11.5   Problem Definition for Borderline Personality Disorder

Dysregulation and Lability of Emotions

- Reactive emotional responses
- Problems with anger and anger expression
- Episodic depression, anxiety, and irritability
- Difficulty maintaining attitude of detachment

Interpersonal Dysregulation

- Relationships are chaotic, intense, and marked with difficulties
- Extreme difficulty letting go of relationships
- Engages in intense and frantic efforts to keep significant others from leaving
- Lack of stable, positive relationships

Behavioral Dysregulation

- Extreme and problematic impulsive behaviors
- Attempts to injure or mutilate self
- Suicide attempts
- Maladaptive problem-solving behaviors

Dysregulation of the Sense of Self

- No "sense of self"
- Feeling empty
- Self-hate and sense of shame

Brief, Cognitive Disturbances Triggered by Stress

- Depersonalization
- Dissociation
- Delusions

ACTIVITY 11.3 _____

Problem Definition from Your Preliminary List

This activity in Appendix III asks you to take the preliminary problem list that you created for Activity 11.1 and practice lumping and splitting until you arrive at a final problem list of 3 to 6 problem titles. If you are a "lumper," you might find it hard to get more than two problems, and if you are a "splitter," the limit of six problems will be difficult.

Standard 7. The problem list is complete and comprehensive.

To assure that the problem list is complete, you need to gather a thorough and comprehensive database. Once you have a database, the best way to evaluate the completeness of the list is through supervision, consultation, and group discussions of the clinical case.

The omission of problems is a much more serious error than the inclusion of too many problems. Often the therapist and client define a single problem and appear to have blinders to many other problems that would be obvious to an outside consultant. One frequent example of this type of narrow focus is with clients who come to therapy because of substance abuse.

A trainee was working with a client who came to therapy because of her excessive drinking (see Table 10.2). The client did not want to set abstinence as a goal, but rather wanted to achieve the goal of moderate drinking. Sessions were dominated by talk about alcohol. The therapist created a case formulation report with *Excessive alcohol use* as the only problem. She brought a tape recording of a session with this client to a supervision group. After listening to a brief segment, the other trainees defined the following additional problems:

* *Shyness and lack of confidence in social situations.*
* *Lack of close friendships.*
* *Unsuccessful in developing intimate romantic relationship with available partner.*
* *Stress from recent geographic relocation and new job.*
* *Unwillingness to consider abstinence as a goal.*

The number of problems on the list must be appropriate to the client's resources and motivation. Not every single imaginable problem will be included: The client may have problems that could be targets for therapy, but which will not be addressed at the present time.

Chapter 12 ————————————————————

SETTING OUTCOME GOALS

An outcome goal describes how the client will be functioning at the end of therapy as a demonstration that the problem has been resolved. Specifying outcome goals is mandatory if you work with managed care companies. For them, the term *outcome goals* refers to "specific goals that the patient must achieve to attain, maintain, and/or reestablish emotional and/or physical health as well as maximum growth and adaptive capabilities" (Goodman et al., 1992, p. 96). The determination of suitable, realistic, attainable goals is an important process between client and therapist. Agreement on goals is an important step in creating the therapeutic contract and assuring adherence to the ethical principle of "informed consent."

Outcome goals need to be specific enough to guide planning and to provide criteria for the termination of therapy. They are essential for evaluating the effectiveness of therapy; without outcome goals, there is no way to hold a therapist accountable for the quality of service. By stating the outcome goal, the therapist knows when to terminate treatment and can evaluate whether progress is occurring. The therapist can estimate the appropriate duration of treatment by calculating the length of time needed to achieve all of the goals.

To create good outcome goals you need cognitive flexibility to move among many levels of abstraction (see Table 2.8 for examples of how to explore cognitive classification systems). Abstract goals need to be made concrete so that success can be recognized. For instance, the goal "satisfying career" could be made much more specific: "a career that allows me to provide service to people, while providing financial security, without interfering with my time with family and leisure activities." At other times, concrete goals need to be made more abstract, as when the client's chosen goal—"to marry a specific woman or gain admission into a specific medical school"—has proved unattainable.

When setting future goals, the therapist's values and cultural beliefs are more influential than perhaps in any other area. As soon as we specify a goal, we are expressing what we believe is desirable, possible, and often necessary for the client's well-being. In clinical work, the nature of the goal conveys a belief about health and pathology. An example of biased goals comes from Freud's analysis of a client he called Dora (S. Freud, 1996). Freud was upset that this young woman terminated therapy prematurely and he berated himself for not having recognized her negative transference in time to prevent her termination. However, feminists who analyzed this case from the perspective of the late twentieth century applaud Dora's decision to leave therapy because they see Freud's goals as serving the dominant men in Dora's life rather than the client's needs. In Freud's era, the desirable goal for a female was to accept the social role of wife and mother, renounce educational and career aspirations, avoid expression of anger, suppress any needs for power, and be submissive and obedient to a husband or father. Therapists need to avoid becoming agents of social conformity in their goal setting and recognize their own biases.

In setting outcome goals:

- Be sure to examine the values related to a stated goal and question whose value system is operating.
- Question whether the client is accepting others' definitions for happiness.
- Recognize when you are imposing your own values.

In discussions of values, here is a question that students usually raise: *What if the client defines a problem and sets a goal for therapy that conflict with my values?*

Therapists do not have to accept all clients who knock on their doors. The problem definition and goal-setting process is a two-way endeavor: Both parties have to agree to the contract. It is essential to make it clear to the client before the first session that you are not "starting therapy" but rather "are going to offer recommendations after an assessment phase," and at that point, your recommendation could be a referral to another therapist.

Here are examples of goals that may conflict with a therapist's values:

- **Problem:** *Stress over extramarital affair.*
- **Goal:** Wants to conduct the affair with less anxiety and deceive spouse more successfully.

- **Problem:** *Frustration over not fulfilling creative potential.*
- **Goal:** Wants to leave children and husband and move to the Left Bank of Paris and pursue a career as an artist.

- **Problem:** *Disappointment over lack of career advancement.*
- **Goal:** Wants to achieve promotion by engaging in fraudulent practices that involve jeopardizing the savings of elderly people.

The therapist needs to discuss with the client the meaning and consequences of the proposed goal. *What are the implications of choosing this goal? Will this cause harm to other people? Is this consistent with your moral code?* The therapist might suggest a problem title worded as *Moral dilemma* and help the client sort out the advantages and disadvantages of different choices. If the client is adamant about wanting to pursue goals that the therapist cannot morally endorse, he or she will need to take steps to terminate the relationship, assuring that ethical duties are met in providing a referral.

BENEFITS OF CLEARLY DEFINED FUTURE GOALS

There are many benefits of having a clearly defined goal, in addition to providing the focus of treatment efforts and the criterion by which to evaluate success.

Instillation of Hope

Think of the contrast between a conversation that focuses on problems (*What's wrong? What's bad in your life? What's causing you pain?*) to one that focuses on future goals (*What do you want? How should things be?*) When the therapist makes the shift from problems to outcomes, he or she conveys that change is possible and that goals will be achieved. This instillation of hope—often discussed as nonspecific factors or placebo effects—is a factor that contributes to positive therapy outcome.

Language of Change

Perhaps this is a different way of describing the previous advantage. Beliefs such as "change is possible" and "I can change" are precursors of successful therapy. Therapists can use language to plant positive suggestions. For instance, questions such as *Imagine what it would be like . . .* can plant the presupposition that change will occur or continue. Clients who are at a precontemplation or contemplation stage shift to the stage of preparation for change once goals are set.

Visualization of a Different Future Makes It Possible

It can be enormously beneficial to help a client draw a mental picture of his or her desired future. Arnold Lazarus (1981) offered the opinion that if people cannot picture themselves performing an act in imagery, they will probably not be able to do it in real life.

Responsibility for Change

Once the client states what he or she wants (the desired future outcome), the therapist has leverage to challenge the client with this question: *Is what you are doing getting you what you want?* This approach is a key element of William Glasser's (1965) reality therapy. Therapists who work with reluctant clients, such as court-referred offenders or adolescents, know to "hook" them into collaborating in therapy by making them identify something they *personally* want. Using an acronym commonly used in business settings, they are aware that to motivate people to change, you need them to ask and answer the question *What's in it for me?* (WIFM).

Goal-Setting Skills

Covey (1994) explains in his book *The 7 Habits of Highly Effective People* that the most important habit is *begin with the end in mind.* People who are successful in life are those who set goals for the future and work toward them: They understand their values and dreams and have a vision of where they want to be in 1 year, 5 years, and 10 years. Effectiveness in setting goals and making plans to implement them can be modeled through good goal setting and treatment planning in therapy.

Psychotherapy Outcome Research

In addition to its benefits to the client and to the management of a specific case, the setting of clear outcome goals is a necessary part of research on the effectiveness of psychotherapy ("outcome research"). If therapists want to empirically test the validity of their treatments, they need to demonstrate the achievement of a clearly specified and measured positive outcome.

HELPING CLIENTS DEFINE "SMART OUTCOMES"

Goal setting usually begins with a focus on the content of the client's presenting problems followed by exploration of how the future would be different when the problem is resolved. However, it is not necessary to begin with a problem focus. Many therapists encourage "solution-focused" approaches, or put an emphasis on "positive psychology" instead of pathology. It can be extremely productive to begin with a focus on the desired future. When the client enters therapy in a demoralized state, the setting of positive, achievable goals can have a profound impact on mood and functioning.

An important data-gathering activity is helping the client to define future goals that are clear, realistic, attainable, and consistent with values, and which do not create further difficulties. Whereas clients usually pour forth their problems without difficulty, they often need prodding, and a good deal of creativity on the clinician's part, to put into words their desired future. Usually the desired outcome will be stated as an abstract noun that is vague and ill defined such as *job satisfaction, security, a comfortable home.* It is all too easy for therapists to hear these terms and assume that we understand what the client means. Part of data gathering is to help the client clarify the meaning of abstract nouns, answering questions like *What specifically does that mean to you?* and *How specifically would we know that you had achieved that goal?* The use of the metamodel skills in Table 2.7 is essential for getting concrete, specific goals. To distinguish between the outcome goal that is a part of the formal case formulation, and the category of data comprising the client's stated wishes and desires, the term *outcome statement* will be used.

> An outcome statement is the client's exact wording of the desired future and answers questions such as *How will things be when the problem is solved?*

Egan (2002) describes three levels of goals in decreasing order of abstractness:

1. *Good Intention:* A vague statement of a desired change: "Clean up my act"; "be more assertive"; "do something about the way we communicate."

2. *General Aim:* The goal becomes specific enough to drive action. You move from vagueness to a more concrete definition of the desired future: "Do something about the way we always argue about unimportant things"; "Take more initiative in the group."

3. *Specific Goal:* The goal is made so specific that, in behavioral terms, it is *operationalized* with concrete descriptions of behavior, thoughts, and feelings. "Use a time-out when anger escalates"; "Make an appointment to discuss it when we are calm and rested."

You help the client move from vague to more specific by framing good questions, paraphrasing, and offering suggestions, always checking to make sure that the outcome meets a set of five criteria:

1. Stated in positives.
2. Within individual's control.
3. Testable: Evidence can be specified.
4. Appropriately contextualized.
5. Ecological.

Practitioners of Neurolinguistic Programming (NLP; Linden, 1998) call an outcome that meets these criteria a "smart outcome." Table 12.1 explains the five criteria and gives examples of questions that will help in forming good outcome statements.

As the therapist asks questions, restates, and explores issues, the outcome statement is transformed from a vague, short statement, to a detailed, expanded description of the desired future. After assuring that the first criterion is met, the order in which the other criteria is achieved can vary. The following example shows the contrast between two different final outcome statements that followed from the same vague initial statement:

Initial statement: A more balanced life.

First example: (Married professional woman without children) I will limit my work week to 35 hours, except in the two busiest seasons. I will attend an exercise class at least 3 times a week. At least twice a month I will go to a concert or other cultural event. I will have a 6-hour block of time every week to take care of housekeeping and bill paying. At least three evenings a week will be unscheduled, for just relaxing at home with my husband.

Second example: (Married mother of two children, ages 2 and 5) I will hire a babysitter three mornings a week so I can go out and engage in activities that are just for me, such as yoga, coffee with a friend, or participation in a book group. I will learn to be more relaxed. I will spend less time on housework and

Table 12.1   Criteria for a "Smart Outcome"

Description	Questions to Elicit Good Outcome Statements
1. Stated in Positives	
Describing a future state in terms of what will be rather than what will not be. Often the person wants change like "get rid of X" or "I would stop X," or "I would no longer have X." The therapist asks questions to change the negative definition to a positive statement—"I would have Y," "Y would be occurring," "I want Y."	What do you want instead of X? What would getting rid of X do for you? What would be happening instead of X? What would you be doing instead of X? What would replace X? How do you want to be different? If the client draws a blank, and keeps answering, "I don't know," try this question: If you knew what you wanted, what would it be?
2. Within Individual's Control	
Outcome statements are worded in terms of the client's own behavior, feelings, and thinking. The therapist helps the client shape an outcome statement for which *success is not dependent on change in another person.* Success has to be defined in terms of self-change. Thus, the outcome is *under the client's control.*	What would you be doing that would *increase your probability* of getting your boss to respect you more? How would you be thinking, feeling, and behaving if this problem were resolved? Imagine that absolutely nothing on earth is going to change that person. Then how would you describe what you want? Because *you can't control* the weather on that day, how else could you word what you want? Would a good wording be "taking the actions necessary to maximize your chances at getting him to change"?
3. Testable: Evidence Can Be Specified	
The outcome is *do-able, realistic, and possible.* The client describes the specific evidence that would show the outcome has been achieved. This means that the outcome is *operationalized:* It is stated in concrete terms rather than abstractions so that there can be no ambiguity or disagreement about whether it is obtained.	What will you see, hear, or feel that will let you know you're achieving your outcome? What else? (pursue more details) How will you know when you have attained your goal? What specific feedback will let you know you're achieving your outcome? How will we know that it is time to stop therapy, or stop working on this particular problem?

(continued)

Table 12.1 *(Continued)*

Description	Questions to Elicit Good Outcome Statements
4. Appropriately Contextualized	
The exact context and circumstances are limited and defined so that the outcome is not too global and broad and so that it is realistic and achievable. You need to challenge all-or-nothing thinking, utopianism, and perfectionism.	When, where, and with whom do you want this outcome?
	It is possible to have this outcome all the time, with everyone?
	Under what circumstances will it be okay for change not to occur, for you to stay the same, or for the problem to continue?
	Do you mean that you will *never* do X or *always* do Y?
	If you can achieve the goal about 85% of the time and accept times when you are not perfect, could that be okay?
5. Ecological	
Promote awareness of interrelated systems: Change in one area of life produces changes in others. Change in an individual disrupts the equilibrium of a family. Positive change in one arena can cause damage in another. The therapist structures a cost-benefit analysis of the stated outcome. This criterion helps you check for the side effects or negative results of change.	Will the desired change make anything worse or create new problems?
	How will having this outcome affect your life? Your family? Your friends? Your health?
	What will happen when you achieve this outcome? What other changes in your life might follow as a consequence?
	How does *not* having this outcome (continuing to have the problem) benefit you?
	What are the advantages and disadvantages of achieving this outcome? Of accepting the status quo and not seeking change?

learn to tolerate a normal amount of messiness and disorder. I will read the Sunday paper and take more of an interest in world events.

The ecological criterion is probably the most challenging. Clients may discover that "they can't have it all" and that choice and compromise are needed. For instance, in certain cultures, marrying someone from outside the culture carries the risk that parents will cut off their relationship with their disobedient child. Choosing to have one parent give up work to stay home with the children means a loss of income and the need to move to a less desirable neighborhood.

The answers to the questions are sometimes very quick and simple, and other times require extensive thought and exploration. As clients examine their problems and outcomes more closely, they acknowledge the benefits and payoffs from staying the same. In exploring the negative consequences of giving up a problem, you may discover evidence of "secondary gains," which refers to the benefits from having symptoms and impairments. Some "payoffs" for mental health problems include getting a family member to provide financial support, postponing the responsibilities of the next stage of life, having an excuse for not achieving exceptional success, controlling a relationship through symptomatic behavior, and avoiding the tedium and annoyances of a 9-to-5 job (**SCE6** addresses benefits of the social role of mental patient).

When the client is struggling with personal choices rather than dealing with impairments or psychiatric symptoms, "staying the same" should be viewed as a successful outcome of therapy.

ACTIVITY 12.1

Developing "Smart Outcomes"

Appendix III contains instructions for conducting an interview with a classmate or a volunteer to achieve a detailed outcome statement that meets all five criteria.

OUTCOME GOALS FOR CASE FORMULATIONS

An intermediate level of abstractness is usually appropriate for the outcome goal for case formulations, unless the problem title pertains to a very limited problem or the duration of therapy is very brief. For instance, if the client has two college acceptances, the goal will be very specific (*choose one college by a certain date*), whereas if the client enters with total confusion about career goals, the outcome goal needs to be more abstract: *Select a career path that is appropriate for her talents and interests.*

Treatment planning manuals are very useful in providing ideas for outcome goals. Table 12.2 gives example of specific goal statements from a treatment planner by Jongsma and Peterson (2003; note that the left column does not give specific problem titles but only names for broad categories of problems).

Another useful source of ideas for outcome goals are competence frameworks that were discussed previously, and are described in charts in Appendix II:

- Chart II.G Domains of Functioning.
- Chart II.H BarOn's Emotional Intelligence—Fifteen Competencies.
- Chart II.I Inventory of Needs.

Four other tables provide useful ideas about possible competence objectives:

1. 3.6 Abilities and Capacities for Optimal Body Functioning.
2. 5.6 Skills-Training Domains.
3. 8.8 Examples of Capacities of a Healthy Self.
4. 8.9 Mature Object Relations.

Table 12.2   Sample Goal Statements

Problem Category	Sample Goal Statements
Dependency	Improved capacity to tolerate being alone.
	A balance between healthy independence and healthy dependence.
	Less dependence on relationships while beginning to meet his/her own needs, build confidence, and practice assertiveness.
Intimate Relationship Conflicts	Awareness of his or her role in relationship conflicts.
	The ability to handle conflicts in a mature, controlled, and assertive way.
	Open, mutually satisfying communication, sexual intimacy, and enjoyable time for companionship in the relationship.
Low Self-Esteem	A consistent, positive self-image.
	Improved self-esteem demonstrated through more pride in appearance, more assertiveness, greater eye contact, and identification of positive traits.
Social Discomfort	Interact socially without excessive fear or anxiety.
	Enjoyment of time spent in selected social activities.
	Reach a satisfying personal balance between solitary time and interpersonal interaction with others.

STANDARDS FOR OUTCOME GOALS

There are four standards to guide the development of good outcome goals for your case formulation.

> **Standard 8.** Outcome goals are directly related to the problem title and are consistent with the client's values.

Outcome goals and problem titles are logically connected: When you read the outcome goal, you should be able to infer the problem title. However, *problem titles do not automatically lead to one correct outcome.* Therefore, outcome statements can be general or offer multiple options. As therapy progresses, the desired future will get clearer:

- **Problem:** *Stress symptoms associated with excessive work commitments.*
- **Possible outcome goals:** Tolerate stress better; cut back on work commitments.
- **Acceptable wording:** The stress symptoms will be reduced. Client will learn to manage stress better and will consider possibility of reducing work commitments.

Although the outcome must be related to the problem title, it is important that it is not too narrowly restricted. The client should not only resolve the immediate reason for seeking therapy but also leave therapy able to manage effectively similar difficulties that arise in the future:

- **Problem:** *Excessive stress over final exams.*
- **Narrow goal:** Stress reduction tools for finals week.
- **Broad goal:** Stress reduction tools for finals week. Decisions to address issues that lead up to excessive stress: work load, study habits, and time management.

Values unavoidably influence the shaping of goals; therapists must be sure that the client's values—some of which are derived from cultural heritage—are respected (Standard 5 addressed the issue of values and biases in problem definition). Sometimes the best outcome goal is one that is vague enough to allow different values to emerge and shape a more specific outcome as therapy progresses. The following example shows how values influence outcome goals.

- **Problem Title:** *Conflict over whether to marry outside of ethnic/religious group.*

Client has been in a secret romantic relationship with a man who is pressuring her to marry him. She believes her parents will "cut her off" if she marries outside their group:

Outcome 1: The client will make a decision based on her own needs and values and feel confident that she can deal with the consequences of familial disapproval and possible rejection.

Outcome 2: The client will understand the importance of her cultural heritage and the difficulties raising children in a mixed marriage. She will accept the need to grieve the current relationship and to seek a partner whom her parents will accept.

Outcome 3: The client will reach a decision after exploring her feelings, thoughts, values, and the costs and benefits of different choices. She will feel able to cope with the negative consequences of whatever decision she makes.

The third outcome is the best. When you write your outcome goal, it might be good practice to see if you could create an outcome goal from a very different value position. If so, you might recognize how you take your own values for granted and have the chance to catch the biases that might otherwise be operating under the surface.

The client's values, desires, and preferences are important in shaping outcome goals, but therapists also have a duty to challenge them, especially when harm will be inflicted on the self or others:

- **Problem:** *Unhappiness in role of mother.*
- **Inappropriate goal:** A "logical" outcome might be "leave children and pursue her own goals for personal fulfillment" but I think that the client needs to hear the goal worded "abandon children and do them irreparable harm."
- **Appropriate goals:** (a) Increased satisfaction with parenting; (b) solve problems that create pain for her in mother role; (c) improve relationships with children; and (d) enjoyment of guilt-free time away from children.

In prior examples, the goals—whether good or bad—were related to the problem title. One of the most significant errors in a case formulation report—and often the first one to meet your eye—is a complete disconnect between the problem title and the outcome goal. When this happens, it is most likely that the outcome goal needs to be adjusted. However, because a good intuition might be guiding your hand, the faulty outcome goal could be a clue that the problem title needs to be improved. Then, after the problem title is changed, the "poor" outcome statement will be appropriate. Here are some examples of unrelated outcome goals.

Example 1

- **Problem:** *Ambivalence about whether to pursue an advanced degree or to secure paid employment.*
- **Unrelated goal:** The client will improve her job search skills.

That outcome goal implies a different problem title, for example, *Difficulty obtaining suitable paid employment,* or, simply, *Poor job search skills.* The outcome goal needs to be changed:

- **Appropriate goal:** The client will resolve the ambivalence and make a choice with which she feels comfortable.

Example 2

- **Problem:** *Difficulty implementing his decision to initiate divorce proceedings.*
- **Unrelated goal:** He will resolve differences and improve the relationship.

The goal ignores that the relationship has been evaluated as negative for the client and assumes that the client should stay in the marriage:

- **Appropriate goal:** He will create and implement a plan to move out, get legal advice, and obtain a divorce.

Yet, the therapist may have collected data supporting the idea that the marriage would not have failed if the couple had sought counseling and that the client is in fact ambivalent about leaving. Perhaps the problem title needs to be modified, with the client's acceptance:

- **Revised problem:** Distress over hostility and blaming in marriage and unwillingness to remain married unless respect and affection are restored to the relationship.
- **New goal:** He will make best efforts to resolve differences and improve the relationship, learn about his own contributions to problems, and pursue a divorce if marriage does not improve.

> **Standard 9.** Outcome goals refer to real-world functioning and do not contain formulation ideas.

Outcome goals are defined in terms of real-world functioning (e.g., love, work, play, or health). The desired change in the client's functioning occurs outside of therapy, not just with the therapist. To assure that this standard is met, ask yourself, as you examine the outcome goal, *How would we evaluate whether this goal is met?* The answer must refer to evidence of change in the client's life outside of therapy. This change encompasses internal, psychological functioning, such as thinking, feeling, sensing, wanting; changes in behavior; and changes in the environment. Most important, *therapists of different theoretical orientations would all approve of the wording of the outcome goal.*

When theoretical concepts enter the outcome goal, you are probably addressing the *process goal,* which belongs in the plan. Your effort was not wasted: you probably produced a good topic sentence for one of the paragraphs in the plan section (see Standard 28). Table 12.3 gives examples of both appropriate and faulty outcome goals so that you can recognize and correct outcome goals that include process goals.

ACTIVITY 12.2

Is It a Process Goal or an Outcome Goal?

The activity in Appendix III gives you a list of goals, and you are asked to correctly identify whether they refer to process or outcome.

> **Standard 10.** Outcome goals are realistic and are not utopian.

Interminable therapy can be based on goals that describe unrealistic ideals of human functioning and are therefore unattainable. Do not create goals based

Table 12.3 Differentiating Outcome Goals and Process Goals

Good Outcome Goals	**Problem:** *Difficulties coping with grief and adjusting to life after spouse's suicide*
	Outcome goals: He will return to better daily functioning and to his prior state of health. He will gradually begin to enjoy life and will set new goals for himself.
	Problem: *Frustration with pattern of relationships with distant, unavailable men*
	Outcome goals: She will be able to identify her needs and develop a realistic plan for meeting her needs in a satisfying, caring, and reciprocal relationship.
	Problem: *Disappointment with parents' lack of involvement with her and her children*
	Outcome goals: She will create an action plan to achieve preferred level of involvement. She will accept whatever relationship results without anger and resentment and find surrogate grandparents for her children, if desired.
Process Goals Inappropriately Placed in Outcome Goals	**Problem:** *Feelings of worthlessness*
	Faulty outcome goals: To come to terms with what I believe is powerful anger toward his father.
	Corrected outcome goal without process goal: Positive feelings about himself.
	Problem: *Difficulty in making a transition from full-time housewife and mother to graduate student*
	Faulty outcome goals: Resolve the guilty feelings that stem from her mother's indoctrination of what a good wife is like.
	Corrected outcome goal without process goal: Satisfaction and balance as student, mother, and wife.
	Problem: *Difficulty knowing her own needs and feelings when faced with major decisions*
	Faulty outcome goals: To overcome the damage to her self from her enmeshed family system.
	Corrected outcome goal without process goal: Improved self-understanding and better decision-making skills.

on the faulty assumption that "normal life difficulties" can be eliminated (hypothesis **C1** addressed the topic of utopian expectations). If absolutes like "always" and "never" are stated or implied, the wording of the goal should be modified.

Three of the most common reasons for unrealistic goals include:

1. The client's agenda to change another person.
2. Standards of perfectionism for behavior, including all-or-nothing thinking.
3. An idealistic belief about how things *should* be.

The Client's Agenda to Change Another Person

- **Problem:** *Frustration with husband's lack of ambition and unwillingness to pursue more lucrative job.*
- **Faulty outcome goal:** Her husband will understand her feelings and will agree to change jobs and live up to his potential.
- **Better outcome goal:** She will increase her understanding of her husband's personality and goals. She will communicate her needs and feelings in an appropriate way. She will differentiate between what can be changed and what can only be accepted in her husband and will deal constructively with anger and frustration.

Standards of Perfectionism for Behavior, Including "All-or-Nothing" Thinking

- **Problem:** *Excessive need for others' approval to feel good about self.*
- **Faulty outcome goal:** Become an independent person who looks inward for sources of approval and who feels good about himself regardless of others' opinions.
- **Better outcome goal:** Learn to tolerate criticism better. Get need for approval met appropriately.

An Idealistic Belief about How Things *Should* Be

- **Problem:** *Dissatisfaction with relationship with mother.*
- **Faulty outcome goals:** Develop a close relationship. Openly discuss with mother issues from early family history.
- **Better outcome goals:** Establish realistic expectations and recognize unrealistic wishes. Create opportunities for increasing closeness and mutual understanding. Cope appropriately with disappointment.

> **Standard 11.** Outcome goals do not contain the "how" of the treatment plan.

Goal statements *should not include the "how" of the intervention*—strategies, procedures, or techniques. This standard overlaps with Standard 9 because both process goals and strategies stem from the formulation. Once a goal statement is made, you should be able to offer strategies from many different orientations or create an integrated strategy. It is important to separate goals (the picture of the desired future) from plans (the means to reach them). People often stifle their ambitions because they are reluctant to set a goal unless they already know how to get there, so you should explain the value of postponing "how" questions.

The following examples illustrate outcome goals that inappropriately include strategies for achieving the outcome goal:

- **Problem:** *Lack of ability to maintain weight loss.*
- **Faulty outcome goal:** Attendance at Weight Watchers meetings.
- **Better outcome goal:** Maintenance of desired weight; ability to initiate weight loss when weight rises.

- **Problem:** *Ambivalence about whether to make commitment to boyfriend.*
- **Faulty outcome goal:** Use the empty-chair technique to have the client get in touch with her feelings.
- **Better outcome goal:** The client will have increased awareness of her feelings and goals. She will feel comfortable with where the relationship is now, or she will take action either to end it or to increase the commitment.

- **Problem:** *Depression following breakup of a romantic relationship.*
- **Faulty outcome goal:** Have the therapist provide the selfobject functions that are lacking in her life. Develop an idealizing transference, which activates early childhood needs.
- **Better outcome goal:** Recover from symptoms of depression. Cope with grief and develop resources to help her deal with this and future losses. Develop increased understanding of the relationship.

ACTIVITY 12.3

Practice Writing Outcome Goals

In the activity in Appendix III, you write appropriate outcome goals for five problem titles. Then, you create outcome goals for the problem titles you created for Maria.

Chapter 13

PRESENTATION OF THE DATABASE

In a traditional report format, the data gleaned from the client (the patient history) is presented in a narrative under specific topics, as illustrated in Appendix II, Chart II.D, with a separate section for *clinical observations.* When you are using the problem-oriented method (POM), and *SOAPing each problem,* the database is presented in two different parts of the report:

1. *Background section prior to the problem list:* This section includes some of the categories of the traditional case history—identifying information, presenting problem (reason for seeking help), and some life history details, which may be subdivided as needed.
2. *After each problem title:* After the problem title and its accompanying outcome goal, data that are relevant to the problem are presented in the subjective (S) and objective (O) categories.

In using the subjective data, objective data, assessment and plan (SOAP) method, it is best to put as much data as possible in the S section under a specific problem title. Use the background section for (a) general information about the client's history and (b) subjective data that would be repeated under different problem titles. Most errors in using the POM format occur from violation of the following important rules:

> You must SOAP *each problem* separately. The data under the problem title must be related to that specific problem.

STANDARDS FOR DATABASE

There are seven standards which apply to the presentation of data in your case formulation.

> **Standard 12.** The database is thorough, comprehensive, and complete: There are sufficient data so that multiple hypotheses can be applied.

- *Thorough:* This means that there are specific details and examples; that the tone is particular, not general; and that the information is concrete rather than abstract or vague.
- *Comprehensive:* This means that the information covers a wide scope and is not limited to one narrow aspect; it is multifaceted rather than one-sided.
- *Complete:* This word is not used to mean being total or entire but rather to mean that nothing essential is lacking and that it has not been shortened by important omissions. The lack of completeness is often recognized when you are able to review a recording (audio or video) of the sessions after reading the database.
- *Sufficient:* The word sufficient reminds you that the purpose of collecting data is to select appropriate hypotheses and design individualized, effective treatment plans. When those goals are accomplished, there are diminishing returns for amassing more information. It is common to discover that the database is insufficient as you write a case formulation report. The process of creating the formulation makes you aware of the need for specific types of information. If you are aware of limits in the data, you should discuss that in the assessment and make the gathering of more data part of the plan. *Incomplete database* can be listed as a separate problem title.

Success in meeting this standard depends on skills in interviewing a client and the amount of time spent with the client. If a case formulation report is based on only one session, the database will naturally have gaps. Judgment about the thoroughness of a database will depend on both the problem title and the specific hypotheses that are chosen. Table 13.1 shows suggested topics for specific problems and hypotheses.

There are several reasons for concluding that the database is not complete:

- You discover that *new* data are introduced in the assessment or plan section (see Standard 20 and Standard 27).

  It is acceptable for data to appear in the two formulation sections (A and P) only when you are *repeating* data that have been presented previously in the database sections (background, S and O). When the therapist remembers data during the creative process of writing the formulation, then he or she must go back and revise the data section, often just by copying and pasting the missing data.

Table 13.1   Suggested Data Topics for Specific Problems and Hypotheses

SAMPLE DATA TOPICS FOR PROBLEM TITLES

Problem: *Difficulty establishing a successful relationship that is committed, intimate, satisfying, stable, and mature*

1. Description of current situation (e.g., a breakup, ambivalence about the current partner, or difficulty choosing between two potential partners)
2. Specific concrete information about how the client and the current/recent partner are/were relating, communicating, and behaving (You need to move from abstract terms like "relationship" to concrete events and experiences.)
3. History of current relationship: early attraction, first date, expectations and feelings, key transitions
4. History of romantic and sexual relationships, starting in adolescence, with sufficient details to support hypotheses about specific patterns
5. Information about the family of origin, the parents' marital relationship(s), and the client's relationships with both parents
6. Information about friends, who are not romantic/sexual partners (to have data to compare how the client relates with people of both genders)

Problem: *Difficulty managing stress*

1. A timeline of specific stressful events, describing them in detail
2. Description of stress reactions (e.g., anxiety, depression, fatigue, irritability, somatic symptoms, substance use, or other forms of self-medication)
3. Concrete description about current activities (e.g., a sample day or a typical week)
4. A BASIC SID of specific stressful situations, including client's cognitive appraisal of stressors and behavioral coping strategies
5. History of past coping with stress, searching for assets as well as deficiencies
6. Information for assessing problem-solving skills
7. Availability of social support
8. Repertoire of relaxation and self-care tools
9. Examination of social context of stressful situations and social relations that reduce or increase stress (friends, family, community)

SAMPLE DATA TOPICS FOR HYPOTHESES

Hypothesis P2: *The client's pattern in intimate relationships is a reenactment of her relationship with her father.*

1. A thorough history of intimate relationships
2. Specific memories about the father and her relationship with him
3. Concrete details and examples from several intimate relationships, to document the presence of the identified pattern
4. Any evidence of the client acting counter to the pattern

Hypothesis BL3: *The client lacks needed communication skills.*

1. Examples of how the client currently communicates in the problematic situation, including quotations
2. Examples of the highest level of skill demonstrated in similar situations
3. In the objective data section, a description of how the client communicates with the therapist
4. Information about the client's cultural group, with attention to its values, norms, and customs about communication

Hypothesis SCE7: *The client's misery at work stems from factors in the environment rather than from personal deficiencies or conflicts.*

1. Concrete description of work environment, including specific examples
2. Information about how coworkers react to the same environment
3. A description of client's functioning in other work environments
4. Examples of the client's cognitive appraisal of the environment to document the absence of faulty information processing

- The assessment hypothesis does not have substantiating evidence in the prior database (see also Standard 19 and Standard 27).

  For example, the following sentence appears in the assessment: *His problem stems from the difficulty he experienced in trying to get his needs met by his mother.* However, the database contained no mention of his relationship with his mother. Because it is inappropriate to assume that every relationship problem is a reenactment of early childhood experiences, it is important to include in the database some anecdotes from childhood or a description of his mother's style of relating. This deficiency in the report can be rectified only by learning to use hypotheses during the session, to guide the gathering of data. If there are no substantiating data, then the hypothesis should be eliminated from the assessment discussion.

- Supervisory sessions or tapes of sessions reveal important data that were not included in the database.

  A benefit of using tapes or written transcripts is that someone else can recognize important omissions. Group supervision, where people from many different perspectives ask questions, also is invaluable for helping the therapist recall facts that never made it to the stage of designing the formulation.

Example 1

A student wrote a very competent case formulation, discussing the client's *Difficulties maintaining intimate relationship* in terms of her mother's example as a role model. However, when I reviewed a tape of the session, I discovered that the client had talked at length about her father's infidelity. This information was never mentioned in the database.

Example 2

Here are quotations from a client whose problem was *Social isolation.* He has been explaining that he distanced himself from people after his mother's death:

> "After she died, I saw a lot of bullshit. I couldn't stand to hear people who didn't care for me before all of a sudden have warmth for me. (15 second pause) People think they can just walk into my life when I'm most vulnerable, who do they think they are? . . . If you put too much stock into people you'll usually get hurt, do you agree? . . . I generally think all people are stupid and selfish. That, when it comes down to it, people will stab you in the back to get their way."

The therapist's failure to include these quotations in the database led her to completely neglect the relevance of hypothesis **C2 (Faulty Cognitive Map).**

The writing of a complete yet concise database can be a time-consuming process. It takes experience and judgment to determine what facts and quotations must be included and what can be summarized. It is better to include too much, and then have the challenge of condensing, rather than writing too little, and risk omitting important data. The writing of a competent database requires a willingness to go through several revisions, and to review tapes (if they exist) and take thorough notes. If a tape is not used, the therapist must allocate time after the session, before seeing the next client, for writing down as much as she can remember, including quotations.

This process can be tedious, yet the payoff is tremendous: The quality of the database contributes directly to the quality of the formulation. Furthermore, the quality of the supervision and consultation you receive will depend on the database. When you want guidance, your consultant, who will not be meeting directly with the client, must have access to a database that is complete and reliable.

> **Standard 13.** Subjective and objective data are appropriately distinguished.

The use of the terms *subjective* (S) and *objective* (O) originated in medical practice: A *symptom* is what the patient reports (subjective) and a *sign* is what the clinician observes on examination (objective). The distinction between subjective and objective data is based on the source of the data. A similar distinction occurs in the courtroom. An ordinary witness gives subjective information (S data) and is prohibited from giving conclusions. An expert witness can give objective opinions (O data). It is up to the jury to reach the verdict (assessment; A). In SOAPing problems, if data come from the client or the client's family, they go in the S section; if they come from a professional expert or objective tests or records (e.g., medical tests—blood tests and brain scans—school or legal records, prior hospital charts, and psychological test results), they go in the O section. You, the therapist, are a professional expert, so your observations of the client's appearance and behavior are viewed as objective data.

> Content—*what* the client tells you—goes in S.
> Process—*how* the client tells it—goes in O.

A common error is to think that subjective means distorted or biased, while objective must mean accurate, true, verifiable, and unbiased. Table 13.2 shows that *both S and O data can be either accurate or inaccurate*. Note that a competent therapist should not have anything in the bottom right box, because *inaccurate objective data* is something that therapists are trained to avoid.

There are two types of errors:

1. Objective data appears in the S section.
2. Subjective data appears in the O section.

Table 13.2   Distinction between Subjective and Objective Data

	True: Accurate, Verifiable, Unbiased	False: Inaccurate, Distorted, Biased
S **Subjective Data** The *source* is the client's words.	The client states: I have three sisters. I completed three years of college. I live alone, with my cat. (If a detective were hired, these statements would be found to be true.)	The client states: Joe is out to get me. (Joe doesn't recall ever meeting her.) I'm an excellent singer. (He can't carry a tune.) My parents were both alcoholics. (They drank only two drinks a week.)
O **Objective Data** The *source* is the therapist's observations.	**All objective data should fall in this category.** The therapist reports: The client is well groomed and fashionably dressed. The client laughed and changed the subject when the topic of her mother came up. The client reacted to me as if she expected negative judgments. (Observers watching a video of the session agree with these conclusions.)	**This category should NOT occur in a competent report.** The therapist reports: The client needed to be prompted with questions and never initiated a topic. (The therapist bombarded the client with questions and never allowed a pause.) The client is overweight. (The client is of normal weight, but the therapist finds any woman above a size 8 to be in need of a diet.)

Error 1: Objective Data Appears in the S Section

For each of the following examples, the part in italics should be moved to the O section.

DESCRIPTION OF NONVERBAL BEHAVIOR

The client's voice was raised in anger as she described a phone conversation in which her mother blamed her for her brother's behavioral problems.

DESCRIPTION OF PROCESS

I probed for details about her early school experience, and the client described *with apparent pleasure* how well she did in elementary school and how the teachers always held her up as an example for other children.

DESCRIPTION OF THERAPIST'S JUDGMENTS OR INTERNAL REACTIONS

With absolutely no compassion or empathy, the client described her husband's depressed mood and impaired functioning since he lost his job.

Error 2: Subjective Data Appears in the O Section

These are examples of data that were incorrectly included in O instead of in S:

SECOND-HAND REPORT OF EVALUATION
BY ANOTHER EXPERT

Jay's former therapist told him that he was "dysthymic and overly sensitive." *(Data came from the client's verbal report, not from the professional's formal report, so they go in S.)*

A FACT THAT CAN BE OBJECTIVELY VERIFIED

She is in a breast cancer survivor group. *(The writer incorrectly thought this was objective because it could have been observed; however, the source of the information was the client's words.)*

THE SOURCE OF INFORMATION IS OTHER
FAMILY MEMBERS

Her mother described her as very sullen, uncooperative, and hostile. *(A family member is not an unbiased professional, so the source is considered subjective.)*

ACTIVITY 13.1

Is It Subjective or Objective Data?

This activity in Appendix III allows you to test your understanding of the distinction between these two categories of data.

> **Standard 14.** Good quotations from the client are included in the subjective data section.

Quotations help the reader see the client as a real person, not just a case, and give a sense of the client's way of speaking, level of insight, and patterns of thinking. Quotations provide evidence to support specific hypotheses, and are especially valuable when using cognitive hypotheses. As is discussed under Standard 15, when the client uses psychological jargon and expresses her own formulation of the problem, it is mandatory to enclose those phrases in quotation marks. When sessions are not taped, the therapist has to take time immediately after the session to capture good quotations from memory.

Movies provide an enjoyable way to practice the skill of integrating quotations. One student used the movie *When Harry Met Sally,* treating Harry as a client with this problem: *Difficulty maintaining an intimate, committed relationship with a woman who both attracts him and can be a good friend.* Here is an excerpt from the subjective section:

> Harry feels he has a "dark side" and he spends "hours and days thinking about death." He believes that "men and women can't be friends because the sex part always gets in the way." When he was single, he would have sex with a woman and afterward think, "How long do I have to lie here and hold her before I can go home?"

When two cases use the same problem title, the quotations help you individualize the formulation. The following examples give subjective data for *Difficulty balancing school work and other aspects of life.*

EXAMPLE 1

Jeff feels that he should take time out every day to do something that he has fun doing. He thinks doing this helps him get through finals without getting stressed out, but he wonders if he is doing enough studying to do well in school. He described his approach to studying: "I usually just get done what needs to get done. There's no reason to stress over problems. If you just worry about them, nothing gets accomplished." He also mentioned that in talking to friends who have completed law school, "They all said it was the hardest time of their lives, but I don't feel like it's that hard."

EXAMPLE 2

Leila feels conflicted between her professional obligations and the obligations to her relationship. Her boyfriend "understands about her school and workload" but often makes weekend plans for the two of them. She has difficulty telling him that she needs to devote most weekends to school. She says that to make up for the lack of time together, he tries to nurture her, but she ends up "feeling smothered." Despite his requests for her to talk about her problems, Leila does not share her feelings of stress with her boyfriend. She "would rather have fun together, than spend the time complaining about something he can't relate to."

Good quotations are important because they provide evidence to support specific hypotheses.

C3 FAULTY INFORMATION PROCESSING AND C4 DYSFUNCTIONAL SELF-TALK

Elisa says she can't go shopping at an upscale store without feeling like everyone is staring at her because she is "so out of place." She imagines people are thinking, "She doesn't belong in here."

C2 FAULTY COGNITIVE MAP AND P2 REENACTMENT
OF EARLY EXPERIENCES

Robin notes that she places high expectations on herself and strives "for perfection in everything." Growing up, she only received appreciation from her father for straight As or a school achievement that earned mention in the local newspaper. Now in graduate school, if she doesn't get the highest score in the class, she winds up "feeling like a failure." She described an interaction with her teacher when she went to argue about her grade, and admitted that her anger was out of proportion. "I felt that nothing I do could ever be good enough."

There are two types of errors for this standard: too few or too many quotations. Omitting important quotations is a more serious error than having too many.

Omission of Necessary Quotations

Quotations are needed when they would clarify the client's meaning, reveal the client's specific self-talk, or dramatize unique aspects of this individual. Note how quotations give the therapist a chance to independently evaluate the validity of the client's judgments. Here are two examples for a description of "verbal abuse":

- Maggie complained that her boyfriend "continually verbally abused" her by calling her "too sensitive," and "messy." (Most people would not call the boyfriend abusive.)
- Maggie complained that her boyfriend "continually verbally abused" her, describing how, after she got a rejection letter from graduate school, he told her she was "a worthless loser who is too stupid to succeed at anything."

Unneeded Quotations

Quotations are not helpful if they do not convey something particular and unique about the client's thinking, feeling, and experience. Relying too much on quotations interrupts the narrative. Sometimes quotations are a way of avoiding the work of creating concise content summaries and of putting your own impressions into words, in the objective data section:

- **Original wording:** The client says her family was "close" and "attended Church every Sunday." Her mother always invited her parents "to a big Sunday dinner."
- **Revised:** The client describes her family as "close," attending Church every Sunday, followed by a big dinner which always included her maternal grandparents.

- **Original wording:** The client stated "I earned a 3.8 average" and described his college as "part of the Ivy League"
- **Revised: S:** The client earned a 3.8 average at an Ivy League university.
- **O:** The client seemed to want to impress the therapist with his superior intelligence.

Standard 15. The subjective section does not include formulation concepts (unless they are quotations from the client).

Mingling formulation ideas with the database is very common in your first draft. By doing so, you show that you are thinking creatively and interpretively about the data rather than summarizing it in a mechanical, unimaginative way. When you review your first draft, you realize that you need to cut and paste the formulation ideas, moving them to the assessment section. You also will need to add concrete examples to the S section, as evidence for your conclusions and explanations.

When the client states his or her thoughts in a way that sounds like a formulation, perhaps by using psychological jargon, it is essential to use quotations to show the reader that it is the client who is doing the formulating, not you. Here is an example of two ways to correct violations of standard 15:

ASSESSMENT ERRONEOUSLY APPEARS IN SUBJECTIVE DATA

S: The client has been the primary caretaker in her family since she was a child. Her parents, especially her mother, were emotionally unavailable so, as a result, she tends to meet her own needs and does not seek assistance from others.

THE FORMULATION CAME FROM THE THERAPIST

S: As a child, the client prepared meals for her parents, felt responsible for cheering her mother up when she was unhappy, took care of getting her younger sister to school and helping her with homework, and made excuses for her father when his alcoholic binges caused him to miss work.

A: The client has been the primary caretaker in her family since she was a child. Her parents, especially her mother, were emotionally unavailable so, as a result, she tends to meet her own needs and does not seek assistance from others.

THE FORMULATION CAME FROM THE CLIENT

S: The client described herself as "the primary caretaker" since she was a child. She explains her difficulty seeking help from others in these words: "Since my mother was emotionally unavailable, I tend to meet my own needs and I don't seek assistance from others."

Sometimes the therapist's opinions and judgments creep into the subjective data section:

EXAMPLE 1: ORIGINAL WORDING

S: He explained that the job he is at now does not pay as much as what he can potentially make in his new venture, which does not seem like a viable option. *(The client thinks it is viable but the therapist is making the judgment that it is not.)*

EXAMPLE 1: CORRECTIONS

S: He explained that the job he is at now does not pay as much as what he can potentially make in his new venture. For over a year he and his friend have discussed starting their own company but "have no idea how we will get the money to start it."

A: His new venture does not seem to be a viable option and a decision to quit his job will have serious consequences for his stability and financial security.

EXAMPLE 2: ORIGINAL WORDING

S: She described how she was nagging him to take a job with her brother, even though it was ridiculously below his educational level. *(The client did not use the term nagging, she just said "I've told him over and over again." The word "ridiculously" definitely conveys the therapist's bias.)*

EXAMPLE 2: CORRECTIONS

S: She described how she repeatedly urged him to take a job with her brother as a delivery truck driver, while he tells her that he prefers to continue looking for a position similar to the middle management position that he previously held.

A: She attempts to get her husband to change in a way that he probably experiences as nagging. She does not directly express her fears to him, nor try to empathically understand his feelings about unemployment.

ACTIVITY 13.2 _____

Find the Assessment in the Subjective Section

In Appendix III, you are given two excerpts from a subjective section and asked to identify one or more sentences that belong in the assessment section.

> **Standard 16.** There is no reference to how and when the information was gathered in the subjective data section; this information, if relevant, goes in the objective section.

The subjective data section is *not* organized in the sequence in which the client told the story.

In writing the S section, you need to remove all phrases that describe the "when" of the client's revelation. If that information is important, it goes in the O section. Very often those details are not important and interfere with a smooth, well-organized narrative of the data (discussed under the next standard).

The subjective data section does not contain details regarding "how" the story was told.

If these details are relevant, they go in the O section. When clinicians write *process notes* for a session, they describe the sequence of the session, and are free to include content, as needed. If you have detailed process notes on the computer, and you want to write a SOAP, you can cut and paste. The content will go to S and those process details that are relevant to the problem title will go to O.

In the following examples, the italicized process details should be eliminated from the S section.

EXAMPLE 1: ORIGINAL WORDING

S: *In the first session, the client was reluctant to talk about her family of origin. However, in the third session,* she described her early experiences with a distant father and an alcoholic mother.

REVISED

S: She described her early experiences with a distant father and an alcoholic mother.

O: It was not until the third session that the client was willing to talk about her family of origin.

EXAMPLE 2: ORIGINAL WORDING

S: *Ann's voice shook with anger* when she told how her sister had seduced her boyfriend 2 years ago. *Her body language showed sadness* when she described their lack of contact for the past 2 years. She stated that she felt frustrated and confused whenever her sister made overtures toward friendship.

REVISED

S: Ann described her lack of contact with her sister following an event 2 years ago when her sister had "seduced" Ann's boyfriend. She stated that she felt frustrated and confused whenever her sister made overtures toward friendship.

O: Ann's voice and body language showed a great deal of anger and sadness while discussing her sister.

> **Standard 17.** The subjective section is well organized and appropriately concise: There is selection, summarization, and condensation of details.

The organization of the database is based on topics, in a logical sequence, *not* (as stated in the prior standard) by the order in which the therapist acquired the information. Paragraphs have good topic sentences, thoughts flow logically, and transitions are clear.

This report format is designed to improve your case formulations—it is not a report for the client's chart. You need to overcome the tendency to omit important data in the interest of being brief. When you have too much, it is relatively easy to go back and summarize, condense, and eliminate unneeded details. When you have too little, it means that you need to go back to a tape of the session and get more information—or if there is no tape, lament the fact that you didn't write detailed notes after each session.

The key to success on this standard is good writing skills: organize, pare down, and aim for clarity. The discussion of writing skills under Standard 25 is also relevant to this standard. The writer must have a good stylebook handy, and my preference is *The Elements of Style* (Strunk & White, 2000). This concise book is organized into brief rules with examples. One of the rules of style most frequently violated is this one: *Omit needless words.* The authors show a comparison between two summaries of *Macbeth:*

Version 1

Macbeth was very ambitious. This led him to wish to become king of Scotland. The witches told him that this wish of his would come true. The king of Scotland at this time was Duncan. Encouraged by his wife, Macbeth murdered Duncan. He was thus enabled to succeed Duncan as king. (6 sentences, 51 words)

Version 2

Encouraged by his wife, Macbeth achieved his ambition and realized the prediction of the witches by murdering Duncan and becoming king of Scotland in his place. (p. 24; 1 sentence, 26 words)

Notice that the two versions contain the same amount of information. By using a concise style with complex sentences, you can pack a great deal into a limited length. Often the subjective section gets very long, not from too much data, but from repetition, excessive detail, and verbosity. It is absolutely essential to plan to revise your first draft of a report and to put effort into writing skills.

> The effort to write good sentences and paragraphs forces you to increase your understanding and do more thinking than you would if you were presenting your ideas in bulleted form.

Use Timelines

To write a well-organized subjective database (background plus S sections), it is absolutely essential to have two detailed timelines in front of you: (1) a recent history and (2) a life history. It is also important to consult a timeline for the historical and cultural events in the client's lifetime—and do research if the client comes from a different culture. As explained in Chapter 2, when the client tells the story, he or she uses different methods to pinpoint the time of a past event: *age* ("I was 12 when"), *date* ("In June of 1997"), *amount of time prior to the present moment* ("Six years ago, we moved"), *and reference to other events* ("When I finished high school"; "When my older sister was 17"; "After working at that job for 9 years"). To get a detailed timeline, you must convert all of those phrases to the client's age. For recent events, in the past year, it is essential to indicate exactly how much time has passed.

Create an Outline

Use of an outline is an amazingly effective way to assure good organization (your high school English teacher *was* right), yet most of us forget to use it. When you see what the topic of a paragraph is supposed to be, it becomes glaringly obvious when items don't fit.

There is no single outline for presenting subjective data that would fit for all clients. Instead, the writer needs to determine which organization will result in the greatest clarity. Table 13.3 illustrates three methods of organization with case examples.

When the subjective data is a well-organized essay, the evidence for different hypotheses will be apparent. The writer has to be careful not to draw the conclusions and get into explanatory mode while writing topic sentences and transitional statements that move a list of facts to a coherent essay. There are many different ways to organize, and a given bit of information can logically fit in different locations, so there is never a single correct way to present the database.

> **Standard 18.** The objective section does not contain theoretical concepts, biased opinions, or formulation discussion.

This standard differentiates objective data from assessment. Because both the objective data and assessment sections contain judgments and opinions, it is important to clarify the different functions of these two sections:

O: An objective section contains data about the client that all therapists, regardless of theoretical orientation, would agree is valid. This section includes more than just a presentation of raw, unprocessed data. Based on professional expertise and mastery of a specific, technical vocabulary, the

Table 13.3   Organizing the Subjective Section

1. CHRONOLOGICAL ORDER OVER THE ENTIRE LIFE SPAN, ENDING WITH THE CURRENT TIME

Problem: *Anxiety while communicating at work, school, and in casual social settings*

A. Description of life history relevant to experiences with anxiety and socializing, including first recollections, experiences with parents, and a highlight from each level of school

B. Description of current problems, using data from all categories of BASIC SID, and providing relevant quotations

C. Description of current situations (contexts/people) in which he communicates with comfort

2. CURRENT SITUATION FIRST, FOLLOWED BY CHRONOLOGICAL ORDER UP TO THE PRESENT

Problem: *Inability to decide if she wants to continue relationship with boyfriend*

A. Description of the client's current dilemma, including quotations to illustrate different voices in her inner conflict and to provide details of pros and cons

B. Summary of this current relationship from when they first met until the present, illustrating both positive experiences and description of problems, using quotations

C. Chronological presentation of her relationship with her parents, describing their stormy marriage, use of alcohol, and ultimate divorce

D. History of her romantic relationships up to the current boyfriend

3. BY TOPIC, WITHOUT REGARD TO CHRONOLOGY

Problem: *Anxiety over husband's impending retirement and proposed geographic move*

A. Description of her husband's unilateral announcement 2 months ago, her reaction, and details of how this decision and the proposed move will impact her and the children

B. Summary of history of marriage and four prior moves, with quotations illustrating frustration at the decision-making process

C. Summary of the core issues that she identifies: complaint that husband is "domineering, controlling, and opinionated" and that he is "violating their contract" that she will have control over the home

D. Description of her concerns about the children, including the negative effects of moving as well as having their "overcontrolling" father become more involved in their lives

E. Illustrate how the client connected her current feelings to her family of origin—"being dominated all the time"

F. Summary of the positive aspects of the change and comments the client made illustrating empathy for husband's desire for freedom therapist makes judgments and offers opinions. Different therapists watching the session from behind a one-way mirror would agree on the judgments offered in this section. There is no attempt to explain the problem or offer suggestions for treatment. This section does not contain concepts that belong to a particular theory, although it does include terms that have technical meaning to members of the mental health professions, such as Mental Status Exam terminology (Chart II.C in Appendix II). The objective section can also include the therapist's reactions such as "I felt as if the client was uncomfortable with my level of warmth," or "I think the client sensed my discomfort when she asked me about my level of experience." These sentences are worded in a personal way and show the therapist's tentativeness.

A: In an assessment section, the therapist explains the problem, using preferred clinical hypotheses. There is room here for creative hunches and disagreement among professionals. The purpose of this section is not to summarize the data but rather to explain the problem and propose ideas that will lead to effective treatment strategies.

You can use your knowledge of *DSM-IV-TR* to clarify the distinction. The behavioral criteria are based on data (S and O) and the diagnosis is an assessment (A). There is one thing the two sections have in common: *They should both be focused on the problem title.* This principle helps in making decisions about what is relevant or irrelevant, necessary or optional, and sufficient or excessive.

In my opinion, the style using the third person (e.g., the client and therapist developed a very good rapport) is awkward; it is more natural to use the word "I," for yourself along with the client's (fictitious) name. This, however, is a matter of personal preference. The following three examples will illustrate appropriate objective data sections. They show different styles and illustrate some of the decisions that are made for this section.

EXAMPLE 1

• **Problem:** *Frustration over repeatedly taking caretaker role in relationships.*

O: Amanda was clearly nervous coming into the sessions. She seemed tense but there was a sense of hope that began to grow as the time passed. She expressed strong feelings of frustration as well as sadness through her words and body language. We developed a very good rapport and I felt very empathically attuned to her. When she told stories or described moments of importance, she primarily used the visual modality. When she recognized connections between her current relationships and her family of origin, she showed satisfaction with herself and me. I think she gained some new insights and she seemed highly motivated to continue in some form of therapy.

The objective data is useful for treatment planning. The client would be a good candidate for insight-oriented psychodynamic therapy and visual imagery techniques. If there had been any signs that the client took on the role of caretaker with the therapist, it would be important to include them.

EXAMPLE 2

- **Problem:** *Conflict about whether to remain in the relationship or break up with her boyfriend.*

O: It was clear to me early in our sessions that Emily was describing two distinct parts of her "self." When speaking about the part of her wanting to remain in the relationship, her voice was powerful and loud. She maintained eye contact with me and appeared confident. In contrast, when she spoke about her unhappiness with Jim, and her strong desire to terminate the relationship, the strength and confidence in her voice diminished, her speech slowed and her posture seemed to shrink. As she described Jim's behavior, she clenched her fists and raised her voice. On occasion, she spoke directly to Jim, putting me in his role. I felt her frustration and anger as my countertransference increased, and I felt myself wanting to side with her.

The objective section appropriately focuses on the problem title. The information definitely justifies the application of hypothesis **P1 Internal Parts and Subpersonalities.** The writer provides clear, concrete descriptions of the nonverbal, emotional messages.

EXAMPLE 3

- **Problem:** *Emotional pain from obesity.*

O: Vera is a short woman, about 5'2", who appears to weigh at least 200 pounds, so the term *obese* is appropriate. She is neatly groomed and chooses clothing that is appropriately sized and styled for her body. She is attractive (not "ugly" as she described herself) with clear skin, fashionably styled hair, and a beautiful smile. She often laughed nervously or made jokes when discussing her weight and size. At other times, she appeared depressed about her weight, exhibiting a frown, downcast eyes, and slumping shoulders.

The objective section provides an observer's picture of the "obesity" mentioned in the title. It also provides evidence that her appraisal of herself as "ugly" is a distortion.

The following is an example of an objective data section that is flawed by the inclusion of assessment ideas, along with an appropriate correction.

- **Problem:** *Dissatisfaction with current job and unrealized ambitions for material success.*

ORIGINAL WORDING

O: It was clear to me in our first session that John is expecting more out of life than what he is putting into it. Because he is smoking marijuana on a daily basis, he is unable to gain the motivation to think clearly about his work.

REVISED

O: John's description of his work was confusing and disorganized. There were times when he would forget what he was saying, and I would have to remind him. He seemed apathetic at times, and did not take initiative but waited for me to direct the session. His explanations for lack of success focused on shortcomings of others.

A: John is expecting more out of life than what he is putting into it. Because he is smoking marijuana on a daily basis, he is unable to gain the motivation to think clearly about his work.

ACTIVITY 13.3

Is It Objective Data or Assessment?

This activity gives you a chance to test your understanding of the distinction between these two sections of a SOAP report.

Chapter 14

A COHERENT INTEGRATIVE ASSESSMENT

In the A section of the SOAP, finally, your own original thinking appears.

The core principle of case formulation is that the treatment plans are a match for the specific client. That means that there is a connection between data, hypotheses, and plans. Chapter 10 described the process of applying hypotheses to data, and then seeking new data to confirm the relevance of the hypothesis. To organize your thoughts and assure a coherent formulation, it is very helpful to develop a three-column chart, as illustrated in Table 14.1 and available as Form I.E in Appendix I. This chart assures that every hypothesis is supported by data and that there is correspondence between the A and P sections of the report. Even though you start with the hypothesis, it is in the middle rather than on the left because in the final report it is also between the data and the plan.

Preparing a formulation is not a linear process, as explained previously. It is possible that an idea for a treatment approach will be the first thing that occurs to you. By using the worksheet, you can assure that you provide the necessary conceptual foundation. The plan idea would go in the right column, you would then need to specify the theoretical foundation for that treatment and make sure that the data of this specific client support your decision.

ACTIVITY 14.1

Using a Three-Column Worksheet

The instructions tell you to use the model in Table 14.1 and prepare a three-column worksheet for (a) Maria and (b) a new client, a classmate, or a volunteer.

As a step toward building competence in case formulations, it is essential that you practice writing a discussion of your integration of clinical hypotheses rather than just listing each one with a sentence or two. You put yourself in the reader's place and realize that you must anticipate questions such as, "How specifically? How do you know? Through what precise mechanism? What is the specific sequence?" After preparing the three-column worksheet, write a brief essay, indicating in parentheses the hypotheses you are choosing.

Table 14.1 Using a Worksheet for Preparing the Formulation

Problem Title: *Difficulties adjusting to new marriage*

Data *S and O:* Data that support the hypothesis	Hypotheses *A:* List in order of importance	Treatment Ideas *P:* Plans consistent with hypothesis
"She is disappointed in me." "When she complained about the food in the restaurant, it was because I'm not earning enough to go to a good restaurant." "When she has a hard day at work, I think she's angry at me."	**C3 Faulty Information Processing** He is mind reading and exhibiting personalization; he seems insightful and catches his own distortions.	Use metamodel questions. Test the evidence: Have him check his assumptions with the spouse. Shift between empathy and confronting.
"A part of me wants to please her, but another part resents her expectations." "When I get into my Pleaser, I feel that I'll never be good enough."	**P1 Internal Parts** He identifies the parts easily. The Pleaser probably stems from relationship with parent (**P2** might also fit).	Use voice dialogue technique to explore each part. Set goals according to what emerges. Allow emotions from the Child parts to be experienced.
Client comes from British background; feelings not expressed at home, people needed to guess. Spouse is Latina and very expressive.	**SCE2 Cultural Context** He exaggerates meaning of negative emotions because they were so rare in his family.	Discuss issue of culture; offer interpretation about roots of his interpretation of feeling (this ties in with **C3**).

STANDARDS FOR ASSESSMENT

The following seven standards will guide you in creating a competent integrative formulation.

> **Standard 19.** The assessment integrates hypotheses that are consistent with the prior database.

It is a major error to write ideas in the assessment discussion that are unrelated to the database. You know this standard is violated when you are reading the assessment and find yourself wondering, "Were there data to support this?" "Where did this idea come from?" or "This doesn't fit the data."

It can also be an error to ignore important information in the database and fail to provide the appropriate hypothesis. Certain leeway is allowed because you cannot include every hypothesis; however, in the assessment discussion you might explain why you are omitting the most obvious hypotheses. Three major errors that therapists could make include an assessment that (1) is not supported by data, (2) is inconsistent with the data, or (3) omits a strong hypothesis.

Assessment Is Not Supported by Data

There are three possibilities:

1. You have the data to justify this explanation, but you forgot to include it in the database. Therefore, you simply need to go back and expand the database.
2. You had a good hunch but failed to gather data to support it. In your next meeting with the client, you explore the hypothesis in an unbiased manner.
3. You fail to find supportive evidence for your choice of that hypothesis, so you need to remove that idea from your assessment discussion. This error occurs when the therapist selects the orientation she wants to use before meeting a new client and is usually accompanied by the second type of error, ignoring data that point to a different hypothesis.

EXAMPLE 1: HYPOTHESIS P3

A trainee applied hypothesis **P3,** using Heinz Kohut's theory of a *disorder of the self.* The student wrote that *the client lacked adequate mirroring from the mother.* The subjective data section lacked any information about early childhood experiences with the mother. Nor was there any description of the mother's personality. There was one single example of the mother's alleged "lack of mirroring": The student wrote in the database: *When the client was a teenager, riding in the car with friends, the mother embarrassed her by talking in a harsh, critical voice.* This example is not only from a much later stage than the early childhood stage of Kohut's theory but also seems like fairly normal behavior for a mother of a teenager. Furthermore, you need more than one example to demonstrate a pattern.

EXAMPLE 2: HYPOTHESIS P1

A student wrote the following in the assessment: *John has many internal parts in conflict. One side of him wants to be independent and the other part is rooted in his desire to help people in a hands-on fashion.* Referring to the subjective data section, there were many details about his desire to live independently, make his own hours, be creative, and make money. There also were many details about how he dislikes his current job as a physical therapy assistant. There was nothing to support the assertion that he had a "desire to help people," an idea seemingly invented by the writer.

Assessment Is Inconsistent with Data

This mistake is more glaring than the prior one: The database contains information that would lead the reader to reject, rather than apply, the chosen hypothesis. Examples of this mistake include (a) minimizing the severity of a problem, (b) ignoring the client's strengths, and (c) faulty understanding of the chosen hypothesis.

THE THERAPIST MINIMIZES THE SEVERITY
OF THE PROBLEM

A period of depression was formulated as "normal anxieties about finishing graduate school," when there were impairments in many areas of functioning, a history of other depressive episodes, and a family history that includes a sibling on antidepressant medication.

THE THERAPIST IGNORES THE CLIENTS'
ASSETS AND STRENGTHS

P3 was selected and the assessment discussion focused on the client's *disorder of the self*. However, there was evidence that contradicted that conceptualization: The client responds well to the normal disappointments, failures, and frustrations of living, had long-lasting relationships with reciprocity, and demonstrated the capacity to empathize with others.

THE THERAPIST'S UNDERSTANDING
OF THE HYPOTHESIS IS DEFICIENT

The assessment section contains this sentence: *His lack of interpersonal skills is rooted in the death of his mother when he was 20.* In the subjective section, he wrote: *When she died he put himself into a shell and didn't speak to anyone about his feelings and distanced himself from his family and friends.* The fact that he withdraws from people after the death of his mother does not demonstrate a skill deficit. There were data that showed good interpersonal skills in high school and college.

Assessment Omits a Strong Hypothesis

The assessment omits mention of a hypothesis that is an exceptionally good fit for data you have collected. This error often overlaps with the prior one: The contradictory data usually points toward a different hypothesis.

EXAMPLE

Review the case of Maria in Appendix III. Do you agree that the fact that her father left on her 12th birthday, never to contact her again, is a significant event that will affect her ability to have trusting relationships with men? This event should be addressed in the assessment discussion, because it contributed to faulty cognitive maps about men and marriage (**C2**), contributes to reenactments of old experiences (**P2**), or has created the need for defenses against unconscious pain (**P4**).

> **Standard 20.** The assessment does not introduce new data.

Standard 20 is the flip side of Standard 12—the database must be complete. *The database must contain every bit of information that is going to contribute to the formulation.* Draw a horizontal line between the O and A sections, and remind yourself—repeatedly—that *all data must first be presented prior to that line.* As long as data appeared prior to that line, they can be repeated in the A section to illustrate a point or provide evidence for an argument.

When you are checking to see if your report meets this standard and notice that the assessment includes data as supportive evidence for an idea, you must take the trouble to go back and review the S and O sections to be sure that the information was initially presented there. In the following example, the sentences in italics must be copied into the appropriate database section.

NEW S DATA APPEARING IN ASSESSMENT

A: Mark also struggles with issues of dysfunctional self-talk. When questioned about his thought process when experiencing anxiety, *Mark revealed his most common thoughts to be: "Don't say something stupid, you will look like an idiot. You just don't have the social skills you need."*

NEW O DATA APPEARING IN ASSESSMENT

A: Linda has a distorted view of her parents, seeing her mother as all bad and her father as all good. She denies feeling that her father abandoned her, even though he failed to protect her from a mother he knew was emotionally and physically abusing her. *Any suggestion I made that her father was perhaps partially responsible for those traumatic years was met with either an excuse or an attempt to change the topic back to her mother.*

As mentioned previously, it is very common for new data to come to mind when you are engaged in the creative process of writing your assessment discussions. Therefore, you need to always allow time to review and revise your completed report.

> **Standard 21.** The focus of the assessment is on the specific problem of the specific client: This is not an abstract essay about a theory.

Once the method is understood, this standard is rarely violated. When errors occur, they usually happen in the first attempt to use the problem-oriented method (POM). It takes time to break habits that developed from being a student. Students are often asked in *Theories of Personality* or *Psychotherapy* courses to write essays about a theorist or about the entire personality of an individual. When students "choose an orientation," they often assume that explaining the orientation will serve to also explain the client. Furthermore, as a student you were rewarded for showing the teacher how much you knew, so you have to transition to a more confident tone, selecting only those ideas that explain the problem and lead to treatment plans.

Two reminders will usually be enough to get you on the right track:

> 1. You SOAP the problem, not the person.
> 2. You explain the problem, not the theory.

The Correct Way

- **Problem:** *Distress over jealousy and conflict in relationship with sister.*

A: Helen and her sister have created different schemas (**C2**) of how they define love from their father. Helen evaluates love in material ways and, because her sister receives more financial help from their father, she tries to make her father feel guilty so that he will give her more material items. Her sister, in contrast, measures love from their father in terms of how much he respects her, and recognizes that he has more respect for Helen, a successful professional. These two different schemas have resulted in a fixed sibling rivalry for the past 10 years.

- **Problem:** *Frustration over failure to find and date women who "meet his standards."*

A: While growing up, Ali's father was a very strong figure in his family's life. In his Jamaican Muslim family (**SCE2**), the mother took care of the home, and the father financially provided for the family. Educated and strong-minded women in that society were not seen as appropriate marriage partners. Despite his avowed desire to have a wife of equal education and intelligence, he rejects women who want equality and are not submissive to his authority. He takes advantage of American cultural norms by having sex with a woman as soon as possible, and then, even though she meets his standards in every way, he views her as unacceptable as a wife because of her lack of modesty and chastity.

The Wrong Way

A student who had mastered the method but was frustrated by its restrictions, began a paragraph in the assessment discussion, "Allow me to digress" and launched into a detailed explanation of a theory, after which he wrote in parentheses, "please disregard if this is killing my paper." In the following examples, the italicized portions in the A section need to be eliminated:

- **Problem:** *Difficulty establishing close, trusting relationship with woman.*

A: The struggle between the desires for intimacy and independence was probably a constant tension in his life and may be at the root of his current problem (**P2, P3, or P4**). His early relationship with his mother was marked by extreme anxiety over separation. *Otto Rank maintained, "Every newborn human comes face to face with his first object, his mother, only to begin gradually to lose her. This primal catastrophe is the harbinger of all the losses and separations that await in human life, and indeed is paradigmatic of all of life's later suffering."*

Suggested rewording: *His pattern of breaking off relationships with women at the point when he starts feeling dependent is his way of protecting himself from reexperiencing the feelings of loss from early disappointments with his mother (**P2**).*

- **Problem:** *Ambivalence over revealing his sexual orientation.*

A: We have a cultural issue working with Dave (**SCE2**). I feel that as American culture evolves over the next several decades we will begin to see the acceptance of diverse subcultures. Today, white, Christian, heterosexual Americans are in the minority in many parts of the country. As 10% of the population, American homosexual males and females have found refuge in large areas of our cities.

Suggested rewording: Dave's level of comfort with living an openly gay lifestyle would be increased if he lived in a geographic location with an active gay community (**SCE7**).

- **Problem:** *Difficulty completing tasks in a timely manner.*

A: In view of Polly's life history and the role models that surrounded her, her level of competence shows her exceptional resilience. *Survival* is an amazing thing. It shows up in detention facilities, rehab centers, and in academia. The reasons why humans shape their survival mechanisms the way they do is beyond the scope of my understanding. Nevertheless, I profoundly respect each individual's means of survival. Life preservers are practical tools that keep us alive. They save us from sinking and come in all shapes and sizes. More importantly, they can slowly be deflated once we realize that we can tread water. *Polly's life preserver is a need for perfection.*

Suggested rewording: She developed the schema "I need to be perfect to survive" (**C2**), an early childhood decision, which contributed to her high achievements, but is now working against her ability to succeed in a high-pressured job where B+ work delivered on time is more highly valued than A+ work that is late. The metaphor of a life preserver would help to challenge her perfectionism.

Another violation of Standard 21 occurs when the assessment discussion does not explain the problem as titled, but instead discusses a different problem.

> When you write your assessment discussion, keep referring back to the problem title.

In the following example, the italicized portions in the A section show that the writer has strayed from the defined problem:

- **Problem:** *Difficulty completing projects that have vague rather than definite deadlines.*

  A: The client's *ambivalence about remaining in her job* or pursuing an entrepreneurial opportunity has its roots in the way her father functioned as a role model.

Clearly, the therapist has in mind this problem: *Difficulty deciding whether to remain in job or pursue an entrepreneurial opportunity.* If the client agrees that this is an issue, a new problem is added. However, a new assessment needs to be written for the original problem.

> **Standard 22.** The writer is not including all possible hypotheses, just the ones that are useful in developing intervention plans.

If you completed the chart illustrated in Table 14.1 in preparation for writing your SOAP, you will have no difficulty adhering to this standard.

In Chapter 10, you were encouraged to brainstorm and "try on" as many hypotheses as you could. When you write a formal report, the assessment section requires selection and exclusion: You need to select the hypotheses, which, in your opinion, *best* fit the data and will lead to the *best* treatment plans. Quality is measured by the effectiveness of the plan, not by the quantity of ideas.

Sometimes, therapists who do a great job applying hypotheses in their sessions and recognizing hypotheses in reviewing transcripts, find themselves blocked when it is time to write the assessment section. They search for ideas for their assessment essay as if they were starting with a blank slate, instead of putting on paper, with precision and clarity, *the exact ideas that have been in their minds when they sit with clients.* A useful strategy, albeit very time consuming, is to transcribe your own tape-recorded sessions, leaving a wide right margin, and write down the hypotheses that come to mind (see Tables 10.2 and 10.3 for examples).

Remember to always check whether there are ideas in the A section that are not followed up in the plan. This standard is the flip side of Standard 27: *Plans follow logically from the prior formulation discussion; new ideas are not introduced.* To achieve the best possible case formulations, study the following principles:

The hypotheses in the assessment and the prescribed intervention are rationally related to each other:

- The assessment provides the rationale for the plan.
- The plan is the experiment that tests the validity of the hypotheses in the assessment.

If you find a lack of consistency between these two sections, these are your options:

- Standard 22—When the assessment section is too broad, you can:
  —Add more ideas to the P section.
  —Eliminate parts of the A section.
- Standard 27—When the plan section is too broad, you can:
  —Add more ideas to the A section.
  —Eliminate parts of the P section.

Standard 23. If theoretical jargon is used, it enhances rather than detracts from understanding and does not contribute to tautological explanations.

Here are two definitions of *tautology:*

1. The saying of the same thing twice over in different words (Concise Oxford Dictionary).
2. Repetition of the sense of word(s) in other unnecessary words (http://www.tiscali.com.uk/reference/dictionaries/difficultwords/data/d0012694.html).

Tautology often occurs when a foreign language or an acronym is used, for example, *The La Brea tar pits* means "the the tar tar pits." When we say the "SUDS scale" we are guilty of tautology because the meaning of that phrase is Subjective Units of Discomfort Scale scale. Tautology frequently arises when we use jargon, which is like a foreign language.

David Levy (1997) dedicated a chapter in his book on critical thinking to "The nominal fallacy and tautologous reasoning: To name something isn't to explain it" (pp. 19–22). Here is an example of circular, tautological reasoning:

The man is so sociable because he's an extravert.
How do you know that he's an extravert?
Because he is so sociable.

Levy explains how diagnostic labels promote tautological explanations:

The cause of her suspiciousness of everybody's motives is Paranoid Personality Disorder.

How do you know that she's got Paranoid Personality Disorder?

By the fact that she's suspicious of everybody's motives.

Once your ears become sensitized to the presence of tautologies, you will notice them in many psychological explanations:

- Her low self-esteem is caused by her negative self-appraisal.

  (Low self-esteem and negative self-appraisal mean exactly the same thing.)

- His ambivalence resulted from mixed feelings toward each option.

  (The definition of ambivalence is mixed feelings.)

- Because of a fused relationship, Jane feels an unhealthy amount of responsibility for her mother's happiness.

  (The only basis for the judgment of a fused relationship was the level of responsibility of the daughter, so there is no justification for a causal statement.)

- His shyness stems from his Social Anxiety Disorder.

  (Unlike a medical diagnosis, a psychiatric diagnosis is not an explanation, which includes etiology: It is only an arbitrary title given to a collection of symptoms and behaviors.)

The lesson from these examples is this:

> Technical terms (jargon) should only be used if they have explanatory power. If the explanation is sufficient without these terms, they should be eliminated.

One of the advantages of removing esoteric jargon from your assessments is that you are learning to express your formulation in words that can easily be shared with your client. This is not to say that you should avoid jargon at all costs—just be sure that you are avoiding circular reasoning and the nominal fallacy. The following sentences give examples of nontautological explanatory sentences that use technical terms:

- The attention that she gets from her peers serves as *a reinforcer* for the behavior that annoys her teacher.
- Her anxiety symptoms were precipitated by the simultaneous occurrence of several *psychosocial stressors:* loss of job, mother's illness, and breakup of a relationship.
- She achieved high levels of academic success despite coming from a very economically disadvantaged background thanks to the influence of several positive *role models.*

> **Standard 24.** The writer is integrating material from the highest level of education thus far attained. Commonsense ideas are appropriate but are not sufficient for explaining the problem.

The explanation of the client's problem should demonstrate knowledge gained from academic courses, clinical supervision, independent reading, and continuing education courses. The evaluation of reports must take into consideration the level of experience of the writer. There usually is dramatic improvement between the first and third attempts at a formulation. Here is an example of improvement in the quality of an explanation through revision:

FIRST DRAFT

Jenny's problem is caused by low self-esteem. She lets her husband walk over her and she doesn't take care of her own needs.

REVISED

Jenny's faulty model of the world (**C2**) contributes to her problem. First, she believes that someone her age "has to take what she can get" in a relationship. She thinks that she is not deserving of anything better in a relationship because she waited so long to get into a marriage. She places her own needs second because she does not believe that she is deserving of happiness.

Even though you have taken many psychology and counseling courses and studied the 28 hypothesis, there is still an important role for common sense and your own life experience in creating good formulations. Here are two examples of assessment discussions that are written in a very natural style, showing how clinical hypotheses and intelligent common sense reasoning get blended together:

EXAMPLE 1

Millie revealed that she wants "everybody to be happy so they don't have bad thoughts." Although a well-intentioned statement, it would be more appropriately spoken by an 8-year-old child than a 22-year-old adult (**P3, C2**). Millie describes her relationship with Leo as confusing because it has bad and good parts. Unfortunately, all adult relationships have positive and negative features and her desire to be involved in a relationship that is only good is another example of her misperceptions about life (**C1**). She became totally disenchanted with one of the men she was dating, and immediately ended the relationship, because he "wanted to talk about depressing things."

EXAMPLE 2

Mary's first experience of love was a relationship that ended after 3 months, and in the 2 years since that painful breakup, she has avoiding dating for fear of getting hurt again. In addition to having unresolved issues related to grief (**CS4**), she seems to be struggling with issues of moving to the next phase in her life (**CS3**). The experiences of a first love and first breakup are normal developmental phases most people go through. This attachment and subsequent loss is a challenging phase, which, although extremely painful, usually creates an opportunity for personal discovery or growth, as well as providing learning experiences for future relationships.

> **Standard 25.** The writer demonstrates professional-level thinking and writing skills to provide a coherent conceptualization.

The main reason for revision is to improve the quality of your ideas, thereby improving the quality of services for the client. Once your ideas are clear to you, you then must put additional time and effort into your writing skills so that your ideas become equally clear to the reader. When someone else will read your writing, you must challenge yourself to think clearly, provide missing links, anticipate objections, and search for better words. When the report is completed to your satisfaction, you still need to allow time for a final revision to correct grammar and spelling. Some suggestions for good writing were presented previously under Database Standard 17.

The Writing Process Can Be Divided into Three Stages

1. *Prewriting:* Getting ready to write. Reviewing instructions. Making preliminary outlines. Getting in the mood.
2. *Free-writing:* Getting your ideas down without caring about grammar and punctuation. Brainstorming, without criticism. Not worrying about getting your ideas in the right section of the report.
3. *Rewriting:* Editing. Searching for the best words to convey your meaning. Improving organization. Consulting a writing style reference book. Proofreading.

Criteria for Good Writing

- *Clarity of ideas:* This involves balancing concrete and specific illustrations with abstract statements.
- *Good organization:* This criterion applies to paragraphs and the entire essay.
- *Analytic thinking:* This criterion requires the use of complex sentences, effective vocabulary, and coherent development of thought.
- *Editing and Proofreading:* These steps involve taking the time to improve sentences and catch errors in grammar, spelling, and punctuation.

Clarity of ideas: A well-written paragraph often begins with a topic sentence that contains abstract ideas, followed by sentences that provide concrete examples and detailed explanations. Here is a brief assessment paragraph that shows both abstract ideas and concrete clarification.

- *Topic sentence:* Cognitive factors (**C2**) play a role in Anat's *ambivalence* about Mark.

- *Clarifying the Term Ambivalence:* She feels torn between wanting to follow her heart and marry Mark and wanting to marry someone her parents approve of (**P1**).

- *Giving Examples of Cognitive Factors*: She highly *values* many of Mark's qualities: he is loyal, dependable, romantic, ambitious, has similar interests, and maturely communicates his feelings. He treats her well, making thoughtful gestures and showing respect for her opinions, in contrast to her former boyfriend. She does not *believe* that his ethnic background is important, but she knows that her parents believe she should marry someone of their ethnic background (**SCE2**). She not only *assumes* that her parents will never give Mark a chance, she has the underlying *schema*, "I can't survive without my parents' approval."

Good organization: Good organization does not come automatically. A good college English text is a great help in improving organization. Bell and Cohn (1976) give advice for good expository writing: *use the techniques of development to clarify, illustrate, or prove your main idea* (p. 17). The following example of a student's assessment section gives a model of good organization. Every broad, general statement of the hypothesis is developed with specific statements that refer to concrete data. The reader is guided along the path of the writer's thinking. The discussion is clear and coherent—and, most important, lays out a foundation for treatment plans.

- **Problem:** *Distress in social encounters at workplace.*

Tom feels that his English speaking ability and his dissimilar cultural background prevent him from feeling comfortable when socializing and speaking English at work.

A: Tom's native culture and his Taiwanese upbringing seem to contribute to his dilemma at work (**SCE2**). Tom was born and raised for the first 10 years of his life in Taiwan, and he is only partially acculturated to the norms of the United States. For an example, Tom mentioned that his colleagues do not understand why he still lives at home with his parents. His colleagues do not understand that it is a Taiwanese tradition for the oldest son to care for his aging parents. It seemed that what his parents have taught him about certain values, morals, and ways of life are not necessarily in agreement with those of his colleagues and the clash of cultures has put Tom in an awkward position at work.

The company that Tom works for has been around for many years and it is quite possible that this specific company has its own customs. It could be possible that Tom's specific working environment is heavily driven by the company's traditions. For an example, Tom stated that most of his immediate colleagues are older Caucasian males. He may not be aware that the demographic makeup at his workplace could establish a company-specific environment that he is not very comfortable with. Thus, he may not necessarily be at odds with the American culture but rather with his company's corporate culture.

Tom could also have an unrealistic expectation of his workplace. His "utopian syndrome" (**C1**) might have led him to believe that the experience of being the only member of his minority group in a predominantly Caucasian work environment would be easy. He might believe that he should be able to "blend" right in or that others should reach out to him to make him comfortable without his having to expend any effort.

Tom appears to be engaged in faulty information processing (**C3**). Throughout all three sessions, I thought Tom's English was very good considering that it is not his native language. His sentences were clear and easily understood. He spoke intelligently and his thoughts were coherent. Based on my experience with him, I do not believe that coworkers would feel uncomfortable communicating with him. He described a situation when he felt uneasy with the silence during a car ride with a colleague. Tom's cognitive distortion of "mind reading" was demonstrated by his belief that it was because of his poor English that his colleague was silent. His colleague's silence while riding in the car could be attributed to other factors. Perhaps the colleague was tired or he was comfortable with the silent car ride. The coworker may have assumed that Tom wanted silence. Tom's erroneous schema (**C2**) that others reject him because of his English speaking ability or his ethnicity may function as a self-filling prophecy: He doesn't speak spontaneously so others assume he has language difficulties and so avoid initiating conversation.

Tom's feeling of being isolated at work could also be explained by his lack of certain interpersonal communication skills (**BL3**). Tom stated that he had surrounded himself with Mandarin-speaking friends and that his social circle has been limited to those with a similar cultural background. Tom is skilled at interacting with these people, outside of his work, in his native language. His hesitation to initiate a casual conversation at work could be attributed to the fact that he has not given himself a chance to practice his socializing skills in English and with non-Chinese Americans.

Analytical thinking: Competence in case formulation skills requires the ability to create an original analysis. In a hierarchy of cognitive skills, the middle range includes descriptions, summaries, and explanations and at the top is the ability to analyze and critically evaluate. Some dictionary meanings of *analyze* are: to examine critically, to bring out the essential elements, and to examine carefully and in detail so as to identify causes, key factors, possible results, and so on. Implied in the term *analyze* is the expenditure of mental effort and the creative combination of ideas.

A high-quality assessment discussion includes speculation, hunches, and logical deduction. The writer demonstrates that he or she is actively engaged in the creative process of conceptualization, applying hypotheses and demonstrating, convincingly, the goodness of their fit. A barrier to demonstrating high-level analytical thinking is the inability to write complex sentences that are linked together with appropriate transitional expressions, besides "and" and "but." Table 14.2 provides a list of commonly used transitional expressions (Bell & Cohn, 1976, pp. 98–99) that will improve the flow of sentences and the quality of analytical writing.

The skeleton of an analytical assessment discussion: An illustration of the bare bones of an assessment discussion is useful—as an example of principles of organization, not a template to substitute for your own creative style. Table 14.3 gives the outline of an assessment that integrates three hypotheses. The opening paragraph states the writer's main thesis. Each subsequent paragraph has a clear topic sentence that is followed by supportive ideas and specific statements. The italicized phrases carry the logic of the writer's argument.

Editing and proofreading: There are many mistakes that appear in written reports that can easily be avoided by using a stylebook (Strunk & White, 2000) and proofreading carefully, without trusting the spell-check feature in word-processing programs. After revising the essay for content and style, proofread the report by printing out a hard copy. Here is an example of an error that could easily have been caught by reading through the finished document:

Table 14.2   Transitional Phrases to Enhance Analytical Writing

Addition	Additionally, again, also, and also, and then, as well, besides, beyond that, equally important, first (second, third, fourth, finally, last, lastly, etc.), for one thing, further, furthermore, in addition, likewise, moreover, next, now, on top of that, over and above that
Comparison	In the same way, likewise, similarly
Contrast	After all, although this may be true, and yet, be that as it may, but even so, for all that, however, in contrast, in other circumstances, in spite of that, nevertheless, nonetheless, on the contrary, on the other hand, otherwise, still, yet
Emphasis	Above all, certainly, especially, in any event, in fact, in particular, indeed, most important, surely
Exemplification	As an example, as an illustration, for example, for instance, in other words, in particular, that is
Reason	For this purpose, for this reason, to this end
Result	Accordingly, as a consequence, as a result, consequently, for that reason, hence, inevitably, necessarily, that being the case, then, therefore, thus
Summary	As has been noted, as I have said, finally, in brief, in other words, in short, in sum, lastly, on the whole, to be sure, to sum up

Adapted from *Rhetoric in a Modern Mode* (pp. 98–99), 3rd ed., by J. K. Bell and A. A. Cohn, 1976, Beverly Hills, CA: Glencoe Press.

Table 14.3 Sample of a Well-Organized Assessment Discussion

Paragraph #1 Thesis Paragraph

Topic sentence: Nicole's ambivalence toward her relationship with Steve *can be explained* in terms of two parts of her personality in conflict (**P1**).

One part of her wants to remain with Steve because of her comfort level and belief that he is trustworthy and dependable (topic for paragraph #2), *whereas* her other part feels insecure in the relationship and engages in destructive behavior (**P2**) to sabotage the relationship (topic for paragraph #3).

It is crucial to understand the cognitive elements (**C2**) that *contribute* to her conflict (topic for paragraph #4).

Paragraph #2

Topic sentence: The part that wants to remain in the relationship *is based on* both positive experiences with Steve *as well as* a reaction to negative experiences with her prior boyfriend.

She has had many positive experiences with him, *particularly* _____ .

As a result, she _____ .

This relationship *is in sharp contrast* to _____ .

For this reason, she maintains the belief (**C2**) that _____ .

Paragraph #3

Topic sentence: The part that wants to destroy the relationship *stems from* early childhood experiences (**P2**).

To summarize negative childhood experiences, _____ .

In addition, her dad left frequently, *creating* _____ .

Therefore, it can be inferred that _____ .

It is as if she's trying to _____ .

Paragraph #4

Topic sentence: Cognitive factors (**C2**) *contribute to* Nicole's ambivalence about her relationship with Steve.

For example, _____ .

However, she also believes _____ .

In contrast, she _____ .

On top of that, there is _____ .

As a consequence, she _____ .

The student needed to change her client's real name to a fictitious name before submitting the report. The client's name was "Ron" and she wanted to use "Sam." She used the "Find and Replace" feature of the word-processing program, but forgot to put a space after the name Ron, so every time those three letters appeared in the report, they were replaced with Sam. Here are two strange words that appeared: *confSamtation, wSamg.* By not making proofreading the final step, the writer not only handed in a document with errors, but revealed the client's identity and violated confidentiality.

Sometimes good writing requires breaking habits from prior educational experiences:

- Concise is not always better.
- You *are* allowed to use the word "I."
- American Psychological Association (APA) manuscript style is for journal articles, not for all psychological writing.

ACTIVITY 14.2

Writing Your Assessment Discussion

The instructions in Appendix III tell you to write organized discussions for the cases you prepared in Activity 14.1.

Chapter 15 ———————————————————————

THE TREATMENT PLAN

This is the first time in this manual that we deal with the "how" of therapy: *What, specifically, will happen in sessions with the client? What skills will the therapist exercise? What technical expertise will the therapist bring to bear on the client's problems? What type of relationship will be created? What specific processes are considered therapeutic?*

The plan describes how the therapist will work with the client to achieve the goals of treatment and resolve the problems. In addition, it is hoped that treatment plans will assure more resilience and competence so that the client can have better resources for coping with future problems. A plan addresses the goals for different stages of therapy and recommends techniques and the creation of a productive therapist-client relationship.

Every previous chapter has been leading up to the main purpose of a case formulation: to create unique treatment plans for each client. Although the plan is the most important, it actually takes less time and effort than other sections: All the work you put into the assessment pays off by having the ideas of the plan flow naturally and logically. Table 15.1 presents the components of treatment plans.

Part II reviewed every hypothesis and gave ideas for plans as well as suggestions for reading. Table 15.2 provides a quick reference to the 28 hypotheses with a few key ideas for treatment plans but is not intended to be a substitute for deeper, comprehensive knowledge of each hypothesis.

In general, clients should leave therapy not only with their current problems resolved, but also with enhanced problem-solving skills for the future. Beitman and Yue (1999) provide a framework for classifying types of goals in terms of the "desired level of change," which is illustrated in Table 15.3.

STANDARDS FOR PLANS

Eight standards provide guidelines for treatment plans. Be aware that as you develop your plans you will often need to check back and review and possibly improve all prior sections of the report.

> **Standard 26**. The plan is focused on resolving the identified problem and achieving outcome goals.

Table 15.1 Components of Treatment Plans

Component	Explanation	Examples
Process Goals The goals for desired in-session experiences, which are based on the therapist's conceptualization. The process goal contains *verb phrases* referring to the therapist's intentions or to the client's experiences.	Process goals keep the focus on the outcome goals, link the explanation (hypothesis) to the plan, and assure appropriate quality of therapist-client relationship. Clear statements of process goals provide good topic sentences for paragraphs in the plan section.	1. Develop rapport and allow client to disclose at her own pace. 2. Listen to both parts of client's inner conflict without suppression. 3. Explain the effects of racial discrimination on client's level of aspirations.
Intermediate Objectives or **Subgoals** These are outcome goals for small achievements and for brief units of time.	Subgoals include: 1. Small steps in quantity. 2. Steps in hierarchy of difficulty. 3. Successive approximations in quality of behavior. 4. Different goals for stages or subphases of therapy.	1. Exercising once a week with the outcome goal of five times a week. 2. Snake phobic will look at pictures of cartoon snakes without anxiety. 3. Achieve good eye contact before learning verbal skills. 4. Battered wife will agree to talk to a shelter representative.
Strategy This is an overall map of the method for achieving a certain goal. Issues in the relationship of the therapist and client are addressed.	Strategies include: 1. Implement a theoretical model of intervention. 2. Integrate several hypotheses. 3. Adopt an empirically validated treatment manual.	1. Use crisis intervention model. 2. Join with the family and develop credibility for specific cultural group. 3. Implement Barlow's manual for Panic Disorder.
Technique or **Procedure** The procedure is a way of implementing the strategy and specifies what the therapist does in a session.	Categories include: 1. Implement a technique. 2. Direct an experiential activity. 3. Provide a specific type of support. 4. Participate as a fellow pilgrim.	1. Systematic Desensitization technique (**BL2**). 2. Direct a voice dialogue activity (**P1**). 3. Supportive listener with bereaved client (**CS4**). 4. Share stories of oppression (**SCE5**).
Format This is the modality of treatment and the specification of people included.	Inclusion of family or community members is appropriate with certain cultural groups. The choice of couple versus individual therapy influences the risk of divorce. Family therapy is usually the treatment of choice when children are involved.	Individual therapy, play therapy with child, group therapy, couple therapy, family therapy, group family therapy, community network therapy, hospital milieu therapy, token economy in institutional setting.

(continued)

Table 15.1   *(Continued)*

Component	Explanation	Examples
Setting This is the location of the meetings between client and therapist.	In choosing to meet outside an office, consider the risk of dual relationships and confused boundaries, but at the same time be flexible enough to accommodate differences in culture and life circumstances. For disorders that involve hospitalization, consider a continuum of care, assuring the least restrictive environment.	Private office; community outpatient clinic; psychiatric hospital; drug or alcohol residential rehabilitation center; day treatment; halfway house; visits to the client's home; in vivo settings, going to the place where the problem occurs; casual informal settings, such as a park; visit to a client who is in a medical hospital.
Duration and Frequency Duration is the length of treatment, often classified as short-term versus long-term and time-limited versus open-ended. Frequency is usually described as number of meetings per week, but "as needed" is an option.	With higher levels of impairment, more frequent sessions and longer treatment are justified. Insurance or finances may limit duration. A maintenance phase may follow an intensive course of treatment. A "dental model" toward therapy involves periodic checkups.	Suggest a minimum of 20 sessions for moderate impairment; "open-ended" for someone not relying on insurance. Make contract for 10 sessions and then review progress. Crisis model (**CS2**) needs a sufficient duration to return the client to prior equilibrium.

Keep focused by writing topic sentences in the plan section that clearly describe process goals and subgoals. The final paragraph of the plan should deal with monitoring progress toward outcome goals.

In reviewing your plan section, you may notice that it has strayed from the stated problem. Because developing a formulation is a creative, nonlinear process, it occasionally happens that as you write the plan, new ideas pop into your head. When you examine the quality of these ideas, you may decide that the wording of the problem title could be improved. Alternatively, you may realize that you have lost your focus and have accidentally written plans for a completely different problem, or worse, for a problem that is not consistent with the data.

Here is an example, using the case of Maria from Appendix III, of a plan that strays from the problem title, two solutions are offered on page 492.

- **Problem:** *Difficulty expressing feelings.*

P: Maria needs to contact Tony and decide if she still has feelings for him. I would help her role-play the phone call in which she suggests they get together for lunch. It is possible that when she has developed better skills in expressing herself, she will be able to improve the quality of that relationship and convince him that they need to date longer, without pressure to make a commitment, for them to discover whether they would be a compatible married couple. If Tony refuses to meet with her, or when they get together, she finds that there is no hope of continuing that relationship, she can feel more satisfied with the closure.

Table 15.2   Treatment Ideas for Twenty-Eight Core Clinical Hypotheses

Hypothesis	Plan Recommendation
I. Biological Hypotheses (B)	
B1 Biological Cause	Medical referral. Assistance coping with illness. Family involvement. Case management approach. Use of community resources for disabilities.
B2 Medical Interventions	Referral for medication consult. Coordination with prescribing physician. Promote compliance. Be careful not to exceed limits of competence in discussing medical issues.
B3 Mind-Body Connections	Psychoeducation. Relaxation training using the SUDS. Specialized techniques: focusing, EMDR, guided imagery, biofeedback.
II. Crisis, Stressful Situations, and Transitions (CS)	
CS1 Emergency	Take immediate action consistent with legal and ethical obligations. Protect client and others (mandatory). Provide support if hospitalization is necessary.
CS2 Situational Stressors	Crisis intervention model. Post-trauma interventions to prevent PTSD. Treatment of PTSD using integration of methods. Teach tools for managing negative emotions and solving problems.
CS3 Developmental Transition	Psychoeducation and normalization. Family intervention when appropriate. Bibliotherapy. Use of support groups.
CS4 Loss and Bereavement	Psychoeducation and normalization. Referral to support group. Treatment of complicated bereavement integrates methods for depression and PTSD. Recommend hospice care for dying patients. Family support. Don't impose rigid model of "right way to grieve."
III. Behavioral and Learning Models (BL)	
BL1 Antecedents and Consequences	Strategy based on behavioral analysis. Increase desired behavior with positive reinforcement. Contingency contracting.
BL2 Conditioned Emotional Response	Deconditioning interventions: desensitization in imagery, in vivo exposure, or flooding techniques. Incorporate relaxation training.

(continued)

Table 15.2 *(Continued)*

Hypothesis	Plan Recommendation
III. Behavioral and Learning Models (BL)	
BL3 Skill Deficits or Lack of Competence	Coaching, behavioral rehearsal, homework for practice, and use of role models. Shaping with successive approximations. Assign reading. Referral to classes.
IV. Cognitive Models (C)	
C1 Utopian Expectations	Psychoeducation. Identify and modify faulty expectations.
C2 Faulty Cognitive Map	Identify cognitive elements. Self-monitoring homework. Use CBT techniques. Discuss origins of early maladaptive schemas. Narrative Therapy. Transactional Analysis to strengthen Adult's ability to evaluate and change dysfunctional map.
C3 Faulty Information Processing	Explain list of errors in thinking (e.g., overgeneralization, all-or-nothing). Use Beck's collaborative empiricism or Ellis's disputation. Self-monitoring homework.
C4 Dysfunctional Self-Talk	Teach Event-Thought-Feeling relationships. Self-monitoring homework. Create and practice alternatives. Implement stress inoculation. Externalize negative "voice."
V. Existential and Spiritual Models (ES)	
ES1 Existential Issues	The "wisdom is in the client." Phenomenological focus. Philosophical discussion. Logotherapy or narrative therapy to create new meaningful stories. Authentic encounter in client-therapist relationship. Use of "here and now."
ES2 Avoiding Freedom and Responsibility	Explain domains of freedom and limitation. Challenge childhood illusions. Reality therapy or TA: Is what you are doing getting you want you want? Confrontation of evasions of freedom. Goal-setting skills, planning, and support during action phase. Teach tools for self-control.

Table 15.2   *(Continued)*

Hypothesis	Plan Recommendation
V. Existential and Spiritual Models (ES)	

ES3 Spiritual Dimension	Help client access spiritual resources.
	Sensitivity to needs of religious and nonreligious clients.
	Promote experimentation in various spiritual paths, including creative arts.
	Integrate Eastern religious methods.
	Consider referral to clergyperson.
	Moral consultation mode.
	Bring spiritual activity into session.

VI. Psychodynamic Models (P)	
P1 Internal Parts and Subpersonalities	Experiential activity to allow different parts to speak.
	Voice dialogue or Gestalt two-chair activity.
	Explore early origins of parts.
	Set goals for specific parts.
	Creative writing and art.
P2 Reenactment of Early Childhood Experiences	Promote emotional experiencing as well as insight.
	Experiential activities: Gestalt empty chair for "unfinished business," imago or emotionally focused therapy with couples, or psychodrama in groups.
	Utilize transference.
P3 Immature Sense of Self and Conception of Others	Psychoanalytic method using selfobject transference, empathic attunement, and sensitive handling of empathic failures.
	Couple therapy.
	Bowen's methods to promote differentiation of self.
	POV activity to build capacity for empathy and taking multiple perspectives.
P4 Unconscious Dynamics	Psychoanalytic method using neurotic transference for emotional reexperiencing.
	Dream interpretation; art therapy; hypnotherapy.

VII. Social, Cultural, and Environmental Factors (SCE)	
SCE1 Family System	Conjoint therapy with multiple clients, with flexibility to see individuals or dyads, as well as the whole system. Techniques from different models (e.g., structural, strategic, or Bowenian).
SCE2 Cultural Context	Modification of traditional methods according to needs of members of different cultures.
	Utilize culture's own healing methods.
	Interventions including family members and wider community.
	Empowerment approaches for groups with history of oppression.

(continued)

Table 15.2 *(Continued)*

Hypothesis	Plan Recommendation
VII. Social, Cultural, and Environmental Factors (SCE)	
SCE3 Social Support	Help client access current supports or develop new support network.
	Community referrals.
	Individualize plan, based on client's preferences for affiliation versus solitude.
	Monitor whether client lacks skills for making friends.
SCE4 Social Role Performance	Psychoeducation.
	Help client find role models and mentors.
	Engage client in problem solving and decision-making.
SCE5 Social Problem is a Cause	Avoid blaming the victim.
	Avoid perpetuating social problem in session. Empowerment methods.
	Explore possibilities of activism.
	Problem-solving methods.
SCE6 Social Role of Mental Patient	Always use least restrictive environment.
	Protect client from stigma.
	Limit-setting with malingerers.
	Address ethical and legal issues.
SCE7 Environmental Factors	Explore "change environment" solution without "pro-psychology" bias.
	Engage in problem solving and planning.

Two Solutions

1. Improve wording of problem title to make it more specific:
   - *Difficulty knowing and asserting her own feelings in an intimate relationship.*
2. Split off a new problem title:
   - *Unresolved feelings and unexamined possibilities for future, regarding prior romantic relationship.*

> **Standard 27.** The plan follows logically from the assessment discussion and does not introduce new data or hypotheses.

Standard 27 is linked with Standard 22. Both standards check for the required logical connection between A and P. The three-column chart illustrated in Table 14.1 (and available as Form I.E in Appendix I) is very useful to check for corre-

Table 15.3   Planning for Different Orders of Change

First-Order Change	
The goal is a *specific change* in the near future in a single instance.	Reduced anxiety during an important interview.
Second-Order Change	
The goal is *pattern change*. The client will have altered a pattern in a way that generalizes to new situations. There is a change in a system, which means new rules operate in the future.	Client learns to alter irrational thoughts that contribute to anxiety and apply anxiety management tools prior to various feared events.
Third-Order Change	
The goal is the patient's *ability to change patterns without the help of the therapist.*	Faced with new problems, the client will have the skills to recognize dysfunctional patterns, relinquish them, and develop and maintain new functional patterns.

spondence between the ideas in each section. Once you have assured that there is sufficient data to support the hypotheses, you can proceed to a two-column, chart, illustrated in Table 15.4, which allows you to organize all of your plan ideas next to each chosen hypothesis.

Table 15.5 shows the alternative use of a two-column method with the plan in the first instead of the second column and is a useful approach for those therapists who intuitively jump to treatment ideas first, and then need to explain the implicit hypothesis that underlies that plan.

These charts are the final step of preparation before writing a full report. The order of ideas in the plan will need to be adjusted to describe the best possible sequence of interventions for the specific client.

> Present hypotheses in the A section in the order of importance. Present ideas in the P section in the order in which they will be implemented.

When you are evaluating a completed case formulation report, you are looking for two types of violations:

1. The plan introduces new ideas that do not have a foundation in the A section.
2. The plan does not follow up ideas that were discussed in the A section.

New Ideas in Plan

Sometimes new assessment ideas appear in the plan that merely extend and embellish a topic that was previously discussed in the assessment section. When this happens, simple "cut-and-paste" revision will solve the problem, moving the new ideas to the place in the assessment discussion where they fit. A more

Table 15.4   Preparing Plan from Completed Assessment Discussion

Problem: *Difficulty establishing healthy committed relationship with men*

Assessment Discussion	Preliminary Ideas for Plan
P2 Reenactment of Early Childhood Experiences It is possible that Emily's pattern of picking emotionally unavailable men is a repetition compulsion in which she seeks men like her father, who emotionally abandoned her. By becoming romantically involved with men who love drugs or work more than they love her, she creates the same situation she experienced in childhood with her father's perpetual absence. By attempting to get these unavailable men to validate that she is lovable, she is unconsciously trying to win the love of her father.	Focus on relationship with father and her unmet needs. Go beyond intellectual awareness, and facilitate intense emotional experience; when emotions from past are in awareness, she won't need to protect herself from them.
BL3 Skill Deficits or Lack of Competence Perhaps Emily does not choose men with whom she will be happy because she never had an adequate model of what healthy love looks like. She therefore never gained the skill set of identifying traits in men that would contribute to a happy relationship. Instead, she selects men who share traits of her father, because that is all she knows of "love."	Use a psychoeducational approach. Recommend readings that illustrate healthy relationships. Have her make a list of her interests, values, and desired traits. As she meets new men, have her evaluate them according to this list. Once she identifies that a man lacks the necessary traits, assess whether she has a problem in terminating the relationship.

serious violation of this standard occurs when new ideas appear in the plan for which there was absolutely no foundation in the assessment. When this occurs, the therapist needs to make a choice: *Either do additional writing in the assessment or delete the new ideas in the plan.*

Example: Supplement the Assessment

- **Problem:** *Frustration over unfair distribution of labor in the apartment shared with three roommates.*
    - —*New idea in plan:* I believe that assertiveness training will help this client.
    - —*Reasoning backward to discover conceptual foundation:* The implied formulation must be that she has a skills deficit or that there is some barrier to using the assertive skills that she has.
    - —*What might be added to assessment:* The client knows what she wants to say to her roommates and has a clear sense of her rights in this situation.

Table 15.5 Identifying the Conceptual Foundation for Chosen Plan

Problem: *Difficulty coping with deaths of two family members within 3-month period*

Elements of Plan	Foundation in Assessment
	CS4 Loss and Bereavement
Use a Rogerian approach, providing a safe relationship for him to identify and explore his feelings. Engage in empathic listening; provide respect and acceptance.	He seems to be numb to the effects of death and loss. He does not seem to be going through any process of grieving. He seems to fear judgment and criticism for showing his vulnerable side.
	BL3 Skill Deficits or Lack of Competence
Assist him in the development of an emotional vocabulary: Use a "how do you feel today?" cartoon to help him identify emotional experiences, or model expression of feelings. Give him cues for spontaneous discussion of feelings and provide positive reinforcement.	He wants to talk about his feelings but is not sure how to go about doing this. He struggles with words when asked to express his feelings. Lack of emotional release may be the result of inexperience in processing emotions or a lack of role models who expressed feelings. This skill deficit is not unusual in men of this culture.
	P2 Reenactment of Early Childhood Experiences
Provide opportunity for him to access and express emotions related to early childhood experiences of rejection and abandonment. Use art techniques to help him access feelings. Suggest use of journal. Consider empty-chair methods if they seem appropriate.	He may have learned to numb himself and ignore emotional pain as a self-protective tactic when he was very young. When he was little, he had no empathic adult to help him express and label his feelings. If the current losses are reactivating feelings from early traumas, this would cause him to resist experiencing painful emotions.

She can verbalize appropriately, in an assertive manner, what would be a constructive approach to discussing this with her roommates, However, she is overcome with anxiety and has many catastrophic fantasies, and these reactions impede her ability to be appropriately assertive.

Example: Eliminate Idea from the Plan

- **Problem:** *Difficulty establishing an intimate relationship with potential marriage partner.*
  —*New idea in plan:* I want the client to do an empty-chair exercise with her father. I think it would help if she expressed to him, in the safety of the therapy room, the hurt and anger she feels over his treatment of her in her childhood.
  —*Reasoning backward to discover conceptual foundation:* What's my formulation? It has to be related to the problem title. I'm not working on her

relationship with her father—he died years ago. So my formulation must provide an explanation of how these unexpressed feelings toward her father are affecting her current relationships. I must provide some links in my discussion.

—*Decision process:* My plan already includes cognitive work on her childhood schemas (**C2**) related to her father; skill building (**BL3**), so she develops trust gradually and protects herself appropriately; and expecting opportunities for some transference to create opportunities for dealing with father (**P2**). Gestalt exercises are not necessary and might interfere with other process goals. I'll eliminate that idea from my plan.

Ignoring Ideas in Assessment

The same type of decision process must occur. Usually, you will add ideas to the plan because presumably the hypothesis was chosen because you believe it is the best match for the client. However, it is possible that, on final review, the formulation is coherent and sufficient without that hypothesis.

Occasionally, on reviewing the final report, you will notice a serious violation. New data appears in the plan.

> When you see data in a report after the O section, you must check the database to be sure that you are repeating prior data, not introducing new information.

This mistake is much easier to catch when you read another person's report because the new information comes as a surprise. When it is your own report, the information is familiar and doesn't jump out at you. The words in italics in the following sample are presenting data for the first time.

> **P:** I would want to address his inner parts (**P1**) and how each is reacting to his brother. George is very familiar with the part of him that feels angry and jealous. I think he needs to get to know better the part of him that feels very nurturing and protective. *When he was a 10-year-old, he went to summer camp with his 6-year-old brother, and when they were away from their parents, he took on the role of loving protector.*

When new data appear in the plan, you must fill the gap in the database and integrate the new data into the assessment section.

> **Standard 28.** There is clarity regarding process goals, intermediate objectives, strategies, specific techniques, relationship issues, and sequencing of interventions.

The amount of detail in a plan will depend on many factors, including:

- *The writer's level of education and clinical experience:* The first practice report of a graduate student for a course will probably be fairly general.
- *The number of completed sessions with the client:* Plans are more specific and detailed when there has been more contact, and therefore more data and greater understanding of the client's needs and preferences.
- *The choice of hypotheses:* Some hypotheses lead to very detailed and specific plans (e.g., **C2** and **BL1**) and others suggest more flexible and open-ended plans (e.g., **ES1**).
- *Time constraints in clinical practice:* An experienced therapist with a heavy caseload will use only a few brief notes.

A trainee should try to write as much detail as possible to consolidate skills and stimulate creative thinking. No matter how heavy the caseload, the trainee should be taking the time to create case formulation reports with extensive detail for at least two clients. Table 15.1, presented at the beginning of this chapter, contains guidelines and examples for the various components of a thorough plan.

The Therapeutic Relationship

The quality of the client-therapist relationship is often taken for granted, and not fully addressed in statements of treatment plans. However, much of what is beneficial in therapy occurs because of a genuine, healthy human relationship. The therapist cannot control what happens but can discuss in the plan what kind of relationship is desirable and what should be avoided. Flexibility and responsiveness to the client's needs must take precedence over a rigid implementation of a treatment protocol (Norcross, 2002). It is assumed that the therapist will attend to issues of rapport and empathy and be ready to repair ruptures in the alliance. Here are some process goals pertaining to the client-therapist relationship:

Develop Rapport and Trust

- I will be careful not to invalidate the client's perceptions.
- I will demonstrate that I am trustworthy and consistent.

Set Boundaries and Limits

- I will set appropriate limits and not tolerate destructive behavior.
- I will self-disclose judiciously when I feel it will be helpful and not be misconstrued as advice.

Provide a Model of a Healthy Human Relationship

- I will be empathically attuned and respond with empathy and nondefensiveness when the client complains of lack of empathy.
- I will be willing to admit errors and show that I am a fallible human being who makes mistakes.

Provide a Corrective Learning Experience

- I will not betray, abandon, or reject the client, thereby disconfirming the client's beliefs that all people will treat him or her in those ways.
- I will tolerate the client's projections but will disconfirm them or instigate an exploration that turns them into a learning opportunity.
- I will model that conflict and disagreement are natural parts of healthy relationships.
- I will provide a corrective relationship that is different from the one provided by the parents.

Specific forms of the client-therapist relationship can be viewed as "procedures" for meeting specific goals:

Build Self-Esteem

- The therapist is *nonpossessive, noncontrolling,* and *validating.*
- The therapist makes it safe for the client to disclose shame-filled experiences.
- The therapist provides the triad of *empathy, warmth,* and *respect.*

Promote Autonomy

- The therapist abstains from telling the client what to do.
- The therapist helps the client struggle with internal conflict, without taking sides.
- The therapist resists becoming a "rescuer" for a client who "plays helpless."

Utilize Transference

- The therapist abstains from self-disclosure to maximize transference distortions.
- The therapist uses "empathic failures" as opportunities for correcting developmental deficits.
- The therapist functions as a "mirroring selfobject" for the client, refraining from interpretations and challenges.

Selecting Procedures for Intermediate Objectives

Beutler (1983) defined *intermediate objectives* as "short-term effects designed to be accomplished by certain therapeutic procedures in the service of final objectives" (p. 121) and defined six categories—two cognitive, three emotional, and one behavioral. Table 15.6 illustrates how each of Beutler's intermediate objectives—which also serve as *process goals*—can be achieved by a

Table 15.6 Procedures for Meeting Intermediate Objectives

Beutler's Objectives	Therapeutic Conversation	Directed Activity
Insight Enhancement Facilitate cognitive understanding (e.g., of unconscious factors, influence of behavior on other people, and early childhood origins of relationship pattern).	Questioning. Reframing. Confrontation (present the client with discrepancies). Interpretation.	Free association on couch. Dream interpretation. Role-playing. Two-chair dialogue.
Perceptual (Cognitive) Change Change faulty thinking patterns, create new perspectives, and develop thinking and reality-testing skills.	Metamodel questions. Information giving. Interpreting and explaining. Socratic questioning.	Self-monitoring instructions. Teach alternative thinking. Evidence gathering to test beliefs.
Emotional Awareness Help the client attend to and focus on sensations and feelings and to provide words for accurate labeling.	Questioning. Reflection of feelings. Commenting on nonverbal behavior. Avoid cognitive, intellectual emphasis.	Focusing. Guided imagery activity. Direction to exaggerate. Art therapy.
Emotional Escalation Move the underaroused client toward action or create catharsis for the person whose emotions have been buried.	Empathic response to "inner child" state. Facilitate strong transference reaction. Role model: Express intense emotions.	Role-playing. Ask the client to speak in present tense. Empty-chair technique.
Emotion Reduction Help the client maintain optimal arousal levels by reducing intense emotions such as anxiety or anger.	Reassurance to reduce anxiety. Teaching and explaining. Empathy and validation. Normalization.	Modify self-talk. Relaxation training. Desensitization. Flooding. Biofeedback.
Behavioral Control (and Skill Development) Enable the performance of desired behaviors under specific circumstances, reduce performance of undesired behaviors, and increase the client's self-control.	Therapist as role model. Explaining. Problem-solving discussions. Advice giving.	Role-playing with feedback and coaching. Use of contingency contract. Self-monitoring of antecedents and consequences.

Source: Eclectic Psychotherapy: A Systematic Approach, by L. Beutler, 1992, Boston, MA: Allyn & Bacon. Reprinted with permission.

variety of techniques from each of two broad strategies: (1) ordinary conversational interaction and (2) directed activity.

Sequencing Interventions

Once you have made choices about desired intervention techniques and procedures, you need to specify the sequence. Using a framework of *stages* is very useful, and your definition of process goals or intermediate objectives can form topic sentences:

- *Beginning stage:* Deal with presenting symptoms and cope with situations that are anticipated in the 1st month, develop a good working relationship, explain the rationale for treatment and elicit cooperation, set the structure for the sessions, and clarify expectations.
- *Middle stage:* Break this stage into substages for longer term therapy. The goals will directly relate to the chosen strategy and specific techniques.
- *End stage:* Reinforce success in achieving goals, assure transfer of learning to future situations, explore feelings about termination and deal with new issues that arise, and prepare for relapse prevention.

Sample Plans

The two samples in Tables 15.7 and 15.8 were created by graduate students doing prepracticum therapy sessions with a classmate or a volunteer. A risk of giving a single sample is that readers will treat it as a desired model. By providing two samples, you can get a sense of differences in style. Table 15.7 provides an example of a treatment plan, identifying in italics the following six components of the treatment plan: *process goal, intermediate objective, strategy, technique, relationship issue, and sequencing of interventions.* The plan in Table 15.8 is presented without marking those elements.

ACTIVITY 15.1 _____

Components of Plans

In Appendix III, using two sample plans, you identify which of the following components is being specified in a designated sentence: outcome goal, process goal, strategy, technique, relationship issue, intermediate objective, or monitoring effectiveness of treatment.

Standard 29. The plan is tailor-made for the specific client: Such factors as gender, ethnicity, and personal values are considered.

Table 15.7 Sequencing of Interventions

Problem: *Difficulty dealing with breakup of a 3-year intimate relationship*

P: The first stage in my plan (*sequencing interventions*) to help Donna through the natural grieving process (*process goal for CS4*) is to allow her to talk about it. I will be patient and accepting and give her all the time she needs to open up and share her feelings (*strategy, relationship issue*). This catharsis (*process goal*) will help her begin the process of gaining closure (*intermediate objective*).

Since B. has completely disappeared from her life and is not allowing her to gain answers as to why he did the things he did, I feel that it would be extremely beneficial to use the empty-chair technique (*technique*). I feel that by imagining B. in the chair in front of her, Donna would be able to ask the questions that have been gnawing at her for months. She can switch chairs to give the answers that she thinks he would give, if he were honest. She will have the opportunity to release feelings about the last few months of the relationship and the period since the breakup (*process goal*).

At this point in therapy, I will need to help her express her anger (*sequencing interventions, process goal*). Because she is extremely uncomfortable exposing these feelings, it will be important to build a safe therapeutic environment and have her realize that I will accept her feelings without disapproval (*relationship issue*). To help her begin expressing her anger, I would have to encourage her at first. I might even use a physical activity, like letting her pound a cushion with a tennis racket (*technique*). I will avoid intellectual discussion of anger at this phase. However, subsequently, when we deal with her schemas and self-talk (*sequencing interventions*), I will help her examine her rules about not expressing anger and always being nice, which both cause anger to build up and prevent her from being appropriately assertive in her intimate relationships (*strategy*). I will have to monitor my own countertransference (*relationship issue*) as I know I get anxious around intense anger, and I have a tendency to avoid feelings by staying on a cognitive level.

In the next stage, Donna will explore why she stayed so long in such a painful relationship (*sequencing interventions, process goal*). I will guide Donna to recall experiences (*strategy*) from her early childhood (**P2**) to discover when she first took on the role of "rescuer" or "pleaser," as she did in her relationship with B. It would be necessary to confront her belief (**C2**) that she must take on these roles. Through identifying the reasons she feels compelled to take care of others (*intermediate objective*), we can begin the process of developing schemas that allow her to care for others without abandoning her own needs (*outcome goal*).

To create a good plan, you need to understand the client's cultural background, personality, developmental level, preferences, and attitudes. This understanding is important for two goals: (1) to develop rapport, assuring that the client feels comfortable enough with you to continue in therapy and (2) to choose strategies and techniques that are best suited for the particular client.

Cultural Issues

The term *culture* refers to a broad range of factors: ethnic and racial group, gender, age group, sexual orientation, national origin, geographic region, and other subgroups in a society (e.g., gangs, white-collar workers, or the military). When cultural factors explain the client's problem, hypothesis **SCE2** is applied. However, even when that hypothesis is not applied, the therapist needs to consider how cultural factors will affect the therapeutic relationship. Research has found that matching the client with a therapist from the same ethnic group will

Table 15.8   Stages of Therapy in the Plan

Problem: *Difficulty deciding whether to stay at her job*

P: Tiffany is very eager to make a decision regarding her job situation. In the first phase, I will make sure that she is allowed to express all of her feelings regarding the difficulties of her work situation. When she is ready to shift to problem solving, the focus will be on the decision-making process and her freedom to choose (**ES2**), along with the need to make a thoughtful rather than impulsive choice. Tiffany needs to consider both her financial responsibilities and her personal happiness. We will have to weigh the pros and cons of quitting. In exploring her options, we will be viewing whether it is possible to improve her satisfaction at work, by changing the way she evaluates the behaviors of her coworkers or by trying new coping strategies.

We would first deal with the stress that she is currently experiencing at the workplace (**CS2**). It will be important to identify the external stressors at work and establish a way of quantifying their intensity. We will focus on environmental factors (**SCE7**) and see if there are aspects of the job that she can modify to make the work environment more tolerable.

When she feels fully understood and her defensiveness is lowered, we will address ways in which her own thinking and behavior have contributed to the stress at her job. I will assist Tiffany in reevaluating her cognitive map (**C2**). At this point, it would be important to educate her on what a utopian thinker is (**C1**), and how this type of thinking interferes with adjustment to any work environment. I will make sure she truly understands that everyone she comes across will not think or act the same way she does and that she will have to be prepared for these human differences and learn to cope with frustration and disappointment.

The next phase of therapy will go deeper in exploring Tiffany's strong reactions to the lack of friendly relationships with her coworkers. We would need to discuss her cultural background (**SCE2**) and her own personal hierarchy of needs. I would also like to discuss the issue of gender because it is common that women place more emphasis on harmonious relationships at work than do men. If she decides that she needs a better social support network (**SCE3**) at work, we will work together to find the proper strategy to make this happen. I will provide guidance and support for her efforts to identify potential friends and to take risks to initiate friendly relationships. It is also possible that by modifying some schemas (**C2**) she can learn to tolerate unfriendly coworkers, if the other aspects of the job are satisfactory.

We will be ready to terminate therapy when she has made a decision to leave her job or to stay because the job is a more positive experience once she has changed her thinking and implemented new strategies for coping. If she decides to leave the job, the insight and coping strategies she will have gained from therapy will help her enter a new job situation with a better chance of making it a success.

have indirect effects on therapy outcome (e.g., the client is more likely to continue after the first session) but does not lead to better outcomes (e.g., more improvement or success in meeting goals):

- *When therapist and client are from the same culture:* Although rapport may be easier to develop, the assumption of similarity with the client carries the risk of not gathering needed data. Transference, both positive and negative, may be stronger when the therapist seems similar to people from the client's childhood.

- *When therapist and client are from different cultures:* The therapist needs to make a special effort to create rapport and develop credibility with the client. The client may have negative stereotypes about the therapist's group (this can include gender, age group, and ethnic group) and may be sensitive to perceived misunderstanding. The treatment plan can address potential issues.

Rapport

A major task of the first session is to build *rapport,* a term that refers to a harmonious, sympathetic relationship. The therapist is "in tune" with the client; the client feels that it is easy to be understood, her concerns are taken seriously, and she is not being judged; and the client and the therapist are on the same team, not in opposition to each other. Variables such as trust, comfort, and safety are associated with good rapport.

Rapport between two people is not automatic: It is the therapist's task to create it. Fortunately, many people are attracted to careers as psychotherapists because they have spent their lives developing the ability to tune in to others. To some degree, it helps for a therapist to be a bit of a chameleon, having the flexibility to adapt to a variety of different personality styles and to be perceived as agreeable, trustworthy, and nonthreatening. Although the therapist's warmth usually contributes to comfort and trust, some clients may feel engulfed and smothered by your customary level of warmth. It is useful to have several possible places where the client can sit, so that you can let the client choose the preferred distance or closeness of seating positions.

Similarly, the level of formality or informality needs to be adjusted for each client and stage of therapy. Generally, in our culture of psychotherapy, therapists dress in professional clothing and call the client by his or her first name. With certain clients, for instance Asian Americans, a higher level of formality is necessary for rapport, whereas with adolescents, rapport may be increased if the therapist wears casual clothing and speaks less formally, without "talking down."

Readiness to Change

Prochaska et al. (1994) created a widely used *stages of change* model: precontemplation, contemplation, preparation, action, and maintenance. The most important distinction is between "precontemplation" (the person doesn't even think that change is necessary) and "contemplation" (she begins to consider it). The therapist needs to recognize the client's stage when entering therapy and adapt process goals accordingly. For instance, the lack of cooperation that we call "resistance" may stem from the therapist's assumption that the client is at a more advanced stage than he is. Factors that facilitate or block the client's progression to the next stage need to be understood for the specific client. As the client progresses to the next stage, the therapy process and goals will change.

Client's Beliefs about Causes and Cures

Jerome Frank, in *Persuasion and Healing* (Frank & Frank, 1991) emphasized that the therapeutic "ritual" will only be effective if it matches the client's belief about what will be beneficial. Sometimes this means that the therapist, having alternate treatment possibilities available, will select the one that best fits with the client's beliefs. For instance, some educated and psychologically minded clients demand an insight-oriented, in-depth exploration of their lives to feel that they are really getting to the root of their problems, and will reject the structured, short-term approach of cognitive restructuring. Flexibility on the therapist's part is important: He or she needs the ability to gratify one client's need for insight and another's preference for quick action.

On other occasions, the client brings beliefs that are incompatible with effective treatment. Clients who are referred to a psychotherapist by their physicians because they fit the category of "somatizer" are very usually firmly convinced that there are physiological causes for the problem and that only a medical intervention is appropriate. In this case, the first process goal must be to educate the client about stress and mind-body connections to persuade the client that psychological interventions will be effective with their (real) somatic complaints.

Understanding the client's belief system is an important component of cultural competence. Whenever possible, therapists should incorporate healing practices and beliefs about health and illness from the client's culture. For instance, a Latino client might benefit from a *curandero* and religious clients can be encouraged to incorporate prayer and ritual with the psychotherapy.

Amount of Structure

Therapists bring different degrees of structure to a single session and the entire course of therapy. The "treatment contract" can be a casual verbal understanding, for example, "you can talk about whatever you want and I'll respond when I have something important to say," or a written document with signatures. Students trained in cognitive-behavior therapy (CBT) expect to run a very structured session: agenda setting at the beginning and homework at the end. At the other extreme, a Rogerian therapist can refuse to provide any structure, expecting the client to lead the session.

At the same time, clients bring their own preferences for more or less structure. Some clients will feel squelched and disrespected by someone following a CBT manual; others will feel frustrated and bewildered with a nondirective therapist, wondering when the therapist is going to start doing something to help. When a certain approach is desired because it is the best possible match for the chosen hypotheses, therapists need to provide a clear rationale that convinces the client that the plan is a good choice. Even then, flexibility is needed so that the structured therapist allows the client to talk freely, without interruption, and the unstructured therapist provides guidance and support.

Level of Authority

Therapists can take roles with clients that vary tremendously in their level of authority. At one extreme is the *therapist as expert authority,* which is what we expect from our physicians and dentists. With these professionals, the client comes with a problem, and the therapist designs a plan and tells the client what to do. At the other extreme is the *therapist as fellow pilgrim,* another struggling human being who will accompany the client on her search for the right path, but who cannot function as a guide or a guru because each person must find the answers within the self. Many options fall between those extremes. One role of intermediate authority is *therapist as collaborative consultant,* which is Beck's approach to CBT.

Clients will bring their preferences in this area, as in others, because of both cultural conditioning and individual difference variables. In considering issues of authority, the client's level of *reactance* (Brehm & Brehm, 1981; Wright, Greenberg, & Brehm, 2004) must be considered. When an individual experiences the threatened loss of a behavioral alternative, the behavior may increase in attractiveness. The resulting reactance is often described by others as being oppositional, defiant, or rebellious, rather than compliant, cooperative, and obedient, but from Brehm's point of view, the person is simply trying to restore freedom. Parents discover they have a child with high reactance when they find they can get him to do what they want by telling him to do the opposite. This strategy is commonly called *reverse psychology,* a method of getting another person to do what one wants by pretending not to want it or to want something else. The client's level of reactance must be considered in issuing directives. Therapists may choose to use *paradoxical* interventions for highly reactant clients: These are directives that have positive outcomes whether they are obeyed or disobeyed.

Client's Level of Development (Maturity)

Allen Ivey (1993) created a developmental framework for treatment planning that is partly based on Piaget's model of cognitive development. Using this framework, the therapist can design strategies appropriate to the client's level and help clients move to the next developmental level. Five of the nine levels that Ivey describes are:

1. *Sensorimotor:* The client describes what is seen, heard, and felt, without organizing the elements, or trying to make sense of them.
2. *Concrete operations:* The client has the ability to describe in linear, sequential form the concrete specifics of a concern, without interpretation.
3. *Early formal operational thinking:* The client is able to identify and think about behavior and thoughts, with awareness of repeating patterns of behavior.
4. *Late formal operational thinking:* The client has the ability to examine patterns of patterns. The client can be led to see larger, consistently repeating patterns in his or her life. The client becomes aware of how he or she constructs his or her own reality.
5. *Dialectical thinking:* The client is able to develop awareness of the impact of his or her family, ethnic background, race and gender on the reality that he or she has constructed.

Hypothesis **P3** addresses the client's level of maturity in terms of the constructs of "self" and "object relations." For instance, an extremely sensitive client who responds to the slightest lapse in the therapist's empathy with anger or withdrawal may be someone who is stuck at a very early level of development.

> **Standard 30.** The plan is appropriate for the treatment setting, contractual agreements, and financial constraints.

The duration and frequency of therapy is an important component of the plan. When the initial contract is not "brief, time-limited" therapy, the duration is often specified as "open-ended," with timing of termination based on achievement of goals or the client's financial and time priorities. Prediction of the necessary duration of therapy is much easier for experienced clinicians: Students have little to rely on except guesswork, the view of their teachers, and what they have read in books.

In writing plans for class assignments, students can describe the ideal approach for a client with unrestricted time and resources. However, in clinical practice, the therapist must consider many realities, including but not limited to:

- Whether the client's insurance coverage limits the number of sessions.
- Whether the clinic uses a short-term therapy model.
- The duration of the therapist's intended training or employment at the clinical setting.
- Client variables, including expectations, motivational levels, financial resources, and availability of time.

A benefit of writing a plan that describes subgoals in sequential order is that time estimates (using a range) can be made for attainment of those objectives. It is very common practice for managed care companies to authorize a set number of sessions, for instance 6 or 10, and then require the therapist to request an authorization for additional sessions. Even without the pressure from these companies, a therapist can contract with the client for a certain number of sessions and then agree to evaluate where they are at that time. Probably most clients are seeking the most efficient and cost-effective method; only a subset of sophisticated clients specifically seek multiyear therapy.

It is only when you use a treatment manual (e.g., Barlow, 2001) that you can be certain of the duration of treatment—and recently, manuals are becoming more flexible, assigning additional modules for clients with special needs. After therapy has begun, many unexpected factors may impede implementation of the original plan, and the plan needs to change to accommodate them.

Frequency and length of sessions should be determined, ideally, by the client's best interest; however, the standard of weekly, 45- to 50-minute sessions is the predominant mode both for the convenience of therapists and clinics, and because of the influence of psychoanalytic thinking about the importance of a strict "frame." Many clients would probably like to be charged by the time they use, and be able to leave early some weeks, and stay longer others, and if a therapist chooses to do this, there would be nothing professionally or ethically wrong with it.

When using the emergency hypothesis (**CS1**), sessions should be scheduled more frequently. When working with families, sessions should be longer than an hour.

Therapists handle the termination phase of therapy in different manners. For long-term psychoanalytic therapy, it is common to allow several months for this phase, and to be prepared for productive material to surface. Some therapists change the frequency of sessions to twice a month and then less frequently, as the client feels more and more ready to cope without regular sessions.

The treatment setting can place restrictions on treatment plans in areas other than duration and frequency of sessions. For instance, some clinics continue to provide separate therapists for parents and children, despite the preponderance of evidence that family therapy is the treatment of choice. Additional constraints exist for students and trainees, depending on the nature of the course or training program they are in and the instructions of their teachers and supervisors.

> **Standard 31.** When there is more than one problem, the therapist addresses issues of priorities, sequencing, and integration of plans.

As indicated in the report outline (Appendix I, Form I.G) when there is more than one problem, there needs to be a final section called *Case Management Discussion,* which shows how the plans for different problems will be integrated. In some cases, this section can be brief, as when the therapist intends to address each problem in sequence. In other cases, when the same treatment methods are used for different problems, it might be best to keep the plan sections for separate problems brief and make the final section more detailed. The following two samples show that a paragraph is sufficient.

A first-year male law student who has three problems: (1) *Concerns about sufficiency of his study strategy,* (2) *Uncertainty over career choice,* and (3) *Difficulty exploring emotional issues with girlfriend.*

Problem 1 must be addressed first, because final exams are imminent. If he does well on finals, he will probably decide that his approach to studying is satisfactory. If he does poorly, a discussion of his strategy will blend with the exploration designed for Problem 2. Because the third problem is a very sensitive topic, the first two problems will be used in early sessions to build the client's trust and to learn more about the client's communication skills in general. For example, if the therapist has the client interview lawyers to investigate the level of job satisfaction they have, the therapist may gain additional perspective as to how he interacts with others.

A 25-year-old foreign student with two problems: (1) *Difficulty initiating relationships and forming friendships in this country* and (2) *Ambivalence about whether to stay in the United States after receiving her degree.*

Tricia's difficulty in initiating relationships (Problem 1) is her major problem and affects all aspects of her life. The ability to form at least one friendship will affect her decision about where to settle. Thus, this problem will be given priority and will be the focus of the first stage of therapy. She will be given in vivo homework that pertains to the lowest item on her hierarchy of anxiety-evoking situations, initiating a conversation with a salesperson at the mall. She can also start reading a recommended book on acculturation. The goal for this first stage is for her to become comfortable in casual conversation with people outside her culture and to be knowledgeable about effects of "culture shock." When she is comfortable with me, we will begin work on exploring her automatic thoughts and core beliefs, and focus more on Problem 2, her indecision about staying in the United States. During this middle stage of therapy, two techniques will be emphasized: *behavioral rehearsal* for difficult situations on the social anxiety hierarchy, and *voice dialogue* for her ambivalence over which country to settle in after she finishes school. Throughout therapy, Tricia will be given homework, as appropriate: journal writing, extra reading, and in vivo assignments to initiate and develop friendships.

> **Standard 32**. The therapist considers community resources and referrals, if appropriate.

Therapists need to be knowledgeable about resources in their community, in the mental health field, and in other sectors of life. It is essential to own the best mental health resource book for your community. For instance, in California, the Resource Directory Group, Inc. (www.resourcedirectory.com) publishes the *Social Service Rainbow Resource Directory* by Glenda Riddick, for major counties, and therapists should have access to the most current volume or the electronic version.

Here are some examples of the topics covered in the resource directory:

- Addictions.
- Battered persons and adult abuse.
- Eating disorders.
- Education.
- Emergency assistance.

- Employment placement.
- Financial/Budgets/Emergency funds.
- Hospice and grief support.
- Housing and tenants rights.
- Immigration and refugees.
- Legal assistance.
- Parenting resources.
- Self-help and support groups.
- Senior services.
- Volunteering opportunities.

Therapists should also have knowledge of web sites that are useful for clients. For instance, a site that offers information, support, and links to other mental health sites is Mental Health Net-Self Help Resources at www.cmhc.com/selfhelp.htm.

The following examples show appropriate use of community resources for specific problems:

- *Substance abuse:* Inpatient treatment for detoxification; residential treatment for 1 month; Alcoholics Anonymous meetings.
- *Loneliness and social isolation:* Social group in church or synagogue; volunteer program; adult education course.
- *Uncertainty about future career path:* Career counseling/vocational testing agency; interviews with alumni, professors, and members of professions; arrange to shadow members of different professions.

> **Standard 33.** Legal and ethical issues are addressed appropriately, if relevant.

Therapists must be knowledgeable about the laws and ethics affecting professional practice. They should own up-to-date texts and reference books on those subjects (e.g., Sales et al., 2005) and attend continuing education courses on topics related to law and ethics. They also need to know experts with whom they can consult, in addition to representatives from the ethics committee of their national and state professional organizations. The APA's Division 42 for Independent Practitioners has resources for members who wish to consult or discuss problematic issues.

Certain legal and ethical issues are addressed during the intake, and are not mentioned in treatment plans. These include:

- Informed consent for treatment.
- Limits of confidentiality.

- Information about the consumer agency to which the client can address complaints.
- The details of the contract for services, including fees, method and timing of payment, and procedures if bills are not paid in a timely manner.
- Release of information forms for insurance companies and for obtaining prior medical/psychological records.

Some of the most common legal and ethical issues in a community counseling center are the following:

Crisis Situations
- Breaking confidentiality for the protection of the client or others.
- Involuntary hospitalization.
- Awareness of therapists' rights when clients become violent toward them.

Therapy with Minors
- Obtaining consent from parents for therapy.
- Obtaining consent from parents for confidential relationship.
- Community referral for pregnancy or HIV issues.
- Dealing with noncustodial parents.

Clients Who Are Victims of Present or Past Abuse
- Mandated reporting of abuser who still poses risk to children.
- Guiding clients to obtain a restraining order.
- Obtaining consent from client to act on information about prior therapist who violated law or ethics.

Risk Management for Therapists
- Assuring appropriate referral when therapist chooses to terminate.
- Developing an appropriate strategy for client who makes sexual overtures.
- Obtaining consent before talking to family members.
- Gathering data about possible child abuse.

Therapists need to be vigilant in recognizing ways that personal biases may contribute to unethical treatment approaches. An example of unethical practice is to engage in treatment to change a client's homosexual orientation to a heterosexual one. The APA ethical guidelines state that discrimination based on sexual orientation is detrimental to mental health and the public good and that therapist have a responsibility to counteract ignorance or unfounded beliefs about sexual orientation. We must realize that when a gay, lesbian, or bisexual seeks a "conversion" treatment, the reason is societal prejudice, family or social coercion, and/or lack of information.

Perhaps the single most important ethical principle is to practice within the limits of your competence. After studying the hypotheses in this book and practicing skills of case formulation, you may discover that you are not yet competent to implement the ideas you write in your plan section. Sometimes good supervision is sufficient for ethical use of new treatment approaches. Other times, a more familiar alternative approach will achieve the desired goals. However, when the client's interests are best served by using the approach you originally selected, referral to an expert is the ethical choice.

One of the biggest frustrations of trainees is to discover that the clinic where they are being trained has barriers to choosing the best treatment for clients, often by insisting on use of a single orientation, by prohibiting certain therapeutic formats such as conjoint therapy, or through ingrained prejudice against the use of medication. In these circumstances, remember that it is your ethical duty to speak up as an advocate for the client's interests.

ACTIVITY 15.2

Evaluation of a Complete Report

For this final activity in Appendix III, you will find a report in the left column. The right column contains the 33 standards. Your task is to evaluate the report and write comments in the right column to give feedback to the student. If you think improvement is necessary, write your suggestion.

The next step is to create your own case formulation reports, ideally using three session's worth of data. After using this method at least three times, the frustration and confusion that many people experience on their first attempt will yield to satisfying feelings of competence and—even more important—success at creating the best possible treatment plan for each client.

APPENDIXES

Appendix I ————————————————————————

FORMS FOR CLINICAL CASE FORMULATIONS

Form I.A   SOAPing a Problem

Identifying Information:

Presenting Problem:

(include reason for volunteering if not a client)

Relevant Background Information:

Form I.A   *(Continued)*

Problem Title:

Outcome Goals:

THE DATABASE

S   Subjective Data

O   Objective Data

THE FORMULATION

A   Assessment

P   Plan

Form I.B   Using the BASIC SID

B Behavior
What the person is doing and not doing; what others can observe; the quality
of skills

A Affect
Internal experience of feelings and the overt verbal and nonverbal expression
of feelings

S Sensation
Awareness of the body; use of senses; sensory data with minimal filtering
through cognition

I Imagery
Mental imagery about past, present, or future; fantasies and dreams

C Cognitive
Constructed meaning; self-talk; beliefs and schemas; information-processing
skills and other mental abilities

Form I.B   *(Continued)*

S Spiritual
Spirit or soul; religion; religious as well as nonreligious aspects of spirituality; creativity; moral issues; and the lack of spirituality

I Interpersonal
Relationships with others; family interaction patterns; membership in social groups; cultural factors; and issues of social injustice

D Drug and Biological
Physiology, biology, genetics, medical issues; use of legal and illegal drugs, including alcohol

Form I.C   Life History Timeline

Pre-birth	Birth	1	2	3	4	5	6	7	8	9	10	11	12
Parents' marriage								**Industry vs. Inferiority**				Best friend?	
Older siblings		Attachment	Walk	Talk	Preschool	Kindergarten			Elementary School				
Cultural background		Feeding issues								Widening social world			
Prenatal health		**Trust**		**Autonomy**	**Initiative**					New role models	Competence, perseverance		
		vs. Distrust		**vs. Shame**	**vs. Guilt**						Enjoyment of work		
				Terrible Twos		Share, cooperate					Pride in doing well		
				Toilet training		Jealousy, rivalry							
				Separation issues		Imagination, play							

13	14	15	16	17	18	19	20	21	22	23	24	25	26	27
Onset of puberty			**Identity vs. Identity Confusion**	**College**				Legal drinking				**Intimacy vs. Isolation**	- - - ???	
	High School		Abstract thinking	Ideological searching				Separation from parents -						
	Peer group dynamics			**Driver's license**		**Employment**				Graduate School?	**Provisional Adulthood**			
			Sexuality	**Graduation**	**Vote**					Commitments: sexual identity, career				
			Falling in love							Mature sexual relationships				

520

28	29	30	31	32	33	34	35	36	37	38	39	40	41	42
	Marriage?	**First Adulthood**	Parenthood?	Cultural pressures, societal norms			Balancing family and career	Pressures of corporate culture / Decisions about family size			**Generativity vs. Stagnation** / "Biological clock" ticking			

43	44	45	46	47	48	49	50	51	52	53	54	55	56	57
	Middle-aged? / 25th high school reunion			**Second Adulthood**	Menopause		AARP membership		Second career?	**Empty nest stage**			**Age of Mastery** / Grandparenthood	

(continued)

Form I.C *(Continued)*

58	59	60	61	62	63	64	65	66	67	68	69	70	71	72
		Retirement planning			Social security eligibility							50th college reunion		
				Great-grandchildren			Medicare	Retirement	**Integrity vs. Despair**	New interests / Estate planning		Increased health risks		
73	74	75	78	79	80	81	82	83	84	85	86	87	88	89
Frequent deaths of peers			Increased dependence on children			Assisted living?			Give up driver's license			Outliving most peers		
90	91	92	93	94	95	96	97	98	99	100	101	102	103	104
Is this, at last, "old age?"												Getting ready to break records		

522

Form I.D   American History Timeline

1900	1901	1902	1903	1904	1905	1906	1907	1908	1909	1910	1911	1912	1913	1914
NEW CENTURY										Ford's Model T			Panama Canal	
													WW I	
					Freud publishes	*Interpretation of Dreams*								

1915	1916	1917	1918	1919	1920	1921	1922	1923	1924	1925	1926	1927	1928	1929
		United States enters WWI			Women get vote		Prohibition				Lindbergh's flight			**Stock market**
														crash
						Roaring '20s								

1930	1931	1932	1933	1934	1935	1936	1937	1938	1939	1940	1941	1942	1943	1944
Great Depression			Hitler comes to power								Pearl Harbor			
			FDR's first term begins								**United States enters WWII**			
									Movie: Gone With the Wind					

(continued)

Form I.D *(Continued)*

1945	1946	1947	1948	1949	1950	1951	1952	1953	1954	1955	1956	1957	1958	1959
Hiroshima														
					Korean War									
					Hawaii and Alaska statehood									
							McCarthy hearings							
							Queen Elizabeth							
									Brown v. Board of Education					
										Soviet troops in Hungary				
									Polio vaccine					
												Sputnik		
		Baseball racially integrated												
					TV: *Jack Benny*									
						I Love Lucy								
									First McDonald's					
										Rock Around the Clock				
											Elvis Presley			
										Bikinis				
													Jet service begins	
													Credit cards	

1960	1961	1962	1963	1964	1965	1966	1967	1968	1969	1970	1971	1972	1973	1974
	Berlin wall up													
			Kennedy assassinated											
				Civil Rights Act										
					War on Poverty									
					Vietnam War -							troops leave		
								Martin Luther King assassinated						
											Supreme Court ends abortion restrictions			
	Peace Corps													
		John Glenn orbits Earth												
			Supreme Court abolishes school prayer											
				Civil rights marches										
				Birth control pills										
					Watts Riot									
						Miranda decision								
									Armstrong on the moon					
											Voting age becomes 18			
										Kent State				
												Watergate		
														Nixon resigns
													Feminist movement	
James Bond movies														
			Feminine Mystique											
				The Beatles										
						First Xerox machine								
								60 Minutes on TV						
												Ms. Magazine		
													MASH on TV	
	Dick Van Dyke Show													
		Bob Dylan												
				Motown music										
							Superbowl I							
									Woodstock					
								Seatbelts on new cars						
										Waterbeds				

1975	1976	1977	1978	1979	1980	1981	1982	1983	1984	1985	1986	1987	1988	1989
				Hostages in Iran		First woman on Supreme court			**Berlin wall down**					
						HIV/AIDS								
Saturday Night Live					*CNN*	Video games	*Cheers* on TV				Compact Discs			
							Commodore 64 home computer							

1990	1991	1992	1993	1994	1995	1996	1997	1998	1999	2000	2001	2002	2003	2004/5
	Gulf War	Stock market boom						Clinton impeachment			**September 11**		War in Iraq	
											Stock market downturn			**Katrina**
	LA riots			LA earthquake			Oklahoma City bombing					**War on Terror**		
												Enron fraud		
			Seinfeld		Microsoft Windows 95					Reality TV shows				

Form I.E   Worksheet for Preparing Formulation

Problem Title:

Data **S & O:** Data that support the hypothesis	Hypotheses **A:** List in order of importance	Treatment Ideas **P:** Consider culture and time frame

Form I.F   Twenty-Eight Clinical Hypotheses
to Use with Your Own Cases

Hypotheses	Space for Data, Questions, and Ideas
I. Biological Hypotheses (B)	
B1 Biological Cause	
B2 Medical Interventions	
B3 Mind-Body Connections	
II. Crisis, Stressful Situations, and Transitions (CS)	
CS1 Emergency	
CS2 Situational Stressors	
CS3 Developmental Transition	
CS4 Loss and Bereavement	
III. Behavioral and Learning Models (BL)	
BL1 Antecedents and Consequences	
BL2 Conditioned Emotional Response	
BL3 Skill Deficits or Lack of Competence	
IV. Cognitive Models (C)	
C1 Utopian Expectations	
C2 Faulty Cognitive Map	
C3 Faulty Information Processing	
C4 Dysfunctional Self-Talk	

(continued)

Form I.F   *(Continued)*

Hypotheses	Space for Data, Questions, and Ideas
V. Existential and Spiritual Models (ES)	
ES1 Existential Issues	
ES2 Avoiding Freedom and Responsibility	
ES3 Spiritual Dimension	
VI. Psychodynamic Models (P)	
P1 Internal Parts and Subpersonalities	
P2 Reenactment of Early Childhood Experiences	
P3 Immature Sense of Self and Conception of Others	
P4 Unconscious Dynamics	
VII. Social, Cultural, and Environmental Factors (SCE)	
SCE1 Family System	
SCE2 Cultural Context	
SCE3 Social Support	
SCE4 Social Role Performance	
SCE5 Social Problem is a Cause	
SCE6 Social Role of Mental Patient	
SCE7 Environmental Factors	

Appendix II —————————————————————————————

USEFUL CHARTS

Chart II.A   Twenty-Eight Core Clinical Hypotheses

I. Biological Hypotheses (B)

B1: The problem has a **Biological Cause:** The client needs medical intervention to protect life and prevent deterioration, or needs psychosocial assistance in coping with illness, disability, or other biological limitations.

B2: There are **Medical Interventions** (e.g., medication, surgery, or prosthetics) that should be considered.

B3: A holistic understanding of **Mind-Body Connections** leads to treatment for psychological problems that focus on the body and treatment for physical problems that focus on the mind.

II. Crisis, Stressful Situations, and Transitions (CS)

CS1: The client's symptoms constitute an **Emergency:** Immediate action is necessary.

CS2: The client's symptoms result from identifiable recent **Situational Stressors** or from a past traumatic experience.

CS3: The client is at a **Developmental Transition,** dealing with issues related to moving to the next stage of life.

CS4: The client has suffered a **Loss and** needs help during **Bereavement** or for a loss-related problem.

III. Behavioral and Learning Models (BL)

BL1: A behavioral analysis of both problem behaviors and desired behaviors should yield information about **Antecedents** (triggers) **and Consequences** (reinforcers) that will be helpful in constructing an intervention.

BL2: A **Conditioned Emotional Response** (e.g., anxiety, fear, anger, or depression) is at the root of excessive emotion, avoidant behaviors, or maladaptive mechanisms for avoiding painful emotions.

BL3: The problem stems from **Skill Deficits**—the absence of needed skills—**or** the **Lack of Competence** in applying skills, abilities, and knowledge to achieve goals.

IV. Cognitive Models (C)

C1: The client is suffering from the ordinary "miseries of everyday life" and has unrealistic **Utopian Expectations** of what life should be like.

C2: Limiting and outdated elements in the **Faulty Cognitive Map** (e.g., maladaptive schemas, assumptions, rules, beliefs, and narratives) are causing the problem or preventing solutions.

C3: The client demonstrates **Faulty Information Processing** (e.g., overgeneralization, all-or-nothing thinking, and mind reading) or is limited by an inflexible cognitive style.

C4: The problem is triggered and/or maintained by **Dysfunctional Self-Talk** and internal dialogue.

Chart II.A   *(Continued)*

V. Existential and Spiritual Models (ES)

ES1: The client is struggling with **Existential Issues,** including the fundamental philosophical search for the purpose and meaning of life.

ES2: The client is **Avoiding** the **Freedom** and autonomy that come with adulthood **and**/or does not accept **Responsibility** for present and past choices.

ES3: The core of the problem and/or the resources needed for resolving the problem are found in the **Spiritual Dimension** of life, which may or may not include religion.

VI. Psychodynamic Models (P)

P1: The problem is explained in terms of **Internal Parts and Subpersonalities** that need to be heard, understood, and coordinated.

P2: The problem is a **Reenactment of Early Childhood Experiences:** Feelings and needs from early childhood are reactivated and patterns from the family of origin are repeated.

P3: Difficulties stem from the client's failure to progress beyond the **Immature Sense of Self and Conception of Others** that is normal for very young children.

P4: The symptom or problem is explained in terms of **Unconscious Dynamics.** Defense mechanisms keep thoughts and emotions out of awareness.

VII. Social, Cultural, and Environmental Factors (SCE)

SCE1: The problem must be understood in the context of the entire **Family System.**

SCE2: Knowledge of the **Cultural Context** is necessary to understand the problem and/or to create a treatment plan that shows sensitivity to the norms, rules, and values of the client's cultural group.

SCE3 The problem is either caused or maintained by deficiencies in **Social Support.**

SCE4: Difficulty meeting demands for **Social Role Performance** contributes to the client's distress and dysfunction.

SCE5: A Social Problem (e.g., poverty, discrimination, or social oppression) **is a Cause** of the problem. Social problems can also exacerbate difficulties stemming from other causes. You must avoid *blaming the victim.*

SCE6: The problem is causally related to disadvantages or advantages to the **Social Role of Mental Patient.**

SCE7: The problem is explained in terms of **Environmental Factors:** Solutions can involve modifying the environment, leaving the environment, obtaining material resources, or accepting what can't be changed

Chart II.B   Thirty-Three Standards for Evaluating Case Formulations

Problem Definition

1. Problems are defined so that they are solvable targets of treatment.
2. Titles refer to the client's current, real-world functioning.
3. Titles are descriptive, designed for a specific client, and are justified by the data.
4. Problem titles do not contain theoretical, explanatory concepts.
5. The therapist is not imposing cultural or personal values in problem definitions.
6. *Lumping* and *splitting* decisions are justified in that they lead to good treatment planning.
7. The problem list is complete and comprehensive.

Outcome Goals

8. Outcome goals are directly related to the problem title and are consistent with the client's values.
9. Outcome goals refer to real-world functioning and do not contain formulation ideas.
10. Outcome goals are realistic and are not utopian.
11. Outcome goals do not contain the "how" of the treatment plan.

Presentation of Database (S & O)

12. The database is thorough, comprehensive, and complete: There are sufficient data so that multiple hypotheses can be applied.
13. Subjective and objective data are appropriately distinguished.
14. Good quotations from the client are included in the subjective data section.
15. The subjective section does not include formulation concepts (unless they are quotations from the client).
16. There is no reference to how and when the information was gathered in the subjective data section; this information, if relevant, goes in the objective section.
17. The subjective section is well organized and appropriately concise: There is selection, summarization, and condensation of details.
18. The objective section does not contain theoretical concepts, biased opinions, or formulation discussion.

Chart II.B *(Continued)*

Assessment (A)

19. The assessment integrates hypotheses that are consistent with the prior database.

20. The assessment does not introduce new data.

21. The focus of the assessment is on the specific problem of the specific client: This is not an abstract essay about a theory.

22. The writer is not including all possible hypotheses, just the ones that are useful in developing intervention plans.

23. If theoretical jargon is used, it enhances rather than detracts from understanding and does not contribute to tautological explanations.

24. The writer is integrating material from the highest level of education thus far attained. Commonsense ideas are appropriate but are not sufficient for explaining the problem.

25. The writer demonstrates professional-level thinking and writing skills to provide a coherent conceptualization.

Plan (P)

26. The plan is focused on resolving the identified problem and achieving outcome goals.

27. The plan follows logically from the prior discussion and does not introduce new data or hypotheses.

28. There is clarity regarding process goals, intermediate objectives, strategies, specific techniques, relationship issues, and sequencing of interventions.

29. The plan is tailor-made for the specific client: Such factors as gender, ethnicity, and personal values are considered.

30. The plan is appropriate for the treatment setting, contractual agreements, and financial constraints.

31. When there is more than one problem, the therapist addresses issues of priorities, sequencing, and integration of plans.

32. The therapist considers community resources and referrals, if appropriate.

33. Legal and ethical issues are addressed appropriately, if relevant.

Chart II.C   Mental Status Exam

Category	Examples
Appearance	General description: Height, build, apparent weight; Person looks stated age, or looks older or younger. Facial expression: Grimacing, smiling, signs of sadness, tension, relaxed, or angry. Vasomotor changes: Blushing or sweating. Odors: Body odor, strong perfume, alcohol. Dress and grooming: Appropriateness, formal, casual, neat and clean, fashionable, sloppy, unusual adornments, well-groomed, poor hygiene, signs of self-neglect. Observable disabilities or disfigurement.
Level of Consciousness	Impaired: Delirious, stuporous, or comatose. Clouded consciousness: Drowsy or appears to be drugged. Normal: Alert, responsive, and lucid.
Orientation	Does the person know who he is (oriented to person); where he is (oriented to place); and the day, date, and time (oriented to time)?
Motor Behavior	Gestures, posture, or signs of tension. Gait when walking; coordination. Fidgeting, restless, pacing, or relaxed. Speed; activity level. Mannerisms or tics.
Interpersonal Behavior	Eye contact; gaze aversion. Possible barriers to communication: Visual or hearing impairment; unfamiliarity with English. Type of relationship formed with interviewer: Quality of rapport, cooperative, guarded, suspicious, hostile, friendly, requests for advice or opinions, submissive, or defensive.
Speech	Rhythm, pitch, modulation, tempo or speed of speech, monotone, pressured, evasive, or hesitant. Speech impediments: Stuttering, stammering, or lisp. Vocabulary: Indicates education, intelligence, or cultural group. If English is not first language: Fluency of speech, presence of an accent. Does client elaborate, answer in monosyllables, or change subject matter abruptly?
Mood and Affect	Emotional behavior: Crying, shouting, or clenching fists. Amount of emotion: Intensity, range, or bluntness. Congruence or incongruence of affect to the content of communication; appropriateness or inappropriateness (e.g., laughing at sad story). Signs of specific emotional states (e.g., anger, fear, anxiety, dysphoria, embarrassment, guilt, shame, or grief).
Perception	Hallucinations. Illusions.

Chart II.C   *(Continued)*

Category	Examples
Thought Content	Symptoms: Delusions, obsessions, phobias, ideas of reference, grandiosity. Danger to self or others: Suicidal or homicidal ideation. Patterns: Self-critical, self-doubting, blaming others, morbid thoughts, preoccupations, and rumination.
Thought Processes	Attention and concentration: Easily distracted or vigilant. Stream of thought: How productive, relevant, or coherent? Organization of ideas: Logical, well-organized storytelling, rambling, circumstantial, tangential, flight of ideas, or loose associations.
Intellectual Functioning	Estimates are based on vocabulary, fund of information, capacity for abstract thinking, ability to learn, or how well client grasps complex ideas offered by therapist.
Memory	Confusion, vagueness, or forgetfulness in session. How well does person remember personal history? How good is memory for early childhood events? Recent events?
Impulse Control	Is client able to control behaviors that are harmful to self and others? Is client able to delay gratification to reach future goals? Poor control: Low frustration tolerance, quick-tempered, or easily offended. Excessive control: Overcontrolled, inhibited, overcautious, or rigid.
Insight	Is client aware that there are problems that need treatment? Does client blame external factors or show awareness of own contribution to difficulties? Quality of self-understanding; Is client psychologically minded?
Judgment	Use of common sense. Does client learn from experience and anticipate consequences of behavior? Does client make self-damaging choices? Quality of decision making, problem solving, and reality testing.

Chart II.D   Client History

Category	Examples
Identifying Information	**Demographic information:** Age, gender, ethnicity, religion, marital status, socioeconomic information, occupation, and number of and ages of children. **Referral information:** Self-referred, referred by physician, condition of probation, or transferred from prior therapist who completed training rotation.
Presenting Problem	**Description of problem in the client's own words.** **Decision to come to therapy:** What brings the client here at this time? Why now? How and why was the decision to come to therapy made? Who, besides the client, is affected by the problem? What type of help is the client seeking? What is the client's overt or implied request? **Focused data gathering:** What are the symptoms or behaviors? Severity of distress? Danger to self or others? **History of problem:** When did it begin? How did it begin? What was occurring when it begin? Acute onset or chronic? First time? Prior episodes of same or similar problem? **Current actions:** What is currently being done? What solutions has the client already tried? Have attempted solutions created new problems?
Current Situation	**Living situation:** With whom? Who is in family? Ask for socioeconomic details about neighborhood, lifestyle, financial hardships, or legal problems. **Current work life:** Occupation, length of employment, nature of work setting, and significant relationships at work. **Social network:** Connection to family of origin, friends, and intimate relationships. **Recent changes or losses:** For self or family members.
Prior Psychological or Psychiatric Problems and Treatment	**Prior mental health difficulties:** Include history of drug and alcohol use, prior episodes of current dysfunction. **Past therapy:** Were you in therapy before? What was it like? How did it end? What did you gain? What was effective? Look for strengths as well as self-defeating patterns in use of therapy. Any hospitalizations? When and for how long? Prior use of psychotropic medication. **Past success with any kind of change process:** Did you have similar problems before? How did you deal with them? Have you ever helped a friend get through a similar situation? You are searching for assets, resources, skills already in the repertoire, and clues to what works, as well as what will not work.

Chart II.D   *(Continued)*

Category	Examples
Family Background	**Cultural and economic facts about parents:** Countries of origin, religion, racial and ethnic identity, level of acculturation, occupations, and economic status.
	Members of family of origin: Two parents or single parent, number of siblings, birth order, involvement with grandparents and extended family; description of each parent and the client's relationship with that parent during different phases of development; quality of parents' relationship; and relationships with siblings. Emotional climate, warmth, communication, discipline, limit setting, dealing with conflict.
	Early developmental history: Place of birth, normal or abnormal pregnancy, planned or unplanned child, any significant delays in developmental milestones; Information about physical, sexual, or emotional abuse in the family.
	Family history: Mental illness, hospitalization, substance abuse, or suicide.
	Significant transitions while growing up: Divorce, illness of parent, death, separation, birth of younger siblings, geographic relocations; transition to adulthood; separation from parents and family home; current relationships with members of family of origin (overlaps with current situation).
Educational and Occupational History	**Performance in elementary, middle school, and high school:** Strengths, weaknesses, special interests, and talents.
	Higher education: Majors, degrees, chronology.
	Overview of employment history: First job, details about career choice. Successes and failures.
	Important transitions: Career changes or major decisions.
	Interpersonal relations in work settings: With peers, bosses, and subordinates.
Social and Sexual History	**Peer relations:** In elementary school and middle school.
	Details about best friends: Quality of relationships, reasons for friendships ending.
	High school: Social life; early dating experiences.
	Significant romantic/sexual experiences: Chronology including details of how they begin and end, and recurring patterns.
	Experiences involving abuse: Information about violence or sexual assault.
	Chronology of significant events: Marriage(s), parenthood, divorce(s), events in family development such as births of children, coping with developmental stages of children, or relationships with grandchildren.
	Recent events: In social network; apart from family.
Other Topics	**Medical history:** Serious illnesses, accidents, surgeries; use of medication.
	Legal history: Criminal record or incarceration.
	Military history: If relevant, include any combat experiences.

Chart II.E　Patient Impairment Lexicon

alexithymia	medical treatment noncompliance
altered sleep	mood lability
anxiety	motor hyperactivity
assaultiveness	obsessions
compulsions	oppositionalism
concomitant medical condition	pathological grief
decreased concentration	pathological guilt
delusions (nonparanoid)	phobia
delusions (paranoid)	physical abuse perpetrator
dissociative states	physical abuse victim
dysphoric mood	promiscuity
eating disorder	psychomotor retardation
educational performance deficit	psychotic thought/behavior
egocentricity	running away
emotional abuse perpetrator	school avoidance
emotional abuse victim	self-esteem deficiency
encopresis	self-mutilation
enuresis	sexual object choice dysfunction
externalization and blame	sexual performance dysfunction
family dysfunction	sexual trauma perpetrator
fire setting	sexual trauma victim
gender dysphoria	social withdrawal
hallucinations	somatization
homicidal thought/behavior	stealing
inadequate healthcare skills	substance abuse
inadequate self-maintenance skills	suicidal thought/behavior
learning disability	tantrums
lying	truancy
manic thought/behavior	uncommunicativeness
manipulativeness	uncontrolled buying
marital/relationship dysfunction	uncontrolled gambling
medical risk factor	

Source: Casebook for Managing Managed Care: A Self-Study Guide for Treatment Planning, Documentation, and Communication, by J. P. Bjork, J. A. Brown, and M. Goodman, 2000, Washington, DC: American Psychiatric Press.

Chart II.F   Problem Categories from a Treatment Planning Manual

ADD-adult	Intimate Relationship Conflicts
Anger management	Legal Conflicts
Anxiety	Low Self-Esteem
Borderline Personality	Male Sexual Dysfunction
Chemical Dependence	Mania or Hypomania
Chemical Dependence-relapse	Medical Issues
Childhood Traumas	Obsessive-Compulsive Behaviors
Chronic Pain	Paranoid Ideation
Cognitive Deficits	Phobia-Panic/Agoraphobia
Dependency	Post Traumatic Stress Disorder
Depression	Psychoticism
Dissociation	Sexual abuse
Eating Disorder	Sleep Disturbance
Educational Deficits	Social Discomfort
Family Conflicts	Somatization
Female Sexual Dysfunction	Spiritual Confusion
Financial Stress	Suicidal Ideation
Grief/Loss Unresolved	Type-A Behavior
Impulse Control Disorder	Vocational Stress

Source: The Complete Adult Psychotherapy Treatment Planner, second edition, by A. E. Jongsma, Jr. and L. M. Peterson, 2003, New York: Wiley.

Chart II.G   Domains of Functioning

	Examples of Skills, Resources, and Assets	Examples of Problems, Weaknesses, and Deficiencies
Health Maintenance	Maintains healthy lifestyle Regular exercise Knowledge about AIDS and safe sex practices	Poor nutrition Excessive drinking Smokes cigarettes
Home Management	Creates comfortable home environment Invests appropriately in house repairs	Excessive clutter and disorder Starts home improvement projects and leaves them incomplete
Financial Status	Pays bills on time Effective investment strategy	Excessive credit card debt No savings No source of income Poor money manager Debts
Academic	Maintains high GPA Chose academic major that is consistent with interests	Poor study habits Lack of clear goals about future career Learning disability Lack of study skills
Employment	Stable employment Feels challenged at work	Inadequate job skills Dissatisfaction with present job Conflict with supervisors Difficulty maintaining job
Legal Status	No criminal record	Income tax not filed Reported child abuser Legally incompetent—needs legal guardian Divorce papers served AWOL Delinquent in alimony/child support payments
Leisure and Recreation	Pursues creative hobby Ability to plan a vacation	Dangerous, thrill-seeking activities Feels guilty about relaxing and taking time off from duties

Chart II.G   *(Continued)*

	Examples of Skills, Resources, and Assets	**Examples of Problems, Weaknesses, and Deficiencies**
Friendship	Makes new friends easily Good tools for handling conflict	Superficial friendships, lacks a confidante No social support in time of crisis
Family	Supportive extended family Balances needs of different people	Excessive dependence on parental approval Poor conflict resolution with spouse
Intimacy	Shares private feelings with significant other Satisfying sexual relationship	Unable to develop trusting relationship Lacks dating skills
Parenting	Shows empathy and respect toward child Able to set age-appropriate limits	Overreacts to normal adolescent steps toward independence Neglectful of child's emotional needs
Communication	Expresses anger appropriately Good listening skills	Bullies when partner disagrees Expects partner to read mind
Cultural Competence	Knowledge of different cultures Tolerant of differences	Difficulties working with members of minority groups Uses racist speech
Life Planning	Effectively managing midlife career change Maintains adequate insurance and savings	No long-term goals Fails to save for retirement

Chart II.H   Bar-On's Emotional Intelligence: Fifteen Competencies

Category	Definition of Competence
Intrapersonal Components	**Emotional Self-Awareness:** *The ability to recognize and understand one's feelings.* **Assertiveness:** *The ability to express feelings, beliefs, and thoughts and defend one's rights in a nondestructive manner.* **Self-Regard:** *The ability to be aware of, understand, accept, and respect oneself.* **Self-Actualization:** *The ability to realize one's potential capacities.* **Independence:** *The ability to be self-directed and self-controlled in one's thinking and actions and to be free of emotional dependency.*
Interpersonal Components	**Empathy:** *The ability to be aware of, to understand, and to appreciate the feelings of others.* **Social Responsibility:** *The ability to demonstrate oneself as a cooperative, contributing, and constructive member of one's social group.* **Interpersonal Relationship:** *The ability to establish and maintain mutually satisfying relationships that are characterized by emotional closeness, intimacy, and by giving and receiving affection.*
Adaptability Components	**Reality Testing:** *The ability to assess the correspondence between what is emotionally experienced and what objectively exists.* **Flexibility:** *The ability to adjust one's emotions, thoughts, and behavior to changing situations and conditions.* **Problem Solving:** *The ability to identify and define problems as well as to generate and implement potentially effective solutions.*
Stress Management Components	**Stress Tolerance:** *The ability to withstand adverse events, stressful situations, and strong emotions without "falling apart" by actively and positively coping with stress.* **Impulse Control:** *The ability to resist or delay an impulse, drive, or temptation to act, and to control one's emotions.*
General Mood Components	**Optimism:** *The ability to look at the brighter side of life and to maintain a positive attitude, even in the face of adversity and negative feelings.* **Happiness:** *The ability to feel satisfied with one's life, to enjoy oneself and others, and to have fun and express positive feelings.*

Adapted from *The BarOn Emotional Quotient Inventory (EQ-I): A Test of Emotional Intelligence*, by R. BarOn, 1997, Toronto, Ontario, Canada: Multi-Health Systems.

Chart II.I   Inventory of Needs

Category of Human Need	Specific Need	Sample Problems
Basic Needs	Survival (oxygen, food, sleep, drink, shelter)	Homeless/lack of money to support self Dementia
	Safety and security	Living in home with violent spouse Lives in neighborhood with high level of gang violence
	Touch and minimal human contact	Social isolation
	Anxiety within tolerable range	Excessive anxiety without external cause
Freedom	Freedom from abuse, coercion, and criticism	Living with critical and domineering parents who fail to respect rights of their adult child
	Freedom with regard to use of time	Frustration with employment situation with unfair demands to work on weekends
	Freedom with regard to use of money	Submits to husband's restrictions on use of money
	Freedom for goal setting	Restricted view of possible career goals
Pleasure and Personal Comfort	Self-esteem	Feelings of inadequacy and low self-worth
	Relaxation	Feels guilty when spends weekend with family instead of going to work
	Leisure, play, and fun	Lack of hobbies
	Creativity	Excessively critical of her creative products
	Structure and order	Fails to manage time effectively
	Privacy	Lives in overcrowded apartment without room of her own
	Stimulation (neither too much nor too little)	Boredom and lack of interests
Social Needs	Inclusion, belonging, affiliation	Loneliness and lack of friends
	Recognition, attention, appreciation	Feels ignored and rejected by family members
	Respect	Distress over abuse and disrespect in intimate relationship

(continued)

Chart II.I *(Continued)*

Category of Human Need	Specific Need	Sample Problems
	Affection	Difficulty establishing a close intimate relationship
	Sharing and cooperation	Inability to seek help when overwhelmed with difficult task demands
	Control	Seeks excessive control over lives of loved ones
	Power	Feels helpless when confronted with strong-willed people
	Autonomy	Inability to say no without guilt when friends and family make demands
	Self-expression	Fails to express needs and grievances in close relationships
	Ritual	Lack of sense of community, feeling isolated during major holidays and cultural celebrations
	Solitude	Difficulty saying no to invitations when he/she would prefer to be alone
	Sexual gratification	Lack of sexual partner
Occupational Needs	Appreciation	Frustrated over supervisor's failure to acknowledge his achievements
	Achievement	Failure to keep job because of poor performance
	Competence	Difficulty completing dissertation in a timely manner
	Challenge	Bored with routine, repetitive tasks at work
	Autonomy	Anger at over-controlling boss who punishes attempts to work independently
	Material compensation	Unable to earn enough money to pay basic bills
	Status and prestige	Depression following being passed over for promotion
	Utilization of specific talents	Frustration with job that requires continual social interaction
Aesthetic and Spiritual Needs	Access to beauty, nature, and creative outlets	Spends time exclusively on activities related to work, duty, and nurturing others
	Connection to Higher Power	Feelings of emptiness and anguish
	Sense of higher purpose and meaning in life	Suicidal thoughts following retirement and death of spouse

Chart II.J Outline for Multiproblem Case Formulation Report

Identifying Data: Age, gender, ethnic or cultural group, marital status, occupation or status in school, living situation, and other descriptive and demographic details.

Reasons for Seeking Therapy: Presenting complaints, the source of referral, and information about whether therapy is voluntary or mandated. For student assignments, when it is not a real client, this section explains why the person agreed to be a volunteer.

Background Information: An organized narrative of the life history, summarizing data that do not fit specifically under a problem title. Data relevant to a specific problem title are best placed in the S section following the problem title. However, when several problems are using the same data, instead of repeating it, you can put it in this section.

Problem List: Problem 1 *(title in bold and italic)*

Problem 2 *(title in bold and italic)*

Each additional problem with number and title

Problem 1 *Title in bold and italic,* **repeated from the prior list,** followed by a few sentences that give concrete details about the problem.

Outcome Goal: A few sentences.

S

O

A

P

Problem 2 *Title in bold and italic,* **repeated from the prior list,** followed by a few sentences that give concrete details about the problem.

Outcome Goal: A few sentences.

S

O

A

P

Additional problems have the same format.

Case Management Discussion: Includes integration of plans, phases of therapy, coordination with other services.

When there is only one problem, the initial problem list and the concluding case management discussion are eliminated.

Appendix III —————————————————

SKILL-BUILDING ACTIVITIES

These activities are given in the order in which they are mentioned in the text, with numbers coded to the relevant chapter. At the end of the activities, answers or samples give you feedback.

ACTIVITY 1.1 WRITING YOUR BASELINE
CASE FORMULATION REPORT

1. Identifying Information

This section contains a summary of demographic information (e.g., age, gender, ethnic group membership, marital status, and employment status) and some facts about physical characteristics and living situation.

2. Relevant Background Information

Give highlights of the life history. Save information that is specifically related to the problem for the *subjective data* section.

3. Problem Title

Select a current personal problem that you would like to understand and resolve. Write a brief, specific title for that problem. After the title, write two or three descriptive sentences. Examples of problems frequently used for this exercise include: *difficulties adhering to weight loss or exercise programs; academic problems such as poor study habits or fear of public speaking; excessive stress; difficulties in a specific relationship, and difficulty making an important decision.*

4. Outcome Goal

In a couple of sentences, present a concrete, specific vision of how things will be in the future when this problem is resolved. Do not include any ideas about "how" to get there, just describe the desired future state.

5. Subjective Data

Summarize all the information that you think is relevant for understanding this problem. Do not repeat what is given in the *background* section.

6. Objective Data

Pretend you are watching a videotape that someone took of you, over the past week. Write a few examples of things you observe that are relevant to the problem title.

7. Assessment

Write an explanation that you think would be helpful in understanding the problem in more depth. After writing your first ideas, review the list of hypotheses to find useful concepts. Do not describe actions to change the problem, just focus on understanding it.

8. Plan

Write some ideas about how you would go about achieving the results that you want. Make sure that these ideas are consistent with what you wrote for the assessment. If they aren't, go back to the assessment and modify it.

(See Appendix IV, pages 580–582, for an example.)

ACTIVITY 2.1 PRACTICE WITH THE BASIC SID

1. **Make copies of the BASIC SID Chart**—Appendix I Form I.B

2. **Yourself as client:** Select a problem that you wish to explore in detail. Write data for each modality.

3. **Interview a friend or a learning partner:** Ask questions that will gather data for each modality. Because this is not a formal interview, it is okay to have the chart in front of you and to write down data as you get answers to your questions.

ACTIVITY 2.2 METAMODEL PRACTICE

Study Table 2.7 very thoroughly before doing this activity and try to complete it without going back to look at the chart.

Instructions

Here are 10 sentences spoken by different clients:

- **Name violation:** Pay attention to the part that is underlined and decide which meta-model violation best fits. *You must use every one of the nine types once, and one of them is used twice* (use these initial: **D, LRI, UV, N, UQ, MO, MR, CE, LP).**

- **Write question:** Write the appropriate question (*Remember not to use the question "Why?"*).

- **Write client answer:** Make up an answer that the client would give that is either "fully specified" or shows a corrective insight.

1. I <u>shouldn't</u> talk about my parent's marriage.

   Name violation:

   Write question:

   Write client answer:

2. I have a hard time with <u>authority figures.</u>

   Name violation:

   Write question:

   Write client answer:

3. I'm feeling very frustrated with our <u>relationship.</u>

    Name violation:

    Write question:

    Write client answer:

4. I <u>can't</u> keep my house clean.

    Name violation:

    Write question:

    Write client answer:

5. She is <u>always</u> blaming me.

    Name violation:

    Write question:

    Write client answer:

6. He <u>makes</u> me very angry.

    Name violation:

    Write question:

    Write client answer:

7. I'm tired of the way he <u>bullies</u> me.

    Name violation:

    Write question:

    Write client answer:

8. <u>You don't appreciate</u> all the work I've done.

   Name violation:

   Write question:

   Write client answer:

9. <u>I feel afraid.</u>

   Name violation:

   Write question:

   Write client answer:

10. <u>You've got to always be the best at everything you try.</u>

    Name violation:

    Write question:

    Write client answer:

Answers: 1. MO 2. LRI 3. N 4. MO 5. UQ 6. CE 7. UV 8. MR 9. D 10. LP

ACTIVITY 10.1 BRAINSTORM HYPOTHESES

You can choose to do this on yourself or with someone you know very well.

1. Start by identifying a problem and give it a title.

2. Create a timeline of the entire life, using age to anchor events to points in time. Draw a separate timeline for recent history.

3. Now go through the list of hypotheses (Appendix II, Chart II.A) and write down the hypotheses that are consistent. Write a few notes to demonstrate your understanding.

(A sample was provided in Chapter 10, page 395.)

ACTIVITY 10.2 APPLY AND TEST HYPOTHESES
WITH CASE VIGNETTES

Each vignette contains enough data so that you can apply several hypotheses. After each vignette, three different hypotheses are indicated. For each hypothesis, provide the following:

- **Explanation:** Write a sentence or two explaining the hypothesis and how it fits the data.

- **A probe to test the hypothesis:** Write, verbatim, a question or statement you would use to gather additional data (or describe another method for gathering data—e.g., homework, referral to an expert, or consulting another information source).

- **New invented data:** Use your imagination and invent new information that the client would give in response to your probe, supporting the usefulness of the hypothesis you are testing (do not repeat data that are in the vignette. You must add something to the story).

- **Add an additional hypothesis:** Write the code and name of a different hypothesis that also fits the data. Then complete the same instructions: Provide an explanation, a probe to test the hypothesis, and new invented data.

(A sample was provided in Chapter 10, page 396. Complete this activity before looking at sample answers on pages 583–588.)

Practice Vignette 1: Celeste—*Depressed and Confused*

Celeste is an 80-year-old widow living in her own condo in a retirement community. Her first husband died 20 years ago, when they first retired and moved to Florida. Her son lives in New York with his wife and children and they visit her once a year. Eight years ago, she married Fred, a man 5 years her junior. She was "ecstatically happy" with their very loving relationship, which included enjoyable sexual intimacy and many social activities with other couples. Fred died suddenly a year ago, just a few months after the death of her only brother. During the first 6 months after Fred's death, her friends were very supportive. Recently, she has been avoiding them. She has noticed that only her widowed women friends seem to have time for her; she feels excluded from activities with married couples. In the past month, according to her friend Estelle, she has been staying in bed much of the day, not bothering to dress. Her son just came for a visit, and he was so alarmed that he brought her to a mental health clinic. She is unkempt and her house is becoming very dirty, whereas previously she was meticulous in her grooming and housekeeping. She feels confused and has become forgetful. She has lost her appetite, and after a lifetime as an avid reader of detective fiction, she no longer can concentrate on a book for more than 10 minutes.

B1 Biological Cause

• **Explanation:**

_____

• **A probe to test the hypothesis:**

_____

• **New invented data:**

_____

SCE3 Social Support Factors

• **Explanation:**

_____

• **A probe to test the hypothesis:**

_____

• **New invented data:**

_____

ES3 Spiritual Dimension

• **Explanation:**

_____

• **A probe to test the hypothesis:**

_____

• **New invented data:**

_____

Title of Additional Hypothesis

- **Explanation:**

_____

- **A probe to test the hypothesis:**

_____

- **New invented data:**

_____

Practice Vignette 2: Allison—*Feels Stuck in a Bad Relationship*

Allison is a 28-year-old stockbroker who says she is "stuck in a bad relationship" and "doesn't know how to deal with it." Steve, her boyfriend of 2 years, is 10 years older than she is, never married, and "very cold and indifferent." He only wants to see her on weekends and has made it clear that he does not want a deeper commitment. Whereas at work she is confident, decisive, and successful, when she is with Steve, she feels very childlike, and passively goes along with whatever he suggests. She cancelled a recent ski trip with a girlfriend because Steve felt uncomfortable about the thought of her not being available. She has dated other men a few times, but as she begins to pull away from Steve, she becomes panicky and depressed, finding the emotional pain intolerable. She also says that she hates dating: "I can't make superficial chitchat, I hate being examined like a piece of meat, and it's just too boring to have to tell my life story over and over again." After a date or two with a new man, she gets very discouraged and decides to "stick with what I've got."

P3 Immature Sense of Self and Conception of Others

- **Explanation:**

_____

- **A probe to test the hypothesis:**

_____

- **New invented data:**

_____

C2 Faulty Cognitive Map

- Explanation:

_____

- A probe to test the hypothesis:

_____

- New invented data:

_____

BL3 Skill Deficits or Lack of Competence

- Explanation:

_____

- A probe to test the hypothesis:

_____

- New invented data:

_____

Title of Additional Hypothesis

- Explanation:

_____

- A probe to test the hypothesis:

_____

- New invented data:

_____

Practice Vignette 3: Cathy—*Indecisive about Future Goals*

Cathy is a very attractive 46-year-old married woman who looks about 32. Her only son is finishing college and her husband, a vice president of a large corporation, has always supported the family and maintained a very high standard of living. She received her teacher's credential 6 years ago because she wanted to teach high school English, but she never sought employment. She volunteers 1 day a week at a hospital, and spends most of her free time "having lunch with her friends and shopping." She feels bored and empty much of the time, and sometimes thinks it would be fun and challenging to own a coffee shop because she loves social interaction so much. She admits that occasionally she thinks, "it's not too late to have another child—at least then I'd feel needed." She came to therapy to deal with confusion over "what to do with the rest of my life."

P1 Internal Parts or Subpersonalities

• **Explanation:**

• **A probe to test the hypothesis:**

• **New invented data:**

ES2 Avoiding Freedom and Responsibility

• **Explanation:**

• **A probe to test the hypothesis:**

• **New invented data:**

SCE1 Family Systems Factors

- **Explanation:**

- **A probe to test the hypothesis:**

- **New invented data:**

Title of Additional Hypothesis

- **Explanation:**

- **A probe to test the hypothesis:**

- **New invented data:**

Practice Vignette 4: James—*Suffering from Writer's Block*

James is a 36-year-old married man who aspires to be a successful novelist. Since he was a teenager, his dream has been to have a book on the *New York Times* bestseller list. He went to a prestigious university and won recognition for his writing talent. He received suggestions from publishers on changes that would make them more interested in his last manuscript, but he refuses to make them, insisting "it is more important to maintain my artistic integrity than to be a commercial success." He is currently working on what he hopes will be the novel that will make him famous, but he is suffering from "severe writer's block." When he sits down to write, his mind goes blank and he develops anxiety symptoms. If he has a few glasses of wine, he relaxes and his thoughts flow. However, when he rereads what he has just written, he becomes extremely critical. His wife, an elementary school teacher, was supportive for the first 5 years of their 6-year marriage, but in the past year she has begun putting pressure on him to "get a real job" and earn money. She is tired of being the breadwinner and wants to have a child as soon as they can afford it.

B2 Medical Intervention

- **Explanation:**

_____

- **A probe to test the hypothesis:**

_____

- **New invented data:**

_____

C4 Dysfunctional Self-Talk

- **Explanation:**

_____

- **A probe to test the hypothesis:**

_____

- **New invented data:**

_____

CS3 Developmental Transition

- **Explanation:**

_____

- **A probe to test the hypothesis:**

_____

- **New invented data:**

_____

Title of Additional Hypothesis

- **Explanation:**

_____

- **A probe to test the hypothesis:**

_____

- **New invented data:**

_____

ACTIVITY 10.3 PROVIDE COMMENTARY FOR A TRANSCRIPT

This brief transcript comes at the beginning of a third session for a client whose problems were:

- **Problem 1:** *Frustration over distant and strained relationship with mother*
- **Problem 2:** *Difficulty establishing romantic relationship*

Use the right column to write your thoughts about relevant hypotheses. You can also write your ideas about the hypotheses that you think the therapist is exploring.

The client opened the session with a story about a frustrating phone call with her father.

T1: How do you think your experience with your parents affected your personality or your current life? **C1:** Um. . . . I'd say being guarded around people. And I would think, like, my total lack of dating probably has a lot to do with my parents.	
T2: How is that? **C2:** (Voice cracks and gets quiet) Well, I have a really hard time trusting men. So, I'm not very open-minded when I meet new people. With friends it doesn't matter, but with guys I'm extremely close-minded and not open to . . . because your friends can only come in so much before they can really hurt you, you know what I mean? Your girlfriends aren't going to necessarily hurt you, but guys . . . if you get into a relationship . . . so I'm very guarded.	
T3: How do you think your parents affected this distrust? **C3:** Um, well, that's interesting . . . well, my dad has never really done anything for me and has just continuously let me down. So in that sense, there's pretty much a direct line. My mom, it's hard to say. Probably, I learned from her, like with my first boyfriend, that you just put up with stuff and you don't walk away. But I don't know if that so much goes today. I mean I learned a lot from that . . . so I think for my mom it was more of an indirect effect.	
T4: Tell me more about that. **C4:** Well with my first boyfriend I stuck around for like 6 years when things were terrible. And the second one, I just didn't know myself. . . . I realized that I compromised all these things about myself because I didn't know myself very well. But after that, I just needed time to figure out who I was, what my boundaries are and what are my likes, dislikes, and all that.	

T5: What do you think now of your ability to be in a relationship? Are you well equipped to be in a relationship? **C5:** Yeah. Well, yeah, I feel like I'm much more self-assured and can offer a lot more as well as just being a more balanced person.	
T6: So you said that you have a hard time letting guys in. What is that like? How do you experience that? **C6:** Um, I can pretty much just . . . I don't know if you follow pop culture, but that whole "he's just not that into you" book that is out . . . like, the concept of not knowing "he's just not that into you"—eludes me. I have so many friends that just date guy after guy and have no concept of why these guys aren't staying around . . . and to me it's just like, they are such an open book. And at least in the beginning, I can tell when a guy is just like, "yeah, I'd do her" and that's the way they're approaching me. Versus a guy that's genuinely interested. But unfortunately when you're a single female in Los Angeles, there's not many guys who are like, "oh, yeah, you seem really nice!" (laughs hard) Yeah, there's not many of those. So of course, the normal outlets of finding guys . . . like I've had three jobs and have met nobody at work. And I have a tremendous amount of single friends who have no single friends.	

ACTIVITY 11.1 USING THE BASIC SID FOR A PRELIMINARY PROBLEM LIST

1. Make a copy of the BASIC SID chart (Appendix I, Form I.B).

2. Read the following database for Maria and write *every single problem* you identify in the appropriate category of BASIC SID. Write a number in front of each problem so you can refer to those numbers in Activity 11.3.

A CASE FOR PRACTICE: *MARIA*[1]

The information is presented in more detail than would actually go into a report, so do not use this as a sample. Several activities will refer to this case.

Identifying Data

Maria is a 22-year-old single Latina woman who lives at home with her 41-year-old mother and her younger sister, Teresa, a 20-year-old college student, two doors away from her maternal grandparents. Two months ago she broke up with her boyfriend of 2 years, Tony. Maria has been employed as a secretary for the same company since graduating from high school 4 years ago. She was referred to this counseling center by the Employee Assistance Program of that company.

Maria, an attractive, slim, dark-haired woman, was dressed neatly for her first interview. Her eyes were puffy and ringed with dark circles. She answered questions and related information about her life history in a slow, flat tone of voice, which had an impersonal quality to it. She sat stiffly in her chair with her hands in her lap, moving very little during the interview.

Presenting Problems

For the past 2 months she has been severely depressed, with frequent crying spells. She said that her depression began after she and her boyfriend Tony broke up. She found it hard to concentrate on her job, had difficulty falling asleep at night, and had a poor appetite. She stated that she had always had occasional periods of "feeling down," but her present feelings of misery were worse than anything she has ever experienced.

Recent History

In the month preceding the breakup with Tony, she experienced a great deal of emotional turmoil in the relationship. Tony was insisting that she decide whether she wanted to marry him or not, and she felt incapable of making a decision. During a dinner date, he unexpectedly told her that he had decided to stop dating her, because she did not seem to have very strong feelings for him. She did not try to explain her feelings but just "felt numb" and asked to be taken home. She did not attempt to contact him, but became increasingly depressed. She was not sure why she was so depressed, but she began to feel as if it were an effort to walk around and go out to work. It became difficult for her to initiate a conversation with others, and many times her lips felt as if they were stiff, and she had to make an effort to move them to speak. She found it hard to concentrate and began to forget things that she was supposed to do. It took her a long time to fall asleep at night and she suffered from bad dreams. She felt constantly tired and loud noises, including conversation or the television, bothered her. She preferred to lie in bed rather than be with anyone, and she often cried when alone.

Maria considers two women at work her "close friends," yet she has not talked to them about her relationship with Tony or about her feelings of depression after the breakup. She was not able to talk these issues over with her sister, who

[1] Adapted from *Case Histories of Deviant Behavior,* third edition (pp. 109–115), by G. R. Leon. Boston: Allyn & Bacon.

she felt was "living in a completely different world" now that she was attending college. She had missed work several times during the past month and had just "sat around the house crying." She went to her family doctor because she was concerned over her lack of energy, but no medical problems were found. She asked the doctor to prescribe something to help her sleep so she would not be so tired and could concentrate better. Because of her absences and poor concentration at work, her boss had told her to see the Employee Assistance counselor.

Background

Maria comes from a family of Guatemalan origin and was raised in the Catholic religion. Both sets of grandparents emigrated from Guatemala and settled in a neighborhood of predominantly Latino ethnic composition. Her parents were born in the United States. Maria's mother finished 3 years of college, but quit when she married her father, because he did not approve of his wife working. Both of the paternal grandparents died when Maria was quite young, and Maria's mother and father separated when she was 12. After moving away, her father had never sent money to support the family, nor had he been heard from since his departure. Her mother, who had been staying at home to raise the children, got a job as a checker in a supermarket and has worked there ever since.

Maria stated that her childhood was very unhappy. Her father, a truck driver, was seldom home, and when he was present, her parents were constantly fighting. Sometimes her father would throw things and shout, while her mother would become sullen and withdrawn and refuse to speak either to her husband or daughters. Maria remembered being puzzled because it seemed that her mother was angry with her, too. She recalls that her mother often told her daughters that she "had ruined her life" by marrying their father.

The happiest times in her childhood were between the ages of 6 and 9, when her father would take the two girls to a park or movie, while his wife went to her parents' home after church. Maria could not remember her mother ever expressing interest in joining them. By the time she turned 10, she recalled that her father "could not be relied on." Many weekends, he went out in the morning and did not return to take the girls on promised outings, coming home late in the evening instead. He always had an excuse and did not understand how disappointed his daughters were.

Maria remembers very clearly the events that led up to her father's desertion of the family. It was her 12th birthday, her mother had baked a cake, and the grandparents and some other relatives were invited for dinner. Her father was supposed to be home after work, and they delayed dinner for about half an hour. When he did not appear, they ate without him. Maria's mother did not make any comments about her husband, but her grandparents were furious. Maria felt worse and worse each time one of her grandparents made a remark, but she tried not to show them how disappointed she was. She also began to worry about whether her father had been hurt in an accident, as he had promised her the day before that he would be sure to be home on time for her birthday party. She made a comment to her mother expressing concern about why her father had not come home, but her mother abruptly changed the subject. When Maria went to bed that evening, her father still had not appeared. She remembered that she had difficulty falling asleep because she was both disappointed and worried about where her father was. Later that night, Maria and her sister were awakened by the sound of her parents arguing. She heard her mother accusing her father of being with another woman, and her father announced that he was moving out. The two sisters said nothing to each other while they heard their father packing, nor did they get out of bed to talk with their parents. They heard the door slam and that was the last contact they had with their father. The next day her mother told the girls that he was not coming back, and she did not want to hear his name mentioned in her house.

Maria recalls that she had felt very guilty when her father left. "If it hadn't been for my birthday, my parents would not have gotten into an argument, and my father would not have gone away," she stated. She revealed that whenever she thought of her father, it was always with a feeling that she had been responsible in some way for his leaving the family. She never communicated this feeling to anyone.

Maria revealed that she had often been troubled with depressed moods growing up. Teresa got better grades in school than Maria did, and their mother always criticized Maria for not doing as well as her younger sister. She began to think that she was not smart enough to get good grades. Maria always became despondent when she got into an argument with her mother. However, these periods of depression usually lasted only about a day and passed when she became involved in some other activity.

Maria indicated that she had always had a number of children to play with and had several friends when she was a teenager. She recalled that, however, it was always very difficult to share her feelings with her friends and tell them about events that were troubling her. Maria and her sister had gotten along fairly well growing up, but they had never confided in each other. She said that she had always had trouble expressing her emotions and she felt that Teresa had the same problem. When they were younger, their only social activities together were going to church and visiting relatives.

Maria had dated a number of boys as a teenager. She said that she had preferred going out with a group rather than being alone with one boy, because in a group she did not feel compelled to carry on a conversation. When she conversed with boys, she worried that they would find her boring. Her mother was not friendly to any of her daughters' friends, and Maria indicated that whenever someone came to the house, she felt embarrassed by her mother's untidy appearance and distant manner.

Maria described her mother as a "constant complainer." Maria feels that her mother had the skills and education for a better type of employment, but her mother claimed that she did not want any other type of work. Nevertheless, she would come home from work each day quite tired and complain about how hard she had worked. She would then put on her robe, cook dinner, and spend the evening watching television. If her daughters tried to converse with her, she told them that she was tired and just wanted to be left alone. She often expressed the belief that she had sacrificed her life to make her children happy and "all she ever got in return were grief and unhappiness." When they began going out on dates, she never asked if they had a good time, but instead just commented on how tired she was because she had waited up for them. She would make disparaging remarks about the boys they had been with and about men in general. The mother's only social activity was church on Sunday and dinner with her parents.

Maria had met Tony at a party 2 years previously, when she was 20 and he was 23. She liked him from the first time they met, but she was very careful not to show her feelings, for fear that he would not be interested in her if he knew that she liked him. She described Tony as a talkative and friendly person, of similar background. She said that he, too, had difficulty expressing his feelings, and that he resorted to kidding around or changing the topic instead of talking about personal matters. They dated off and on for a number of months and then started to see each other exclusively until the time of their breakup. She stopped attending church when she started dating Tony and admits that she has lost the religious feelings she had as a child.

Four months before they stopped dating, Tony got a job promotion and said that he wanted to marry Maria. Maria enjoyed being with Tony, but she was troubled by her mother's attitude toward him. Her mother did not seem to like Tony and was very cold and aloof whenever he came to the house. When she tried to discuss the topic of marriage, her mother said "all men are nice before they get married, but later their true nature comes out."

Maria was confused about her feelings toward Tony and about his feelings toward her. She was not sure whether she loved him, but she knew she would be unhappy if they stopped seeing each other. Maria had never told Tony about the events that occurred at the time her father left the family or about her fear that she would end up in a situation similar to her mother. When she asked him how he felt about her, Tony became annoyed and said it was obvious what his feelings were because he wanted to marry her. After Tony broke up with her on a dinner date, Maria was upset, but also "relieved that he made the decision for me."

ACTIVITY 11.2 IS IT A PROBLEM TITLE OR AN ASSESSMENT IDEA?

Decide if each of the following client goals is a problem title (**P**) or an assessment idea (**A**; a title for the explanation).

1. Difficulty initiating conversations with new acquaintances.

2. Maladaptive conditioned responses to authority figures.

3. Unmet needs for a mirroring selfobject.

4. Overweight.

5. Overeats from emotional hunger for stimulation and nurturance.

6. Biologically based alcohol addiction.

7. Depressed mood following divorce of parents.

8. Depressed mood caused by divorce of parents.

9. Lack of courage for major life changes.

10. Plays role of identified patient for dysfunctional family.

Answers: 1. P 2. A 3. A 4. P 5. A 6. A 7. P 8. A 9. A 10. A

ACTIVITY 11.3 PROBLEM DEFINITION FROM
YOUR PRELIMINARY LIST

Using the problem list that you created for Maria in Activity 11.1, define your formal list of problem titles. Aim for a minimum of 3 and a maximum of 6. When you have decided on your final list, write the numbers of all the items on the preliminary list under the title. *Every problem must be accounted for, and the same preliminary problem can appear under more than one problem title.*

Class Activity

In groups of between three and five people, compare your problems lists. Work together as a group to come up with a final problem list that you all would endorse. Take time to word the titles so that they are clear and specific. When the entire class reconvenes, each group will presents its list of problems. Discussion focuses on decisions to *lump* or *split*.

ACTIVITY 12.1 DEVELOPING "SMART OUTCOMES"

Interview a member of class or a friend and help him or her develop an outcome that meets the five criteria of a "smart outcome." Write down, verbatim, the initial statement. Ask questions, as necessary, to shape the outcome into a "smart" one. Be sure to paraphrase frequently, as the outcome is modified. Each time the outcome is modified, write down a new outcome statement. Evaluate the final statement to see if it meets the five criteria.

ACTIVITY 12.2 IS IT A PROCESS GOAL OR AN OUTCOME GOAL?

Decide if each of the following client goals is a process goal (**P**), an outcome goal (**O**), or an unacceptable goal (**X**):

1. To deal effectively with her child when she is feeling angry.

2. To access the anger she felt as a child toward her mother.

3. To set realistic goals for channeling creative talents.

4. To make a decision regarding career choice and the balance of work and leisure.

5. To build relationships that are supportive and to terminate relationships with critical, abusive people.

6. To become a fully integrated person.

7. To successfully resolve the transference.

8. To feel a sense of equality with others.

9. To help the client change faulty motivation.

10. To be free of stress.

Answers: 1. O 2. P 3. O & P 4. O 5. O 6. X 7. P 8. O 9. P 10. X

ACTIVITY 12.3 PRACTICE WRITING OUTCOME GOALS

Part I: Problem Titles

For each of the five problems, write an appropriate outcome goal that does not contain explanatory concepts or jump to conclusions about the assessment or treatment strategy. Compare your answers with others who are doing the same activity.

1. *Feelings of inadequacy in new role as clinical trainee.*

2. *Frustration and hurt in friendship where she feels exploited and unappreciated.*

3. *Inability to resolve conflicts with spouse combined with excessive angry outbursts.*

4. *Boredom and frustration over lack of challenge in well-paying, secure job.*

5. *Fails to comply with medically necessary exercise and diet.*

Part II: The Case of Maria

Select three problem titles that you wrote for Maria and write outcome goals.

ACTIVITY 13.1 IS IT SUBJECTIVE DATA
OR OBJECTIVE DATA?

1. A client whom you believe is an accurate reporter is giving you details about his life history. You get a large number of facts that you know can be verified: the name of the college and the degree received could of course be verified by transcript; date and place of birth can be documented with a passport or birth certificate. Is this objective enough to go in **O**? _____

2. The clinician's observations belong in the **O** section. That makes sense when these observations are reliable and unbiased. But what if the therapist is having a countertransference reaction and has an inaccurate perception of the client? Or what if the therapist is from a different culture and draws wrong conclusions about the meaning of nonverbal behavior? Wouldn't you want to put this material in the **S** section? _____

> *Answers:* 1. No, the source is the client. The data go in S. 2. No, the source is not the client. These faulty conclusions do not belong in the database.

ACTIVITY 13.2 FIND THE ASSESSMENT IN
THE SUBJECTIVE SECTION

After each paragraph, taken from a subjective section, write the number of the sentence(s) that belong in the assessment section.

A. 1. His addiction to marijuana started when he was in his late teens. **2.** His marijuana consumption may be a reason why he holds such unrealistic goals for himself. **3.** He stated, "I think that smoking weed helps me relax and think about what I need to get done." **4.** When asked how it affects his decision-making process, he said, "I don't think it has any negative consequences except for a little dry mouth, it doesn't affect the way I decide on things." **5.** He is relying too much on his impulses and very little on his practical nature. _____

B. 1. She never told her family about the abuse. **2.** At the time it was happening, she thought that no one would believe her. **3.** She feels that she could never tell her family now because they would judge her and think that she is "damaged goods." **4.** She feels that she is a "fraud and a liar" because she has told everyone that she is still a virgin. **5.** Unspoken family rules about sex have contributed to her feeling that she could never tell her family what happened. **6.** She states that sex was never discussed in her home. _____

Answers: A. 2, 5 B. 5

ACTIVITY 13.3 IS IT OBJECTIVE DATA OR ASSESSMENT?

You are in the audience at an interdisciplinary case conference in a hospital setting. Members of many different professions are discussing a 68-year-old female inpatient with a diagnosis of Major Depressive Disorder. For each of the following comments, decide if it would fit in **O** or **A**.

1. **Psychiatrist:** *Her short-term memory is impaired and she has poor concentration.*
2. **Counselor:** *She lost the will to live after her child died.*
3. **Psychologist:** *Her full scale IQ is 160.*
4. **Nurse:** *She sits in ward meetings looking at the floor and she doesn't say a word.*
5. **Occupational Therapist:** *I caught her trying to take sharp scissors out of the room.*
6. **Marriage and Family Therapist:** *Her symptoms are an expression of the dysfunctional marital relationship, and we should definitely have her husband come in for conjoint therapy.*
7. **Physician:** *We have ruled out an endocrine disorder.*

Answers: 1. O 2. A 3. O 4. O 5. O 6. A 7. A

ACTIVITY 14.1 USING A THREE-COLUMN WORKSHEET

Part I: Use the model in Table 14.1, and a three-column worksheet (Form **I.E** in Appendix I) to write down your selected hypotheses, supporting data, and treatment ideas for Maria's problem: *Difficulty establishing intimate, trusting relationship with a man.*

Part II: Using either a new client or an interview with a classmate, write each problem title on a three-column worksheet, and enter supporting data, hypotheses, and treatment ideas in the appropriate columns.

ACTIVITY 14.2 WRITING YOUR ASSESSMENT DISCUSSION

Referring to the charts you prepared in Activity 14.1, write assessment sections for one or two problems. Evaluate these essays according to the standards and recommendations for good writing from Chapter 14. When you are finished, meet with others who are doing this same activity and offer each other feedback.

ACTIVITY 15.1 COMPONENTS OF THE PLAN

Here are two examples of plans. Decide for the *preceding sentence* which term (or terms) apply.

Outcome Goal (OG).

Process Goal (PG).

Strategy (S).

Technique (T).

Relationship Issue (RI).

Intermediate Objective (IO).

Monitoring Effectiveness of Treatment (ME).

Sample 1

I will help her explore her relationships with her mother and father and help her see connections between these early experiences and current patterns in her marriage **1.** _____ It will be crucial that I maintain an empathic stance and function as a mirroring selfobject for Sandra. **2.** _____ I will acknowledge the importance of her needs and experiences, allowing her to experience validation, and I will encourage her awareness of unmet needs and painful emotions of her childhood. **3.** _____ I will make sure that both emotional experiencing and cognitive insight occur in a safe, empathic relationship with me. During the early stages of therapy, she will be trying to meet my needs and provide what she thinks I want. **4.** _____ A first sign of growth will be when she is able to express her disagreement and hurt feelings at the moment they occur. **5.** _____ Through temporary breakdowns in my empathic understanding, she will develop more empathy for herself and will, for the first time, experience a relationship with someone who can admit she is wrong, accept her anger without retaliating, and validate her experience instead of telling her that her feelings are wrong. **6.** _____ Gradually, she will transfer her new expectations and communication skills to her relationship with her husband. **7.** _____

Answers: 1. PG 2. S & RI 3. S and PG 4. RI 5. IO 6. RI 7. OG and ME

Sample 2

My strategy will change when he demonstrates the ability to examine himself and see things from another's point of view. **1.** _____ I will begin to challenge some of his cognitive distortions. **2.** _____ I will use questioning to ask him for evidence that exists for his various assumptions (that his boss will try to prove him incompetent). **3.** _____ I will teach him the errors of mind reading and catastrophizing, and help him to recognize when he engages in those processes. **4.** _____ As homework, I will give him a cognitive monitoring chart. There will be a column where he would be required to dispute beliefs and indicate rational beliefs to replace the irrational ones. **5.** _____ Because he and I have different cultural backgrounds, I will monitor my own cultural biases and encourage him to educate me about his culture. **6.** _____ I will encourage him to evaluate beliefs in terms of his cultural upbringing as well as his self-defined value system. **7.** _____

Answers: 1. IO 2. S 3. T 4. T & S 5. T 6. RI 7. S

(If you have different answers from the answer key, discuss them with people who are doing the same activity.)

ACTIVITY 15.2 EVALUATION OF A COMPLETE REPORT

The left column contains a report that was written based on one session with a classmate. The right column contains the 33 standards, placed next to the section to which they apply. Your task is to evaluate the report and write comments in the right column to give feedback to the student. If you think improvement is necessary, write your suggestion.

Identifying Data

The client, Tami is a 24-year-old single woman of Middle Eastern descent, enrolled as a full-time student in a graduate psychology program, living with her aunt and uncle, and receiving financial support from her parents.

Background

The only child of an affluent businessman and his college-educated wife, she moved with her parents to a large eastern city when she was a baby. She lived at home while attending undergraduate school. She came to a city 3,000 miles from her home to enter a master's program in psychology. She has been living with her aunt and uncle and her parents have been providing financial support for school. She has been living there for 8 months and has 2 months left before she completes her graduate degree and returns to her parents' home. Although she has cordial relationships with her classmates when she is at school, she has not formed any friendships and engages in no social activities, except meals with her aunt and uncle and other relatives who live in the area.

Problem Title: *Conflict with aunt and uncle over living style*

The client is frustrated by expectations and general living conditions imposed on her while living as a guest in her relatives' house.

Review the entire report and return to this section:

If you would change the problem title, write the new title here:

If you would split this problem, write an additional problem title here:

17. The subjective section is well organized and appropriately concise: There is selection, summarization, and condensation of details.

1. Problems are defined so that they are solvable targets of treatment.
2. Titles refer to the client's current, real-world functioning.
3. Titles are descriptive, designed for a specific client, and are justified by the data.
4. Problem titles do not contain theoretical, explanatory concepts.
5. The therapist is not imposing cultural or personal values in problem definitions.
6. Lumping and splitting decisions are justified in that they lead to good treatment planning.
7. The problem list is complete and comprehensive.

Outcome Goals

One possible goal is that the client will resolve the conflict with her relatives: She might choose to improve communication and negotiate changes in her living situation. It is also possible that the conflict will no longer bother her if she can develop a more serene attitude during the remaining 2 months. In either case, she will attain greater clarity on her values and the choices she is making.

If you would change the outcome goals, write your thoughts here:

Subjective Data

Tami's problem reportedly began when she moved into her aunt and uncle's house in September of this year. She explained that because she would be attending school in California for 1 year, her relatives offered her a room in their home. She related that she did not want to stay with them, citing "different people have different living styles" and "I knew this was going to happen." However, she did move in with them to satisfy her parents, and to guard against "appearing ungrateful." She related how certain things about them really bother her and that they are "starting to do things." Tami described how they are moody, not very cheerful, and seem to be hiding things from her. She justified the previous statement by explaining they are not as open as her relatives back home and that they are not as comfortable to be with as her parents. She expanded by describing her uncle and aunt as "quiet" and "reserved," contrasting them with her parents who are "always laughing and more freestyle."

The client recounted several bothersome incidents that happened while

8. Outcome goals are directly related to the problem title and are consistent with the client's values.

9. Outcome goals refer to real-world functioning and do not contain formulation ideas.

10. Outcome goals are realistic and are not utopian.

11. Outcome goals do not contain the "how" of the treatment plan.

12. The database is thorough, comprehensive, and complete: There are sufficient data so that multiple hypotheses can be applied.

13. Subjective and objective data are appropriately distinguished.

14. Good quotations from the client are included in the subjective data section.

15. The subjective section does not include formulation concepts (unless they are quotations from the client).

staying at her uncle and aunt's home. In one instance, she explained that when her uncle had bronchitis, he asked her to wash his dishes because he wasn't feeling well. He said, "you know I'm not feeling well, if you ever see any dishes in the sink you could wash them." The client felt her uncle was "way out of line" with this request. Another unpleasant incident occurred when she went to the grocery store to buy certain foods that she enjoys and which her relatives do not stock. Her uncle was very offended and said, "What, do you think we can't afford it?" In addition, the client complained that she is not given her phone messages. She made that discovery after she asked her boyfriend why he hadn't called for such a long time, and he explained that he had left messages twice with her aunt. The client reported that when she spoke to her uncle about the situation he made excuses for his wife, explaining she is tired after work, and intimating that it is Tami's responsibility to ask for her calls by commenting, "maybe you should check with us." Furthermore, the client expressed anger and frustration at the fact that she has no phone in her room. She explained that she has no privacy and is forced to use the phone in the kitchen if she wants to make or take a call.

Finally, the client commented that the breaking point has arrived because they are "imposing" on her now. She supported her claim by describing how her uncle and aunt are pressuring her into taking a vacation with them for the July 4 weekend. The client explained that she really has no desire to go and that it would set her behind in her schoolwork. However, she related "I should just go already. If I don't go it will be even worse ... they're doing all this planning, and they'll be upset if I can't go."

Tami explained that she deals with the situations that she finds herself in

16. There is no reference to how and when the information was gathered in the subjective data section; this information, if relevant, goes in the objective section.

17. The subjective section is well organized and appropriately concise: There is selection, summarization, and condensation of details.

by "playing by their rules." She maintains that she does this just to get through the next 2 months without rocking the boat. She described that now she tells her uncle what groceries she needs or buys herself some treats to eat at school and doesn't bring them home. The client explained that she feels obligated to be a good guest for her parents' sake. In response to the suggestion that she could speak up to her uncle and aunt, she offered, "I would be worried that it would reflect badly on my parents." She further explained that in their culture it would be viewed as disrespectful. At one point, the client confessed that if she were to speak up it should have been done much earlier. However, as soon as she said that, she added, "It would look bad, my parents would look bad, and my parents are very important to me." She spoke of her closeness to them and of how "they come first."

Objective Data

Her facial expression and body language convey a sense of ease and relaxation. She was dressed neatly and exuded strength and confidence despite her petite frame. She answered questions and related information about her situation in a soft voice. At the beginning of the session, she spoke in a calm, careful manner that evolved into expressions of appropriate emotions. As the session progressed she became more animated, using hand gestures and body language to communicate her thoughts and feelings. She was very open to discussing different aspects of her problem situation. However, when I proposed the idea of expressing her complaints in an assertive manner to her relatives, she was adamant about not being willing to do that. She was very assertive with me, expressing her feelings and rejecting my suggestion in a polite, but firm way.

18. The objective section does not contain theoretical concepts, biased opinions, or formulation discussion.

Assessment

First, the conflict with her aunt and uncle can be assessed cognitively. Tami admits that "different people have different living styles." Therefore, with her complaints about her relatives' behavior, she is demonstrating utopian expectations (**C1**): It is unrealistic to expect that there will be no conflicts or frustrations. While bothersome, these incidents would not be producing the intensity of her emotional response if it were not for her interpretations of these and other incidents. There must be faulty, maladaptive beliefs contributing to the intensity of her feelings (**C2**).

In discussing her relatives, she demonstrates mind reading (**C3**). Without discussing with them whether she should accompany her aunt and uncle on a weekend vacation, she had decided that they will be upset if she decides not to join them. Furthermore, overgeneralization contributes to her cognitive errors. She believes that they get offended and defensive if she doesn't accept everything they offer her, based on earlier incidents (i.e., the grocery incident). From my perspective, it was faulty information processing to treat an invitation to go on a vacation as if it fell in the same category as a demand to do dishes.

In addition, Tami is operating under a maladaptive schema that most likely has its origin in early childhood (**C2, P2**). This schema can be called the "pressure of being the only child." It seems that many of her thoughts and actions hinge on her ability to make her parents happy or unhappy. She cannot make any mistakes because she thinks that she is their only chance for happiness. The implied belief that "It is my duty to make sure my parents are happy, no matter how much I'm suffering" may also demonstrate mind reading of her parents. I neglected to

19. The assessment integrates hypotheses that are consistent with the prior database.

20. The assessment does not introduce new data.

21. The focus of the assessment is on the specific problem of the specific client: This is not an abstract essay about a theory.

22. The writer is not including all possible hypotheses, just the ones that are useful in developing intervention plans.

23. If theoretical jargon is used, it enhances rather than detracts from understanding and does not contribute to tautological explanations.

24. The writer is integrating material from the highest level of education thus far attained. Commonsense ideas are appropriate but are not sufficient for explaining the problem.

get necessary data, but I would want to get information about what they say when she discusses her complaints with them.

From my own belief system, it would seem sensible to communicate with her aunt and uncle. However, this is an unthinkable solution from her model of the world, because if she speaks out it will reflect poorly on her parents, and then they will be unhappy, which will make her feel guilty. In her implicit cost-benefit analysis, the pain of that guilt outweighs any benefits she can imagine from being assertive.

She is unable to discuss with her uncle and aunt her thoughts and feelings about their rules and expectations while she is living at their home because it is perceived as disrespectful by cultural standards (**SCE2**). To evaluate Tami's situation, I would need more understanding of her culture. From her point of view, her beliefs are based on her culture. Another way to look at it, however, is that she defends her beliefs by calling them cultural standards, thus avoiding taking responsibility for examining deeper sources of her fear of confronting her relatives. She explained that she is suppressing her wants and needs so as not to disgrace her parents. As long as she adamantly insists that she is just following cultural rules, it is difficult to explore more personal explanations and dynamics.

The problem also has environmental causes (**SCE7**). She is unable to talk to her parents, boyfriend, and friends in her home because she does not have the privacy of a telephone in her room. A simple solution might be obtaining a cell phone. Her distress over her living situation is exacerbated by her social isolation: Her situation might not appear so unbearable if she had social support (**SCE3**).

25. The writer demonstrates professional-level thinking and writing skills to provide a coherent conceptualization.

Plan

If I were to continue to see Tami, I would study her culture, both through reading and consultation.

Tami's assumption that she is responsible for her parents' happiness needs to be explored in more depth. Perhaps dispelling this myth would enable her to deal with her problem with her aunt and uncle more constructively. I might explore other situations in which she has let her parents down to point out that it is not fatal. Moreover, I would recommend more communication with her parents. Because she is unable to discuss her current situation over the phone with her parents (due to lack of privacy), I would suggest she keep a journal of daily events or problems she would like to discuss with her parents and then mail them a letter or a copy of the journal. She might get a response from her parents acknowledging her situation as a large burden (thus providing social support) and their concern for her happiness (possibly by talking to her uncle and aunt about the situation or by helping her make other living arrangements).

26. The plan is focused on resolving the identified problem and achieving outcome goals.

I would address the mind reading and overgeneralization by explaining the concepts and indicating under what circumstances she is using them. These are important for Tami to be aware of because they are maintaining her problem. I would want to explore her values and "rules" for family living. In doing this, I would need to be aware of my own countertransference: I think her uncle is right and she should have done his dishes when he was sick. I would really need to understand her background. As an only child with affluent parents, did she have any household chores?

27. The plan follows logically from the prior discussion and does not introduce new data or hypotheses.

28. There is clarity regarding process goals, intermediate objectives, strategies, specific techniques, relationship issues, and sequencing of interventions.

29. The plan is tailor-made for the specific client: Such factors as gender, ethnicity, and personal values are considered.

Even though she refuses to consider communicating her complaints directly to her aunt and uncle, I would want to use therapy time to have her pretend to talk to them. In this way, I could assess her assertive skills and see if her anger interferes with her expressing herself appropriately. Perhaps with further discussion, we could do some behavioral rehearsal during our sessions.

If her goal is to maintain a more serene attitude for the next 2 months, she could learn cognitive skills and relaxation methods to reduce her emotional distress. Even though there are only 2 months left in this situation, I would want her to leave therapy with tools that will help her when she again lives outside her parents' home, as when she gets married or if she chooses a roommate situation after returning home.

30. The plan is appropriate for the treatment setting, contractual agreements, and financial constraints.

31. When there is more than one problem, the therapist addresses issues of priorities, sequencing, and integration of plans.

32. The therapist considers community resources and referrals, if appropriate.

33. Legal and ethical issues are addressed appropriately, if relevant.

Appendix IV

EXAMPLES

SAMPLE SOAP FOR ACTIVITY 1.1: WRITING YOUR BASELINE CASE FORMULATION REPORT

SAMPLE ANSWERS FOR ACTIVITY 10.2: APPLY AND TEST HYPOTHESES WITH CASE VIGNETTES

MARIA: A SAMPLE CASE FORMULATION REPORT

Sample SOAP for Activity 1.1:
Writing Your Baseline Case Formulation Report

STUDENT'S CASE FORMULATION REPORT FOR HIS
OWN PROBLEM (DATA CHANGED TO PROTECT ANONYMITY)

1. Identifying Information

I am a 23-year-old Caucasian male and have a younger sister who is 17. My parents are in their early 50s; my father is a biology professor and my mother is a homemaker. I moved to the opposite coast from my parents to go to college and stayed here to go to graduate school in psychology. I am unmarried and live alone. I am a full-time student, financing my education through an inheritance from my grandparents and student loans.

2. Background Information

My father does not respect the field of psychology and belittles the professors in that department at his university. I am deeply interested in studying psychology because of my long-standing interest in helping people. My GPA in undergraduate school was 3.8, and I am maintaining a 4.0 in my master's program.

3. Problem: *Daily academic procrastination*

I fail to keep up with weekly reading assignments for courses. I make plans to study but then make different choices for my time. I only do school work in concentrated short time periods (cramming) before deadlines.

4. Outcome Goal

Either adherence to a study schedule that is continuous throughout the semester rather than just prior to exams, or acceptance of cramming, without guilt.

5. Subjective Data

In elementary school, my mother would quiz me for exams and check my homework every day. In fifth grade, I told her I didn't want her help anymore. Upset with me, she accepted my decision, but still asked each day whether I'd finished my homework before she would let me read for fun or play with friends. It was a cardinal rule in our house that one couldn't play until one's work was done. I resented this rule immensely. From sixth grade onward, I had trouble turning assignments in on time. In sixth grade, I received a C+ in a course because of fifteen late assignments, although I produced A-quality work. I was repeatedly told that it was unacceptable to do anything less than my best. In junior high and high school, I would lie to my parents that my homework was done when in fact it was not. I would then secretly stay up all night before a big paper or an exam in order to get good grades to keep my parents off my back. I was very afraid of my parents' anger and disapproval. In college, I finally had the freedom to play before I worked. I became adept at knowing when it was the last possible moment to start a paper and still get a good grade on it. With two exceptions, I completed every paper on time, usually functioning well on less than 3 hours sleep when necessary.

Procrastination has the following costs: I often get sick after finals; I feel very stressed the week before a big test or paper; I don't enjoy the leisure time that I gain from procrastination because I feel guilt ridden and exhausted; I know my work is not as good as it would be if I took more time. There are definitely payoffs for my pattern of procrastination: I like the "adrenaline high" I get from leaving things to the last minute and then working furiously to complete the project. I also feel intellectually and personally powerful that I can do so well academically in such a limited amount of time. I have made numerous attempts to stop procrastinating, but I don't like the resulting feelings of boredom and depression from being cooped up. I engage in "goofing off" to improve my mood and return to my pattern of cramming at the last minute.

6. Objective Data

(What an imaginary observer would have noted from interviewing me and videotaping samples of my behavior during the past month.)

- When he talks about his father, he raises his voice and clenches his fist.
- He stayed at his desk reading for 1 hour and 10 minutes for a course he likes, but only lasted 20 minutes for a course that he finds boring.
- During a cram session prior to an exam, he stayed at his desk for 3 hours. During that time, there were distracting noises in the room to which he did not react. He terminated that work session appearing more, rather than less, energetic than when he began.

7. Assessment

I will not be able to achieve my outcome goal if I don't sort out my ambivalence about whether to change my study habits or whether to continue with the strategy (which I label procrastination) that I employ. I can identify different internal parts (**P1**). The "responsible" part of me identifies with my parents' values and wants to do work on time. The "fun lover" in me rejects my parents' values and wants to have fun. By procrastinating but still doing well in my courses, both parts have a voice, and, in fact, seem to have achieved a good compromise. In addition to exploring these two parts and examining the goals they can agree on, I need to examine the "self-punishing" internal voice that nags me to stop procrastinating.

There are many schemas and assumptions that contribute to my procrastination problem (**C2**). I find myself labeling myself "a bad person" if I don't "do my best." At the same time, I believe that always doing my work first makes me "boring." A great deal of dysfunctional self-talk (**C4**) interferes with my ability to sit down at my desk and start working, unless I am very close to the deadline. I have the skills (**BL3**) to concentrate and produce above average academic products.

In conducting a behavioral analysis (**BL1**) of the procrastination behavior, I notice that there are many rewards for this strategy. I am rewarded by the adrenaline rush and feelings of potency that follow cramming. If I do not find those highs elsewhere in my life, I will keep engaging in procrastination in order to get that reward. Many other people get those highs from their romantic or social life, whereas I have been fairly solitary for many years. There are no rewards for studying early and in a steady, regular schedule.

The procrastination could be looked at as a compromise between the desires to both defy and please my parents. It is possible that the intensity of my guilt and anxiety over my procrastination behavior could stem from an unconscious desire to punish myself for defying my parents (**P4**). By not doing my work first and by not doing my absolute best, I symbolically reject my parents. This defiance causes me to unconsciously feel that I don't deserve their love. My mother checking my schoolwork and my dad's lectures when I didn't do my best gave me the message that I was not worthy of love if I wasn't a responsible high achiever.

8. Plan

First, I will commit to experiment with a new approach to schoolwork that involves using a time schedule and rewarding myself for sticking to it (**BL1**). I will agree to try this approach for a week, keeping a daily journal. In the journal, I will write down verbatim my self-talk (**C4**) and identify the different inner parts (**P1**). I will also record my emotional states. I will set up a contingency contract so that I reward myself for sticking to my new study schedule, in order to offset the loss of post-cramming highs. I will be sure to spend my post-dinner free time in ways that are rewarding and stimulating.

I will use cognitive techniques to challenge schemas (**C2**): "What specifically do you mean by 'boring'?" "How specifically does not doing your best cause you to be a bad person?" Each answer would be followed up with other questions until the fundamental core beliefs are exposed and can be challenged with evidence (e.g., friends who do their work first and are not boring).

If the cognitive and behavioral strategies are not effective, then I will explore my internal parts (**P1**). I will have my different inner parts engage in dialogue and reach decisions that they can all endorse. A dialogue between the Responsible and the Fun Lover parts of my self will yield greater clarity about each internal part's purposes and hopes. A dialogue with a Child part might yield greater awareness of unconscious beliefs about my love-worthiness (**P4**). This awareness would free me from the need to unconsciously act out. Some empty-chair exercises in which I speak directly to my parents might also help me become conscious of any desire to punish myself for not living up to my parents' demands. I think other Gestalt exercises will be helpful when I raise my voice or clench my fist: I suspect that there is anger toward my parents, especially toward my father, which needs to be experienced.

It is possible that after this course of therapy, I will freely choose my current pattern of cramming before deadlines. Instead of calling it "procrastination," I'll label it "my preferred strategy for time management." In that case, I will not be feeling guilty and will stop nagging and torturing myself during my free time.

Sample Answers for Activity 10.2: Apply and Test Hypotheses with Case Vignettes

I have collected answers to this activity from various students.

CELESTE

B1 Biological Cause

- **Explanation:** Celeste's memory impairment and confusion may be signs of the onset of a medical disorder such as Alzheimer's.
- **Probe:** Celeste was referred to a neurologist for brain imagining and a neuropsychologist for a neuropsychological assessment.
- **New invented data:** Celeste's brain imaging results indicated that she did have plaques and fissures indicative of Alzheimer's disease. The neuropsychological assessment was congruent with the brain imaging results and showed that she had major impairments with her working memory.

SCE3 Social Support

- **Explanation:** Celeste's isolation and resulting symptoms of depression are related to the breakdown in her social support system since she lost her husband and her only sibling. She no longer "fits in" with the other married couples, and her other friends who are not widowed are not able to make time for her now.
- **Probe:** Celeste, can you tell me how you felt when you have been able to spend time with your friends since your husband's death?
- **New invented data:** According to her, she was feeling "down," but overall the experience was a positive one because she was able to "get out and live a little." She further reported that she misses her friends because they make her feel so good and they are supportive with the loss that she is going through.

ES3 Spiritual Dimension

- **Explanation:** The loss of her husband has deeply hurt her soul, and she now lacks the deep connection that she once had, and it makes her feel alone in the world.
- **Probe:** Celeste, can you tell me about any spiritual beliefs that you have?
- **New invented data:** Celeste reported that she has lost faith in God after her husband died. She stated "how can I believe in a higher power when I keep losing those closest to me?"

C3 Faulty Information Processing

- **Explanation:** Celeste believes that her married friends do not want to be around her because she is no longer "one of the couples" (mind reading). She thinks that the only friend who wants to spend time with her is her widowed friend despite evidence that her other friends have made an effort to see her. These faulty cognitions have negatively impacted her mood and caused her to isolate herself.
- **Probe:** Can you tell me about the last time you spoke with one of your friends whom you used to spend a good deal of time with?
- **New invented data:** Celeste says, "My friends called me two weeks ago to go out to the movies, but I knew they didn't really want to spend time with me, it was a sympathy call, so I just stayed in and kept to myself. I don't want sympathy."

ES1 Existential Issues

- **Explanation:** She has been forced to face the death of her husband and brother and is struggling with questions about meaning and fairness in life. She is also now facing the reality of her aging and the imminence of her own death.
- **Probe:** Tell me about your thoughts about life and death.
- **New invented data:** She mentions that she thinks there is no hope of any happiness left; it's all downhill until she dies.

CS4 Loss and Bereavement

- **Explanation:** Although some time has passed since the death of her husband and her brother, she may still be going through the grieving process. The changes in her grooming and housekeeping, her staying in bed all day, and her lack of joy in previously pleasurable activities, such as reading and being with her friends, all could be indications of depression related to her unresolved grief.
- **Probe:** When your husband died, how did you deal with your grief?
- **New invented data:** She says that she tried not to let herself feel her feelings and just kept busy as much as possible.

ALLISON

P3 Immature Sense of Self and Conception of Others

- **Explanation:** Allison needs Steve to ease the emotional pain of being alone. She never learned to soothe herself and whenever she tries to function without a relationship, she feels the abandonment feelings of a 2-year-old child.
- **Probe:** How would you describe the feelings when you break up with him?
- **New invented data:** She says "it feels like abandonment, like when I was little and having a bad dream and I'd cry and cry, but my mother didn't come."

C2 Faulty Cognitive Map, Sample 1

- **Explanation:** Allison believes that she cannot leave this relationship with Steve. She views dating as a negative thing that is boring. She gives up after only a few dates, suggesting a schema that "things should come easy."
- **Probe:** What would happen if you left this relationship with Steve?
- **New invented data:** "I would end up all alone. Deep down I believe I'm unlovable and that if a man really spent more time with me than Steve does, he would reject me."

C2 Faulty Cognitive Map, Sample 2

- **Explanation:** She gets discouraged after dates, so decides to stick with what she's got. This implies that she doesn't think she deserves better.
- **Probe:** Tell me more about why you stay with him.
- **New invented data:** "I can't do any better."

BL3 Skill Deficits or Lack of Competence

- **Explanation:** Allison lacks the necessary communication and interpersonal skills to interact with men. Maybe Steve is satisfied with her because he has very limited needs for intimacy but when she tries to date other men, she doesn't listen at all or talks in a way that is a huge turnoff to others.
- **Probe:** Can you tell me about the last date that you went on with someone other than Steve?
- **New invented data:** Allison proceeds to describe her last date where she "just sat there" because she did not know what to say to her date. When he attempted to initiate conversation, she answered with one word answers. She admitted that she never asked him questions or showed interest in him.

C4 Dysfunctional Self-Talk

- **Explanation:** Allison stated that she is "stuck in a bad relationship." By saying this to herself, she feels helpless. She also stated that she "doesn't know how to deal with it," yet another dysfunctional message that perpetuates her lack of problem solving.
- **Probe:** Can you tell me more about what you tell yourself about your relationship with Steve?
- **New invented data:** "I tell myself that I shouldn't complain, I should just stick it out and it'll get better. I tell myself that he won't listen to me, so what's the use of trying to talk about it."

C3 Faulty Information Processing

- **Explanation:** She assumes that new dates look at her like "meat."
- **Probe:** How specifically do you know they think that?
- **New invented data:** "I can just tell. All men are like that."

P2 Reenactment of Early Childhood Experiences

- **Explanation:** She has selected a man who is like her father and she is copying her mother's role.
- **Probe:** What were your parents like?
- **New invented data:** Her mother and father had a similar relationship; her father was cold and distant and her mother made him the center of her world and always asked his permission to go do things with her friends.

CATHY

P1 Internal Parts and Subpersonalities

- **Explanation:** She has raised her son and filled the role of stay-at-home mother perfectly. She was successful in the role of student, earning a teaching credential. However, she has never developed the part of her that wants to be a successful career woman.
- **Probe:** Let's do an activity where I can hear from each of the parts of your inner conflict. We can hear from the "good mother" and the "business owner."
- **New invented data:** As Cathy expresses her desire to own a business, she reported hearing an inner, critical voice that was telling her "You can't succeed at a business. You're not smart enough." She recognized that when she was ready to get a job as a teacher, the "inner critic" put her down and told her she was not competent.

ES2 Avoiding Freedom and Responsibility

- **Explanation:** She has raised her family but has been protected by her husband from having to choose a career or focus on anything except her son. She has shared little in the responsibilities of adulthood, leaving that to her husband. With her son gone, she is facing for the first time the adult decision of fulfilling her desire for a place in the world. Having another baby would postpone her confrontation with freedom, and this is an attractive option, at times, because it's familiar.
- **Probe:** I wonder if it is scary for you to take risks and go down a path that isn't familiar.
- **New invented data:** She admits that she wants to say safe and is finding all kinds of excuses to avoid experiencing herself as separate and free. Her husband is really supportive of her finding new interests in life, but she shows insight that she is playing a game and pretending that he really needs her at home.

SCE1 Family System

- **Explanation:** Her role as stay-at-home wife satisfies her husband's desire to be the only breadwinner and his desire to maintain control. If she makes efforts to change the marital equilibrium, he exerts pressure to keep her in the familiar role, or maybe he begins to develop symptoms.

- **Probe:** How does your husband react when you talk about starting a business?
- **New invented data:** "He gets agitated and picks a fight. He puts me down and says I'm not competent enough. Once when I took a job in my friend's company, he started getting anxiety attacks, so I stopped working."

CS3 Developmental Transition

- **Explanation:** Her "empty nest syndrome" is a difficult transition, and she will need to develop new social supports and new outlets for the energies she has been directing toward her family.
- **Probe:** Have you heard the term *empty nest?*
- **New invented data:** Cathy said that she has heard that term, but that she does not want to face the fact that she is no longer needed as a mother.

SCE2 Cultural Context

- **Explanation:** Cathy's problem is very typical of upper middle-class women of her cohort who were raised by stay-at-home mothers. She has fulfilled the cultural rules for wife and mother, and there was nothing available in her cultural background to prepare her for any other role.
- **Probe:** Tell me about your cultural background and the roles that most women fill.
- **New invented data:** "I come from a very traditional Italian background, where most families have lots of children and women stay home and do cooking and entertaining. My mother was very shocked when we only had one child, and she always tells me that my role is to please my husband."

ES1 Existential Issues

- **Explanation:** Cathy is searching for a path with meaning. She is so used to paying attention to the needs of others and doing what she is "supposed to do" that it is very hard for her to figure out her own true wants. She might be very happy with her current lifestyle if she weren't trying to live up to some external standard.
- **Probe:** Is it possible that you are trying to live up to standards of what other people say you should do, instead of pursuing your own true desires?
- **New invented data:** Cathy admits that she is really happy with the freedom to enjoy her friends and spend money on things that she wants, but she thinks that she "should" do something serious. When she realizes that she is truly free to make her own choices, she gets a panicky feeling.

JAMES

B2 Medical Intervention

- **Explanation:** James appears to have symptoms of anxiety that may best be treated by having him see a psychiatrist for a medication evaluation. He attempts to reduce his anxiety by drinking, which is somewhat effective, but it may lead to a larger problem if he continues.

- **Probe:** Can you tell me how anxious you felt over the past few months?
- **New invented data:** James relates that his anxiety has been constant for the past few months and nothing he does seems to reduce it; his fingernails are almost gone, and he sometimes suffers from shortness of breath.

C4 Dysfunctional Self-Talk

- **Explanation:** He is talking to himself in a way that increases his anxiety, interferes with his writing, and prevents him from making reasonable compromises with prospective publishers.
- **Probe:** What do you say to yourself when you review what you've written?
- **New invented data:** "You're no good. You're a fraud."

CS3 Developmental Transition

- **Explanation:** The pressure from his wife may be interpreted as a sign that she is developmentally ahead of him, ready to start a family, and that he is trying to stay in the stage of young adulthood, where life still holds unlimited possibilities.
- **Probe:** Can you tell me more about your thoughts about parenthood?
- **New invented data:** James relates that he feels totally unready and he wants to gain more of an identity: "Almost like I need to take care of me, before I take care of children."

ES2 Avoiding Freedom and Responsibility

- **Explanation:** James has fallen short of his goal to become a great writer. His anxiety is a result of his awareness that he is responsible for his current life position and no one (including his wife) can "make him successful." His anxiety will worsen if he doesn't find a way to confront adult responsibility.
- **Probe:** Can you tell me more about the feeling you have about the choices that you have made?
- **New invented data:** James acknowledges that he has been free to choose his path thus far, and that he has not been living up to his responsibility to contribute to the family's financial well-being.

P4 Unconscious Dynamics

- **Explanation:** James may be unconsciously reenacting a childhood pattern. He is striving to be superior and unwilling to settle for less. If he tries to examine the situation using mature problem-solving skills, he is unable to be reasonable because there are defense mechanisms operating.
- **Probe:** Can you tell me about a recent dream?
- **New invented data:** He reports a dream and I ask him to associate to the different parts of it. He gives some of his thoughts and they trigger a memory of early childhood experiences. He now has a hunch that somehow he is trying to triumph over his brother, who was their father's favorite.

Maria: A Sample Case
Formulation Report

This sample shows the use of the case formulation method for the case of Maria (pp. 562–565). Data are reorganized below to fit the desired SOAP format for three problems, with a little imaginary data added to fill in the objective data sections. Three problems are defined.

Identifying Data

Maria is a 22-year-old single Latina woman who lives with her 41-year-old mother and her younger sister, Teresa, a 20-year-old college student, two doors away from her maternal grandparents. Maria has been employed as a secretary for the same company since graduating from high school 4 years ago.

Reasons for Seeking Therapy

Her boss referred her to the Employee Assistance Program (EAP) of her company because of absences and poor concentration at work. These problems began 2 months ago following the breakup of a relationship with her boyfriend of 2 years. The EAP counselor referred her to this counseling center.

Background

Maria is the older of two girls born to Latino Catholic parents who married right after high school. Both sets of grandparents emigrated from Guatemala and settled in a predominantly Latino neighborhood. The paternal grandparents died when Maria was young, but her maternal grandparents have always been an active part of her family.

Maria stated that her childhood was very unhappy. Her father, a truck driver, was seldom home, and when he was present, her parents were "constantly fighting." Sometimes her father would "throw things and shout," while her mother would become "sullen and withdrawn" and refuse to speak to either her husband or daughters. Maria recalls that her mother often told her daughters that she "had ruined her life" by marrying their father, who had demanded that she drop out of college after completing 3 years.

The happiest times in her childhood were between the ages of 6 and 9, when her father would take the two girls to a park or movie while her mother, who expressed no interest in joining them, went to her parents' home after church. By the time she turned 10, Maria recalled that her father "could not be relied on" because he failed to return home, as promised, to take his daughters on outings. A very significant event in Maria's childhood was her 12th birthday, when her father missed her birthday party despite having promised to be there. When she expressed her worry, her mother changed the subject. She and her sister overheard the fight her parents had in the middle of the night, when her mother accused her father of infidelity, and her father packed up and left without saying anything to his daughters. The girls did not discuss what happened, and the following morning their mother told them that their father was not coming back and she "did not want to hear his name mentioned in her house." Her father never sent money to support the family, nor has he been heard from since his departure. Maria recalls that whenever she thought of her father, it was always with a feeling that she had been responsible in some way for his leaving the family: "If it hadn't been for my birthday, my parents would not have gotten into an argument and my father would not have gone away," she stated.

After the departure of her father, her mother got a job in a supermarket and has worked there ever since. Maria described her mother as a "constant complainer" who would come home tired from work each day, complain about how hard she had worked, and spend the evening watching television. If her daughters tried to converse with her, she told them that she was tired and just wanted to be left alone. She often expressed the belief that she had sacrificed her life to make her children happy and "all she ever got in return were grief and unhappiness." Maria feels that her mother had the skills and education for a better type of employment but her mother claimed that she did not want any other type of work. Maria indicated that whenever someone came to the house, she felt embarrassed by her mother's untidy appearance and distant manner.

Problem List

> **Problem 1:** *Depression following breakup of relationship*
> **Problem 2:** *Difficulty establishing intimate, trusting relationship with a man*
> **Problem 3:** *Lack of a confidante and social support*

Problem 1: *Depression following breakup of relationship*

Maria has symptoms of acute depression that are contributing to absenteeism and poor work performance.

Outcome Goals

Her depressed mood will be alleviated and she will be attending work regularly and functioning effectively at work. She will have the ability to cope better with loss and disappointment in the future.

S: Maria said that her depression began 2 months ago, after the breakup of her relationship with her boyfriend Tony. During the month preceding the breakup, Tony had been insisting that she decide whether she wanted to marry him or not, and she felt incapable of making a decision. During a dinner date, he unexpectedly told her that he had decided it was time for him to move on and stop dating her, because she did not seem to have very strong feelings for him. She did not try to explain her feelings to him but just "felt numb" and asked to be taken home. She did not attempt to contact him.

Following that event, she had difficulty falling asleep at night, had bad dreams, and had a poor appetite. She felt constantly tired, loud noises bothered her, she preferred to lie in bed rather than be with anyone, and she often cried when alone. It became difficult for her to initiate a conversation with others, and many times her lips felt as if they were stiff, and she had to make an effort to move them to speak. It was an effort to walk around and go to work, and at work, she had difficulty concentrating. She had missed work several times during the past month and had just "sat around the house crying." She went to her family doctor because she was concerned over her lack of energy, but no medical problems were found. She asked the doctor to prescribe something to help her sleep so she would not be so tired and could concentrate better.

She stated that she "was not sure why she was so depressed." She had always had occasional periods of "feeling down," but her present feelings of misery were worse than anything she had ever experienced. Her depressed moods in childhood were associated with her mother criticizing her for not doing as well in school as her sister Teresa did. She began to think that she "was not smart enough to get good grades." She always became despondent when she got into an argument with her mother, but those moods usually lasted "only about a day," and passed when she became involved in some other activity. When Maria was feeling intense feelings of disappointment, as when her father did not show up for her birthday party, she kept them to herself.

O: Maria, an attractive, slim, dark-haired woman, was dressed neatly for her first interview. Her eyes were puffy and ringed with dark circles. She answered questions and related information about her life history in a slow, flat tone of voice, which had an impersonal quality to it. Even when she shared the painful details of her father's departure, she spoke in a monotone. She sat stiffly in her chair with her hands in her lap, moving very little during the interview.

A: The onset of Maria's depression corresponds to the loss of a significant 2-year relationship (**CS4**). She seems stuck at a stage of numbness, not having expressed emotions that are usually associated with grieving. There are several risk factors for development of major depression unless she gets prompt intervention: She lacks understanding of the relationship between the loss and her response (she stated she "was not sure why she was so depressed"). Because she never emotionally dealt with her father's desertion, she is carrying "unfinished business" from that earlier loss (**P2**); and she lacks social support (**SCE3;** the social support issue is addressed under Problem 3).

Maria's skills deficits in accessing, understanding, and expressing her feelings prevent her from moving forward in dealing with the loss of her boyfriend (**BL3**). Her mother never helped her deal with sadness and anger from her father's disappearance, and was, in fact, a role model for depressive behaviors and emotional withdrawal instead of healthy coping with loss and disappointment. Furthermore, her mother was a role model for passivity and martyrdom, never teaching Maria's to pursue happiness in friendships, employment, or romantic relationship.

Many underlying schemas **(C2)** contribute to and maintain Maria's current depression. She has a faulty cognitive map for coping with disappointment: In her family, she learned "don't talk about it" and "pretend nothing happened." There are cognitive barriers to being happy that stem from her mother's influence: "If my mother disapproves of a man, I can't be happy with him," "I need my mother's permission to be happy," or "Because I ruined my mother's life, I need to atone by being as miserable as she is." Based on her father's desertion, she believes "If someone leaves me, it's my fault." Her mother's constant criticism and negative comparisons to her sister led to the core belief "I am no good and don't deserve to be loved." Thus, the loss of a boyfriend taps into deep feelings of worthlessness, shame, and guilt.

The treatment for her depression should not cut off emotional experience but rather should deepen it. There will be resistance to experiencing painful emotions: When she says she doesn't know why she is depressed, she is avoiding facing the pain of being rejected and deserted. I suspect that once she begins to let herself experience those painful feelings related to Tony, she will tap into the pain of her father's desertion. Because Maria wanted sleeping medication from her physician, she may decide that she wants antidepressants (**B2**) to make the pain go away. I will need to persuade her that she needs to deal with the trauma of her father's desertion to reduce her risk for future depression, and that for the sake of these long-term benefits, she needs to have the courage to face emotional pain. Unless she deals with that trauma emotionally, she will be likely to reenact it in her adult life: repeatedly finding a man who will leave her, and ending up depressed but unable to talk about it (**P2**).

P: The major strategy for helping her cope with her depression is to explore her feelings and let her express emotions surrounding the loss (**CS4**). I will explain that her symptoms are a normal response to a loss, and provide a rationale for how talking about her feelings can help reduce the somatic symptoms. Maria will need a moderate amount of structure because of her low skill level in emotional expression (**BL3**). I will want to create a safe relationship, use empathic responses, and model emotional expression in my voice and words. I will definitely use specific feeling words to help her develop an emotional vocabulary. I will assign homework to read about grief (e.g., Colgrove, Bloomfield, & McWilliams, 1976) and give her journal assignments to write about her thoughts and feelings before and after the breakup. I hope that the benefits she gets from putting feelings into words and expressing her pain to an empathic, caring person will correct her faulty belief that it is better not to talk about problems. I will monitor her report of sleep, appetite, energy level, concentration, and work attendance to assure that the humanistic strategy is effective and that a medication referral is not necessary.

Cognitive interventions will be integrated with an empathic humanistic approach (**C2**). For instance, when she says, "It's my fault that Tony broke up," I'll ask her to examine the evidence and to consider alternate explanations. We will examine her relationship with her mother, and I will help her identify and challenge the core schemas of worthlessness that she has developed from her mother's words and actions. I will help her develop a more positive cognitive map, which will include the beliefs, "I deserve to be happy," and "I am not responsible for my mother's happiness."

When she has developed some trust in me and feels safe expressing feelings, I will help her explore the loss of her father (**P2**), not only because of the faulty beliefs that she developed but to give her a chance to deal emotionally with the pain she was never able to express. It may be beneficial for her to do the Gestalt exercise of imagining her father in an empty chair and expressing her feelings directly to him. I anticipate that there will be tears and anger, and I hope to help her empathize with the sad, lonely child that she was, who was in no way to blame for her parents' conflict and her father's poor character. When she is able to access and understand her feelings about her father, she will have insight into how those buried feelings were activated by Tony's sudden breakup. She is able to separate her grief reaction to the loss of a recent relationship from reactions to the traumatic desertion by a father.

Problem 2: *Difficulty establishing an intimate, trusting relationship with a man*

Maria's only long-term relationship ended 2 months ago. She was indecisive about her feelings toward Tony, never developed trust for him, and was unable to openly share her thoughts and feelings.

Outcome Goals

Maria will be able to communicate on a personal level, understanding the needs and feelings of the other person as well as her own. She will be able to select men for dating who are trustworthy and make her feel emotionally safe.

S: As a teenager, Maria preferred going out with a group rather than being alone with one boy, because in a group she did not feel compelled to carry on a conversation. When she dated boys, she worried that they would find her boring. Her mother never asked if she or her sister had enjoyed their dates and would make disparaging remarks about the boys they had been with and about men in general.

Maria met Tony at a party 2 years ago, when she was 20 and he was 23. She liked him from the first time they met, but she was very careful not to show her feelings, for fear that he would not be interested in her if he knew that she liked him. She described Tony as a talkative and friendly person, of similar background. She said that he, too, had difficulty expressing his feelings, and that he resorted to kidding around or changing the topic instead of talking about personal matters. They dated off and on for a number of months and then started to see each other exclusively until the time of their breakup. Maria enjoyed being with Tony but she was troubled by her mother's attitude toward him. Her mother did not seem to like Tony and was very cold and aloof whenever he came to the house. Four months prior to when they stopped dating, Tony got a job promotion and said that he wanted to marry Maria. When she tried to discuss the topic of marriage, her mother said "all men are nice before they get married, but later their true nature comes out."

Maria was confused about her feelings toward Tony and about his feelings toward her. She was "not sure whether she loved him," but she knew she would be unhappy if they stopped seeing each other. Maria had never told Tony about the events that occurred at the time her father left the family, or about her fear that she would end up in a situation similar to her mother's. When she asked him how he felt about her, Tony became annoyed and said it was "obvious what his feelings were, because he wanted to marry her." After several confrontations over whether she would marry him or not, he broke up with her on a dinner date (see Problem 1 for additional data about the breakup). Maria stated that she was both relieved and upset that Tony had forced the issue and essentially made the decision for her.

O: She answered questions but did not take any initiative. Her content focused on facts and behaviors rather than on feelings. When asked to guess what Tony was thinking and feeling before they broke up, she stared blankly and was unable to generate any hunches.

A: Maria's difficulty with intimacy is not limited to romantic relationships; she has never had a trusting, intimate relationship with anyone. She lacks competence in a broad array of skills that are necessary for developing a healthy relationship (**BL3**); she has defended herself against vulnerability because of the circumstances of her father's desertion (**P4**); she has faulty schemas about men and marriage and a low opinion of her own worth (**C2**); and she is dependent on her mother's approval and has never advanced to a stage of relying on her own judgment and values (**CS3, SCE2, SCE1**).

As described under Problem 1, she lacks the ability to access and express her emotions (**BL3**). She also lacks skills of understanding how another person thinks and feels and of stimulating and making personal disclosures. Because of her lack of basic communication skills, her appraisal of herself as a boring conversationalist may be accurate. She also lacks decision-making competence, which involves knowing what she wants, being able to evaluate alternative choices, and experiencing herself as an active creator of her life instead of a passive object of other people's decisions.

To be able to have a satisfying intimate relationship with a man, she will have to deal with the loss of her father and what that has meant for her ability to be vulnerable, trust men, and view herself as worthy of love. She did not know if she loved Tony: Either she was staying in a minimally satisfying relationship because of low expectations of a loving relationship, or she was protecting herself from being hurt by numbing her loving feelings. The source of either difficulty is in the trauma of being deserted by her father. Unconsciously, she is defending against the emotional pain he caused and the belief that she must be unlovable to have him never contact her again (**P4**). She is comfortable with a superficial, distant relationship because it allows her to maintain her defenses against feeling emotional needs and to feel protected from rejection and abandonment. If a relationship got closer, it would stir up the painful feelings from her childhood. She needs to be able to access those feelings in a safe setting and develop the courage to be vulnerable with a trustworthy person.

Maria has developed many schemas that prevent a satisfying intimate relationship (**C2**). Her father's departure caused her to believe that she is not lovable. Even before he left, she was developing the belief that "men can't be trusted," based on his unreliable behavior. Her mother's opinions also contributed to her negative beliefs about men and marriage: The belief that men are nice before they marry but then turn bad is a powerful barrier to commitment. She believes that she will end up like her mother if she gets married: abandoned by the man she trusted. That belief would function as a self-fulfilling prophecy if it were not modified. Furthermore, Maria has faulty schemas of responsibility. She feels responsible for her mother's happiness (because her mother blames her for her unhappiness) and so she needs her mother's seal of approval to enter marriage.

Maria is at the chronological age when most women in our culture begin to move away from their family of origin and make independent judgments about what will make them happy (**CS3**). She seems developmentally much younger than her age—more like someone in mid-adolescence who has never rebelled against her mother, and who does not have enough of a self-identity to be ready for intimacy. I need to learn more about her culture (**SCE2**). In Latino families, it may be the norm for the woman to depend on her mother's approval of her choice of mate. For Maria to make the developmental transition to readiness for marriage, her mother may need to become involved as an ally; otherwise, she will sabotage her daughter's movement toward intimacy and independence (**SCE1**).

P: A major component of therapy will be building a strong therapist-client relationship. This will be the first time that Maria will experience a trusting, emotionally open relationship with another human being. In the process of talking about her relationships, her mother and family system, her cultural values, and the loss of her father, she will be building skills (**BL3**) of communication and "feeling awareness." I will use self-disclosure to help her experience how people communicate in intimate relationships and will occasionally ask her to take the role of the other people in her stories—her mother, sister, or boyfriend—to help her develop perspective-taking skills. I hope to facilitate an emotional catharsis regarding the failure of both parents to give her the love, validation, and support she needed. She will develop insight into her defensive strategies as she expresses vulnerable feelings that she has buried (**P4**).

Then, I can help her challenge the faulty beliefs that she has adopted about her own worth as well as her responsibility for both the departure of her father and her mother's happiness (**C2**). As she becomes clearer about her own needs and her right to be happy, I will have her revisit her relationship with Tony. She may discover that this was not a very intimate relationship, and that she did not have strong feelings; in that case, she will be clearer about what she wants as she starts dating. Alternatively, she may realize that she did have deeper feelings but was not yet able to trust or express her needs and feelings. Then, we could explore the possibility of her contacting him and talking about her new realizations.

As Maria begins to date, therapy sessions will focus on her experiences with men and the reactions from her mother. I will use opportunities to build skills (**BL3**), perhaps role-playing how to communicate her feelings or maintain an interesting conversation. I predict her mother will try to sabotage her happiness and separation; in that case, I will teach Maria about family systems concepts (**SCE1**) and give her options for responding to her mother that are compatible with her values. We may consider having her mother come for a few conjoint sessions so that I could try to enlist the mother's support in helping her daughter through this developmental transition (**CS3**). Perhaps the mother could see the benefits of therapy for herself. If it becomes clear that Maria's mother is not going to approve of any man and is not supportive of her daughter's development, I can help Maria challenge the cultural rules that make her subordinate to her mother's judgment (**CS2**). We could explore whether her grandparents could provide support to counter her mother's disapproval.

Problem 3: *Lack of a confidante and social support*

Maria does not have close friends and maintains a distant relationship with her sister. She does not confide in the people she calls "friends" and had no social support while she was deciding about a marriage proposal and coping with a breakup. She no longer attends church, which is a potential source of support.

Outcome Goals

Maria will have one or two people in whom she confides and can turn to for support in times of loss and disappointment. She will decide if she wants to be involved in a community or religious group that provides social support.

S: Maria considers two women at work her "close friends," yet she never talked to them about her relationship with Tony or about her feelings of depression after the breakup. She was not able to talk these issues over with her sister, who she felt was "living in a completely different world" now that she was attending college.

Maria indicated that she had always had a number of children to play with and had several friends when she was a teenager. She recalled, however, that it was always very difficult to share her feelings with her friends and tell them about events that were troubling her. Maria and her sister "got along fairly well" growing up, but they had never confided in each other. She said that she had always had trouble expressing her emotions, and she felt that Teresa had the same problem. As described in the Background section, the two sisters never talked with each other about their father's departure. Maria never expressed to anyone her feelings of guilt over her father's leaving. When the sisters were younger, their only social activities together were going to church and visiting relatives. Maria stopped attending church when she started dating Tony and admits that she has lost the religious feelings she had as a child.

O: Maria answered all questions and seemed motivated to share personal information. However, she gave short answers and did not elaborate unless she was prompted. It is hard to determine what her conversational skills would be like if she were not depressed.

A: Maria needs friends, but there are only casual acquaintances in her life. Having friends would (a) serve as a buffer against depression (Problem 1), (b) give her experiences in trust and vulnerability in a safer context than a romantic relationship, and (c) provide fun and pleasure in her free time, which is currently dominated by contact with a depressed, complaining mother.

Her lack of skills in emotional expression and conversation (**BL3**), a deficiency mentioned under both prior problems, prevents her from turning casual acquaintances at work into real friends. Her beliefs about being "less than" others (**C2**) would lead her to doubt that others would be interested in her problems or would want to spend time with her outside of work. Her younger sister is a potential source of support, but cognitive factors serve as barriers: There were rules growing up about not communicating about their shared loss, and Maria believes that "if my sister is in college, she can't be interested in me."

Because religion can be a powerful source of support (**ES3**), I need to find out more about her feelings about her religion. It is possible that she might want to explore other churches, besides the one her mother and grandparents attend, to find a community of young singles of similar backgrounds and values.

P: I believe that a good client-therapist relationship will give her a model of the processes that are part of friendships. I will explain to her the benefits of friendship and social support and suggest that she select two people from work with whom she would like to become closer. We could rehearse how she would propose getting together (**BL3**) and practice conversational skills to bring more intimate subjects into the relationship. I would encourage her to talk to her sister and test her beliefs (**C2**) that she and her sister have nothing in common. A discussion of religion (**ES3**) might lead her to build a support system through a church. Because Maria is comfortable in group activities, it might be helpful to encourage her to find a group in the community that gives her a chance to practice communication skills and initiate friendship, as well as develop new interests or creative talents.

Case Management Discussion

A warm and empathic therapeutic relationship is fundamental for helping Maria to express feelings, develop trust in another person, and build relationship skills. Because Maria is currently in a crisis, I would recommend twice-a-week sessions for the first few weeks. The first goal is resolving the depression (Problem 1) and getting her back to her prior level of functioning through encouraging her to share feelings, conducting cognitive interventions, and teaching her about grief reactions. Through our conversations, I will be encouraging her to express herself fully and put her experiences into words. I will be accepting of her level of skills and avoidance and monitor my countertransference if I begin to feel impatient. I don't want her to feel that she is getting a "bad grade" in therapy or that I am critical of her, like her mother is. Preliminary discussion of social support (Problem 3) might lead her to take steps to create more closeness in her friendships or with her sister. Among her potential friends, there may be better role models than her mother for coping with emotions. If her mood and functioning do not improve, a medication consult will be advised.

After the crisis of her depression is resolved, sessions will be changed from twice weekly to weekly. We will deal with the deeper issues of her childhood, especially the loss of her father and the lack of support from her mother. I will be monitoring several aspects of her functioning: her awareness of her feelings, reduction in fear of feeling deeply, ability to freely disclose at a personal level, modification of her core schema of worthlessness and her negative beliefs about men, correction of her faulty sense of responsibility for her father's disappearance and mother's unhappiness, and conversational skills. We will focus on outside relationships as well as using our own relationship to help her understand how other people think and feel.

As therapy progresses, I anticipate that she will report positive progress in developing friendships and experiencing moments of intimacy and trust with other people. When she describes difficult interpersonal experiences, we can use therapy to practice communication skills. For instance, if her mother disparages a man she is dating, we can address how she can talk to her mother. As she becomes more mature and independent, her mother may attempt to sabotage her growth. At such time, we will consider having conjoint sessions with her mother. As Maria's self-worth improves and her social contact with her sister increases, she may express interest in college courses and a more interesting career. I will support her autonomy as she makes decisions. As we near termination, we can decrease the frequency of sessions, instead of ending abruptly. At the end of therapy, Maria will have a strong sense that she is entitled to be happy, can cope effectively with loss and disappointment, and can attract good friends and potential partners.

References ———————————————————————————————————

Adler, A., Ansbacher, H. L., & Ansbacher, R. R. (Eds.). (1989). *Individual psychology of Alfred Adler: A systematic presentation in selections from his writings.* New York: HarperCollins.

Aguilera, D. (1998). *Crisis intervention: Theory and methodology* (8th ed.). Saint Louis, MO: Mosby.

Ainsworth, M. D. S. (1982). Attachment: Retrospect and prospect. In C. M. Parkes & J. Stevenson-Hinde (Eds.), *The place of attachment in human behavior* (pp. 3–30). New York: Basic Books.

Alberti, R., & Emmons, M. (1995). *Your perfect right.* San Luis Obispo, CA: Impact.

Alvord, M. K., & Grados, J. J. (2005). Enhancing resilience in children: A proactive approach. *Professional Psychology: Research and Practice, 36*(3), 238–245.

American Cancer Association. (2005). *Coping with grief and loss.* Retrieved August 26, 2005, from http://documents.cancer.org/6036.00.

American Psychiatric Association. (2002). *Diagnostic and statistical manual of mental disorders* (4th ed., text rev.). Washington, DC: Author.

American Psychological Association. (2000). *Guidelines for psychotherapy with lesbian, gay, and bisexual clients.* Washington, DC: Author. Retrieved September 4, 2005, from http://wpa.apa.org/pi/lgbc/guidelines.html.

Ancis, J. R. (Ed.). (2004). *Culturally responsive interventions: Innovative approaches to working with diverse populations.* New York: Brunner-Routledge.

Anderson, A. J. (1997). Therapeutic program models for mentally ill chemical abusers. *International Journal of Psychosocial Rehabilitation, 1*(1), 21–33.

Assagioli, R. (1971). *Psychosynthesis.* New York: Penguin.

Axness, M. W. (1998). *Affirming the adoptee's reality: A way to intimacy.* Retrieved August 27, 2005, from http://www.naturalchild.com/guest/marcy_axness.html.

Bader, E., & Pearson, P. T. (1988). *In quest of the mythical mate: A developmental approach to diagnosis and treatment in couples therapy.* New York: Brunner/Mazel.

Baker, H. S., & Baker, M. N. (1987). Heinz Kohut's self psychology: An overview. *American Journal of Psychiatry, 144,* 1–9.

Bandler, R., & Grinder, J. (1990). *The structure of magic: A book about language and therapy.* Palo Alto, CA: Science and Behavior Books.

Bandura, A. (1977). *Social learning theory.* Englewood Cliffs, NJ: Prentice-Hall.

Bandura, A. (1989). Human agency in social cognitive theory. *American Psychologist, 44,* 1175–1184.

Barkley, R. A. (1997). *Defiant children: A clinician's manual for assessment and parent training* (2nd ed.). New York: Guilford Press.

Barlow, D. H. (Ed.). (2001). *Clinical handbook of psychological disorders: A step-by-step treatment manual* (3rd ed.). New York: Guilford Press.

Bar-On, R. (1997). *The BarOn Emotional Quotient Inventory (EQ-I): A test of emotional intelligence.* Toronto, Ontario, Canada: Multi-Health Systems.

Basch, M. (1980). *Doing psychotherapy.* New York: Basic Books.

Bass, E., & Davis, L. (1988). *The courage to heal: A guide for women survivors of child sexual abuse.* New York: Harper & Row.

Bass, E., & Thornton, L. (Eds.). (1983). *I never told anyone: Writing by women survivors of child sexual abuse.* New York: Harper & Row.

Bavarsky, A. (2000). *The soulful art.* Unpublished doctoral dissertation, Ryokan College, Los Angeles.

Beahrs, J. O. (1986). *Limits of scientific psychiatry.* New York: Brunner/Mazel.

Beck, A. T. (2000). *Prisoners of hate: The cognitive basis of anger, hostility, and violence.* New York: Perennial Currents.

Beck, A. T., Emery, G., & Greenberg, R. L. (1985). *Anxiety disorders and phobias: A cognitive perspective.* New York: Basic Books.

Beck, A. T., Freeman, A., & Davis, D. D. (2003). *Cognitive therapy of personality disorders* (2nd ed.). New York: Guilford Press.

Beck, A. T., Rush, A. J., Shaw, B. F., & Emery, G. (1979). *Cognitive therapy of depression.* New York: Guilford Press.

Beck, A. T., & Weishaar, M. (2000). Cognitive therapy. In R. Corsini & D. Wedding (Eds.), *Current psychotherapies* (6th ed.). Itasca, IL: F. E. Peacock.

Becker, E. (1973). *The denial of death.* New York: Free Press.

Beitman, B. D., & Yue, D. (1999). *Learning psychotherapy: A time-efficient, research-based, and outcome-measured psychotherapy training program.* New York: Norton.

Bell, J. K., & Cohn, A. A. (1976). *Rhetoric in a modern mode* (3rd ed.). Beverly Hills, CA: Glencoe Press.

Ben-Ari, A., Winstok, Z., & Eisikovits, Z. (2003). Choice within entrapment and entrapment within choice: The challenge facing battered women who stay. *Families in Society: Journal of Contemporary Human Services, 84,* 539–546.

Bergin, A. E., & Garfield, S. L. (1993). *Handbook of psychotherapy and behavior change* (4th ed.). New York: Wiley.

Berne, E. (1996). *Games people play: The basic handbook of transactional analysis.* New York: Ballantine Books.

Beutler, L. (1983). *Eclectic psychotherapy: A systematic approach.* New York: Allyn & Bacon.

Beutler, L. E., Machado, P. P. P., & Neufeldt, S. A. (1994). Therapist variables. In A. E. Bergin & S. L. Garfield (Eds.), *Handbook of psychotherapy and behavior change* (4th ed., pp. 229–269). New York: Wiley.

Beveridge, K., & Cheung, M. (2004). A spiritual framework in incest survivors treatment. *Journal of Child Sexual Abuse, 13*(2), 105–120.

Bisson, J. I., & Deahl, M. P. (1994). Psychological debriefing and prevention of post-traumatic stress: More research needed. *British Journal of Psychiatry, 165,* 717–720.

Bjork, J. P., Brown, J. A., & Goodman, M. (2000). *Casebook for managing managed care: A self-study guide for treatment planning, documentation, and communication.* Washington, DC: American Psychiatric Press.

Blatner, A. (2000). *Foundations of psychodrama: History, theory and practice* (4th ed.). New York: Springer.

Bohart, A., & Greenberg, L. S. (Eds.). (1997). *Empathy reconsidered: New directions in psychotherapy.* Washington, DC: American Psychological Association.

Bonanno, G. A., & Field, N. P. (2001). Examining the delayed grief hypothesis across 5 years of bereavement. *American Behavioral Scientist, 44*(5), 798–816.

Bowen, M. (1994). *Family therapy in clinical practice.* Lanham, MD: Aronson.

Bowlby, J. (1988). *A secure base: Parent-child attachment and healthy human development.* New York: Basic Books.

Braun, M. J., & Berg, D. H. (1994). Meaning reconstruction in the experience of parental bereavement. *Death Studies, 18,* 105–112.

Brehm, S. S., & Brehm, J. W. (1981). *Psychological reactance: A theory of freedom and control.* New York: Academic Press.

Brenner, C. (1982). *The mind in conflict.* Madison, WI: International Universities Press.

Bretherton, I. (1992). The origins of attachment theory: John Bowlby and Mary Ainsworth. *Developmental Psychology, 28,* 759–775.

Brodzinsky, D. M., & Schechter, M. D. (1990). *The psychology of adoption.* London: Oxford University Press.

Brom, D., Kleber, R. J., & Hofman, M. C. (1993). Victims of traffic accidents: Incidence and prevention of post-traumatic stress disorder. *Journal of Clinical Psychology, 49*(2), 131–139.

Buber, M. (1970). *I and thou.* New York: Touchstone.

Burns, D. D. (2005). *Scared stiff: Fast effective treatment for anxiety disorders.* Portola Valley, CA: Institute for the Advancement of Human Behavior.

Busby, D. M. (Ed.). (1996). *The impact of violence on the family: Treatment approaches for therapists and other professionals.* Needham Heights, MA: Allyn & Bacon.

Cain, D. J., & Seeman, J. (Eds.). (2001). *Humanistic psychotherapies: Handbook of research and practice.* Washington, DC: American Psychological Association.

Cameron, J. (2002). *The artist's way: A spiritual path to higher creativity.* New York: J. P. Tarcher.

Cameron-Bandler, L. (1985). *Solutions.* Moab, UT: Real People Press.

Camus, A. (1991). *The myth of Sisyphus and other essays* (Reprint ed.). New York: Vintage Books.

Canter, L., & Petersen, K. (1995). *Teaching students to get along.* Santa Monica, CA: Canter & Associates.

Caplan, G. (1964). *Principles of preventive psychiatry.* New York: Basic Books.

Carlson, D. L. (1994). *Why do Christians shoot their wounded? Helping (not hurting) those with emotional difficulties.* Downers Grove, IL: InterVarsity Press.

Cassidy, J., & Shaver, P. R. (Eds.). (1999). *Handbook of attachment: Theory, research, and clinical applications.* New York: Guilford Press.

Castaneda, C. (1985). *Teachings of Don Juan: A Yaqui way of knowledge* (Reprint ed.). New York: Washington Square Press.

Centers for Disease Control and Prevention. (2001). *Revised guidelines for HIV counseling, testing, and referral* (Morbidity and Mortality Weekly Report). Retrieved September 29, 2005, from htpp://www.cdc.gov/mmwr/PDF/RR/RR5019.pdf.

Christensen, A., & Jacobson, N. (2000). *Reconcilable differences.* New York: Guilford Press.

Clum, G. A. (1990). *Coping with panic.* Belmont, CA: Wadsworth.

Colgrove, M., Bloomfield, H. H., & McWilliams, P. (1976). *How to survive the loss of a love.* New York: Bantam Books.

Comas-Diaz, L., & Greene, B. (Eds.). (1994). *Women of color: Integrating ethnic and gender identities in psychotherapy.* New York: Guilford Press.

Cope, S. (1999). *Yoga and the quest for the true self.* New York: Bantam Books.

Courtois, C. A. (1996). *Healing the incest wound: Adult survivors in therapy* (Reprint ed.). New York: Norton.

Cousins, N. (1979). *Anatomy of an illness as perceived by the patient.* New York: Norton.

Covey, S. (1994). *The 7 habits of highly effective people.* New York: Simon & Schuster.

Cozolino, L. (2002). *The neuroscience of psychotherapy: Building and rebuilding the human brain.* New York: Norton.

Cross, W. (1971). The Negro to Black conversion experience. *Black World, 20,* 13–27.

Dana, R. H. (2002). Mental health services for African Americans: A cultural/racial perspective. *Cultural Diversity and Ethnic Minority Psychology, 8*(1), 3–18.

Datillio, F. M. (Ed.). (1998). *Case studies in couple and family therapy: Systemic and cognitive perspectives.* New York: Guilford Press.

Demitrack, M. A., & Abbey, S. E. (Eds.). (1999). *Chronic fatigue syndrome: An integrative approach to evaluation and treatment.* London: Guilford Press.

Doherty, W. J. (1996). *Soul searching: Why psychotherapy must promote moral responsibility.* New York: Basic Books.

Dresser, N. (2005). *Multicultural manners: Essential rules of etiquette for the 21st century* (Rev. ed.). Hoboken, NJ: Wiley.

Egan, G. (2002). *The skilled helper* (7th ed.). Belmont, CA: Brooks/Cole.

Ellis, A. & Grieger, R. (Eds.). (1977). *Handbook of rational-emotive therapy.* New York: Springer.

Elwyn, T. S., Ahmed, I., & Burns, J. A. (2002). *Factitious disorder.* Retrieved September 23, 2005, from http://emedicine.com/med/topic3125.htm.

Emmelkamp, P. M. (1994). Behavior therapy with adults. In A. E. Bergin & S. L. Garfield (Eds.), *Handbook of psychotherapy and behavior change* (4th ed., pp. 379–427). New York: Wiley.

Emmelkamp, P. M. G. (2004). Behavior therapy with adults. In M. J. Lambert (Ed.), *Bergin and Garfield's handbook of psychotherapy and behavior change* (5th ed., pp. 393–446). Hoboken, NJ: Wiley.

Epstein, M. (1995). *Thoughts without a thinker: Psychotherapy from a Buddhist perspective.* New York: Basic Books.

Erickson, C. D., & Al-Timimi, N. R. (2004). Counseling and psychotherapy with Arab American clients. In T. B. Smith (Ed.), *Practicing multiculturalism: Affirming diversity in counseling and psychotherapy* (pp. 234–254). Boston: Pearson Education.

Erikson, E. (1993). *Childhood and society* (Reprint ed.). New York: Norton.

Eskander, E. N., Cosgrove, G. R., & Rauch, S. L. (2001). *Psychiatric neurosurgery overview.* Retrieved September 17, 2005, from http://neurosurgery .mgh.harvard.edu/functional/Psychosurgery2001.htm.

Fadiman, A. (1998). *The spirit catches you and you fall down.* New York: Farrar, Straus and Giroux.

Ferster, C. B. (1973). A functional analysis of depression. *American Psychologist, 28,* 857–870.

Firestone, R. W. (1997). *Combating destructive thought processes: Voice therapy and separation theory.* Thousand Oaks, CA: Sage.

Fisher, D., & Ahern, L. (2005). *People can recover from mental illness* (Newsletter of National Empowerment Center, Inc.). Retrieved September 20, 2005, from www.power2u.org/recovery/people_can.html.

Foa, E. B., Keane,T. M., & Friedman, M. J. (Eds.). (2000). *Effective treatments for PTSD*. New York: Guilford Press.

Fowler, D. R., & Longabaugh, R. (1975). The problem-oriented record. *Archives of General Psychiatry, 32,* 831–834.

Framo, J. L. (1972). Symptoms from a family transactional viewpoint. In C. J. Sager & H. S. Kaplan (Eds.), *Progress in group and family therapy* (pp. 271–308). New York: Brunner/Mazel.

Frank, J. D., & Frank, J. B. (1991). *Persuasion and healing: A comparative study of psychotherapy* (3rd ed.). Baltimore: Johns Hopkins University Press.

Frankl, V. E. (1997). *Man's search for meaning* (Rev. ed.). New York: Pocket Books.

Freedman, J., & Combs, G. (1996). *Narrative therapy: The social construction of preferred realities*. New York: Norton.

Freud, A. (1967). *Ego and the mechanisms of defense: The writings of Anna Freud* (Rev. ed., Vol. 2). Guilford, CT: International Universities Press.

Freud, S. (1996). *Three case histories*. New York: Touchstone.

Fromm, E. (1941). *Escape from freedom*. New York: Holt, Rinehart and Winston.

Galinsky, E. (1987). *The six stages of parenthood*. New York: Addison-Wesley.

Gendlin, E. T. (1982). *Focusing* (Reprint ed.). New York: Bantam.

Gendlin, E. (1996). *Focusing-oriented psychotherapy: A manual of the experiential method*. New York: Guilford Press.

Genskow, J. (1996). *Responding to loss: A practical framework* (Polio Network News). Retrieved August 27, 2005, from www.post-polio.org/ipn/pnn12-3.html.

Gitlin, M. J. (1996).*The psychotherapist's guide to psychopharmacology* (2nd ed.). New York: Free Press.

Gladwell, M. (2005). *Blink: The power of thinking without thinking*. New York: Little, Brown.

Glasser, W. (1965). *Reality therapy: A new approach to psychiatry*. New York: Harper & Row.

Goffman, E. (1963). *Stigma: Notes on the management of spoiled identity*. Englewood Cliffs, NJ: Prentice-Hall.

Goldenberg, I., & Goldenberg, H. (2000). *Family therapy: An overview*. Belmont, CA: Brooks/Cole.

Goldfried, M., & Davison, G. C. (1994). *Clinical behavior therapy* (Expanded ed.). New York: Wiley.

Goleman, D. (1995). *Emotional intelligence: Why it can matter more than IQ*. New York: Bantam Books.

Gonzalez, A. R., Gonzalez, F. J., & Aguirre, M. V. F. (2001). Rehabilitation and social insertion of the homeless chronically mentally ill. *International Journal of Psychosocial Rehabilitation, 5,* 79–100.

Goodman, M., Brown, J. A., & Deitz, P. M. (1992). *Managing managed care: A mental health practitioner's survival guide.* Washington, DC: American Psychiatric Press.

Gottlieb, M. M. (1999). *The angry self: A comprehensive approach to anger management.* Phoenix, AZ: Zeig, Tucker & Co.

Gottman, J. (2002). *The relationship cure: A 5 step guide to strengthening your marriage, family, and friendships.* New York: Three Rivers Press.

Goulding, R., & Goulding, M. (1979). *Changing lives through redecision therapy.* New York: Grove Press.

Graber, K. (1991). *Ghosts in the bedroom: A guide for partners of incest survivors.* Deerfield Beach, FL: Health Communication.

Greenberg, L. S., Watson, J. C., & Lietaer, G. (1998). *Handbook of experiential psychotherapy.* New York: Guilford Press.

Greenstone, J. L., & Leviton, S. C. (1993). *Elements of crisis intervention: Crises and how to respond to them.* Belmont, CA: Brooks/Cole.

Grof, C., & Grof, S. G. (1990). *The stormy search for the self: A guide to personal growth through transformational crisis.* Los Angeles: J. P. Tarcher.

Haley, J. (1993). *Uncommon therapy: The psychiatric techniques of Milton H. Erickson, M.D.* (Reprint ed.). New York: Norton.

Haley, J. (1997). *Leaving home: The therapy of disturbed young people.* New York: Brunner/Mazel.

Hammer, A. L. (Ed.). (1996). *MBTI applications.* Palo Alto, CA: Consulting Psychologists Press.

Hendrix, H. (1988). *Getting the love you want: A guide for couples.* New York: Henry Holt.

Hill, M. A. (2005). *Healing grief through art: Art therapy bereavement group workshops.* Retrieved August 28, 2005, from www.drawntogether.com/healing.htm.

Hipple, J. L., & Hipple, L. B. (1983). *Diagnosis and management of psychological emergencies.* Springfield, IL: Charles C Thomas.

Hoff, B. H. (1999). *The faulty Duluth model.* Retrieved August 22, 2005, from http://www/menweb.org/batdulut.htm.

Holmes, T. H., & Rahe, R. H. (1967). The social readjustment rating scale. *Journal of Psychosomatic Research, 11,* 213–218.

Horowitz, M. J. (1992). *Stress response syndromes* (2nd ed.). New York: Aronson.

House, J. S. (1981). *Work, stress, and social support.* Reading, MA: Addison-Wesley.

Houston, B. K. (1987). Stress and coping. In C. R. Snyder & C. E. Ford (Eds.), *Coping with negative life events: Clinical and social psychological perspectives* (pp. 373–399). New York: Plenum Press.

Howard, G. S. (1991). Culture tales: A narrative approach to thinking, cross-cultural psychology, and psychotherapy. *American Psychologist, 46,* 187–197.

Husted, D. S., & Shapiro, N. A. (2004). A review of the treatment for refractory obsessive-compulsive disorder: From medicine to deep brain stimulation. *CNS Spectrums, 9,* 833–847.

Hutchins, L., & Kaahumanu, L. (Eds.). (1991). *Bi any other name: Bisexual people speak out.* Boston: Alyson.

Hyman, B. M., & Pedrick, C. (2005). *The OCD workbook: Your guide to breaking free from obsessive-compulsive disorder.* Oakland, CA: New Harbinger.

Ingram, B. L. (1990). *Psychological factors facilitating the adjustment of immigrants: Americans in Israel.* Unpublished manuscript, The Jewish Agency, Department of Immigration and Absorption, Jerusalem, Israel.

Ireland, M. S. (1993). *Reconceiving women: Separating motherhood from female identity.* New York: Guilford Press.

Ivey, A. (1993). *Developmental strategies for helpers: Individual, family, and network interventions.* North Amherst, MA: Microtraining Associates.

James, J. W., & Friedman, R. (1998). *The grief recovery handbook: The action program for moving beyond death, divorce, and other losses.* New York: Harper-Collins.

James, M., & Jongeward, D. (1996). *Born to win: Transactional analysis with Gestalt experiments.* New York: Addison-Wesley.

Johnson, J., & Preston, J. D. (2004). *Clinical psychopharmacology made ridiculously simple* (5th ed.). Miami, FL: Medmaster.

Johnson, S. M. (2004). *The practice of emotionally focused couple therapy: Creating connection* (2nd ed.). New York: Brunner-Routledge.

Jongsma, A. E., & Peterson, L. M. (2003). *The complete adult psychotherapy treatment planner.* Hoboken, NJ: Wiley.

Kahn, M. (1997). *Between therapist and client: The new relationship* (2nd ed.). New York: Freeman.

Karlsson, R. (2005). Ethnic matching between therapist and patient in psychotherapy: An overview of findings, together with methodological and conceptual issues. *Cultural Diversity and Ethnic Minority Psychology, 11*(2), 113–129.

Katz, C. L., & Pandya, A. (Eds.). (2004). *Disaster psychiatry: A closer look—Psychiatric clinics of North America.* New York: Elsevier.

Kazdin, A. E., & Whitley, M. K. (2003). Treatment of parental stress to enhance therapeutic change among children referred for aggressive and antisocial behavior. *Journal of Consulting and Clinical Psychology, 71*(3), 504–515.

Kelly, G. (1955). *The psychology of personal constructs.* New York: Norton.

Klass, D., Silverman, P. R., & Nickman, S. L. (Eds.). (1996). *Continuing bonds: New understandings of grief.* Washington, DC: Taylor and Francis.

Klerman, G., & Weissman, M. M. (Eds.). (1993). *New applications of interpersonal psychotherapy.* Washington, DC: American Psychiatric Press.

Knapp, S. E., & Jongsma, A. E. (2004). *The parenting skills treatment planner.* Hoboken, NJ: Wiley.

Kohut, H., & Wolf, E. S. (1978). The disorders of the self and their treatment: An outline. *International Journal of Psycho-Analysis, 59,* 413–425.

Koplewicz, H. S., Cloitre, M., Reyes, K., & Kessler, L. S. (2004). The 9/11 experience: Who's listening to the children. *Psychiatric Clinics of North America, 27*(3), 491–504.

Kopp, S. (1976). *If you meet the Buddha on the road, kill him* (Reprint ed.). New York, Bantam.

Koss, M. P., & Harvey, M. R. (1991). *The rape victim: Clinical and community interventions.* Thousand Oaks, CA: Sage.

Krajeski, J. (1986). Psychotherapy with gay men and lesbians: A history of controversy. In C. Cohen & T. Stein (Eds.), *Contemporary perspective on psychotherapy with lesbians and gay men* (pp. 9–26). New York: Plenum Press.

Kubler-Ross, E. (1997). *On death and dying* (Reprint ed.). New York: Scribner.

Kushner, H. S. (1981). *When bad things happen to good people.* New York: Avon Books.

Kwan, K. L., & Sodowsky, G. R. (1997). Internal and external ethnic identity and their correlates: A study of Chinese American immigrants. *Journal of Multicultural Counseling and Development, 25,* 51–67.

Kyrouz, E., Humphreys, K., & Loomis, C. (2002). A review of research on the effectiveness of self-help mutual aid groups. In B. J. White & E. J. Madera (Eds.), *The self-help group sourcebook: Your guide to community and online support groups* (7th ed.). Denville, NJ: Saint Clares Health Services.

Laborde, G. (1987). *Influencing with integrity.* Palo Alto, CA: Syntony.

Lai, Y. M., Hong, C. P. H., & Chee, C. Y. I. (2000). Stigma of mental illness. *Singapore Medical Journal, 42*(3), 111–114.

Lakein, A. (1996). *How to get control of your time and your life* (Reprint ed.). New York: New American Library.

Lam, A. G., & Sue, S. S. (2001). Client diversity. *Psychotherapy, 38,* 479–486.

Lambert, M. J. (Ed.). (2004). *Bergin and Garfield's handbook of psychotherapy and behavior change* (5th ed.). Hoboken, NJ: Wiley.

Lambert, M. J., Garfield, S. L., & Bergin, A. E. (2004). Overview, trends and future issues. In M. J. Lambert (Ed.), *Bergin and Garfield's handbook of psychotherapy and behavior change* (5th ed., pp. 805–821). Hoboken, NJ: Wiley.

Lambert, M. J., & Ogles, B. M. (2004). The efficacy and effectiveness of psychotherapy. In M. J. Lambert (Ed.), *Bergin and Garfield's handbook of psychotherapy and behavior change* (5th ed., pp. 139–193). Hoboken, NJ: Wiley.

Lange, A. J., & Jakubowski, P. (1978). *Responsible assertive behavior: Cognitive/behavioral procedures for trainers.* Champaign, IL: Research Press.

Lazare, A. (1976). The psychiatric examination in the walk-in clinic: Hypothesis generation and hypothesis testing. *Archives of General Psychiatry, 33,* 96–102.

Lazarus, A. A. (1981). *The practice of multimodal psychotherapy.* New York: McGraw-Hill.

Lazarus, R., & Folkman, S. (1984). *Stress, appraisal, and coping.* New York: Springer.

Leiter, M. P., & Maslach, C. (2005). *Banishing burnout: Six strategies for improving your relationship with work.* San Francisco: Jossey-Bass.

Lepore, S. J., & Smyth, J. M. (2002). *The writing cure: How expressive writing promotes heath and emotional well-being.* Washington, DC: American Psychological Association.

Levine, P. A. (1997). *Waking the tiger: Healing trauma.* Berkeley, CA: North Atlantic Books.

Levinson, D. J. (1986). *The seasons of a man's life* (Reprint ed.). New York: Ballantine Books.

Levy, D. (1997). *Tools of critical thinking: Metathoughts for psychology.* Needham Heights, MA: Allyn & Bacon.

Lewinsohn, P. M., Antonuccio, D. O., Steinmetz, J. L., & Teri, L. (1984). *The coping with depression course: A psychoeducational course for unipolar depression.* Eugene, OR: Castalia.

Liberman, R. P. (Ed.). (1992). *Handbook of psychiatric rehabilitation.* Boston: Allyn & Bacon.

Lindemann, E. (1944). Symptomology and management of acute grief. *American Journal of Psychiatry, 101,* 141–148.

Linden, A. (1998). *Mindworks: Unlock the promise within—NLP tools for building a better life.* New York: Berkeley Publishing Group.

Linehan, M. M. (1993a). *Cognitive-behavioral treatment of borderline personality disorder.* New York: Guilford Press.

Linehan, M. M. (1993b). *Skills training manual for treating borderline personality disorder.* New York: Guilford Press.

London, P. (1989). *No more secondhand art: Awakening the artist within.* Boston: Shambhala.

Lubit, R., Rovine, D., Defrancisci, L., & Eth, S. (2003). Impact of trauma on children. *Journal of Psychiatric Practice, 9,* 128–138.

Lundberg, G. D. (1998). Dawn's early light to twilight's gleaming. *Journal of the American Medical Association, 280,* 1618–1619.

Mahler, M., Pine, F., & Bergman, A (1975). *The psychological birth of the human infant.* New York: Basic Books.

Mahoney, M. J. (1974). *Cognition and behavior modification.* Cambridge, MA: Ballinger.

Marsalla, A. J., & Christopher, M. A. (2004). Ethnocultural considerations in disaster: An overview of research, issues, and directions. *Psychiatric clinics of North America, 27,* 521–539.

Martell, C. R., Addis, M. E., & Jacobson, N. S. (2001). *Depression in context: Strategies for guided action.* New York: Norton.

Maslach, C. (2003). *Burnout: The cost of caring.* Cambridge, MA: Malor Books.

Masterson, J. (1990). *The search for the real self: Unmasking the personality disorders of our age*. New York: Touchstone Books.

Matsakis, A. (2003). *The rape recovery handbook: Step-by-step help for survivors of sexual assault*. Oakland, CA: New Harbinger.

May, R. (1995). Black and impotent: The life of Mercedes. In D. Wedding & R. J. Corsini (Eds.), *Case studies in psychotherapy* (2nd ed., pp. 137–148). Itasca, IL: F. E. Peacock.

McCullough, D. (2005). *1776*. New York: Simon & Schuster.

McGoldrick, M., Gerson, R., & Shellenberger, S. (1999). *Genograms: Assessment and intervention* (2nd ed.). New York: Norton.

McGuire, P. A. (2000). New hope for people with schizophrenia. *Monitor on Psychology, 31*(2). Retrieved September 22, 2005, from http://www.apa.org/monitor/feb00/schizophrenia.html.

McKay, M., Davis, M., & Fanning, P. (1995). *Messages: The communication skills book* (2nd ed.). San Luis Obispo, CA: New Harbinger.

McLoyd, V. C. (1998). Socioeconomic disadvantages and child development. *American Psychologist, 53*, 185–204.

McNally, R. J., Bryant, R. A., & Ehlers, A. (2003). Does early psychological intervention promote recovery from posttraumatic stress? *Psychological Science in the Public Interest, 4*(2), 45–79.

McWhirter, E. H. (1994). *Counseling for empowerment*. Alexandria, VA: American Counseling Association.

McWilliams, N. (1999). *Psychoanalytic case formulation*. New York: Guilford Press.

Medical Economics. (Ed.). (2005). *Physicians' desk reference* (59th ed.). Montvale, NJ: Thomson Healthcare.

Meichenbaum, D. (1977). *Cognitive-behavior modification: An integrative approach*. New York: Plenum Press.

Menninger, K. (1973). *Whatever became of sin?* New York: Bantam Books.

Metzger, D. (1976). It is always the woman who is raped. *American Journal of Psychiatry, 133*(4), 405–408.

Miller, A. (1981). *The drama of the gifted child: How narcissistic parents form and deform the emotional lives of their talented children*. New York: Basic Books.

Miller, M. D., Wolfson, L., Frank, E., Cornes C., Silberman, R., Ehrenpreis, L., et al. (1998). Using Interpersonal Psychotherapy (IPT) in a combined psychotherapy/medication research protocol with depressed elders: A descriptive report with case vignettes. *Journal of Psychotherapy Practice and Research, 7*, 47–55.

Mitchell, J. T., & Everly, G. S. (2001). *Critical incident stress debriefing: An operations manual for CISD, defusing, and other crisis intervention services* (3rd ed.). Ellicott City, MD: Chevron.

Mitchell, S. A. (1996). *Freud and beyond: A history of modern psychoanalytic thought* (Reprint ed.). New York: HarperCollins.

Mozak, H. H. (2000). Adlerian psychotherapy. In R. J. Corsini & D. Wedding, D. (Eds.), *Current psychotherapies* (6th ed., pp. 54–98). Itasca, IL: F. E. Peacock.

Muller, E. D., & Thompson, C. L. (2003). The experience of grief after bereavement: A phenomenological study with implications for mental health counseling. *Journal of Mental Health Counseling, 25*(3), 183–203.

Myers, D. G. (1989). Mental health and disaster: Preventive approaches to intervention. In R. Gist & B. Lubin (Eds.), *Psychosocial aspects of disaster* (pp. 190–228). New York: Wiley.

National Hospice and Palliative Care Organization. (2005). *History of hospice care.* Retrieved August 27, 2005, from http://nhpco.org/i4a/pages/index.cfm?pageid=3285.

Neiburg, H. A., & Fischer, A. (1982). *Pet loss.* New York: Harper & Row.

Neimeyer, R. A. (2000). Searching for the meaning of meaning: Grief therapy and the process of reconstruction. *Death Studies, 24*(6), 541–558.

Neugarten, B. L. (1996). *The meanings of age: Selected papers.* Chicago: University of Chicago Press.

Ney, P. G. (1994). The effects of pregnancy loss on women's health. *Social Science and Medicine, 38*(9), 1193–1200.

Norcross, J. C. (Ed.). (2002). *Psychotherapy relationships that work: Therapist contributions and responsiveness to patient needs.* New York: Oxford University Press.

Novaco, R. W. (1986). *Stress inoculation for anger and impulse control: A treatment manual.* Tampa: University of South Florida, The Louis de la Parte Florida Mental Health Institute.

Oliver, J., & Ryan, M. (2004). *Lesson one: The ABCs of life—The skills we all need but were never taught.* New York: Simon & Schuster.

Orange, D. M., Atwood, G. E., & Stolorow, R. D. (1998). *Working intersubjectively: Contextualism in psychoanalytic practice.* Hillsdale, NJ: Analytic Press.

Pachankis, J. E., & Goldfried, M. R. (2004). Clinical issues in working with lesbian, gay, and bisexual clients. *Psychotherapy: Theory, Research, Practice, Training, 41*, 227–246.

Parks, C. M., & Weiss, R. A. (1995). *Recovery from bereavement.* New York: Aronson.

Peck, S. (2003). *The road less travelled: A new psychology of love, traditional values and spiritual growth* (25th anniversary ed.). New York: Touchstone.

Perls, F. (1973). *The Gestalt approach.* Palo Alto, CA: Science and Behavior Books.

Peter, L. J. (1969). *The Peter principle.* New York: Morrow.

Phillips, K. A. (2003). Somatoform and factitious disorders. *American Journal of Psychiatry, 160*(3), 606–607.

Piaget, J. (2002). *Language and thought of the child* (2nd ed.). New York: Routledge.

Pines, F. (1990). *Drive, ego, object, and self: A synthesis for clinical work.* New York: Basic Books.

Pipher, M. (1999). *Another country: Navigating the emotional terrain of our elders.* New York: Riverhead Books.

Pittman, F. (1998). *Grow up! How taking responsibility can make you a happy adult.* New York: St. Martin's Griffin.

Polster, E. (1995). *A population of selves: A therapeutic exploration of personal diversity.* New York: Jossey Bass.

Pope, K. S., & Brown, L. S. (1996). *Recovered memories of abuse: Assessment, therapy, forensics.* Washington, DC: American Psychological Association.

Prochaska, J. O., Norcross, J. C., & DiClemente, C. C. (1994). *Changing for good: The revolutionary program that explains the six stages of change and teaches you how to free yourself from bad habits.* New York: Morrow.

Progoff, I. (1992). *At a journal workshop* (Rev. ed.). New York: Tarcher.

Pryor, K. (1999). *Don't shoot the dog! The new art of teaching and training* (Rev. ed.). New York: Bantam Books.

Reich, W. (1980). *Character analysis* (3rd ed.). New York: Farrar, Straus and Giroux.

Reinecke, M. A., & Freeman, A. (2003). Cognitive therapy. In A. S. Gurman & S. B. Messer (Eds.), *Essential psychotherapies* (pp. 224–271). New York: Guilford Press.

Reitz, M., & Watson, K. W. (1992). *Adoption and the family system: Strategies for treatment.* New York: Guilford Press.

Richards, P. S., & Bergin, A. E. (2000). *Handbook of psychotherapy and religious diversity.* Washington, DC: American Psychological Association.

Rigazio-DiGilio, S. A., Ivey, A. E., Kunkler-Peck, K. P., & Grady, L. T. (2005). *Community genograms: Using individual, family, and cultural narratives with clients.* New York: Teachers College Press.

Ritter, K. I., & Terndrup, A. I. (2002). *Handbook of affirmative psychotherapy with lesbians and gay men.* New York: Guilford Press.

Roberts, A. R. (1998). *Battered women and their families* (2nd ed.). New York: Springer.

Robin, A., Schneider, M., & Dolnick, M. (1976). The turtle technique: An extended case study of self-control in the classroom. *Psychology in the Schools, 13,* 449–453.

Rodgers, J. E. (1992). Psychosurgery: Damaging the brain to save the mind (*Psychology Today Magazine*). Retrieved September 18, 2005, from http://cms.psychologytoday.com/articles/pto-19920301-000030.html.

Root, M. P. P. (Ed.). (1996). *The multiracial experience: Racial borders as the new frontier.* Thousand Oaks, CA: Sage.

Rosenhan, D. L. (1973). On being sane in insane places. *Science, 179,* 250–258.

Rowan, J. (1990). *Subpersonalities: The people inside us.* London: Routledge.

Ryan, W. (1976). *Blaming the victim* (Rev. ed.). New York: Vintage Books.

Sales, B. D., Miller, M. O., & Hall, S. R. (2005). *Laws affecting clinical practice.* Washington, DC: American Psychological Association.

Savin-Williams, R. C. (2001). *"Mom, Dad. I'm gay": How families negotiate coming out.* Washington, DC: American Psychological Association.

Scharff, J. S., & Scharff, D. E. (1995). *The primer of object relations therapy.* New York: Aronson.

Schnarch, D. (1998). *Passionate marriage: Love, sex, and intimacy in emotionally committed relationships.* New York: Owl Books.

Schore, A. (2003). *Affect regulation and the repair of the self.* New York: Norton.

Schwartz, R. C. (1995). *Internal family systems therapy.* New York: Guilford Press.

Seligman, M. (2002). *Authentic happiness: Using the new positive psychology to realize your potential for lasting fulfillment.* New York: Free Press.

Servaty-Seib, H. L. (2004). Connections between counseling theories and current theories of grief and mourning. *Journal of Mental Health Counseling, 26*(2), 125–146.

Shafranske, E. P. (Ed.). (1996). *Religion and the clinical practice of psychology.* Washington, DC: American Psychological Association.

Shapiro, D. (1965). *Neurotic styles.* New York: Basic Books.

Shapiro, F. (1996). *Eye movement desensitization and reprocessing (EMDR): Basic principles, protocols and procedures.* New York: Guilford Press.

Shear, K., Frank, E., Houck, P. R., & Reynolds, C. F. (2005). Treatment of complicated grief: A randomized controlled trial. *Journal of the American Medical Association, 29*(21), 2601–2608.

Sheehy, G. (1977). *Passages: Predictable crises of adult life.* New York: Bantam Books.

Sheehy, G. (1996). *New passages: Mapping your life across time.* New York: Ballantine Books.

Shiraev, E., & Levy, D. (2004). *Cross-cultural psychology: Critical thinking and contemporary applications.* Boston: Pearson Education.

Shure, M. B., & Spivack, G. (1980). Interpersonal problem solving as a mediator of behavioral adjustment in preschool and kindergarten children. *Journal of Applied Developmental Psychology, 1,* 29–44.

Siegel, D. J. (2001). *The developing mind: How relationships and the brain interact to shape who we are.* New York: Guilford Press.

Smith, M. J. (1975). *When I say no, I feel guilty.* Toronto, Canada: Bantam.

Smith, T. B. (2004). *Practicing multiculturalism: Affirming diversity in counseling and psychotherapy.* Boston: Pearson Education.

Snow, K. (1992). *Writing yourself home: A woman's guided journey of self discovery.* Berkeley, CA: Conari Press.

Spector, A. R. (2004). Psychological issues and interventions with infertile patients. *Women and Therapy, 27*(3/4), 91–205.

Sperry, L. (2001). *Spirituality in clinical practice: Incorporating the spiritual dimension in psychotherapy and counseling.* New York: Brunner-Routledge.

Sperry, L., & Shafranske, E. (2004). *Spiritually oriented psychotherapy.* Washington, DC: American Psychological Association.

St. Clair, M. (1996). *Object relations and self-psychology: An introduction* (3rd ed.). Belmont, CA: Brooks/Cole.

Stern, D. N. (1985). *The interpersonal world of the infant: A view from psychoanalysis and developmental psychology.* New York: Basic Books.

Stern, D. N. (1998). *Diary of a baby.* New York: Basic Books.

Stevens, A. (1999). *On Jung.* Princeton, NJ: Princeton University Press.

Stevenson, H. C., & Renard, G. (1993). Trusting ole' wise owls: Therapeutic use of cultural strengths in African-American families. *Professional Psychology: Research and Practice, 24,* 433–442.

Stone, H., & Stone, S. (1993). *Embracing your inner critic: Turning self-criticism into a creative asset.* San Francisco: Harper.

Stone, H., & Stone, S. L. (1989). *Embracing our selves: The voice dialogue manual.* Novato, CA: New World Library.

Storr, A. (1989). *Solitude: A return to the self* (Reprint ed.). New York: Ballantine Books.

Stroebe, M., Schut, H., & Stroebe, W. (2005). Attachment in coping with bereavement: A theoretical integration. *Review of General Psychology, 9*(1), 48–66.

Stroebe, M. S., Hansson, R. O., Stroebe, W., & Schut, H. (Eds.). (2001). *Handbook of bereavement research: Consequences, coping, and care.* Washington, DC: American Psychological Association.

Stroebe, M. S., & Schut, H. (2001). Models of coping with bereavement: A review. In M. S. Stroebe, R. O. Hansson, W. Stroebe, & H. Schut (Eds.), *Handbook of bereavement research: Consequences, coping, and care* (pp. 375–403). Washington, DC: American Psychological Association.

Stroebe, W., Schut, H., & Stroebe, M. S. (2005). Grief work, disclosure, and counseling: Do they help the bereaved? *Clinical Psychology Review, 25*(4), 395–414.

Strunk, W., & White, E. B. (2000). *The elements of style* (4th ed.). New York: Longman.

Stuart, R. B. (1972). *Slim chance in a fat world: Behavioral control of obesity.* Champaign, IL: Research Press.

Stuart, R. B. (1980). *Helping couples change: A social learning approach to marital therapy.* New York: Guilford Press.

Sue, D. W., & Sue, D. (2002). *Counseling the culturally diverse: Theory and practice* (4th ed.). Hoboken, NJ: Wiley.

Sue, S. (1998). In search of cultural competence in psychotherapy and counseling. *American Psychologist, 53*(4), 440–448.

Sullivan, H. S. (1968). *The interpersonal theory of psychiatry.* New York: Norton.

Synergy Project. (2005). *HIV voluntary counseling and testing: Skills training curriculum—Participant's manual.* Retrieved September 28, 2005, from www.synergyaids.com/documents/VCT_ParticipantsManual.pdf.

Tannen, D. (2001). *You just don't understand: Women and men in conversation.* New York: HarperCollins.

Terman, M., & Terman, J. S. (2005). Light therapy for seasonal and nonseasonal depression: Efficacy, protocol, safety, and side effects. *CNS Spectrums, 10,* 647–663.

Thase, M. E., & Jindal, R. D. (2004). Combining psychotherapy and psychopharmacology for treatment of mental disorders. In M. J. Lambert (Ed.), *Bergin and Garfield's handbook of psychotherapy and behavior change* (5th ed., pp. 743–766). Hoboken, NJ: Wiley.

Thompson, C. E. (2004). Awareness and identity: Foundational principles of multicultural practice. In T. B. Smith (Ed.), *Practicing multiculturalism: Affirming diversity in counseling and psychotherapy* (pp. 35–56). Boston: Pearson Education.

Tinsley-Jones, H. (2003). Racism: Calling a spade a spade. *Psychotherapy: Theory, Research, Practice, Training, 40,* 179–186.

Tseng, W.-S., & Streltzer, J. (Eds.). (2004). *Cultural competence in clinical psychiatry.* Washington, DC: American Psychiatric Publishing.

Vace, N. A., DeVaney, S. B., & Brendel, J. M. (2003). *Counseling multicultural and diverse populations: Strategies for practitioners* (4th ed.). New York: Brunner-Routledge.

Walker, L. (1984). *The battered woman syndrome.* New York: Springer.

Wanderer, Z., & Ingram, B. L. (1990). Physiologically monitored implosion therapy of phobias. *Phobia Practice and Research Journal, 3*(2), 61–76.

Watson, D. L., & Tharp, R. G. (2001). *Self-directed behavior: Self-modification for personal adjustment* (8th ed.). Belmont, CA: Wadsworth Publishing.

Watzlawick, P., Weakland, J., & Fisch, R. (1974). *Change: Principles of problem formation and problem resolution.* New York: Norton.

Webster-Stratton, C., & Hammond, M. (1997). Treating children with early-onset conduct problems: A comparison of child and parent training interventions. *Journal of Consulting and Clinical Psychology, 65*(1), 93–109.

Weed, L. L. (1971). The problem-oriented record as a basic tool in medical education, patient care, and clinical research. *Annals of Clinical Research, 3*(3), 131–134.

Wheelis, A. (1975). *How people change.* New York: Harper Colophon.

White, M., & Epston, D. (1990). *Narrative means to therapeutic ends.* New York: Norton.

Whitfield, C. L. (1987). *Healing the child within: Discovery and recovery for adult children of dysfunctional families.* Deerfield Beach, FL: Health Communications.

Wiggins, J. G. (2004). *Comparing standards of mental health care: Combined psychotherapy/pharmacotherapy versus usual medical services.* Retrieved September 18, 2005, from www.division42.org/MembersArea/IPfiles/Sum04/prof_practice/wiggins.php.

Wilkinson, C. B., & Vera, E. (1989). Clinical responses to disaster: Assessment, management, and treatment. In R. Gist & B. Lubin (Eds.), *Psychosocial aspects of disaster* (pp. 229–267). New York: Wiley.

Williams, R., & Williams, V. (1993). *Anger kills.* New York: Harper Perennial.

Winnicott, D. W. (1965). *Maturational processes and the facilitating environment: Studies in the theory of emotional development.* New York: International Universities Press.

Witztum, E., & Goodman, Y. (2004). Rewriting stories of distress. In J. R. Ancis (Ed.), *Culturally responsive interventions: Innovative approaches to working with diverse populations* (pp. 143–173). New York: Brunner-Routledge.

Wolf, E. (1988). *Treating the self: Elements of clinical self-psychology.* New York: Guilford Press.

Wolpe, J. (1958). *Psychotherapy by reciprocal inhibition.* Stanford, CA: Stanford University Press.

Wolpe, J. (1995). A complex case. In D. Wedding & R. J. Corsini (Eds.), *Case studies in psychotherapy* (2nd ed., pp. 111–116). Itasca, IL: F. E. Peacock.

Wong, E. C., Kim, B. S. K., Zane, N. W. S., Kim, I. J., & Huang, J. S. (2003). Examining culturally based variables associated with ethnicity: Influence on credibility perceptions of empirically supported interventions. *Cultural Diversity and Ethnic Minority Psychology, 9*(1), 88–96.

Worden, J. W. (1991). *Grief counseling and grief therapy: A handbook for the mental health practitioner* (2nd ed.). New York: Springer.

Wright, R. A., Greenberg, J., & Brehm, S. S. (2004). *Motivational analyses of social behavior: Building on Jack Brehm's contributions to psychology.* Hillsdale, NJ: Erlbaum.

Yalom, I. D. (1980). *Existential psychotherapy.* New York: Basic Books.

Yalom, I. D. (1990). *Love's executioner, and other tales of psychotherapy.* New York: Perennial.

Yalom, I. D. (1995). *Theory and practice of group psychotherapy* (4th ed.). New York: Basic Books.

Yi, K., & Shorter-Gooden, K. (1999). Ethnic identity formation: From stage theory to a constructivist narrative model. *Psychotherapy: Theory, Research, Practice, Training, 36,* 16–26.

Young, J. (1999). *Cognitive therapy for personality disorders: A schema-focused approach* (3rd ed.). Sarasota, FL: Professional Resource Press.

Young, M. A. (1989). Crime, violence, and terrorism. In R. Gist & B. Lubin (Eds.), *Psychosocial aspects of disaster* (pp. 229–267). New York: Wiley.

Zane, N., Morton, T., Chu, J., & Lin, N. (2004). Counseling and psychotherapy with Asian American clients. In T. B. Smith (Ed.), *Practicing multiculturalism: Affirming diversity in counseling and psychotherapy* (pp. 190–214). Boston: Pearson Education.

Zuckerman, E. L. (2000). *Clinician's thesaurus: The guidebook for writing psychological reports* (5th ed.). New York: Guilford Press.

Zuckerman, E. L. (2003). *The paper office: Forms, guidelines, and resources to make your practice work ethically, legally, and profitably.* New York: Guilford Press.

Author Index

617

Subject Index